MANAGERIAL ECONOMICS

K. RAMA MOHANA RAO
M.Com., MBA, Ph.D.

Vice Chairman
AP State Council of Higher Education
Government of Andhra Pradesh
Sr. Professor (Retd.)
Department of Commerce and Management Studies
Andhra University, Visakhapatnam
Andhra Pradesh

CHANDRA SEKHAR PATRO
M.Com., MFM, MBA, Ph.D.

Assistant Professor
Department of Management Studies
Gayatri Vidya Parishad College of Engineering (Autonomous)
Visakhapatnam, Andhra Pradesh

TECHSAR™
NEW DELHI

Published and Printed by
Techsar Pvt. Ltd.
4435-36/7, Ansari Road, Daryaganj
New Delhi-110 002 (India)
E-mail: tech_info@techsarworld.com
Website: www.techsarworld.com

ISBN: 978-93-90620-02-9

Reprint 2025

Preface

In the fast changing business environment due to advancements in technology and global access, decision making has become a multifaceted managerial task. The growing complexity of decision variables are reflected by the managerial problems related to market evaluation, production planning, pricing, marketing, financing, human resource management and business planning considering the existing business conditions and economic perspectives such as demand, supply, cost, pricing, market structure, competition, profit, growth, resource mobilisation, optimisation, and other factors of production.

Managerial Economics deals with the use of economic principles and concepts for managerial decision making. This is naturally reflected in the approach adopted in the book where a concerted effort has been made to impart various concepts of micro– and macroeconomics. All the relevant topics are included to provide a comprehensive understanding to the readers as to make use of economics effectively in managerial decisions and utilising resources optimally. The book is divided in nine sections such as introduction to managerial economics, demand analysis and forecasting, production and supply analysis, cost analysis and cost control, market structure and price-output decisions, pricing decisions, profit analysis, macroeconomics and business decisions, and modern managerial economics.

The popularity of the subject and usefulness for the graduation and postgraduation courses in managerial economics has encouraged to take up the task of writing this book. We have made a fresh attempt by adding new features and presenting the text in simplest form to the possible extent. More questions and answers, trends and viewpoints are added. The book offers complete coverage of all the topics encountered in actual managerial decision making and covered in Managerial Economics course in a modular format. Thus, allowing a great deal of flexibility in the choice of topics that any teacher or student may wish to cover.

Salient features:

- The book integrates various concepts and ideas from the fields of economics and other subjects, which have bearing on managerial decision making and policy formulation within the business unit.
- The text gives a number of suitable examples, including large number of review questions, objective type questions and exercises.
- Provides relevant material for class discussions, assignments and examination point of view.
- Focuses on the concepts related to macroeconomics and business decisions, economic optimisation techniques and modern approaches to managerial economics.
- The text makes minimum use of mathematical and statistical techniques to suit the basic knowledge of subject without sacrificing the metrical dimension of the subject.

This book emphasises on conceptual clarity and simplified presentation. By integrating the economic theory with business practice, it aims at providing a unifying framework for managerial decision making. It comprehensively covers all the aspects that impinge upon economic decision making of modern business units. This text would be helpful for the students of Commerce, Management, Economics, Engineering, Law, and other social science disciplines. It is also useful to the practising managers.

K. Rama Mohana Rao
Chandra Sekhar Patro

Acknowledgements

The work of this magnitude cannot be done without the support of many resourceful personalities. We sincerely acknowledge the support and encouragement of our family members and friends. We also express our deep gratitude to all those people who have directly and indirectly contributed their efforts in bringing out this book.

We are grateful to Prof. Hrushikesava Rao and Dr. U. Adinarayana for their valuable contributions. The concepts used in the text are developed by many economists around the world. We express our grateful thanks to all of them for their wonderful contribution to the field of Economics, particularly Managerial Economics.

K. Rama Mohana Rao
Chandra Sekhar Patro

Contents

Chapter

1 Concept and Scope of Managerial Economics

LEARNING OBJECTIVES

After studying this chapter, you should be able to understand:

- concept of managerial economics;
- features of managerial econaomics;
- scope of managerial economics; and
- links of managerial economics with other disciplines.

1.1. CONCEPT OF MANAGERIAL ECONOMICS

The primary goal of every business organisation is to achieve growth in profit and growth in business. The theories of economics provide a foundational base for the achievement of the business goals. Managerial economics, therefore, gained prominence in business management. Managerial economics is referred to as the study of economic theories, principles and tools of economic analysis used in the process of decision making and solving managerial problems. Managerial economics helps to perform two key managerial functions such as decision making and forward-planning. Decision making refers to the process of selecting one action from two or more alternative courses of action, whereas forward-planning is the projected blueprint of operations with their costs and benefits.

Joel Dean (1951) observed that managerial economics shows how economic analysis can be used in formulating policies and strategies. Managerial economics bridges the gap between traditional economic theory and real business practices in two ways:

- It provides several tools and techniques to enable the manager to become more competent to take decisions in specific situations.
- It serves as an integrating force by establishing interrelationships and interdependency among various economic activities of a business unit.

Managerial economics is a combination of two different disciplines, i.e., economics and management. Let us understand the philosophy of economics as well as management in the following paragraphs.

1.1.1. Economics

The term "economics" derives from the Greek word "Oikonomia" which means "household". Economics is the study of individuals as they live, act, move and believe in the normal life. The basic function of economics is to study human behaviour as a relationship between numerous wants and scarce means having alternative uses. Every human being aims at earning money and spending it to satisfy his/her needs and wants such as food, clothing, shelter, etc., from time to time. Such activities of earning and spending money are called "economic activities". Therefore, Economics is mainly concerned with the description and analysis of economic problems faced by individuals, organisations and nations.

Classical economists like Adam Smith, David Ricardo, John Stuart Mill, Thomas Robert Malthus, and others; socialist economist like Karl Marx; neo-classical economists like Alfred Marshall, A.C. Pigou and Lionel Robbins; and modern economists like J.M. Keynes, A. Samuelson, and others have made considerable contributions to the development of economics. The classical and neo-classical economists have been broadly classified economics into four major concepts as:

1. Wealth concept
2. Welfare concept
3. Scarcity concept
4. Growth concept

1. **Wealth Concept:** The wealth concept of economics believes that human beings try to maximise their wealth through economic activities. During the eighteenth century, Adam Smith, who is regarded as the father of Economics, in his famous book An Enquiry into the Nature and Cause of Wealth of Nation (1776), defined economics as "an enquiry into the nature and causes of wealth". Economics is the study to find how wealth is created and utilised for human needs. Much importance is given to the creation of wealth in an economy and believed that the economic prosperity of any nation depends only on the accumulation of wealth. Thus, according to this concept wealth is the ultimate goal of an individual. However, in real life wealth is not regarded as the ultimate goal of the life of an individual. There are many other goals related to family, society, growth, well-being, etc., make the individual take up many economic activities. Therefore, the purpose of economic activity is to create 'surplus' or 'profit' to satisfy the maximum possible wants by sacrificing minimum possible resources.
2. **Welfare Concept:** The welfare concept believes that the economic activities of human beings are beyond wealth and towards the welfare of self and society. Dr Alfred Marshall, one of the greatest economists of the nineteenth century, defined "Economics as the study of individual's actions in the ordinary business of life, and it enquires how an individual earns income and uses it". This concept

published in the book Principles of Economics, in 1890, shifted the focus from wealth to human welfare. It emphasises wealth as a means of satisfying human wants, not as an end of human activities. This concept gave primary importance to human welfare and secondary importance to wealth. Therefore, on one side it is the study of wealth and on the other side, it is the study of human welfare also. The welfare concept of economics was also criticised by saying that the scope of economics is beyond wealth and human welfare.

3. **Scarcity Concept:** The scarcity concept of economics believes that human beings are in search of finding better ways of utilising resources. Every resource will have multiple uses and applications. As natural resources are limited in nature, human beings try to optimise the value of such resources. Prof. Lionel Robbins developed the concept of economics in his book, An Essay on the Nature and Significance of Economic Science during 1932. Robbins referred to "Economics as the science that studies human behaviour as a relationship between ends and scarce means which have alternative uses". This concept shifted the focus of economics from the creation of wealth to human behaviour in the application of resources. The concept states that the human wants are unlimited and if one want is satisfied another want crops up, but the means for satisfying these wants are limited. Therefore, human beings set priorities and efficiently use scarce resources for satisfying their needs and wants.
4. **Growth Concept:** Growth concept of economics believes that the economic activities of human beings are towards the achievement of growth in life. It reflects on the continuous pursuit of individuals for betterment, growth and development. John Maynard Keynes (1936) referred to economics as the "study of the administration of scares resources and the determinants of income and employment". Paul Anthony Samuelson (1947) presented the growth-oriented concept of economics, "as the study of how man and society choose, with or without the use of money to employ scarce productive resources, which could have alternative uses, to produce various commodities over time and distribute them for consumption now and in the future among various people and groups of society." The growth-oriented concept is considered modern and is concerned with:

1. Determining the pattern of employing scarce resources to produce goods over time.
2. The pattern of present and future consumption of resources.
3. Analysing costs and benefits of the pattern of resource allocation.
4. Distribution of resources among various persons and groups in society for use and consumption.

Thus, the growth theory of economics is considered the most comprehensive of all the concepts of economics. This theory is inclusive of all the philosophies propagated by classical and neo-classical economists. It addresses the growth and developmental issues of both developed and developing economies. As such this concept is regarded as the modern philosophy of economics.

1.1.2. Microeconomics and Macroeconomics

Economic theory has two most important branches referred to as microeconomics and macroeconomics.

1. **Microeconomics:** Microeconomics is the study of individuals', households' and organisations' behaviour in decision making and allocation of resources. Microeconomics is concerned with the factors that affect individuals' economic choice, the factors influencing their choices, and effect of their decisions on the individual markets by affecting price, supply and demand. It applies to the marketing of goods and services and deals with individual and economic issues. The relevant microeconomic theories are the theory of the firm, the theory of consumer behaviour (demand), production and cost theory (supply), price theory, and market structure and competition theory. Microeconomics deals with forecasting of demand, supply and demand of products and services in a market, pricing, cost analysis, and provides a solution to the economic problems.
2. **Macroeconomics:** Macroeconomics is the study of 'aggregate' or 'total level' of economic activities of a nation. It studies the flow of economic resources or factors of production (such as land, labour, capital, organisation and technology) to the ultimate households through business units. It deals with problems relating to national income, inflation, unemployment, economic growth, business cycles, balance of payments, fiscal and monetary policies.

The study of microeconomics and macroeconomics are complementary to each other. To have a comprehensive understanding of economics, one has to study both, microeconomics and macroeconomics.

1.1.3. Management

Management deals with principles which help in decision making under uncertainty and improves the effectiveness of an organisation. Every business unit must be well managed to achieve its objectives. Management includes several functions such as planning, organising, staffing, directing, and controlling. A manager is a person who gets the things done through people in an organisation. Managers in their day-to-day activities are always confronted with several issues such as how much quantity is to be supplied, at what price should the product be made or whether it should be bought from outside, how much quantity is to be produced to make a given amount of profit, how to achieve high-quality products and services with minimum resources, how to optimise the value of the use of resources and so on. Therefore, knowledge of economics particularly managerial economics is essential for a manager to optimise the costs and revenues of the business unit.

Managerial economics defined by various economists

Author	Definition
M. H. Spencer & Louis Siegelman (1959)	Managerial economics is the integration of economic theory with business practice to facilitate decision making and forward planning by management.
Edurin Mansfield (1975)	Managerial economics is concerned with the application of economic concepts and economic analysis to the problem of formulating rational managerial decisions.
Eugene F. Brigham & James L. Pappas (1974)	Managerial economics is the application of economic theory and methodology to business administration practice.
Michael Baye (1994)	Managerial economics is the study of how to direct scarce resources in a way that most effectively achieves a managerial goal.
DC Hague (1969)	Managerial economics is a fundamental academic subject which seeks to understand and to analyse the problems of business decision making.
James R McGuigan & R Charles Moyer (1975)	Managerial economics is the application of economic theory and methodology to decision making problems faced by both public and private institutions.
Evan J. Douglas (1987)	Managerial economics is concerned with the application of economic principles and methodologies to the decision making process within the firm or organisation. It seeks to establish rules and principles to facilitate the attainment of the desired economic goals of management.

1.2. FEATURES OF MANAGERIAL ECONOMICS

Managerial economics originated from economics as well as management and therefore, it involves the basic characteristics of economics and management. Managerial economics is a special discipline which integrates the economic theory with business practice for decision making and forward planning. The following are the features of managerial economics:

1. Close to microeconomics
2. Normative approach
3. Action oriented
4. Application oriented
5. Multidisciplinary approach
6. Evaluation of alternatives for decision making
7. Perspective planning
8. Assumptions and limitations

1. **Close to microeconomics**: It is difficult to draw a line between microeconomics and managerial economics. The difference is found in terms of the scope of coverage of issues. Microeconomics deals with the behaviour of individuals and business units in the allocation of scarce resources and the relationship between individuals and business units. Managerial economics, on the other hand, focuses on finding solutions to different managerial problems of a business unit from an economic perspective. It helps a business unit in allocating productive resources for achieving maximum output with minimum cost and maximum profit.
2. **Normative approach:** Normative economics provides a perspective of the expected outcome by judging investment projects, statements, and scenarios. Normative economics mostly concerns with the ideologies and describes what ought to be rather than facts based on cause and effect relationships. Managerial economics is a part of normative economics as its focus is more on suggesting choice and action but less on explaining what has happened. It explains desirability or undesirability of a situation for the benefit of an organisation. It deals with goal formulation, the achievement of goals, future planning, policy making, decision making besides optimal utilisation of available resources.
3. **Action oriented:** Managerial economics is concerned only with those decisions which are made to achieve the objectives of a business unit. It provides various alternatives to select the best choice for attaining the goals of an organisation. Managerial economics suggests the course of action for the business problems from the available alternatives for an optimal solution.
4. **Application oriented:** Managerial economics drives the organisations to get activated in resolving problems at the right time and to the benefit of the organisation. All the issues covered under managerial economics are application oriented and aim at achieving desired results. Managerial economics is judged by its ability to help the managers to make better decisions.

5. **Multidisciplinary:** Managerial economics takes inputs from micro- and macroeconomics, management, mathematics, statistics, accountancy, psychology, behavioural sciences, sociology and so on.
6. **Evaluation of alternatives for decision making:** Evaluation of alternatives is essential to find out the best alternative. The quality of decision making primarily depends upon the way in which the alternatives are evaluated. Managerial economics supports the manger in finding the right methods and appropriate quantitative techniques to evaluate each of the alternatives in terms of costs and benefits. This helps the manager to decide the best alternative to achieve the organisational goals.
7. **Perspective planning:** Perspective planning is a blueprint of objectives, tasks and targets for long-term growth of a business unit. The basic purpose of a perspective plan is to provide a policy framework for the design and development of various programmes and activities within the orbit of the business unit's goals. Managerial economics is essentially used in the development of a perspective plan of a business unit.
8. **Assumptions and limitations**: Managerial economics deals with the activities of a business unit and analyses economic factors under specific situations following certain assumptions. Each analysis is valid only for the specific situation and conditioned by the assumptions and limitations. Therefore, the economic analysis of one situation cannot be generalised or universalised. The analysis changes with the situation or the assumptions or the limitations.

1.3. SCOPE OF MANAGERIAL ECONOMICS

The scope of managerial economics is wider as it deals with the problems related to both business and non-business units. Managerial economics focuses to find an optimal solution for a managerial problem. The managerial economist makes use of certain principles, concepts, tools and techniques of economics and other related disciplines to find the optimum solution to managerial problems like production decisions, make-buy decisions, inventory decisions, investment decisions, human resource management, controlling costs, profit planning, determining the price of goods and services, marketing problems, etc.

Managerial economics helps in estimating the product demand, planning of production schedule, deciding the input combinations, estimation of the cost of production, achieving economies of scale and increasing the returns to scale. It also includes determining the price of the product, analysing market structure to determine the price of the product for profit maximisation, which helps them to control and plan capital in an effective manner. The scope of managerial economics covers two areas of decision making:

(a) Operational / internal issues
(b) Environmental / external issues

1.3.1. Operational / Internal Issues

The following are the operational issues of a business unit:

1. Demand analysis
2. Profit analysis
3. Capital or investment decisions
4. Cost analysis
5. Pricing decisions
6. Production and supply analysis
7. Economic forecasting and planning

1. **Demand analysis:** Demand analysis is a fundamental requirement for demand management. Business units need to develop strategies to match supply with estimated demand. It may need to initiate programmes to scale up the demand to match the capacity if the estimated demand is less than the required demand. In the case of overflowing demand situation, the business unit should find out ways to upscale the supply capacity either from its resources or from outside resources. Demand analysis helps in identifying the various factors influencing the product demand and provides guidelines for manipulating demand. The demands for the business unit's product would change in response to change in price, consumer's income, tastes, etc., which are the determinants of demand. The impacts of these are assessed and decisions are taken to maximise the profits.
2. **Profit analysis:** The business units are generally organised to make profits and are taken as an important measure of the business unit's success. Profit planning becomes necessary under the conditions of uncertainty. There are several techniques such as break-even analysis, cost reduction, cost control, and ratio analysis to ascertain the level of profits. Break-even analysis is concerned with profit planning, i.e., if a business unit produces less than break-even point (BEP) it gets losses. Similarly, cost reduction and control deal with strategies to reduce wastages and reduce costs.
3. **Capital or investment decisions:** The business units often find it difficult to make decisions related to capital investment. These decisions require sound knowledge and expertise in various

economic aspects. To make sound capital investment decisions, a business unit needs to determine various aspects, such as the cost of capital and rate of return. The manager has to calculate the profitability of investment and properly allocate the capital. Availability of capital from various sources like equity capital, banks, institutional finance, etc., may help to undertake large-scale operations. The success of the business unit depends upon the proper analysis of the capital project and selecting the best one.

4. **Cost analysis**: A study of economic costs, combined with the data drawn from the business unit's accounting records, can yield significant cost estimates which are useful for management decisions. An element of cost uncertainty exists because all the factors determining costs are not known and are uncontrollable. The factors causing variation in costs must be identified and allowed for if management is to arrive at cost estimates which are significant for planning purposes. The determinants of estimating costs, the relationship between cost and output, the forecast of cost and profit are very vital to a business unit.
5. **Pricing decisions:** Pricing is an important area of managerial economics. The profit goals of the business unit can be reached through appropriate and accurate pricing decisions. The key areas are price determination in various market structures such as monopoly, oligopoly, and monopolistic, determination of pricing method, price differentiation, product-line pricing and competitive pricing. Pricing is guided by cost concepts, profit concepts, organisational objectives and government policies. The pricing policies and strategies of a business unit guide the manager to take appropriate pricing decisions in varied situations.
6. **Production and supply analysis:** Production and supply analysis refers to factors of production used in an organisation. Production inputs such as land, labour, capital, organisation and technology play a vital role in the economics of production. The factors of production otherwise called inputs may be combined in a particular way to yield the maximum output. When the prices of inputs fluctuate, a business unit may be forced to work out a different combination of inputs to ensure that this combination becomes the least cost combination. The main areas under production analysis are production function, the least-cost combination of factor inputs, the law of variable proportions, factor productiveness, returns to scale, cost concepts and classification, cost-output relationship and linear programming. The supply analysis also plays an important role and aspects to be considered undersupply analysis include supply schedule, the law of supply and the elasticity of supply.

7. **Economic planning and forecasting:** Economic planning and forecasting provide essential basis for business planning and occupies a strategic place in managerial economics. The business unit operates in an environment dominated by external and internal factors. The external factors include demographic factors, technological factors, socio-cultural factors, natural resources, government policies and competition. Internal factors include policies and procedures relating to production, human resources, finance, marketing, research and development. The analysis of external and internal factors is useful in economic planning and forecasting of an organisation.

1.3.2. Environmental / External Issues

Environmental issues refer to the general business environment in which the business unit operates. The following are the issues related to the economic environment:

1. The type of economic system prevailing in the country.
2. The general trend in production, employment, income, prices, savings and investments.
3. Trends in the working of financial institutions like banks, financial corporations, insurance companies, etc.
4. The magnitude and trends in foreign trade.
5. The trends in human resources and capital market.
6. The economic policies of the government such as industrial policy, monetary policy, fiscal policy, price policy, regulatory mechanisms, etc.

1.4. LINKS WITH OTHER DISCIPLINES

Managerial economics takes support from many disciplines for providing effective support to managers in planning and decision making. The disciplines such as economics, management, accounting, mathematics, statistics, operations research, computer science, psychology, and other technology and social sciences provide immense support to the managerial economist in functioning effectively.

1. **Economics:** Managerial economics has been described as economics applied to decision making. Economics deals with theoretical concepts whereas managerial economics deals with the application of these theories in real-life situations. Managerial economics takes the relevant theoretical support from macroeconomics and mostly connected to microeconomics. The problems of an individual or a business unit are the basis for managerial economics. Without taking

support from economics it may not be possible to a managerial economist to perform the specific functions in an organisation.

2. **Management:** Management refers to the process of planning, organising, leading and controlling the activities of an organisation and using the resources to achieve the set objectives. Management theories bring out the behaviour of the business unit in its efforts to achieve some predetermined objectives. The objectives of the business unit and the managerial behaviour are subject to change with changes in the business environment and circumstances. Therefore, the knowledge of management theory and practice contributes significantly in taking the right decisions at the right time. A managerial economist should know management principles and practices related to marketing, finance, human resources, production, technology, etc., for achieving the desired performance.
3. **Accounting:** Accounting deals with systematic and comprehensive recording of financial transactions of a business unit. It is referred to as the process of summarising, analysing and reporting transactions to stakeholders, regulators and tax collection entities. Accounting information is one of the principal sources of data required by a managerial economist. It provides information related to costs, revenues, receivables, payables, profit and loss, preparation of financial statements, analytical and critical evaluation of financial performance. It also aids the top management in reviewing policies and taking vital management decisions.
4. **Mathematics:** Mathematical concepts and techniques are widely used in economic logic to solve managerial problems. Mathematical methods also help to estimate and predict the economic factors for decision making and forward planning. The tools and techniques of mathematics like logarithms, exponentials, geometry, vectors, input-output tables, algebra and calculus, etc., are widely used. Advanced techniques like linear programming, inventory models and game theory are also used. Therefore, the knowledge of mathematics is essential for a managerial economist.
5. **Statistics:** Statistics deals with various techniques that are useful for analysing the cause and effect relationships for a given variable or phenomenon. Statistical tools such as probability, averages, correlation, regression, measures of dispersion, interpolation, time series, etc., are used in collecting data and analysing it. Managerial economist needs statistical tools in more than one way to analyse situations comprehensively and to draw relevant inferences. A

managerial economist gathers information in the form of statistical data for the demand of a product, production levels, inputs used, advertisement expenditure, etc., and applies statistical tools for comprehending the situation and to design an action plan.

6. **Operations research:** Operations research deals with the application of advanced analytical methods to find out optimal or near-optimal solutions for complex management problems. It emphasises on the human-technology interface and focuses on practical applications. It employs mathematical modelling, statistical analysis and mathematical optimisation. The operations research models such as linear programming, queuing, transportation, inventory model, optimisation techniques, etc., are extensively used for solving managerial problems.
7. **Computer science:** The entry of computers changed the way of the functioning of the organisations. Computer science has a great influence on managerial economics. Computers are used in data and account maintenance, inventory and stock controls and supply and demand predictions. It stores the data in the database and the data can be retrieved whenever required by a managerial economist. It helps the management in sorting out data and information appropriately and at an unimaginable speed.
8. **Psychology:** Consumer psychology is the basis on which managerial economist acts upon. How consumers understand and react when there is a change in price, supply, income, product features, etc., and its consequential effect on demand or profits is the main focus of the study of managerial economics. The discipline of psychology helps in understanding the behavioural implications, attitudes and motivations of each of the microeconomic variables such as consumer, supplier, investor and employee.

1.5. SUMMARY

- Managerial economics is referred to as the study of economic theories, logic and tools of economic analysis, used in the process of decision making and solving business problems.
- The classical and neo-classical economists classified economics into four major concepts as wealth concept, welfare concept, scarcity concept, and growth concept.
- Wealth concept of economics states that human beings try to maximise their wealth through economic activities.
- Welfare concept believes that the economic activities of human beings are beyond wealth and towards the welfare of self and society.

- The scarcity concept studies human behaviour as a relationship between ends and scarce means which have alternative uses.
- The growth concept of economics refers to the study of the administration of scarce resources and the determinants of income and employment.
- Economic theory has two most important branches referred to as microeconomics and macroeconomics.
- Microeconomics is the study of individuals, households' and organisations' behaviour in decision making and allocation of resources.
- Macroeconomics is the study of 'aggregate' or 'total level' of economic activities of a nation.
- Management refers to the science and art of getting things done through people in formally organised groups.
- The important features of managerial economics are close to microeconomics, normative approach, action oriented, application oriented, multidisciplinary, evaluation of alternatives for decision making, prospective planning, and assumptions and limitations.
- The scope of managerial economics covers two areas of decision making such as operational / internal issues and environmental / external issues.
- The operational issues of a business unit are demand analysis, profit analysis, capital or investment decisions, cost analysis, pricing decisions, production and supply analysis, and economic forecasting and planning.
- The environmental issues are the type of economic system prevailing in the country, the trend in production, employment, income, prices, savings and investments, trends in the working of financial institutions like banks, financial corporations, insurance companies, etc., magnitude and trends in foreign trade, trends in human resource and capital market, and economic policies of the government.
- The most important disciplines on which managerial economics operates are economics, management, accounting, mathematics, statistics, operational research, computer science, psychology, and other technology and social sciences.

SHORT ANSWER QUESTIONS

1. Define managerial economics.
2. Describe the wealth concept.
3. What is the welfare concept?
4. Explain the scarcity concept of economics.
5. Write a short note on growth concept.
6. What is microeconomics?

7. What is macroeconomics?
8. Define management.

ESSAY ANSWER QUESTIONS

1. "Managerial economics is the application of economic theory to business management." Discuss.
2. What is managerial economics? Explain the features of managerial economics.
3. Discuss the scope of managerial economics.
4. What are the operational issues of managerial economics? Explain.
5. Managerial economics is a multidimensional discipline. Explain.

FILL IN THE BLANKS

1. The famous book A*n Enquiry into the Nature and Cause of Wealth of Nation* was written by ___________.
2. Welfare definition of economics was given by ___________.
3. The scarcity concept of economics was proposed by ___________.
4. Decision making and ___________ are the fundamental activities of managerial economics.
5. The book *The Nature and Significance of Economic Science* was introduced in the year _________.
6. The study of the total level of economic activities of a nation is called _________.
7. Profit planning becomes necessary under the conditions of _________.
8. The business unit operates in an environment dominated by external and _________ factors.

Answers:

1. Adam Smith
2. Alfred Marshall
3. Lionel Robbins
4. Forward planning
5. 1932
6. Macroeconomics
7. Uncertainty
8. Internal

MULTIPLE-CHOICE QUESTIONS

1. The book *Principles of Economics* was introduced by:
   (A) Prof. Lionel Robbins (B) Dr. Alfred Marshall
   (C) Adam Smith (D) Lord J. M. Keynes
2. Which of the following concept was proposed by Prof. Lionel Robbins?
   (A) Scarcity concept (B) Welfare concept
   (C) Growth concept (D) Wealth concept
3. Which of the following do not fall under microeconomics?
   (A) Demand theory (B) Cost theory
   (C) Supply theory (D) Gross domestic product

4. The nature of managerial economics is
   (A) Descriptive (B) Normative
   (C) Subjective (D) Objective
5. Managerial economics takes the help of one of the following disciplines.
   (A) Zoology (B) Operations research
   (C) Biotechnology (D) History
6. The study of individuals', households' and organisations' behaviour in decision making and allocation of resources is called:
   (A) Macroeconomics (B) Economic activities
   (C) Microeconomics (D) Non-Economic activities
7. Operational issues are also referred to as:
   (A) Environmental issues (B) External issues
   (C) Internal issues (D) Workplace issues
8. Which one of the following deals with systematic and comprehensive recording of financial transactions about a business?
   (A) Statistics (B) Economics
   (C) Management (D) Accounting

Answers:

1. B	2. A	3. D	4. B	5. B
6. C	7. C	8. D		

REFERENCES

1. Baye, Michael R. (1994). *Managerial Economics and Business Strategy.* New York: McGraw-Hill.
2. Brigham, E. F. & Pappas, J. L. (1974). *Managerial Economics.* London: Holt, Rinehart and Winston.
3. Dean, Joel. (1951). *Managerial Economics.* New York: Prentice-Hall Inc.
4. Douglas, E. J. (1987). *Managerial Economics: Analysis and Strategy.* Prentice-Hall.
5. Dwivedi, D.N. (2015). *Managerial Economics* (8th Edition). New Delhi, India: Vikas Publishing House Pvt. Ltd.
6. Gupta, G.S. (2017). *Managerial Economics.* New Delhi, India: Tata McGraw-Hill.
7. Hague, D. C. (1969). *Managerial Economics: Analysis for Business Decisions.* Wiley.
8. Hirschey, M. (2009). *Managerial Economics* (12th Edition). USA: South-Western Cengage Learning.
9. Keynes, J. M. (1936). *The General Theory of Employment, Interest and Money.* London, UK: Palgrave Macmillan.
10. Mansfield, E. (1975). *Microeconomics: Theory/Applications.* New York: W.W. Norton & Co.

11. Marshall, A. (1890). *Principles of Economics.* London: Macmillan.
12. McGuigan, J. R. & Moyer, R. C. (1975). *Managerial Economics: Private and Public Sector Decision Analysis*. Dryden Press.
13. Mehta, P. L. (2007). *Managerial Economics: Text and Cases*. New Delhi, India: Sultan Chand & Co.
14. Robbins, Lionel. (1932). *An Essay on the Nature and Significance of Economic Science.* London: Macmillan & Co. Limited.
15. Samuelson, Paul A. (1947). *Foundations of Economic Analysis.* Enlarged edn. 1983. Harvard University Press.
16. Smith, Adam. (1776). *An Inquiry into the Nature and Causes of the Wealth of Nations.* London: W. Strahan.
17. Spencer, M. H. & Siegelman, L. (1959). *Managerial Economics: Decision Making and Forward Planning.* Richard D., Irwin, Inc., Homewood, Illionous.
18. Thomas, C. R. & Maurice, S. C. (2016). *Managerial Economics: Foundations of Business Analysis and* Strategy. New York, NY: McGraw-Hill Education.
19. Varshney, R. L. & Maheswari, K. L. (2014). *Managerial Economics.* New Delhi, India: Sultan Chand & Sons.

Chapter

2 Roles and Responsibilities of a Managerial Economist

LEARNING OBJECTIVES

After studying this chapter, you should be able to understand:

- importance of managerial economics;
- the managerial economist,
- tasks performed by managerial economist;
- role of a managerial economist in managerial decision making; and
- responsibilities of a managerial economist.

2.1. IMPORTANCE OF MANAGERIAL ECONOMICS

Managerial economics is the science of allocation of available resources to a business unit in such a way that the scarce resources yield optimum results. It is fundamentally concerned with the art of making rational choices to yield maximum return out of minimum resources and efforts. Managerial economics is essentially applied economics in the field of management. It relates to the economic aspects of managerial decision making and forward planning. Milton H. Spencer and Louis Siegelman (1959) described the importance of managerial economics in five organisational and industrial perspectives. They are:

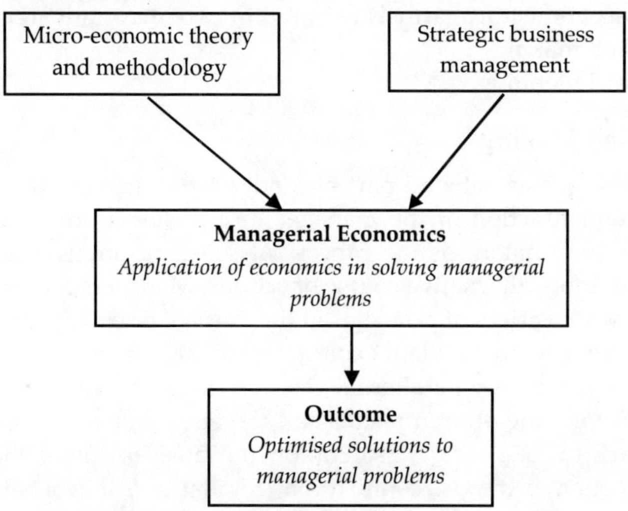

Figure 2.1. Importance of managerial economics

1. Relating traditional theoretical concepts with actual business conditions.
2. Basis of business policies.
3. Forecasting appropriate economic quantities.
4. Estimating economic relationships.
5. Knowing substantial external forces.

Managerial economics is concerned with the aspects and tools of economic analysis, and therefore, it is relevant to the decision making process. Managerial economics is the outcome of the integration of two disciplines such as microeconomic theory and methodology, and strategic business management. In other words, it is the application of economics in solving managerial problems. The intended outcome of managerial economics is to achieve optimised solutions to managerial problems (Figure 2.1).

2.2. THE MANAGERIAL ECONOMIST

The managerial economist is the person who assists the management in providing and analysing economic information for managerial decision making. The quality of the managerial decisions greatly depends upon the effective role played by the managerial economist. Many multinational companies around the globe take the support of expert managerial economists for continuation in the business in the presence of intense competition and also to achieve growth objectives. Major companies in India also recruit managerial economists for the purpose. The support of managerial economist primarily is required in two important areas:

1. Decision making
2. Forward planning

2.2.1. Decision Making

Decision making is an integral part of modern management theory. The most important function of the manager in a business unit is decision making. Decision making is the process of selecting one solution from among two or more alternative course of actions. Managers are constantly faced with a wide variety of problems in the areas of pricing, product, cost control, asset management, plant expansion, etc. Managers have to choose the best among the various alternatives, which can be most effectively used for achieving the desired results and targets. While taking decisions it is necessary to take into consideration the business units'objectives, resources, economic trends, competition, regulations, the behaviour of beneficiaries, and the responses of all the stakeholders. A speedy, accurate, sufficient, relevant and reliable information analysed using advanced analytical methods will be of immense help to the managers in making decisions. A managerial economist is the right person to extend valuable support to the management in this respect.

2.2.2. Forward Planning

Business units are future oriented and the future of a business unit is uncertain as it operates under the conditions of risk and uncertainty. Risk and uncertainty can be minimised only by making an accurate forecast and plan accordingly. Managerial economist helps the business unit in making plans for the future effectively. He possesses the knowledge of micro- and macroeconomics and therefore, is capable of understanding and estimating the trends of the business environment in which the business unit is operating.

2.3. TASKS OF MANAGERIAL ECONOMIST

The tasks of managerial economist are presented in Figure 2.1. The most important tasks are economic intelligence, research, expert analyst of the business environment, a supporter of decision making, economic analyst of internal operations, advisor, consultant, reviewer, forecaster, and integrator.

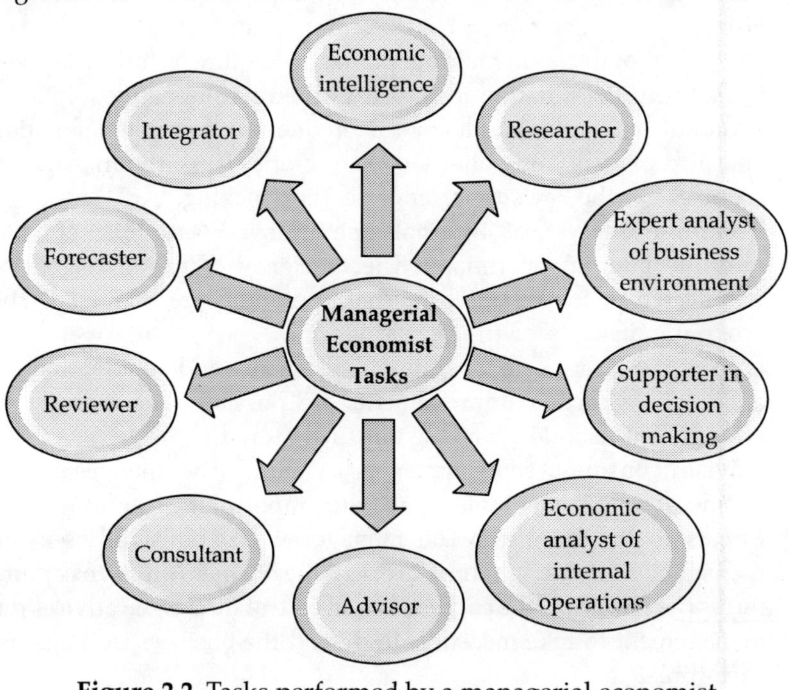

Figure 2.2. Tasks performed by a managerial economist

1. **Economic intelligence:** One of the important tasks of a managerial economist is to collect economic intelligence and provide it to management. Global trends of the business are monitored by various business units and they publish reports periodically. Some reports may be available at free of cost and some are priced ones. These trends in the business environment need to be monitored, and the useful information relating to the present business and the future plans of the company should be identified. The managerial economist is expected to keep in touch with a variety of sources of information. He has to collect, classify, and supply relevant information to the management for taking qualitative decisions.
2. **Researcher:** The managerial economist not only collects facts related to business trends and changes in the environment but also interprets such facts to draw useful conclusions for the business. In case of specific need, the managerial economist carries out research empirically to have a broader understanding of the business problem and to suggest measures for improvement in business.
3. **Expert analyst of business environment:** The managerial economist is considered to be a person with a high level of expertise in analysing the business environment. Economic analysis of the business environment is vital for developing business plans and also in designing strategies to face competition.
4. **Supporter of decision making:** Managers require technical support in analysing the situation and also in evaluating alternative solutions. Economic analysis plays a key role in defining a problem situation and also in evaluating alternative solutions. Thus, the managerial economist is the key supporter of decision making.
5. **Economic analyst of internal operations:** Every business has multiple internal operations. The efficiency of the management is reflected in the way the internal operations are managed. The economic analysis of the performance of each of the operations is important to locate operational problems and to identify the areas where further improvements are possible. The managerial economist is useful in carrying out such exercise.
6. **Advisor:** Business environment is dynamic. The changes in the business environment may generate opportunities or may pose threats to the business. The managerial economist advises the management at the right time to orient the business units, to capture the opportunities at the earliest, and in case of threats, he advises the management to take measures to defend the business unit against such threats.

7. **Consultant:** Many a time the managers are in confusion to decide a course of action to solve a problem. Particularly in strategic decision making managers often feel little uncertain over some estimations. In such circumstances, a managerial economist serves as the right person in providing consultancy to the management.
8. **Reviewer:** The managerial economist conducts periodic reviews of different economic activities of the business unit and submits reports to the relevant managers. These reviews are useful to ensure the functioning of the business unit as per the plans.
9. **Forecaster:** One of the key functions of the managerial economist is to forecast the changes based on past trends. These forecasts are essential for preparing future plans.
10. **Integrator:** Business units perform multiple tasks by way of work distribution to various divisions. Each division prepares plans and executes them as per the goals of the business unit. Sometimes there may be inter-departmental conflicts in setting goals. For example, the production department may set a goal to develop a high-quality low pricing product as an indicator of their high-level performance. The marketing department, on the other hand, may want to introduce a low quality and low price product by sensing the potential demand. The goals of these two departments will conflict. In such situations, the managerial economist acts as an integrator to align the goals of all divisions towards achieving the overall performance of the business unit.

2.4. ROLE OF A MANAGERIAL ECONOMIST

A managerial economist plays a very important role by assisting the management in using the specialised skills and sophisticated techniques required to solve the difficult problems of successful decision making and forward planning. Managerial economist monitors the economic trends that are relevant to the vision and mission of the company. The managerial economist continuously tries to acquire the data and information on the following issues:

1. The economic policy of a country including monetary policy, fiscal policy, tax policy, foreign policy, industrial policy, welfare policy, and policy of prioritised development of the economy.
2. Monitoring national economic trends, prices, changes in national income, output, the volume of trade, the directions of change, opportunities generated, and the emerging threats to the business.
3. Monitoring global economic trends.

4. Analysing demographic studies and identifying shifts in population in terms of age, sex, income, and occupation.
5. Changes in purchasing power of the population, consumption behaviour, and orientation towards spending future incomes.
6. The demand prospects in the existing as well as new markets, the study of market potential and sales potential of the existing as well as proposed products and services.
7. Analysing and projecting market opportunities for the company in domestic and international markets for different products and services.
8. Identifying the factors influencing the demand for products and services in different market segments.
9. Analysing various supply sources to optimise input costs and to ensure uninterrupted supply of inputs.
10. Analysing various cost concepts and suggesting appropriate cost concepts for different products in different situations.
11. Study the intensity of competition, changing trends in competition structures, and suggesting appropriate strategic options to the management.
12. Assisting in the development of perspective plans towards the achievement of long-term goals of the business unit.
13. Closely monitoring the government philosophy and policy to track newly generating opportunities, and also in formulating growth strategies.
14. Helping the management in an optimal allocation of resources towards maximisation of profit.
15. Helping the management in making investment decisions such as capital budgeting, analysing and evaluating sources of funds, credit rating, risk analysis, investment portfolio and so on.
16. Development of production schedules to ensure effective operations by eliminating waste of materials as well as time.
17. Reporting economic trends and relevant information regularly and periodically to different managerial personnel at the right time to make them take decisions effectively. Undertaking research studies on the impact of various policies and programmes of the business unit related to the market and society.
18. Helps in finding an appropriate choice of pricing methods and also in formulating timely pricing strategies for different market segments.
19. Assists management in profit planning and formulating policies for profit maximisation.
20. Helps in designing programmes for corporate social responsibility.

The specific role of a managerial economist can be identified with internal factors as well as external factors. The jobs performed by a managerial economist are presented hereunder:

1. **Internal factors** lie within the scope and operations of a business unit and hence, they are within the control of management. The managerial economist can help the management in making decisions regarding the internal operations of the business unit concerning the problems such as:
   - Identifying the factors influencing the cost structure.
   - Minimisation of costs.
   - Demand forecasting.
   - Pricing and investment plans.
   - Production schedule.
   - Profit budgeting.
   - Adoption of appropriate technology.
   - Sales promotion techniques.
   - Inventory control.
   - Utilisation of manpower.
2. **External factors** lie outside the control of management because they are external to the business unit, and are said to be part of the business environment. The key tasks of a managerial economist are to make an extensive study of the following business environments and external factors that are affecting the business unit's interest in present and future.
   - Level and growth of national income.
   - Influence of the global economy on the domestic economy.
   - Trade cycle.
   - Volume of trade.
   - Balance of payments.
   - Nature and changes in financial markets.
   - Competition scenario at the national and global level.
   - Trends in technology changes.
   - Trends in the availability of factors of production.
   - Research trends.
   - Trade regulations.
   - Exchange regulations.
   - International relations.
   - Cultural and social changes.
   - Environmental laws.
   - Pressure groups and their influence on government policy.

These factors have to be thoroughly analysed by the managerial economist and solutions are to be identified to different problems. A managerial economist has to gather the economic data, analyse the related information about the business environment, and prepare necessary documents on the problems faced by the business unit and industry. In the case of industries moving to rapid technological advancements, the manager may have to make a continuous assessment of the impact of changing technology on the business environment. The manager may need to evaluate the capital budget in the light of short-term and long-term financial, profit and market potential. Thus, in practice, a managerial economist has many roles to perform by undertaking detailed statistical analysis in the business.

2.5. RESPONSIBILITIES OF A MANAGERIAL ECONOMIST

The managerial economist has significant responsibilities towards a business unit. The information provided by the managerial economist forms the basis for managerial decision making. Therefore, the quality of the decision of the management depends upon the quality of the work performed by the managerial economist. The environment is full of opportunities. The dynamic changes in the business environment create many opportunities and also pose threats. If an opportunity is not identified at the right time the business unit may either lose it permanently or may lose its early entrant advantage. Similarly, if the threats are not identified and analysed at the appropriate time the business unit may have to pay a heavy penalty in the form of failure. The responsibility of the managerial economist is to monitor closely such changes and appraise the management to initiate progressive/protective measures. Managerial economist helps the management in achieving internal efficiency as well as external efficiency. Internal efficiency refers to achieving targeted goals on every internal activity whereas external efficiency refers to the activities that are designed to connect the business unit with the external environment. A managerial economist can better serve the management by identifying the main objectives of the business unit and earn the required profit on its invested capital.

Most management decisions necessarily concern the future, which is rather uncertain. Therefore, a managerial economist must identify his responsibility to make a successful forecast. By making the best possible forecasts and through constant efforts to improve, a managerial economist can aim at minimising the risks involved in uncertainties. This enables the management to follow a more orderly course of business planning. The managerial economist should be willing to take fairly positive statements about impending economic developments. These can be based upon the best possible information and analysis. The management's confidence in a managerial economist increases more quickly and thoroughly with a record of successful forecasts, well known in advance and modestly evaluated when the actual results become available.

2.6. SUMMARY

- Managerial economics is fundamentally concerned with the art of making rational choices to yield maximum return out of minimum resources and efforts.
- Managerial economics is the outcome of the integration of two disciplines such as microeconomic theory and methodology, and strategic business management.
- A managerial economist is a person who assists the management in providing and analysing economic information for managerial decision making.
- Decision making is the process of selecting one solution from among two or more alternative course of actions.
- Managerial economist helps the business unit in making plans for the future effectively.
- The tasks performed by a managerial economist are economic intelligence, research, expert analyst of the business environment, a supporter of decision making, economic analyst of internal operations, advisor, consultant, reviewer, forecaster, and integrator.
- A managerial economist plays an important role by assisting the management in using the specialised skills and sophisticated techniques required to solve the difficult problems of successful decision making and future planning.
- The specific role of the managerial economist can be identified with internal factors as well as external factors.
- The internal factors lie within the scope and operations of a business unit and hence, they are within the control of management.
- The external factors lie outside the control of management because they are external to the business unit, and are said to be part of the business environment.
- The responsibility of the managerial economist is to monitor closely such changes and appraise the management to initiate progressive/protective measures.

SHORT ANSWER QUESTIONS

1. What is forward planning?
2. Write a short note on the managerial economist.
3. Define decision making.
4. What is economic intelligence?
5. What is the role of a managerial economist as an integrator?
6. What are the internal factors affecting a business unit?

ESSAY ANSWER QUESTIONS

1. Explain the importance of managerial economics in decision making.
2. What is the significance of a managerial economist in decision making and forward planning? Discuss.
3. Discuss the various tasks performed by a managerial economist.
4. Describe the role of a managerial economist in decision making.
5. Explain the responsibilities of a managerial economist towards a business unit.

FILL IN THE BLANKS

1. The factors which lie within the scope and operations of a business unit are known as __________.
2. The dynamic changes in the business environment create many opportunities and __________.
3. The responsibility of the managerial economist is to monitor changes and appraise the management to initiate __________ measures.
4. The activities that are designed to connect the business unit with the external environment are known as __________.
5. Managerial economics is concerned with the aspects and tools of __________.
6. Risk and __________ can be minimised by making an accurate forecast.

Answers:

1. Internal
2. Threats
3. Progressive
4. External efficiency
5. Economic analysis
6. Uncertainty

MULTIPLE-CHOICE QUESTIONS

1. The process of selecting one solution from among two or more alternative course of actions is called:
   (A) Forward planning (B) Economic analysis
   (C) Decision making (D) Microeconomics
2. The factors that are within the control of the management are known as:
   (A) Internal factors (B) Environmental factors
   (C) External factors (D) Economic factors

3. Which of the following is not an internal operational problem?
   (A) Demand forecasting (B) Production schedule
   (C) Balance of payments (D) Inventory control
4. Which one of the following is not an external factor affecting the business unit?
   (A) Level and growth of national income
   (B) Volume of trade
   (C) International relations
   (D) Pricing and investment plans

Answers:

1. C 2. A 3. C 4. D

REFERENCES

1. Dean, J. (1968). *Managerial Economics.* New Delhi, India: Prentice-Hall of India Private Limited.
2. Dwivedi, D.N. (2015). *Managerial Economics* (8th Edition). New Delhi, India: Vikas Publishing House Pvt. Ltd.
3. Gupta, G.S. (2017). *Managerial Economics.* New Delhi, India: Tata McGraw-Hill.
4. Maheswari, Y. (2012). *Managerial Economics.* New Delhi, India: PHI Learning.
5. Mansfield, E. (1975). *Microeconomics: Theory/Applications.* New York: W.W. Norton & Co.
6. Mithani, D. M. (2010). *Managerial Economics.* Mumbai, India: Himalaya Publishing House Pvt. Ltd.
7. Salvator, D. & Rastogi, S. K. (2016). *Managerial Economics.* New Delhi, India: Oxford.
8. Spencer, M. H. & Siegelman, L. (1959). *Managerial Economics: Decision Making and Forward Planning.* Homewood, Illionous: Richard D., Irwin, Inc.
9. Thomas, C. R. & Maurice, S. C. (2016). *Managerial Economics: Foundations of Business Analysis and Strategy.* New York: McGraw-Hill Education.
10. Varshney, R. L. & Maheswari, K. L. (2014). *Managerial Economics.* New Delhi, India: Sultan Chand & Sons.
11. Webster, T. J. (2003). *Managerial Economics: Theory and Practice.* California, USA: Academic Press (Elsevier).

Chapter

3 Managerial Economics and Business Decisions

LEARNING OBJECTIVES

After studying this chapter, you should be able to understand:

- basic economic tools in managerial economics;
- the meaning of decision making;
- steps involved in the decision making process; and
- factors influencing the managerial decision making process.

3.1. BASIC ECONOMIC TOOLS IN MANAGERIAL ECONOMICS

Economic theory offers a variety of concepts and analytical tools that can be of considerable assistance to the managers for solving their business related problems. The following are the basic economic tools for decision making:

1. Opportunity cost principle
2. Incremental principle
3. Time perspective principle
4. Discounting principle
5. Equi-marginal principle

3.1.1. Opportunity Cost Principle

The opportunity cost principle is useful in decision making as it involves a choice between different alternative courses of action. The opportunity cost is the cost of sacrificing an alternative to that of someone taken as a decision. According to Benham & Benham (2001), "the opportunity cost of anything is the next best alternative could be produced instead by the same factors or by an equivalent group of factors, costing the same amount of money." Opportunity cost, therefore, represents the benefits or revenue foregone by pursuing one course of action rather than another. For example, the opportunity cost of holding Rs. 1000 as cash in hand for one year is equal to the 10% rate of interest which would have been earned had the money been kept as a fixed deposit in a bank. The opportunity cost of the time as an entrepreneur devotes to his own business is equal to the salary he could earn by seeking employment. The opportunity cost of using a machine to produce one product is equal to the earnings forgone which would have been possible from other products. Therefore, it is clear that opportunity cost requires the measurement of sacrifices.

If a decision involves no sacrifice, its opportunity cost is nil. Though the opportunity cost is not recorded in the books of accounts, it is an important consideration in business decisions.

3.1.2. Incremental Principle

The incremental principle is another important concept in managerial economics. Incremental costs are the costs incurred for taking up an expansion project to the existing concern. For example, the cost of creating additional space by constructing one or two floors over the ground floor will be less than the cost of constructing a new building of the same space. In the words of Haynes, Mote & Paul (1970), "the incremental concept involves estimating the impact of the decision on alternatives on costs and revenues, stressing the changes in the total cost and total revenue that result from changes in prices, products, producers, investments or whatever may be at stake in the decision." There are two fundamental concepts involved in incremental principle:

1. *Incremental cost concept* is referred to as the change in total cost due to expansion or taking up a new project.
2. *Incremental revenue concept* is referred to as the change in total revenue resulting from such decisions.

A decision is obviously a profitable one if:

- It reduces cost more than revenues.
- It decreases some costs more than it increases others.
- It increases revenue more than the costs.
- It increases some revenues more than it decreases others.

There are certain limitations to the incremental concept:

- This principle cannot be generalised because the observed behaviour of the firm is always varies.
- This principle can be applied only when there is excess capacity in the concern.
- This principle is applicable only during a short period.

3.1.3. Time Perspective Principle

The time element in economic theory was introduced by Alfred Marshall (1890). The time perspective principle states that the costs and revenues of a managerial decision vary between short period and long period. Therefore, while taking decisions the impact of a decision in the short run on revenues and costs and in the long run on revenues and costs shall be estimated. The important problem in decision making is to maintain the right balance between the long run- and short-run considerations. For example, an order for 5000 units comes to management's attention. The customer is willing to pay Rs. 4 per unit or Rs. 20,000 for the whole lot but not more. The short-run incremental cost (ignoring the fixed cost) is only Rs.3 Therefore, the profit is Re.1 per unit. If the other customers come to know about this low price, they may demand a similarly low price. Such customers may complain of being treated unfairly and feel discriminated against. A decision should take into account both the short-run and long-run effects on revenues and costs and maintain the right balance between long-run and short-run perspectives.

3.1.4. Discounting Principle

Discounting principle is an extension of the concept of time perspective. As the future is unpredictable, there is a lot of risk and uncertainty in future. One of the fundamental ideas in economics is that a rupee tomorrow is worth less than a rupee today. For example, a sum of money on hand can earn a return as compared to the same amount of money available at the end of the period. Therefore, it is referred to as:

$$FV = PV^*(1 + r)^t$$

where,

FV is the future value (future time),

PV is the present value (value at t),

r is the discount (interest) rate, and

t is the time between the future value and present value.

For example, a person is offered a choice to make between a gift of Rs. 1000 today or Rs. 1,000 next year. Naturally, he will choose Rs. 1000 today. This is true for two reasons. First, the future is uncertain and there may be uncertainty in getting Rs. 1000 if the present opportunity is not availed of. Secondly, even if he is sure to receive the gift in future, today's Rs. 1000 can be invested to earn interest, say, at Rs.100 per cent so that, one year after the Rs. 1000 of today will become Rs. 1,100 whereas, if he does not accept Rs.1000 today, he will get Rs.1000 only in the next year. Naturally, he would prefer the first alternative because he is likely to gain by Rs.100 more.

3.1.5. Equi-Marginal Principle

Equi-marginal principle deals with the allocation of available resources among alternative activities. According to this principle, the input should be allocated in such a manner that the value added by the last unit is the same in all cases. This principle provides a base for maximum exploitation of all the inputs of a firm to maximise the profit. This principle is also known as the *principle of maximum satisfaction*. The main objective is to allocate resources where they are most productive. The equi-marginal principle can be applied in different areas of management for eliminating wastage in useless activities, effective budgeting, optimum allocation of capital resources, multi-product pricing, allocating money for research, etc. For instance, a firm has 100 units of labour at its disposal. The firm is engaged in four activities, which need labour services, viz., A, B, C and D. It can enhance any one of these activities by adding more labour but sacrificing in return the cost of other activities. If the value of the marginal product is higher in one activity than another, then it should be assumed that an optimum allocation has not been attained. Hence, it would be profitable to shift labour from low marginal value activity to high marginal value activity, thus increasing the total value of all products taken together.

3.2. DECISION MAKING

Decision making is an essential and primary function of modern management. A manager is expected to make decisions for solving day-to-day problems and to make the business unit ready to take challenges in the future. A decision is a choice from among a set of alternatives. The word 'decision' is derived from the Latin words 'de ciso' which means 'a cutting away or a cutting off' or in a practical sense' to come to a conclusion'. A decision may be defined as "a course of action which is consciously chosen from among a set of alternatives to achieve the desired result." The decision represents a balanced judgment and a commitment to action. Decisions are made to achieve goals through suitable follow-up actions.

3.3. DECISION MAKING PROCESS

The decision making process prescribes some rules and guidelines as to how a decision should be taken or made. This involves many steps logically arranged. Peter Drucker (1955) was the first to strongly advocate the scientific method of decision making in *The Practice of Management*. According to him, the decision making process involves six steps as shown in Figure 3.1.

1. **Identify/Define the Problem**

   Identification of the real problem of a business unit is the first step in the process of decision making. It is rightly said that a problem well defined is a problem half solved. Information relevant to the problem should be gathered, so that critical analysis of the problem is possible. This is how the problem can be diagnosed. A clear distinction should be made between the problem and the symptoms of a problem which may cloud the real issue. Similarly, while diagnosing the real problem a manager should consider the causes of the problem and find out whether they are controllable or uncontrollable. Finally, the manager should be able to identify the variables connected with the problem to take some corrective measures in the form of decisions. The manager must be capable of identifying and eliminating all other variables which are not part of the problem.

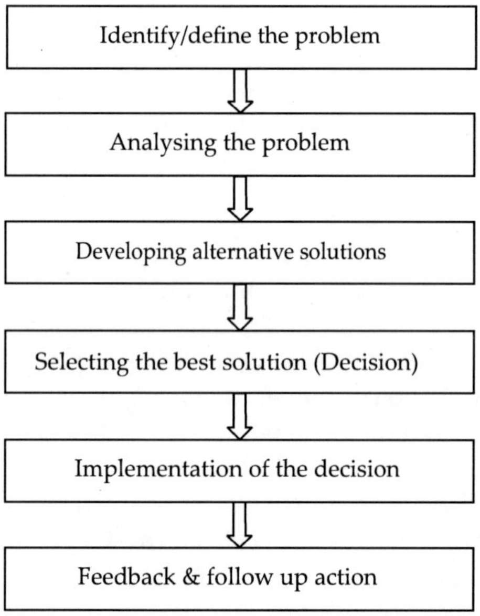

Figure 3.1. Decision making process

2. **Analysing the Problem**
   After defining the problem, the next step in the decision making process is to analyse the problem in depth. The variables identified shall be analysed in the light of the role of each variable in creating the problem. It is necessary to develop a model or a flowchart interconnecting different variables and their contribution to the problem directly or indirectly. The problem analysis provides a clear depiction of the people/ processes that are responsible for the problem and corrective actions are necessary to resolve the problem. The problem diagnosis will be complete when the problem is comprehensively analysed. The problem analysis is useful not only to the decision maker but also to all those involved in the problem in understanding and also getting ready for responding to a solution. While analysing the problem the manager may need to interact with persons at various levels, consult experts in the relevant field, and collect sufficient and relevant information relating to the problem.

3. **Developing Alternative Solutions**
After defining the problem and analysing its nature, the next step is the development of alternative courses of action. It is believed that there will be no problem without a solution and every problem will have multiple solutions. Every alternative solution is capable of solving the problem but the effectiveness of solving a problem differs with each alternative. While developing alternative courses of action the manager has to take into consideration the business unit's goals, its vision, the current business scenario, intensity of competition, expected outcome, chances of disturbance, impact on other departments in the business unit, the acceptability, the desirability and so on.
4. **Selecting the Best Solution**
After developing alternative solutions, the next step in the decision making process is to select an alternative that seems to be most rational for solving the problem. Each alternative needs to be analysed and evaluated in the light of organisational interests. The cost-benefit analysis of each alternative has to be conducted in the light of the present and future perspectives. Non-monetary costs and non-monetary benefits of each alternative also need to be analysed. In the analysis and evaluation of alternatives, the managers use econometric models, statistical and mathematical models, and other relevant techniques. After conducting a systematic analysis of each alternative the best alternative will be selected as the solution to the problem. The best alternative will be given which offers relatively higher benefits to the business unit over sacrifices.
5. **Implementation of the Decision**
After the selection of the best course of action, the next step is to develop an action plan for effective implementation of the decision. Without such action, the decision will remain merely a declaration of good intentions. The action plan involves:
   - Listing the tasks for the execution of thc dccision.
   - Identifying the people responsible to undertake the tasks of listing.
   - Fixing the time frame for execution of the tasks.
   - Fixing up the roles of supervisors and their accountability.
   - Time schedules for periodic reviews.
   - Follow-up.
6. **Feedback and follow-up action**
Feedback is the last step in the decision making process. The manager has to make built-in arrangements to ensure feedback for continuously testing actual developments against the expectations.

It is like checking the effectiveness of the implementation process. Feedback is possible in the form of organised information, reports and personal observations. Feedback is necessary to decide whether the decision already taken should be continued or be modified in the light of changed conditions.

Every step in the decision making process is important and needs proper consideration by managers. This facilitates quality in decision making. The quality of decision making should be always superior. On the other hand, faulty/irrational decisions are always dangerous. Therefore, managers need to follow the decision making process systematically using relevant techniques of analysis and ensure the right decisions at the right time for organisational effectiveness.

3.4. FACTORS INFLUENCING THE DECISION MAKING PROCESS

Many factors influence the decision making process. These factors impact directly or indirectly the quality of decisions. The managers, therefore, should understand the influence of various factors on the problem on hand while taking decisions. The following are the factors that influence the managerial decision making process:

1. Adequacy of data and information
2. Dynamics of the environment
3. Competency of the decision maker
4. Personal bias in decision making
5. Interrelationships with other functions

1. **Adequacy of data and information:** For rational decision making accurate, reliable and complete information about various aspects of the problem under investigation is necessary. The possible future trends can be estimated with the help of such information. However, adequate and reliable information may not be available at the time of decision making. As a result, decisions become defective or irrational. Such a decision may prove to be faulty over time. This is how the decisions become irrational to a certain extent.
2. **Dynamics of the environment:** Decisions are based on information available about various environmental variables. However, the variables are many and complex. They may be related to political, economic, social and other aspects. It is not possible to study all such variables in-depth due to inadequate information or data. This leads to inaccuracy in decision making and the decisions taken may not fully rational.

3. **Competency of the decision maker:** A decision maker should be expert, knowledgeable, intelligent and matured. He needs vision and capacity to imagine a possible future situation. In the absence of such qualities, he may not be able to make rational decisions. Similarly, the decision taken may not be rational if the decision maker fails to follow all necessary steps required for scientific decision making. A hasty decision or decision taken without full use of all mental faculties may not be fully rational. Thus, decisions are likely to be less rational if the decision maker lacks the capacity to make rational decisions.
4. **Personal bias in decision making:** Decision making should be always impartial and also favourable to the organisation. The decision against organisation but favourable to a decision maker or other employees will be unfair. Such a decision will not be rational. Similarly, every decision maker has his background in the form of personal beliefs, attributes, preferences, likes and dislikes and so on. A decision maker is expected to keep these elements away while taking management decisions. However, decisions are not fully rational when such personal element comes in the picture.
5. **Interrelationships with other functions:** Managerial decisions are interlinked and interdependent. A manager has to make adjustments or compromises while making decisions. For example, for reducing the price, some compromise with the quality may be necessary. A manager takes one decision which is rational at the same time makes some compromise in the other decision. As a result, another decision is not likely to be fully reasonable. As business decisions are interlinked, this brings an element of irrationality in some decisions.

3.5. SUMMARY

- The basic economic tools used for managerial decision making are opportunity cost principle, incremental principle, time perspective principle, discounting principle, and equi-marginal principle.
- The opportunity cost principle is useful in decision making as it involves a choice between different alternative courses of action.
- Incremental costs are the costs incurred for taking up an expansion project to the existing concern.
- The time perspective principle states that the costs and revenues of a managerial decision vary between short period and long period.
- Discounting principle states that there is a lot of risk and uncertainty in future. The rupee tomorrow is worth less than a rupee today.

- Equi-marginal principle states that input should be allocated in such a manner that the value added by the last unit is the same in all cases.
- Decision making is an essential and primary function of modern management where a manager is expected to make decisions for solving day-to-day problems and make the business unit ready to take challenges in the future.
- The steps involved in the decision making process are identifying the problem, analysing the problem, developing alternative solutions, selecting the best solution, implementating the decision, and feedback and follow up action.
- The factors influencing managerial decision making process are the adequacy of data and information, dynamics of the environment, competency of the decision maker, the personal bias in decision making, and interrelationships with other functions.

SHORT ANSWER QUESTIONS

1. Define decision making.
2. What is the opportunity cost principle?
3. Explain the discounting principle.
4. Write a short note on time perspective principle.

ESSAY ANSWER QUESTIONS

1. Explain the basic economic tools used in managerial economics.
2. What is the decision making process? Explain the steps involved in the decision making process.
3. Explain the factors influencing the managerial decision making process.
4. What are the principles of managerial economics? How far are these principles followed in the present managerial economic scenario?

FILL IN THE BLANKS

1. The change in total cost due to expansion or taking up a new project is called __________.
2. The principle that deals with the allocation of available resources among alternative activities is called __________.
3. A decision is a choice from among a set of __________.
4. Cost-benefit analysis of each alternative has to be conducted in the light of present and __________ perspectives.
5. Adequate and reliable information may not be available at the time of __________.

Answers:

1. Incremental cost concept
2. Equi-marginal principle
3. Alternatives
4. Future
5. Decision making

MULTIPLE-CHOICE QUESTIONS

1. The cost of sacrificing an alternative to that of someone taken as the decision is called:
   (A) Discounting principle (B) Equi-marginal principle
   (C) Opportunity cost principle (D) Incremental principle
2. The time element in economic theory was introduced by:
   (A) W. W. Haynes (B) Alfred Marshall
   (C) Hanes, Mote and Paul (D) Adam Smith
3. The costs incurred for taking up an expansion project to the existing business unit is:
   (A) Incremental costs (B) Incremental revenue
   (C) Opportunity cost (D) Future costs
4. Peter Drucker advocated the scientific method of decision making in the:
   (A) Principles of management (B) Practice of management
   (C) Economic theory (D) Principles of economics
5. Discounting principle is an extension of the concept of:
   (A) Decision making (B) Economic analysis
   (C) Marginal cost (D) Time perspective

Answers:

1. C 2. B 3. A 4. B 5. D

REFERENCES

1. Baye, Michael R. (1994). *Managerial Economics and Business Strategy.* New York: McGraw-Hill.
2. Benham, A. & Benham, L. (2001). The costs of exchange. *2000: Institutions, Contracts and Organizations: Perspectives from New Institutional Economics.* Edward Elgar, Cheltenham, 367-375.
3. Drucker, P. F. (1955). "Management Science" and the manager. *Management Science,* 1(2), 115-126.
4. Dwivedi, D. N. (2015). *Managerial Economics* (8th Edition). New Delhi, India: Vikas Publishing House Pvt. Ltd.
5. Gupta, G. S. (2017). *Managerial Economics.* New Delhi, India: Tata McGraw-Hill.
6. Haynes, W. W., Mote, V. L. & Paul, S. (1970). *Managerial Economics: Analysis and Cases.* Bombay: Vakils, Feffer & Simons Pvt. Ltd.
7. Marshall, Alfred. (1890). *Principles of Economics.* London: Macmillan.
8. Samuelson, W. F. & Marks, S.G. (2012). *Managerial Economics* (7th Edition*).* Hoboken, New Jersey: John Wiley & Sons, Inc.
9. Spencer, M. H. & Siegelman, L. (1959). *Managerial Economics: Decision Making and Forward Planning.* Homewood, Illionous: Richard D., Irwin, Inc.

Chapter

4 Theories of the Firm

LEARNING OBJECTIVES

After studying this lesson, you should be able to understand:

- the growth, societal, and profit-making objectives of a business unit;
- profit maximisation theory of a business unit;
- Marris' growth rate maximisation and Williamson's managerial theories;
- Baumol's sales revenue maximisation theory; and
- Simon's satisficing and Cyert & Marks behavioural theories.

4.1. INTRODUCTION

Theory of a firm refers to the purpose of the business unit for its existence, goals and objectives, behaviour, performance, identity, market share, the vision and mission and the strategies to achievement. Economists are often critical in understanding the theory of the firm. Many studies facilitated the knowledge of description and analysis of market performance. But, in understanding the behaviour and organisation of business units the economists face problems. In managing a business unit, the managers focus on problem solving and forward planning. They try to find the best ways to allocate scarce resources among competing uses to optimise the results.

The main function of a business unit is to use scarce productive resources to produce products/services demanded by the market. It is done by converting productive inputs into consumable or usable outputs in the form of products/services. The vision and mission of the business unit formulated by the owners will guide the manner in which productive resources are combined and organised to achieve organisational objectives. The management of the business unit selects the productive resources and design the activities as per the plan of production and marketing of products/services. For taking up the production process, the business unit needs many resources such as capital, human resources, technology, organisational system, equipment, materials and spare parts, etc. Mobilising the resources at the right time and to the right cost is a challenging task. Further, it has to face competition from the producers of similar products or substitutes in the market. The changing business environment further makes the business unit to introduce changes to either exploit opportunities or to face threats. Thus, managing the business unit is to manage scarce resources for achieving optimal business results.

As per the traditional theory of economics a business unit mobilises the required resources and transform them into products/services as demanded by consumers. The volume of trade of business units depends upon the demand for such products/services at a given point of time. Large size business units have economies of scale and therefore, they can produce at a lower cost compared to small business units. The cost of production is governed by the technology used, and the quantity produced. The prices of the products/services are influenced by market structure. The ultimate aim of the business unit is to make profits. Profit is the difference between the revenue and the costs. Economists assume that profit maximisation is the main objective of the business unit. The theory of the firm has been developed with an assumption that the objective of rational business units is profit maximisation. They pursue this objective under technical and market constraints.

4.2. OBJECTIVES OF A BUSINESS UNIT

Every business unit will set its business objectives and design all its activities towards achieving the objectives. The objectives demonstrate the purpose for which the business unit is established. The objectives of a business unit can be broadly categorised as:

1. Growth objectives
2. Societal objectives
3. Profit making objectives

4.2.1. Growth Objectives

No business unit prefer to stay at the same level. They want to grow further and further. Growth orientation is the fundamental focus of every business unit. Assessing growth opportunities includes planning new businesses, downsizing, and terminating older businesses, is the first step in this direction. Growth opportunities can be of three types. Business units need to identify opportunities for growth within the current businesses. This approach is called a search for *intensive opportunities*. Business units may find *integrative opportunities* wherein they identify opportunities to build or acquire businesses related to current businesses. In certain situations, they may explore *diversification opportunities* to add attractive unrelated businesses. These three approaches are not mutually exclusive. Business units may work out for exploring these opportunities simultaneously.

1. **Intensive growth:** One of the main objectives of a business unit is to find various opportunities for improving the existing business. It considers the strategic growth opportunities in terms of existing products and new products, and existing markets and new markets.

First, the business units can opt for the *market penetration strategy* to identify the market share of its existing products in current markets. Secondly, they may adopt a *market development strategy* to find or develop new markets for existing products. Thirdly, they may use a *product development strategy* for developing new products or new product features of potential interest to its existing markets. They can offer a single product in two or more quality variations. Later, the business units can review the potential opportunities to develop new products for new markets in a diversification strategy. Therefore, intensive growth strategies offer several opportunities for business units to increase their sales and achieve the desired growth level.

2. **Integrative growth:** A business unit can achieve growth by increasing sales and profits through backward, forward, or horizontal integration within the industry. *Backward integration* means that a business unit acquires one or more of its suppliers, to gain more control. *Forward integration* means that a business unit acquires some wholesalers or retailers, especially if they are highly profitable to achieve greater control over the distribution of its products. *Horizontal integration* means that a business unit acquires one or more competitors to become a major supplier or leader in product supply.
3. **Diversification growth:** Diversification growth is preferred when good opportunities exist outside the scope of the present businesses. In the dynamic business environment, some new businesses may become attractive in terms of profit and growth. Business units may desire to exploit the emerging opportunities to strengthen the business though they do not fall under the current business portfolio. Several types of diversifications are possible.
   (a) The business unit can follow the *concentric strategy.* Under this strategy, business units introduce new products which are synergic with production technology or marketing of the existing product lines. For example, the business unit is having established business in childcare products, it can introduce mother-care products using concentric strategy. The same distribution network and brand image can be used to promote new products.
   (b) The business unit can follow the *horizontal strategy.* Under this strategy, business units introduce unrelated new products to current customers. For example, if a mobile phone manufacturer starts producing laptops, mixer and grinders, dryers, etc., the business unit is adopting a horizontal strategy.

(c) The business unit can follow *conglomerate strategy.* Under this strategy, the business units introduce altogether entirely new businesses that have no relationship between current business and its resources. For example, a business unit producing footwear may enter the software industry.

4.2.2. Societal Objectives

Business units cannot run in isolation with society. The requirements of the society are the foundational base for the existence of a business. Therefore, profit making or profit maximisation cannot be the sole objective of the business. They have to pay back or share the benefits with the society. Many business units realised that societal acceptance is essential for the survival and growth of any business in the long run. Business units should have societal objectives with a clear direction of offering benefits to the society. It is rational to the society to expect some benefits from the business units as they use scarce resources belong to society. Business units should not indulge in harming the society by way of introducing harmful products, unfair practices, and unwholesome activities. In such cases, there is a danger of public reaction against the business unit. The societal objectives of a business unit include:

1. New product innovations that enhance the quality of life of consumers.
2. The utilisation of natural resources optimally by avoiding waste and allocating them to appropriate and correct usage.
3. Creation of customer value in terms of utility, perception and possession.
4. Employment generation through extension and expansion.
5. Protecting and preserving the environment.
6. Adhering to social norms and promoting values and ethics.

4.2.3. Profit Making Objectives

Many businessmen believe that the core philosophy of business units is to make profits. They try to put all possible efforts to generate higher value than what is expended in the production process. Such excess value is called profit. Profit objectives of all business units are not similar. They vary according to a variety of situations. Supply, demand, innovativeness, competition, government policy, nature of the product, legal protection, market segment, brand image, etc., are some of the factors influencing the profit objectives. Broadly profit objectives can be classified into the following categories:

- Profit maximisation in the short run.

- Profit maximisation in the long run.
- Revenue for survival.

4.3. PROFIT MAXIMISATION THEORY

The traditional objective of business units is profit maximisation. The theories based on the objective of profit maximisation are derived from the neo-classical marginalist theory of the business unit. The common concern of such theories is to predict optimal price and output decisions which maximise the profit of the business unit. In essence, the theories based on the profit maximisation suggest that business unit seeks to make the difference between total revenue and total cost as large as possible. However, one pertinent question at this point is: do the business units aim at maximising profit in the long run or the short run? The basic valuation model of the business unit is based on the fundamental assumption that the business unit seeks to maximise its profit in the long run.

According to this model, a business unit seeks to maximise its discounted present value. To arrive at an estimate of discounted present value of the business unit, future profits are reduced by a discount factor or weight, to make future profits comparable with present profits. The major problem in this model is that the choice of weights that largely depends on the time preference taken by the business unit, i.e., comparison of present profits to future profits.

4.3.1. Short-run and Long-run Profit Maximisation Hypothesis

The short-run profit maximisation hypothesis is that the business unit maximises profit at a point where marginal cost (MC) and marginal revenue (MR) of producing and selling a product are equal. The additional revenue generated by selling an additional unit is called marginal revenue (MR) and the additional cost incurred for producing an additional unit is called marginal cost (MC). Thus, a business unit maximises profit when MR = MC. Based on this condition, if the MC curve intersects the MR curve from below, the total profit (i.e., $\pi = TR - TC$) will be maximum. However, if the periods are dependent (i.e., if current decisions or actions affect future decisions of the business unit) short-run profit maximisation may lead to inaccurate decisions due to lack of provision for the future. For instance, a business unit can make higher profits at present by not replacing capital goods, delaying payment, etc., all of which will surely reduce the size of future profits.

By contrast, if profits are independent in different periods, long-run profit maximisation would simply amount to maximising the series of short-term profits. But such a situation does not prevail in the real world. All business units which have made huge capital investments will observe that profits in different periods are interdependent. There is a trade-off between short-term and long-term profit. If more or a steady flow of profit is derived in the long run, adequate provision has to be made for depreciation (capital consumption) and short-term dues are to be cleared. If more profit is to be made in the short run, some long-term profit has to be sacrificed.

The short-run profit maximisation hypothesis is illustrated in Figure 4.1. The total cost (TC) and total revenue (TR) are shown on the Y-axis and output on the X-axis. The business unit produces OQ level of output for which TR = OR and TC = OP and the gap between the two (P & R) is maximum. Q is indeed the profit maximising level of output. The slope of the TR curve measures MR and the slope of the TC curve measures MC. At points A and B, two curves have the same slope. Thus, at OQ, MR = MC. This can be verified by passing two tangents, one through A and the other through B and ensuring that they are parallel.

The total cost curve is always nonlinear and is not related to the market structure. The slope of the revenue curve depends on the elasticity of demand and is dependent on the market structure. Since most real-life markets are imperfectly competitive, it is assumed that the revenue function is nonlinear. Subtracting the TC from TR, the total net profit curve (π) is derived which cuts the X-axis where TR = TC. Thus, the top of the profit hill is reached when Q is the level of output that is produced and sold.

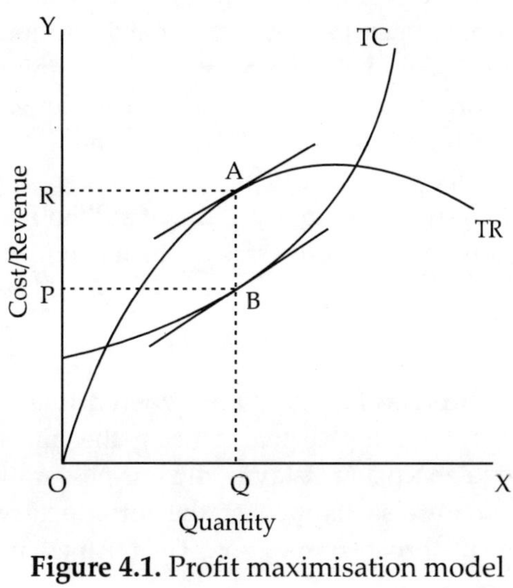

Figure 4.1. Profit maximisation model

In Figure 4.1 the business unit produces OQ units and makes total revenue of OR by charging a price of OROQ. At this stage, the total profit is 'PR' which is maximum. The hypothesis is based on several assumptions. The decision maker is supposed to have relevant information about cost and revenue based on which an optimal decision can be made. Secondly, the decision maker is assumed to have sufficient power to take the decision and implement it appropriately. However, the external or market forces that are beyond the control of a business unit are the major determinants for making optimal decisions on price and quantity.

The equilibrium of the profit maximising business unit occurs simultaneously on the input and output sides. A business unit which is maximising its profit by choosing an output where marginal cost (MC) equals marginal revenue (MR) is simultaneously minimising the cost of producing that output or maximising the output subject to cost constraint. From the above hypothesis, two important rationales may be provided for maximising profit.

First, in a single owner business unit, where the entrepreneur is both owner and manager, maximising profit will maximise his income. For a given amount of effort, this is considered to be rational behaviour, irrespective of the structure of the market or competition. If the magnitude of profit varies with the amount of entrepreneurial effort expended, and effort has negative utility for the entrepreneur, rational behaviour would dictate something else. He must find an optimal trade-off between the effort and the profit to maximise entrepreneurial utility which is unlikely to lead to maximum profit.

Secondly, the impact of competition from rival business units forces the entrepreneur to maximise profits. Profit maximisation, therefore, is not an aspect of discretionary behaviour but rather a compelled necessity. The entrepreneur is forced to maximise profit for his long-term survival. Thus, the justification for profit maximisation depends upon the nature of competition. If competition is absent (as in monopoly) there are no such pressures, although the previous argument still holds. Under highly competitive conditions the entrepreneur has to maximise profit just for survival.

4.3.2. Income for Survival

Business units may face certain situations wherein the place of profit making survival becomes the objective. During the times of recession, business units try to keep up a just stay in the business until the situation turns favourable. It may also happen at the introductory stage of the business unit, facing cut-throat competition. The business units try to earn at least a minimum revenue that can meet their variable expenses. This objective is to protect the interests of shareholders and the employees. The present and future returns depend on the continued existence of the business unit.

4.3.3. Criticism of Profit Maximisation Theory

The profit maximisation hypothesis developed during 1874-1890 by Leon Walras, W. S. Jevons and Alfred Marshall is the basis of the neoclassical (marginalist) theory of the business unit. From the early 1930s, it has been subject to various criticisms. Critics argued that profit maximisation is not the only objective of a business unit. Modern business units and their managers also pursue certain other objectives. Thus, profit maximisation as the only objective of a business unit is no longer an acceptable hypothesis. Being dissatisfied with both of the justifications, modern economists and management specialists have suggested various alternatives to profit maximisation. The following arguments bear relevance in this context:

1. ***The emergence of oligopoly.*** In the inter-war period, it became increasingly apparent, especially in industrially advanced countries, that the modern economy was dominated by an oligopoly, a market structure characterised by the existence of a few large business units. In several industries, the structure has become gradually more and more concentrated (through a merger or amalgamation) so that a few large (dominant) business units accounted for a major portion of an industry's output. In such environments, there was hardly any pressure on each business unit to maximise profit independently. Instead business unit arrived at joint profit maximisation through such devices as collusions and cartels. Alternatively, the pressure from rival business units was not strong enough to dictate profit maximisation as an inevitable objective for each business unit.
2. ***Separation of ownership from management.*** In 1932, Berle and Means challenged, through their pioneering work, the argument that the business unit would seek to maximise profits (even though it was necessary due to competitive pressure). They discarded profit maximisation as a rational behaviour because of an alleged break-in the identity of the purpose of the manager and his business unit.

4.4. MARRIS' GROWTH RATE MAXIMISATION THEORY

The managerial theory of the business unit was introduced by Robin Marris in 1963. The theory states that the managers do not prefer to maximise profits rather they seek to maximise the balanced growth rate of the business unit. Maximisation of balanced growth rate means maximisation of the rate of growth of demand for products and the rate of growth of capital supply. According to the theory, the balanced growth rate is:

$$G = G_d = G_C$$

where,

G refers to balanced growth

G_d refers to the growth rate of demand for the product

G_C refers to the rate of growth of the capital supply

The ultimate goal of a manager is to maximise the balanced growth (G). Accordingly, there are two constraints in maximising the balanced growth rate such as managerial constraint and financial constraint. Managerial constraint refers to the strength of the managerial team and their skills. Financial constraint refers to the three ratios like debt-asset ratio, liquidity ratio, and retention ratio. Debt-asset ratio (D/A) refers to the relationship between debt (D) and total assets (A). Liquidity ratio (L/A) shows the relationship between liquid assets (L) and the total assets (A). Retention ratio (π_r/π) refers to the relationship between retained profits (π_r) and the total profits (π). These financial variables determine the job security of the managers. When the financial ratios cross the limits, the business unit is exposed to the risk of being acquired by others and also influence on mangers job security. Therefore, managers need to consider job security constraint while making business decisions. Some variables in Marris' model particularly in the manager's utility function such as salaries, status, and power are strongly correlated with the rate of growth of demand for the products. Therefore, managers' salaries will be higher and they will have more power and value. The higher the salaries and power, the faster will be the rate of growth of the business units. On the other hand, the higher growth of a business unit also ensures better job security to the managers.

Therefore, the utility of the mangers (U_M) function can be stated as:

$$U_M = f(G_D, S)$$

where,

U_M refers to the utility of mangers

G_D refers to the rate of growth of demand for the output of the business unit

S refers to the measure of job security of managers

On the other hand, the utility of owners (U_O) depends on the growth of capital supply which is positively correlated with the growth of profits. Thus, the owner's utility function can be stated as:

$$U_O = f(G_C)$$

where,

U_O refers to the utility of owners

G_C refers to the rate of growth of capital supply

According to the model, the growth rate of capital is subject to the constraint set by the capacity of the managerial team. The job security of the manger is determined by the weighted average of three financial ratios, viz., debt-asset ratio, liquidity ratio, and profit retention ratio. These financial ratios reflect the manager's financial policy. Further, there is a saturation level for job security. After this saturation level, marginal utility from the extra job security is zero, and below this level, marginal utility from extra job security is infinite. With this constraint of job security, managerial utility function becomes:

$$U_M = (G_D)\,\bar{S}$$

where,

U_M refers to the utility of managers

$\bar{S}$ refers to the job security that acts as a constraint for utility maximisation of managers

G_D refers to the rate of growth of demand for the output of the business unit

Managers maximise their utility, i.e., growth of demand for output subject to this job security constraint. Financial constraint is reflected in the job security constraint of a manager. The manager's utility (U_M) function includes variables such as salaries, status, power and job security, while the owner's utility (U_O) function oincludes variables such as profits, the volume of output, size of capital, share of the market and public image. Thus, managers want to maximise their utility, while the owners seek the maximisation of their utility.

$U_M = f$ (salaries, power, status, job security)

$U_O = f$ (profits, capital, output, market share, public esteem)

Marris states that the difference between the goals of managers and the goals of the owners may not be very wide due to the reason that most variables appearing in both functions are strongly correlated with a single variable, i.e., size of the business unit. Thus, in the Marris model, the managerial team constraint and the job security constraint are reflected in a financial constraint.

4.4.1. The Managerial Constraint

Marris admits that there exists a definite limit on the rate of efficient managerial expansion. There is a ceiling to the growth of the business unit set by the capacity of its managerial team at a given point of time. The managerial capacity can be increased by hiring new managers, but there is a definite limit to the rate at which management can expand and remain competitive. The decision making and the planning of business activities are the results of teamwork involving the manager's cooperation. Coordination and cooperation require experience. A new manager needs time to get fully ready before joining the team for the efficient functioning of the business unit. Thus, although the managerial ceiling is diminishing gradually, the process cannot be speeded up.

Research and development (R&D) department which contributes new ideas and new products plays an important role in the growth of a business unit. The kind of investment and the expertise of the human resource employed, the kind of positive teamwork determines the quality outcome of the department. Thus, the managerial constraint and the R&D capacity of the business unit set limits to the growth rate of demand (G_D) and the growth rate of capital supply (G_C).

4.4.2. The Job Security Constraint

Managers of business units also will have concern for their job security. They prefer to enter into service contracts as a protective measure. They do not take high-risk decisions with a fear that if something goes wrong they may be dismissed by the owners. On the other hand, if there is a downfall in the performance of the company, the shareholders may change the managers or may sell the business unit. In both cases, the manager's job will be at risk. Therefore, the managers try to take only calculated risks in decision making. They do not involve risky investments. They try to ensure optimal levels in leverage ratio, liquidity ratio, and retention ratio.

4.4.3. Equilibrium of the Business Unit

The managers aim at the maximisation of their utility, which is a function of the growth of demand for the products of the business unit. The shareholders aim at the maximisation of their utility which assumes to be a function of the rate of growth of the capital supply. A business unit is said to be in equilibrium when the maximum balanced growth rate is attained. Thus,

$$G_{(max)} = G_D = G_C$$

In operational terms, it is redefined as:

$$G_D = f(d, k) \text{ and } G_C = \bar{r}(P)$$

where,

d refers to a diversification of product

k refers to the success rate of new products

$\bar{r}$ refers to financial security ratio assumed to be a constant proportion of profit (P)

4.4.4. Criticism of the Model

The managerial theory is regarded as an important theory of the firm as it introduces financial ratios as decision variables for setting the goals of the business unit. An important contribution of the theory is that it provides for reconciliation between utility functions of the managers and owners. However, this theory is criticised on certain grounds. The theory assumes that the cost, price and profit are given. The critics disagree by stating this as unrealistic. They say that price determination by the business unit is ignored. Further, the theory is criticised on the ground that the theory has not taken into consideration the interdependency of decisions of business units, particularly under oligopolistic market conditions.

4.5. WILLIAMSON'S MANAGERIAL THEORY

A full-fledged managerial theory of the business unit has been put forward by O.E. Williamson (1963). He emphasised that managers are motivated by their self-interest and they maximise their utility function. The objective of utility maximisation by the managers is subject to the constraint that after-tax profits are large enough to pay acceptable dividends to the shareholders and also to pay for economically necessary investments. It may, however, be pointed out that utility maximisation by the self-interest seeking managers is possible only in a corporate form of business units where there is a separation between ownership and management.

According to Williamson, the utility function of the self-seeking managers depends on salaries and other forms of monetary compensation, number of staff under their control , management slack, and the magnitude of discretionary investment expenditure by the manager.

4.5.1. Williamson's Managerial Discretional Model

Williamson has distinguished the three concepts of profits, viz., actual profits (π), reported profits (π_r) and minimum profits (π_o). Actual profits are the differences between total revenue (R) and production costs (C) minus expenditure on staff (S). Thus, it can be denoted as:

$$\pi = R - C - S$$

where,

R represents the total sales revenue
C represents the production cost
S represents the staff expenditure

Reported profit (π_r) is the difference between actual profits (π) and non-essential managerial expenditure as represented by management slack (M). Thus, it is denoted as:

$$\pi_r = \pi - M$$

where,

π_r represents the reported profit

π represents the actual profit

M represents the management slack

Since, $$\pi = R - C - S$$

$$\pi_r = R - C - S - M$$

Minimum profits (π_o) are the amount of profits (after tax) which are required to be paid as acceptable dividends to satisfy the shareholders. If the shareholders do not get reasonable dividends, they may sell their shares, thereby exposing the business unit to the risk of being taken over by others or they will vote for the dismissal of the top management. Both of these actions by the shareholders will reduce the job security of the top managerial team. Hence, managers must provide minimum profits in the form of dividends to satisfy the shareholders to promote their job security. To meet this goal, the reported profits must be large enough to be equal to the minimum profit (π_o) plus the tax to be paid to the government. Thus,

$$\pi_r \times \pi_O + T$$

Discretionary profits (π_D) are the actual profits minus minimum profits and tax to be paid. Thus, it can be represented as:

$$\pi_D = \pi - \pi_O - T$$

where,

π_D represents the discretionary profits

π represents the actual profits

π_O represents the minimum profits

T represents the tax to be paid to the government

Discretionary profits should be carefully distinguished from discretionary investment. Discretionary profits are the amount left after minimum profits (π_O) and tax (T) are deducted from actual profits (π_D) = ($\pi - \pi_O$ – T). The discretionary investment (I_D) is the result of subtracting reported profits from minimum profits and tax. Thus, discretionary investment (I_D) is represented as:

$$I_D = \pi_r - \pi_O - T$$

where,

π_R represents the reported profits

π_O represents the minimum profits

T represents the tax to be paid

Since the difference between reported profits (π_R) and actual profits (π) arises due to management slack, discretionary profits can be stated as:

$\pi_D = I_D$ + Expenditure due to management slack

Thus, if management slack is zero

$$\pi_R = \pi \text{ and } \pi_D = I_D$$

4.5.2. Managerial Utility Maximisation

As stated above, Williamson clubs the first two variables, salary and other monetary compensations received by the manager and the number of staff under his control into a single variable. Therefore, the utility of a manager is a function of the following three variables:

$$U = U(S, M, I_D)$$

where,

U represents utility function

S represents the monetary expenditure on staff including salaries of the managerial team

M represents the management slack

I_D represents the amount of discretionary investment

Maximisation of the utility function is subject to the minimum profit constraint. Therefore, the level of profits incurred must be such to pay satisfactory profit to shareholders and pay for economically necessary investment (not included in discretionary investment). In Williamson's managerial model, price is regarded as a function of output, the expenditure on staff and a demand shift parameter. Thus,

$$P = P(X, S, E)$$

where,

P represents the price function

X represents the output level in a period

S represents the expenditure on staff

E represents the demand shift parameter

To present a simplified Williamson's managerial model, it is assumed that expenditure on account of managerial slack (M) is zero. Given this, the managerial utility function becomes

$$U_M = f(S, I_D)$$

When management slack (M) is zero, then reported profits equal actual profits, then

$$I_D = \pi - \pi_O - T$$

Substituting this formulation in managerial utility function:

$$U_M = f(S, I_D)$$

Thus, the following is the simplified model of managerial function which has to be maximised subject to a constraint. Thus,

$$\text{Maximise } U_M = f(S, I_D)$$
$$\text{Subject to } \pi_r \geq \pi_O + T$$

However, there is substitutability between S and I_D. Given the actual profit (π), S can be increased only by reducing I_D, and vice versa. Therefore, in an attempt to maximise their utility function, managers find an optimum combination of S and I_D. This is the point of equilibrium. Thus, Williamson model lays stress on the managerial discretion in determining not only output and price but also the level of staff expenditure and managerial emoluments.

Williamson's model also suffers from certain weaknesses. This model does not deal satisfactorily with the problem of the interdependence of business units under oligopolistic competition. This model is applicable only where rivalry is not strong. In the case of strong rivalry, this model does not hold appropriate.

4.6. BAUMOL'S SALES REVENUE MAXIMISATION

W.J. Baumol proposed the maximisation of sales revenue model in 1959 as an alternative model to profit maximisation objective. The sales revenue maximisation model exposes the dichotomy between ownership and management in large business units. The dichotomy allows managers to set their goals other than profit maximisation goal. The assumption is that given an opportunity, the managers may choose to maximise their utility function. The reasons for managers' utility function of maximisation through sales revenue are:

1. Managers' salary and other benefits are more closely related to sales revenue than to profits.
2. Banks and financial institutions lay great emphasis on sales revenue while financing business units.
3. The trend in sales revenue is the indicator of the performance of the business unit. It helps in handling the employees' problem of awarding efficiency and penalising inefficiency.
4. Increasing sales revenue enhances the prestige, status, and perks of managers while profits go to the owners.
5. Managers find profit maximisation a difficult objective to fulfil consistently over time and at the same level, as profits may fluctuate with changing conditions.
6. Growing sales strengthen the competitive spirit of the business unit in the market, whereas, decreasing sales may put the survival of the business at risk.

4.6.1. Single Product Model without Advertising

Sales maximisation implies achieving the highest level of total revenue. Generally, the total revenue equals the number of units (Q) multiplied by price (P) per unit (Q*P). The total revenue curve is derived as per the demand curve using different prices and related demand. In Figure 4.2,

TR represents the total revenue curve. Due to downward sloping demand curve, TR curve reaches its peak for output level (Q_3) where the change in revenue due to one more unit of sale of output is equal to zero, that is, the slope of the curve is zero. The sales beyond this point lead to a reduction in total revenue (TR). TC represents the total cost curve. The difference between TR and TC is the profit which is represented below in the profit curve. At output level, Q_1 and Q_4 profits are zero as TR = TC at both those levels of output. The profit curve reaches its peak at Q_2 where the difference between TC and TR is highest and the slopes of both curves are same as evident from the parallel line drawn at point L and M. At this level of output, firm earns P_1 level of profit.

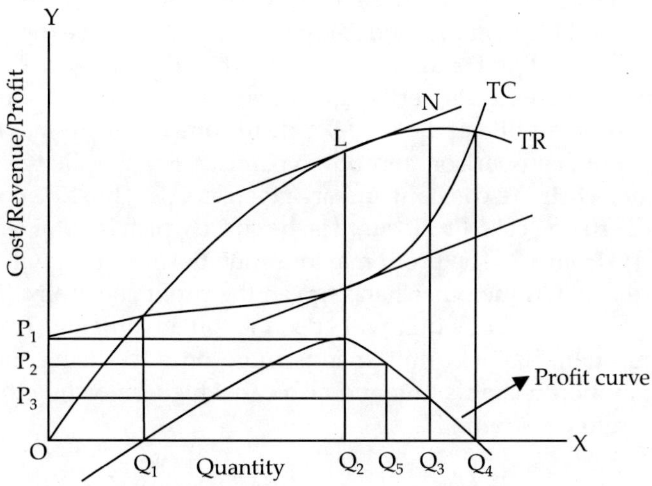

Figure 4.2. Single product model without advertising

In Baumol's model, the business unit is a sale maximiser, but it must also earn a minimum level of profit. The business unit needs minimum profits to support future sales. Further, these profits are essential for a business unit for paying dividends on share capital and for meeting other financial requirements. Thus, minimum profits serve as a constraint on the maximisation of a business unit's revenue. Maximum sale revenue depends on the minimum acceptable level of profit. If the business unit acceptance profit is P_2, the business unit will produce Q_3 which maximises sales revenue. At this level, the business unit earns a P_2 level of profit. If minimum acceptance level of profit increase and it is P_3, in this case, the business unit is not able to earn maximum sales revenue because at this level business unit will produce Q_5 level of output which is less than Q_3 that maximises total revenue. Profit maximising level of output is Q_2 and sales maximising business unit will produce a higher level of output compared to profit maximiser. The sales maximiser will sell the product at a lower price as compared to the profit maximiser. The sale maximiser will earn a lower profit as compared to profit maximiser.

4.6.2. Single Product Model with Advertising

Baumol has further shown that the profit constraint under sales maximisation is also effective in advertising and thereby increases the business unit's revenue. One key assumption of the model is that revenue always increases with advertising expenditure. Therefore, it is not possible to attain sales maximising equilibrium without profit constraint as a business unit can always increase its sales by increasing advertising. In Figure 4.3, expenditure on advertising is taken on the horizontal axis, and total revenue, costs and profit on the vertical axis. TR is the total revenue curve, TC is the total cost curve, and A represents advertising expenditure.

An oligopolist will prefer to increase its sale by advertising rather than by a cut in prices. Increased advertising always increases sales of a business unit as per the assumption of the model. Sale maximiser always has higher advertising cost in comparison to profit maximiser. For simplicity assume that production costs are constant and are given as C_1C. Thus, TC contains costs plus advertising cost. Profit curve is the curve which is obtained from subtracting TC from TR. The profit maximisation business unit will spend A_1 on advertising. On the other hand, given the profit constraint (P_1) the sales maximisation business unit will spend A_2 on advertising. Thus, the sales maximisation business unit spends more on advertising than the profit maximisation business unit and also earns higher revenue than the latter at the profit constraint, P_1.

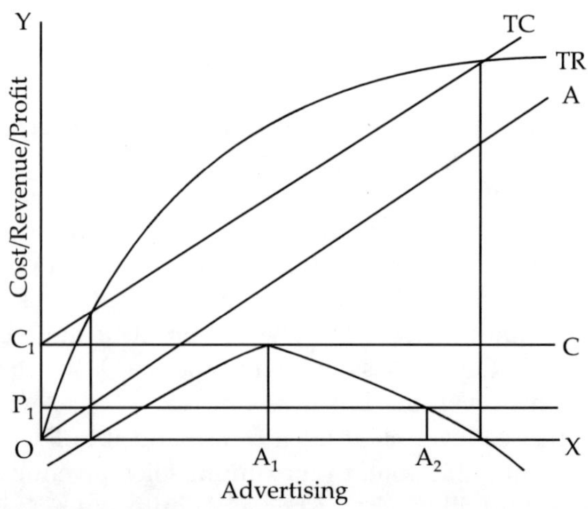

Figure 4.3. Single product model with advertising

4.6.3. Arguments in favour of Sales Maximisation Objective

1. **More realistic:** The goal of maximisation of sales is a more realistic one. The business units accord more importance to the goal of sales maximisation than profit maximisation. It is so because the success of a business unit is generally judged by its total sales.
2. **More practical:** Revenue maximisation theory is more practical. It is so because the goal of revenue (sales) maximisation leads to more production which, in turn, leads to a fall in price. As a result, consumers' welfare is promoted.
3. **Availability of loans:** At the time of sanctioning loan to a business unit, financial institutions mainly consider its sales. Prospects of loans are bright for such business units as have large total sales.
4. **Strong position in the market:** Maximum sales of a business unit represent its strong position in the market. Sales of a business unit will be large only when consumers like its products. Business units will enjoy more competitive power with a larger share of total sales in the market. All these features are indicative of the progress of the business unit.
5. **More advantageous to managers:** Sales maximisation is advantageous to managers as their credibility enhances in the market. Maximum sales are a reflection of the competence of the managers. It has a favourable effect on their wages. Business units are in a position to offer higher wages to the employees. Consequently, employer-employee relations become more cordial. It is the constant endeavour of the managers to maximise the sales of the firm after attaining a given level of profit.

4.6.4. Criticism of Sales Maximisation Model

Baumol's sales maximisation hypothesis is criticised on the following reasons:

1. The evidence regarding the empirical validity of sales revenue maximisation objective is uncertain.
2. If total cost function (TC) intersects the total revenue function (TR) before it reaches its maximum level, Baumol's theory collapses.
3. In the long run, sales maximisation and profit maximisation objectives converge into one. In the long run, sales maximisation tends to yield only normal profits which turn out to be maximum under competitive conditions.

4.7. SIMON'S SATISFYING BEHAVIOUR MODEL

The satisfying behaviour model was proposed by H. A. Simon in 1955. This model states that while taking business decisions the managers are constrained by factors like incomplete information, inadequate data and uncertain future. The management determines a 'satisfactory aspiration level' based on its experience and judgment about future uncertainty. Therefore, they seek the second-best solution which is called satisfying behaviour. The satisfying behaviour model suggests that a manager will aim for a satisfactory level of profit maximisation and a satisfactory level of cost rather than cost minimisation.

If the satisfactory aspiration level is achieved easily, the expiration level is revised upwards. If the satisfactory aspiration level is not achieved, the management indulges in 'search behaviour' to find the reasons for the deviations from the aspiration level. Simon suggests that if the satisfactory state is not achieved even by lowering the aspiration level and the search behaviour, the behaviour pattern of managers becomes that of apathy or aggression.

The **advantages** of this theory are:

1. The model explains a certain real-world situation. For example, the business units generally use make-up pricing to generate reasonable profits rather resort to marginal cost pricing to maximise profits.
2. The model is consistent with the theory of motivation where human action is a function of drives and it terminates when drives are satisfied.

The **disadvantages** of this theory are:

1. The model lacks correctness and complete information. It does not identify the types of information that are sought by a business unit and the nature of 'incompleteness' the information suffer from.
2. The model fails to appreciate the difference between information about conditions and information about changes in conditions. It is the information regarding changes in conditions that is vitally more important.
3. 'Satisfactory level' is a subjective concept. It depends on many factors like industry, the economic situation, the nature of top management, the perception of the decision makers, etc.

4.8. CYERT AND MARCH BEHAVIOURAL THEORY

The behavioural model of the business unit proposed by Simon was subsequently elaborated by R.M. Cyert and J.E. March in 1963. This theory focuses on the way decisions are made in the large multi-product business units under uncertainty in an imperfect market. The theory is based on the internal structure of such business units, analyses the organisational problems of such business units and the effects of these problems on the managerial decision making process. They explain the difference in reactions of different business units, to the same set of external forces in terms of the differences in internal organisational factors.

Cyert and March consider the business unit as a multi-goal, multi-decision organisational coalition. It consists of various groups associated with the business unit like managers, workers, shareholders, customers, suppliers, bankers, lawyers, accountants and so on. Each group has its own set of goals. They point out that the most significant groups in the decision making are: shareholders and workers. The behaviour theory of the business unit starts with a recognition that individual members of the coalition business unit have different goals to that of the organisation coalition. The business units are determined by the demands of individuals in the coalition. The top management in the corporate business unit enjoys the ultimate authority to perform the goals of the business unit.

According to Cyert and March, there are five major goals of a business unit. They are production goal, inventory goal, sales goal, market share goal, and profit goal. The production department sets the production goals in such a way that smooth running of the production process is ensured, production time is evenly distributed, and production capacity is optimally utilised. The inventory department sets the inventory goals to ensure adequate stocks of raw materials, and the smooth flow of raw materials and other inputs to different job points. The goals of the sales department are to promote sales of the total output generated at reasonable prices. The department may also set market share goal to consolidate its position in the market. The top management of the business unit sets the profit goal to meet the expectations of the shareholders and other stakeholders.

Like individual goals, the objectives of the business unit also change over a period. As the number of goals of the business unit increases, the decision making process becomes increasingly complex and consequently the efficiency of decision making decreases. The goals of the business unit are eventually decided by the top management through continuous consultations with various groups of the coalition. The top management tries to accommodate as many of the conflicting demands as possible.

Cyert and March model is a satisfying business unit theory that compares the business unit's performance with the set goals. In case the goals have not been met a search activity begins to find out the reasons for the non-fulfilment of the target. If it is found that non-fulfilment was due to factors outside the control of the business unit, a downward revision of the goals likely for the next period is made. In the organisation coalition, if there is often a conflict of goals it needs to be overcome. Thus, Cyert and March suggested two ways in which the conflict can be avoided:

- Conflict may be phased out over time in the sense that they are dealt with one by one, as they arise.
- Conflicts may be segregated to diffuse their impact on the whole organisation. Each conflict may be restricted to its respective department and decisions can be taken accordingly.

In the process of decision making, the following controversial points create doubts about the merits of the behavioural theory:

1. Investment decisions are usually based on long-term considerations which this theory ignores in its eagerness to avoid the role of uncertainty in decision making.
2. An adjustment of aspiration levels when costs and demand adjustment fail implies that any performance of the business unit can be considered satisfactory. This is a questionable proposition because the downward revision of the goals to lower satisfying levels may not be acceptable to various groups despite the business unit's claim that it did its best under the circumstances.
3. By constant revision in the satisfying level, the criterion on which the top management sets the goals of the business unit loses its relevance.
4. Estimates of costs and rules of their upward or downward adjustment are simplistic and mechanical.
5. Forecast of demand in the current period is simply the extrapolation of the demands in the previous periods in estimating current demand, no allowance is made for future uncertainty.

4.8.1. Criticism of the Model

Cyert and March based their theory on four actual case studies and two experimental studies conducted with hypothetical business units. It is thus, obvious that their attempt to develop a generalised behavioural theory of business unit is flawed by lack of adequate empirical evidence. The behaviour theory suffers from the following weaknesses and criticisms.

1. The behavioural theory follows a simulation approach to analyse the working of a multi-product business unit. Simulation is a predictive technique and is not appropriate for explaining the behaviour of the business unit.
2. The behavioural theory is concerned with the short run which is unrealistic for dealing with uncertainty. The business unit must take a long-run view of the environment.

3. The behavioural theory does not deal with the equilibrium of the industry.
4. The theory does not explain the interdependence of the business units.
5. The behavioural theory does not examine the implications of potential and real threats to established business units.
6. The behavioural theory suggests a multiplicity of goals for a modern corporate which is incorrect and misleading.
7. The theory attempts to resolve the problem of oligopolistic interdependence by assuming tacit collusion of business units which is not valid in all cases. An oligopolistic theory may also be non-collusive.
8. The adjustment of aspiration levels downward, whenever the goals are unstable, implies that there is no objective criterion to judge the satisfactory performance.
9. Search is usually problem oriented and on this issue, the behavioural theory takes an unrealistic position.

4.9. SUMMARY

- Theory of a firm refers to the purpose of the business units for its existence, goals and objectives, behaviour, performance, identity, market share, the vision and mission and the strategies to achievement.
- The theory of the firm has been developed with an assumption that the objective of rational business units is profit maximisation.
- The objectives of a business unit can be broadly categorised as growth, societal and profit making objectives.
- Assessing growth opportunities includes planning new businesses, downsizing, and terminating older businesses, is the first step in this direction. Growth opportunities are classified as intensive growth, integrative growth, and diversification growth.
- Intensive growth refers to the strategic growth opportunities in terms of the existing products and new products and the existing markets and new markets. The business units can opt for strategies such as market penetration, market development, and product development.
- A business unit can achieve integrative growth by increasing sales and profits through backward, forward, or horizontal integration within the industry.
- Diversification growth is preferred when good opportunities exist outside the scope of the present businesses. It includes concentric, horizontal, and conglomerate strategies.

- Business units should have societal objectives with a clear direction of offering benefits to society for the survival and growth of any business in the long run.
- Profit maximisation objective suggests that business unit seeks to make the difference between total revenue and total cost as large as possible. A business unit seeks to maximise its discounted present value.
- The short-run profit maximisation hypothesis is that the business unit maximises profit at a point where marginal cost (MC) and marginal revenue (MR) of producing and selling a product are equal.
- If profits are independent in different periods, long-run profit maximisation would simply amount to maximising the series of short-term profits.
- The equilibrium of the profit maximising business unit occurs simultaneously on the input and output sides. A business unit which is maximising its profit by choosing an output where marginal cost (MC) equals marginal revenue (MR) is simultaneously minimising the cost of producing that output or maximising the output subject to cost constraint.
- Business units may face certain situations wherein the place of profit making survival becomes the objective. During the times of recession, business units try to keep up a just stay in the business until the situation turns favourable.
- The managerial theory of the business unit was introduced by Robin Marris in 1963. The theory states that the managers do not prefer to maximise profits rather they seek to maximise the balanced growth rate of the business unit. The balanced growth rate is $G = G_d = G_C$.
- The ultimate goal of the manager is to maximise the balanced growth (G). Accordingly, there are two constraints in maximising the balanced growth rate such as managerial constraint and financial constraint.
- According to the theory, managers want to maximise their utility, while the owners seek maximisation of their utility. $U_M = f$ (salaries, power, status, job security) and $U_O = f$ (profits, capital, output, market share, public esteem). A business unit is said to be in equilibrium when the maximum balanced growth rate is attained ($G_{(max)} = G_D = G_C$).
- Williamson's managerial theory emphasised that managers are motivated by their self-interest and they maximise their utility function. The objective of utility maximisation by the managers is subject to the constraint that after-tax profits are large enough to pay acceptable dividends to the shareholders and also to pay for economically necessary investments.

- Williamson has distinguished the three concepts of profits, viz., actual profits (π), reported profits (π_r), and minimum profits (π_O). The discretional model was denoted as $\pi = R - C - S$.
- Williamson managerial utility maximisation clubs the two variables, salary and other monetary compensations received by the manager and the number of staff under his control into a single variable. Therefore, the utility of a manager is a function denoted as $U = U(S, M, I_D)$. Maximisation of the utility function is subject to the minimum profit constraint.
- Williamson model lays stress on the managerial discretion in determining not only output and price but also the level of staff expenditure and managerial emoluments.
- The sales revenue maximisation model proposed by Baumol exposes the dichotomy between ownership and management in large business units. The assumption is that given an opportunity, the managers may choose to maximise their utility function.
- In Baumol's model, the business unit is a sales maximiser, but it must also earn a minimum level of profit. The business unit needs minimum profits to support future sales. Further, these profits are essential for a business unit for paying dividends on share capital and for meeting other financial requirements. Thus, minimum profits serve as a constraint on the maximisation of a business unit's revenue.
- Baumol has shown that the profit constraint under sales maximisation is also effective in advertising and thereby increases the business unit's revenue. One key assumption of the model is that revenue always increases with advertising expenditure. Therefore, it is not possible to attain sales maximising equilibrium without profit constraint as a business unit can always increase its sales by increasing advertising.
- The satisfying behaviour model was proposed by H. A. Simon in 1955. This model states that while taking business decisions the managers are constrained by factors like incomplete information, inadequate data and uncertain future.
- Simon suggests that if the satisfactory state is not achieved even by lowering the aspiration level and the search behaviour, the behaviour pattern of managers becomes that of apathy or aggression.
- Cyert and March in 1963 proposed behavioural theory that focuses on the way decisions are made in the large multi-product business units under uncertainty in an imperfect market. The theory is based on the internal structure of such business units, analyses the organisational problems of such business units and the effects of these problems on the managerial decision making process.

- There are five major goals of a business unit like production goal, inventory goal, sales goal, market share goal, and profit goal. The model is a satisfying business unit theory that compares the business unit's performance with the set goals.

SHORT ANSWER QUESTIONS

1. What are the societal objectives of a business unit?
2. Write a short note on profit maximisation theory.
3. Define managerial constraint.
4. Explain managerial utility maximisation.
5. What are the reasons for managers' utility function of maximisation?
6. Explain the single product model without advertising.
7. What are the arguments in favour of sales maximisation objective?
8. Write a short note on Simon's satisfying behaviour model.

ESSAY ANSWER QUESTIONS

1. Discuss the different objectives of a business unit.
2. What is profit maximisation? Explain the short-run and long-run profit maximisation hypothesis.
3. Elucidate Marris' growth rate maximisation theory and equilibrium of the business unit.
4. Explain how managers maximise their utility function under Williamson's managerial discretional model.
5. Describe the Baumol's sales revenue maximisation model.
6. Explain the advantages and disadvantages of satisfying behaviour model proposed by Simon.
7. Discuss how decisions are made in the large multi-product business units under uncertainty in an imperfect market.

FILL IN THE BLANKS

1. In managing a business unit, the managers focus on problem solving and __________.
2. The prices of the products/services are influenced by __________.
3. Under __________ strategy, business units introduce unrelated new products to current customers.
4. When the MC curve intersects the MR curve from below, the total profit will be __________.
5. In profit maximisation theory, a business unit seeks to maximise its discounted __________.
6. The two constraints in maximising the balanced growth rate are financial and __________.
7. The job security of the manger is determined by the weighted average of __________ ratios.

8. Financial constraint is reflected in the _________ constraint of a manager.
9. The amount of profits (after tax) which are required to be paid as acceptable dividends to satisfy the shareholders is called _________.
10. The actual profits minus minimum profits and tax to be paid are known as _________.
11. The sales revenue maximisation model was proposed by _________.
12. The sale maximiser will earn a lower profit as compared to _________ maximiser.
13. Simon's satisfying behaviour model was proposed in the year _________.
14. The business units are determined by the demands of individuals in the _________.

Answers:

1. Forward planning
2. Market structure
3. Horizontal
4. Maximum
5. Present value
6. Managerial
7. Financial
8. Job security
9. Minimum profit
10. Discretionary profit
11. W.J. Baumol
12. Profit maximiser
13. 1955
14. Coalition

MULTIPLE-CHOICE QUESTIONS

1. Which one of the following growth strategy offers several opportunities for business units to increase their sales and achieve the desired growth level?
(A) Intensive (B) Integrative
(C) Diversification (D) Market penetration
2. Which growth strategy is preferred when good opportunities are outside the scope of the present businesses?
(A) Centralisation (B) Homogeneous
(C) Diversification (D) Integrative
3. Under which strategy, business units introduce new products which are synergic with production technology or marketing of existing product lines?
(A) Conglomerate (B) Concentric
(C) Horizontal (D) Vertical
4. When a business unit acquires one or more of its suppliers to gain more control it is called:
(A) Backward integration (B) Horizontal integration
(C) Forward integration (D) Market integration
5. When the business units introduce altogether entirely new businesses that have no relationship between current business and its resources, it is referred to as:
(A) Horizontal (B) Vertical
(C) Concentric (D) Conglomerate

6. The business unit maximises profit at a point where:
   (A) MR = MC (B) MR > MC
   (C) MR < MC (D) MR ≠ MC
7. The growth rate maximisation theory was introduced by:
   (A) Leon Walras (B) W. S. Jevons
   (C) Robin Marris (D) Alfred Marshall
8. A business unit is said to be in equilibrium when the _______ balanced growth rate is attained.
   (A) Minimum (B) Maximum
   (C) Optimum (D) Favourable
9. Williamson's managerial theory was put forward in the year:
   (A) 1936 (B) 1968
   (C) 1966 (D) 1963
10. The difference between actual profits and non-essential managerial expenditure as represented by management slack is called:
    (A) Minimum profit (B) Maximum profit
    (C) Reported profit (D) Management slack
11. Which model exposes the dichotomy between ownership and management in large business units?
    (A) Sales revenue maximisation (B) Profit maximisation
    (C) Revenue maximisation (D) Wealth maximisation
12. The satisfying behaviour model was proposed by:
    (A) W.J. Baumol (B) R.M. Cyert
    (C) J.E. March (D) H. A. Simon
13. Which model suggests that a manager will aim for a satisfactory level of profit maximisation and a satisfactory level of cost rather than cost minimisation?
    (A) Satisfying behaviour model
    (B) Sales maximisation model
    (C) Williamson's discretionary model
    (D) Growth rate maximisation model

Answers:

1. A	2. C	3. B	4. A	5. D
6. A	7. C	8. B	9. D	10. C
11. A	12. D	13. A		

REFERENCES

1. Baumol, W.J. (1959). *Business Behaviour, Value and Growth.* New York: Macmillan.
2. Baumol, W. J. (1985). *Economic Theory and Operations Analysis.* New Delhi: Prentice-Hall of India Pvt. Ltd.
3. Cyert, R. M. & March, J. G. (1963). *A Behavioural Theory of the Firm.* Engleward Cliffs, New Jersey: Prentice-Hall.

4. Holmstorm, B. R. & Tirole, J. (1989). Theory of the firm. *Handbook of Industrial Organisation,* 1(61-133).
5. Marris, R. (1963). A model of the "managerial" enterprise. *The Quarterly Journal of Economics,* 77(2), 185-209.
6. Marris, R. (1963). *Theory of Managerial Capitalism.* New York: Macmillan.
7. Marris, R. (1998). Managerial theories of the firm. In *Managerial Capitalism in Retrospect* (pp. 108-121). Palgrave Macmillan, London.
8. Simon, H. A. (1955). A behavioural model of rational choice. *Quarterly Journal of Economics,* 99-118.
9. Simon, H. A. (1956). Rational choice and the structure of the environment. *Psychological Review,* 63(2), 129.
10. Williamson, O. E. (1963). Managerial discretion and business behavior. *The American Economic Review,* 53(5), 1032-1057.
11. Williamson, O. E. (1967). The Economics of Discretionary Behaviour: Managerial objectives of theory of the firm. Chicago: Markhamm.
12. Kotler, P. & Keller, K. L. (2012). *Marketing Management,* 14th edition. Upper Saddle River, New Jersey: Prentice-Hall.
13. Berle, A. & Means, G. (1932). *The Modern Corporation and Private Property*. New York: Macmillan.
14. Mehta, P.L. (2007). *Managerial Economics: Text and Cases*. New Delhi, India: Sultan Chand & Co.
15. Gupta, G. S. (2017). *Managerial Economics.* New Delhi, India: Tata McGraw-Hill.
16. Marshall, Alfred. (1890). *Principles of Economics.* London: Macmillan.
17. Dwivedi, D. N. (2015). *Managerial Economics* (8th Edition). New Delhi, India: Vikas Publishing House Pvt. Ltd.
18. Thomas, C. R. & Maurice, S. C. (2016). *Managerial Economics: Foundations of Business Analysis and Strategy*. New York: McGraw-Hill Education.
19. Varshney, R. L. & Maheswari, K .L. (2014). *Managerial Economics.* New Delhi, India: Sultan Chand & Sons.

Chapter

5 Theory of Demand

ÑLEARNING OBJECTIVES

After studying this chapter, you should be able to understand:

- the concept of demand and demand distinctions;
- demand situations at a market place;
- demand function and its determinants;
- the law of demand and its assumptions and exceptions; and
- shifts along the demand curve.

5.1. CONCEPT OF DEMAND

The term *demand* finds meaning contextually. The demand for product 'x' in a market and the demand for product 'x' among the middle-income group have different meanings. One has to find the meaning based on the variables like time, place, segment, period, product variant, etc. The major effort of any company is to manage demand to their favour. Conceptually, every product will have some demand generated if it is offered in the right market. However, the automatically generated demand may not be sufficient to achieve organisational goals. Business units want sufficient demand as to their capacity to produce goods and/or services. Demand is an external factor and therefore, companies cannot control demand. They can only manage internal resources to meet the challenges in finding sufficient demand for their products and services. For this purpose companies need to understand the characteristics of demand, the factors influencing the demand, the trends, the relationship between the market factors and demand, the change dimensions, etc., and forecast demand with the help of technical methods. Demand forecasting is essential for developing plans for the future.

Demand is one of the most important economic decision variables. The analysis of demand fora business unit's product/service plays an essential role in the following areas besides many other situational variables:

1. determining the size and pattern of the market,
2. profit of the business unit,
3. demand and supply conditions of inputs and outputs,
4. production planning,
5. sales and profit targeting,
6. revenue maximisation,
7. pricing policies,

8. inventory management,
9. advertisement and marketing strategy,
10. financial strategy,
11. human resource strategy,
12. growth strategy,
13. competition strategy, and
14. research and development.

Generally, consumers desire to possess several products or services, but all of them may not be willing and able to buy the products or avail the services. Demand means the number of goods or services which the consumers would buy in the market at a given time and given place. Every want supported by the willingness and ability to buy constitutes a demand for a particular product or service.

A product/service is said to have demand when the following three conditions are satisfied:

- desire to have a product/service;
- ability to pay; and
- willingness to have such product/service.

For example, Mercedes Benz car may be desired by many car lovers. If they do not have the ability to buy such a car the desire cannot create demand. The desire and ability should be accompanied by the person's willingness to buy the car. Thus, the demand for a product/service is its quantity which consumer is willing and able to buy at various prices during the given time.

Definitions of demand

Author	**Definition**
F. Benham (1939)	The demand for anything, at a given price, is the amount of it, which will be bought per unit of time at that price
James E. Hibdon (1969)	Demand means the various quantities of goods that would be purchased per time at different prices in a given market

5.1.1. Demand Schedule and Demand Curve

A demand schedule is a tabular statement showing different quantities of a product that can be bought at different prices during a specified time. It represents the functional relationship between the price of a product and its quantity demanded. The demand schedule for an individual is called individual demand schedule (IDS). The demand schedule for the whole or aggregate market is called market demand schedule (MDS).

The graphical representation of the demand schedule is called a demand curve. It shows the relationship between the price of a product and its quantity demanded. There are two types of demand curves, viz., individual demand curve (IDC) and market demand curve (MDC). A demand curve may be linear or nonlinear depending upon the nature of the demand function (Figure 5.1).

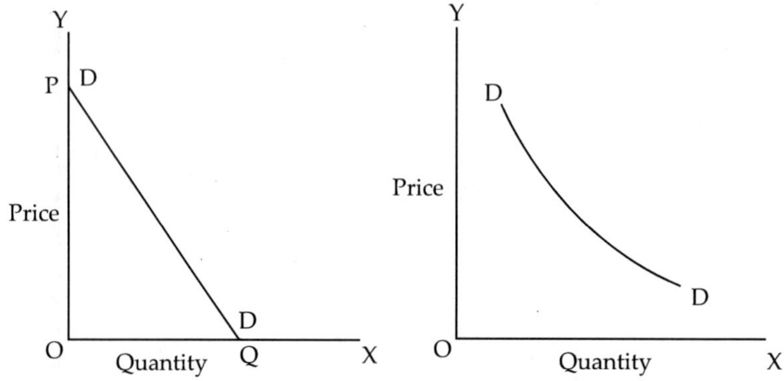

Figure 5.1. Linear and nonlinear demand curve

5.1.2. Price and Demand

Price is the fundamental and essential factor in determining the quantity of demand. The demand for a product and its price are inversely related. If the price of a product increases, the quantity demanded decreases. If the price decreases, more quantity of products will be bought and the demand increases. Thus, the prevailing price for a product or service is an important determinant of demand.

1. **Individual demand:** Individual demand refers to the quantity demanded of a product by a particular consumer at various prices. For example, Person-X's demand for apples at different prices (Table 5.1).

Table 5.1. Individual demand schedule

Price of apple	Person-X's demand
20	3
17	4
14	5

In the form of a graph it will look like as shown in Figure 5.2.

2. **Market demand:** The demand for the total or aggregate market at various prices for a product is known as market demand. It is shown by the market demand schedule and demand curve. A market demand schedule is achieved by adding all the individual

demand schedules. For example, Person-X's & Person-Y's combined demand for apples at different prices is shown in Table 5.2.

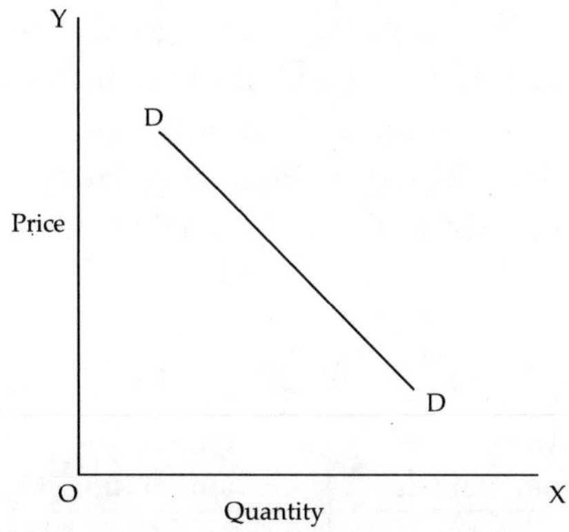

Figure 5.2. Individual demand curve

Table 5.2. Market demand schedule

Price of apple	Person-X's demand	Person-Y's demand	Market demand
20	3	1	4
17	4	2	6
14	5	4	9
10	6	5	11

In the form of a graph it will look like as shown in Figure 5.3.

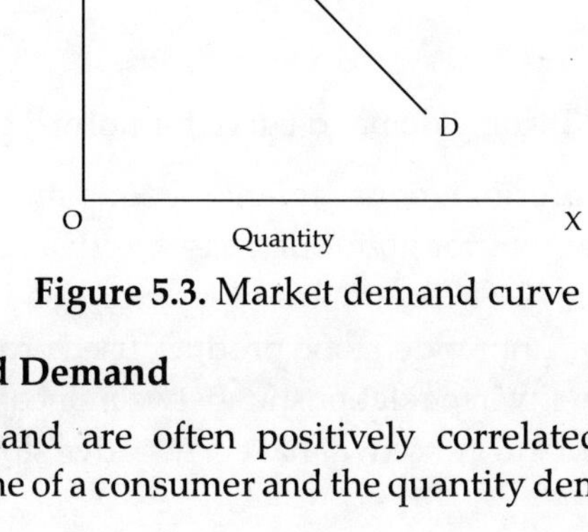

Figure 5.3. Market demand curve

5.1.3. Income and Demand

Income and demand are often positively correlated. The relationship between the income of a consumer and the quantity demanded of a product can be established on an assumption that other factors like price, taste, nature, etc., remain constant. The relationship varies in case of demand for normal goods and demand for inferior goods.

1. **Demand for normal goods:** Normal goods are those goods for which the demand increases with a rise in income of the consumer and decreases with a fall in income when other things remain constant (Table 5.3). The income-demand curve will have an upward slope (Figure 5.4). Examples of normal goods are bread, wheat, milk, etc.

Table 5.3. Income demand schedule for normal goods

Income of consumer (Rs.)	Quantity demanded (units)
10,000	100
20,000	200
30,000	300

In the form of a graph it will look like as shown in Figure 5.4.

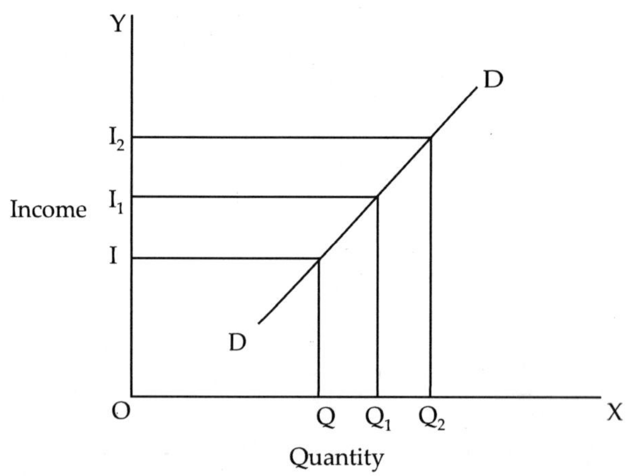

Figure 5.4. Income demand curve for normal goods

2. **Demand for inferior goods:** Inferior goods are low-cost goods. The demand for inferior goods decreases with a rise in consumer's income (Table 5.4). The examples of inferior goods are low priced plastic products, unbranded food product, used products, etc. In this case, there is an inverse relationship between income and demand. The income demand curve will have a negative slope (Figure 5.5).

Table 5.4. Income demand schedule for inferior goods

Income of consumer (Rs.)	Quantity demanded (units)
10,000	100
20,000	50
30,000	25

In the form of a graph it will look like as shown in Figure 5.5.

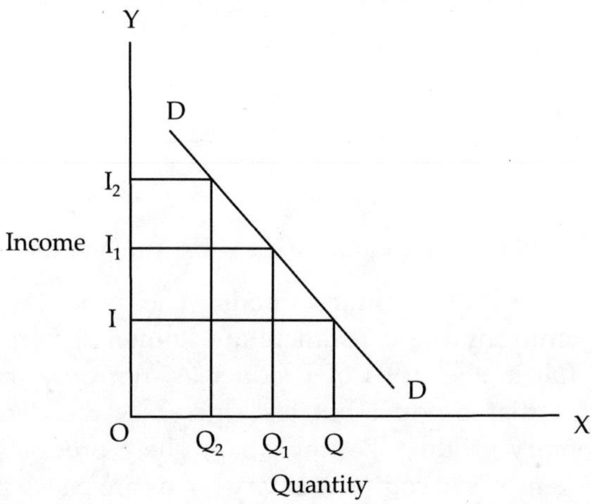

Figure 5.5. Income demand curve for inferior goods

5.1.4. Price of Related Goods and Demand

The demand for a product may change when there is a significant change in the price of related products. For example, the demand for coffee may change when there is a significant change in the price of tea, as the products coffee and tea are related from the point of view of consumers. This kind of change is called *cross demand.* It indicates how the prices of related goods are affected by a change in the quantity demanded. Cross demand generally takes place with substitute goods and complementary goods.

1. **Demand for substitute goods:** The products that can be used in place of other products are known as substitute goods. With a rise in the price of product 'A' the demand for it decreases and the demand for its related product 'B' increases (Table 5.5). Examples of substitute goods are tea & coffee, bread & rice, Pepsi & Coke, etc.

Table 5.5. Demand schedule for substitute goods

Price of coffee (Rs.)	Demand for tea (units)
100	20
200	25

In the form of a graph it will look like as shown in Figure 5.6.

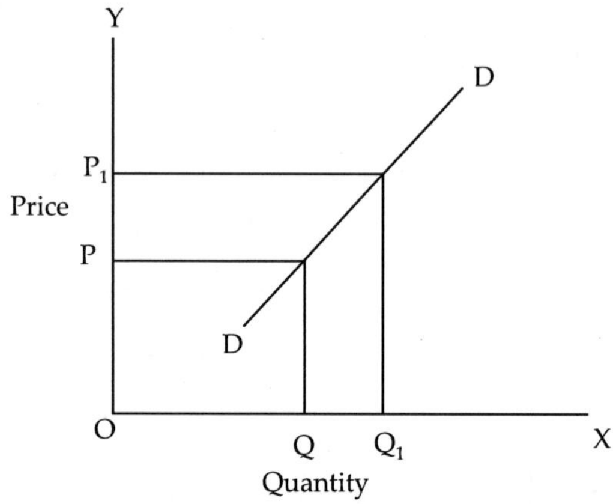

Figure 5.6. Demand curve for substitute goods

2. **Demand for complementary goods:** The products which are required jointly by the consumers are known as complementary goods. A fall in the price of product 'A' not only increases the demand for that product but also increases the demand of its complementary product 'B' (Table 5.6). These products have joint demand. Examples of complementary goods are pen & paper, car & petrol, printer & cartridge, etc.

Table 5.6. Demand schedule for complementary goods

Price of petrol (Rs.)	Demand for car (units)
100	20
200	10

In the form of a graph it will look like as shown in Figure 5.7.

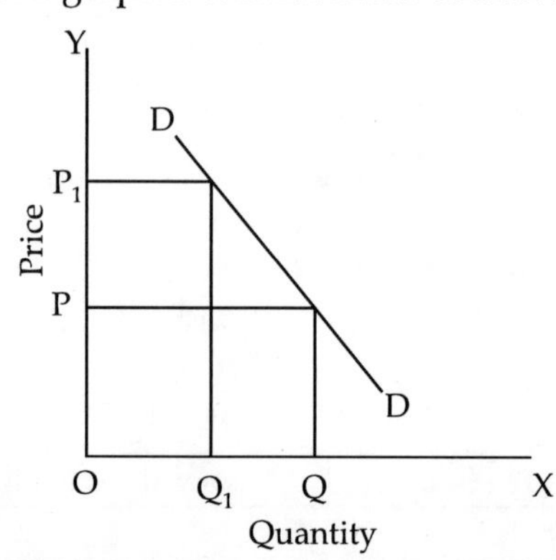

Figure 5.7. Demand curve for complementary goods

5.2. DEMAND DISTINCTIONS

The concept of demand generally implies at a given price of a product or service. The behaviour of the demand will not be similar to different kinds of products and services. The study of demand distinctions will help in understanding different variations in the nature of demand. The following are the demand distinctions.

1. Consumer goods and producer goods
2. Durable goods and perishable goods
3. Short-run demand and long-run demand
4. Firm demand and industry demand
5. Autonomous demand and derived demand
6. New demand and replacement demand
7. Total market demand and segment market demand

1. **Consumer Goods and Producer Goods:** Consumer goods refer to such products and services which are used or consumed by individuals to satisfy their needs and desires. These are available for ultimate consumption or use. These goods give direct satisfaction to the consumer. For example, food products like bread, mango, rice, milk, etc.

   Producer goods are the goods which can be used for the further process of production of goods or services to earn income. These goods yield satisfaction indirectly. These are used to produce consumer goods. For example, machinery, tractor, etc.

   There are certain cases where a product may be both a producer good and also a consumer good. For instance, a farmer having ten bags of paddy may use five bags for his consumption and another five bags as seeds for the next crop. In such a case, paddy is both producer and consumer good. The demand for producer goods is indirect, whereas the demand for consumer goods is direct. It is also possible that consumer good for one can become producer good for another. A microwave oven at home is a consumer good and the same in a hotel is a producer good. Therefore, the classification of goods as consumer goods and producer goods is based on the user rather than the product.

2. **Durable Goods and Perishable Goods:** The distinction between durable goods and perishable goods is necessary for analysing demand. Both consumer and producer goods may be of perishable and non-perishable nature. Durable goods are those goods whose total utility is not exhausted in single or short-run use. Such goods can be used continuously over a period of time. Durable goods may be consumer goods as well as producer goods. Durable consumer

goods include clothes, shoes, house furniture, refrigerators, scooters, and cars, etc. The durable producer goods include mainly the items under fixed assets such as building, plant and machinery, office furniture and fixture, etc.

Perishable goods are the goods which can be used only once such as food items and their total utility is exhausted in a single use. Perishable goods have a short lifespan. This category of goods can be grouped under perishable consumer and producer goods. All food items such as drinks, ice creams, bread, butter, soap, gas, kerosene, coal and cosmetics fall under consumer perishable goods category whereas, goods such as raw materials, fuel and power, finishing materials and packing items fall under producer perishable goods category.

3. **Short-run Demand and Long-run Demand:** Short-run demand refers to the demand for a product in a short period. Some products such as fashion consumer goods, goods of seasonal use and inferior substitutes during the scarcity period of superior goods will have demand only for a short period. The demand for umbrella, raincoats, gumboots, cold drinks and ice creams is of seasonal nature, the demand for such goods lasts till the season lasts. Some goods of this category are demanded for a very short period, i.e., 1-2 weeks, for example, new year greeting cards, candles and crackers on occasion of Diwali, etc.

   The long-run demand refers to the demand for a product, which exists over a long period. The change in long-term demand is visible only after a long period. Most generic goods have long-term demand. For example, the demand for many consumer and producer goods, durable and non-durable goods may sustain for a long period, though their different varieties or brands may have only short-term demand. The long-run demand depends on the long-term income trends, availability of better substitutes, sales promotion, consumer credit facility, etc.

4. **Firm Demand and Industry Demand:** A firm is a single business unit. The quantity of a business unit's yield that can be sold at a given price over a period refers to the demand for a business unit's product. The industry refers to a group of business units carrying on similar business activity. The aggregate demand for the product of all business units of the industry is known as the marketdemand or demand for the industry's product. For example, the market of cars, radios, TV sets, refrigerators, scooters, toilet soaps and toothpaste, all belong to this category of markets.

In the case of monopoly, the industry is the one-business unit industry and the demand for a business unit's product is the same as that of the industry. In the case of perfect competition, products of all business units in the industry are homogeneous and price for each business unit is determined by industry.

5. **Autonomous Demand and Derived Demand:** When a product is demanded in a market independently such demand is called autonomous demand. The demand for such a product does not depend on any other product. Autonomous demand arises as a result of the demonstration effect, the rise in income, an increase in population and advertisement of new products. For example, the demand for consumer goods is autonomous.

   The demand for a product that arises because of the demand for some other product is called derived demand. For example, demand for land, fertilizer and agricultural tools and implements are derived demands, since the demand for such goods depends on the demand for food. Similarly, the demand for steel, bricks, cement, etc., is a derived demand because it is derived from the demand for houses. To look more closely at the distinction between the two kinds of demand, the demand for the house is autonomous demand and demand for units like bricks, sand, cement, iron, etc., are derived demands.

6. **New Demand and Replacement Demand:** New demand refers to the demand for new products sold in the market and it is an addition to the existing stock. For example, cars, bikes, etc.

   Replacement demand refers to the products purchased to replace the existing products or the parts therein. It may also be referred to the demand resulting out of replacing the existing assets with the new ones. For example, spare parts, machines, etc. Many companies announce exchange schemes for TV's, refrigerator, washing machines and so on to trigger replacement demand.

7. **Total Market Demand and Segment Market Demand:** The total demand for a product in a given region is called total market demand. For example, sugar is demanded by households and a variety of industrial users like sweet making industry, soft drink industry, milk products, pharmaceuticals, etc.

   The demand for a product by anyone of the business unit or industry among others from the given region is called segment market demand. For example, demand for sugar by sweet making industry.

   If the market is large in terms of geographical spread, the product uses, distribution channels, customer sizes or product varieties, and if any one or more of these differences were significant in terms of the product price, profit margins, competition, seasonal patterns or cyclical sensitivity, then it may be worthwhile to distinguish the market by specific segments for a meaningful analysis. In that case, the total demand would mean the total demand for the product from all market segments while a particular market segment demand would refer to the demand for the product in that specific market segment.

5.3. DEMAND SITUATIONS AT MARKETPLACE

The response from the consumers for different products in the market may not be similar to the demand for a product depends upon a variety of factors. Companies have to understand and analyse demand situations and act accordingly to achieve organisational objectives. The following are different demand situations a business unit may face when a product is introduced.

1. **Negative demand:** When the targeted customers have negative reactions to a product offer then such demand is called negative demand. The target persons will have negative perceptions of either features or the promised utilities of a product, perceived dangers and negative effects on their life. The companies have to understand the reasons for negativity and work out strategies to convert the negative demand into positive demand. Many products have faced negative demand when they were introduced and after the successful strategic approach by the business units, the same products became the most sought after products in the market. The examples are pressure cookers, cooking gas, hair dye, condoms , contraceptives, etc.
2. **No demand:** Products will face no demand situation when targeted persons do not show any interest in buying such products. They may not have negative feelings against such products, but they don't buy due to indifference. Many imitative products or me-too products face no demand situation in the market. To convert no demand into positive demand companies have to establish a strong driving reason for preferring the product. The driving reason may be in the form of price, an additional benefit of the product, innovativeness, extra features, etc. The target persons should value such reason to prefer the product over other existing products.
3. **Latent demand:** Latent demand is the demand unexploited. Latent demand exists in all product categories due to the reason the best product is not available to the consumers. It is believed that every

purchase by a consumer involves some amount of compromise between the desired product and the available product. Any significant improvement in the existing product class finds demand automatically. For example, if somebody introduces a motorbike which gives a thousand kilometres mileage per litre without an increase in price and the other features, the demand for such product is expected to automatically exist. Companies have to understand the concept of latent demand and continuously work for offering significant improvements to the existing products or developing products for unmet needs.

4. **Seasonal demand:** Some products will be in demand over a season. Such demand is called seasonal demand. The products such as woollen clothes, umbrellas, and raincoats have seasonal demand. Seasonal demand creates many problems for business units. They have to face problems such as laying-off employees during leanseason, the fixed expenses will continue to incur, higher storage costs, increased prices, and reduced margins. The success of the companies depends upon how effectively they convert seasonal demand into regular demand. For example, fans and refrigerators used to have seasonal demand for a long period. The companies worked out appropriate marketing strategies to convert the demand for such products as regular demand. If the seasonal demand is due to climatic conditions of a region, the companies have to find markets in such other regions also where different climatic conditions exist during the same season to spread the demand.
5. **Irregular demand:** When demand for products is highly irregular and fluctuating the business unit faces many challenges in managing production schedules, and in controlling costs. Irregular demand situation is undesirable from the point of view of any business unit. Business units can handle irregular demand in two ways. One is to influence the market to use the product during slack periods and the other is to design production schedules matching the peak and slack periods. Both the options are difficult to execute. Electricity boards in various states worked out a strategy of offering discounts/concessions to users during slack periods. Industrial consumers responded positively for such kind of offer and shifted their production schedules accordingly to save electricity charges. This measure to a greater extent helped to balance the demand for electricity. Road transport corporations worked out a strategy of designing a schedule of trips according to the variations in demand. They could reduce a lot of waste due to such scheduling.

6. **Falling demand:** When a company experiences a falling demand for any product in the market, it has to study the reasons for such a decline in sales and take appropriate measures to arrest the decline immediately. The falling demand situation demoralizes the sales personnel and promotes a negative image to the product and the business unit in the market. Therefore, immediate response from the company to correct the situation is necessary.
7. **Full demand:** Full demand means that the company could able to sell all the products produced without any problem. Full demand situation is the most desirable situation for any producer. However, the company cannot relax when full demand situation is existing in the market. Competitors may enter at any point and take away the market share or any dynamic change in the market may shift the demand from the existing product to an altogether new product class. Therefore, the challenge for the companies during a full demand situation is to retain the same situation for a long period.
8. **Overfull demand:** This situation arises when the demand for a product exceeds the supply. Overfull demand though appears very positive, it attracts many competitors to enter the market. If the supply is not matched with the growing demand some consumers remain unserved and they get highly disappointed for not having the products. The negative feeling of such people turns positive towards competitive products when they are available. Therefore, companies have to handle overfull demand quickly in a short period. They may expand the supply or may outsource the production. Some companies design strategies to discourage people to buy products or to buy products in large quantities. Strategies like increase in price, limiting the order size, introducing a quota system, reservation system, etc., will be used. Such strategies can only be used for a short period and if they are continued for a long period it works out very badly for the future of the organisation.
9. **Unwholesome demand:** Not all products and services offered by producers to the market are good to society. Some products or services affect society badly either in terms of a value system or health system. The demand for such products and services which are not good for the health of the society is called unwholesome demand. Companies with such products/services will not have a longer life. They may be closed as per the law of land or the public may revolt against such products and see that the business is closed.

5.4. DETERMINANTS OF DEMAND

1. **Price of the product (P):** The price of the product is one of the most important determinants of demand in the long run and the only determinant in the short run. The price and quantity demanded of a product is inversely related. The quantity demanded of a product at a given point of time increases when its price falls and decreases when its price increases, on an assumption that other factors remaining constant.
2. **Income of the consumer (I):** Income is the basic determinant of quantity demanded of a product, as it determines the purchasing power of the consumer. In general, people with higher disposable income spend a larger amount on goods and services than those with lower income. The relationship between income and demand is closer than other determinants. While other determinants of demand, i.e., product's price and the price of its substitutes are more significant in the short run, income as a determinant of demand is important in both short run and long run.
3. **Tastes and preferences (T):** Consumers' tastes and preferences play an important role in determining the demand for a product. Usually, the tastes and preferences of the people depend on their lifestyle, fashion, beliefs, social customs, age, sex, habits, religious values, and the general levels of living in society. A change in these factors influences positively or negatively the consumers' tastes and preferences. As a result, consumers either reduce or give up the consumption of certain goods/services or add new ones to their consumption pattern.
4. **Price of related goods (P_R):** The demand for a product is also affected by the changes in the price of related products. The related goods may be substitutes or complementary. In the case of substitutes, the relation between the demand for a product and the price of its substitute is of a positive nature. Similarly, in the case of complementary goods, there is an inverse relationship between the demand for a product and the price of its complementary product.
5. **Expected change in price (E_p):** Consumers' expectations regarding the future prices and supply position of goods play an important role in determining the demand for goods/services in the short run. If consumers expect a rise in the price of a product, they would buy more of it at its current price to avoid the pinch of the rise in future. On the contrary, if consumers expect a fall in the price of certain goods, they postpone the purchase of such goods to take advantage of lower prices in future, particularly in the case of non-essential

goods. This behaviour of consumers reduces the current demand for the goods whose prices are expected to decrease in future.

6. **Expected change in income of consumers (E_I):** The expectation of the consumers regarding the future change in income also changes the demand for some goods and services. If consumers expect a fall in income, they may postpone the present consumption which will affect the current demand for the product. On the other hand, if the rise in income is expected, the consumer may take some purchase decisions expecting a future inflow of money. They may also switch over from inferior goods that are used at present to superior goods.
7. **Size of the population (S_P):** The increase in population in any economy increases the demand for goods and services. The total domestic demand for a product of mass consumption depends on the size of the population. Given the price, per capita income, taste and preference, etc., the larger the population, the larger the demand for a product/service and vice versa.
8. **Distribution pattern of national income (D):** The distribution pattern of national income is also an important determinant of demand for a product. If the national income is evenly distributed, the market demand for normal goods will be more. If the national income is unevenly distributed, i.e., if the majority of the population belongs to the lower-income groups, market demand for essential goods, including inferior ones, will be more whereas the demand for other kinds of goods will be relatively less.
9. **Advertisement costs (A):** Advertisement costs are incurred to promote the sale of the product. Advertisements help in increasing demand for a product as they inform the potential consumers about the benefits, product features, availability, superiority over rival products, and by influencing consumers' choice against the rival products. The impact of such advertisements shifts the demand upward to the right. In other words, the other factors remaining the same and the increase in expenditure on advertisement leads to an increase in the volume of sales of a product.
10. **Other factors (O):** The change in other factors such as nature, quality and quantity of a product also influences the demand for the product from time to time.

5.5. DEMAND FUNCTION

Demand function describes the relationship between demand and its determinants. It explains how much quantity of goods are brought at alternative prices of goods and its related goods, alternative income levels, and alternative values of other variables. It is possible to develop a function to measure the relationship between demand and specific determinants. Such a function is called demand function. The demand function for a product can be formulated as:

$$Q_d = f(P, I, T, P_R, E_P, E_I, S_P, D, A, O)$$

where,

Q_d refers to the quantity of demand
f refers to the function of various determinants
Price of the product (P)
The income level of the Consumer (I)
Tastes and preferences of the consumer (T)
Prices of related goods (P_R)
Expected change in the price of a product (E_P)
Expected change in income of the consumer (E_I)
Size of the population (S_P)
Distribution to national Income (D)
Advertising costs (A)
Other factors affecting demand (O)

5.6. LAW OF DEMAND

The law of demand shows the functional relationship between the price of a product and the quantity demanded of a product in the market with an assumption that all the other demand determinants remain same or do not change in a given point of time. For instance, an individual may purchase 5 dozens of apples at Rs.100 per dozen. If the price of apples increases to Rs. 200 per dozen, the person may buy less quantity of apples as the person is conditioned by budget limitations. Thus, the demand for apples reduces with the increase in price. As such, there will be an inverse relationship between the price and quantity demanded a product.

The law of demand states that "Ceteris paribus (other things remaining the same), higher the price the lower the demand and vice versa." The law is stated primarily in terms of the price and quantity relationship. The quantity demanded is inversely related to its price.

Definitions of the law of demand

Author	Definitions
A. Marshall (1890)	The law of demand: demand increases with a fall in price and diminishes with a rise in price.
Paul Samuelson (1947)	If a greater quantity of a good is thrown in the market then other things being equal, it can be sold only at a lower price.

5.6.1. Assumptions of the Law of Demand

The law of demand is based on certain assumptions:

1. No change in consumers income or remain constant.
2. Consumers' taste and preferences remain the same.
3. No change in the availability and the price of the related products (i.e., complementary and substitute goods).
4. No change in the population and its structure.
5. The demand for the product should be continuous.
6. There are no expectations of the consumers about changes in the future price and income level.

When all other determinants are assumed to be constant, the law of demand establishes the relationship between price and quantity of demand of a product. The demand curve slopes downwards from left to right. It indicates that with a fall in the price of a product the quantity demanded increases and vice versa.

5.6.2. Why the Demand Curve Slopes Downwards?

The demand curve slopes downwards from left to right (i.e., a negative slope). There are many causes for the downward sloping of the demand curve:

1. Law of diminishing marginal utility
2. The principle of equi-marginal utility
3. Income effect
4. Substitution effect
5. Different uses of a product
6. Consumer psychology

1. **Law of diminishing marginal utility:** When the consumer buys more and more of a product, the marginal utility of the additional units consumed decreases. Therefore, a consumer may purchase a larger amount of a product when it is priced low as the marginal utility of the additional unit decreases. If the price of the product increases, the consumer may restrict its consumption.
2. **The principle of equi-marginal utility:** The consumers arrange their purchases in such a way that the marginal utility is equal in all their purchases. If it is not equal, they may alter their purchases until the marginal utility is equal.
3. **Income effect:** A change in the demand arising due to change in income of a consumer owing to change in the price of a product is called income effect. When the price of the product decreases, the real income of the consumer increases. The consumer will spend this increased income either to buy an additional quantity of the same product or other commodities.

4. **Substitution effect:** The change in demand due to a change in the relative price of a product is called substitution effect. The relative price of a product refers to its price in relation to the prices of other commodities. When the price of a product 'A' falls, it becomes cheaper. Therefore, the consumer will substitute product 'A' for another product which is of a higher price. This leads to an increase in demand for the product 'A'.
5. **Different uses of a product:** Some products serve more than one purpose. If the price of such a product is high, its use will be restricted only for an important purpose. For example, when the price of tomato is high, it will be used only for cooking purpose. When it becomes cheaper, it may be used for preparing jams, pickles, etc.
6. **Consumer psychology:** Consumers buy more of a product when its price decreases. Falling prices attract new consumers. When the price of a product decreases the number of consumers of the product increases. This leads to a rise in the demand for the product.

5.7. EXCEPTIONS TO THE LAW OF DEMAND

The law of demand states that an increase in the price of a product leads to a fall in quantity demanded of the product and vice versa. In some exceptional cases, the fall in the price of a product may not result in an increase in demand and vice versa. This situation is paradoxical in nature and regarded as an exception to the law of demand. In other words, exceptions to the law of demand refer to conditions where the law of demand is not applicable. In the case of exceptions, the demand curve shows an upward slope and is referred to as the exceptional demand curve. Figure 5.8 shows an exceptional demand curve.

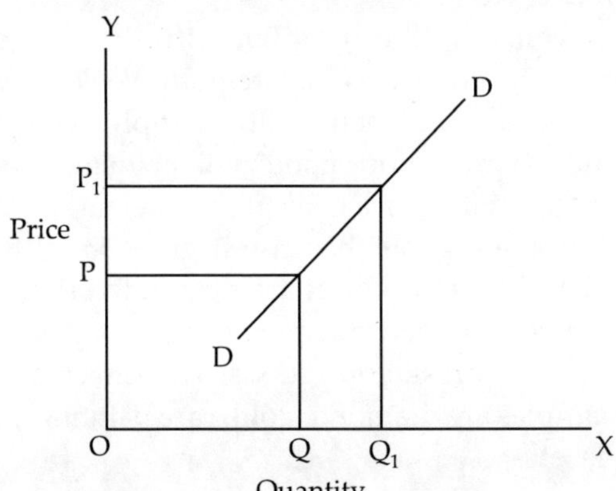

Figure 5.8. Exceptional demand curve

The following are a few exceptions to the law of demand.

1. Inferior goods (Giffen paradox)
2. Conspicuous consumption
3. Conspicuous necessities
4. Consumers' ignorance
5. Expected changes in prices
6. Extraordinary situations
7. Changes in tastes and fashion
8. Demonstration effect

1. **Inferior goods (Giffen paradox):** According to Giffen's paradox, the inferior goods stand as an exception to the law of demand. When the price of inferior good falls, the demand may not increase, instead the consumers buy the same quantity and use the savings for the purchase of better goods. Sir Robert Giffen (1837-1910), conducted a study on the expenditure pattern of the workers in Ireland. He found an exceptional behaviour that when there was an increase in the price of potatoes, there was more demand for it. The working class people of Ireland used to have potatoes and meat as daily consumption, potato being their main food. When there was an increase in the price of potato, the same quantity was consumed, as it was an essential item. To buy the same quantity of potato, they had to spend more money and less money was available for buying meat. Due to that, the consumption of meat became less. This led to less satisfaction and less calorie content in the food. These workers wanted to compensate for this and purchased more potato. Therefore, Giffen indicated this position as a paradox as it is operating against the law of demand. Other examples are bread, cloth, broken rice, etc.
2. **Conspicuous consumption (Veblen effect):** This exception is named after the economist, Thorstein B. Veblen. According to Veblen (1899), the law of demand will not apply in the case of costly items. Demand for prestigious goods will be demanded more with a rise in price. When the price goes up, the demand will rise, as the rich people buy these goods because it gives social distinction or prestige to them. These products are demanded even if the prices go up. If the prices fall, poor people will also buy and hence, they no longer remain as prestigious goods. This effect is called Veblen effect. The examples are diamond, gold, rare paintings, vintage cars, antique goods, etc.
3. **Conspicuous necessities:** Certain commodities have turned into necessities of modern life. Consumers purchase these commodities

despite their high prices. Thus, conspicuous necessities are an exception to the law of demand. For example, the demand for TVs, automobiles, refrigerators, etc., is generally high despite their increasing prices. These things have become the symbol of status for the consumers. So, these goods are purchased despite their rising prices.

4. **Consumers' ignorance:** Consumers' ignorance is another factor that works against the law of demand. When the consumers do not have the knowledge of previous price or the price of substitute products, they may go on buying irrespective of price changes. Some consumers perceive a relationship between price and quality. When prices increase the consumers believe that they are getting improved quality products and therefore, they are not sensitive to price changes. For example, at fairs and exhibitions, the visitors are impulsive and they do not have the opportunity to refer prices. Therefore, the factors other than price mostly influence the demand for products.
5. **Expected changes in prices (speculative effect):** The law of demand does not operate in case of speculative demand. When there is an expectation of a further rise in the price of a product or service, the demand increases more and more even with a rise in price. Similarly, if there is an expectation that the price of a product or service may fall in the future the demand also falls. For example, in the stock market, the demand for shares goes up with the increase in price when the buyers expect a further rise in prices and vice versa.
6. **Extraordinary situations (emergencies):** During extraordinary situations such as emergency, wars, famines, riots, floods, strikes, etc., the consumers exhibit abnormal purchase behaviour and buy products at any price available in the market. Due to the fear of scarcity of products the consumers' buy more at higher prices. On the other hand, during the depression, the fall in prices is not a sufficient condition for consumers to buy more as there will be a fall in their income during the period of depression.
7. **Changes in tastes and fashion:** The changes in consumer needs, fashion, taste, preferences, customs, beliefs, etc., are also responsible to make the law of demand ineffective. The quantity demanded may not be related to the change in price in such cases. For example, when a digital camera replaces a normal manual camera, no amount of reduction in the price of the latter is sufficient to clear the stocks.

Digital cameras, on the other hand, will have more customers even though its price may be going up. The law of demand, therefore, becomes ineffective in such cases.

8. **Demonstration effect:** It refers to a tendency of low-income groups to imitate the consumption pattern of high-income groups. The consumers buy a product to imitate the consumption of their neighbours even if they do not have sufficient purchasing power.

5.8. SHIFT IN DEMAND

When changes in demand are due to factors other than the price it is called the shift in demand. If the price remains constant, the increase in income of a person allows him to buy more products for liberal consumption and vice versa. The factors such as tastes and preferences, price of related goods, expected change in price and income, size of the population, advertisements, distribution of national income, and other factors such as nature, quality and quantity also cause a shift in the demand curve.

1. **Increase in demand:** Due to factors other than price when more quantity is demanded at the same price, it is referred to as an increase in demand. Technically, the increase in demand may be due to higher quantity at the same price or same quantity at a higher price. The demand curve shifts towards the right or upwards.

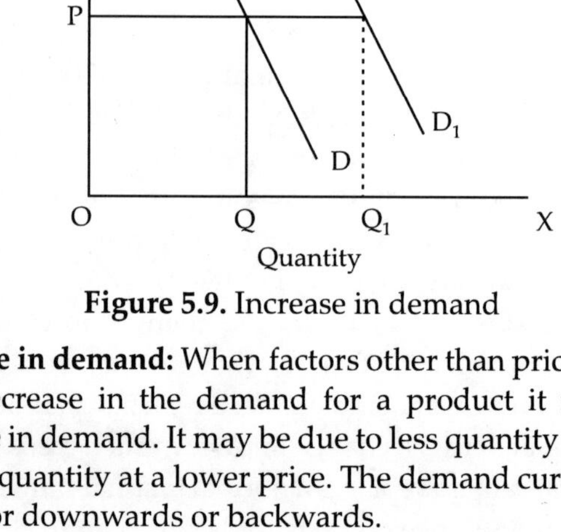

Figure 5.9. Increase in demand

2. **Decrease in demand:** When factors other than price are responsible for a decrease in the demand for a product it is referred to as decrease in demand. It may be due to less quantity at the same price or same quantity at a lower price. The demand curve shifts towards the left or downwards or backwards.

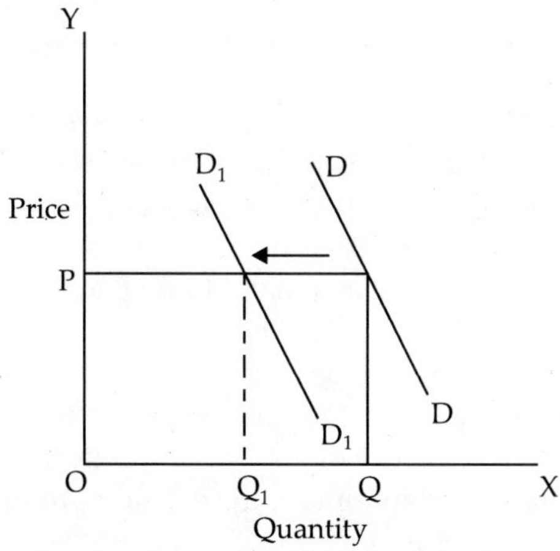

Figure 5.10. Decrease in demand

5.9. SUMMARY

- The demand for a product is a schedule of the quantity that consumers would be willing to purchase at all possible prices at a given point of time.
- A product or service is said to have demand when the conditions of desire to have a product/service, ability to pay, and willingness to have such product/service are satisfied.
- A demand schedule is a tabular statement showing different quantities of a product that can be bought at different prices during a specified time.
- The demand curve shows a graphical representation of the relationship between the price of a product and its quantity demanded.
- Individual demand refers to the quantity demanded of a product by a particular consumer at various prices. The demand for the total or aggregate market at various prices for a product is known as market demand.
- Consumer goods refer to such products and services which are used or consumed by individuals to satisfy their needs and desires. Producer goods are the goods which can be used for the further process of production of goods or services to earn income.
- Durable goods are those goods whose total utility is not exhausted in single or short-run use. Perishable goods are the goods which can be used only once such as food items and their total utility are exhausted in a single use.

- Short-run demand refers to the demand for a product in a short period. The long-run demand refers to the demand for a product, which exists over a long period.
- The quantity of a business unit's yield that can be sold at a given price over a period refers to the demand for a business unit's product. The aggregate demand for the product of all business units of the industry is known as the market demand or demand for the industry's product.
- When a product is demanded in a market independently such demand is called autonomous demand. The demand for a product that arises because of the demand for some other product is called derived demand.
- New demand refers to the demand for new products sold in the market and it is an addition to the existing stock. Replacement demand refers to the products purchased to replace the existing products or the parts therein.
- The total demand for a product in a given region is called total market demand. The demand for a product by anyone of the business unit or industry among others from the given region is called segment market demand.
- The different demand situations a company may face when a product is introduced are negative demand, no demand, latent demand, seasonal demand, irregular demand, falling demand, full demand, overfull demand, and unwholesome demand.
- The various determinants of demand are the price of the product, income of the consumer, tastes and preferences, price of related goods, expected change in price, expected change in income of the consumes, size of the population, the distribution pattern of national income, advertisement costs, and other factors.
- Demand function describes the relationship between demand and its determinants.
- The law of demand shows the functional relationship between the price of a product and its quantity demanded in the market with an assumption that all the other demand determinants remain same or do not change in a given point of time.
- The causes for the downward sloping of the demand curve are the law of diminishing marginal utility, the principle of equi-marginal utility, income effect, substitution effect, different uses of a product, and consumer psychology.
- There are a few exceptions to the law of demand such as inferior goods, conspicuous consumption, conspicuous necessities, consumers' ignorance, expected changes in prices, extraordinary situations, changes in tastes and fashions, and demonstration effect.

- Due to factors other than price when more quantity is demanded at the same price, it is referred to as an increase in demand. When factors other than price are responsible for a decrease in the demand for a product it is referred to as a decrease in demand.

SHORT ANSWER QUESTIONS

1. Define the term demand.
2. What are demand schedule and demand curve?
3. Write a short note on individual demand and market demand.
4. What are consumer goods and producer goods?
5. Write a short note on total demand and segment market demand.
6. What is Giffen paradox?
7. Write a short note on the Veblen effect.
8. What is the shift in demand?

ESSAY ANSWER QUESTIONS

1. What is demand? Explain the concept of demand with suitable examples.
2. Discuss the relationship between income and demand with examples.
3. Explain how the prices of related goods are affected by a change in the quantity demanded.
4. Discuss the various demand distinctions with suitable illustrations.
5. Elucidate the different demand situations a business unit may face when a product is introduced.
6. What is the demand function? Explain the various demand determinants.
7. Discuss why the demand curve slopes downwards from left to right.
8. Define the law of demand. Explain the exceptions to the law of demand.

FILL IN THE BLANKS

1. Law of demand states that price and demand are __________ related.
2. Giffen goods are also known as __________.
3. When changes in demand are due to factors other than the price it is called __________.
4. Demand curve slopes downwards from __________.
5. Pepsi and Coke are __________ goods.
6. The demand schedule for the whole or aggregate market is called __________ schedule.
7. Car and petrol are __________ goods.
8. The graphical representation of the demand schedule is called __________.
9. The products which are used or consumed by individuals to satisfy their needs and desires are known as __________.
10. When the targeted customers have negative reactions to a product then such demand is called __________.

11. The products such as woollen clothes, umbrellas, and raincoats will have__________ demand.
12. Milk and vegetables are perishable goods. (T/F)
13. Steel and cement are derived goods. (T/F)
14. The income demand curve for inferior goods will have a positive slope. (T/F)
15. Overfull demand arises when the demand for a product exceeds the supply. (T/F)
16. The demand for a product may change when there is a significant change in the price of related products. (T/F)

Answers:

1. Inversely
2. Inferior goods
3. Shift in demand
4. Left to right
5. Substitute
6. Market demand
7. Complementary
8. Demand curve
9. Consumer goods
10. Negative demand
11. Seasonal
12. True
13. True
14. False
15. True
16. True

MULTIPLE-CHOICE QUESTIONS

1. The demand curve is:
   (A) Horizontal straight line to X-axis
   (B) Horizontal straight line to Y-axis
   (C) Slopes downwards from left to right
   (D) Slopes upwards from left to right
2. Tomato is categorised as:
   (A) Durable goods (B) Perishable goods
   (C) Perennial goods (D) Temporary goods
3. The income demand curve for normal goods will have an:
   (A) Upward slope (B) Downward slope
   (C) Upward movement (D) Negative slope
4. The products that can be used in place of other products are known as
   (A) Inferior goods (B) Superior goods
   (C) Complementary goods (D) Substitute goods
5. The goods which can be used for the further process of production to earn income are called:
   (A) Consumer goods (B) Producer goods
   (C) Multi-user goods (D) Normal goods
6. The demand for a product by anyone of the business unit or industry among others from the given region is called:
   (A) Firm demand (B) Industry demand
   (C) Total market demand (D) Segment market demand

7. When the business unit can sell all the products produced without any problem then it is:
   (A) Full demand (B) Latent demand
   (C) Overfull demand (D) Falling demand
8. When the consumer buys more and more of a product, the marginal utility of the additional units consumed will:
   (A) Increase (B) Decrease
   (C) Remain constant (D) Rise
9. Which one of the following is not an exception to the law of demand?
   (A) Conspicuous consumption (B) Conspicuous necessities
   (C) Size of the population (D) Consumers' ignorance
10. The demand for a product that arises because of the demand for some other product is called:
    (A) Derived demand (B) Autonomous demand
    (C) New demand (D) Replacement demand

Answers:

1. C	2. B	3. A	4. D	5. B
6. D	7. A	8. D	9. C	10. A

REFERENCES

1. Benham, F. (1939). *Economics: A General Textbook for Students.* London: Sir Issac Pitman & Sons Ltd.
2. Drucker, P.F. (1955). "Management Science" and the manager. *Management Science,* 1(2), 115-126.
3. Hibdon, J.E. (1969). *Price and Welfare Theory.* McGraw Hill.
4. Kishtainy, N. & Abbot, G. (2012). *The Economics Book* (1st Edn.). New York [N.Y.]: DK Pub.
5. Marshall, Alfred. (1890). *Principles of Economics.* London: Macmillan.
6. Mote, V.L., Paul, S. & Gupta, G.S. (2001). *Managerial Economics: Concepts and Cases.* New Delhi, India: Tata McGraw Hill Publishing Company Ltd.
7. Samuelson, Paul A. (1947). *Foundations of Economic Analysis.* Enlarged Edn. 1983. Harvard University Press.
8. Thomas, C.R. & Maurice, S.C. (2016). *Managerial Economics: Foundations of Business Analysis and Strategy.* New York: McGraw-Hill Education.
9. Varshney, R.L. & Maheswari, K.L. (2014). *Managerial Economics.* New Delhi, India: Sultan Chand & Sons.
10. Veblen, T.B. (1899). *The Theory of the Leisure Class.* New York: MacMillan.

Chapter

6 Elasticity of Demand

LEARNING OBJECTIVES

After studying this chapter, you should be able to understand:

- the concept of elasticity of demand;
- factors affecting the elasticity of demand;
- types of elasticity of demand;
- degrees and measures of different elasticity of demand; and
- significance of elasticity of demand.

6.1. INTRODUCTION

Business units try to understand not only the direction of change in demand but also the degree of change in demand. The direction, as well as the degree of change in demand for a product, helps the business units to work out strategies to achieve desired profit and market share. The concept of the law of demand describes the direction of change in quantity demanded. Elasticity of demand, on the other hand, describes the degree of change in quantity demanded. The demand for a product is influenced by many factors. For example, the demand for a product is influenced by changes in the price, changes in the price of related products, changes in the income level of consumers, and so on. However, it is not sufficient for business units to only be aware of the factors that influence the demand for a product. The business units need to measure the extent to which these factors affect demand.

Elasticity is such a measure to know how much will be the change in quantity demanded by a proportionate change in its determinants either independently or combined. The demand for a product can be elastic, inelastic or unitary. The concept of elasticity of demand is of paramount importance for business organisations as their pricing and profit-making strategies depend upon this information. The government of a country also requires information on the elasticity of demand to formulate various tax related policies.

6.2. CONCEPT OF ELASTICITY OF DEMAND

The concept of elasticity was first introduced by Alfred Marshall (1890), who is regarded as the major contributor to the theory of demand, in his book: *Principles of Economics*. The elasticity of demand explains the relationship between a change in the price of a product and a consequent change in quantity demanded. Elasticity is the most commonly used measurement of the demand function to find the effects of changes in any of its determinants. The best measure of this responsiveness is the proportional or per cent change in the variables.

Definitions of elasticity of demand

Author	Definition
Alfred Marshall (1890)	The elasticity (or responsiveness) of demand in a market is great or small accordingly as the amount demanded increases much or little for a given fall in the price and diminishes much or little for a given rise in price. Elasticity is the ratio of the percentage change in one variable relative to the percentage change in another variable. $\text{Elasticity} = \frac{\text{Percentage change in the dependent variable}}{\text{Percentage change in the independent variable}}$
Richard Lipsey (1997)	The elasticity of demand is the ratio of the percentage change in demand to the percentage change in the price.
K E Boulding (1941)	The elasticity of demand is the percentage change in the quantity demand which would result in one per cent change in price.
Joan Robinson (1934)	The elasticity of demand at any price or any output is equal to the proportional change of amount demanded in response to a small change in price divided by the proportional change in price.

According to Boulding and Robinson, the following formula for calculation of the elasticity of demand is derived as:

$$\text{Elasticity} = \frac{\text{Percentage change in demand}}{\text{Percentage change in the price of the product}}$$

6.2.1. Elastic Demand and Inelastic Demand

A change in demand for a product need not be proportional to the change in the price. Therefore, the elasticity of demand is divided into elastic and inelastic demands.

- When the percentage change in the price of a product leads to a higher percentage of change in quantity demanded, it is called elastic demand. For example, when the price of a TV falls by 5 per cent and the demand for TV increased by more than 5 per cent then the demand is called elastic.
- A large change in the price of a product is followed by a small change in quantity demanded or no change in demand, it is called inelastic demand. For example, if the price of salt increases by 5 per cent and the

demand for salt is either not affected or falls only by less than 5 per cent, it is called inelastic demand.

6.3. FACTORS AFFECTING THE ELASTICITY OF DEMAND

The various factors affecting the elasticity of demand (Figure. 6.1) are:

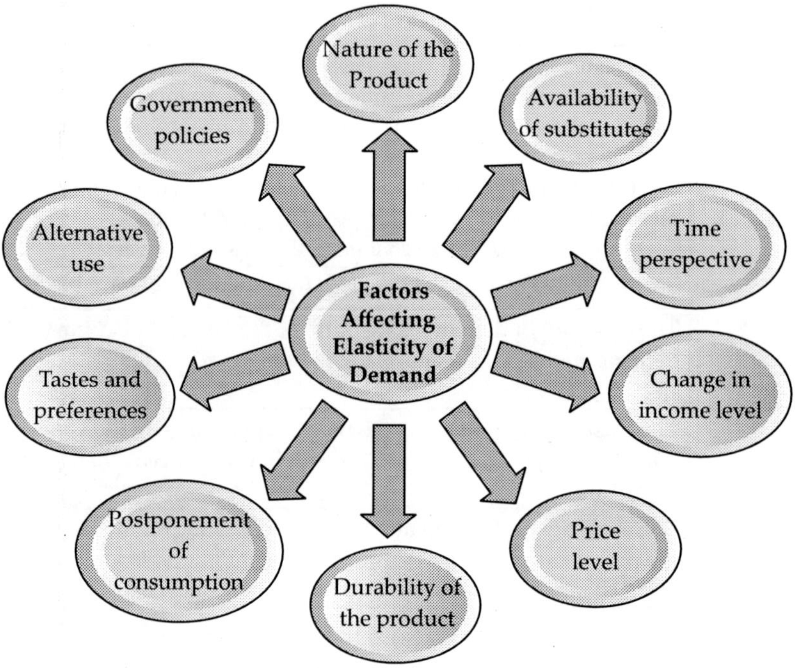

Figure 6.1. Factors affecting elasticity of demand

1. **Nature of the product:** Based on nature, products can be classified as luxuries, comforts and necessities. The demand for luxury products (high-priced cars, refrigerators, diamonds, gold, etc.) is more elastic than the demand for necessities and comforts because consumption of luxury products can be dispensed with or postponed when price increases. On the other hand, consumption of necessary products (rice, clothes, vegetables, sugar, etc.) cannot be postponed and hence, their demand becomes inelastic. Comforts have more elastic demand than necessities and less elastic than luxuries. The elasticity of demand varies from person to person, time to time and place to place.
2. **Availability of substitutes:** One of the most important determinants of elasticity of demand for a product is the availability of its close

substitutes. The higher the degree of the closeness of the substitutes, the greater is the elasticity of demand for a product. For example, Maaza and Slice may be regarded as close substitutes for each other. If the price of one of these product increases, the other product becomes relatively cheaper. Therefore, consumers buy more of relatively cheaper products, and less of the costlier one, when all other determinants remaining constant. On the other hand, sugar and salt do not have their close substitute and hence, their price elasticity is lower.

3. **Time perspective:** Time perspective also plays an important role in determining the elasticity of demand. In the short run, when the consumption of a product cannot be postponed, its demand will be less elastic. In the long run, if the price rises, people may find other ways to reduce the consumption of the product. So, the demand for a product, in the long run, is elastic when other things remain constant. For example, if the price of electricity increases, it is very difficult to cut back its consumption in the short run. However, if the rise in price continues, the consumer may plan for substitutes like gas, heater, fluorescent bulbs, etc., and use less electricity. Thus, the elasticity of demand will be greater in the long run than in the short run.
4. **Change in income level:** Elasticity of demand depends on the income level of the consumer. The rich and the poor are not equally affected by the change in price. The poor people are more affected than the rich. Because of the high income, rich people buy the same amount of an expensive product in response to a rise in price. For example, with a rise in the price of Boost, poor people buy other products which are relatively cheaper than Boost. Thus, for rich people, the demand for Boost is inelastic whereas for poor people the demand for the Boost is elastic.
5. **Price level:** The demand for high priced products is elastic whereas, the low priced products are said to have inelastic demand. High priced products are luxury products and low priced products are necessaries. Luxurious products are mainly consumed by people with high-income levels. For example, if the price of a smart TV falls from Rs. 70,000 to Rs. 60,000 the price comes to the reach of the people who were unable to buy at the old price. Thus, with a rise or fall in price, the quantity demanded of smart TVs remarkably falls or rises. But, if the price of salt increases from Rs.10 to Rs.15, it accounts for no such remarkable fall in the quantity demanded.
6. **The durability of the product:** The demand for durable products is elastic whereas, the demand for non-durable products is inelastic.

Durable products are used over a long period and the utility is destroyed continuously. Once a durable product is bought, the buyer doesn't require it for a long period. Thus, the change in price cannot influence the demand and the demand becomes inelastic. On the other hand, non-durable or perishable goods are consumed repeatedly. Any change in price affects demand. Thus, the demand for perishable goods is elastic.

7. **Postponement of consumption:** The demand for products whose consumption can be postponed for some time is elastic. For example, the products like refrigerator, television, air conditioner, etc., can be postponed if the prices of such products are not within the reach of the consumers. On the other hand, the demand for necessities such as food grains, medicines, books and milk cannot be postponed. Thus, the demand for those commodities is inelastic.
8. **Tastes and preferences:** When a consumer is particular about the tastes, habits, fashion, and preferences, the product is said to be inelastic. Repeated and stable use of a product by a person forms a habit and it cannot be avoided. Thus, in such a case the consumption of the product cannot be withheld despite the rise in price. Thus, the demand for habitual products (example: toothpaste, tea, coffee, etc.) is fairly inelastic.
9. **Alternative use:** The demand for the products having more than one application or use is said to be elastic. All the uses or applications of the product may not be of the same importance to the consumers. In the case of a rise in price, the product will be used for the most important needs only. When the price falls, the product will be used for many applications. Therefore, the demand for such a product will be elastic.
10. **Government policies:** When the government policies are liberal towards a product, the demand is elastic and vice versa. The government, in the interest of the lower-income group consumers, closely monitors the prices of certain products such as food products and to control price fluctuations such products are distributed through fair- price shops in large quantities to bridge the demand-supply gap. Such a measure stabilises the price and the demand becomes inelastic.

6.4. TYPES OF ELASTICITY OF DEMAND

The elasticity of demand measures the responsiveness of demand for a product with a change in any of its determinants such as the price, income of consumers, and availability of substitutes. Therefore, economists have divided the elasticity of demand into four main categories:

1. Price elasticity of demand
2. Income elasticity ofdemand
3. Cross elasticity of demand
4. Advertisement elasticity of demand

6.5. PRICE ELASTICITY OF DEMAND

Alfred Marshall was the first economist to introduce the concept of price elasticity of demand. Price elasticity of demand measures the changes in quantity demanded of a product as against the change in price. It is the ratio of the percentage change in quantity demanded to the percentage change in price. The price elasticity is always negative because of the inverse relationship between price and quantity demanded. However, as per convention, the negative sign is ignored while calculating the price elasticity of demand.

$$\text{Price elasticity (ep)} = \frac{\text{Proportionate/percentage change in quantity demand for product 'X'}}{\text{Proportionate/percentage change in the price of product 'X'}}$$

The formula is mathematically presented as:

$$ep = \frac{(Q_2 - Q_1)/Q_1}{(P_2 - P_1)/P_1} \text{ or } \frac{\Delta Q}{\Delta P} \times \frac{P}{Q}$$

where,

ΔQ = change in quantity demanded or difference, $Q_2 - Q_1$

ΔP = change in price or difference, $P_2 - P_1$

P = initial price of the product

Q = initial quantity demanded of the product

For example, a business unit sells a product at a price of Rs. 500 and the quantity demanded is 20 units. The business unit decided to reduce the price to Rs. 400, as a result, there is an increase in demand by 30 units. In this case, the price elasticity of demand can be computed as follows:

where,

$$P = \text{Rs. } 500$$
$$Q = 20 \text{ units}$$
$$\Delta P = \text{Rs. } 100\ (500 - 400)$$
$$\Delta Q = 10 \text{ units } (30 - 20)$$

By substituting these values in the formula:

$$E_P = \frac{10}{100} \times \frac{500}{20} = 0.25$$

Thus, the elasticity of demand is 0.25.

6.5.1. Degrees of Price Elasticity of Demand

The extent of responsiveness of demand with a change in the price does not remain the same in all circumstances. The demand for a product can be elastic or inelastic, depending on the rate of change in the demand with respect to a change in the price of a product. The demand elasticity can be classified into five categories based on the degree of response to the change in price.

1. Perfectly elastic demand
2. Perfectly inelastic demand
3. Relatively elastic demand
4. Relatively inelastic demand
5. Unitary elastic demand

1. **Perfectly elastic demand:** When a small change (rise or fall) in price leads to an infinite or large change (rise or fall) in quantity demanded, it is called perfectly elastic demand. Under such type of elasticity of demand, a small rise in price results in a fall in demand to zero, while a small fall in price causes an increase in demand to infinity. Thus, it is also referred to as *infinite elasticity of demand* and denoted as $E_P = \infty$. In perfectly elastic demand, the demand curve will be a horizontal straight line, i.e., parallel to X-axis as shown in Figure 6.2.

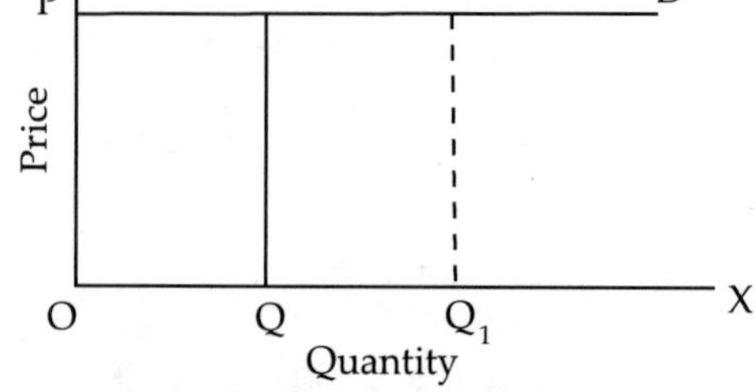

Figure 6.2. Perfectly elastic demand

The demand curve (D) is a horizontal straight line or parallel to X-axis. It shows that the increase or decrease in demand will not be due to a change in price.

2. **Perfectly inelastic demand:** When a change (rise or fall) in the price of a product does not bring any change (fall or rise) in the quantity demanded, the demand is called perfectly inelastic demand. In this case, even a large change in price fails to bring about a change in quantity demanded or demand remains constant. It is also referred to as *zero elasticity of demand* and denoted as $E_p = 0$. A perfectly inelastic demand curve is represented as a vertical straight line, i.e., parallel to Y-axis as shown in Figure 6.3.

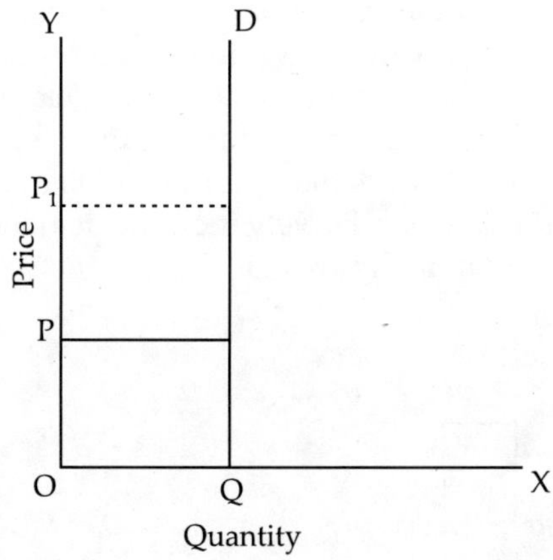

Figure 6.3. Perfectly inelastic demand

The demand curve (D) is parallel or vertical to Y-axis. When price increases the quantity demanded remains the same. In other words, the response of demand to a change in price is nil.

3. **Relatively elastic demand:** When a percentage change (fall or rise) in price results in greater than the percentage change (rise or fall) in

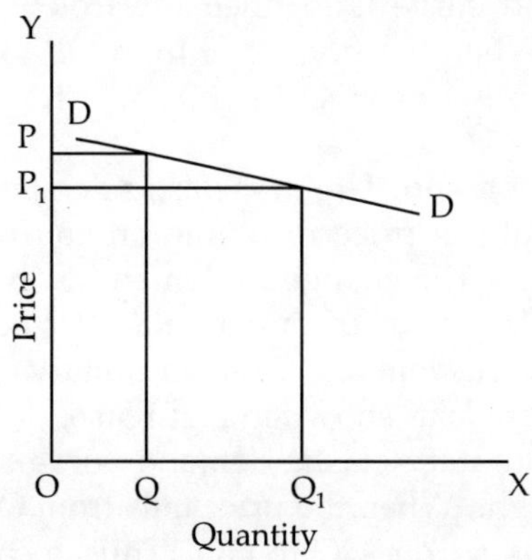

Figure 6.4. Relatively elastic demand

quantity demanded, the demand is said to be relatively elastic. In other words, a small change in price leads to a large change in the quantity demanded. Therefore, the elasticity of demand is *greater than one* and denoted as $E_p > 1$. The demand curve of relatively elastic demand gradually slopes downwards as shown in Figure 6.4.
Here, the demand curve is inclined to X-axis or the curve will be flatter. When the price falls from 'OP' to 'OP$_1$', the amount demanded increases from 'OQ' to 'OQ$_1$' which is larger than the change in price.

4. **Relatively inelastic demand:** When a major percentage of change (fall or rise) in price results in a minor percentage of change (rise or fall) in demand, the demand is said to be relatively inelastic. In other words, the change in demand is less than the change in price. Therefore, the elasticity of demand is *less than one* and denoted as $E_p < 1$. The demand curve of relatively inelastic demand rapidly slopes downwards as shown in Figure 6.5.

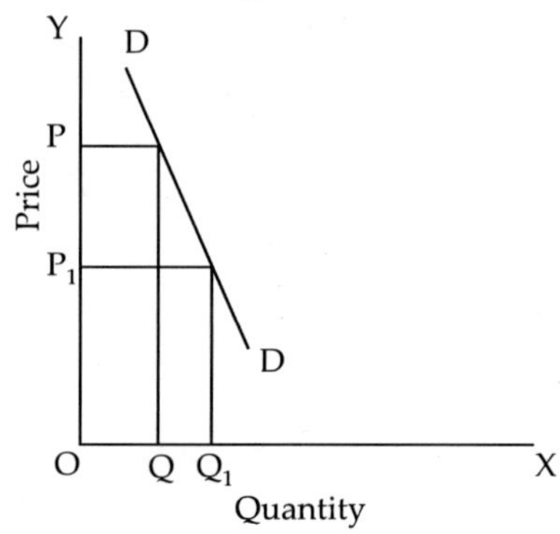

Figure 6.5. Relatively inelastic demand

Here, the demand curve is inclined towards Y-axis or the curve will be steeper. When the price falls from OP to OP$_1$, the amount demanded increases from OQ to OQ$_1$, which is smaller than the change in price.

5. **Unitary elastic demand:** Unitary elastic demand occurs when a change (rise or fall) in price results in an equivalent change (fall or rise) in demand. The change in demand is exactly equal to the change in price. The value of unitary elastic is equal to one and is denoted as $E_p = 1$. The demand curve for unitary elastic demand is a rectangular hyperbola as shown in Figure 6.6.
Here, DD is the unitary elastic demand curve sloping uniformly from left to the right. When the price falls from OP to OP$_1$ quantity demanded increases from OQ to OQ$_1$. Thus, a change in price has resulted in an equal change in quantity.

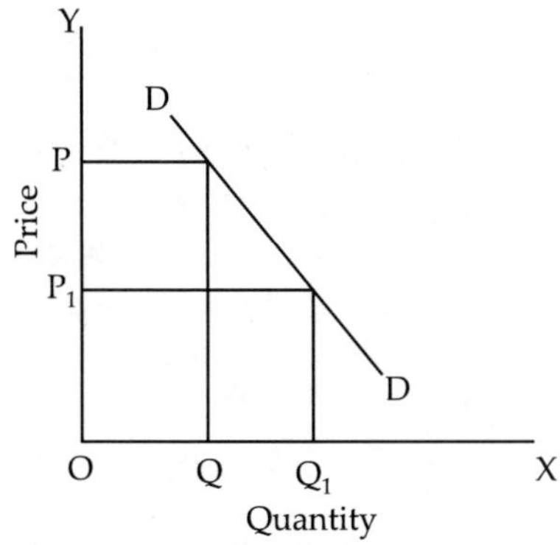

Figure 6.6. Unitary elastic demand

6.5.2. Measurement of Price Elasticity of Demand

In practical applications, it is not sufficient to determine whether the demand for a product or service is elastic or inelastic. A business unit needs to estimate the numerical value of the change in quantity demanded with respect to change in the given price for taking business decisions. The numerical value of price elasticity of demand for a product can be measured by various methods. There are four methods of measuring price elasticity of demand.

1. Percentage method
2. Total outlay method
3. Point elasticity method
4. Arc elasticity method

1. Percentage Method

In this method, the percentage change in demand and percentage change in price is compared. This method is also known as the *ratio method.* The price elasticity of demand is shown as a ratio of proportionate change in quantity demanded to the price of the product. This method can also be treated as an analytical approach.

E_P = Percentage change in demand / Percentage change in price

$$E_P = \%\Delta Q/\%\Delta P$$

where,

$\%\Delta Q$ = percentage change in demand $(Q_2 - Q_1)$

$\%\Delta P$ = percentage change in price $(P_2 - P_1)$

In this method, three values of E_p can be obtained:

- If the percentage change in demand is equal to a percentage change in price, it is unitary elastic ($E_p = 1$).
- If the percentage change in demand is greater than the percentage change in price, then the demand is elastic ($E_p > 1$).

- If the percentage change in demand is less than the change in price, the demand is inelastic ($E_p < 1$).

2. Total Outlay Method

The total outlay method was introduced by Alfred Marshall. According to this method, the price elasticity of a product is measured on the basis of the total amount of money spent (total expenditure) by consumers on the consumption of that product. It is also known as a *total expenditure* or *total revenue method.* The price elasticity can be measured by comparing consumers' expenditure or outlay before the change in the price with that of after change in the price. In the total outlay method, three cases are considered:

(i) When a fall in the price of a product leads to a greater increase in the quantity demanded resulting in the rise of total expenditure, the elasticity of demand is more than one ($E_p > 1$) as shown in Table 6.1.

Table 6.1. Total outlay-More than elastic demand

Price (Rs.)	Quantity (units)	Total expenditure (Rs.)
20	10 Pens	200
10	30 Pens	300

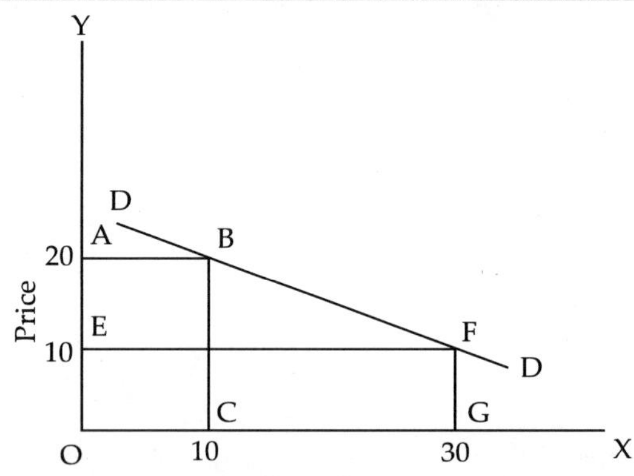

Figure 6.7. Total outlay-More than elastic demand

If the same is represented in the form of a graph it will be like as shown in Figure 6.7. Since OEFG is greater than OABC it implies that a change in quantity demanded is proportionately more than the change in price. Hence, the demand is elastic (i.e., more than one).

(ii) When a percentage fall in price rises the quantity demanded a product so much as to leave the total expenditure unchanged, the elasticity of demand is said to be unitary ($E_p = 1$) as shown in Table 6.2.

Table 6.2. Total outlay - Unitary elastic demand

Price (Rs.)	Quantity (units)	Total expenditure (Rs.)
10	30 Pens	300
5	60 Pens	300

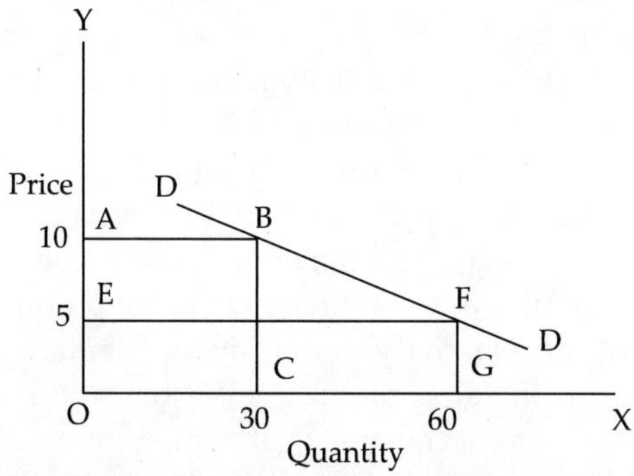

Figure 6.8. Total outlay-Unitary elastic demand

If the same is represented in the form of a graph it will be like as shown in Figure 6.8. Here, OABC = OEFG which implies that the change in quantity demanded is proportionately equal to change in price. So, the price elasticity of demand is equal to one ($E_p = 1$).

(iii) When a percentage fall in price rises the quantity demanded of a product to cause a decrease in total expenditure, the demand is said to be inelastic or less than one (Table 6.3). It is denoted as $E_d < 1$.

Table 6.3. Total outlay-Less than elastic demand

Price (Rs.)	Quantity (units)	Total expenditure (Rs.)
5	60 pens	300
2	100 pens	200

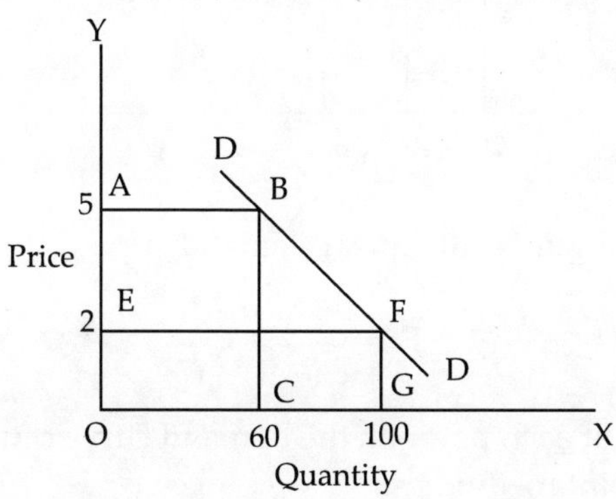

Figure 6.9. Total outlay-Less than elastic demand

If the same is represented in the form of a graph it will be like as shown in Figure 6.9. Since OEFG is smaller than OABC, this implies that the change in quantity demanded is proportionately less than the change in price. Hence, the price elasticity of demand is less than one or inelastic.

3. Point Elasticity Method

The measurement of elasticity at a specific point on the demand curve is called point elasticity. The point elasticity method is also called 'geometric method' or 'slope method'. The point elasticity of demand is defined as "the proportionate change in the quantity demanded of a product as a result of small proportionate change in price." The points at which elasticity is measured are lower and upper segments of the curve. The point price elasticity of demand is measured on linear curves and non-linear curves.

(i) Measurement of elasticity on a linear demand curve: If the demand curve is linear (straight line), it has a unitary elasticity at the midpoint. The total revenue is at a maximum at this point. Any point above the midpoint has an elasticity greater than one, ($E_d > 1$). The point below the midpoint shows the elasticity as less than one ($E_d < 1$). The Figure 6.10 shows the measurement of a linear demand curve.

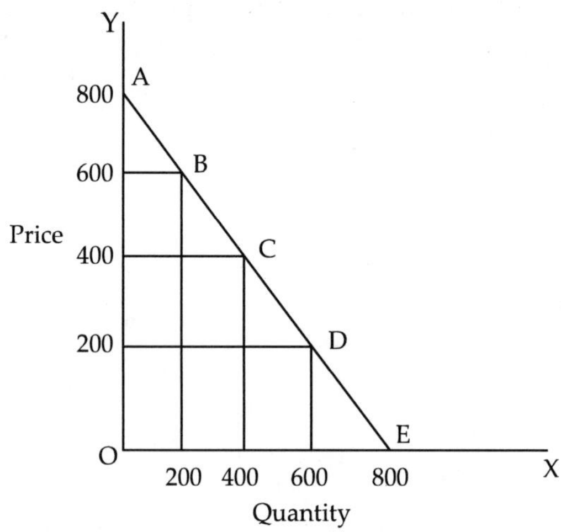

Figure 6.10. Linear demand curve

$$E_d = \frac{\%\Delta Q}{\%\Delta P} \times \frac{P}{Q}$$

The elasticity at each point on the demand curve can be traced with the help of point method as:

$$E_d = \frac{\text{Lower segment}}{\text{Upper segment}}$$

1. Elasticity of demand at point D = $\frac{DG}{DA} = \frac{400}{400}$ = 1 (unity)
2. Elasticity of demand at point E = $\frac{GE}{EA} = \frac{200}{600}$ = 0.33 (<1)
3. Elasticity of demand at point C = $\frac{GC}{CA} = \frac{600}{200}$ = 3 (>1)
4. The elasticity of demand at point A is infinity.
5. At point G, the elasticity of demand is zero.

(ii) Measurement of elasticity on a nonlinear demand curve: When the demand curve is nonlinear, the elasticity at a point can be measured by drawing a tangent to the demand curve at the point of the price. The magnitude of elasticity at the point is arrived at by dividing the lower part of the tangent with the upper part of the tangent. Figure 6.11 shows that DD is a nonlinear demand curve. To measure elasticity at point P, the tangent MN is drawn on the demand curve.

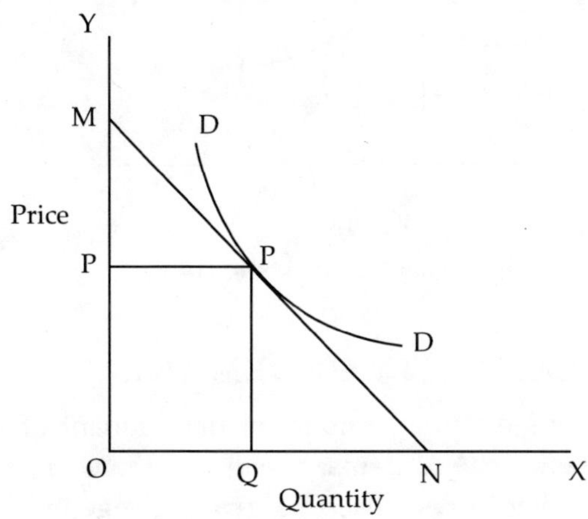

Figure 6.11. Nonlinear demand curve

4. Arc Elasticity Method

Under this method, elasticity is measured over an arc of the demand curve. For example, as shown in Figure 6.12, when the price of a product is P, the demand for the product is Q. When price changes to P_1, the demand also changes to Q_1. To measure elasticity, the average of prices ($P_1 - P/2$) and the average of demand ($Q_1 - Q/2$) will be taken. The formula for measuring elasticity is:

$$E_d = \frac{\Delta Q}{\Delta P} \times \frac{P_1 + P}{Q_1 + Q}$$

where,

ΔQ denotes a change in quantity
ΔP denotes a change in price
Q signifies the initial quantity
Q_1 denotes a new quantity
P stands for the initial price
P_1 denotes the new price

The arc elasticity concept yields only rough or approximate measures. In case of high fluctuations in prices and consequent variations in demand, the arc elasticity gives a broad idea of elasticity of demand.

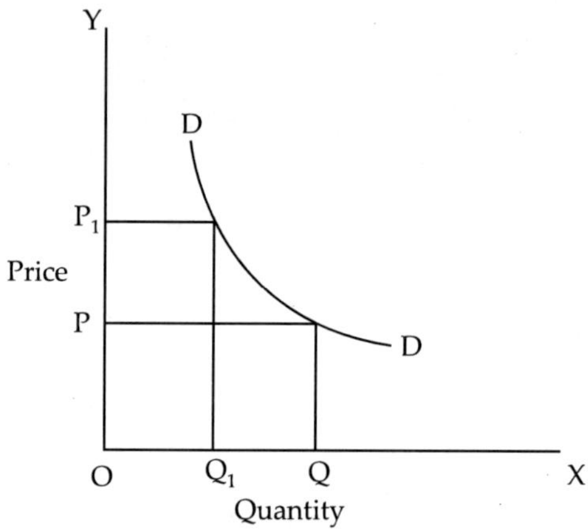

Figure 6.12. Arc elastic curve

6.6. INCOME ELASTICITY OF DEMAND

The income of consumers is an important determinant of demand for a product. Income elasticity of demand refers to the change in quantity demanded of a product in response to a given change in income of the consumer.

Mathematically, the income elasticity of demand can be stated as:

$$\text{Income elasticity} = \frac{\text{Proportionate change in quantity demanded of a product}}{\text{Proportionate change in consumer's income}}$$

The formula for calculating income elasticity of demand is:

$$E_I = \frac{(Q_2 - Q_1)/Q_1}{(I_2 - I_1)/I_1} \text{ or } \frac{\Delta Q}{\Delta I} \times \frac{I}{Q}$$

where,

ΔQ = change in quantity demanded or difference, $Q_2 - Q_1$

ΔI = change in income or difference, $I_2 - I_1$

I = initial income of the consumer

Q = initial quantity demanded

For example, if the apples demanded by an individual increased from 25 units to 35 units due to increase in monthly income from Rs. 10,000 to Rs. 25,000, the income elasticity of demand will be:

ΔI = 25,000 – 10,000 = Rs. 15,000

ΔQ = 35 – 25 = 10 units

I = Rs. 10,000

Q = 25 units

$$E_I = \frac{\Delta Q}{\Delta I} \times \frac{I}{Q} = \frac{10}{15,000} \times \frac{10,000}{25} = 0.27$$

Thus, the income elasticity of demand is 0.27.

6.6.1. Degrees of Income Elasticity of Demand

The income elasticity of demand varies for different products and under different situations. The income elasticity of demand is positive for superior products and negative for inferior products. Based on numerical value, the income elasticity of demand is classified into three groups:

1. Positive income elasticity
2. Zero income elasticity
3. Negative income elasticity

1. **Positive income elasticity (E_I > = 0):** When a percentage change in income of a consumer increases leads to proportionate change in demand of a product, the income elasticity of demand is said to be positive. This is possible in case of normal products. This can be further classified into three types:
   (a) Income elasticity greater than one
   (b) Income elasticity less than one
   (c) Income elasticity equal to one
   (a) **Income elasticity is greater than one ($E_I > 1$):** When a percentage change in demand is greater than the percentage change in income, a greater portion of income is spent on a product with an increase in income, it is said to be greater than one.

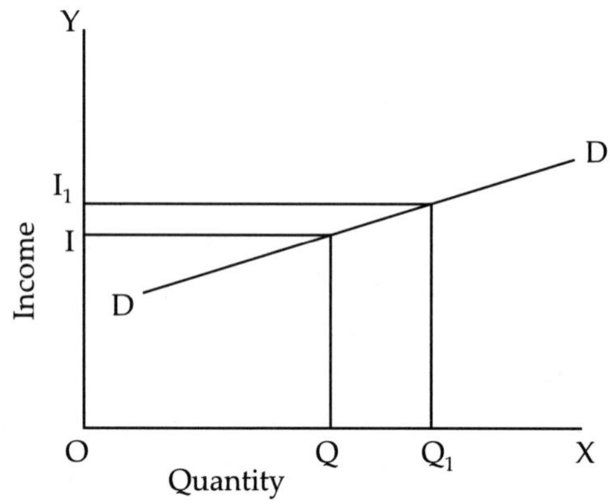

Figure 6.13. Income elasticity greater than one

In Figure 6.13, DD is the curve representing positive income elasticity of demand, i.e. greater than one. The curve is slanting upwards from left to right, which shows a greater increase in quantity demanded (Q to Q_1) as a result of the rise in income (I to I_1).

(b) Income elasticity less than one (E_I < 1): This occurs when the percentage change in quantity demanded of a product is less than the percentage change in income.

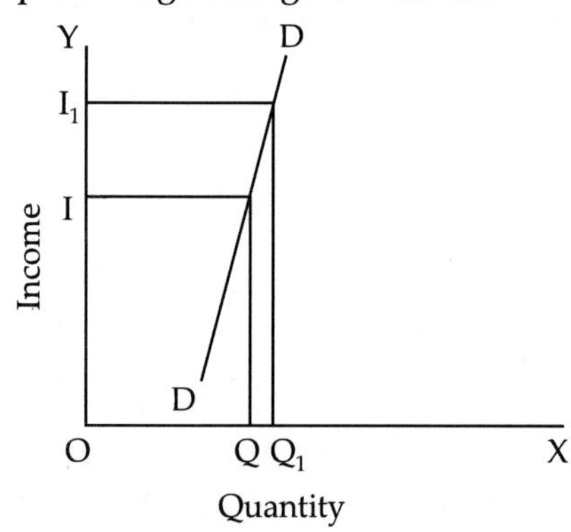

Figure 6.14. Income elasticity less than one

In Figure 6.14, DD is the curve representing positive income elasticity of demand, i.e., less than one. The curve is moving upwards from left to the right, slanting marginally slowing a low increase in quantity demanded (Q to Q_1) as a result of the rise in income (I to I_1).

(c) Income elasticity equal to one (E_I = 1): When the proportion of income spent on a product remains the same or when the percentage change in income is equal to the percentage change in demand, income elasticity is unitary.

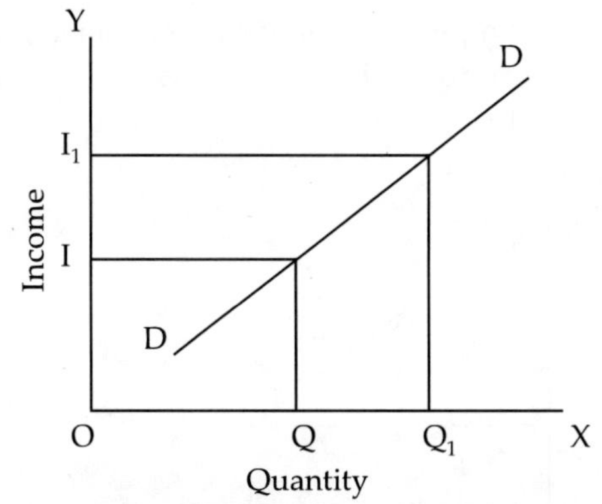

Figure 6.15. Unitary income elasticity

In Figure 6.15, DD is the curve representing unitary elasticity of demand. The curve is moving upwards from left to the right, which shows an equal increase in quantity demanded (Q to Q_1) and income (I to I_1).

2. **Zero income elasticity of demand (E_I = 0):** When a change in income of a consumer does not bring any change in the demand for a product, the income elasticity of demand is zero. It occurs for utility products such as salt, kerosene, electricity, etc.

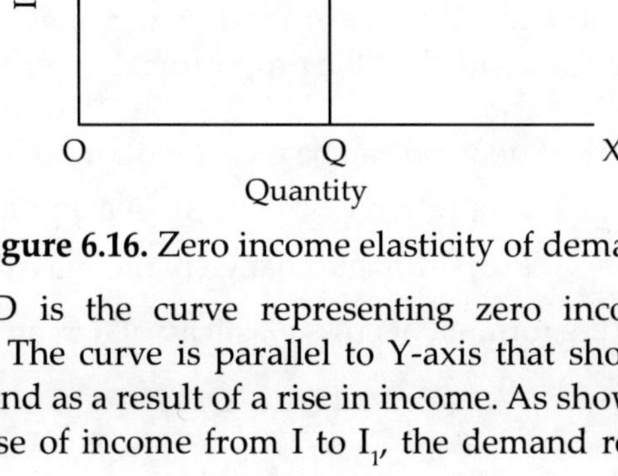

Figure 6.16. Zero income elasticity of demand

Here, DD is the curve representing zero income elasticity of demand. The curve is parallel to Y-axis that shows no change in the demand as a result of a rise in income. As shown in Figure 6.16, with a rise of income from I to I_1, the demand remains the same, i.e., Q.

3. **Negative income elasticity of demand ($E_I < 0$):** In the case of inferior products, the income effect beyond a certain level of income becomes negative. This implies that as the income increases, instead of buying more of a product the consumer buys less and switches on to a superior product. The income elasticity of demand in such cases will be negative.

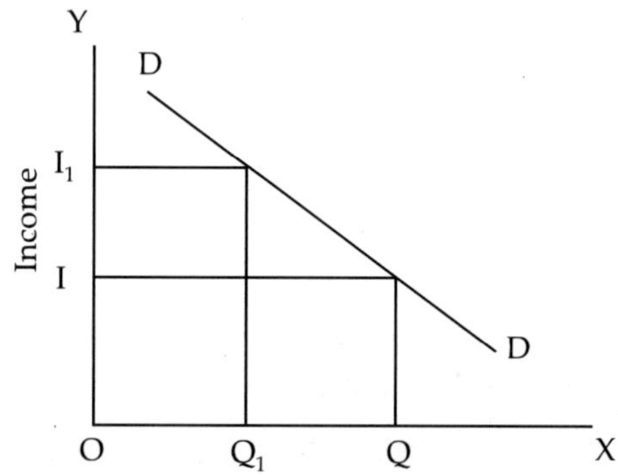

Figure 6.17. Negative income elasticity of demand

Here, DD is the curve representing negative income elasticity of demand. The curve is sloping downwards from left to right, which shows a decrease in the demand as a result of the rise in income. As shown in Figure 6.17, with a rise in income from I to I_1 the demand falls from Q to Q_1.

6.7. CROSS ELASTICITY OF DEMAND

The cross elasticity of demand can be defined as a measure of a change in the quantity demanded a product as a result of a change in the price of related products which may be a substitute or complementary product. The cross elasticity of demand is the proportional change in the quantity demanded of product X divided by the proportional change in the price of the related product Y.

The cross elasticity of demand can be measured as:

$$\text{Cross elasticity } (E_c) = \frac{\text{Proportionate change in demand for product 'X'}}{\text{Proportionate change in the price of product 'Y'}}$$

Mathematically, the formula of cross elasticity of demand is stated as:

$$E_c = \frac{(Qx_2 - Qx_1)/Qx_1}{(Py_2 - Py_1)/Py_1} \text{ or } \frac{\Delta Q_x}{\Delta Q_y} \times \frac{P_y}{Q_x}$$

where,

ΔQ_x = change in quantity demanded or difference, $Qx_2 - Qx_1$

ΔP_y = change in price or difference, $Py_2 - Py_1$

P_y = initial price of product Y

Q_x = initial quantity demanded product X

For example, the quantity of demanded detergent cakes has increased from 600 units to 700 units with an increase in the price of detergent powder from Rs. 150 to Rs. 200. The cross elasticity of demand between the two products will be:

$\Delta Q_x = 700 - 600 = 100$ units

$\Delta P_y = 200 - 150 =$ Rs. 50

$P_y = 150$

$Q_x = 600$ units

$$E_c = \frac{100}{50} \times \frac{150}{600} = 0.5$$

Thus, the cross elasticity of demand is 0.5.

6.7.1. Degrees of Cross Elasticity of Demand

Cross elasticity of demand is always referred with substitute and complementary products. The greater the cross elasticity the more related are the two products. The cross elasticity will be zero if the two products have no relationship. The cross elasticity of demand can be classified into the following three types:

1. Positive cross elasticity
2. Negative cross elasticity
3. Zero cross elasticity

1. **Positive cross elasticity (E_c > 0):** When an increase in the price of a related product results in an increase in the demand for the main product and vice versa, the cross elasticity of demand is said to be positive. Cross elasticity of demand is positive in the case of substitute products. The substitute products like Pepsi and Coke have positive cross elasticity because the increase in the price of Pepsi may increase the demand of Coke, and the consumer may shift from the consumption of Pepsi to Coke or vice versa. Thus, the cross elasticity of demand for the two products is greater than zero.

   Figure 6.18 shows the positive cross elasticity of demand. When the price of product Y is increased from P to P_1 and the price of product X is constant, the quantity demanded product X increases from Q to Q_1.

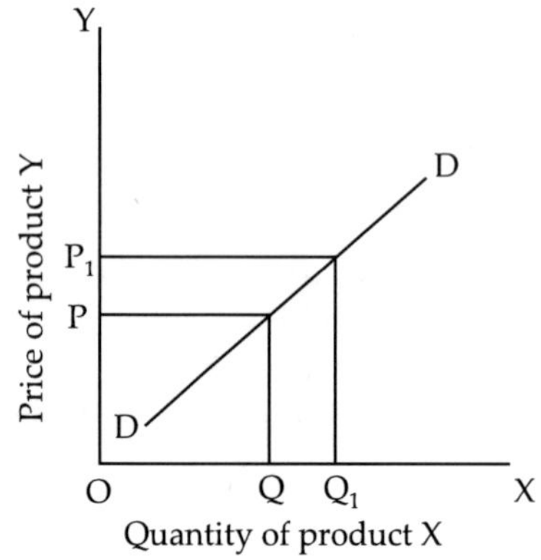

Figure 6.18. Positive cross elasticity

2. **Negative cross elasticity (E_C < 0):** When an increase in the price of a related product results in the decrease of the demand of the main product and vice versa, the elasticity of demand is said to be negative. The cross elasticity is negative if the commodities are compliments. Complementary products (car and petrol) have negative cross elasticity because an increase in the price of the car will reduce the quantity demanded of petrol. So, cross elasticity is found here, negative which is less than zero.

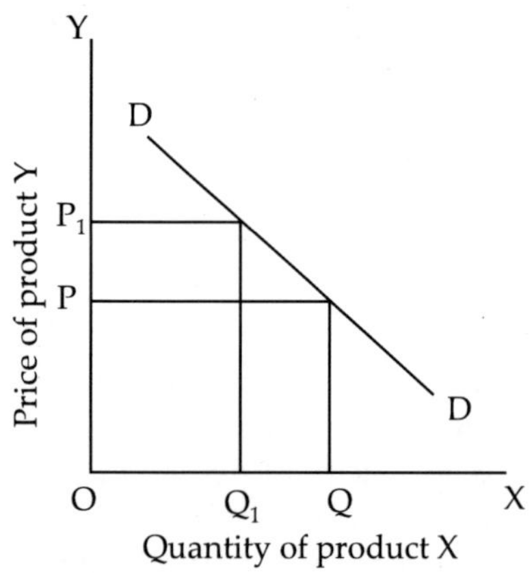

Figure 6.19. Negative cross elasticity

Figure 6.19 shows the negative cross elasticity of demand. When the price of product Y is increased from P to P_1 and the price of product X is constant, the quantity demanded product X decreases from Q to Q_1.

3. **Zero cross elasticity of demand (E_C = 0):** When a proportionate change in the price of a related product does not bring any change

in the demand for the main product, the negative elasticity of demand is said to be negative. For instance, an increase in the price of the car does not affect the demand for cloth. Thus, cross elasticity of demand is zero in the case of independent products or when substitutability does not exist.

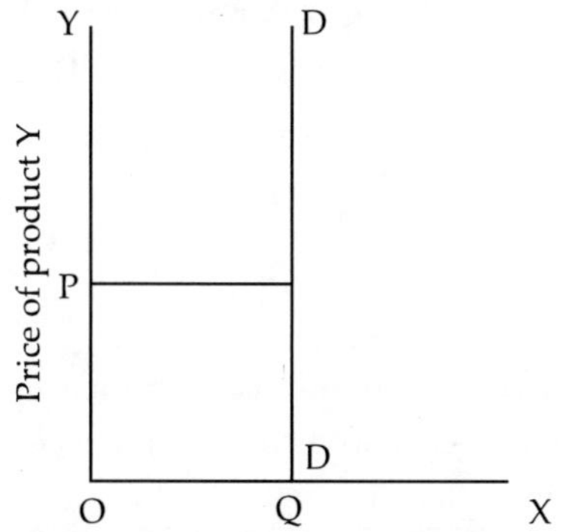

Figure 6.20. Zero cross elasticity

Figure 6.20 shows the zero cross elasticity of demand. When the price of product Y increases the quantity demanded product X remains constant. Thus, the concept of cross elasticity of demand helps the business units to forecast the effect of a change in the price of a product on the demand for its substitutes and complementary products. Moreover, it helps an organisation to anticipate the degree of competition in the market.

6.8. ADVERTISING / PROMOTIONAL ELASTICITY OF DEMAND

The products of a business unit reach the market through promotional communication. Many a time the success or failure of a product depends upon how effectively the consumers are communicated. Therefore, every business unit spends a certain amount on the advertisement and other promotional activities intending to create awareness among customers and persuade them to buy the product. There exists a relationship between the amount spent on advertisement and promotional activity and the demand generated. The companies want to measure the degree of relationship between the two variables for effective allocation budgetary resources for generating desired demand. Advertisement elasticity of demand measures the responsiveness of quantity demanded due to a change in advertising costs. Promotional elasticity of demand is positive as the demand increases with an increase in advertising expenditure. This ratio lies between 0 and ∞ (infinity). The advertising elasticity of demand can be measured by using the following formula.

$$\text{Advertising elasticity } (E_A) = \frac{\text{Proportionate change in quantity demanded of a product}}{\text{Proportionate change in advertising expenditure}}$$

The formula is mathematically presented as:

$$E_A = \frac{(Q_2 - Q_1)/Q_1}{(A_2 - A_1)/A_1} \text{ or } \frac{\Delta Q}{\Delta A} \times \frac{A}{Q}$$

where,

ΔQ = change in quantity demanded or difference, $Q_2 - Q_1$

ΔA = change in advertisement cost or difference, $A_2 - A_1$

A = Initial advertisement costs

Q = Initial quantity demanded

For example, the quantity demanded of a product has increased from 500 units to 600 units with an increase in the advertisement expenditure from Rs. 200 to Rs. 250. The promotional elasticity of demand will be:

$\Delta Q = 600 - 500 = 100$ units

$\Delta A = 250 - 200 =$ Rs. 50

A = Rs. 200

Y = 500 units

$$E_c = \frac{100}{50} \times \frac{200}{500} = 0.8$$

Thus, the promotional elasticity of demand is 0.8.

6.8.1. Degrees of Advertising Elasticity of Demand

By measuring the advertisement elasticity of demand, an organisation can determine the optimum level of advertisement expenditure. The different types of advertising elasticity of demand are:

1. Perfectly elastic demand
2. Perfectly inelastic demand
3. Relatively elastic demand
4. Relatively inelastic demand
5. Unitary demand

1. **Perfectly elastic demand:** If a small change in advertising costs leads to an infinitely or large change in quantity demanded, it is called perfectly elastic demand. It is also referred to as infinite elasticity of demand. It is denoted as $E_A = \infty$.

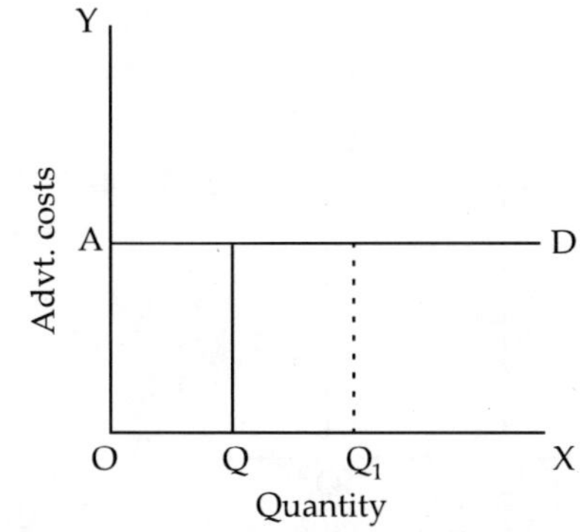

Figure 6.21. Perfectly elastic demand

Figure 6.21 shows that the demand curve DD is a horizontal straight line or parallel to X-axis. It shows that the increase or decrease in demand will not be due to the change in advertisement costs, where the demand rises from OQ to OQ_1 and so on.

2. **Perfectly inelastic demand:** If a change in the advertising costs of a product does not bring any change in the quantity demanded, it is called perfectly inelastic demand. It is also known as zero elasticity of demand. It is denoted as $E_A = 0$.

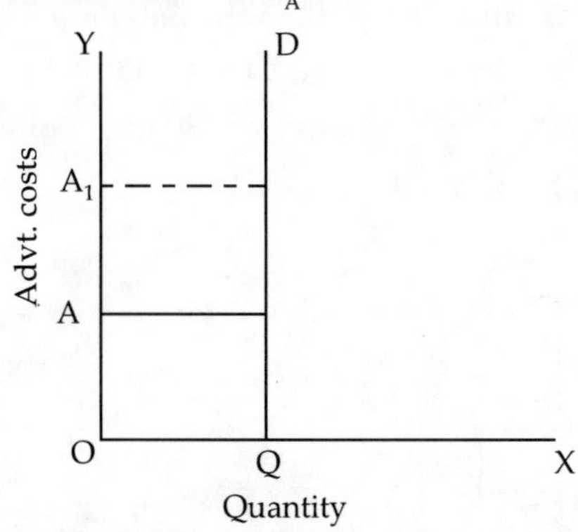

Figure 6.22. Perfectly inelastic demand

Figure 6.22 shows that the demand curve D is parallel or vertical to Y-axis. When advertising costs increase from OA to OA_1, the quantity demanded remains the same.

3. **Relatively elastic demand:** When a proportionate change in advertising costs results in greater than the proportionate change in quantity demanded, it is called relatively elastic demand. Here, the elasticity of demand is greater than one, denoted by $E_A > 1$.

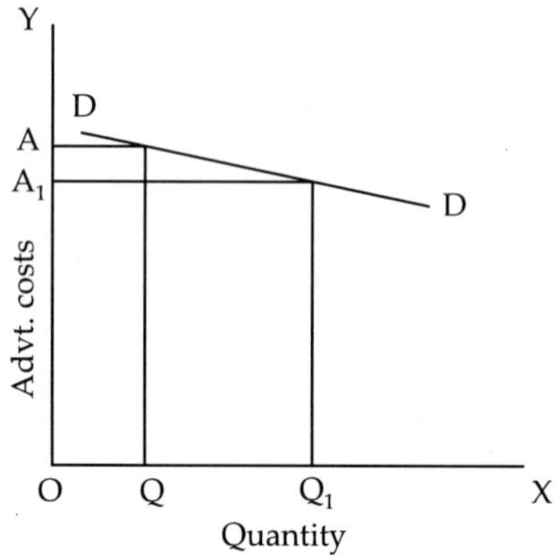

Figure 6.23. Relatively elastic demand

Figure 6.23 shows that the demand curve DD is inclined to X-axis. When the advertisement costs decreased from OA to OA_1, the quantity demanded increases from OQ to OQ_1 which is larger than the change in advertisement costs. Thus, the change in advertising costs leads to more than proportionate change in quantity demanded.

4. **Relatively inelastic demand:** When a proportionate change in advertising costs results in less than the percentage or proportionate change in quantity demanded, it is called relatively inelastic demand. Here, the elasticity of demand is less than one and denoted as $E_A < 1$.

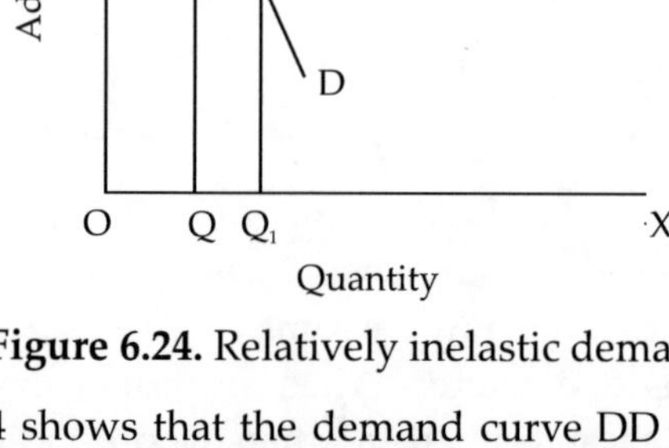

Figure 6.24. Relatively inelastic demand

Figure 6.24 shows that the demand curve DD is inclined towards Y-axis. When advertising costs fall from OA to OA_1, the quantity demanded increases from OQ to OQ_1. Thus, the change in advertising costs leads to less than proportionate change in quantity demanded.

5. **Unitary elastic demand:** Unitary elastic demand occurs when a change in advertising costs results in an equivalent change in demand. The value of unitary elastic is equal to one and is denoted as $E_A = 1$.

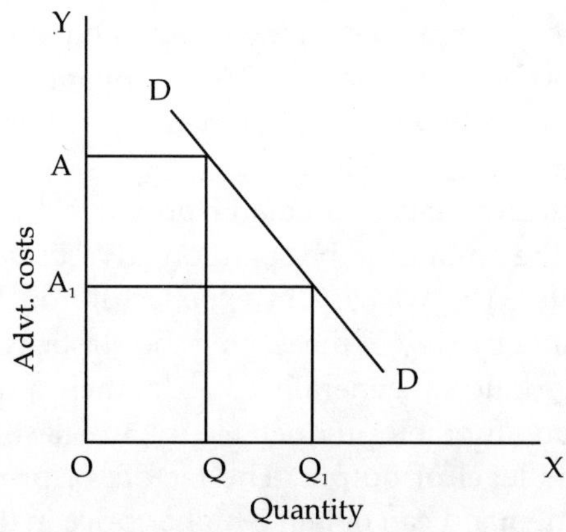

Figure 6.25. Unitary elastic demand

In Figure 6.25, DD is the unitary elastic demand curve sloping uniformly from left to the right. When the advertising costs fall from OA to OA_1 quantity demanded increases from OQ to OQ_1. Thus, a change in advertising costs has resulted in an equal change in quantity.

6.9. SIGNIFICANCE OF ELASTICITY OF DEMAND

The concept of elasticity of demand is much of practical importance to the business units in determining and measuring the demand for their products and services. The significant aspects of elasticity of demand are:

1. Price fixation
2. Price discrimination
3. Advertisement
4. Production
5. International trade

1. **Price fixation:** Price is one of the key determinant factors of demand. The prices fixed for any product must suit the market conditions, i.e., the consumers' expectations and prices of competing brands. Before launching a product into the market, the business unit must carefully analyse the price elasticity to achieve marketing

goals. A failure in fixing the right price may lead to failure of the product in the market. Therefore, the measure of elasticity helps the organisations to fix prices to various products and services under different market conditions.

2. **Price discrimination:** The elasticity of demand may not be uniform in all the segments of the market. In some segments the reaction to price change may be very high, in some segments, it may be moderate, in some segments it may be low and in some segments, there may not be any change. The companies can use price discrimination by differentiating segments based on their response to price changes.
3. **Advertisement:** Elasticity of demand provides a guideline to the producers for the amount to be spent on advertisement to achieve optimum results. The wastage in expenditure on advertisements can be eliminated by way of measuring the elasticity of demand.
4. **Production:** Producers generally decide their production level based on demand for their product. Hence, the elasticity of demand helps to fix the level of output. The factors of production which have inelastic demand can obtain a higher price in the market than those having elastic demand.
5. **International trade:** Elasticity of demand helps in deciding the terms of trade, i.e., the rate at which domestic products are exchanged for foreign products. The rate of foreign exchange is considered on the elasticity of imports and exports of a country. A country benefits from exports of products which have inelastic demand by selling them at a higher price, and in case of elastic demand, it can achieve high turnover at a lower price.

6.10. SUMMARY

- The elasticity of demand explains the relationship between a change in the price of a product and a consequent change in quantity demanded.
- When the percentage change in the price of a product leads to a higher percentage of change in quantity demanded, it is called elastic demand.
- A large change in the price of a product is followed by a small change in quantity demanded or no change in demand, it is called inelastic demand.
- The various factors affecting the elasticity of demand are nature of the product, availability of substitutes, time, change in income level, price level, the durability of the product, postponement of consumption, tastes and preferences, alternative uses, and government policies.

- The elasticity of demand is divided into four main categories, i.e., price elasticity of demand, income elasticity of demand, cross elasticity of demand, and advertisement elasticity of demand.
- Price elasticity of demand measures the changes in quantity demanded of a product as against the change in price.
- The price elasticity of demand is classified into five categories such as perfectly elastic demand, perfectly inelastic demand, relatively elastic demand, relatively inelastic demand, and unitary elastic demand.
- The methods of measuring price elasticity of demand are percentage method, total outlay method, point elasticity method, and arc elasticity method.
- In the percentage method, the percentage change in demand and percentage change in price is compared.
- In total outlay method, the price elasticity of a product is measured based on the total amount of money spent (total expenditure) by consumers on the consumption of that product.
- The measurement of elasticity at a specific point on the demand curve is called point elasticity.
- Income elasticity of demand refers to the quantity demanded of a product in response to a given change in income of the consumer.
- The income elasticity of demand is classified as positive income elasticity, zero income elasticity, and negative income elasticity.
- The cross elasticity of demand is the proportional change in the quantity demanded of product X divided by the proportional change in the price of the related product Y.
- The cross elasticity of demand can be classified as positive cross elasticity, negative cross elasticity, and zero cross elasticity.
- Advertisement elasticity of demand measures the responsiveness of quantity demanded due to a change in advertising costs.
- The different types of advertising elasticity of demand are perfectly elastic demand, perfectly inelastic demand, relatively elastic demand, relatively inelastic demand, and unitary demand.
- The significant aspects of elasticity of demand price fixation, price discrimination, advertisements, production, and international trade.

SHORT ANSWER QUESTIONS

1. What is the price elasticity of demand?
2. What is the income elasticity of demand?
3. Write a short note on cross elasticity of demand.
4. What is promotional elasticity demand?
5. Write a short note on the total expenditure method.

ESSAY ANSWER QUESTIONS

1. What do you understand by the elasticity of demand? Explain the factors affecting it.
2. What is the price elasticity of demand? Elucidate the degrees of price elasticity of demand.
3. Explain the various methods of measuring the price elasticity of demand diagrammatically.
4. What is the advertising elasticity of demand? Discuss the effect of advertising expenses on company profits.
5. Explain the concept of income elasticity of demand. What are the different degrees of measuring income elasticity?
6. What is the cross elasticity of demand? Briefly explain the degrees of cross elasticity of demand.
7. Explain the significance of elasticity of demand.

FILL IN THE BLANKS

1. When the percentage change in the price of a product leads to a higher percentage of change in quantity demanded, it is called _________ demand.
2. A change in the price of a product does not bring any change in the quantity demanded the demand is called _________.
3. The demand curve for unitary elastic demand is a _________.
4. The total outlay method was introduced by _________ .
5. The change in quantity demanded of a product in response to a given change in the income of the consumer is known as _________ of demand.
6. The income elasticity of demand will be negative in the case of _________ goods.

Answers:

1. Elastic
2. Perfectly inelastic demand
3. Rectangular hyperbola
4. Alfred Marshall
5. Income elasticity
6. Inferior

MULTIPLE-CHOICE QUESTIONS

1. If a percentage change in the quantity demanded is equal to the percentage change in price, it is known as:
   (A) Infinite elasticity
   (B) Relatively elastic
   (C) Unit elasticity
   (D) Relatively inelastic
2. The income elasticity of demand is referred to as the:
   (A) Percentage change in quantity demanded to the percentage change in income
   (B) Percentage change in income to the percentage change in price
   (C) Percentage change in the quantity demanded to the percentage change in price
   (D) Percentage change in the advertising expenditure to the percentage change in price

3. The concept of price elasticity of demand was first introduced by:
   (A) Adam Smith (B) Alfred Marshall
   (C) Jone Robinson (D) K E Boulding
4. When a small change in price leads to an infinite or large change in quantity demanded, it is called:
   (A) Perfectly elastic demand (B) Perfectly inelastic demand
   (C) Relatively elastic demand (D) Relatively inelastic demand
5. Percentage method is also known as:
   (A) Geometric method (B) Point method
   (C) Ratio method (D) Total outlay method
6. The measurement of elasticity at a specific point on the demand curve is called:
   (A) Arc elasticity (B) Point elasticity
   (C) Total expenditure method (D) Mathematical method
7. When a change in income of a consumer does not bring any change in the demand for a product, it is:
   (A) Zero income elasticity of demand
   (B) Positive income elasticity of demand
   (C) Negative income elasticity of demand
   (D) Infinite income elasticity of demand
8. A proportional change in the quantity demanded of product X to a proportional change in the price of product Y is referred to as:
   (A) Price elasticity of demand (B) Cross elasticity of demand
   (C) Relatively elastic demand (D) Income elasticity of demand

Answers:

1. C	2. A	3. B	4. A	5. C
6. B	7. A	8. B		

REFERENCES

1. Boulding, K.E. (1941). *Economic Analysis.* New York: Harper & Brothers.
2. Dean, J. (1968). *Managerial Economics.* New Delhi, India: Prentice-Hall of India Private Limited.
3. Dwivedi, D. N. (2015). *Managerial Economics* (8th Edition). New Delhi, India: Vikas Publishing House Pvt. Ltd.
4. Kotler, P. (1984). *Marketing Management: Analysis, Planning, and Control.* New York: Prentice-Hall, Inc.
5. Lipsey, R. (1997). *Microeconomics, Growth and Political Economy.* Edward Elgar Publishing.
6. Marshall, Alfred (1890). *Principles of Economics.* London: Macmillan.
7. Mehta, P. L. (2007). *Managerial Economics: Text and Cases.* New Delhi, India: Sultan Chand & Co.

8. Mithani, D.M. (2010). *Managerial Economics*. Mumbai, India: Himalaya Publishing House Pvt. Ltd.
9. Robinson, J. (1934). The economics of imperfect competition. *Journal of the Royal Statistical Society*, 97(4), 671-674.
10. Thomas, C. R. & Maurice, S. C. (2016). *Managerial Economics: Foundations of Business Analysis and Strategy*. New York: McGraw-Hill Education.
11. Varshney, R. L. & Maheswari, K. L. (2014). *Managerial Economics.* New Delhi, India: Sultan Chand & Sons.

Chapter

7 Demand Forecasting

LEARNING OBJECTIVES

After studying this chapter, you should be able to understand:

- meaning and importance of demand forecasting;
- factors influencing demand forecasting;
- classification and objectives of demand forecasting;
- steps in demand forecasting; and
- limitations of demand forecasting.

7.1. CONCEPT OF DEMAND FORECASTING

Business units need to have an idea of future demand for their products and services to develop plans for production and also design strategies to create demand. Market demand is an external element and influenced by many factors. Business units cannot control demand but can develop strategies to manipulate demand. Therefore, they will try to estimate the demand for the future by way of demand forecasting.

Demand forecasting refers to an objective assessment of the demand in future. The demand forecast is a sales estimate of a product/service either in terms of money or physical units for a defined future period under a business plan or programme of a business unit and under a set of economic and environmental forces. Demand forecasting is helpful not only at the business unit level but also at the industry level. It is an essential element to make business decisions to foresee the future and act accordingly. Demand forecasting enables a business unit to arrange for the required inputs as per the predicted demand, without any wastage of materials and time. Thus, accurate demand forecasting is essential for a business unit to enable it to produce the required quantities at the right time and to arrange well in advance for the various factors of production.

Definitions of demand forecasting

Author	Definition
Cundiff and Still (1971)	Demand forecasting is an estimate of sales during a specified future period based on a proposed marketing plan and a set of particular uncontrollable and competitive forces.
Philip Kotler (1984)	The company sales forecast is the expected level of company sales based on a chosen marketing plan and assumed marketing environment.

Evan J. Douglas (1987)	Demand estimation (forecasting) may be defined as a process of finding values for demand in future periods.

7.1.1. Levels of Demand

Demand can be forecasted by the business units either internally by making estimates or externally through specialised consultants or market research agencies. Demand forecasting can be done at the business unit level, industry level, or economy level.

- At the business unit level, the demand is forecasted for the products and services of an individual business unit for the future.
- At the industry level, the collective demand for the products and services of all the business units in a particular industry is forecasted.
- At the economy level, the aggregate demand for products and services in the economy as a whole is anticipated.

7.2. IMPORTANCE OF DEMAND FORECASTING

Demand forecasting is vital to the management of every business unit. It provides insight into the business unit's capital investment and expansion decisions. The following are the important aspects of demand forecasting:

1. Management decisions
2. Evaluation of sales
3. Quality and quantity controls
4. Financial estimates
5. Avoiding surplus and inadequate production
6. Ensuring stability
7. Significance for the government

1. **Management decisions:** An effective demand forecast facilitates the management to take appropriate steps in the factors that are pertinent to decision making such as plant capacity, raw-material requisites, space and building requirements and availability of labour and capital. Manufacturing schedules can be drafted in compliance with the demand requisites in this manner cutting down on the inventory, production and other related costs.
2. **Evaluation of sales:** Demand forecasting smoothen the process of evaluating the efficiency of the sales department. Sales forecasting refers to the estimation of sales figures for a business unit for a given period. Demand forecasting helps in predicting the sales figures by considering historical sales data and current trends in the market.
3. **Quality and quantity controls:** Demand forecasting is an essential and valuable instrument in the control of the management of a

business unit to provide finished goods of good quality and quantity at the right time with the least amount of expenditure.

4. **Financial estimates:** As per the sales level and production functions, the financial requirements of a business unit can be calculated using various techniques of demand forecasting. Also, it needs a little time to acquire revenue on practical terms. Sales forecasts will, as a result, make it possible for arranging adequate resources on practical terms and in advance as well.
5. **Avoiding surplus and inadequate production:** Demand forecasting is necessary for old and new business units. It is somewhat essential if a business unit is engaged in large-scale production of goods and the development period is extremely time consuming in the course of production. In such situations, an estimate regarding future demand is essential to avoid inadequate and surplus production.
6. **Ensuring stability:** Demand forecasting helps a business unit to stabilise its operations by initiating the development of suitable business policies to meet cyclical and seasonal fluctuations of an economy.
7. **Significance for the government:** At the macro-level, demand forecasting is valuable to the government as it aids in determining targets of imports as well as exports for various products and preparing for the international business.

7.3. FACTORS INFLUENCING DEMAND FORECASTING

The various factors that influence the process of demand forecasting are shown in Figure 7.1.

1. **Existing economic conditions:** Demand forecasting can be affected by the changing price levels, national and per capita income, consumption pattern of consumers, saving and investment practices, employment level, etc., of an economy. Thus, it is important that the existing economic conditions should be assessed to align demand forecasting with current economic trends.
2. **Existing conditions of business unit:** The internal environment of a business unit also affects demand forecasting. Within the business unit, the demand forecasting is affected by various factors, such as plant capacity, product quality, product price, advertising and distribution policies, financial policies, etc.
3. **Existing industrial conditions:** The assessment of demand for a business unit's products and services is also affected by the existing conditions of the industry, i.e., the concentration of an industry increases the level of competition, which directly affects the demand for products and services of different business units in the industry.

In such a case, demand forecasted by the business units may be faltering.

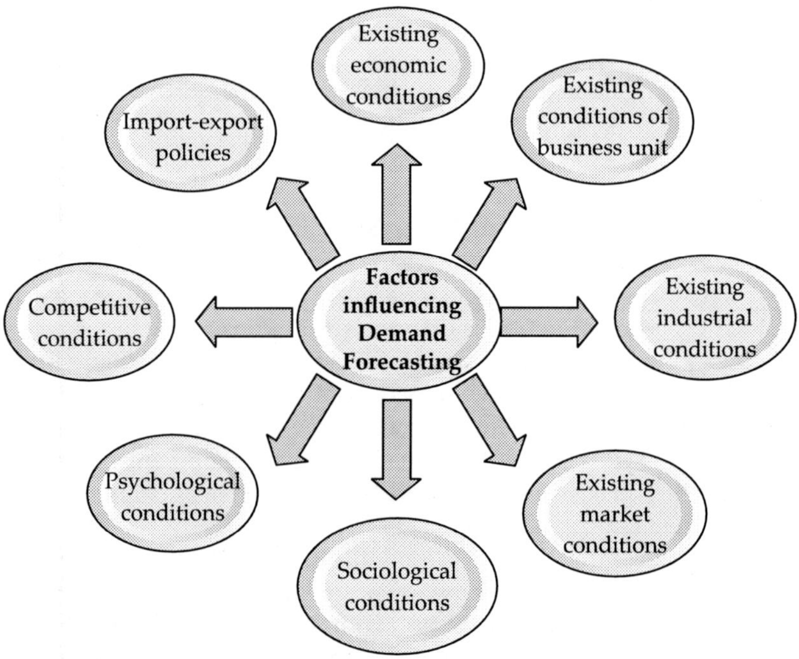

Figure 7.1. Factors influencing the process of demand forecasting

4. **Existing market conditions:** Changes in market conditions, such as a change in the price of goods, change in consumers' expectations, tastes and preferences, change in the price of related goods, and change in the income level of consumers also influence the demand for a business unit's products and services.
5. **Sociological conditions:** Sociological factors such as size and density of population, age group, size of family, family life cycle, education level, family income, social awareness, etc., largely impact demand forecasts of a business unit.
6. **Psychological conditions:** Psychological factors such as changes in consumer attitude, habits, fashion, lifestyle, perception, cultural and religious beliefs, etc., affect the demand forecast of a business unit to a large extent.
7. **Competitive conditions:** A market consists of several business units offering similar products. This gives rise to competition in the market, which affects demand forecasted by business units.
8. **Import-export policies:** The demand for export-import goods is directly affected by changes in factors, such as import and export

control, terms and conditions of import and export, import/export policies, import/export conditions, etc.

7.4. CLASSIFICATION OF DEMAND FORECASTS

Demand forecasting is an attempt to predict future demand based on past data under conditions of uncertainty. In this context, the various methods of demand forecasting will come to the rescue of the decision maker. Demand forecasting occupies importance for production, planning, product scheduling, inventory planning and so on. The demand forecasts are classified as follows:

1. Active and passive forecasts
2. Short-run and long-run forecasts
3. Company and industry forecasts
4. Micro-level and macro-level forecasts

1. **Active and passive forecasts:** Active forecasting is a method of forecasting the demand on the consideration that a business unit is likely to initiate some action like changes in product quality, size, price, etc. Passive forecasting is based on the assumption that the same product will be offered without any changes.
2. **Short-run and long-run forecasts:** Short-run forecasting normally extends up to one year. These forecasts are useful for product scheduling, inventory planning, mobilisation of working capital, etc. Long-run forecasts extend beyond one year. They are helpful in capital budgeting, product diversification, personnel recruitment, etc.
3. **Company and industry forecasts:** Forecasting the demand for the products of a particular business unit is company forecasting. These are business unit-specific and designed to serve the individual business units in planning their policies. Industry forecasting forecasts the demand for the products of the industry as a whole. The association of manufacturers or trade associations undertake them and serve the needs of all the business units in the industry.
4. **Micro-level and macro-level forecasts:** Micro-level forecasting may take the form of company forecasting or industry forecasting. Macro-level forecasting, on the other hand, is concerned with forecasting general economic environment and business conditions in the country as a whole. The national income growth rates, production indices, price indices provide useful insights into the future demand for most of the products. Governmental business units provide the base data to forecast the demand.

7.5. OBJECTIVES OF DEMAND FORECASTING

The main objectives of demand forecasting are categorized as short-term objectives and long-term objectives.

7.5.1. Short-Term Objectives

The short-term objectives of demand forecasting are:

1. Drafting of production policy
2. Drafting the price policy
3. Appropriate supervision of sales
4. Organising finances

1. **Drafting of production policy:** Demand forecasts facilitate drafting appropriate production policy so that there may not be any discrepancy between future demand and supply of a product. This can also ensure:
   (a) Routine supply of materials
   (b) Best possible use of machines
   (c) Regular availability of labour
   (a) Routine supply of materials: Demand forecasting assists in figuring out the preferred volume of production. The essential prerequisite of raw materials in future can be calculated based on such forecasts. This guarantees a regular and continuous supply of the materials in addition to managing the amount of supply at the economic level.
   (b) Best possible use of machines: Demand forecasting, also expedites cutting down inactive capacity because only the necessary amount of machines and equipment are set up to meet future demands.
   (c) Regular availability of labour: As soon as demand forecasts are made, skilled and unskilled workers can be organised well beforehand to meet the future production plans.
2. **Drafting the price policy:** Demand forecasts facilitate the management to prepare a few suitable pricing systems so that the level of price does not rise or fall to a great extent during a depression or inflation.
3. **Appropriate supervision of sales:** Appropriate demand forecasts are made area wise and based on the forecasts the sales targets for different regions are set. This abets the calculation of sales performances.
4. **Organising finances:** Based on the demand forecast, an individual can find out the monetary requirements of the business unit to bring about the desired output. This can make it possible to cut down on the expenditure of acquiring funds.

7.5.2. Long-Term Objectives

If the demand forecast period is more than a year, in that case, it is called a long-term forecast. The following are the key goals of such forecasts:

1. To resolve on production ability
2. Labour requirements
3. Production planning

1. **To resolve production ability:** Long-term decisions are intertwined with capacity variations by adding or discarding capacity in the form of capital assets manufacturing plants, new technology implementation, etc. The business units that are extremely small or large might not be in the financial interest of the business. Inadequate capacity can hasten declining delivery performance, needless rise in work-in-process and disturb sales personnel and those in the production unit. By examining the demand pattern for the product as well as the forecasts for the future, the business unit can prepare for its desired capacity of output.
2. **Labour requirements:** Spending on labour is one of the most vital elements of cost of production. Dependable and correct demand forecasts facilitate the management to evaluate suitable labour requirements. This can ensure the best labour supply and uninterrupted production procedures.
3. **Production planning:** Long-term production planning can aid the management in organising long-term finances on practical terms and conditions.

Long-term sales forecast facilitates the management to take few policy decisions of importance and any mistake in it could be extremely different or costly to be corrected. Therefore, the success of a business unit usually is contingent upon the quality and authenticity of sales forecasting methods.

7.6. STEPS IN DEMAND FORECASTING

Demand forecasting is an intricate exercise and conducted systematically and meticulously. To achieve the desired results, it is important that demand forecasting is done systematically. Demand forecasting involves the following steps as shown in Figure 7.2.

1. **Identification of the objective:** The first step in demand forecasting is the identification of the objective or purpose for which the forecasting is undertaken. The forecaster should be clear about the uses of forecast data on how it is related to forward planning and corporate planning by the business unit. The objective can

be specified on the basis of short-term or long-term demand for a product, industry demand to a business unit, and whole market demand to a market segment.

2. **Determining the time perspective:** Depending on the objective of the business unit, the demand can be forecasted for a short period (1-3 years) or long period (beyond 10 years). If a business unit performs long-term demand forecasting, it needs to take into consideration constant changes in the market as well the economy.

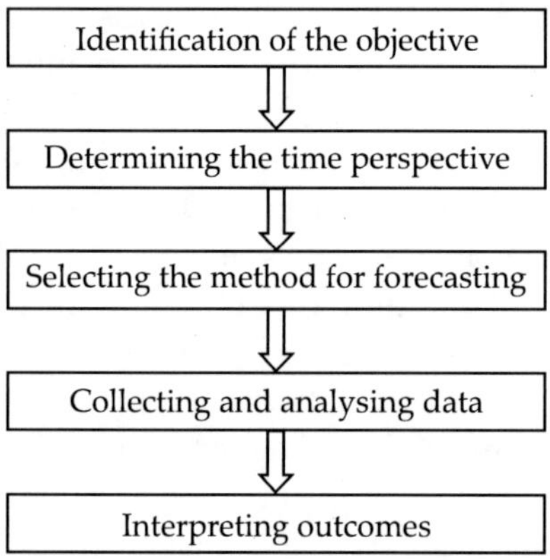

Figure 7.2. Steps in demand forecasting

3. **Selecting the method for forecasting:** This is a very crucial step in forecasting demand. There are various methods of demand forecasting for different products depending upon their nature. However, all methods are suitable for all types of demand forecasting. However, the choice of technique has to be logical and appropriate for it is a very critical choice. Depending on the objective, time, availability of data, and experience and expertise of the demand forecaster the business unit needs to select the best suitable method of forecasting demand.
4. **Collecting and analysing data:** After selecting the demand forecasting method, the data needs to be collected. Data can be gathered either from primary or secondary sources or from. As data is collected in the raw form, it needs to be analysed to derive meaningful information out of it.
5. **Interpreting outcomes:** This is the final step in demand forecasting. After the data is analysed, it is used to estimate the demand for the predetermined years. Generally, the results obtained are in the form of equations, which need to be presented in a comprehensible format.

7.7. LIMITATIONS OF DEMAND FORECASTING

Demand forecasting is based on the analysis of past and present actions for determining the future course of action. The events or occurrences in the past may not always be reliable to base the future predictions on them. Although demand forecasting has wide applicability in a business unit, there are certain limitations associated with demand forecasting.

1. Lack of past sales data
2. Impractical assumptions
3. Cost incurred
4. Change in buyer's preferences
5. Lack of knowledge
6. Psychological factors

1. **Lack of past sales data:** The past sales figures may not always be available with a business unit. In the case of a new product, the past sales data is not available. Thus, new sales data is required for demand forecasting which can be cumbersome and challenging for a business unit.
2. **Impractical assumptions:** Demand forecasting is based on various assumptions which may not always be consistent with the current market conditions. In such a case, relying on these assumptions may produce incorrect forecasts.
3. **The cost incurred:** A business unit incurs certain costs during the demand forecasting such as implementation cost, labour cost, and administrative cost, etc. These costs may be very high depending on the complexity of the forecasting method selected and the resources utilised. Thus, it becomes difficult for new business and small-scale business units to perform demand forecasting.
4. **Change in buyers' preferences:** Buyers' tastes and preferences change with a change in the current fashion trends. This limits the use of demand forecasting as it is generally based on historical trend analysis.
5. **Lack of knowledge:** Demand forecasting requires effective skills, ability, knowledge and experience of the personnel while forecasting demand. In the absence of trained experts, demand forecasting becomes a challenge for the business. If the responsibility of demand forecasting is assigned to untrained personnel, it could bring huge losses to the business unit.
6. **Psychological factors:** Consumers usually prefer a particular type of product over others. However, the factors such as changes in economic policy, fear of strikes and natural disasters could affect the buyer's psychology. In such cases, the outcomes of forecasting may no longer remain relevant for the period.

7.8. SUMMARY

- Demand forecasting is referred to as an objective assessment of the demand in future. It is an essential element to make business decisions to foresee the future and act accordingly.
- The important aspects of demand forecasting are management decisions, evaluation of sales, quality and quantity controls, financial estimates, avoiding surplus and inadequate production, ensuring stability, and significance for the government.
- The factors influencing the process of demand forecasting are the existing economic conditions, conditions of the business unit, industrial conditions, market conditions, sociological conditions, psychological conditions, competitive conditions, and import-export policies.
- The demand forecasts are classified as active and passive forecasts, short-run and long-run forecasts, company and industry forecasts, and micro-level and macro-level forecasts.
- The main objectives of demand forecasting are categorized as short-term objectives and long-term objectives.
- The short-term objectives of demand forecasting are drafting of production policy, drafting the price policy, appropriate supervision of sales, and organising finances.
- The drafting of production policy can ensure routine supply of materials, best possible use of machines, and regular availability of labour.
- The long-term objectives of demand forecasting are to resolve production ability, labour requirements, and production planning.
- The steps involved in demand forecasting are the identification of the objective, determining the time perspective, selecting the method for forecasting, collecting and analysing data, and interpreting outcomes.
- The limitations associated with demand forecasting are lack of past sales data, impractical assumptions, cost incurred, change in buyer's preferences, lack of knowledge, and psychological factors.

SHORT ANSWER QUESTIONS

1. What is demand forecasting?
2. What are the different levels of demand?
3. Write a short note on active and passive forecasts.
4. What are the short-run and long-run forecasts?
5. Distinguish between the-micro level and macro-level forecasts.
6. What are company and industry forecasts?

ESSAY ANSWER QUESTIONS

1. Define demand forecasting. Explain the important aspects of demand forecasting.

2. Briefly explain the factors that influence the process of demand forecasting.
3. Discuss the various steps involved in forecasting demand of a product.
4. What is meant by demand forecasting? Explain the main objectives of demand forecasting.
5. Elucidate the limitations associated with demand forecasting of a product.

FILL IN THE BLANKS

1. The forecasting concerned with the general economic environment and business conditions in the country as a whole is called _________ forecasting.
2. Estimation of sales figures of a business unit for a given period is referred to as _________ forecasting.
3. An estimate regarding the future demand is essential to avoid inadequate and _________ production.
4. Forecasting the demand for the products of a particular business unit is _________ forecasting.
5. Drafting the price policy is a _________ objective.
6. Determining the time perspective is the _________ step of demand forecasting.
7. The knowledge of the future demand for a product or service in the market is gained through the process of _________.
8. The use of demand forecasting is not affected by the change in consumers' tastes and preferences or psychological factors. (True/False)
9. Demand forecasting is useful to the consumer. (True/False)
10. Demand forecasting is used in the short and long run. (True/False)

Answers

1. Macro-level
2. Sales
3. Surplus
4. Company
5. Short term
6. Second
7. Demand forecasting
8. False
9. False
10. True

MULTIPLE-CHOICE QUESTIONS

1. The forecasting based on the assumption that the same product will be offered without any changes is called:
   (A) Active forecasting
   (B) Passive forecasting
   (C) Micro-level forecasting
   (D) Macro-level forecasting
2. Which one of the following is not a short-term objective?
   (A) Drafting production policy
   (B) Drafting the price policy
   (C) Production planning
   (D) Organising finances

3. The final step in demand forecasting is:
   (A) Collecting and analysing data
   (B) Interpreting outcomes
   (C) Determining the time perspective
   (D) Selecting the best method of forecasting
4. When the aggregate demand for products and services in the economy as a whole is anticipated, it is called:
   (A) Business unit level forecasting
   (B) Industry-level forecasting
   (C) Company-level forecasting
   (D) Economy-level forecasting
5. The forecasts useful for product scheduling, inventory planning, and mobilisation of working capital are known as:
   (A) Short-run forecasts (B) Long-run forecasts
   (C) Company forecasts (D) Industry forecasts
6. Demand forecasting is helpful not only at the business unit level but also at:
   (A) Individual level (B) Industry level
   (C) Firm level (D) Institutional level

Answers:

1. B 2. C 3. B 4. D 5. A
6. B

REFERENCES

1. Douglas, E. J. (1987). *Managerial Economics: Analysis and Strategy.* New York: Prentice-Hall.
2. Edward W. Cundiff, E. W. & Still, R. R. (1971). *Basic Marketing: Concepts, Decisions and Strategies.* New York: Prentice-Hall.
3. Kotler, P. (1984). *Marketing Management: Analysis, Planning, and Control.* New York: Prentice-Hall, Inc.
4. Varshney, R. L. & Maheswari, K. L. (2014). *Managerial Economics.* New Delhi, India: Sultan Chand & Sons.
5. Webster, T. J. (2003). *Managerial Economics: Theory and Practice.* California, USA: Academic Press (Elsevier).
6. Wilkinson, N. (2005). *Managerial Economics: A Problem-solving Approach.* Cambridge, UK: Cambridge University Press.
7. Baye, Michael R. (1994). *Managerial Economics and Business Strategy.* New York: McGraw-Hill.
8. Dean, Joel. (1951). *Managerial Economics.* New York: Prentice-Hall, Inc.
9. Gupta, G. S. (2017). *Managerial Economics.* New Delhi, India: Tata McGraw-Hill.

Chapter

8 Demand Forecasting Methods

LEARNING OBJECTIVES

After studying this chapter, you should be able to understand:

- qualitative methods of demand forecasting;
- quantitative methods of demand forecasting;
- demand forecasting for a new product; and
- criteria for good demand forecasting.

8.1. METHODS OF DEMAND FORECASTING

The methods of demand forecasting are many. Various qualitative and quantitative methods of demand forecasting are used by business organisations. Selection of appropriate method of demand forecasting is an important decision. The choice of a method often depends upon data availability, the urgency of forecast, accuracy level required, cost, and other factors. Demand forecasting methods range from the simple to the extremely complex. There is no unique method which always guarantees the best result. Different business units rely on different methods to forecast demand for their products or services for a future time period depending on their requirements and budget.

Demand forecasting methods are broadly grouped into two types (Figure 8.1). One method, that is, qualitative method is used to obtain information about the intentions of the consumers through collecting opinions of different groups of people. The other method is a quantitative method which uses past experience as a guide and extrapolates past statistical relationships to suggest the level of future demand. The qualitative demand forecasting method is also called a *survey method* or *opinion polling method*. The quantitative demand forecasting method is also called a *statistical method*. Some business units also use judgement method for demand forecasting.

8.2. QUALITATIVE METHODS (SURVEY METHODS)

Qualitative methods rely on collecting data on the buying behaviour of consumers through conducting consumer surveys or by collecting opinion from experts in order to forecast the demand. These methods are generally used to make short-term forecasts of demand. When sufficient historical data for statistical analysis is not available, it may become necessary to perform marketing research in which the analyst obtains certain information directly from the consumer or from experts. For example, when a new product is introduced, the business unit will not be having any past experience therefore, statistical database on the product will not be available. In such a case, the business unit can only depend upon qualitative methods for forecasting demand. When changes are expected in qualitative variables such as consumer needs, tastes, preferences or expectations, and when market experimentation is necessary the business units often use qualitative methods of demand forecasting. The following are the qualitative methods for demand forecasting.

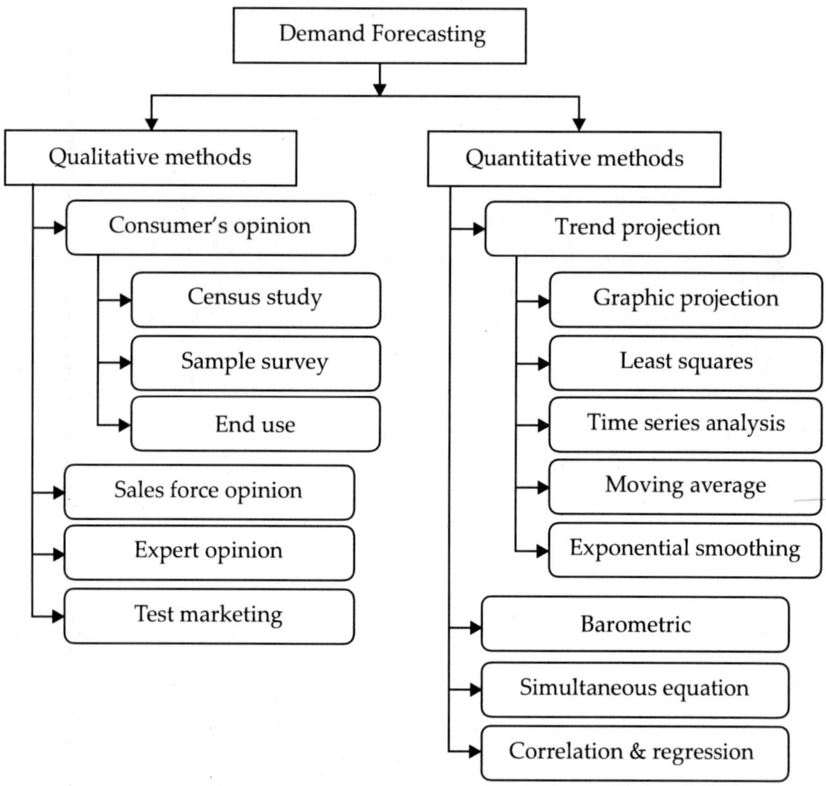

Figure 8.1. Methods of demand forecasting

8.2.1. Consumers Opinion

Consumers/buyers are the ultimate purchase decision makers. Therefore, they decide the demand for products/services. Collection of data on consumers' opinion is considered the most effective method because of the reason that the information is collected directly from the consumers or users. Consumer surveys are used to ask the present and potential buyers about their buying behaviour through different ways like face-to-face interactions, telephone conversations, direct mails, internet, spot survey, etc. The buyers are asked for their reaction to changes in demand variables such as price, income, the process of related goods, advertising expenses, etc., and also about the expectation regarding future prices, income, substitutes, inflation, etc. Consumer survey can be done in the following ways.

(a) Census study: Under this method, the forecaster undertakes a complete survey of all the consumers of the product/service to forecast demand. When the total population of buyers (present and potential) in a nation or region are surveyed for the collection of required data and information, it is known as the *census method*. This method is not preferred when the total number of buyers is very large due to time, cost, and other limitations. When the universe is large it involves a long time to cover all the consumers. In addition, the cost of the demand forecast will be very high and also there is a possibility of measurement errors. Therefore, the census method is used when the population is small like organisation buyers or premium segment of the market. For example, if there are 'n' consumers and their demand for product 'x' in the forecast period are $x_1, x_2, x_3, \ldots x_n$, the sales forecast would be:

$$X = x_1 + x_2 + x_3 + \ldots x_n$$

Merits

1. Direct response from the ultimate consumers/users.
2. The sales forecast is relatively accurate compared to other methods.
3. Suitable for products having a small number of consumers.
4. Collection of information from all the consumers and therefore, no sampling errors.

Demerits

1. It is costly and time consuming.
2. Based on opinions which may not be true when comes to actual purchase behaviour.
3. Not feasible for products having a large number of consumers.
4. A consumer may not reveal his purchase plan due to personal privacy.

(b) Sample survey: Under this method, the forecaster selects a few consumers/buyers out of the total population for the collection of data and information. A sample survey is used when the universe is large and when the business unit wants a quick forecast at limited expense. If the sample survey is conducted systematically in a larger population, the results would be more accurate than the census study.

When only a portion/group of the total population of buyers (present and potential) in a region is surveyed, it is called a sample survey. For example, there are 10,000 consumers of product 'x', the forecaster may choose only 500 consumers, then the probable demand for the selected units are $x_1, x_2, x_3, \ldots x_{500}$ respectively. The total demand will be:

$$X = n_1x_1 + n_2 x_2 + n_3 x_3 + \ldots n_{500} x_{500}$$

Merits

1. Easier than census study and less costly.
2. Limited data and measurement errors.
3. Yields good results if the sample is appropriate.
4. The most appropriate method for products with mass markets.

Demerits

1. The sample itself is an error.
2. The accuracy of the results depends upon the selection of a representative sample.
3. The results of the sample data will be generalised to forecast demand which may not be accurate.
4. The larger the sample size, the more the time required and more the expenses.
5. The data may be inaccurate, in case of non-cooperation from the sample consumers.

(c) **End-use method:** End-use method is also called a user expectation method. Under this method, the list of several users of the product under forecasting is prepared. The users are then asked to reveal their individual purchasing patterns. A complete product demand forecast is ascertained based on such information. This method is suitable for industrial products such as raw materials or intermediary products because unlike consumer goods these are limited in number and can be surveyed exhaustively. The industrial buyers are generally clustered in the industrial areas and can be accessed easily, whereas in the case of the consumer goods the buyers are widely scattered. It is very difficult to reach household consumers directly. The end-user method is very effective in knowing the buying organisation's likely consumption of the product and its future buying plans.

Merits

1. Forecasts are directly from the end user.
2. Perfectly suitable for the industrial market.
3. The forecast will be highly accurate as the information is provided by professionally qualified experts.
4. It is less expensive and less time consuming.

Demerits

1. Difficult to get information as many organisations keep future plans confidential.
2. The respondents do not know about their consumption patterns and might be reluctant disclose their buying plans.
3. Difficult to develop forecasts in the light of rapid changes in the business environment.
4. Impact of changes in competition cannot be reflected in forecasting.

8.2.2. Sales Force Opinion (Collective Opinion)

The sales personnel are very close to the consumers and dealers. In the sales force opinion method, the business unit will extract the opinions of the sales team which is on the pay rolls of the business unit about the future demand for the product. However, care should be taken before forming an opinion based on the information from the sales force in estimating future demand. The opinions of the sales team should not be taken on the face value as an ambitious salesman gives an overestimate of the demand for the product while a sceptic sales person, fearful of of higher sales targets, may prefer to quote a lesser forecast. This can be resolved by maintaining a track record of accomplishment of the previous targets and achievements of each member of the sales team and make necessary adjustments in the sales forecast of each sales person to arrive at an overall sales forecasting.

Merits

1. This method is inexpensive.
2. The opinion of the company's sales personnel is dependable.
3. It is less time consuming.
4. It is based on the value judgment of the salesmen.
5. It is useful for forecasting demand for new products.

Demerits

1. Sales personnel may be ambitious or casual in estimating future sales. It affects the accuracy of the forecast.
2. It is subject to the bias of reporting agency.

3. Its accuracy depends on the forecasting ability of the reporting salesmen.
4. It can't be relied upon for long-term business forecasting.

8.2.3. Expert Opinion (Delphi Method)

Expert opinion is a method of collecting opinion from experts on future demand for products/services of a business unit. Experts are the outside persons and they do not have any interest in the results of a particular survey. Therefore, unbiased estimates can be obtained through this method. This method is best suited under the conditions of the non-existence of data or when a new product is launched or for predicting the demand under conditions of technological changes. The popular technique used for the collection of opinion from experts is the Delphi technique. This technique is first used by Rand Corporation in the USA for predicting the demand under conditions of intractable technological changes. Experts may differ in their views and therefore, it is difficult to prepare a final forecast taking a different estimate of the experts. The Delphi technique facilitates an agreement of all the experts involved by following a systematic approach.

Delphi technique is a forecasting process in which questionnaires are sent to a panel of experts in multiple rounds. First, the independent estimates of demand from each expert are obtained. Then the estimates of one expert will be passed on to other experts to seek their reactions. Several rounds of questionnaires are sent out to the group of experts, and the anonymous responses are aggregated and shared with the group after each round. The experts are requested to adjust their answers in subsequent rounds, based on their interpretation to the responses of other members in the group. The experts' responses shift as rounds are completed based on the information brought forth by other experts participating in the analysis. Finally, the Delphi technique seeks accurate estimate through a consensus of all the experts.

Merits

1. This method is simple and easy to understand.
2. Forecasts are based on experts' opinion.
3. It is an inexpensive method and less time consuming.
4. This method is more appropriate for forecasting demand for new products.

Demerits

1. Opinions and intuitions are highly subjective.

2. Personal estimates are likely to be biased.
3. Results may be distant from reality.
4. This method is not useful for long-term forecasts.

8.2.4. Test Marketing

Business units resort test marketing while launching a new product or likely to change the design or model of the existing products. This is also known as *controlled experimentation method* as the product is likely to be launched in a segmented market to identify its demand potential. Test marketing is taken up to know the initial response of the target consumers on a new product or new changes in the product or new composition of the marketing mix. The selection of the market for testing is a crucial decision. The market selected should be such that it represents all geographical, economic, sociological and demographic features of the total market. Test marketing can be undertaken in a single market or different markets with different features of the product. The marketing offer including product, price, distribution and promotion strategy, will be tested to know the acceptability of the target consumers. Based on the results of the test marketing, the business unit may introduce certain modifications before launching the product commercially in the total market. Thus, test marketing is highly useful in rectifying errors if any and to confidently approach the total market.

Merits

1. Demand is estimated on the basis of actual purchases.
2. Opportunity to modify marketing offer as per the expectations of the consumers.
3. Provides information on variations in response from different segments.
4. Minimises errors in the introduction of new products or changes in the existing products.

Demerits

1. It is very expensive and time consuming.
2. It is risky as the competitors will know about the product in advance.
3. It is very difficult to find heterogeneous markets for test marketing.
4. There is no guarantee that the consumers will respond similarly to that of the test market.

8.3. QUANTITATIVE METHODS (STATISTICAL METHODS)

Quantitative methods for demand forecasting usually make use of statistical tools. All statistical approaches of forecasting project the historical information into the future. These are based on the assumption that future patterns tend to be extensions of past ones. One can make useful predictions by studying the past-behaviour, i.e., the demand determinants responsible in the past will also be operative to the same extent in future. The following are the statistical methods for demand forecasting.

8.3.1. Trend Projection Method

Trend projection methods analyse the past data for projecting the future. It takes into consideration the historical data for a significantly long period and projects the trend by using statistical and mathematical models. The following are different techniques used for demand forecasting under trend projection method.

(a) Time Series Analysis

Time series analysis is one of the most popular techniques used by business units for the projection of demand. This technique can be used for only such products that are in existence for a significant period in the market and the sales data is available. Some companies maintain detailed sales record item wise as well as territory wise. These sales records are useful to make demand forecasting. The information available should be complete in all respects such as product related, segment-wise, price vs. demand, distribution, promotion, quality vs. demand, etc. Such information is known as time series data. The time series data is composed of four items.

1. **Trend component (T):** Trend indicates the general tendency of the data and is known as a long period data or secular trend. This can be either upward or downward depending on the behaviour. The data over a long period ranging from five to 10 years or more will be used to determine the trend.
2. **Cyclical component (C):** The data relating to a long period of time may include wide variations caused by economic cycles like boom, depression, and recovery. Such variation in data is called the cyclical component. The presence of a cyclical component in the data makes the sales graph of a business unit move upward and downward. The cyclical component of data is an important factor for predicting future demand.
3. **Seasonal component (S):** Seasonal component refers to demand variations in different seasons of a year for a product/service. The products such as umbrellas, woollen clothes, agricultural products,

etc., may have seasonal demand in markets. Trend projections necessarily consider the seasonal character of the demand for the product/service.

4. **Erratic component (E):** Demand variations are significant in some specific situations like strikes, riots, wars, natural disasters, etc. This is called erratic component in trend. The presence of erratic trend makes the forecasting process more complex and difficult.

Time series involves a process of classifying original sales series (y) into components T, C, S, and E. The four components of the time series data are related in an additive or multiplicative function. It can be projected in a graph, i.e., sales on Y-axis and time on the X-axis.

Sales = f (T, C, S, E)

In an additive function: Sales = T + C + S + E

In a multiplicative function: Sales = T × C × S × E

The business units can use either additive or multiplicative function. The trend value will be the same but the seasonal and irregular variable values of sales data vary in both the functions. By fitting a trend line to the time series data demand forecast can be obtained.

(b) Trend Line by Observation

Fitting trend line by observation involves plotting the actual sales data on a chart and estimating the future demand by carefully observing the behaviour of the data in the past. This method of forecasting trend is easy and quick as it involves the plotting of data in a graph. For example, the sales data of a business unit ABC Ltd. is shown in Table 8.1. Under this method time is shown on X-axis and sales on the Y-axis. The sales data is plotted on the graph as shown in Figure 8.2 joining them by a straight line. This method is fully subjective in nature. The extension of the graph is imaginary and does not follow any logical base.

Example:

Table 8.1. Sales data of ABC Ltd.

Year	2013	2014	2015	2016	2017	2018
Sales (Rs. lakh)	50	60	54	70	64	72

(c) Least Square Method

The method of least square is one of the forms of mathematical regression analysis. It finds the line of best fit for a set of data and provides a visual demonstration of the relationship between data points. Each data point represents the relationship between a known independent variable and an unknown dependent variable. The least square method is used to predict the behaviour of dependent variables. This method provides a rationale for the placement of a line of best fit among data points. It creates a straight line that minimises the differences in observed value and anticipated value. The least square method begins with a set of data points to be plotted on X-axis and Y-axis in a graph. Dependent variables are shown on the vertical Y-axis and independent variables are shown on the horizontal X-axis. By applying the least square method, the equation for the line of best fit will be formed.

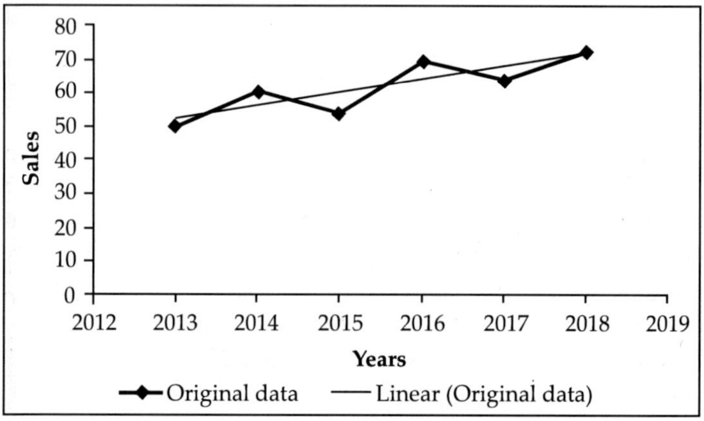

Figure 8.2. Forecasting by a trend line

The determination of the line of best fit using the least square method is based on an equation that establishes the relationship between data points. Certain statistical formulae are used to find the trend line which fits the available data. The formula used for fitting the trend line is:

$Y = a + bx$

where,

Y = future sales

x = period for a certain product

a = Y-axis intercept, i.e., constant

b = coefficient of the determining variable x

The values of a & b can be calculated as:

$$\Sigma y = Na + bx$$
$$\Sigma xy = a\Sigma x + b\Sigma x^2$$

where,

N = Number of years or months for which data is available.

Example:

The sales data of a company for 10 years starting from 2009 to 2018 are as given below. Fit a linear regression equation anddraw a trend line to estimate sales for the years 2019 and 2020.

Year	Sales (Tonnes)
2009	215
2010	240
2011	304
2012	441
2013	539
2014	900
2015	1332
2016	1175
2017	1264
2018	980

Solution:

The calculation of ΣX, ΣY, ΣXY and ΣX^2 are shown in the following table.

Year	X	Sales (Y)	XY	X^2
2009	1	215	215	1
2010	2	240	480	4
2011	3	304	912	9
2012	4	441	1,764	16
2013	5	539	2,695	25
2014	6	900	5,400	36
2015	7	1332	9,324	49
2016	8	1175	9,400	64
2017	9	1264	11,376	81
2018	10	980	9,800	100
	$\Sigma X = 55$	$\Sigma Y = 7{,}390$	$\Sigma XY = 51{,}366$	$\Sigma X^2 = 385$

$$\Sigma Y = na + b\Sigma X \quad \text{...(i)}$$

$$7{,}390 = 10a + 55b$$

$$\Sigma XY = a\Sigma X + b\Sigma X^2 \quad \text{...(ii)}$$

$$51{,}366 = 55a + 385b$$

$$7{,}390 = 10a + 55b \quad \text{...(i)}$$

$$51{,}366 = 55a + 385b \quad \text{...(ii)}$$

Equation (i) x 7 $\quad 51{,}730 = 70a + 385b \quad$ ...(iii)

Equation (iii) – (ii) $\quad 364 = 15a$

$$a = 24.27$$

Substitute value of 'a' in equation (i)

$$7{,}390 = 242.7 + 55\,b$$
$$55b = 7{,}390 - 242.7$$
$$55b = 7{,}147.3$$
$$b = 130$$
$$Y = a + b\,x$$
$$Y = 242.7 + 130x$$
$$\text{Sales for } 2019 = 242.7 + 130(11) = 1{,}672.7 \text{ tonnes}$$
$$\text{Sales for } 2020 = 242.7 + 130(12) = 1{,}802.7 \text{ tonnes}$$

Therefore, the sales projected for the year 2019 is 1672.7 tonnes and 2020 is 1802.7 tonnes. The sales from 2009 to 2020 are shown in Figure 8.3.

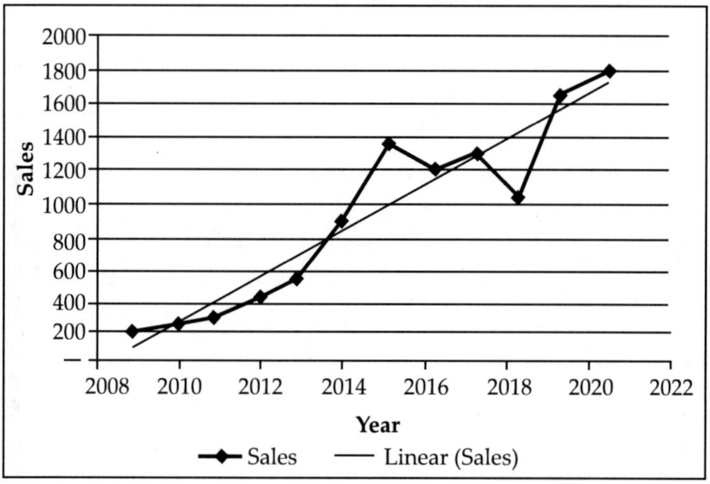

Figure 8.3. Trend in sales

(d) Moving Average Method

Moving average is a useful technique for forecasting long-term trends. It is also called a *simple smoothing technique* of trend analysis. Moving average is obtained by calculating the mean for a specified set of values. These values are used to forecast the next period. The moving average is one of the popular technical indicators used to predict future data in time series analysis. One can calculate the moving average for any specific period of time.

For example, if moving average for sales data of the twenty-year period is needed, first of all, one should decide the time period for moving average. It can be a five-year moving average, or four-year moving average, or three-year moving average or any specific time interval. Stock market analysts will often use a 50 or 200-day moving average to study the trends in the stock market and to forecast the trends for the future.

An average represents the middle value of a set of numbers. In moving average, the middle value of the data (average) is calculated several times for different subsets of data. For example, to calculate a two-year moving average for a data set from 2015, 2016, 2017 and 2018, the averages for the subsets can be calculated as 2015/2016, 2016/2017 and 2017/2018. Moving averages are generally plotted on a graph for better visualisation. This method can be used to determine the trend values for given data without going into complex mathematical calculations. The period depends on the nature of characteristics in the time series.

A moving average is an average of some fixed or pre-determined number of observations which moves through the series by dropping of a top item of the previous averaged group and adding the next item below in each successive average. The calculation depends upon the period which can be either odd or even. In the case of odd order period (3,5,7,....) the average of the observations is calculated for the given period and the calculated value is written in front of central value of the period, e.g., for a period of 5 years, the average of the values of five years is calculated and is recorded against the third year. Thus, in the case of five-year moving averages, the first two years and last two years of the data will not have an average value. If the period of observations is even, e.g., four years, then the average of the four-yearly observations is written between the second year and third-year values, after centring done by finding the average of the paired values. The even order periods create the problem of centring between the periods. Due to this reason, generally odd order periods are preferred for calculating moving averages. The calculated values of the moving averages become the basis for determining the expected future values. In this method, equal weightage is assigned to all the periods chosen for average.

Example:

The following are the annual sales of a product during the period 2009-2018. Find the trend of sales using 3 yearly moving averages.

Year	Sales in units	Year	Sales in units
2009	12,000	2014	17,000
2010	15,000	2015	19,000
2011	14,000	2016	20,000
2012	16,000	2017	22,000
2013	18,000	2018	25,000

Solution

The trend values can be calculated in the following tabular form.

Year	Sales (in units)	Three year moving total	3 yearly moving average trend values (in units)
2009	12,000		
2010	15,000	41,000	41,000/3 = 13,700
2011	14,000	45,000	45,000/3 = 45,000
2012	16,000	48,000	48,000/3 = 16,000
2013	18,000	51,000	51,000/3 = 17,000
2014	17,000	54,000	54,000/3 = 18,000
2015	19,000	56,000	56,000/3 = 18,700
2016	20,000	61,000	61,000/3 = 20,200
2017	22,000	67,000	67,000/3 = 22,300
2018	25,000		

The three yearly moving averages for the given data can be calculated as the following:

Sales for the first three-year period

2009 = 12,000 units
2010 = 15,000 units
2011 = 14,000 units

The three yearly moving total is: 12,000 + 15,000 + 14,000 = 41,000

The moving average is: 41,000/3 = 13,700 units

(e) Exponential Smoothing

In simple moving average, the past observations are weighted equally whereas in exponential smoothing functions are used to assign exponentially decreasing weights for newest to oldest observations. In other words, the older the data, the lesser the weightage is given for the data. The newer data is considered more relevant and therefore, is assigned higher weightage. Smoothing parameters (smoothing constants) are usually denoted by α to determine the weights for observations.

This method is an improvement over the simple moving averages method. Unlike in the moving averages method, all the time periods are assigned weights in order that the nearest one gets higher weight and distant one gets lower weight. This method proves more realistic when the data is consistent all through the year, unaffected by wide seasonal fluctuations. It is used for short-run demand forecasts.

The formula for exponential smoothing is:

$$S_{t+1} = \alpha S_t + (1 - \alpha)\, Sm_t$$

where,

S_{t+1} = exponentially smoothed average for a new year

S_t = actual data in the most recent past

Sm_t = most recent smoothed forecast

α = smoothing constant

If the smoothing constant (α) is higher, higher weight is given to the most recent information. The value of α varies between 0 and 1 inclusive and the exact value of α is determined by the magnitude of random variations. If the magnitude of random variations is large, lower value to α is assigned and vice versa. However, it is considered that a value between 0.1 and 0.2 is more appropriate in most of the cases.

Example

A company provides the data related to the sales of shaving cream for the last 7 months as follows:

Month	1	2	3	4	5	6	7
Demand	32	39	43	48	51	54	59

Forecast the demand for eighth month using exponential smoothing method with a smoothing constant of 0.1.

Solution:

The demand forecasting for eighth month can be computed as follows:

$$S_{t+1} = \alpha S_t + (1 - \alpha)\, Sm_t$$

$$\alpha = \text{smoothing constant} = 0.1$$

$$1 - \alpha = 1 - 0.1 = 0.9$$

Using exponential smoothing with a smoothing constant of 0.1, it can be observed that:

$S_1 = Sm_1 = 32$

$S_2 = 0.1S_2 + 0.9Sm_1 = 0.1(39) + 0.9(32) = 32.70$ or 33

$S_3 = 0.1S_3 + 0.9Sm_2 = 0.1(43) + 0.9(32.70) = 33.73$ or 34

$S_4 = 0.1S_4 + 0.9Sm_3 = 0.1(48) + 0.9(33.73) = 35.16$ or 35

$S_5 = 0.1S_5 + 0.9Sm_4 = 0.1(51) + 0.9(35.16) = 36.74$ or 37

$S_6 = 0.1S_6 + 0.9Sm_5 = 0.1(54) + 0.9(36.74) = 38.47$ or 38

$S_7 = 0.1S_7 + 0.9Sm_6 = 0.1(59) + 0.9(38.47) = 40.52$ or 41

Therefore, the demand forecast for eighth month S_8 is: 41

The overall exponential smoothing average is:

$$SD = [(32 - 39)^2 + (33 - 43)^2 + (34 - 48)^2 + (35 - 51)^2 + (37 - 54)^2 + (38 - 59)^2]/6$$

$$= 221.53 \text{ or } 222$$

8.3.2. Barometric Method

The barometric method of forecasting is used to forecast the trend in overall economic activities. It uses the time series data on economic activities in key sectors of the economy. Intelligent analysis and understanding of the time duration and the amplitude of cyclical ups and downs in the selected indicators provide useful information regarding the future behaviour of overall cyclical movements. The barometric method can also be used to forecast demand prospects. It may not forecast the exact quantity demanded, but it is useful to predict the directions of change.

The barometric method is used in some of the developed countries for predicting business cycles situation. For this purpose, some countries construct what are known as *'diffusion indices'* by combining the movement of a number of leading series in the economy, so that turning points in business activity could be discovered well in advance. The leading indicator method does not tell anything about the magnitude of the change that can be expected in the lagging series, but only the directionof change.

8.3.3. Regression Method

For demand forecasting, regression analysis is the most commonly used method. Under the regression method, the demand function for a product is estimated. As per the demand function, demand is the dependent variable and the variable(s) that determine the demand is/are the independent variable(s). When only one variable determines the demand, it is called a single variable demand function. In such a case, simple regression techniques are used. In the case of multiple variables determine the demand, it is called a multi-variable demand function. In such a case, multiple regression is used.

The equation to calculate simple regression is: $Y = a + bX$

where,

Y = Estimated value of Y for a given value of X

b = Amount of change in Y produced by a unit change in X

a and b = Constants

The equation to calculate multiple regression: $Y = a + b_1X_1 + b_2X_2$

where,

Y (dependent variable) = Estimated value of Y for a given value of X_1 and X_1

X_1 and X_2 = Independent variables

b_1 = Amount of change in Y produced by a unit change in X_1

b_2 = Amount of change in Y produced by a unit change in X_2

a, b_1 and b_2 = Constants

8.3.4. Simultaneous Equations Model

Demand forecasting under this method involves the estimation of several simultaneous equations. Unlike, the regression technique which is based on the assumption of one-way causation (independent variables cause variations in the dependent variables, and not vice versa), the simultaneous equations model enables simultaneous interaction between the dependent and independent variables. Therefore, the simultaneous equation model is considered a systematic and complete approach to demand forecasting.

8.3.5. Judgemental Approach

Business units often follow a judgemental approach to forecast demand. Under this method, the manager by using the available resources and personal experience makes a judgement regarding the future demand for a product/service. This method is not a scientific method and therefore, subjected to many technical errors. However, in certain situations, the judgemental method is considered most appropriate. The following are the situations where management prefers judgemental approach for forecasting demand.

1. Historical data for a significantly long period of time is not available.
2. Turning points in terms of policies or procedures or causal factors cannot be precisely determined.
3. Sales fluctuations are wide and significant.
4. Sophisticated statistical methods may not cover all the significant factors that affect demand.

8.4. DEMAND FORECASTING FOR A NEW PRODUCT

Demand forecasting for new products is quite different to that of established products. The business units will not have any past experience or past data as the product is introduced for the first time in the market. Demand forecasting is an essential strategic input for the existing as well as new products. Therefore, it is necessary to forecast taking into consideration the economic and competitive characteristics of the product. Joel Dean (1968) suggested the following six approaches to forecast demand for new products.

1. Evolution approach
2. Substitute approach
3. Opinion poll approach
4. Sales experience approach
5. Growth curve approach
6. Vicarious approach

1. **Evolution approach:** Under this approach, the demand for a new product is considered an outgrowth of an existing product. For example, the demand for new Pulsar, which is a modified version of an old Pulsar, can most effectively be projected based on the sales of the old Pulsar. Thus, when a new product is evolved from the old product, the demand conditions of the old product can be considered a basis for forecasting the demand for the new product.

In the case of an innovative product, the demand characteristics of the closely related products will be used for forecasting demand.

2. **Substitute approach:** When a new product serves as a substitute for the existing product, the demand for the new product may be estimated on the basis of market trends of the existing products. The growth in demand for existing products can be estimated on the basis of intelligent forecasts. The independent variables that influence the demand for its substitutes will also be identified. After that strategies will be designed to slice out a portion of demand for the new product. For example, liquid soap is a substitute for hard cake soap. The demand for liquid soap can be forecasted using a substitute approach.
3. **Opinion poll approach:** Under this approach, the opinion of the potential buyers is collected either by direct contact or through the use of samples of the new product. This information is finally used to forecast the demand for the new product.
4. **Sales experience approach:** A business unit may offer a new product for sale in some selected markets such as supermarket and retail stores in cosmopolitan cities for a specific period. Based on the sales experience in such markets the demand for the product will be projected for the entire market.
5. **Growth curve approach:** According to this approach, first, the rate of growth and the ultimate level of demand for the existing product will be estimated. Based on such estimates the demand for new product and its pattern of growth will be estimated. For example, an automobile business unit, while introducing a new version of a car will study the growth of demand for the existing cars in similar categories to forecast demand for the new car.
6. **Vicarious approach:** A business unit will survey consumers' reactions to a new product indirectly through getting in touch with some specialised and informed dealers who have good knowledge about the market, about the different varieties of the product already available in the market, the consumers' preferences, etc. Based on such information the demand for the new product will be forecasted. This approach helps in making a more efficient estimation of future demand as the information is provided by highly experienced persons.

The six approaches discussed above are not mutually exclusive. The management can use one approach or a combination of a few approaches for forecasting demand for a new product. The use of multiple approaches will help to cross-check the forecast of each approach with the other and to arrive at the right conclusion.

8.5. CRITERIA FOR GOOD DEMAND FORECASTING

Different methods of demand forecasting have their own merits and limitations. While choosing a method for forecasting the managerial economist should check for suitability as per the following nine criteria.

1. **Accuracy:** Accuracy is the most important criterion of a demand forecast, even though cent per cent accuracy about the future demand cannot be assured. The accuracy of a forecasting method is assessed based on its past results. The past forecasts using a particular method and the real demand for the product is compared to establish the accuracy levels of the method.
2. **Plausibility:** The forecasting method used, and the assumptions made should be clear and consistent in providing results to the management.
3. **Simplicity:** The method of demand forecasting should be simple, understandable and easy to use with the existing knowledge.
4. **Durability:** The method used for demand forecasting should be capable of future applications. The consistency in the relationships of the variables considered and the stability underlying such relationships, for instance, the relation between price and demand, advertisement and sales, the level of income and the volume of sales, and so on is important.
5. **Flexibility:** The business environment will be dynamic and as such the demand forecasting method should have the flexibility to become adaptable to meet the changing conditions.
6. **Suitability:** The method selected should be suitable for the specific needs of the company or the product or the market.
7. **Economy:** The cost of demand forecasting using a method should not be more than the benefits of demand forecasting for an organisation.
8. **Quickness:** It should be capable of yielding timely and useful results.
9. **Scalability:** The demand forecasting method should be capable of facilitating upscaling technically to suit the changing requirements.

8.6. SUMMARY

- Demand forecasting methods are broadly classified as qualitative method and quantitative method.
- Qualitative methods rely on collecting data on the buying behaviour of consumers through conducting consumer surveys or by collecting opinion from experts in order to forecast demand.

- When the information is collected directly from the consumers or users it is called the consumer opinion method of forecasting demand.
- When the total population of buyers (present and potential) in a nation or region is surveyed for the collection of required data and information, it is known as the census method.
- A sample survey is used when the universe is large and when the business unit wants a quick forecast at limited expense.
- In the end-use method, the list of several users of the product under forecasting is prepared and is asked to reveal their individual purchasing patterns.
- In the sales force opinion method, the business unit will extract the opinions of the sales team which is on the payrolls of the business unit about the future demand for the product.
- Expert opinion is a method of collecting opinion from experts on future demand for products/services of a business unit.
- Test marketing is taken up to know the initial response of the target consumers on a new product or new changes in the product or new composition of the marketing mix.
- Quantitative methods for demand forecasting usually make use of statistical tools and are based on the assumption that future patterns tend to be extensions of past ones.
- Trend projection methods consider the historical data for a significantly long period and project the trend by using statistical and mathematical models.
- Time series analysis technique can be used for only such products that are in existence for a significant period in the market and the sales data is available.
- Fitting trend line by observation involves plotting the actual sales data on a chart and estimating the future demand by carefully observing the behaviour of the data in the past.
- Least square is one of the forms of mathematical regression analysis. It finds the line of best fit for a set of data and provides a visual demonstration of the relationship between data points.
- Moving average is an useful technique for forecasting long-term trends. It is obtained by calculating the mean for a specified set of values.
- Exponential smoothing functions are used to assign exponentially decreasing weights for newest to oldest observations.
- The barometric method can be used to forecast the trend in overall economic activities. It uses the time series data on economic activities in key sectors of the economy.

- In the regression method, the demand function for a product is estimated, where demand is the dependent variable and the variable(s) that determine the demand is/are the independent variable(s).
- Simultaneous equations model enables simultaneous interaction between the dependent and independent variables.
- In the judgmental method, the manager by using the available resources and personal experience make a judgment regarding the future demand for a product/service.
- The six approaches to forecasting demand for new products are evolution approach, substitute approach, opinion poll approach, sales experience approach, growth curve approach, and vicarious approach.
- The criteria for good demand forecasting involve accuracy, plausibility, simplicity, durability, flexibility, suitability, economy, quickness, and scalability.

SHORT ANSWER QUESTIONS

1. List the methods of demand forecasting.
2. Outline the trend projection method of demand forecasting.
3. What is the Delphi method?
4. Write a short note on consumer opinion method.
5. Briefly explain the least square method of forecasting demand.
6. What is test marketing? List its merits.

ESSAY ANSWER QUESTIONS

1. What is the criterion of good demand forecasting?
2. Discuss critically the different methods of demand forecasting.
3. What are the survey methods of demand forecasting? Explain its merits and demerits.
4. Explain the trend projection methods of forecasting demand with illustrations.
5. What are the quantitative methods of forecasting? Explain.
6. What are the various methods of forecasting demand for a new product?

FILL IN THE BLANKS

1. Qualitative methods of forecasting demand are also known as __________ methods.
2. Survey methods are generally used to make __________ forecasts of demand.
3. When only a group of the total population of buyers in a region is surveyed, it is called __________.
4. Quantitative methods for demand forecasting make use of __________ tools.

5. The least square method is used to predict the behaviour of _________ variables.
6. Moving average is an useful technique for forecasting _________ trends.
7. Sales force opinion method is based on the value judgment of the salesmen. (True/False)
8. A graphical method is a qualitative method of demand forecasting. (True/False)

Answers:

1. Survey
2. Short-term
3. Sample survey
4. Statistical
5. Dependent
6. Long-term
7. True
8. False

MULTIPLE-CHOICE QUESTIONS

1. Quantitative methods of demand forecasting are also referred to as:
   (A) Survey methods (B) Statistical methods
   (C) Standard methods (D) General methods
2. When the forecaster undertakes a complete survey of all the consumers of the product to forecast demand it is called:
   (A) Census study (B) Sample survey
   (C) End-use method (D) Trial survey
3. End-use method of forecasting demand is also called :
   (A) Sales force opinion method (B) Collective opinion method
   (C) User expectation method (D) Test marketing
4. Delphi technique was first used by Rand Corporation in:
   (A) India (B) USA
   (C) China (D) Japan
5. Which one of the following component is not included in the time series analysis technique of demand forecasting?
   (A) Seasonal (B) Erratic
   (C) Cyclical (D) Political
6. When a manager forecasts demand with the available resources and personal experience it is called:
   (A) Judgmental approach (B) Controlled experiments
   (C) Expert opinion method (D) Multivariable approach

Answers:

1. B 2. A 3. C 4. B 5. D
6. A

REFERENCES

1. Alhabeeb, M.J. & Moffitt, L.J. (2013). *Managerial Economics: A Mathematical Approach.* New Jersey : John Wiley & Sons, Inc.

2. Baye, M. (2000). *Managerial Economics & Business Strategy* (1st Edn.). Boston: Irwin/McGraw-Hill.
3. Douglas, Evan, J. (1970). *Managerial Economics: Theory Practice and Problems.* N.J : Prentice Hall, Inc.
4. Dwivedi, D.N. (1999). *Managerial Economics.* New Delhi: Vikas Publishing House Pvt. Ltd.
5. Geetika, Ghosh, P. & Choudhury, P. (2008). *Managerial Economics* (1st Edn). New Delhi: Tata McGraw-Hill.
6. Hague, D. C. (1969). *Managerial Economics: Analysis for Business Decisions.* Wiley.
7. Haynes, W. W., Mote, V. L. & Paul, S. (1970). *Managerial Economics: Analysis and Cases.* Bombay: Vakils, Feffer & Simons Pvt. Ltd.
8. Hooda, R. P. (2000). *Statistics for Business and Economics,* McMillan India Ltd.
9. Keita, L. (1992). *Science, Rationality, and Neoclassical Economics* (1st Edn.). Newark: University of Delaware Press.
10. Lipsey, R. (1997). *Microeconomics, Growth and Political Economy.* Edward Elgar Publishing.
11. Mansfield, E. (1975). *Microeconomics: Theory/Applications.* New York: W.W. Norton & Co.

Chapter

9 Production Analysis

LEARNING OBJECTIVES

After studying this chapter, you should be able to understand:

- concept of production and production function;
- law of variable proportions and returns to scale;
- production function with two variable inputs;
- least-cost combination of inputs; and
- Cobb-Douglas production function.

9.1. INTRODUCTION

Production is an essential economic activity that satisfies the wants and needs of consumers and increases consumer usage of goods and services. Production theory explains the principles based on which business units take decisions on the quantity of each product to be produced, how much of raw material, fixed capital and labour it employs and uses during a specified period. Production refers to all activities involved in the production of goods and services. The activities include borrowing capital to set up or expand production facilities, hiring workers, purchase of raw materials, quality control, and so on. The major factors of production are land, capital, labour, organisation and technology. Every business unit tries to utilise these five factors of production optimally to achieve maximum output. The production function explains the technical relationship between inputs and output. It enables an business unit to achieve maximum output with the given combinations of factors of production in a particular period.

9.2. CONCEPT OF PRODUCTION

Production can be defined as the process of converting the inputs into outputs. A production is an act of creating value that satisfies the wants of the individuals. Organisations engage in production for earning a profit, which is the difference between the cost incurred and the revenue generated. Therefore, a business unit's production decision depends on its cost and revenue. According to C.E. Ferguson (1969), the theory of production consists of how the producer, given the state of technology, combines the inputs to produce a definite quantity of output in an economically efficient manner.

The main aim of the production function is to generate maximum output with given inputs. For attaining the maximum output, inputs are combined in more than one way. The most efficient combination is chosen from different combinations. The decision in choosing the right combination depends upon the selection of inputs, quantities available, allocation of budget, input prices, accessibility, demand for outputs, production resources and so on.

The inputs of production can be classified into fixed inputs and variable inputs.

1. **Fixed inputs:** Fixed factors are those factors which do not change with an increase or decrease in the quantity of output. The fixed inputs include land and buildings, machinery and computer systems, fixed equipment, and other fixed expenses.
2. **Variable inputs:** Variable factors are those factors which change with increase or decrease in the quantity of output. The variable inputs include raw materials, spare parts, labour, power, and other variable expenses.

9.2.1. Time Periods for the Business Unit

The production is often explained in terms of time periods. The time periods are classified as follows:

- **Very short period:** A business unit is said to be in a very short period when the only way to increase output is by using the existing stocks of inputs.
- **Short seriod:** A business unit is said to be in a short period when it can increase its output by expanding the use of variable inputs such as hiring more workers but not by increasing its fixed factors. In a short period, business units do not use extra fixed inputs such as the construction of additional space, acquiring new machinery, etc., to increase the output. Therefore, in a short period, the changes in production can be taken up on a limited scale.
- **Long period:** A business unit is said to be in a long period when it can make arrangements for increasing or decreasing its scale of operations. If the business unit requires an increase in output it can do so by expanding its production capacity. It can procure land and buildings, machinery, and all other inputs sufficiently because it has adequate time to do so. On the other hand, if the business unit wants to reduce the output, it can plan other products to avoid idle capacity or it can scale down the entire capacity without losing significantly.
- **Very long period:** A whole industry is said to be in a very long period when there is a significant change in the use of technology or major shifts in consumer behaviour. For example, e-applications, technology adaptations require a sufficiently long period to introduce

changes in the business unit. In a very long period, business units may plan for business diversification, modification of product portfolio, and entry into new markets and/or new market segments either nationally or globally. Such decisions have a major impact on the production function of the business unit.

9.3. PRODUCTION FUNCTION

The production function expresses a functional relationship between quantities of inputs and outputs. It shows how and to what extent output changes with variations in inputs during a specified period. The production function may be defined as the functional relationship between physical inputs (i.e., the factors of production) and physical outputs (i.e., the number of goods produced).

Definitions of production function

Author	Definition
Koutsoyiannis (1975)	The production function is purely its inputs and output technical relation which connects factor.
George J Stigler (1953)	The production function is the relationship between the rates of inputs of productive services and the rate of output. It is the economist's summary of technical knowledge.

Thus, a production function includes a wide range of inputs like land, labour, capital, organisation, and technology. Algebraically, it may be expressed in the form of an equation as:

$$Q = f(L, La, K, O, T)$$

where,

Q = for the output of a good per unit of time

F = functional relationship

L = land (or natural resources)

La = labour (or employees)

K = capital (or investment)

O = organisation (or management)

T = technology

The production function with many inputs cannot be depicted on a diagram. Moreover, given the specific values of the various inputs, it becomes difficult to solve such a production function mathematically. Therefore, economists use a two-input production function. If only two inputs, labour and capital are considered the production function assumes the form:

$$Q = f(L, K)$$

According to Michael R. Baye (1994), the production function is that function which defines the maximum amount of output that can be produced with a given set of inputs. The production function as determined by technical conditions of production may be rigid or flexible. The former relates to the short-run and the latter is related to the long-run decisions. The production function can be classified as:

1. Production function with one variable input factor
2. Production function with two variable input factors
3. Production function with all variable input factors

9.3.1. Characteristics of the Production Function

The following characteristics of the production function can be identified:

1. It is the relation between physical inputs and outputs.
2. It is the development of a combination of inputs to produce maximum output.
3. It is to ensure organisational efficiency in production processes to minimise wastage and costs.
4. It enables efficient and timely production process.
5. Use of appropriate technology and skilled human resource.
6. Efficient monitoring and quality control.
7. Facilitation of timely production of required output.

Therefore, the production function can be defined as "the kind of relationship between inputs factors and output to ensure maximum output with minimum inputs, timely and qualitative output with efficient processing and cost control".

9.3.2. Importance of Production Function

The production function is of great help to a manager or business economist. The important managerial uses of production function are outlined below.

1. **Determine the least cost factor combination:** The production function is a guide to the entrepreneur to determine the least cost factor combination. Profit can be maximised only by minimising the cost of production. To minimise the cost of production, inputs are to be substituted. The production function helps in substituting the inputs.
2. **Determine the optimum level of output:** The production function helps to determine the optimum level of output from a given quantity of input. In other words, it helps to arrive at the producer's equilibrium.
3. **Production planning:** The production function helps the entrepreneur (or management) to plan for the production.

4. **Decision making:** Production function is very useful to the management to make decisions regarding cost and output. It also helps cost control and cost reduction. In short, production function helps both in the short-run and long-run decision making processes.

9.4. LAW OF VARIABLE PROPORTIONS

The law of variable proportions is one of the three laws of production. This law was first explained by Sir Edward West in his book, *Essay on the Application of Capital to Land,* in 1815. The law of variable proportion states that, if one factor is used more and more (variable), keeping the other factors constant, the total output will increase at an increasing rate in the beginning and then at a diminishing rate and eventually decreases absolutely. Thus, the law of variable proportions shows the production function with one input factor variable while keeping the other input factors constant.

Definitions on law of variable proportions

Author	**Definition**
K. E. Boulding (1941)	As we increase the quantity of any one input which is combined with a fixed quantity of the other inputs, the marginal physical productivity of the variable input must eventually decline.
G.J. Stigler (1953)	As equal increments of one input are added, the inputs of other productive services being held, constant, beyond a certain point the resulting increments of the product will decrease, i.e., the marginal product will diminish.
F. Benham (1939)	As the proportion of one factor in a combination of factors is increased, after a point, first the marginal and then the average product of that factor will diminish.
Alfred Marshall (1890)	An increase in the capital and labour applied in the cultivation of land causes, in general, less than proportionate increase in the amount of produce raised unless it happens to coincide with an improvement in the art of agriculture.

The law shows the effect of variations in factor proportion on output. When one factor varies and the other factors are fixed, the proportion between the fixed factor and the variable factor will vary, (for example, land and capital will be fixed in the short run, while labour will be variable). Thus, the law is called the law of variable proportions. It is also known as the law of proportionality, the law of diminishing returns, or the law of non-proportional outputs.

According to the law of variable proportions, there are three types of product, viz., total product, average product, and marginal product.

1. **Total product (TP):** The level of output produced with a given amount of input.
2. **Average product (AP):** The output produced per unit of the variable input (AP = Quantity/variable input).
3. **Marginal product (MP):** The change in total output due to an additional unit of the variable input.
   - The marginal product of labour = $\Delta Q/\Delta L$ (i.e., change in the quantity produced to a given change in the labour).
   - The marginal product of capital = $\Delta Q/\Delta K$ (i.e., change in the quantity produced to a given change in the capital).

9.4.1. Assumptions of the Law

The law of variable proportions is based on the following assumptions:

1. Only one factor is considered variable while other factors are considered constant.
2. All units of the variable factors are homogeneous.
3. There is no change in technology.
4. It is possible to vary the proportions when different inputs are combined.
5. It assumes a short-run situation, as in the long run, all factors are variable.

The product is measured in physical units, i.e., in quintals, tonnes, etc., because the use of money in measuring the product may show increasing rather than decreasing returns, if the prices of the product rise, even though the output declines.

9.4.2. Three Stages of the Law of Variable Proportions

There are three stages in the law of variable proportions. Table 9.1 shows the three stages of the law of variable proportions.

Table 9.1. Output in physical units (For example: Wheat in quintals)

Stage	Fixed factor (Capital)	Variable factor (Labour)	Total product (TP)	Average product (AP)	Marginal product (MP)
Stage I	1	1	10	10	10
	1	2	24	12	14
	1	3	39	13	15
	1	4	56	14	17

	1	5	70	14	14
Stage II	1	6	78	13	8
	1	7	84	12	6
	1	8	84	10	0
Stage III	1	9	81	9	–3
	1	10	70	7	–11

From the table, it can be observed that both the average and marginal products increase initially and then decline. The total product increases at an increasing rate until the employment of the 4th unit of labour. Beyond the 4th unit of labour, the marginal product is diminishing. The marginal product declines faster than the average product. When the 7th unit of labour is employed, the total product reaches the maximum level. For the 8th unit of labour, the marginal product is zero and at the 9th unit of labour, the marginal product is negative. Thus, when more and more units of labour are combined with other fixed factors, the total product and average product increases first at an increasing rate and then at a diminishing rate.

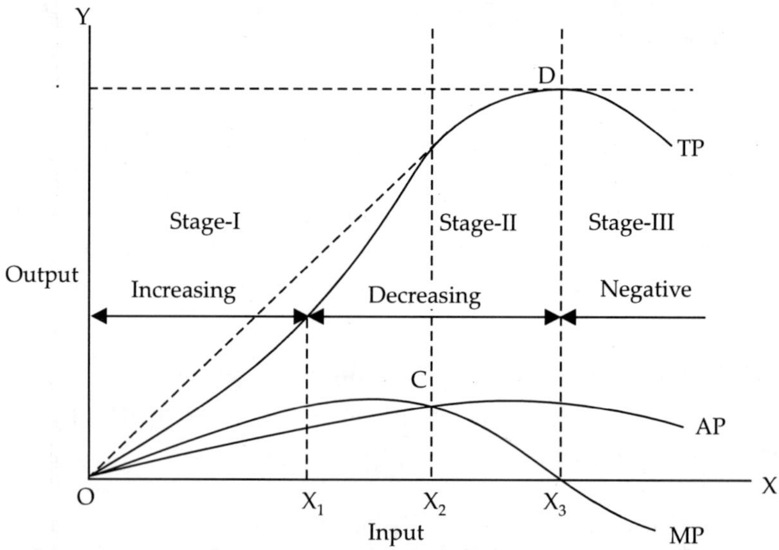

Figure 9.1. Three stages of production function

The stage-wise description of the production function with one variable input factor (Figure 9.1) helps us to analyse the outcomes and to take appropriate decisions. The quantity of the variable input factor is measured on the X-axis, and the total product, average product and marginal product are measured on the Y-axis.

Stage-I: Increasing Returns

In stage-I, the behaviour of the total product curve, marginal product curve and the average product curve will not be similar. The total product (TP) curve shows an increasing trend in this stage. Though in the beginning, the TP curve registers slow growth rate, it will grow faster after some time. The marginal product (MP) curve reaches its peak at X_1 input and at point F, afterwards, the MP curve shows a decreasing trend. The average product (AP) curve shows an increasing trend right from the beginning until the end of the stage. The point at which the MP curve and AP curve intersect (point C) that point is considered an endpoint of stage-I. Thus, during stage-I the TP curve continues to increase, the MP curve reaches its peak and starts declining, and the AP curve goes on increasing to intersect with the MP curve.

Stage-II: Diminishing Returns

The second stage begins with the declining growth rate of TP curve, the steep decline of the MP curve and the AP curve remains constant. During this stage, the TP curve reaches its peak at point D. The MP curve touches the *X*-axis at X_3. Thus, this stage is referred to as diminishing returns.

Stage-III: Negative Returns

Stage-III begins with the decline in the TP curve, the negative growth of the MP curve and a marginal decline in the AP curve. The feature of this stage is that all three curves show a negative trend. This stage is referred to as the stage of negative returns.

9.5. ISOQUANT

A production function with two variable inputs can be represented by isoquants. The term 'Iso' derives from a Greek word which means 'equal' and the term 'quant' is derives from a Latin word which means 'quantity'. Isoquant means equal quantity throughout the production process. It is defined as a curve which shows different combinations of two inputs producing the same level of output. Isoquant shows all possible combinations of the two inputs (say, labour and capital) capable of producing equal or a given level of output.

A producer may not be certain about different combinations of inputs that require producing the same level of output. The indifference on the part of the producer can be described in the form of 'Iso product curve' or 'product indifference curve' or 'equal product curve' or 'production function with two variable inputs'.

9.5.1. Assumptions of an Isoquant

The assumptions of an isoquant curve are as follows:

- Only two-factor inputs (Ex: capital and labour) are employed for producing a product.
- The two factors are divisible in nature.
- The two factors are substitutable to each other. The production function is of variable proportion rather than a fixed proportion.
- The production technology is unchanged for a specific period.
- Factors of production can be divided into two parts.

The example shown in Table 9.2 explains the isoquant schedule.

Table 9.2. Isoquant schedule

Combinations	Capital	Labour	Output (units)
A	1	20	1000
B	2	15	1000
C	3	11	1000
D	4	8	1000
E	5	6	1000

The isoquant schedule (Table 9.2) shows the five possible combinations of input. All the five combinations yield the same level of output, i.e., 1000 units. The combination-A with 20 units of labour and 1 unit of capital produce 1000 units. Combination-B with 15 units of labour and 2 units of capital also produce 1000 units and so on. All combinations are equally possible because all of them produce the same level of output.

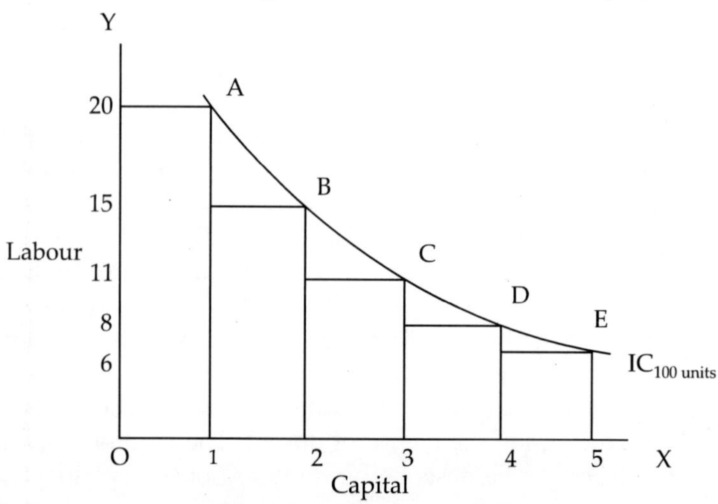

Figure 9.2. Isoquant curve

When these combinations of labour and capital are plotted in a graph, it is known as an isoquant curve (Figure 9.2). The units of capital are measured on the horizontal axis and units of labour on the vertical axis. The five combinations of *A, B, C, D,* and *E* are plotted on the graph. Here, it is assumed that the level of technology remains constant and the input can be substituted for each other. If the quantity of labour is reduced, the quantity of capital must be increased to produce the same level of output. Thus, an isoquant shows various combinations of the two inputs in the existing state of technology which produce the same level of output.

9.5.2. Isoquant Map or Equal Product Map

An isoquant map consists of several isoquants showing a set of equal product curves at different production levels. The curves on the right side of $IQ_{1000\ units}$ represent a higher level of output. The distance of an isoquant from the origin shows the relative levels of output. The farther the isoquant from the origin the greater will be the level of output. The isoquant map is shown in Figure 9.3.

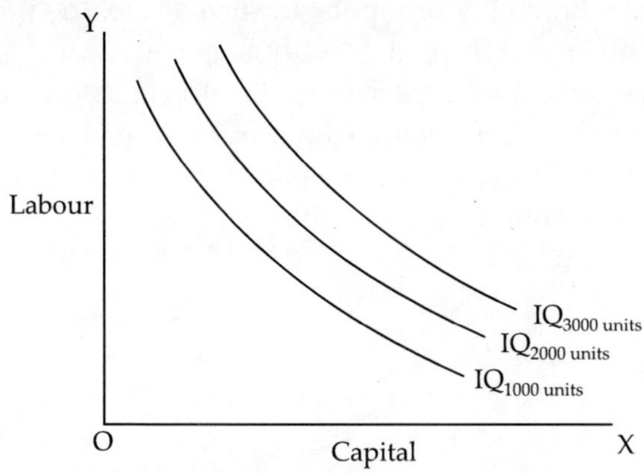

Figure 9.3. Isoquant map

9.5.3. Features of Isoquants

The following are the important features of isoquants:

1. **Slopes downward from left to right:** This implies that the isoquant is a negatively sloped curve. This is because in the combination of two variables if the quantity of one variable factor K (capital) is increased, the quantity of another variable factor L (labour) gets reduced for generating the same level of output or vice versa.
2. **Do not intersect or touch each other:** Each isoquant curve represents a particular level of output. An isoquant curve right to the previous

curve represents the higher output. Therefore, the two isoquant curves never intersect.

3. **Convex to the origin:** The isoquant curve is convex to the origin because of the marginal rate of the technical substitution effect. This shows that factors of production are substitutable for each other and with the increase in the quantity of one factor reduces the quantity of the other factor to have the same level of production.
4. **Isoquants need not be parallel to each other:** Isoquant curves need not be parallel to each other due to the reason that the technical substitution to the variable factors may vary in different isoquant curves.

9.5.4. Types of Isoquants

Isoquants assume different shapes depending upon the degree of substitutability of inputs under consideration. The following are the four types of isoquants.

1. **Linear isoquants:** Linear isoquants are possible when there is perfect substitutability of inputs. In such a case, the production is possible either with capital or with labour or with a combination of both. For example, a given output of 100 units can be produced by using only capital or only labour or by several combinations of labour and capital. Isoquants, therefore, are the linear straight lines as shown in Figure 9.4.

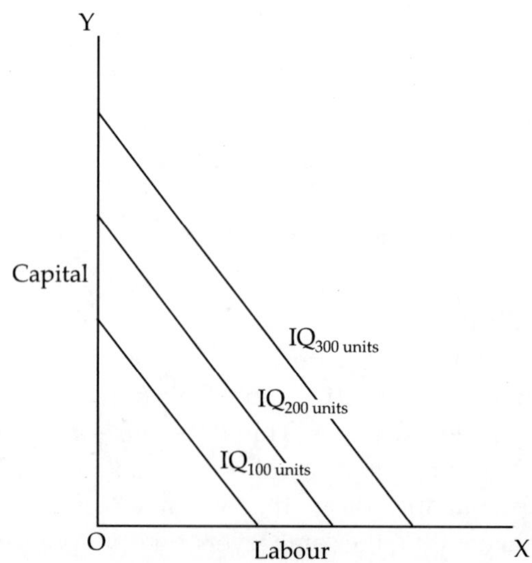

Figure 9.4. Linear isoquants

2. **Input-output isoquant:** In case of complete non-substitutability between the factors of inputs, the isoquant curve takes the form of right angle isoquant. For example, to produce a bicycle, two wheels and one frame are required. It is not possible to substitute wheels for frames or vice versa. Input-output isoquant is also known as 'Leontief isoquant' or 'right-angle isoquant'. Figure 9.5 shows the input-output iso-quant curve.

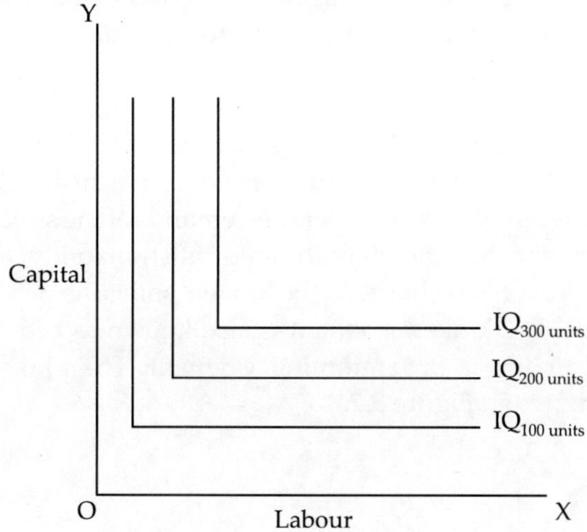

Figure 9.5. Leontief isoquant

3. **Smooth convex isoquant:** This form of isoquant assumes substitutability of inputs but, the substitution is not perfect. For example,

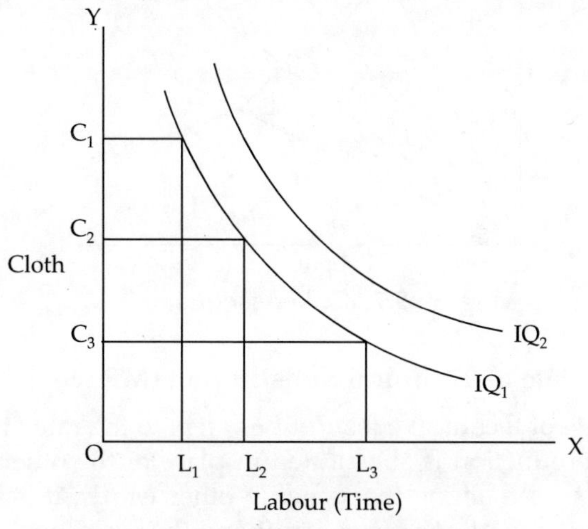

Figure 9.6. Smooth convex isoquant

a tailor uses cloth (C_1) liberally if the time (L_1) available for making a shirt is very less to make his time more productive. If the tailor is given more time (L_2) he/she may enhance the efficiency in cutting the cloth and therefore, the shirt is made with less cloth (C_2) by reducing wastage. If the time (L_3) available to the tailor is enhanced further the shirt will be made with the minimum possible cloth (C_3) and the wastage is eliminated. Therefore, an increase in labour from L_1 to L_2 leads to a decrease in the input of cloth from C_1 to C_2. A further increase in labour from L_2 to L_3 results in the reduction of cloth used from C_2 to C_3. Figure 9.6 shows the smooth convex isoquant curve.

4. **Kinked Isoquant:** In production function, some input factors may have limited substitutability. In such a case, the business unit has to choose between processes as per the demands of the situation. When two factors of production have limited substitutability, the isoquant curve takes a kinked shape. At the kinked point, the production will be efficient. The kinked isoquant is also known as activity analysis iso-quant or linear programming isoquant. The kinked isoquant curve is shown in Figure 9.7.

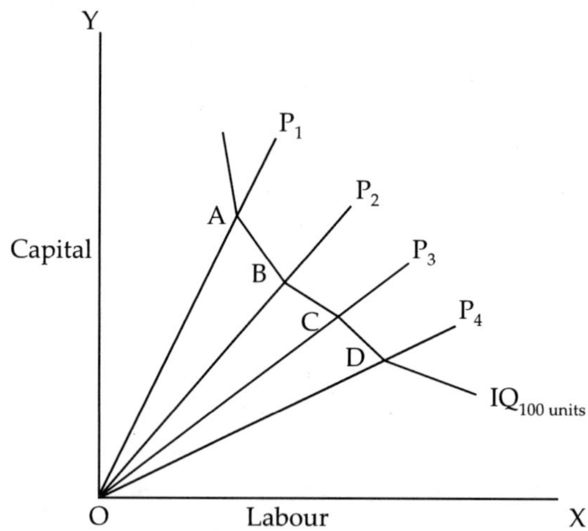

Figure 9.7. Kinked isoquant

9.5.5. Marginal Rate of Technical Substitution (MRTS)

The marginal rate of technical substitution refers to the rate at which one input factor of production is substituted in place of the other factor, the quantity of output remaining the same. In other words, it is the ratio of change in the quantity of one-factor input and the corresponding change in the quantity of other factor input to keep the same level of output. For example, in terms of inputs of capital (K) and labour (L), the MRTS can be calculated as:

$$\text{MRTS} = \frac{\text{Change in one input}}{\text{Change in other input}} = \frac{\Delta K}{\Delta L}$$

Table 9.3. Possible combinations

Combinations	Capital	Labour	MRTS
A	1	20	—
B	2	15	5:1
C	3	11	4:1
D	4	8	3:1

$$\text{MRTS} = \frac{2-1}{20-15} = \frac{1}{5} = 1{:}5$$

Table 9.3 presents the ratio of MRTS between two input factors, capital and labour. A decrease of 5 units in labour is compensated by an increase in one unit of capital, i.e., 5:1. The marginal rate of technical substitution explains the ratio of marginal productivity of labour to the marginal productivity of capital. The slope of the isoquant is technically known as the MRTS in production.

9.5.6. Isocost

An isocost line indicates different combinations of two input factors which the business unit can buy at given prices with a given amount of money.

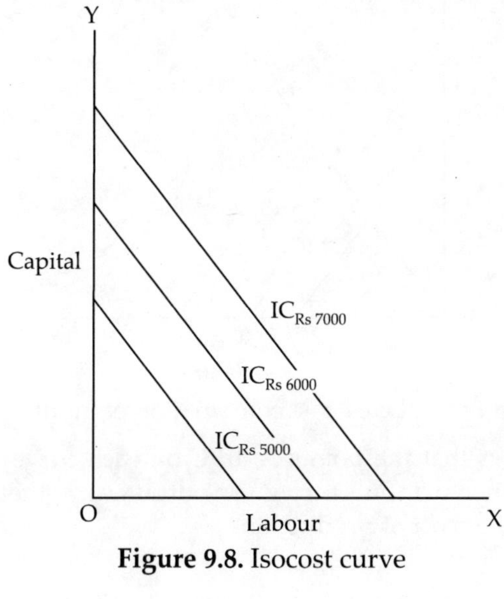

Figure 9.8. Isocost curve

If the production changes the total cost also changes. Thus, isocost shows the prices of the two factors and the total amount of money spent on production.

For example, a business unit decides to spend Rs. 5000 on two input factors, capital and labour. If the weekly wage of a worker is Rs. 50, the business unit can employ 100 workers. Similarly, if one unit of capital costs Rs. 20, the business unit buys 250 units. Thus, the business unit can spend the whole amount of Rs. 5000 either on labour (100 workers) or on capital (250 units) or partly on labour and partly on capital. If the business unit decides to spend a higher amount on the two input factors the isocost curve moves upward (Figure 9.8).

9.5.7. Least Cost Combination of Inputs

The isoquant shows different combinations of two input factors producing the same level of output. However, the producer will not accept all combinations. The choice of the combination depends upon its maximum contribution to the profit. It is possible only by maximising the output at minimum cost. Therefore, the optimum input combination which incurs the least cost will be preferred. The optimum or least-cost combination is that combination where the average cost of production is the minimum. This is the producer's equilibrium. This can be found out by combining the business unit's production function and cost function. The production function is represented by isoquant and cost function is represented by an isocost curve.

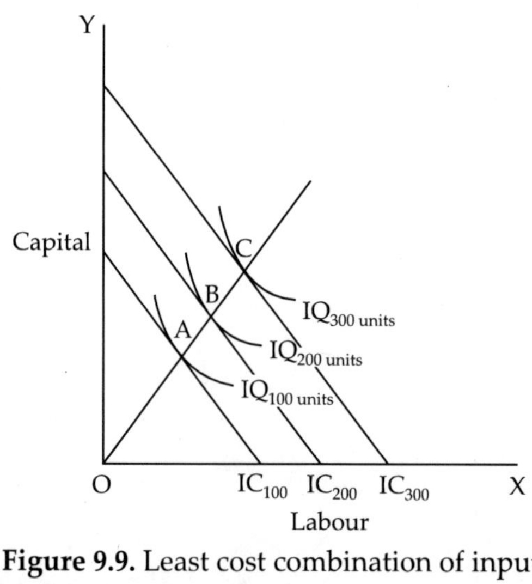

Figure 9.9. Least cost combination of inputs

Figure 9.9 shows that the points A, B, C on each curve represent the least-cost combination of inputs for a given output. Any other combination will result in a higher cost of production.

9.6. LAW OF RETURNS TO SCALE

The law of variable proportion assumes the behaviour of output in such a way that when one input factor is variable and the other factors are held constant. Such an assumption is valid only in the short run. But in the long run, all input factors become variable. In the words of Roger Miller (1959), "Returns to scale refer to the relationship between changes in output and proportionate changes in all factors of productions." To meet a long-run change in demand, the business unit increases its scale of production by using more space, more machines and labourers in the factory. When all input factors change in the same proportion, the behaviour of output is analysed with laws of returns to scale. Thus, the law of returns to scale is a long-run analysis.

9.6.1. Assumptions of the Law

The law of returns to scale assumes that:

1. All factors of production excluding business unit are variable in the long run.
2. Technological changes are absent.
3. The output or returns are measured in physical terms.

The returns to scale are categorised as increasing returns to scale, constant return to scale, and decreasing returns to scale. Table 9.4 shows the returns to scale in physical units when two input factors such as capital and labour change in the long run.

Table 9.4. Returns to scale in physical units

Units of labour	Units of capital (Rs. '000)	Total product	Change in output	Scale
1	2	4	–	Increasing
2	4	10	6	
3	6	18	8	
4	8	28	10	Constant
5	10	38	10	
6	12	48	10	
7	14	56	8	Decreasing
8	16	62	6	

From Table 9.4, it can be observed that the total production increases continuously, whereas, the change in output (marginal product) initially increases, becomes constant and then declines. The total product increases at an increasing rate until the employment of the 4th unit of labour and 8 units of capital. Beyond that level, the total product increases in a proportionate manner and the change in output remains constant. After a certain level, i.e., employing 7 units of labour and 14 units of capital the total product and marginal product declines. Thus, when more and more units of labour and capital are employed, the total production increases first at an increasing rate and then at a diminishing rate. The change in output also initially increases with a change in input factors labour and capital, then becomes constant and when more and more input factor is introduced the marginal product declines. Figure 8.10 shows the graphical representation of the law of returns to scale.

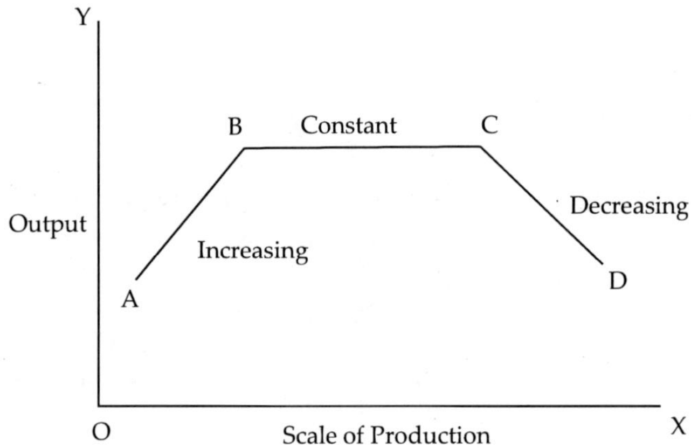

Figure 9.10. Law of returns to scale

Stage 1: Increasing returns to scale

During this stage, the increase in inputs in a given proportion leads to an increase in output in a greater proportion. In other words, a proportionate increase in all factors of production results in more than proportionate increase in output. For example, if the inputs are increased by 40%, the output will be increased by more than 40%.

The reasons for increasing returns to scale are given below.

1. **Specialisation and division of labour:** When the scale of the business unit is expanded there is a wide scope of specialisation and division of labour. Work can be divided into small tasks and workers can be concentrated to a narrower range of processes for which specialised equipment can be installed. Thus, with specialisation, efficiency increases and returns to scale increases.
2. **Internal economies:** As the business unit expands, it enjoys internal economies of production. It may be able to install better machines,

sell its products more easily, borrow money cheaply, procure the services of the more efficient manager and workers, etc. All these economies help in increasing the returns to scale more than proportionately.

Stage 2: Constant return to scale

In this stage, the increase in inputs in a given proportion increases the output in the same proportion. For example, if inputs are increased by 40%, the output also increases by 40%. There will not be any additional output as in the case of stage-I during this stage. However, the proportion of change in input, as well as output, will be constant during this stage.

The reasons for constant returns to scale are:

1. As the business unit expands further, internal economies are counterbalanced by internal diseconomies.
2. The benefits of specialisation and division of labour reach to its maximum and therefore, there will not be any additional advantage with further expansion from the stage-I position.

Stage 3: Decreasing returns to scale

Decreasing returns to scale is otherwise known as the law of diminishing returns. This is an important law of production. If the business unit continues to expand beyond the stage of constant returns, the stage of diminishing returns to scale will start operating. A proportionate increase in all input factors results in less than proportionate increase in output. For example, if inputs are increased by 40%, the output increases by less than 40%.

The reasons for diminishing returns to scale:

1. Expansion beyond a particular point affects the control system of the business unit.
2. Coordination problems and internal communication problems arise.
3. Diseconomies will associate with the increased scale of all input factors.

9.7. COBB-DOUGLAS PRODUCTION FUNCTION

The Cobb-Douglas production function is widely used to represent the relationship of output with inputs. This concept was proposed by Knut Wicksell (1851-1926) and tested against statistical evidence by Cobb and Douglas in 1928. The American ex-senator and economist Paul H. Douglas and mathematician Charles W. Cobb published a study in which they modelled the growth of the American economy during the period

1899-1922. They considered a simplified view of the economy in which production output is determined by the amount of labour involved and the amount of capital invested. While many other factors were affecting economic performance, their model proved to be remarkably accurate. The inputs are capital and labour.

The Cobb-Douglas production function is expressed as:

$$Q = bL^{\alpha}C^{\beta}$$

where,

Q = total output (monetary value of all goods produced in a year)
L = labour input (total number of person-hours worked in a year)
K = capital input (monetary worth of all machinery, equipment, and buildings)
b = total factor productivity
α and β = output elasticity of labour and capital, respectively.

The function estimated by Cobb and Douglas is:

$$Q = 1\ L^{0.75}\ C^{0.25}$$
$$R^2 = 94.09$$

This production function shows that a 1% change in labour input, with the capital remaining constant, is associated with a 0.75% change in output. Similarly, a 1% change in capital, with the labour remaining constant, is associated with a 0.25 % change in output. The coefficient of determination (R^2) means that 94% of the variations on the dependent variable (P) were accounted for, by the variations in the independent variables (L and C). If labour (L) and capital (K) are each increased by 20%, then production (P) increases by 20%. Thus, Cobb-Douglas production function indicates constant returns to scale, i.e., if the factors of production are each increased by 1% the output also increases by 1%.

9.8. SUMMARY

- Production refers to all activities involved in the production of goods and services.
- Production theory explains the principles based on which business units take decisions on the quantity of each product to be produced, how much of raw material, fixed capital and labour it employs and uses during a specified period.
- The inputs of production can be classified into fixed inputs and variable inputs.
- The production function expresses a functional relationship between quantities of inputs and outputs.
- The major factors of production are land, capital, labour, organisation and technology.

- The important managerial uses of production function are determining the least cost factor combination, determine the optimum level of output, production planning, and decision making.
- The law of variable proportion states that, if one factor is used more and more (variable), keeping the other factors constant, the total output will increase at an increasing rate in the beginning and then at a diminishing rate and eventually decreases absolutely.
- The three stages of the law of variable proportions are increasing returns, decreasing returns, and negative returns.
- Isoquant is defined as a curve which shows different combinations of two inputs producing the same level of output.
- An isoquant map consists of several isoquants showing a set of equal product curves at different production levels.
- The important features of isoquants are slopes downward from left to right, do not intersect or touch each other, convex to the origin, and isoquants need not be parallel to each other.
- Linear isoquants are possible when there is perfect substitutability of inputs.
- In the case of complete non-substitutability between the factors of inputs, the iso-quant curve takes the form of right angle isoquant.
- Smooth isoquant assumes substitutability of inputs but, the substitution is not perfect.
- When two factors of production are having limited substitutability, the isoquant curve takes a kinked shape.
- The marginal rate of technical substitution refers to the rate at which one input factor of production is substituted in place of the other factor, the quantity of output remaining the same.
- An isocost line indicates different combinations of two input factors which the business unit can buy at given prices with a given amount of money.
- The optimum or least-cost combination is that combination where the average cost of production is the minimum.
- The law of returns to scale refers to the relationship between changes in output and proportionate changes in all factors of production.
- The three stages of the law of returns to scale are increasing, constant, and decreasing returns.
- Cobb-Douglas production function considered a simplified view of the economy in which production output is determined by the amount of labour involved and the amount of capital invested. The Cobb-Douglas production function is expressed as $Q = b\ L^{\alpha}C^{\beta}$

SHORT ANSWER QUESTIONS

1. Define production.
2. What are the characteristics of the production function?
3. What are the features of isoquants?
4. Write a short note on MRTS.
5. Briefly explain the kinked isoquant.
6. What are the assumptions of the law of variable proportions?
7. What is an isocost?

ESSAY ANSWER QUESTIONS

1. What are isoquants and isocosts? Analyse how the producer reaches the least-cost combination of inputs with suitable example.
2. What is Cobb-Douglas production function? Explain it is helpful to a manufacturer in production decisions.
3. Explain the concept of production. Discuss the production time periods of a business unit.
4. Define the production function? Explain the characteristics and importance of production function.
5. Define the law of returns to scale. What is the significance of increasing, decreasing and constant returns to scale?
6. What is the law of variable proportions? Explain the three stages with an illustration.
7. Discuss the different isoquants with suitable diagrams.

FILL IN THE BLANKS

1. The process of converting inputs into outputs is known as __________.
2. The law of production studied under short-run production is called ____________.
3. The stage of production in which the total output increases, but the marginal product starts declining with the increase in one input factor is __________ returns to scale.
4. A constant return to scale implies the situation in which an increase in output is _________to the increase in factor inputs.
5. Profit is the difference between revenue and cost. (True/ False)
6. L-shaped isoquant is the case of perfect substitutes. (True/ False)

Answers:

1. Production
2. Law of variable proportions
3. Diminishing
4. Equal
5. True
6. False

MULTIPLE-CHOICE QUESTIONS

1. In the first stage of the production function with one variable input, the average product is:

(A) greater than the total product
(B) greater than the marginal product
(C) less than the marginal product
(D) greater than the total product

2. Marginal product is referred to as:
   (A) additional production obtained by the addition of two units
   (B) additional production obtained by the addition of one unit
   (C) additional production obtained by the reduction of one unit
   (D) additional production obtained by the reduction of two units
3. Wages are a return for:
   (A) Land (B) Labour
   (C) Capital (D) Organisation
4. Rent is a return on:
   (A) Land (B) Technology
   (C) Capital (D) Enterprise
5. Compute MRTS, when one combination of factor X and factor Y is 1 and 20 and another combination of is 2 and 12.
   (A) 1:10 (B) 1:8
   (C) 2:22 (D) 1:12
6. Isoquant refers to the curve in which the
   (A) production is the same for different combinations of two factors
   (B) production is not the same for different combinations of two factors
   (C) production is the same for different combinations of one factor
   (D) production is the same for different combinations of one factor
7. The Isocost line is:
   (A) Horizontal straight line to X-axis
   (B) Downward sloping curve
   (C) Parallel straight line to Y-axis
   (D) Upward sloping curve
8. Least-cost combination of two factors of production is:
   (A) where the isocost line is tangent to isoquant curve
   (B) where the isocost line intersects isoquant curve
   (C) where two isocost lines overlap each other
   (D) where two isoquant lines overlap each other
9. Isoquant means:
   (A) Downward sloping
   (B) Do not interest
   (C) Convex to origin
   (D) Equal quantity
10. The full form of MRTS is:
    (A) Marginal rate of technical substance
    (B) Marginal right of technical substance
    (C) Marginal rate of technical substitution
    (D) Mechanical rate of technical substitution

11. Which one of the following is not a feature of isoquant curve?
    (A) slopes upwards from right to left
    (B) slopes downwards from left to right
    (C) do not intersect or touch each other
    (D) convex to the origin

Answers:

1. C	2. B	3. B	4. A	5. B
6. A	7. B	8. B	9. D	10. C
11. A				

REFERENCES

1. Ahuja, H.L. (2008). *Managerial Economics.* New Delhi: S Chand Publications.
2. Baye, Michael R. (1994). *Managerial Economics and Business Strategy.* New York: McGraw-Hill.
3. Benham, F. (1939). *Economics: A General Textbook for Students.* London: Sir Issac Pitman & Sons Ltd.
4. Boulding, K.E. (1941). *Economic Analysis.* New York: Harper & Brothers.
5. Cobb, C.W. & Douglas, P.H. (1928). "A theory of production". *American Economic Review,* 18 (Supplement), 139-165.
6. Douglas, E.J. (1987). *Managerial Economics: Analysis and Strategy.* New York: Prentice-Hall.
7. Dwivedi, D.N. (1999). *Managerial Economics.* New Delhi: Vikas Publishing House Pvt. Ltd.
8. Ferguson, C.E. (1969). *The Neoclassical Theory of Production and Distribution.* Cambridge University Press.
9. Gupta, G.S. (2017). *Managerial Economics.* New Delhi, India: Tata McGraw-Hill.
10. Koutsoyiannis, A. (1975). *Modern Microeconomics.* London: The Macmillan Press Ltd.
11. Mansfield, E. (1975). *Microeconomics: Theory/Applications.* New York: W.W. Norton & Co.
12. Marshall, Alfred. (1890). *Principles of Economics.* London: Macmillan.
13. Miller, R.F. (1959). "A note on the theory of investment and production". *The Quarterly Journal of Economics,* 73(4), 672-681.
14. Stiglar, G.J. (1953). *Theory of Price.* New York: The Macmillan Co.
15. West, E. (1815). *Essay on the Application of Capital to Land.* McMaster University Archive for the History of Economic Thought.

Chapter

10 Supply Analysis

LEARNING OBJECTIVES

After studying this chapter, you should be able to understand:

- concept of supply and supply function;
- determinants of supply;
- the law of supply, its assumptions and exceptions;
- supply curve movements and elasticity of supply; and
- factors influencing the elasticity of supply.

10.1. THE CONCEPT OF SUPPLY

Supply refers to the quantity of a product available in the market for sale at a specified price and time. In other words, supply is referred to as the willingness of a seller to sell the specified quantity of a product at an agreed price and time. The supply of a product is influenced by various determinants such as availability of inputs, production capacity, government regulations, accessibility to other factors of production, business strategy, demand, technology, etc. The law of supply states the relationship between the supply of a product and price. Producers increase the supply of products when prices are on the increase and thereby maximise their profits. Thus, the supply of a product increases with an increase in price and decreases with a decrease in price when other things remain constant.

Definitions of supply

Author	Definition
Albert L. Meyers (1940)	Supply is a schedule of the amount of a product that would be offered for sale at all possible prices at any one instant of time, or during any one period of time, for example, a day, a week, a month, a year and so on, in which the conditions of supply remain the same.
McConnell et al. (2009)	Supply is a schedule which shows the various amounts of a product which a particular seller is willing and able to produce and make available for sale in the market at each specific price in a set of possible prices during a given period.
Anatol Murad (1958)	Supply refers to the quantity of a product offered for sale at a given price, in a given market, at a given time.

From the above definitions, it can be assumed that supply has three important aspects:

- The price at which quantities are supplied differs from one location to the other.
- Supply is the quantity that suppliers are willing to offer during a specific period (per day, per week, per month, etc.).
- Supply depends upon the stock and the market price of a product.
- The quantity of product, price, and time are the three essential factors for determining supply. For example, a seller offers a product at Rs. 100 per piece in the market. In this case, only product and price are specified and it cannot be treated as supply. However, there is another seller who offers the same product at Rs. 110 per piece in the market for the next six months. In this case, product, price and time are specified, thus, it is supplied.

10.2. SUPPLY FUNCTION

The functional representation of the relationship between supply and its various determinants is known as supply function. In a supply function, supply is the dependent variable and the determinants of supply are independent variables. The supply function of a product represents the quantity of the product that would be supplied at a given price, levels of technology, input prices and all other factors that influence supply. A supply function can be represented as:

$$S_X = f(P_X, C, T, G, E)$$

where,

S_X = Supply of x product

P_X = Price of x product

C = Cost of production (wages, rent, interest, and price of raw materials)

T = State of technology

G = Government policy regarding regulations, taxes and subsidies

E = Factors outside the economic sphere (exogenous factors)

A business unit's supply function (S_X) for a product X can be simplified by holding constant the values of all variables other than the price of the product. Thus,

$$S_X = f(P_X)$$

A linear supply function is written in the form of:

$$Q_S = a + bP$$

where,

Q_S = the quantity supplied

a = the level of supply independent of price

P = the market price of the product

b = the coefficient of price elasticity (It is the change in demand of a product in response to change in price. It can be elastic, perfectly elastic, inelastic, or perfectly inelastic based on the coefficient.)

For example, if the supply of product X = 10 + 2 (P) and if the market price is Rs. 20, then, the quantity supplied is:

$$Q_S = 10 + 2(20) = 50 \text{ units}$$

10.3. DETERMINANTS OF SUPPLY

Supply does not remain constant all the time in the market. Many factors influence the supply of a product in the market. Generally, the supply of a product depends on its price and cost of production. Thus, it can be said that supply is the function of price and cost of production. The factors that influence the supply are called the determinants of supply. The determinants of supply are given below.

1. **Availability of inputs** determines the supply of the products. Some input materials are scarce or in limited supply or regulated supply. In such cases, though there is a demand for products and the prices are favourable, supply cannot be increased beyond the point.
2. **Production capacity** of a business unit is the limitation for supply in the short run. However, in the long run, the business unit may go for expansion of production capacity and thereby increase the supply of products.
3. **Government regulations** often influence supply conditions. The government policy towards permitting the production of certain products limits the supply. The government policies towards taxation, exports, imports, pricing, subsidies, the ceiling on production capacity, etc., will influence the supply conditions of different products.
4. **Accessibility to other factors of production** influence the supply position of various goods and services. The availability of electric power, water, and other support services, skilled human resource, and other resources required for production influences the supply position.
5. **Business strategy** of organisations also determines the supply position of products. A business unit may target the premium market in the beginning to make more profits. In such a case, the business unit will go for restricted supply. If the company targets the mass market then huge quantities of supply are required. The competitive environment also influences the business unit to be strategic in the supply of products.

6. **Demand and supply** are positively correlated. The higher the demand, the higher will be supply and vice versa, when other things remain constant.
7. **Transportation and storage** facilities also influence the supply position. If the products are to be imported from other countries, transportation and warehousing facilities play an important role in determining supply position at various points of time. The distance between the production point and consumption point, transport infrastructure and the mode of transport, storage and warehousing facilities are the critical determinants of supply positions.
8. **Prices of related products** and complementary goods also influence the supply of a product to a large extent. For example, if the price of related products increases, the demand for the main product increases and therefore, the producers try to produce maximum quantities to fill the demand-supply gap.
9. **Technology** used in production also influences the supply position. Mechanisation and automation increase the production capacity and therefore, producers can increase supply in a short period also. The technological innovations have revolutionised production processes and facilitated not only the production of large quantities in the shortest period possible, but also facilitated the variations in production at lowest cost and time.
10. **Exogenous factors** such as weather conditions, floods and droughts, epidemics, etc., cause fluctuations in the supply of goods, particularly of agricultural goods. Fire, war, and earthquakes may destroy productive assets of a product and affect future supplies.
11. **Firm's expectation about price changes** influences the decisions of supply by business units. If they expect an increase in price in future, they will keep the product in storage and wait for grabbing the opportunity. Thus, they will release only a limited quantity to the market. In case they expect to fall in price in future, the business units try to sell the total quantity at the earliest, and therefore, they will release full supply to the market.
12. **Market structure** in which a business unit is operating influences the supply. If there is a monopoly in the industry, the manufacturer may restrict the supply of goods to raise the prices of goods and increase profits. In a monopolistic competitive market, there would be a large of a number of sellers and hence, no single seller can influence the supply of a product.

10.4. THE LAW OF SUPPLY

The law of supply explains the relationship between the price and the supply of a product. According to the law, the quantity supplied increases with a rise in the price of a product and vice versa while other factors remain constant. The other factors include customer preferences, size of the market, size of the population, etc. The law of supply states a direct relationship between the price of a product and its supply. Therefore, both price and supply curves move in the same direction. The law of supply can be better understood with the help of 'supply schedule' and 'supply curve'.

- **Supply schedule:** Supply schedule can be defined as a tabular representation of the law of supply. It represents the quantities of a product supplied by a supplier at different prices and periods, keeping all other factors constant. Supply schedule can be prepared for an individual supplier or a market.
- **Supply curve:** The graphical representation of the supply schedule or the quantities of a product supplied by a supplier at different prices and periods is called the supply curve.

10.4.1. Supply by an Individual

Supply by an individual represents the quantities of a product supplied by an individual business unit at different prices during a specific period, assuming other factors remain unchanged. For example, a business unit supplies a product of 200 units per month at a price of Rs. 5 per unit. As the price rises to Rs. 10, the business unit increases its supply to 600 units. Further, when the price increases to Rs. 15 and later to Rs. 20, the quantity supplied also increased to 1000 units and 1400 units respectively. Therefore, the individual supply schedule indicates that the quantity supplied increases with a rise in price as shown in Table 10.1.

Table 10.1. Individual supply schedule

Price (Rs. per kg.)	Quantity supplied (units per month)
5	200
10	600
15	1000
20	1400

Figure 10.1 shows the supply curve when the supply is made by an individual business unit. The slope of the curve moves upward to the right. It shows the direct relationship between supply and price, i.e., increase in supply along with the rise in prices.

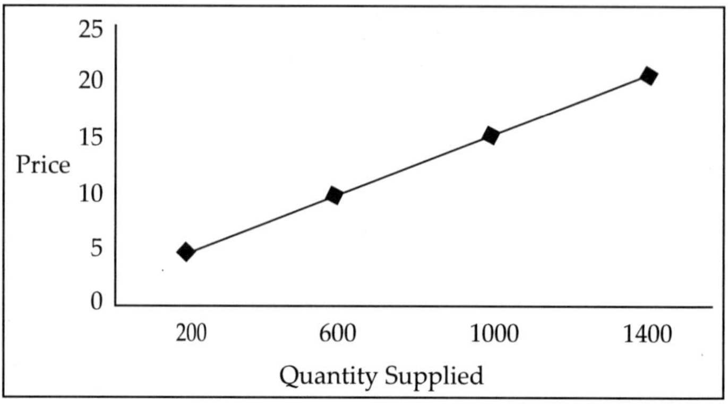

Figure 10.1. Individual supply curve

10.4.2. Market Supply

The market supply represents the quantities of a product supplied by all business units or suppliers in the market at different prices during a specific period, while other factors are constant. Table 10.2 shows the market supply schedule. For example, market supply is calculated by combining the quantities supplied by business units X and Y. When the product is priced at Rs. 5 the market supply of the product is 10,000 kg per month. When the price rises to Rs. 10 the market supply increases to 20,000 kg. Further, when the price increases to Rs. 15 and later to Rs. 20, the quantity supplied also increased to 27,000 kg and 32,000 kg, respectively. Thus, a rise in the price of the product increases the market supply.

Table 10.2. Market supply schedule

Price (Rs. per kg.)	**Quantity supplied (kg. per month)**		**Market supply (kg. per month)**
	Business unit X	**Business unit Y**	
5	3000	7000	10,000
10	8000	12,000	20,000
15	12,000	15,000	27,000
20	15,000	17,000	32,000

Figure 10.2 depicts the market supply curve. The slope of the curve moves upwards to the right. It shows the direct relationship between supply and price, i.e., increase in supply along with the rise in prices.

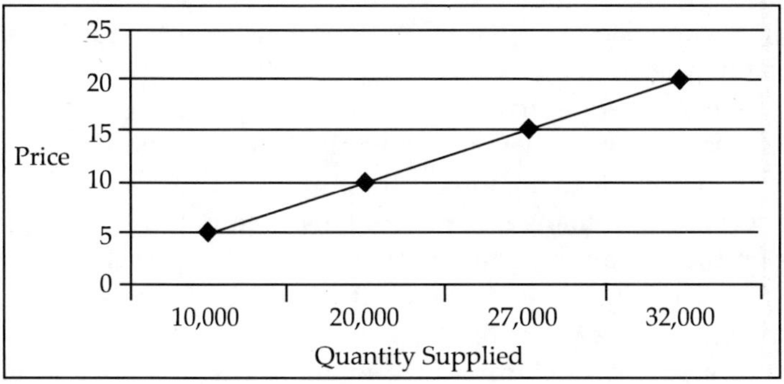

Figure 10.2. Market supply curve

10.4.3. Assumptions of the Law of Supply

The law of supply has the following assumptions.

- The income of buyers and sellers remains unchanged.
- The product is measurable and available in small units.
- The tastes and preferences of buyers remain unchanged.
- The cost of all factors of production does not change over a period of time.
- The time period under consideration is short.
- The technology used remains constant.
- The producer is rational.
- Natural factors remain stable.
- Expectations of producers and the government policy do not change over a period of time.

10.4.4. Exceptions to the Law of Supply

According to the law of supply, if the price of a product increases, the supply of the product also rises and vice versa. However, there are certain conditions where the law of supply is not applicable. In such cases, the supply of a product falls with an increase in the price of the product at a particular point of time. Some important exceptions to the law of supply are discussed below.

1. **Agricultural products:** The law of supply does not apply to agricultural products. The production of these products depends on many factors which are uncontrollable such as climate, availability of fertile land, qualitative seeds, fertilisers and chemicals, water, and human resources. Further, the production is seasonal in case of many products. Therefore, the supply of agricultural products cannot be increased beyond a limit in a short period. Thus, a rise in the price for certain agricultural products will not increase the supply beyond a limit.

2. **Auction goods:** Auctions goods are offered for sale through bidding. The auction can take place due to various reasons, for instance, a bank may auction the assets of a customer in case he fails in payment of debts over some time. Thus, the supply of these goods cannot increase or decrease beyond a limit. In the case of these goods, a rise or fall in price does not impact the supply.
3. **Expectation of change in prices:** Law of supply is not applicable when there is an expectation of change in the prices of a product in the near future. For instance, if the price of wheat rises and is expected to increase further in the next few months, sellers may not increase supply and store huge quantities with a hope of getting more profits at the time of a price rise.
4. **Supply of labour:** The law of supply fails in the case of labour. After a certain point, the rise in wages does not increase the supply of labour. At higher wages, labour prefers to work for lesser hours. This happens due to a change in preference of labour for leisure hours.

10.5. MOVEMENTS IN THE SUPPLY CURVE

The change in quantity supplied occurs due to rise or fall in product prices while other factors are constant. Change in supply refers to an increase or decrease in the supply of a product due to various determinants of supply other than price. Change in quantity supplied can be measured by the movement of the supply curve, while the change in supply is measured by shifts in the supply curve. The terms, change in quantity supplied refers to expansion or contraction of demand, while the change in supply means to increase or decrease in demand.

10.5.1. Expansion and Contraction of Supply

When there are large quantities of a product supplied at higher prices, it is known as expansion or extension of supply. The contraction of supply occurs when smaller quantities of goods are supplied even at reduced prices.

In Figure 10.3, quantity supplied at price OP_1 is OQ_1. When the price rises from OP_1 to OP_2, the quantity supplied also increased from OQ_1 to OQ_2, which is represented by the upward movement from A_1 to A_2. This upward movement is known as the expansion of supply. On the contrary, a fall in price from OP_1 to OP_3 resulted in a decrease in supply from OQ_1 to OQ_3. The movement from A_1 to A_3 in the supply curve moving downwards is known as the contraction of supply. Thus, the movement from A_1 to A_2 is the representation of the expansion and the movement from A_1 to A_3 is the representation of contraction of the quantity supplied.

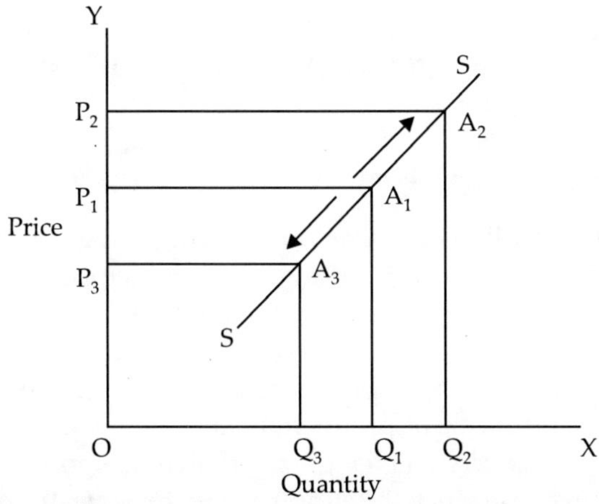

Figure 10.3. Expansion and contraction of supply

10.5.2. Increase and Decrease in Supply

An increase in supply takes place at a given price when a supplier is willing to offer large quantities of products in the market due to various reasons such as improvement in production technology, fall in prices of factors of production, and reduction in taxes. On the other hand, a decrease in supply occurs at the same price when a supplier is willing to offer small quantities of products in the market due to increase in taxes, low agricultural production, high costs of labour, unfavourable weather conditions, etc.

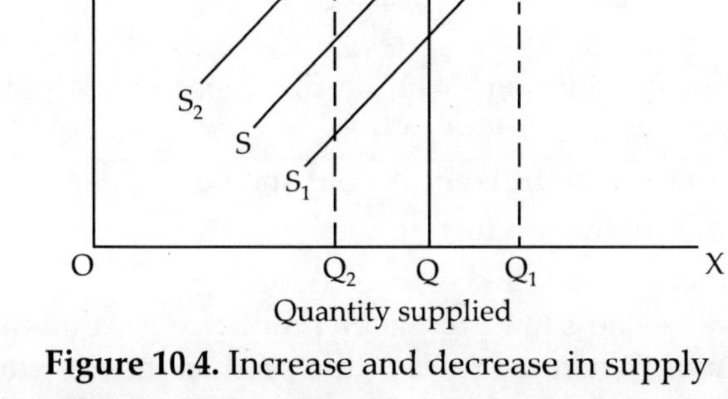

Figure 10.4. Increase and decrease in supply

Figure 10.4 illustrates the changes in supply curve due to an increase or decrease in supply. The SS curve indicates the supply at a given price in the market. When supply increases from OQ to OQ_1, the supply curve shifts from left to right which is indicated by a shift from SS to S_1S_1. In case of a decrease in supply from OQ to OQ_2, the supply curve shifts from right to left indicating a shift from SS to S_2S_2.

10.6. ELASTICITY OF SUPPLY

The elasticity of supply is referred to as the responsiveness of the quantity supplied with respect to a change in the price of a product. It is a measurement of change in quantity supplied with a certain change in the price of a product. It is also called *price elasticity* of supply. The elasticity of supply is influenced by a number of factors such as the nature of a product, production technology, scale of production, and time period.

When the quantity supplied changes more than proportionately to the change in the price of a product, the supply is said to be elastic. If the change in price leads to less than proportionate change in quantity supplied of a product, the supply is said to be relatively inelastic. For example, if one per cent change in the price of potato leads to 5 per cent change in its quantity supplied, the supply of potato is elastic. On the other hand, if one per cent change in the price of potato leads to less than one per cent change in quantity supplied is relatively inelastic. Thus, the elasticity of supply is a measure of the degree of change in the quantity supplied of a product in response to a change in its price.

Mathematically, the elasticity of supply is expressed as:

$$\text{Elasticity of supply} = \frac{\text{Percentage change in quantity supplied of a product}}{\text{Percentage change in the price of a product}}$$

The formula for elasticity of supply is expressed as:

$$E_S = \frac{\Delta S}{\Delta P} \times \frac{P}{S}$$

ΔS = change in quantity supplied or difference in the old and new quantity

ΔP = change in price or difference in old and new price

P = initial price of the product

S = initial quantity supplied of the product

For example, a business unit supplies a product of 500 units at the price of Rs. 4000 per unit. When the price of the product increases to Rs. 5000 per unit, the supply of the product increases to 650 units. The elasticity of supply of the product is:

$P = \text{Rs. } 4000$

$\Delta P = \text{Rs. } 1000 \text{ (Rs. } 5000 - \text{Rs. } 4000)$

$S = 500 \text{ units}$

$\Delta S = 150\ (650 - 500)$

$$E_S = \frac{150}{1,000} \times \frac{4000}{500} = 1.2$$

Thus, the elasticity of supply is greater than one.

10.7. FACTORS INFLUENCING ELASTICITY OF SUPPLY

The various factors influencing the elasticity of supply are described below.

1. **Nature of the product:** The most important determinant of the elasticity of supply is the nature of the product. Based on nature, the products can be classified as perishables and durables. Perishable products cannot be inventoried and therefore, their supply does not respond similarly to the change in price. Hence, the supply of perishable products is inelastic in nature. Durable products can be stored for a long period and their supply responds to the change in prices. Thus, the supply of durable products is elastic.
2. **Time perspective:** The supply of a product mostly depends upon its production. Production involves a time lag which may vary from a few days to years. Moreover, the increase in production of a product may require capacity expansion of a business unit. Thus, the supply of a product may be less elastic in the short run, as time progresses supply may become more elastic.
3. **Production technology:** If the production technology is simple, less expensive, and upgradation takes less time, it is possible to increase production in the short run. The supply of products, in that case, is generally elastic in nature. If the production technology is complex, expensive and time consuming, it may not be possible to change the supply in response to varying price-demand conditions in the short run. Supply of such products would generally be less elastic or inelastic.
4. **Estimation of future prices:** Future expectations of price changes may also influence the supply of a product. If the producers expect rise in prices of a product in future they reduce the supply of the product to the market and may resort to keeping in stock with an expectation of gaining profit in future.

10.8. TYPES OF ELASTICITY OF SUPPLY

The degree of change in the quantity supplied of a product with respect to a change in price varies under different situations. Based on the rate of change in price, the elasticity of supply is classified into five categories:

1. Perfectly elastic supply
2. Perfectly inelastic supply
3. Relatively elastic supply
4. Relatively inelastic supply
5. Unitary elastic supply

1. **Perfectly elastic supply:** The supply of a product will not change at a given price in the perfectly elastic market. Therefore, the supply curve is horizontal at a given price. In perfectly elastic supply, a small rise in price results in an increase in supply to the infinity whereas, the supply becomes zero with even a slight fall in the price. It is also referred to as *infinite elasticity of supply*. It is denoted as $E_S = \infty$.

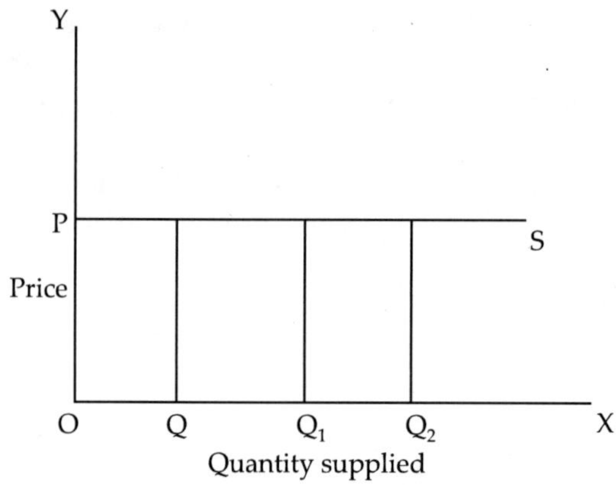

Figure 10.5. Perfectly elastic supply

Figure 10.5 shows that the supply curve S is a horizontal straight line or parallel to X-axis. It shows that the supply may increase from OQ to OQ_1 or OQ_2 and so on at a given market price. A minor increase in price may raise the supply to the infinity while a minor decrease in price may make the supply zero.

2. **Perfectly inelastic supply:** When a change (rise or fall) in the price of a product does not bring any change (fall or rise) in the quantity supplied, it is called perfectly inelastic supply. In this case, the supply remains constant irrespective of change in price. It is also referred to as *zero elasticity of supply*. It is denoted as $E_S = 0$.

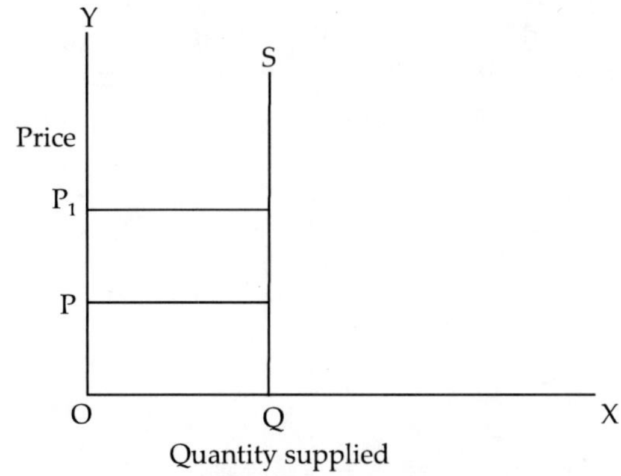

Figure 10.6. Perfectly inelastic supply

Figure 10.6 shows that the supply curve S is parallel or vertical to Y-axis. When price increases from OP to OP_1, the quantity supplied remains the same. In other words, the response of supply to a change in price is nil.

3. **Relatively elastic supply:** When a percentage change in the quantity supplied is more than the percentage change in the price of a product, it is called relatively elastic supply. In this case, the elasticity of supply is more than one. It is denoted as $E_S > 1$.

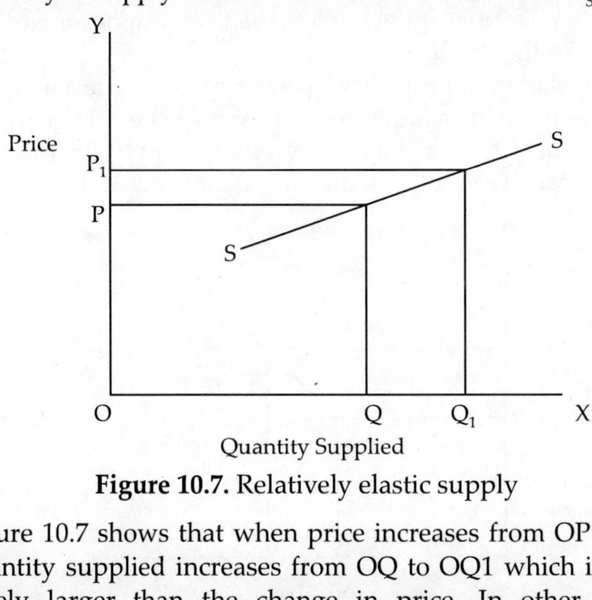

Figure 10.7. Relatively elastic supply

Figure 10.7 shows that when price increases from OP to OP1, the quantity supplied increases from OQ to OQ1 which is proportionately larger than the change in price. In other words, the proportionate change in quantity supplied is more than the proportionate change in the price of the product.

4. **Relatively inelastic supply:** When a percentage change in the quantity supplied is less than the percentage change in the price of the product, it is called relatively inelastic supply. In this case, the elasticity of supply is less than one. It is denoted as $E_S < 1$.

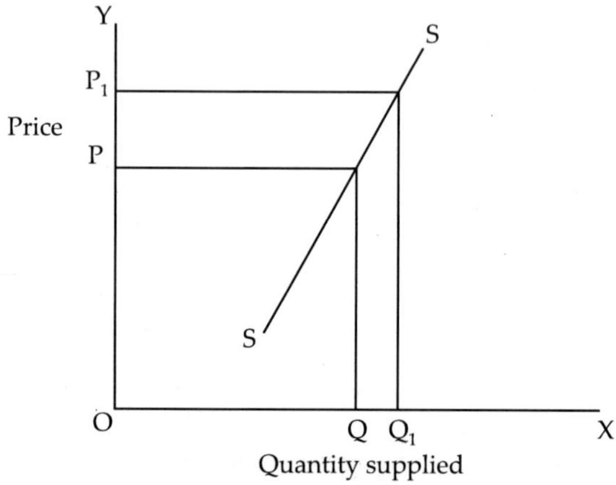

Figure 10.8. Relatively inelastic supply

Figure 10.8 shows that when price increases from OP to OP_1, the quantity supplied increases from OQ to OQ_1 which is proportionately less than the change in price. In other words, the proportionate change in quantity supplied is less than the proportionate change in the price of the product.

5. **Unitary elastic supply:** When the proportionate change in the quantity supplied is equal to the proportionate change in the price of a product, it is called unitary elastic supply. In this case, the supply elasticity is equal to one. It is denoted as $E_S = 1$.

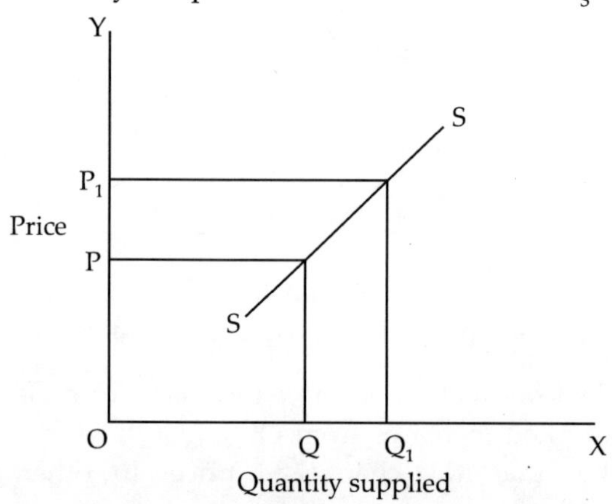

Figure 10.9. Unitary elastic supply

Figure 10.9 shows that when price increases from OP to OP_1, the quantity supplied increases from OQ to OQ_1 that means the change in price, as well as supply, is proportionate to each other. In other words, the proportionate change in quantity supplied is equal to the change in the price of the product.

10.9. SUMMARY

- Supply is referred to as the willingness of a seller to sell the specified quantity of a product at an agreed price and time.
- Supply function is the functional representation of the relationship between supply and its various determinants. It can be represented as $S_X = f(P_X, C, T, G, E)$.
- The various determinants influencing the supply of a product in the market are the availability of inputs, production capacity, government regulations, accessibility to other factors of production, business strategy, demand, transportation and storage, prices of related products, technology, exogenous factors, firm's expectations about price changes, and market structure.
- The law of supply refers to the relationship between the price and the supply of a product, while other factors remain constant.
- A supply schedule is the tabular representation of quantities of a product supplied by a supplier at different prices and periods, keeping all other factors constant.
- The supply curve is the graphical representation of the quantities of a product supplied by a supplier at different prices and periods.
- Supply by an individual represents the quantities of a product supplied by an individual business unit at different prices during a specific period, assuming other factors remain unchanged.
- The market supply represents the quantities of a product supplied by all business units or suppliers in the market at different prices during a specific period, while other factors are constant.
- The important exceptions to the law of supply are agricultural products, auction goods, the expectation of change in prices, and the supply of labour.
- Expansion of supply occurs when large quantities of a product supplied at higher prices and contraction of supply occurs when smaller quantities of goods are supplied even at reduced prices.
- An increase in supply takes place at a given price when a supplier is willing to offer large quantities of products in the market.
- A decrease in supply occurs at the same price when a supplier is willing to offer small quantities of products in the market.

- The elasticity of supply is a measure of the degree of change in the quantity supplied of a product with a certain change in the price of a product.
- The various factors influencing the elasticity of supply are the nature of the product, time period, production technology, and estimation of future prices.
- The elasticity of supply is classified into five categories such as perfectly elastic supply, perfectly inelastic supply, relatively elastic supply, relatively inelastic supply, and unitary elastic supply.

SHORT ANSWER QUESTIONS

1. Define supply.
2. What are the determinants of supply?
3. What do you understand by the law of supply?
4. What are the exceptions to the law of supply?
5. What is the supply schedule and supply curve?
6. Write a short note on market supply.

ESSAY ANSWER QUESTIONS

1. What is supply function? Explain the various determinants of supply.
2. What is the law of supply? Explain its assumptions and exceptions.
3. Discuss the movements along the supply curve with suitable examples.
4. Briefly explain the concept of supply by individual and market supply.
5. What is the elasticity of supply? Explain the factors influencing the elasticity of supply.
6. Elucidate different types of elasticity of supply with a diagrammatic illustration.

FILL IN THE BLANKS

1. The willingness of a seller to sell the specified quantity of a product within a particular price and period is called __________.
2. The graphical representation of supply schedule is called __________.
3. When a proportionate change in the price of a product increases/decreases of quantity supplied, it is called ________.
4. The functional representation of the relationship between supply and its various determinants is known as __________.
5. The quantities of a product supplied by all business units in the market at different prices during a specific period, while other factors are constant is __________.
6. Supply is said to be ____________ when $E_S < 1$.
7. The price at which quantities are supplied remains the same at all locations. (True/False)

8. Change in quantity supplied can be measured by the movement along the supply curve. (True/False)
9. A shift in the supply or demand curve also shifts the equilibrium point. (True/False)
10. If the shift in the supply curve is greater than the demand curve, equilibrium price falls and output rise. (True/False)

Answers:

1. Supply
2. Individual supply schedule
3. Perfectly elastic supply
4. Supply function
5. Market supply
6. Relatively inelastic supply
7. False
8. True
9. True
10. True

MULTIPLE-CHOICE QUESTIONS

1. Which one of the following is not an assumption of supply?
   (A) The period under consideration is short
   (B) The technology used keeps changing
   (C) The producer is rational
   (D) Natural factors remain stable
2. The change that occurs when smaller quantities of goods are supplied even at reduced prices is:
   (A) Contraction of supply (B) Increase in supply
   (C) Expansion of supply (D) Decrease in demand
3. A supply curve passing through the origin will have elasticity
   (A) Less than 1 (B) More than 1
   (C) Only One (D) Zero
4. Supply curve passing through any point on Y-axis (price) will have the elasticity of:
   (A) Less than 1 (B) More than 1
   (C) Just one (D) Zero
5. A perfectly elastic supply curve will be:
   (A) Parallel to Y-axis (B) Parallel to the X-axis
   (C) U shaped (D) Downward sloping
6. Which one of the following is not a factor in the market supply of a product?
   (A) Cost of production (B) Number of buyers
   (C) Market price of the product (D) Price of related products
7. The minimum price that a supplier expects to make available for a specific quantity of sale is called:
   (A) Demand price (B) Administered price
   (C) Cost price (D) Supply price
8. Which one of the following is not a factor of quantity supplied?
   (A) Price of the goods (B) Price of the related goods
   (C) Cost of production (D) Consumers disposal income

9. According to the law of supply:
   (A) the higher the price higher the production of the product
   (B) the higher the price the lower the cost of production
   (C) the lower the price the lower the demand for the product
   (D) the higher the price higher the quantity the seller is prepared to supply in the market
10. Which one of the following is not an exception to the law of supply?
   (A) Agricultural products (B) Auction goods
   (C) Supply of labour (D) Consumer preferences

Answers:

1. B	2. A	3. A	4. B	5. A
6. C	7. D	8. B	9. A	10. D

REFERENCES

1. Dean, J. (1951). *Managerial Economics* (1st Edn.). New York: Prentice-Hall.
2. Graham, P. & Bodenhorn, D. (1980). *Managerial Economics* (1st Edn.). Reading, Mass: Addison-Wesley Pub. Co.
3. McConnell, C.R., Brue, S.L. & Flynn, S.M. (2009). *Economics: Principles, Problems and Policies.* New York, NY: McGraw-Hill Irwin.
4. Meyers, A.L. (1940). *Elements of Modern Economics.* New York: Prentice-Hall Press.
5. Murad, A. (1958). *Economics: Principles and Problems.* Littlefield, Adams.
6. Peterson, H.C., Lewis, W.C. & Jain, S.K. (2005). *Managerial Economics* (4th Edition). New Delhi: Pearson Education.
7. Pindyck, R.S. & Rubinfeld, D.L. (2009). *Microeconomics* (7th Edn). New Jersey: Pearson Prentice Hall.
8. Salvatore, D. (2006). *Managerial Economics in a Global Economy.* USA: Oxford University Press.

Chapter

11 Cost Analysis

LEARNING OBJECTIVES

After studying this chapter, you should be able to understand:

- meaning of cost and various determinants of cost;
- cost concepts involved in the managerial decision making process;
- role of cost-output relationship in determining the optimum level of production; and
- short-run and long-run cost-output relationship.

11.1. INTRODUCTION

In managerial decision making alternative courses of action are evaluated based on cost-benefit analysis. The historical costs are recorded in books of accounts. These costs are useful as standards of reference but not directly useful for managerial decisions. It is a fact that every business unit looks forward to taking up gainful activities in future. That means whatever activity that is taken up should yield more revenue than the cost. It requires a system that optimises the use of resources (factors of production) to ensure the cost of production to be the lowest and promote the products in the market to gain maximum revenue. They can make higher profits by achieving a larger gap between the cost of production per unit and the revenue per unit. Managerial decisions are made for the future which is not certain. Therefore, in the place of historical costs, they need cost estimates which reflect the consequential changes in future. In other words, the managerial economist needs future costs of various input factors rather than the costs recorded in the accounting books.

It is not simple to estimate the costs of various alternative programmes for decision making. It involves guessing future happenings under different plans. It requires an understanding of different cost concepts and cost behaviour patterns in different situations. Then only a managerial economist can develop economic analysis for each alternative production programme.

The value of an item in the factors of production depends upon the purpose for which it is used and therefore, differs with the economic situation of each alternative course of action. For example, a piece of equipment may have different values in terms of disposal price, replacement cost, the value in the current job, and value in alternative jobs. It is appropriate to pick up the right/relevant value of each variable to be more accurate in economic analysis. It is necessary, therefore, to have absolute clarity of alternative programmes involved in the choice and also an understanding of differences among alternatives. It is necessary to establish cost-output relations in the short run as well as in the long run. Further, it is also necessary to examine the variations in costs if the business unit goes for multiple product operations.

This chapter presents briefly the cost determinants which are considered the root of the problems of cost analysis. Further, it deals with different cost concepts and cost-output relations in the short run as well as in the long run.

11.2. COST DETERMINANTS

The cost of a product is the result of a combination of many cost factors. The changes in the combination of the cost factors will result in a change in cost behaviour. For estimation of costs for different alternative production programmes, it is necessary to establish a functional relationship of cost to each of the major factors of production. The understanding of such relationships will help the managerial economist to develop a variety of combinations of cost factors and work out cost estimates. To understand the behaviour of the cost it is necessary to identify the determinants of cost. There are a few determinants that are considered important to manufacturing business units. The following are the key determinants of cost in a manufacturing unit.

1. **Price of input factors:** The prices of input factors are not fixed forever. They go on changing as per the changes in the business environment. The material prices, for example, changes according to the demand and supply positions which vary from time to time. Similarly, the wage rates of the labour change due to inflation or government regulation or demand-supply variations. The changes in input factors not only change the cost of production but also may influence the combination of labour, material and capital in a production schedule. The managerial economist, therefore, needs to anticipate the possible changes in the prices of input factors may be by using statistical tools for projection or by closely following the business trends of various input factors.
2. **Lot size:** Lot size refers to the size of a single production job. Production costs vary with lot size. It is important to know the optimum lot size that results in the lowest cost per unit. Variations in lot size result in variations in cost per unit of output.

3. **Technology:** The technology and cost relationships are becoming vital in business decisions in recent years. Worldwide changes in technology are happening at an unimaginable pace. The technological advancements in material science, computerisation, machinery and equipment, and digitisation brought many changes in production systems and cost of production. Artificial intelligence, for example, is creating wonders by supporting systems to optimise the use of resources and in enhancing the scale of efficiency. Therefore, the choice of technology, the level of technology, and its operational efficiency influence the cost of production significantly.
4. **Size of plant:** It refers to the physical size of the plant. The cost of production varies with the size of the plant. Large size plants can produce large quantities and thereby, gain economies of scale. In the case of business units with a small size, the plant cannot gain the economies of scale. Therefore, cost per unit of production is lower in large size business units and higher in small size business units.
5. **Rate of output:** Rate of output refers to the utilisation of fixed plant. The fixed expenses are common irrespective of the use of the fixed plant. If the plant is used to its full capacity, the per unit cost of this factor will be the lowest. If the plant is utilised partially due to the incurrence of fixed cost per unit would be higher. Therefore, the cost per unit varies with the rate of output.
6. **Output stability:** When the output is stable for a considerable period, the processes can be standardised and as such the business units can achieve a high level of process efficiency and the benefits of the division of labour. Frequent variations in production may lead to changes in the work process in quick successions and thereby impact the work efficiency. Therefore, output stability leads to cost efficiency while output instability may lead to an escalation of cost of production.
7. **Efficiency:** Efficiency in this context refers to managerial efficiency in making choices and also in executing processes effectively. There will be many choices at every level of using different factors of production, and also in finding the right combinations. For example, the output of a product can be increased by increasing the number of machine-hours per day, the speed of machines, the number of days of operation. It can also be done by adding similar new machines and also by installing high capacity machines. Selecting the right option, taking into consideration financial, legal, workers' behaviour, reactions from unions, and other impacting factors is not easy and requires a high level of efficiency in judgement.

11.3. COST CONCEPTS

Cost concepts are important for managerial decision making. The selection of cost concept for economic analysis of an alternative course of action depends upon the situation in which the business decisions are made. Sometimes, actual full costs may be relevant while sometimes, only marginal costs are relevant. As the word 'cost' has multiple meanings in varied situations, the managerial economist needs to identify the relevant cost concept suitable to the situation. He may need to identify different combinations of cost ingredients for different kinds of managerial problems. The following are some of the important cost concepts useful to the managerial economist.

1. Outlay costs and opportunity costs
2. Fixed costs and variable costs
3. Short-run costs and long-run costs
4. Incremental costs and sunk costs
5. Traceable costs and non-traceable costs
6. Out-of-pocket costs and book costs
7. Controllable costs and non-controllable costs
8. Historical costs and replacement costs
9. Accounting costs and economic costs
10. Escapable costs and unavoidable costs
11. Past cost and future costs

1. Outlay costs and opportunity costs

Outlay costs are those that involve financial expenditure. These expenses are recorded in the books of accounts. The outlay cost includes wages, payments made for the purchase of raw materials, machinery, operating expenses, etc. These costs are called actual costs or real costs.

Opportunity costs are in the form of foregone profits from the alternative use of limited resources for a particular purpose. These costs represent the sacrificed alternatives. Therefore, opportunity costs are never recorded in the books of accounts. For example, a machine may be used for producing alternatively product A or product B or product C. The managerial economist while deciding the use of the machine for a product, he has to necessarily work out the profitability of producing each of the products. If the machine is to produce product A, it means that the opportunity to produce product B or product C is forgone. To choose product A for the machine, the managerial economist needs to sacrifice the production of product B and product C. Therefore, the opportunity cost of choosing product A is the possible profit to be earned from either product B or product C. The choice, therefore, depends not upon the profit generated from product A, but on the comparative analysis of profits foregone from product B or product C. Product A becomes the choice only when it generates higher profits by using the limited resources compared to other alternatives.

The concept of opportunity cost has a much wider meaning and usefulness in various situations. Some benefits are calculable and some are not measurable. For example, a person got two job options after completing graduation. Job-1 allows him to do the job in his locality and the pay package is Rs. 20 lakh per annum. Job-2 requires him to work at a distant place and the pay package is Rs. 30 lakh per annum. If we take only the revenue benefit it is very easy to conclude which option is the best. But if we look at the opportunity costs, there are so many issues which are not financially calculable but play a significant role in decision making. In the case of job-1, the intangible benefits associated with the form of known location, social relations, continuing with family, zero lifestyle risks, friends and social identities, etc. On the other hand, in job-2 many intangible costs may be associated such as unknown location, break-in social relations, staying away from family members and friends, new food habits, new accommodation and neighbourhood, etc. In the assessment, if the person finds the value of the intangible benefits associated with job-1 is more than the difference in pay from job-2, he may prefer job-1. Thus, the managerial economist needs to analyse the opportunity costs in a broader perspective using both measurable costs and non-measurable costs.

2. Fixed costs and variable costs

Fixed costs are those, which are fixed in volume for a given production capacity irrespective of the volume of production. For example, the fixed costs of a 1000 unit capacity plant are Rs. 1,50,000 per month. The cost remains the same whether the business unit produces 100 units or 500 units or 1000 units. That is the reason these costs are called fixed costs. If the business unit utilises the capacity fully then the fixed cost per unit will be the lowest. If the production is below the full capacity, the fixed cost per unit increases accordingly. The examples of fixed costs are salaries to permanent employees, rent, depreciation, insurance, interest, cost of utilities such as electricity, water, phones, etc.

The variable costs, on the other hand, vary with the volume of production. The variable cost per unit remains unchanged irrespective of the volume of production. For example, if the variable cost per unit is Rs. 5 and the business unit decides to produce 500 units, the total variable cost would be Rs. 2500. In case, the production volume is increased to 1000 units, the total variable cost becomes Rs. 5000. The examples of variable costs are raw materials, spare parts, lubricants, piece-rate labour, etc. The distinction between fixed costs and variable costs is important in planning production and in analysing cost variations with changes in the volume of operations.

3. Short-run costs and long-run costs

The difference between short-run costs and long-run costs is related to the period. In the short run, a business unit cannot expand its production capacity by changing its size and scale of production. In the long run, the business unit can make desirable changes in the size and scale of production. In the short run, there will be fixed costs and variable costs, whereas, in the long run, all costs are variable. Fixed costs have no impact on short-run costs, only variable costs and revenues affect short-run production. Variable costs change with the output. The short-run costs increase or decrease based on variable cost. In the short run, the volume of production cannot be increased beyond a point due to capacity limitations. In the long run, the business unit can expand or reduce the capacity depending upon the forecasts. Long-run costs are, therefore, the costs incurred when a business unit changes its production level over time in response to expected changes in the market demand. It is possible to design a combination of outputs of desired quantity at the lowest possible cost, in the long run, taking the advantage of economies of scale.

4. Incremental costs and sunk costs

Incremental costs are the additional costs incurred due to change in the level of operations of a business unit. The changes may be adding a new product, the distribution channel, new machines, workspace, etc. Sunk costs, on the other hand, are the costs that are not affected with change in the level of operations in a business unit. The sunk costs remain the same irrespective of the change in volume of operations.

The concept of incremental costs and sunk costs does not apply for a new business unit. These concepts apply for an already existing business unit intending to change its operations. The distinction between these two concepts is important to recognise when the managerial economist evaluates the alternatives. The incremental costs vary with different alternatives, whereas, the sunk costs remain the same for all the alternatives. The final decision, therefore, is influenced by the variations in incremental costs of alternatives.

5. Traceable costs and non-traceable costs

Traceable costs are the direct costs which can easily be identified with the product. The material, labour, and the expenses that are used for producing a specific product or process are traceable costs.

Non-traceable costs are indirect costs which are not traceable with a specific product or process. These costs are shared with other products and processes. It is not possible to exactly identify some cost items with any of the products or processes as the inputs are common for multiple products. For example, for operating air services, the cost of the runway, airport equipment, staff, etc., cannot be assigned to one passenger. These are common costs for all services and not identifiable with any one of the services.

6. Out-of-pocket costs and book costs

Out-of-pocket costs are the costs that involve current cash payments. Book costs are the costs recorded in books of accounts. Some book costs do not require current cash payments, for example, depreciation. Out-of-pocket costs can be fixed costs or variable costs. The salary paid to the administrative staff is fixed cost, whereas, the amount paid for the purchase of raw material is a variable cost. But both the costs are out-of-pocket costs. Some out-of-pocket costs are traceable and some are non-traceable. The payment for electric power bill is not directly traceable, whereas, payment to piece-rate workers is traceable. The distinction between out-of-pocket costs and book costs is made primarily to know the business unit's cash position.

7. Controllable costs and non-controllable costs

The classification of costs as controllable and non-controllable depends upon the managerial position and the discretion of the manager in planning and controlling activities. Non-controllable costs at one management level may be controllable costs at a higher level of management. All costs are controllable at one management level or the other as they are assignable to some executives and make them responsible for control. The degree of controllability of costs depends upon the delegation of authority and the managerial efficiency.

8. Historical costs and replacement costs

Historical cost is the cost of an asset recorded at the time of acquiring the asset in the books of accounts. It is the original price paid for the asset. The historical cost of assets is used for accounting purposes. Valuation based on historical cost gives a poor projection of the future cost particularly when there is a substantial change in the price level over some time. Therefore, the historical cost will not provide realistic estimation for management when they are planning for replacement of the asset.

Replacement cost is the price currently paid to replace the existing asset. The concept of replacement cost is relevant when financial statements have to be adjusted for inflation. Replacement costs reflect the current value of the assets and therefore, the management can properly assess the value of the business unit close to the reality.

9. Accounting costs and economic costs

Accounting costs are recorded in the books of accounts to prepare the balance sheet and profit and loss statements which are intended for the legal, financial and tax purposes of the business unit. The accounting concept is a historical concept. It records what has happened. The past cost data revealed by the books of accounts does not help very much in decision making as it requires the realistic estimation of future costs.

The economic concept considers accounting costs as a basis to estimate future costs and revenues. The managerial decision making takes the support of the economic analysis of accounting costs and the projection of such costs in future. When the accountant describes what has happened, the economist aims at projecting what will happen. Accounting data ignores implicit or imputed cost. The economist considers decision making costs. For this, different cost concepts relevant to different kinds of problems are considered. The cost distinctions such as opportunity and outlay costs, short-run and long-run costs, and replacement and historical costs are made from the economic viewpoint.

10. Escapable costs and unavoidable costs

The management tries to identify escapable costs in times of economic problems and when the management wants to cut the expenses to the bottom. During the period of recession, all software companies have taken up austerity measures and cut the costs of many facilitating and supporting activities. These costs fall under discretionary costs and it is very difficult to estimate the impact of cutting down of such costs. The manager has to prioritise the costs and find out the costs that will have less impact on performance. Downsizing employment, withdrawal of transport facility to some cadres of employees, reduction in organisational comforts, reduction in socialisation expenses are some of the examples of escapable costs. The management generally considers escapable costs as a temporary measure until the situation gets improved.

Unavoidable costs are the costs that are to be incurred compulsorily to complete a project. These costs are beyond the discretion of managers.

11. Past and future costs

Past costs are actual costs incurred in the past. These costs are recorded in the books of account. Future costs are those costs which are to be incurred in the near future. Future costs are the estimated costs.

11.4. PRODUCTION COSTS

There are seven types of production costs calculated for the purpose of managerial decision making.

1. Total cost (TC)
2. Total fixed cost (TFC)
3. Total variable cost (TVC)
4. Average fixed cost (AFC)
5. Average variable cost (AVC)
6. Average total cost (ATC)
7. Marginal cost (MC)

1. **Total cost (TC):** Total cost is the aggregate of expenditures incurred by the firm in producing a given level of output. Total cost includes a total fixed cost (TFC) and total variable cost (TVC) for a given volume of output. Symbolically, it can be expressed as TC = TFC + TVC.
2. **Total fixed cost (TFC):** Total fixed cost is the sum of fixed cost items incurred during a specific period. TFC remains the same at all levels of output in the short run.
3. **Total variable cost (TVC):** The total variable cost is the sum of the cost incurred on variable inputs in the production. The variable cost is fixed per unit and varies with the volume of output.
4. **Average fixed cost (AFC):** Average fixed cost is the total fixed cost divided by total units of output. Therefore,

$$AFC = \frac{TFC}{Q}$$

   where, Q stands for the number of units of the product. TFC stands for a total fixed cost. Thus, average fixed costs are the fixed cost per unit of output.
5. **Average variable cost (AVC):** Average variable cost is the total variable cost divided by total units of output. Thus,

$$AVC = \frac{TVC}{Q}$$

   where Q stands for the number of units of the product, TVC stands for total variable cost, TFC stands for a total fixed cost. Thus, the average variable cost is the variable cost per unit of output.
6. **Average total cost (ATC):** Average total cost or average cost is the total cost divided by total units of output. Thus,

$$ATC = \frac{TC}{Q} = \frac{TFC + TVC}{Q}$$

Since,

$$\frac{TFC}{Q} = AFC \quad \frac{TVC}{Q} = AVC$$

Therefore,

$$ATC = AFC + AVC$$

Hence, the average total cost can be computed simply by adding average fixed cost and average variable cost at each level of output.

7. **Marginal cost (MC):** Marginal cost is the cost incurred for producing an extra unit of output. It can also be calculated by dividing the change in total cost by the one unit change in output. Symbolically, it can be expressed as:

$$MC = \frac{\Delta TC}{\Delta Q}$$

where, ΔTC denotes a change in total cost and ΔQ denotes the change in quantity.

11.5. COST-OUTPUT RELATIONS

Cost-output relations play an important role in business decisions relating to cost minimisation, profit prediction, pricing, promotion, profit maximisation and optimisation of output. Cost-output relations are specified through a cost function. The cost function is derived basically from the production function. The relationship between output and costs is expressed in terms of the cost function. It is a function of input prices and the quantity of output produced.

The time factor is very important in cost theory. In the long run, it is assumed that all input factors such as buildings, machinery, supervisory personnel, materials, and labour can be completely adapted to achieve minimum total cost using the total capacity of the plant. In the short run, on the other hand, it is assumed that some input factors such as plant, machinery, supervisory personnel, etc., are fixed in nature. They are not adaptable to the changes in the rate of output within a short period. Thus, in the short run, only some input factors are variable in response to changes in the rate of output. To sum up we can say that in the short run partial adaptation of input factors is possible whereas, in the long run, total adaptation is possible.

11.5.1. Short-run Cost-Output Relationship

The cost-output relationship in the short run depends upon the proposition between cost and a set of independent variables. The independent variables include the volume of production, prices of input services, size of a production lot, and different product varieties. The independent variables vary with the type of manufacturing operation. However, the rate of output is the most commonly used variable. The cost-output function is determined based on current operations assuming that all other independent variables are constant. Once the cost-output function is determined, it is used for estimating the future cost of production at various levels by adjusting the cost function to the changes in factors such as wage rates, material prices, and lot size.

One of the important factors to be considered in the analysis of short-run cost behaviour is the characteristics of fixed equipment. The important consideration is the extent of segmentation possible in the fixed equipment. It is necessary to identify the potentiality of variations in the rate of flow of output without changing the proportions of variable inputs in fixed equipment. Therefore, whether the technical nature of the fixed equipment facilitates a wide range of variations or not has to be decided. If the fixed equipment facilitates then a wide range of choice in machine hours used per week will be available to the producer. The degree of segmentation will not be similar to all plants. It varies from none to complete and continuous segmentation. In steel plants, a blast furnace is operated continuously and in such case no segmentation is possible. In the packaging industry, some machines can be used completely segmenting the input resources. Discontinuous segmentation occurs when the production processes depend upon labour contracts, technical nature of the equipment, dependency on suppliers for spare parts, managerial problems, and other external problems.

There are three sources of segmentation of fixed equipment. They are physical divisibility, time segmentation, and speed segmentation. When a business unit has a large number of homogeneous units, *physical divisibility* of work is possible. Unit-wise segmentation of work is possible when machines are physically divisible. *Time segmentation* refers to the allocation of several hours for each machine in each shift and the number of machine-hours allocated for each product. *Speed segmentation* is possible when the nature of the fixed equipment allows using at varying speeds. The machines may be operated sometimes at high speed and sometimes and low speed. Speed segmentation permits continuous variability in-plant use.

The short-run cost-output relationship can be better understood with Figure 11.1. The basic analytical cost concepts used in the analysis of cost behaviour are total, average and marginal costs. The concepts ATC, AFC and AVC give only a static relationship between cost and output in the sense that they are related to a given output.

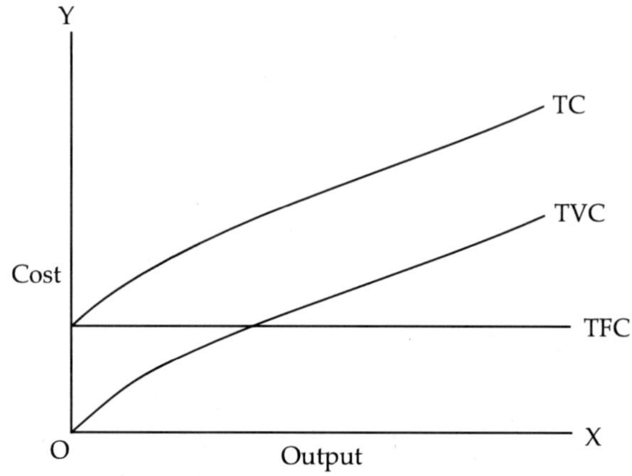

Figure 11.1. Short-run cost-output relationship

In Figure 11.1, OX represents the quantity of output and OY represents the cost of production. The TFC curve is a horizontal straight line indicating that the fixed cost remains unchanged at different output levels. The TVC curve moves upwards as the variable cost increases with the increase in the volume of output. As TFC remains constant, an increase in TC means an increase in TVC only. Therefore, the gap between TVC and TC will always be the same. Thus, the TC curve shows the same pattern of behaviour to that of the TVC curve.

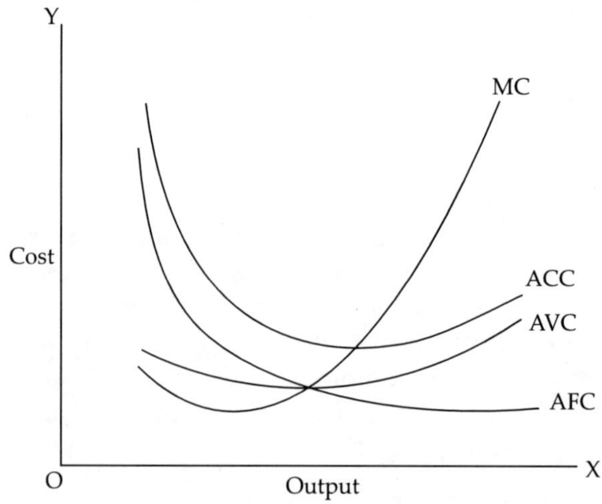

Figure 11.2. Short-run cost curves

Figure 11.2 shows the relation between the various costs and output more clearly. The AFC curve continues to fall as output rises from lower levels to higher levels. This is because the total fixed cost is spread over more and more units as output increases. TVC increases with the increase in production since more raw materials, labour, power, etc., would be required for increasing output. But, the AVC curve (i.e.,variable cost per unit) falls in the beginning and rises afterwards. This is due to the operation of the law of variable proportions.

The behaviour of the AC curve depends upon the behaviour of the AVC and AFC curves. In the initial stage of production, both AFC and AVC are declining. Hence, AC also declines. AFC continues to fall with an increase in output while AVC declines initially due to some scale economies and then rises after a point due to dis-economies of scale. So, as long as AFC and AVC decline AC will also decline. But after a certain point, AVC starts rising. If the rise in AVC is less than the decline in AFC, the AC continues to decline. When the rise in AVC is more than the drop in AFC, AC begins to rise. The lower end of the AC curve thus, turns up and gives it a U-shape. That is why AC curves are U-shaped. The least-cost combination of inputs is indicated by the lowest point in the AC curve, i.e., where the total average cost is the minimum. It is the short-run stage of optimum output. It may not be the maximum output level. It is the point where per unit cost of production will be the lowest.

A downward trend in the MC curve shows increasing marginal productivity (i.e., decreasing marginal cost) of the variable input. Similarly, an upward trend in the MC curve shows the rate of increase in TVC, on one hand, and the decreasing marginal productivity (i.e., increasing marginal cost) of the variable input on the other. MC curve intersects both AVC and AC curves at their lowest points.

The relationship between AVC, ATC and AFC can be summed up as follows:

1. If both AFC and AVC fall, AC will also fall because: AC = AFC + AVC
2. When AFC falls and AVC rises:
    (a) AC will fall when the fall in AFC is more than the rise in AVC
    (b) AC remains constant if the fall in AFC is equal to the rise in AVC
    (c) AC will rise when the fall in AFC is less than the rise in AVC.

11.5.2 Long-run Cost-Output Relationship

In the long run, a business unit can increase or decrease its output according to its demand by having more or less of all the required factors of production. The business units can expand the scale of their operation in the long run by expanding the production capacity and by purchasing larger quantities of all the inputs. Thus, in the long run all factors become variable. The long-run cost-output relations, therefore, imply the relationship between total cost and total output.

In the long run, a business unit has several alternatives regarding the scale of operations. The expansion of the scale of operations generally takes place in a phased manner as per the requirement in the market from time to time. For each scale of production or plant size, the business unit has a separate short-run average cost curve. Hence, the long-run average cost curve is composed of a series of short-run average cost curves. A short-run average cost (SAC) curve applies to only one plant whereas the long-run average cost (LAC) curve takes into consideration many plants. At any given time, the business unit has only one size of the plant which remains fixed during that period. Any increase in production in that period is possible only with that plant capacity. That plant has a corresponding average cost (SAC) curve. But in a long period, the business unit can move from one plant size to another. Each plant has its corresponding SAC curve.

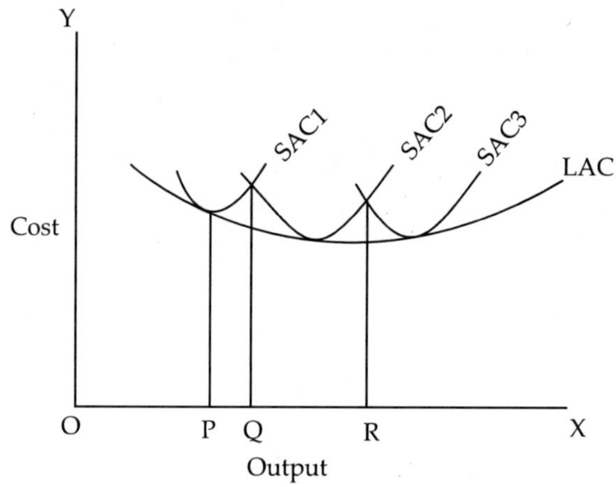

Figure 11.3. Long-run cost-output relationship

The long-run cost-output relationship is shown in Figure 11.3 by the LAC curve. To draw an LAC curve, it is necessary to start with a number of SAC curves. In Figure 11.3 it is assumed that there are only three sizes of plants, i.e., small, medium and large, SAC1 refers to the average cost curve for the small plant, SAC2 for the medium size plant and SAC3 for the large size plant. If the business unit plans to produce OP units or less, it will choose the small plant. For an output beyond OQ, the business unit will opt for medium size plant. Even if an increased production is possible with small plant production beyond OQ but it will increase the cost of production per unit. For an output (OR) the firm will choose the large plant. Thus, in the long run, the firm has a series of SAC curves. The LAC curve drawn will be tangential to the three SAC curves, i.e., the LAC curve touches each SAC curve at the lowest point. The LAC curve is also known as *envelope curve* as it envelopes all the SAC curves. No point on any of the LAC curve can ever be below the LAC curve. It is also known as planning curve as it serves as a guide to the entrepreneur.

The plant which yields the lowest average cost of production will be selected. LAC can, therefore, be defined as the lowest possible average cost of producing any output, when the management has adequate time to make all desired changes and adjustments. In the longrun, the demand curve of the firm depends on the law of returns to scale.

The law of returns to scale states that, if a firm increases the quantity of all inputs simultaneously and proportionately, the total output initially increases more than proportionately, but afterwards increases less than proportionately. It implies that when production increases, the per unit cost of production decreases initially and later shows an increasing trend. This means the LAC curve falls initially until a point and then rises subsequently. Like SAC curve, the LAC curve also is U-shaped, but it will be always flatter than SAC curves. The U-shape implies lower and lower average cost in the beginning until the optimum scale of the firm is reached and successively higher average cost after that. The increasing return is experienced on account of the economies of scale or advantages of large-scale production. Increase in scale makes possible increased division and specialisation of labour and more efficient use of machines. After a certain point, the increase in production makes management more difficult and less efficient resulting in less than proportionate increase in output.

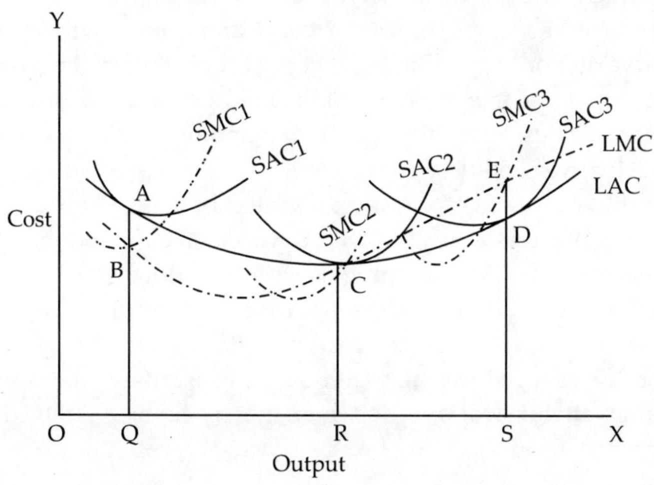

Figure 11.4. Long-run marginal cost curve

The long-run marginal cost curve represents the cost of an additional unit of output when all the inputs vary. The long-run marginal cost curve (LMC) is derived from the short-run marginal cost (SMC) curves. LMC curve intersects LAC curve at its lowest point C. There is only one plant size whose minimum SAC coincides with the minimum LAC and LMC.

$$SAC2 = SMC2 = LAC = LMC$$

The point C also indicates the optimum scale of production of the business unit in the long run or optimum output. The optimum output level is the level of production at which the cost of production per unit, i.e., AC is the lowest. The optimum level is not the maximum profit level. The optimum point is where AC = MC. Hence, C is the optimum point.

11.6. LEARNING CURVE

Economists have identified learning as one of the factors that contributes to the fall in average cost over a period of time. The learning curve was first described by psychologist Hermann Ebbinghaus in 1885 and is used to measure production efficiency and to forecast costs. The philosophy behind this is that any employee irrespective of the position takes time initially to learn how to carry a specific work. When the task is repeated, the employee learns the methods and techniques to complete it quickly and easily. Therefore, the amount of time needed to repeat the work will be less than what it is used to be in the beginning. When the employee gains more and more experience, he/she gains competence to complete the work at the minimum possible time. Thus, learning increases worker efficiency and enhances productivity. The learning curve is also known as experience curve, cost curve, efficiency curve and productivity curve. The learning curve demonstrates that the cost per unit of output decreases over time with the increase in experience of the employees. The learning curve is used by the business units in production planning, cost estimations, and preparing delivery schedules.

The learning curve is graphically presented in Figure 11.5. The X-axis shows cumulative total output over a successive period and Y-axis shows the cost per unit. The learning curve slopes downwards indicating the cost per unit of output declines with increased output over time as the business unit learns from its experience. The fall in the cost is steep initially and the cost reduces at a later stage, as learning from the initial lot of production for workers and manager is high. As they become more efficient at production with experience, the cost does not reduce considerably at the later stage.

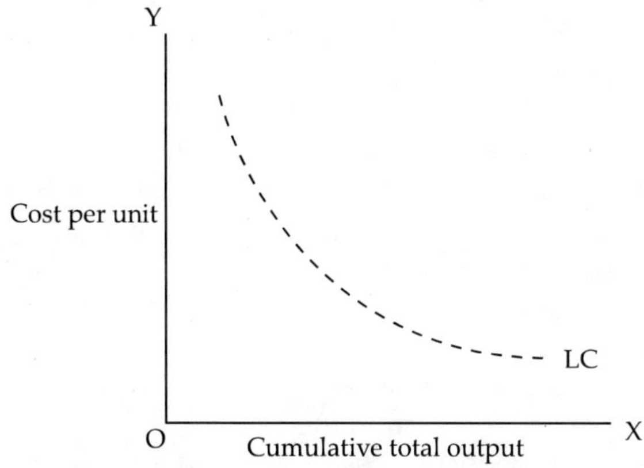

Figure 11.5. Learning curve

The concept of "learning curve" is different from that of "economies of scale" as economies of scale refer to the decline in the cost per unit of output due to increase in the scale of operations, while in the learning curve cost per unit of output reduces due to increase in productivity of employees as a result of learning.

11.7. SUMMARY

- The key determinants of cost in a manufacturing unit are the price of input factors, lot size, technology, size of the plant, rate of output, output stability, and efficiency.
- Outlay costs are those costs that involve financial expenditure. These expenses are recorded in the books of accounts.
- Opportunity costs are in the form of foregone profits from the alternative use of limited resources for a particular purpose.
- Fixed costs are those costs, which are fixed in volume for a given production capacity irrespective of the volume of production. The variable cost per unit remains unchanged irrespective of the volume of production.
- In the short run, a business unit cannot expand its production capacity by changing its size and scale of production. In the long run, it can make desirable changes in the size and scale of production.
- Incremental costs are the additional costs incurred due to change in the level of operations of a business unit. Sunk costs are the costs that are not affected by a change in the level of operations in a business unit.
- Traceable costs are the direct costs which can easily be identified with the product. Non-traceable costs are indirect costs which are not traceable with a specific product or process.

- Out-of-pocket costs are the costs that involve current cash payments. Book costs are the costs recorded in books of accounts.
- Historical cost is the cost of an asset recorded at the time of acquiring the asset in the books of accounts. Replacement cost is the price currently paid to replace the existing asset.
- Accounting costs are recorded to prepare the balance sheet and profit and loss statements which are intended for the legal, financial and tax purposes of the business unit.
- The economic concept considers accounting costs as a basis to estimate future costs and revenues.
- Past costs are actual costs incurred in the past. Future costs are those costs which are to be incurred in the near future.
- The seven types of production costs calculated for managerial decision making are: total cost, total fixed cost, total variable cost, average fixed cost, the average variable cost, average total cost, and marginal cost.
- The relationship between output and costs is expressed in terms of the cost function.
- The cost-output relationship in the short run depends upon the proposition between cost and a set of independent variables. The independent variables include the volume of production, prices of input services, size of a production lot, and different product varieties.
- In the long run, a business unit can increase or decrease its output according to its demand by having more or less all the required factors of production.
- The learning curve demonstrates that the cost per unit of output decreases over time with the increase in experience of the employees.

SHORT ANSWER QUESTIONS

1. What is cost?
2. What does the opportunity cost mean?
3. Write a short note on the following:
   (a) Fixed costs and variable costs
   (b) Controllable costs and non-controllable costs
   (c) Out-of-pocket and book costs
   (d) Incremental and sunk costs
   (e) Historical and replacement costs
4. Briefly explain the cost function.
5. Write a short note on the productivity curve.

ESSAY ANSWER QUESTIONS

1. Define cost. Discuss in detail the various determinants of cost.

2. Explain how the cost concepts are important for managerial decision making.
3. "Cost-output relations play an important role in business decisions." Explain.
4. Explain the short-run cost-output relationship with suitable illustration.
5. Elucidate the long-run cost-output relationship with diagrams.
6. Discuss the various production costs involved in managerial decision making.
7. What is the learning curve? Explain its importance in increasing workers efficiency.

FILL IN THE BLANKS

1. Opportunity costs represent the sacrificed _________.
2. Traceable costs are the _________ costs.
3. The historical cost of assets is used for _________ purposes.
4. The price currently paid to replace the existing asset is _________.
5. The total cost divided by total units of output is referred to as _________.
6. The cost incurred for producing an extra unit of output is called _________.
7. Cost-output relations are specified through _________.
8. The LAC curve is also known as _________ curve.
9. Opportunity costs are recorded in the books of accounts. (T/F)
10. The variable costs vary with the volume of production. (T/F)
11. Out-of-pocket costs involve future cash payments. (T/F)
12. The long-run marginal cost curve is derived from the short-run marginal cost curves. (T/F)

Answers:

1. Alternatives
2. Direct
3. Accounting
4. Replacement cost
5. Average total cost
6. Marginal cost
7. Cost function
8. Envelope
9. False
10. True
11. False
12. True

MULTIPLE-CHOICE QUESTIONS

1. Outlay costs are also known as:
   (A) Actual costs (B) Opportunity costs
   (C) Alternative costs (D) Variable costs
2. The additional costs incurred due to change in the level of operations of a business unit are referred to as:
   (A) Economic costs (B) Incremental costs
   (C) Fixed costs (D) Operational costs

3. The costs that are not affected by the change in the level of business operations are:
   (A) Sunk costs (B) Accounting costs
   (C) Short-run costs (D) Long-run costs
4. The sum of the cost incurred on variable inputs in the production is:
   (A) Total variable cost (B) Average variable cost
   (C) Total cost (D) Marginal cost
5. The relationship between output and costs is expressed in terms of:
   (A) Demand function (B) Supply function
   (C) Production function (D) Cost function
6. Which one of the following is not a source of segmentation?
   (A) Physical divisibility (B) Time segmentation
   (C) Product segmentation (D) Speed segmentation
7. The allocation of several hours for each machine in each shift and number of machine-hours allocated for each product is called:
   (A) Time segmentation (B) Continuous segmentation
   (C) Machine segmentation (D) Discontinuous segmentation
8. The gap between TVC and TC will always be:
   (A) Increasing (B) Same
   (C) Decreasing (D) Greater
9. The concept of the learning curve was first described by:
   (A) Hermann Ebbinghaus (B) Alfred Marshall
   (C) Frederick Benham (D) Edwards West
10. The AC will rise when the fall in AFC is less than the rise in:
   (A) ATC (B) AVC
   (C) TVC (D) TFC

Answers:

1. A	2. B	3. A	4. A	5. D
6. C	7. A	8. B	9. A	10. B

REFERENCES

1. Ahuja, H.L. (2008). *Managerial Economics.* New Delhi: S. Chand Publications.
2. Besanko, D.A. & Braeutigam, R.R. (2011). *Micro Economics* (4th Edition). New Jersey: John Wiley & Sons, Inc., Hoboken.
3. Dean, Joel. (1951). *Managerial Economics*. New York: Prentice-Hall, Inc.
4. Dwivedi, D.N. (2015). *Managerial Economics* (8th Edition). New Delhi, India: Vikas Publishing House Pvt. Ltd.
5. Hooda, R.P. (2000). *Statistics for Business and Economics.* McMillan India Ltd.
6. Hirschey, M. (2009). *Managerial Economics* (12th Edition). USA: South-Western Cengage Learning.

7. McConnell, C.R., Brue, S.L. & Flynn, S.M. (2009). *Economics: Principles, Problems and Policies.* New York, NY: McGraw-Hill Irwin.
8. Rees, H. (2017). *Managerial Economics*. USA: Library Press.
9. Salvatore, D. (2006). *Managerial Economics in a Global Economy.* USA: Oxford University Press.
10. Webster, T.J. (2003). *Managerial Economics: Theory and Practice.* California, USA: Academic Press (Elsevier).
11. Varshney, R.L. & Maheswari, K.L. (2014). *Managerial Economics.* New Delhi, India: Sultan Chand & Sons.

Chapter

12 Scale of Economies

LEARNING OBJECTIVES

After studying this chapter, you should be able to understand:

- concept of economies of scale;
- internal economies of scale;
- external economies of scale; and
- diseconomies of scale.

12.1. ECONOMIES OF SCALE

The economies of scale refer to the reduction in costs with an increase in the scale of operation. When a business unit expands its scale of operations there will be many economies associated with the expansion. These economies can be classified into internal economies and external economies. Internal economies are those economies that generate due to changes in the scale of internal operations. External economies are the economies that generate because of the changes in the external environment. Figure 12.1 shows the details of economies of scale.

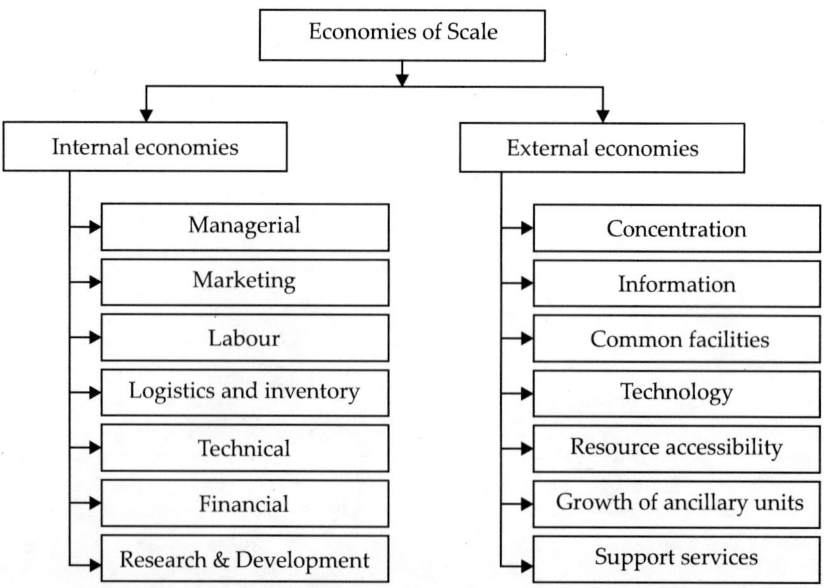

Figure 12.1. Classification of economies of scale

12.2. INTERNAL ECONOMIES

A business unit can achieve internal economies with the expansion of the scale of operations in many areas. The important areas where the possibility of internal economies with the increase in the scale of operations are managerial, marketing, labour, logistics and inventory, technical, financial, and research & development.

1. Managerial economies

With the expansion of operations a business unit can afford to use specialists to perform and manage the various departments. The effective management techniques such as decentralisation, division of labour, departmentalisation, specialisation, effective communication systems, and control systems, can be applied to achieve a high rate of efficiency in organisational performance. Delegation of authority and responsibility, training and development of human resources, advanced strategies for business operations, e-applications, and adoption of modern managerial techniques such as artificial intelligence, machine learning, data analytics, networking, and digitalisation of processes, can be used to generate higher performance outputs. The enhanced managerial efficiency results in huge economies to the business organisations. Size of the business unit certainly matters in achieving a high level of managerial economies.

2. Marketing economies

The size of the business unit and the marketing expenditure per unit are correlated. The smaller the size of the business unit the higher the marketing expenses per unit and vice versa. The business unit with large-scale operations will get an identity in the market. The distributors are attracted to the business unit and accept the distribution at a lower margin compared to a small business unit. Marketing expenses such as sales personnel expenses, advertising expenses, expenditure on sales promotion, direct marketing, and publicity campaign, are shared and the per unit marketing expenditure will be less with a larger quantity. The business unit can take up strategies to push the product through distributors or pull the market by influencing directly the customers. The cost of market development will be economical if the size is substantial.

3. Labour economies

The larger the business unit, the larger its opportunities to employ highly qualified and skilled employees. They can ensure the right man to the right job. It not only eliminates wastage but also enhances the work efficiency of the employees. The labour cost per unit will be reduced with a high rate of productivity and reduced wastage. The large business units can introduce teamwork and train the employees in contemporary skills. The specialised and skilled employees not only perform the work better but also introduce creative changes in work processes. The strength in human resources helps the organisation to grow further and develop a competitive advantage in the market. Thus, the higher the scale of operations, the business units likely to get economies of scale through employees.

4. Logistics and inventory economies

The members in the supply chain will respond positively and try to build relationships with business units considering the size and scale of operations. The larger the size, the more positive the relations with the members of the supply chain. The business unit will gain many benefits such as the supply of raw materials in suitable specifications at desired quality and quantity, and at the appropriate time. The price of the inputs will be less when the size of the order is large. By placing large orders to the suppliers, the business units will get the advantage of low price without compromising quality. The economies in the transportation of large size quantities of materials are common in business. The business unit can have their own logistics resources or they can hire the services to their advantage when transportation in bulk is undertaken.

The business unit can employ the practices of inventory management and inventory control with the increase in the scale of operations. The objective of inventory management is to reduce the cost of inventory and ensure effective supply of materials to the place of their use. Therefore, the logistics and inventory economies are associated with the scale of operations.

5. Technical economies

Business units with large scale operations can employ state-of-the-art technology to reap higher benefits. They can employ sophisticated machinery, introduce full or partial automation, e-practices, advanced software, and continuously upgrade the production and management systems. The advancements of technology reduce the per-unit cost of production significantly and make the organisation highly competitive in the market. It is a proven fact that the business unit that employs technology can offer the products at a competitive price due to economies through technology.

6. Financial economies

Business units require finance. The large-scale business units can get financial support from creditors at lower interest rates compared to small business units. Liberal lending from the public as well as private financial institutions is available for large-scale operators. The creditworthiness of business units is correlated with the scale of operations. Therefore, large-scale operations yield financial economies.

7. Research & development economies

Business units undertake research for introducing improvements in the processes and to innovate new formulations. Breakthroughs in business are possible with research and development. The business units with large-scale operations can have their research and development department to support the processes and also to develop new products. Small size business units, on the other hand, are less likely to have their research and development department due to financial constraints. Therefore, the business units with large-scale operations are capable of reaping benefits from research and development, and through that reduce the cost of production per unit.

12.3. EXTERNAL ECONOMIES

External economies are the economies, the business units get from the outside business environment. When a large number of business units are established in a locality there will be many common facilities developed in the location and such facilities will benefit the organisations. There are many other economies a business unit can achieve from the external environment with the increase in the scale of operations. These are economies of concentration, information, common facilities, technology, resource accessibility, growth of ancillary units, and support services.

1. Economies of concentration

The expansion of an industry consisting of many business units producing similar units may result in the exploration of new and cheaper sources of raw material, machinery and other types of capital equipment. The concentration of business units helps the business units to fight for policy changes in their favour and additional facilities.

2. Economies of information

In the present-day competitive environment, information plays a key role in the success of the business. Business units having an effective flow of qualitative, sufficient, right and timely information will have a competitive advantage. Large organisations may have an information centre inside. Such a centre may not be sufficient to track developments and trends in the business environment. The industry can set up an information centre which may communicate information through publication of e-journals or other sources for the benefit of business units established in the locality. The services of highly qualitative business analysts can be availed at a very low cost with such centres.

3. Economies of common facilities

Many common facilities will develop when a large number of business units are established in a particular locality. Common facilities will cost less compared to the development of facilities independently. The facilities such as transportation, storage and warehousing, power supply, water resources, hospitality services, health care, security, and the like can be developed as common facilities for the use of all the business units.

4. Economies of technology

When business units are expanding their scale of operations the organisations supplying technology will focus upon introducing improvement in technology and the development of new technology suitable for the higher scale of business operations with a focus on achieving higher economies. They will find a growing demand for technology and tries to provide technology at a competitive price due to the fear of new entrants on the technology front.

5. Economies of resource accessibility

If the business units are located close to the supply centres of raw materials and spare parts they will have many economies. There will be a lot of migrations of labour to industrial locations from rural areas in search of employment. Therefore, the business units can easily find the human resource of varied skill levels and at a reasonable cost. It is easier for the business organisations to expand or reduce the workforce as per the demand of the situations by way of promoting hiring practices in the locations.

6. Economies of growth of ancillary industries

With the growth of an industry, several ancillary industries may specialise in the production of raw materials, tools and machinery, etc. They can provide them at a lower price to the main industry. Likewise, some business units may get developed processing the waste products of the industry and making some useful product out of it. This will tend to reduce the cost of production in general.

7. Economies of support services

Many support services will develop in an industrial locality as they find demand from business units. Highly skilled and specialised services will be available at relatively less cost per unit to the business units. Service outsourcing became one of the most economical practices in the present-day business. GIG workforce is on the rise many countries in the world offering specialised services without any long-term commitments. Hire and discard human resource services are highly economical to manufacturing as well as service organisations.

12.4. DISECONOMIES OF SCALE

Economies of increasing size do not continue indefinitely. After a certain point, any further expansion of the size leads to diseconomies of scale. For example, the expansion of human resource beyond a point reduces the performance of the workers. This is the problem with many public sector organisations in India. The state-run passenger transport organisations are incurring huge losses while private passenger transport organisations are making huge profits due to variations in employee engagement. The following are the diseconomies associated with expansion beyond the desirable point.

1. Labour problems
2. Poor teamwork
3. Lack of coordination
4. Difficulty in fund raising
5. Scarcity of resources
6. Increased risk

1. **Labour problems:** Continuous labour problems due to unionism, demand for more facilities and welfare measures, indiscipline, disputes, and so on may interrupt the workflow in the organisation. The labour problems sometimes may lead to the temporary closure of the production units.
2. **Poor teamwork:** Large organisations often face problems with teamwork. The hierarchical system, the power associated with positions, and inter-personnel conflicts may result in poor performance of different teams.
3. **Lack of coordination:** Lack of coordination among various departments, functions, and the workforce may result in poor performance of the organisation. Large organisations face the problem of poor coordination of the workforce due to the volume and complexity of operations.
4. **Difficulty in fund raising:** Expansion of scale of operations require financial strength and the business units may find it difficult to mobilise adequate finances for expansion. They may need to borrow funds at a higher rate of interest to execute their expansion plans.
5. **Scarcity of resources:** When the resources are limited in supply, expansion beyond a point demands more resources and a business can have such resources only at a higher price.
6. **Increased risk:** The production output beyond a specific quantity creates many marketing problems. It is very difficult to sell all the products at the desired price. The expansion beyond a point

enhances the risk of failure in the marketing front. To sell the products the company may need to introduce offers or reduce the price. In such a case, the revenue per unit will be lower and the company may get reduced profits or may incur a loss.

12.5. SUMMARY

- Economies of scale are referred to as the reduction in costs with an increase in the scale of operation.
- Internal economies are those economies that generate due to changes in the scale of internal operations.
- External economies are the economies that generate because of the changes in the external environment.
- The important areas where the possibility of internal economies with the increase in the scale of operations are managerial, marketing, labour, logistics and inventory, technical, financial, and research & development.
- The economies business units can achieve from the external environment are economies of concentration, information, common facilities, technology, resource accessibility, growth of ancillary units, and support services.
- Diseconomies of scale occur when any further expansion of the size beyond a certain limit is anticipated by the business unit.
- The diseconomies associated with expansion beyond the desirable point are labour problems, poor teamwork, lack of coordination, difficulty in fundraising, scarcity of resources, and increased risk.

SHORT ANSWER QUESTIONS

1. What are internal economies?
2. Write a short note on external economies.
3. Brief explain diseconomies of scale.

ESSAY ANSWER QUESTIONS

1. What are economies of scale? Explain different types of internal and external economies of scale.
2. Discuss the various internal economies with suitable examples.
3. Explain the concept of diseconomies of scale.

FILL IN THE BLANKS

1. The economies that generate because of the changes in the external environment are called __________.

2. The cost of market development will be _________, if the size is substantial.
3. The labour cost per unit will be reduced with a high rate of productivity and reduced _________.
4. Small size business units are less likely to have their research and development department due to _________ constraints.

Answers

1. External economies
2. Economical
3. Wastage
4. Financial

MULTIPLE-CHOICE QUESTIONS

1. A business unit is located in a remote place and in around, it has no other company for a distance of 25 km. What economy will the company lose?
   (A) Economies of support services
   (B) Economies of information
   (C) Economies of concentration
   (D) Economies of resource accessibility
2. Business units doing similar kind of business and located at one particular place will have the facility of setting up research and development facilities. This economy of operation is known as:
   (A) Economies of technology
   (B) Economies of common facilities
   (C) Economies of finance
   (D) Economies of research & development
3. Functional specialisation ensures minimum wastage and decreases the cost of production in the long run. Such economies are known as:
   (A) Managerial economies
   (B) Labour economics
   (C) Technical economies
   (D) Marketing economies
4. Where large amounts are borrowed from the financial institutions, the banks consider giving reduced interest rates. Such economies are known as:
   (A) Economies of support services
   (B) Commercial economies
   (C) Financial economies
   (D) External economies

Answers

1. C 2. D 3. A 4. C

REFERENCES

1. Baye, M. (2000). *Managerial Economics & Business Strategy* (1st Edn.). Boston: Irwin/McGraw-Hill.

2. Besanko, D.A. & Braeutigam, R.R. (2011). *Micro Economics* (4th Edition). New Jersey: John Wiley & Sons, Inc., Hoboken.
3. Dean, J. (1951). *Managerial Economics* (1st Edn.). New York: Prentice-Hall.
4. Dwivedi, D.N. (1999). *Managerial Economics*. New Delhi: Vikas Publishing House Pvt. Ltd.
5. Geetika., Ghosh, P. & Choudhury, P. (2008). *Managerial Economics* (1st Edn.). New Delhi: Tata McGraw-Hill.
6. Graham, P. & Bodenhorn, D. (1980). *Managerial Economics* (1st Edn.). Reading, Mass.: Addison-Wesley Pub. Co.
7. Gupta, G.S. (2017). *Managerial Economics*. New Delhi, India: Tata McGraw-Hill.
8. Mehta, P.L. (2007). *Managerial Economics: Text and Cases*. New Delhi, India: Sultan Chand & Co.

Chapter

13 Cost Control and Cost Reduction

LEARNING OBJECTIVES

After studying this chapter, you should be able to understand:

- concept of cost control and budgetary control;
- different cost control techniques;
- areas of applying cost control techniques; and
- cost reduction and its techniques.

13.1. COST CONTROL

Cost control is a process of identifying and reducing possible business costs in all stages of business operations. It is an essential element for the successful functioning of a business unit. The long-run success of a business unit depends on its ability to earn profits. Profit, on the other hand, depends on the selling price and the cost of production. The selling price is not within the control of a business unit, whereas, many costs are under its control. Therefore, the business units should aim at utilising the resources at the minimum cost. Cost control is a means for a better and economical way of carrying out business activities. In other words, cost control is the reduction in the percentage of costs and an increase in the percentage of profits.

Cost control deals with the reduction in specific expenses and effective utilisation of every rupee spent. Cost control helps a business unit to improve its profitability and competitiveness. Profits may be significantly reduced despite an increase in sales volume in the absence of cost control. Large sales volume may not necessarily mean a high profit. It may create a false sense of profitability, while in reality, the increasing costs are eating up profits. Cost control may also assist a business unit in reducing its costs and subsequently reduce the prices of its products. A reduction in prices of a business unit increases its competitiveness. Cost control involves the determination of standards, ascertaining actual results comparing the standards, analysis of the variances, and deciding the course of corrective and preventive action.

The features of cost control are:

1. It helps the business unit to improve its profitability and competitiveness.
2. In the absence of cost control, profits may be drastically reduced despite a large and increasing sales volume.

3. It is indispensable for achieving greater productivity.
4. Cost control may also help a business unit in reducing its costs and thus reduce its prices.
5. If the price of the product is stable and reasonable, it can maintain higher sales and thus employment of the workforce.

13.2. BUDGETARY CONTROL

A budget is an estimated financial statement of income and expenses for a specified period. It refers to the formulation of the plan for the given period in numerical terms. Therefore, budgetary control is a system that uses budgets as a means for planning and controlling all business activities. Budgetary control is the process of preparing budgets for the future period and compare with the actual performance with standards specified. The comparison of budgeted figures with actual figures helps the management to identify the differences and take corrective actions at the proper time.

Definitions of Budgetary Control

Author	Definition
George R. Terry (1960)	Budgetary control is a process of comparing the actual results with the corresponding budget data to approve accomplishments or to remedy differences by either adjusting the budget estimates or correcting the cause of the difference.
J.L. Brown and L.R. Howard (1969)	Budgetary control is a system of controlling costs which includes the preparation of budgets, coordinating the departments and establishing responsibilities, comparing actual performance with the budgeted and acting upon results to achieve maximum profitability.

13.2.1. Objectives of Budgetary Control

The main objectives of budgetary control are:

1. Identifying the financial objectives of a business unit.
2. Planning to achieve the identified objectives.
3. Coordinating and organising various department activities.
4. Efficient and economical operation of departments and cost centres.
5. Assigning the role and responsibility of employees in the departments.
6. Increasing profitability through a reduction of wastage.
7. Centralising the control system and correcting variances from the set standards.

13.2.2. Advantages of Budgetary Control

Budgetary control is an important tool of a business unit to control costs and to maximise profits. The advantages of budgetary control are:

1. **Profit maximisation:** Budgetary control aims at maximising the profits of the business unit. The business units plan effectively and coordinate the various departmental activities to achieve the set objectives. Proper control is initiated over the capital and revenue expenditures. The resources are also utilised optimally to the best possible to generate higher revenue.
2. **Coordination:** The functioning of each department and sector is coordinated effectively. The budgets of one department influence the budgets of another department. Therefore, the coordination of executives and their subordinates is necessary for achieving budgeted targets.
3. **Specific goals:** The plans, policies and goals are determined by the top management of a business unit. Each department is assigned a certain target to be achieved during a particular period. The efforts of each department combined will help to achieve the common goal of the business unit.
4. **Performance measurement tool:** Budgetary control acts as a tool by setting targets to each department for measuring managerial performance. The budgeted targets are compared with the actual results and deviations are identified. The performance of each department is reported to the management. This method enables the introduction of management by exception.
5. **Economy:** The planning of various expenses to be incurred will be done systematically so that the business units can maintain the economy in their spending. The funds and resources will be used optimally. The benefits derived by the business unit will ultimately extend to industry and then to the national economy. The national resources also will be used economically and wastage will be eliminated.
6. **Identifying Weaknesses:** The deviations in budgeted and actual performance enable the top management in determining the weak areas of the business unit. Thus, necessary actions can be taken on those aspects where there is a deviation in the performance.
7. **Corrective measures:** The management will be able to take necessary corrective measures whenever there are any discrepancies in the performance of the business unit. The deviations will be regularly reported to the top management for necessary action at the earliest.

In the absence of a budgetary control system, the deviations in the performance may be determined only at the end of the financial period.

8. **Responsiveness:** Budgetary control creates awareness among the employees. By setting targets, the employees are made responsible for achieving the goals of the business unit. The employees are made aware of the work they are expected to do and they continue with the work uninterruptedly.
9. **Cost reduction:** In the present competitive business environment, budgetary control plays a significant role in reducing the costs of the business unit. Every businessman tries to reduce the cost of production to increase sales and generate maximum revenue. The business units try to go with the combinations of products/services where the profitability is more.
10. **Incentive schemes:** Budgetary control enables the business units to introduce proper incentive schemes of remuneration to the personnel. The comparison of budgeted and actual performance enables the management to offer such schemes.

13.2.3. Limitations of Budgetary Control

Despite many benefits of budgetary control, some limitations are:

1. **Uncertain future:** Uncertainty is the basic character of the future. Business units may follow the systematic procedure in forecasting the future, many a time they find substantial deviations. Budgets represent estimations for the future period. The conditions assumed to happen in future may change. Such changes upset the budgets because they are prepared based on certain assumptions. The uncertainties about the future limit the utility of the budgetary control system.
2. **Budgetary revision:** When assumptions on future happenings do not become reality, the budgets prepared need to be revised. If the revision of targets is frequent it will reduce the value of budgets.
3. **Discourage competent personnel:** Under the budgetary control system, the targets are assigned to every individual in the business unit. The general tendency of personnel will be to achieve that assigned targets only. There may be some competent personnel who can exceed the targets but feel contented after reaching the targets. As a result, budgets may serve as constraints on managerial initiatives.
4. **Difficulties in coordination:** The effectiveness of a budgetary control system depends upon coordination among the departments. The performance of one department will influence the results of

other departments. To overcome the difficulty of coordination, the management should introduce a 'budgetary officer' to coordinate with all the departments. However, all the business units cannot afford to appoint a budgetary officer. Lack of coordination among the departments may result in poor performance of the business unit.

5. **Departmental conflicts:** Budgetary control may lead to conflicts among functional departments. The departmental managers may be concerned about their department goals without thinking about the overall goal of the business unit. Each department seeks to obtain a maximum allocation of funds and thus, raises a conflict among the different departments.
6. **Management support:** The effectiveness of a budgetary control system depends upon the support extended by the top management of a business unit. The management should be passionate about a budgetary control system and provide the necessary support for its effective implementation. In the absence of such support extended by the management, the system may collapse.

13.3. COST CONTROL TECHNIQUES

The following are the tools that are used for controlling cost:

1. Standard costs and budgets
2. Ratio analysis
3. Value analysis
4. Method study

1. Standard Costs and Budgets

The technique of standard costing has been developed to establish standards of performance for producing products or delivering services. These standards serve as an objective and a basis for comparing with actual costs in measuring the performance. The analysis of variance between actual and standard costs will set the responsibility for non-standard performance, and focus on the areas where cost improvement is required by analysing the source of loss and inefficiency.

This is based on the principle of controlling by exception. Instead of focusing on each cost element, attention should be given to certain costs in which significant variances from the specified standard occur. The purpose of standard costs is to create better cost awareness and aid in controlling the cost by directing attention to specific areas where the action is required. The business units which have an immediate concern, the variances would indicate whether any action is to be taken. The business units need to ensure that the costs can be controlled when they are incurred and at the time of occurrence of events. At the same time, it is necessary to identify the nature of costs, whether they are controllable or uncontrollable.

Therefore, it is important to understand the difference between controllable and uncontrollable costs. The controllable costs are incurred by the internal structure of a business unit for various processes and therefore, can be controlled by the management. Uncontrollable costs are influenced by the external structure of the business unit and these costs are not under the control of the management. These costs include prices of raw material, spare parts, capital items, distribution costs, etc. The classification of controllable and uncontrollable costs can be done for a particular business unit only. The variances between budgeted and actual costs may also be controllable and uncontrollable.

For example, if the material cost variance is due to a rise in price, then it cannot be controlled by a production manager. But if the cost variance is due to unnecessary usage, necessary control measures are possible by the manager. The top management can also decide whether they should intervene in the matter and take corrective measures. Sometimes, variances may be so significant due to failure in setting standards. In such cases, a complete reappraisal of the standard costs may be needed. If the variances are always favourable, it means that the standards have not been fixed efficiently. Standard costing can also provide the means for actual and standard cost comparison by type of expense, by department or by cost centre. The yields and spoilage can be compared with the standard allowance for loss. Labour operations and overheads also can be checked for efficiency.

Budgets are another effective technique of controlling cost, especially for controlling the overhead costs. This technique is known as flexible or variable budgets. Flexible budgets act as a basis for determining costs that are anticipated at various levels of business operations. It provides a flexible standard for comparing the costs of the actual volume of activity with the cost of the standard volume of activity. The variances can then be analysed and necessary action can be taken in the matter. The scientific establishment of standards of performance through standard costs and budgets has not only provided better cost control but has led to cost reduction in many business units. This has been the case especially in such organisations where standards were tied to wage-incentive plans and improvement in control is part of a general programme of better management.

2. Ratio Analysis

Ratio analysis is a statistical technique that measures the relationship between two figures or values. This relationship may be expressed as a rate (costs per rupee of sales), as a per cent (cost of sales as a percentage of sales), or as a proportion. Ratios are commonly used in analysing the financial statements for a period of operations. Ratios provide standards of comparison for appraising the performance of a business unit. Ratio analysis can be used for controlling cost in two ways:

- A businessman may compare the business unit's ratios for the period under scrutiny with similar ratios of the previous periods. Such a comparison would help him identify areas that need special attention.
- A businessman can compare his ratios with the standard ratios in the industry. Standard ratios are averages of the results achieved by different business units in the same line of business.

If these comparisons reveal any significant differences, the management shall analyse the reasons for these differences and can take appropriate action to remove the causes responsible for the increase in costs. Some of the most commonly used ratios for cost comparisons are given below:

- Gross profit/Sales
- Not profit/Sales
- Net profit/Total assets
- Sales/Total assets
- Production costs/Costs of sales
- Selling costs/Costs of sales
- Administration costs/Costs of sales
- Sales/Inventory or turnover
- Material costs/Production costs
- Labour costs/Production costs
- Overhead/Production costs

3. Value Analysis

Value analysis is a cost control technique used for improving the value of a product or process by understanding its constituent components and their associated costs. It seeks improvements to the components by either minimising their cost or increasing the value of the functions without diminishing quality, reliability, performance and appearance. This technique eliminates the unnecessary costs which add neither to quality nor the appearance of the product. According to Society of American Value Engineers (SAVE), "Value analysis is the systematic application of recognised techniques which identify the function of a product or services establish a monetary value for the function and provide the necessary function reliability at that lowest overall cost."

It is a rational and structural process that includes:

(a) Functional analysis that identifies the source for the existence of a product or its components.

(b) Creatively analysis for generating new and improved alternative methods.

(c) Measurement for evaluating the value of present and future models.

Value analysis is the process of reducing the cost of the prescribed function without sacrificing the required standards of performance. The emphasis is, first, on the identification of the required function and, secondly, on the determination of the best way to perform it at a lower cost. Value analysis is a supplementary method in addition to the existing cost reduction techniques.

The concept of value analysis has a close relationship with value engineering. Value engineering is a systematic method to improve the value of products and services by using an examination of the function. Value analysis deals with the tasks done by the purchasing department in this direction, whereas value engineering deals with the tasks done by the engineers in this area. Generally, the purchasing department approaches the engineering department and the vendor for solutions to business problems. Value analysis requires full cooperation from the business unit's expertise in design, purchase, production and costing. If necessary, it also requires support from the vendor and other business unit's expertise. Some of the significant practices of cost reduction through value analysis are:

- Abandonment of tailored products where standard components can perform.
- Dispensing with facilities not specified or not required by the customer.
- Use of technology-enabled new and cheaper materials in place of traditional materials.

Cost control applies to the costs that can be altered by the business unit at any point in time. Sometimes non-controllable costs exceed controllable costs thereof restricting the scope of profit improvement through cost control. However, attempts can be made to influence uncontrollable costs also. Further, instead of buying a component, a business unit may decide to make the conversion possible.

4. Method Study

Method study is the technique of subjecting work to systematic and critical evaluation of the existing and proposed ways of doing the work. This is one of the key techniques to achieve productivity improvement. Work-study helps to investigate all the factors and enables the management to get the work done efficiently and economically. Method study aims at analysing and evaluating all those conditions which influence the performance of a given task. It was initially designed for the analysis and improvement of repetitive manual work. However, method study can be used for all types of activities at all levels of a business unit. The main objectives of method study are:

- To analyse all the factors affecting the performance of a given task.
- To develop and install work methods which make optimum use of the materials and human resources.
- To establish appropriate standards for measuring work performance.

13.4. AREAS OF COST CONTROL

There are three main areas of cost control: materials, labour and overheads.

1. Materials

Several techniques can be applied to reduce the cost of materials. If proper care is taken while purchasing the materials, a business unit can get quantity discounts. Sometimes, in addition to the cost of materials, reduction may be sought on freight charges. Generally, the business units attempt to buy from the cheapest source by inviting bids/quotations. Sometimes, it is possible to have more economical substitutes for raw materials. Many a time, by making some improvements in product design also leads to a reduction in material usage. It is desirable to focus on the areas where the saving potential is the maximum. Making or buying components/spare parts from an outside source is another area for reducing the cost of raw materials. Business units may find it beneficial to manufacture certain parts and components in their factory rather than buying them from other sources. In some cases, there may be a specific advantages in purchasing spares and components from an outside source because suppliers may deliver goods at low cost with high quality.

Exploration of the possibilities of the use of standardised parts and components and the utilisation of waste and by-products may also lead to a significant reduction in the cost of materials. Inventory control is another area where the cost of materials can be minimised. It is possible to maintain the investment in inventories at the lowest amount consistent with the production and the sales requirements of the business unit. The cost of carrying inventories ranges from 15% to 20% per annum on account of interest on capital, insurance, storage and handling charges, breakage, physical deterioration, pilferage and obsolescence. Further, 50% of the gross working capital may be locked up in inventories. Some important ways of reducing the cost of inventories are:

- Superior production planning.
- Identifying dependable sources of supplies for the prompt delivery of materials.
- Reducing the slow moving materials and dropping obsolete materials.

- Improved flow of parts and materials leading to increased machine utilisation and shorter manufacturing cycles.

Packaging constitutes a significant quantity of raw materials and the total manufacturing expenses. Business units should make attempts to minimise the packaging. For example, instead of discarding containers that the materials come in, they can be used for shipping the finished goods. Similarly, the manufacturing business unit's such as cars and motorbikes may request its customers to return the containers in which goods were sent so that they could be used again. This helps in minimising the packaging cost.

2. Labour

The cost incurred towards wages is one of the major cost items. Business units prefer a reduction in wages for reducing labour costs. However, reduction in wages may not be a desirable option to reduce the cost of production. Contrary to this, experts advise an increase in wages as an incentive to motivate the workers to raise their productivity. Such a measure will reduce wage cost per unit. A reduction in labour costs is possible by proper selection and training, improvement in productivity and by automation, wherever possible. Work-study might result in a lot of savings by reducing overtime and idle time and providing better workloads. Improvement in working conditions may reduce absenteeism and thus reduce costs per unit. Scrutiny of overtime may reveal substantial scope for savings.

All efforts must be made to reduce the wastage of human effort. Wastage of human effort may be due to lack of coordination among various departments by having more workers than necessary, ·under-utilisation of the existing manpower, shortage of materials, improper scheduling, absenteeism, poor methods and low morale. Attempts must be made to secure the cooperation of employees in cost reduction by inviting suggestions from them. These suggestions should be carefully examined and implemented if found satisfactory. Some business units have a suggestion box scheme and employees who come out with good suggestions receive awards. These suggestions may either lead to savings or improve safety and work convenience. The basic idea is to motivate workers and make them perceive working in the business unit as a participative endeavour.

3. Overheads

Factory overheads can be reduced by the selection of exactly suitable and qualitative equipment, judicious use of space and equipment, maintenance of equipment and minimisation of the cost of power, lighting, water, and other utilities. Product design plays an important role in optimising the expenses and minimising wastages. Effective planning of movements of materials can minimise transportation cost. It can also be analysed whether it would be economical to use own transport or hired transport. To reduce costs, the business units can hire transport services rather than owning them, because the purchase and maintenance of transport services can be more expensive. Thus, by keeping a smaller workforce and by introducing a contract rate linked to a safe delivery schedule it is possible to ensure speedy point-to-point delivery of products.

Reduction of wastes can also minimise manufacturing costs considerably. A certain amount of waste and spoilage is unavoidable because employees make mistakes, machines get out of order, and sometimes raw materials may be defective. However, attempts can be made to reduce these mistakes and faulty handling to the minimum. The amount of waste and spoilage depends upon several factors such as product complexity, the age of the plant and machinery, and the expertise and experience of the workers. Wastes can be reduced considerably by educating operators in the causes and cure of the wastes. Bad debt losses can be reduced considerably by selecting customers carefully, and keeping an eye on the receivables. Concentrating on areas and media can reduce advertising costs, which give the best results. Selling costs can be controlled by improving the supervision and training of salesmen, rearrangement of sales territories, preplanning salesmen's routes and calls and redirecting of the sales efforts, to achieve a more economic product mix. It is possible to save selling costs by the use of warehouses, making bulk shipments to the warehouses and giving faster deliveries to the customers.

13.5. COST REDUCTION

Cost Reduction is a process which aims to lower the per unit cost of a product manufactured or service rendered without affecting its quality. It can be done by using new and improved methods and techniques. It ascertains substitute ways to reduce the production cost of a unit. Thus, cost reduction is an important measure for the maximisation of profits of the business unit. Cost reduction strategy aims to eliminate unnecessary expenditure in areas like production process, storage, selling and distribution of the product, etc.

13.5.1. Cost Reduction Techniques

Techniques for reducing the cost cover a wide range of activities are given below.

1. **Organisation and methods:** Organisation and methods are referred to as a systematic assessment of activities to improve the effective utilisation of human and other material resources. This technique is concerned with improving the managerial work, organising the activities, and usage of methods and procedures. Organisation and method services include analysis of the activities such as organisation, activity, information, interviewing, systems design, flowcharting, etc.
2. **Materials handling:** Materials handling is an important technique of cost reduction. The production processes require materials to be moved from one stage to another stage. Materials handling is concerned with two principal aspects such as the flow of materials, and the methods used in transferring the materials.
3. **Variety reduction:** Variety reduction technique can be applied to the production process. It certainly has more effect if applied in the right place and the right time. Variety reduction consists of four stages through which the cost of production can be reduced. These include materials and components schedule, product analysis into components, identification of common components, and product redesign for production.
4. **Cost-benefit analysis:** The cost-benefit analysis is the most popular and appropriate technique of reducing the costs. This enables the business unit in making accurate investment decisions to attain optimum allocation of resources. This analysis involves the enumeration, comparison and evaluation of benefits and costs involved in the production of a business unit. In this method, the cost-benefit ratio is the measure for evaluating the business unit.
5. **Production control:** Production control refers to the attitude of the management towards the efficient organisation of men, machines and materials to produce a product of the right quality in the shortest time at minimum cost. Control over production cost can be initiated in four main sections like planning, programming, scheduling, and control.
6. **Product design:** A well designed product performs the function for which it is designed, facilitates easy use and has a pleasant appearance. The qualities of good design are durability, reliability, quality, safety, simplicity, and maintainability.
7. **Materials control:** Materials control is a key activity that covers an extensive range of tasks from the moment of designing the product to its final delivery stage. It ensures a systematic control over purchasing, storing, material handling, issuing and consumption to

minimise the cost. The key focus should be on reducing the material handling costs for any business unit. These costs include reducing the travel time and distance of material, paring equipment costs, avoiding damage and improving storage capacity. Controlling material handling costs increases productivity and enhances the profitability of a business unit. Certain techniques are used at planning, procuring and holding stages of materials that facilitate effective material cost control.

8. **Quality control:** The main function of quality control is to ensure minimum defective products. For example, in a manufacturing plant, quality control is designed to inspect each item to make sure that it is produced according to the specific standards. It helps the business units to create an environment in which both the management and employees strive for perfection. When quality measures are applied consistently over a period, it can reduce costs throughout the business unit, especially in the areas of scrap, rework, field service, and warranty cost reduction.
9. **Automation:** One of the key options for cost reduction followed by business units particularly after the industrial revolution is automation. It reduces the human element in the organisation. Automation introduced major technological changes in production processes and costs. It changed the face of industry and commerce. Automation helped to increase speed and large-scale production. The reasons for introducing automation are cost reduction and quality enhancement.
10. **Terotechnology:** Terotechnology is referred to as the technology of installation, commissioning, maintenance, replacement and removal of plant machinery and equipment. It is a combination of technical, managerial, financial, engineering and other practices, applied to physical assets in the detection of economic life cycle costs. The cost of obtaining, operating and maintaining physical assets for their productive life is known as the life-cycle cost. The various aspects covered under by terotechnology in cost reduction are ownership cost of physical assets, low material costs, minimum breakdown costs, and enhanced quality and efficiency.

13.6. SUMMARY

- Cost control is a process of identifying and reducing possible business costs in all stages of business operations. It is an essential element for the successful functioning of a business unit. Cost control deals with reduction in specific expenses and effective utilisation of every rupee spent.

- Cost control helps a business unit to improve its profitability and competitiveness. Cost control involves determination of standards, ascertaining actual results comparing the standards, analysis of the variances, and deciding the course of corrective and preventive action.
- Budgetary control is the process of preparing budgets for the future period and compare with the actual performance with standards specified.
- The advantages of budgetary control are profit maximisation, coordination, specific goals, performance measurement tool, economy, identifying weaknesses, corrective measures, responsiveness, cost reduction, and incentive schemes.
- Some of the limitations of budgetary control are uncertain future, budgetary revision, discouraging competent personnel, difficulties in coordination, departmental conflicts, and management support.
- The technique of standard costing has been developed to establish standards of performance for producing products or delivering services. These standards serve as an objective and a basis for comparing with actual costs in measuring the performance. The purpose of standard costs is to create better cost awareness and aid in controlling the cost by directing attention to specific areas where the action is required.
- Ratio analysis is a statistical technique that measures the relationship between two figures or values. Ratios provide standards of comparison for appraising the performance of a business unit.
- Value analysis is a cost control technique used for improving the value of a product or process by understanding its constituent components and their associated costs. It seeks improvements to the components by either minimising their cost or increasing the value of the functions without diminishing quality, reliability, performance and appearance.
- Method study is the technique of subjecting work to systematic and critical evaluation of the existing and proposed ways of doing the work. This is one of the key techniques to achieve productivity improvement. Method study aims at analysing and evaluating all those conditions which influence the performance of a given task.
- There are three main areas of cost control. They are materials, labour and overheads.
- Several techniques can be applied for reducing the cost of materials. If proper care is taken while purchasing the materials, a business unit can get quantity discounts. Sometimes, in addition to the cost of materials, reduction may be sought on freight charges.

- A reduction in labour costs is possible by proper selection and training, improvement in productivity and by automation, wherever possible.
- Factory overheads can be reduced by the selection of exactly suitable and qualitative equipment, judicious use of space and equipment, maintenance of equipment and minimisation of the cost of power, lighting, water, and other utilities.
- Cost reduction is a process which aims to lower the per unit cost of a product manufactured or service rendered without affecting its quality. It ascertains alternatives to reduce the production cost of a unit.
- The various cost reduction techniques are: organisation and methods, materials handling, variety reduction, cost-benefit analysis, production control, product design, materials control, quality control, automation and terotechnology.

SHORT ANSWER QUESTIONS

1. What are the objectives of budgetary control?
2. What are standard costs?
3. Write a short note on ratio analysis.
4. Explain the main objectives of method study.
5. What is meant by cost reduction?
6. What is meant by terotechnology?
7. What are the important ways of reducing the cost of inventory?

ESSAY ANSWER QUESTIONS

1. What do you mean by cost control? Explain.
2. Define budgetary control. Explain its advantages and disadvantages of cost control.
3. Discuss the techniques used for controlling cost.
4. Explain how standard cost and budgets are useful for controlling cost.
5. What is value analysis? Discuss the significant practices of cost reduction through value analysis.
6. What are the three main areas of cost control? Explain its significance in controlling the cost of a business unit.
7. Describe the techniques for reducing the cost of a wide range of activities.

FILL IN THE BLANKS

1. The process of identifying and reducing possible business costs in all stages of business operations is called _________.
2. An estimated financial statement of income and expenses for a specified period is called _________.
3. The process of preparing budgets for the future period and compare with the actual performance with standards specified is _________.

4. Budgetary control aims at maximising the __________ of the business unit.
5. Budgetary control acts as a tool by setting targets to each department for measuring __________ performance.
6. The process of reducing the cost of the prescribed function without sacrificing the required standards of performance is called __________.
7. The technique of subjecting work to systematic and critical evaluation of the existing and proposed ways of doing the work is __________.
8. Effective planning of movements of materials can minimise __________ cost.
9. Reduction of material wastes can minimise __________ costs considerably.
10. Ascertaining alternatives to reduce the production cost of a unit is called __________.
11. Variety reduction technique can be applied to the __________ process.
12. Controlling material handling costs increases productivity and enhances __________.

Answers

1. Cost control
2. Budget
3. Budgetary control
4. Profits
5. Managerial
6. Value analysis
7. Method study
8. Transportation
9. Manufacturing
10. Cost reduction
11. Production
12. Profitability

MULTIPLE-CHOICE QUESTIONS

1. A reduction in the percentage of costs and an increase in the percentage of profits is known as:
   (A) Material control (B) Production control
   (C) Cost control (D) Supply control
2. A system that uses budgets as a means for planning and controlling all business activities is referred to as:
   (A) Budgetary control (B) Process control
   (C) Management control (D) Sales control
3. Standard costs are based on the principle of:
   (A) Controlling by default (B) Controlling by exception
   (C) Controlling by uniformity (D) Controlling by conformity
4. Which budgets act as a basis for determining costs that are anticipated at various levels of business operations?
   (A) Fixed budget (B) Constant budget
   (C) Master budget (D) Flexible budget
5. The statistical technique that measures the relationship between two figures or values is:
   (A) Trend analysis (B) Comparative analysis
   (C) Ratio analysis (D) Structured analysis

6. A cost control technique used for improving the value of a product or process by understanding its constituent components and their associated costs is:
   (A) Value analysis (B) Profit analysis
   (C) Management analysis (D) Financial analysis
7. The process of lowering the per unit cost of a product manufactured or service rendered without affecting its quality is called:
   (A) Cost estimation (B) Quality maximisation
   (C) Cost reduction (D) Cost analysis
8. A systematic assessment of activities to improve the effective utilisation of human and other material resources is:
   (A) Organisation and methods (B) Cost-benefit analysis
   (C) Variety reduction (D) Work measurement
9. The attitude of management towards the efficient organisation of men, machines and materials to produce a product of the right quality in the shortest time at minimum cost is:
   (A) Product design (B) Quality control
   (C) Production control (D) Automation
10. The cost of obtaining, operating and maintaining physical assets for their productive life is known as:
   (A) Production cost (B) Life-cycle cost
   (C) Storage cost (D) Manufacturing cost

Answers:

1. C	2. A	3. B	4. D	5. C
6. A	7. C	8. A	9. C	10. B

REFERENCES

1. Benham, A. & Benham, L. (2001). "The costs of exchange. *2000: Institutions, Contracts and Organizations: Perspectives from New Institutional Economics*. Edward Elgar, Cheltenham, 367-375.
2. Brigham, E.F. & Pappas, J.L. (1974). *Managerial Economics*. London: Holt, Rinehart and Winston.
3. Brown, J.L. & Howard, L.R. (1969). *Principles and Practice of Management Accountancy*. Mcdonald & Evans.
4. Dean, J. (1968). *Managerial Economics*. New Delhi, India: Prentice-Hall of India Private Limited.
5. Dwivedi, D.N. (2015). *Managerial Economics* (8th Edition). New Delhi, India: Vikas Publishing House Pvt. Ltd.
6. Gupta, G.S. (2017). *Managerial Economics*. New Delhi, India: Tata McGraw-Hill.
7. Leftwich, R.H. & Eckert, R.D. (1966). *The Price System and Resource Allocation* (No. 04; HB221, L4 1966.). New York: Holt, Rinehart and Winston.

8. Mehta, P.L. (2007). *Managerial Economics: Text and Cases.* New Delhi, India: Sultan Chand & Co.
9. Peterson, H.C., Lewis, W.C. & Jain, S.K. (2005). *Managerial Economics* (Fourth Edition). New Delhi: Pearson Education.
10. Salvatore, D. & Rastogi, S.K. (2016). *Managerial Economics.* New Delhi, India: Oxford University Press.
11. Terry, G.R. (1960). *Principles of Management.* Homewood IL: Richard D. Irwin.
12. Varshney, R.L. & Maheswari, K.L. (2014). *Managerial Economics.* New Delhi, India: Sultan Chand & Sons.
13. Watson, D.S. & Mary, A.H. (1978). *Price Theory and its Uses.* Boston: Houghton Mifflin.
14. Webb, S.S. (1976). *Managerial Economics.* Boston: Houghton Mifflin.

Chapter

14 Perfect Competition

LEARNING OBJECTIVES

After studying this chapter, you should be able to understand:

- concept of market structure and its features;
- concept and features of perfect competition;
- pricing under perfect competition;
- price-output determination in the short run and long run; and
- criticisms of perfect competition.

14.1. MARKET STRUCTURE

The market is referred to a group of present and potential buyers in a region where the exchange of goods and services takes place between buyers and sellers at an agreed price. The word 'market' derives from the Latin word 'marcatus' or 'marcart', which means 'to trade'. Market structure is referred to as a group of industries characterised by a number of sellers and buyers, level of competition, degree of differentiation in products, and the conditions for entry and exit of business units. The analysis of market structure helps the business units in understanding the functioning of different business units under different circumstances and in making effective business decisions. It is essential for business units to understand the competitive environment in the targeted market to determine the product to be offered, price, distribution, and promotion of products/services. According to Pappas and Hirschey (1987), "Market structure refers to the number and size distribution of buyers and sellers in the market for a good or service." The market structure for a product/service not only includes business units and individuals currently engaged in buying and selling but also the potential entrants.

The structure of a market is analysed based on the most important factor, i.e., competition. The market structure can be classified as a perfectly competitive market and imperfectly competitive market. A perfectly competitive market presents a highly desirable market situation wherein everything happens as per market situations fairly. Neither buyers, nor sellers can influence market proceedings. No one can exploit the other party. Everything happens rationally and everyone will have equal opportunities in buying and selling. Perfect competitive conditions are highly desirable as it ensures equity among sellers as well as buyers. The concept of perfect competition, however, remained in the vision of the economists but never found as a reality. The imperfection in market conditions is experienced all the time in all the markets. The degree of imperfection, however, varies from market to market, product to product, situation to situation, and time to time. In an imperfectly competitive market, the sellers and buyers try to influence each other with differentiated and unique offers with an objective of exploiting the situation for maximisation of profits. The activities of competitors vary as per the degree of imperfection existing in the market.

The market structure is based on the following features:

1. **Sellers concentration:** It refers to the number of sellers of a product/service in a market and their respective market shares.
2. **Buyer concentration:** It refers to the degree to which a small number of buyers purchase a major share of the total sales of a business unit.
3. **Product differentiation:** It refers to offering uniquely different products/services to the target market compared to competitive brands and the other brands of the producer.
4. **Restrictions to enter a market:** The entry and exit conditions for business units are not similar to all the markets. They vary as per the degree of imperfection in the market. In some cases, only one business unit may be allowed to enter the business. A few business units may be permitted to do the business in some markets. There may be free entry to any business unit to take up the business in some markets. The policy of the government, the economic conditions, the capital requirement, speciality in technology, expert human resources, scarcity of raw materials, etc., are some of the reasons for restrictions to enter into a market.

14.2. PERFECT COMPETITION

Perfect competition refers to a market structure where competition among the sellers and buyers prevails in its most perfect form. In a perfectly competitive market, a single market price prevails for the product/service, which is determined by the forces of total demand and total supply in the market.

Definitions of perfect competition

Author	Definitions
Brander & Spencer (1992)	Perfect competition is the name given to an industry or to a market characterised by a large number of buyers and sellers all engaged in the purchase and sale of a homogeneous commodity, with perfect knowledge of market price and quantities, no discrimination and perfect mobility of resources.

Leftwich & Eckert (1966)	Perfect competition is a market in which there are many firms selling identical products with no firm large enough relative to the entire market to be able to influence the market price.
Bilas (1971)	The perfect competition is characterised by the presence of many firms. They all sell identical products. The seller is a price taker, not price maker.
Stigler (1957)	Perfect market competition prevails when there are indefinitely many traders having full knowledge of all offer and bid prices, acting independently in a perfect market.

14.3. FEATURES OF PERFECT COMPETITION

The important features of a perfectly competitive market are:

1. Existence of a large number of buyers and sellers
2. Homogeneous products
3. Free entry and exit
4. Absence of government regulation
5. Absence of artificial restrictions
6. Mobility of factors of production
7. Perfect knowledge about markets
8. Absence of transport costs

1. **Existence of a large number of buyers and sellers:** There must be a large number of business units in the industry. Each business unit supplies only a small part of the total quantity offered in the market. As a result, no individual business unit can influence the price. Similarly, buyers are also numerous. Hence, no individual buyer has any influence on the market price. The price of the product is determined by the collective forces of market demand and supply. The business unit is only a price taker.
2. **Homogeneous products:** In a perfectly competitive market, the product of any one business unit is identical to the products of all other business units. The technical characteristics of the product, as well as the services associated with its sale and delivery, are identical. The products are homogeneous in the sense that they are perfect substitutes from the buyer's point of view. The sellers do not spend on advertisement, publicity like promotional activities due to the reason that no business unit gets a specific identity in the market.
3. **Free entry and exit:** There are no barriers to entry or exit from the market. Entry or exit may take time but business units have freedom of movement in and out of the market. When the business units earn

abnormal profits, many new business units will enter the market and compete for sharing the profits. Similarly, if the business units in the industry are incurring losses some of them will leave the industry which will reduce the supply of the industry and will thus, lead to increase in price and wipe away the losses.

4. **Absence of government regulation:** In perfect competition, there is no government intervention in the form of tariffs, subsidies, the relationship of supply and demand.
5. **Absence of artificial restrictions:** The major feature of the perfect competition is the non-existence of any artificial restrictions on the demand, supply, price of goods and factors of production in the market. There must not be any external intervention in price fixation and any controls on the product.
6. **Mobility of factors of production:** The factors of production are free to move from one business unit to another throughout the economy. It is also assumed that workers can move among different jobs. Raw materials and other factors are not monopolised and labour is not unionised. In short, there is perfect competition in the market for factors of production.
7. **Perfect knowledge about markets:** It is assumed that all sellers and buyers have complete knowledge of the conditions of the market. This knowledge refers not only to the prevailing conditions in the current period but in all future periods as well. Information is free and costless. There will be an unrestricted free flow of information to all the buyers and sellers. Under these conditions uncertainty about future developments in the market is ruled out.
8. **Absence of transport costs:** Another important feature of a perfectly competitive market is that there will be no transportation costs to the buyers, as uniform price prevails throughout the market. The existence of a single uniform price is an essential feature of a perfectly competitive market. Therefore, a buyer needs to incur transportation costs to find the seller as the products are available everywhere in the market.

14.4. PRICING UNDER PERFECT COMPETITION

Under a perfectly competitive market, the price for a product is determined by the market as a whole consisting of both buyers and sellers. Hence, the consumer's total demand for a product in the market at various prices constitutes the industry demand curve and the total quantity of all the sellers constitutes the industry supply curve. The demand curve for a business unit is horizontal and perfectly elastic.

14.4.1. Equilibrium of the Industry

Equilibrium is the state of an economy where the aggregate demand for products and services is equal to the aggregate supply of products and services. When there is a change in any one or group of variables creates an excess demand or supply, it is called disequilibrium. A sudden change in the variables is called economic shock. In microeconomics, market equilibrium is considered relevant. In perfect competition, price is determined at the market equilibrium point where the demand equates supply in a particular market. In other words, at the market equilibrium price, everything brought to the market by the producers will be purchased by the buyers. No seller tries to set the price higher than the market equilibrium price as such an attempt will yield no sales. On the other hand, no rational producer tries to sell at a price lower than the market equilibrium price due to the fact that the producer can sell the produce at the market equilibrium price. Figure 14.1 illustrates the way in which the market reaches the equilibrium point under competitive conditions.

Table 14.1. Equilibrium of an industry

Price per unit	Demand	Supply	Pressure on price
5	20	40	Fall
4	25	35	Fall
3	30	30	Neutral
2	32	27	Rise
1	35	25	Rise

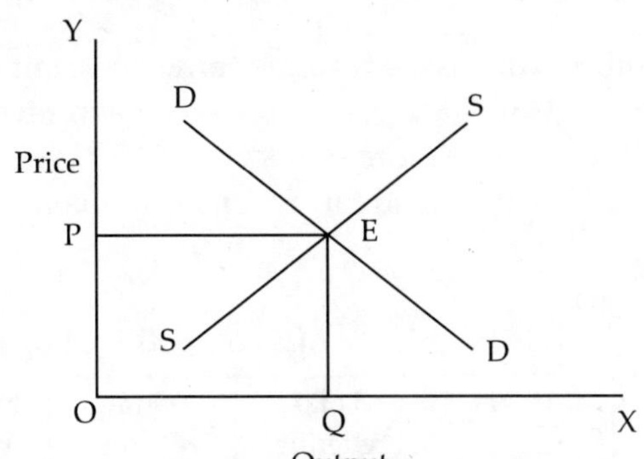

Figure 14.1. Equilibrium of an industry

As shown in Figure 14.1, OP is the equilibrium price and OQ is the equilibrium quantity. The equilibrium price is the price at which both demand and supply are equal and therefore, no buyer or seller is dissatisfied as there is no point of exploitation from either side. If the price were to be fixed at any other level, higher or lower, demand remaining the same, there would not be equilibrium in the market. Likewise, if the quantities of goods were greater or smaller than the demand, there would not be equilibrium in the market.

As such, the line P acts as a demand curve for the business unit as the demand curve of each business unit is perfectly elastic. All the business units can sell as much or as little output as they like along the horizontal price line. Since the price is given, a competitive business unit has to adjust its output to the market price to earn maximum profit.

14.4.2. Equilibrium of a Business Unit

The basic assumption of economic theory is that the business units attempt to maximise profits. They continue to increase production until they reach a point where the cost of producing an additional unit is equal to the revenue generated by the additional unit. Therefore, a business unit is said to be in equilibrium when it maximises profit. The output which gives maximum profit to the business unit is called equilibrium output.

Under perfect competition, the revenue of a business unit depends upon several units sold at the market price. As the price is determined by market forces, the average revenue generated by the sale of products will be equal to marginal revenue generated by the sale of an additional unit. Therefore, Price = AR = MR

The revenue function of a business unit is:

- **Total revenue:** It refers to the earnings earned by producing and selling 'n' number of units. Total revenue (TR) = Price per unit (P) × No. of units sold (Q)
- **Average revenue (AR):** It is the revenue earned per unit sold. AR = TR/Q
- **Marginal revenue (MR):** MR refers to a change in revenue because of producing and selling one more unit.

Table 14.2 illustrates the trends in revenue of a competitive business unit.

Table 14.2: Trends in revenue of a competitive business unit

No. of units	Price	Total revenue	Average revenue	Marginal revenue
1	10	10	10	–
2	10	20	10	10
3	10	30	10	10

4	10	40	10	10
5	10	50	10	10
6	10	60	10	10
7	10	70	10	10

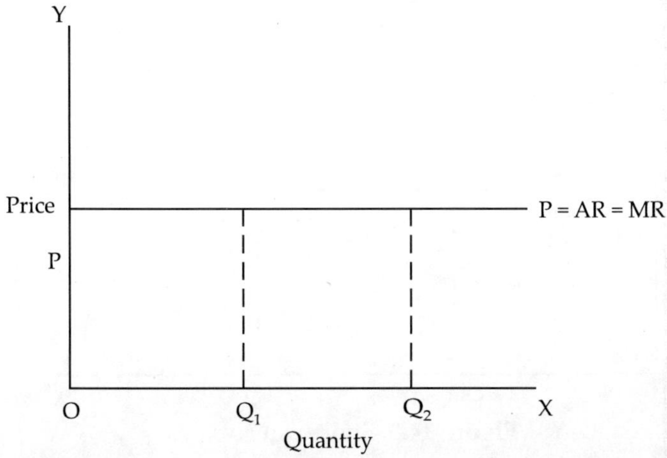

Figure 14.2. Demand curve under perfect competition

Figure 14.2 shows the demand curve under perfection competitive market. The market price OP is determined by the market forces of the total demand and the total supply. The business units have to accept this price as given and as such, they are price-takers rather than price-makers. They may not venture to increase the price above OP because of the fear of losing their customers to other business units. They do not try to sell the product below OP because they can sell all the products at the OP. They will try to sell as much as they can at the price OP. Thus, at OP the AR is equal to MR.

14.5. PRICE-OUTPUT DETERMINATION IN THE SHORT RUN

In the short run, the business units cannot expand their production capacity. The fixed costs remain constant at any level of production. The business units will be in equilibrium by maximising profits. The business unit earns profits when the average cost (AC) and marginal cost (MC) are less than the price. The demand curve of the business units is horizontal at the price determined by the industry (Price = AR = MR) known as average revenue curve (ARC) because all the products are sold at the same price. When AR is constant it will coincide with MR. P is the demand curve representing Price = AR = MR. AC and MC are average and marginal cost curves. The business unit gets profit as long as MC is less than MR. The business unit reaches equilibrium at a point where MC is equal to MR. The business unit may earn abnormal/supernormal profits in the short run which is indicated by PERS (Figure 14.3).

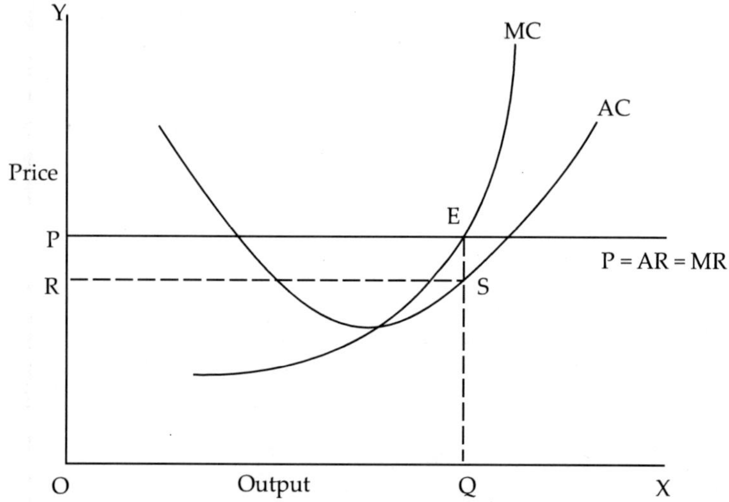

Figure 14.3. Short-run curve

14.6. PRICE-OUTPUT DETERMINATION IN THE LONG RUN

A business unit can make desired changes in factors of production in the long run. Further, new business units may enter or the existing business units may leave the industry during the long run. Therefore, a business unit attains equilibrium when AC = MC = AR = MR.

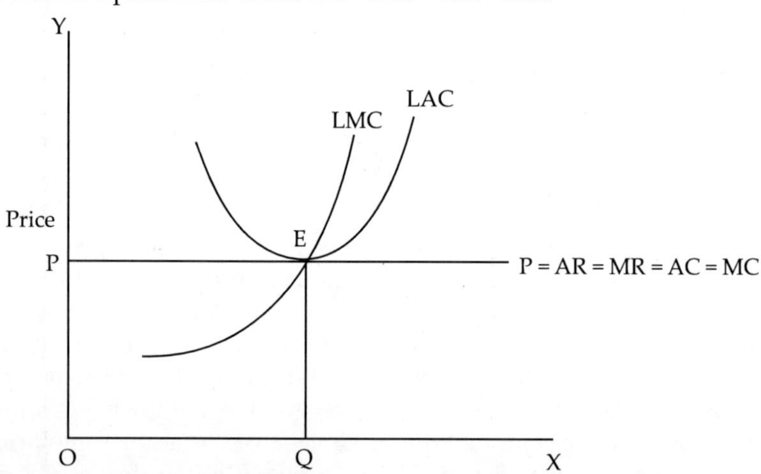

Figure 14.4. Long-run curve

In the long run, the equilibrium position of the business unit satisfies two conditions:

(a) MR = MC

(b) AR = AC

Figure 14.4 shows that the AC curve must be tangential to the AR curve at the lowest point. QP is the price and also the equilibrium point where the long-run average cost (LAC) is the lowest. The long-run marginal cost (LMC) curve passes through the minimum point of the LAC curve. E is an equilibrium point at which a business unit produces OQ output and sells at OP. Therefore, if the market price is below the LAC curve of the business unit, it incurs losses.

14.7. CRITICISMS OF PERFECT COMPETITION

The perfect competition model is considered the most desirable one basically for two reasons. In the first place, the perfect competition ensures maximum welfare to the consumers. The free movement factors of production provide an opportunity to optimise the use of the resources and the consumers get as much quantity as they desire at a given price. In the second place, the perfect competition model drives the business units to work for attaining the most efficient size and thereby maximise their profits. The business units have to work for cost minimisation by way of effective use of resources. However, the perfect competition model is criticised by many as it is unrealistic.

The criticisms are mostly levelled against some of the assumptions of perfect competition. Though there is an agreement on the presence of a large number of buyers and sellers in the market, the assumption that they remain passive and only become takers of the market price is very much criticised. In reality, every business unit tries to offer differentiated products and play games with the quantity of production, and pricing. They try to exploit the dynamic market conditions into their favour. Another criticism is on the determination of the price. The critics argue that in the absence of price maker, who will decide the market price. If the price maker is present in the market then the perfect competition model is appropriate to describe a centralized market economy rather than the decentralized one. Such a model, therefore, represents more of communism than capitalism.

The assumption that the buyers and sellers have perfect knowledge about markets is criticised as such condition is far from reality. The influence of other environmental factors on market dynamics is not considered in the perfect competition model. The critics argue that the perfect competition model is an imaginary one and such competitive conditions were never experienced in the past, existing at present or can be predicted in future.

14.8. SUMMARY

- A market refers to a group of present and potential buyers in a region where the exchange of goods and services takes place between buyers and sellers at an agreed price.
- The market structure can be classified as a perfectly competitive market and imperfectly competitive market.
- The features of a market structure are sellers' concentration, buyers' concentration, product differentiation, and restrictions to enter a market.
- Perfect competition refers to a market structure where competition among the sellers and buyers prevails in its most perfect form.
- The important features of a perfectly competitive market are the existence of a large number of buyers and sellers, homogeneous products, free entry and exit, absence of government regulation, absence of artificial restrictions, mobility of factors of production, perfect knowledge about markets, and absence of transport costs.
- In a perfectly competitive market, the price for a product is determined by the market as a whole consisting of both buyers and sellers.
- Equilibrium is the state of an economy where the aggregate demand for products and services is equal to the aggregate supply of products and services.
- Disequilibrium occurs when there is a change in any one or group of variables. It creates an excess demand or supply.
- In the short run, the business unit earns profits when the average cost (AC) and marginal cost (MC) are less than the price.
- The demand curve of the business units is horizontal at the price determined by the industry (Price = MR = AR) known as average revenue curve (ARC) because all the products are sold at the same price.
- In the long run, a business unit can make desired changes in factors of production. A business unit attains equilibrium when AC = MC = AR = MR.
- The business units have to work for cost minimisation by way of effective use of resources. However, the perfect competition model is criticised by many as it is unrealistic.

SHORT ANSWER QUESTIONS

1. Define a market.
2. Write a short note on equilibrium.
3. Define perfect competition.
4. What is the market structure?
5. What are the features of market structure?

ESSAY ANSWER QUESTIONS

1. What is perfect competition? Explain the features of a perfectly competitive market.
2. Describe the equilibrium of a business unit and industry in a perfectly competitive market.
3. Discuss the price-output determination in the short run and long run in a perfectly competitive market.
4. "The perfect competition model is criticised by many as it is unrealistic." Discuss.

FILL IN THE BLANKS

1. The degree to which a small number of buyers purchase a major share of the total sales of a business unit is called _________.
2. The price of the product is determined by the collective forces of market _________.
3. The business unit is only a price _________.
4. The state of an economy where the aggregate demand for products and services is equal to the aggregate supply of products and services is called _________.
5. A sudden change in the variables is called _________.
6. The output which gives maximum profit to the business unit is called _________.
7. The revenue of a business unit depends upon several units sold at _________.
8. In the short run, the business units will be in equilibrium by _________ profits.
9. In perfect competition, there is no government intervention in the form of tariffs, subsidies. (T/F)
10. Artificial restrictions on the demand, supply, price of goods and factors of productions exist in the market. (T/F)

Answers

1. Buyers concentration
2. Demand and supply
3. Taker
4. Equilibrium
5. Economic shock
6. Equilibrium output
7. Market price
8. Maximising
9. True
10. False

MULTIPLE-CHOICE QUESTIONS

1. Which one of the following is not a feature of perfect competition?
   (A) Homogeneous products
   (B) Free entry and exit
   (C) Absence of artificial restrictions
   (D) Government interference

2. The demand curve for a business unit in perfect competition is:
   (A) Perfectly elastic (B) Perfectly inelastic
   (C) Relatively elastic (D) Relatively inelastic
3. In a perfectly competitive market, the price for a product is determined by:
   (A) Consumer (B) Seller
   (C) Market (D) Business unit
4. When there is a change in any one or group of variables creating an excess demand or supply, it is called:
   (A) Equilibrium (B) Disequilibrium
   (C) Economies (D) Diseconomies
5. The equilibrium price is the price at which both demand and supply are:
   (A) Equal (B) Negative
   (C) Positive (D) Optimistic
6. In the short run, a business unit earns a profit when the average cost and marginal cost are less than:
   (A) Cost (B) Price
   (C) Revenue (D) Expenditure
7. In the short run, the business unit reaches equilibrium at a point where:
   (A) MC = MR (B) MC > MR
   (C) MC < MR (D) AC = AR
8. In the long run, a business unit attains equilibrium when:
   (A) AC = AR & MC > MR (B) AC = MC > AR = MR
   (C) AC = MC = AR = MR (D) AC = MC & AR > MR

Answers

1. D	2. A	3. C	4. B	5. A
6. B	7. A	8. C		

REFERENCES

1. Bilas, R.A. (1971). *Microeconomic Theory.* McGraw-Hill Companies.
2. Brander, J. & Spencer, B. (1992). *Tariff Protection and Imperfect Competition.* Imperfect competition and international trade, (107-119).
3. Dean, J. (1968). *Managerial Economics.* New Delhi, India: Prentice-Hall of India Private Limited.
4. Dwivedi, D.N. (2015). *Managerial Economics* (8th Edition). New Delhi, India: Vikas Publishing House Pvt. Ltd.
5. Hirschey, M. (2009). *Managerial Economics* (12th Edition). USA: South-Western Cengage Learning.
6. Leftwich, R.H. & Eckert, R.D. (1966). *The Price System and Resource Allocation* (No. 04; HB221, L4 1966.). New York: Holt, Rinehart and Winston.

7. Mehta, P.L. (2007). *Managerial Economics: Text and Cases*. New Delhi, India: Sultan Chand & Co.
8. Pappas, J.L. & Hirschey, M. (1987). *Managerial Economics*. Dryden Press.
9. Robinson, J. (1934). The economics of imperfect competition. *Journal of the Royal Statistical Society*, 97(4), 671-674.
10. Stigler, G.J. (1957). Perfect competition, historically contemplated. *Journal of Political Economy*, 65(1), 1-17.

Chapter

15 Monopoly

LEARNING OBJECTIVES

After studying this chapter, you should be able to understand:

- the concept and causes of monopoly;
- features and barriers of monopoly;
- pricing under monopoly; and
- price-output determinants in short run and long run.

15.1. CONCEPT OF MONOPOLY

The word 'monopoly' derives from two Greek words 'monos' which means' alone or single' and 'poly' means 'to sell'. A monopoly is a unique situation where a particular individual or business unit is the only supplier of that product. It is a single seller or a business unit having a significant market power to charge high prices. Market power is the ability to increase the price of the product above the marginal cost without losing the customers. Although many monopolists are big business houses, size is not a distinctive characteristic of a monopoly. A small business unit may also have the monopoly power to raise the price in a market. Monopoly is the highly imperfect market structure wherein the objective is typically to maximise profit by producing less quantity of output and selling them at higher prices. A monopoly can be established by a government, or private business units, or an integration of both. Examples for monopoly are Indian Railways, post for stamps, postcards, envelopes, postal orders, etc.

Definitions of monopoly

Author	Definition
Joel Dean (1951)	A monopoly is a market in which a product of lasting distinctiveness is sold. The product has distinctive products recognised by its buyers and the distinctiveness lasts over many years.
Ferguson (1972)	A pure monopoly exists when there is only one producer in the market. There are no direct competitors.
Koutsoyiannis (1954)	Monopoly is a market situation in which there is a single seller, there are no close substitutes for the product it produces, and there are barriers to entry.

15.2. CAUSES OF MONOPOLY

The basic reasons for a monopoly are:

1. Control over raw materials
2. Efficiency in production
3. Public interest
4. Economies of scale
5. Legal restrictions

1. **Control over raw materials:** Monopoly may exist due to control of the entire supply of the raw materials required to produce the product. For example, a single owner of diamond mines in a country will be a monopolist.
2. **Efficiency in production:** A business unit achieves the status of monopoly due to its distinctive efficiency in production. In imperfect market conditions, the efficiency in production may be the result of long experience, innovative ability, availability of finance, low marketing cost, managerial efficiency, etc. As a result, the business unit gains higher competitive strength and no other business unit ventures to enters the business for fear of making losses.
3. **Public interest:** A government granted monopoly or legal monopoly is another source of monopoly which is sanctioned by the state. In case of risky ventures or the production requires a long gestation period or requirement of a very high level of investment, the government considering the public interest may permit a private monopoly or establish a government monopoly. For example, Railways require a huge investment to lay tracks, build platform and stations and have long gestation periods it should reach a large number of customers before a business unit can make a profit necessitating government intervention.
4. **Economies of scale:** The economies of scale is the technical cause for the emergence of monopoly in some product areas in an unregulated market. The monopoly emerged out of this factor is called a natural monopoly. In some industries economies of scale over a sufficiently large range of output leaves only one business unit to operate.
5. **Legal Restrictions:** A monopoly may emerge from the patent or copyright that restricts other business units to enter into the business. Intellectual Property is a property which allows the holder to exercise his market power. At the same time competition, law and policy are meant to attack unfair monopoly. In an idealist market situation, consumers would benefit without IP which conveys a kind of limited monopoly in the short run. As per the intellectual

property rights act 2011, Copyright act 1957, Patents act 1970, and Indian Competition Act 2002, a monopolist restricts other business units to enter into the market.

15.3. FEATURES OF MONOPOLY

The important features of a monopoly are:

1. Single business unit/Sole supplier
2. No close substitutes
3. A large number of buyers
4. Monopoly is a price maker
5. Barriers for entry of new business units
6. Restricted supply of products

1. **Single business unit/Sole supplier:** In a monopoly market the total supply of the product is controlled by a single person or a business unit as it deals with a particular product. The business unit represents the industry as a whole which has complete control over the supply of a product. No buyer can influence the price of the product.
2. **No close substitutes:** There will be no close substitutes and no competitors in the market for the product.
3. **A large number of Buyers:** There may be a large number of buyers to buy the products under monopoly.
4. **Monopoly is a price maker:** Under monopoly market structure the producer/seller is the price maker, not the price taker because of the fact that a monopolist has full control over the supply of the product. The monopolist can fix whatever price he chooses.
5. **Barriers for entry of new business units:** Under the monopoly market structure no other business unit can enter the market due to the presence of barriers. The barriers may be the requirement of huge investment, very long gestation period, government restrictions, exclusive ownership of raw materials, and so on.
6. **Restricted supply of products:** The monopoly can at a given point of time decides either the price of a product or the quantity for the product, not both.

15.4. BARRIERS OF MONOPOLY

Monopolies in different product categories derive market power from barriers to entry conditions that prevent or greatly hinder a likely competitor. The barriers to entry can be broadly classified into three types. These are economic, legal and deliberate barriers.

1. **Economic barriers:** The economic barriers include economies of scale, high capital requirements, cost advantages and technological superiority.
2. **Legal barriers:** Legal rights can provide an opportunity to monopolise the market of a product/service. Intellectual property rights, including patents and copyrights, give a monopolist exclusive control of the production and selling of certain products. Property rights may give a business unit exclusive control of the materials necessary to manufacture a product.
3. **Deliberate actions:** A business unit wanting to create a monopoly in a market may engage in various types of deliberate actions to exclude competitors or eliminate competition. Such actions include collusion, lobbying governmental authorities, and by force.

15.5. PRICING UNDER MONOPOLY

A monopoly has complete control over the supply of a product in the market and can fix the price of a product at will. Under monopoly, there is no distinction between a business unit and an industry, because the entire industry consists of a single business unit. Therefore, the demand curve of the business unit constitutes the demand curve of the entire industry. The demand curve of the monopoly equates with average revenue (AR) curve and slopes downward which implies that if the high prices are set by the monopolist, the demand will fall.

Under monopoly, the AR curve and marginal revenue (MR) curve are different from each other. However, both of them slope downward. The MR is always less than AR because of the law of demand. As shown in Table 15.1, AR is equal to price and MR is less than AR (MR < AR).

Table 15.1. AR and MR under monopoly

No. of units sold (Q)	Price (P)	Total Revenue (TR = P*Q)	Average Revenue (AR = TR / Q)	Marginal Revenue (MR)
1	30	30	30	30
2	27	54	27	24
3	24	72	24	18
4	21	84	21	12
5	18	90	18	6
6	15	90	15	0
7	12	84	12	–6

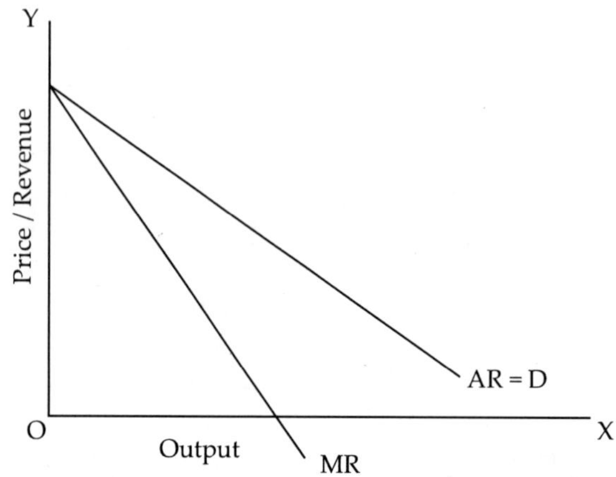

Figure 15.1. AR and MR curves under monopoly

15.6. PRICE-OUTPUT DETERMINATION IN THE SHORT RUN

In the short run, a monopolist acts like any other business unit. A monopolist will maximise profits by producing the quantity of output that equates marginal cost (MC) and marginal revenue (MR). This depends upon the relation between price (P) and average total cost (ATC). A monopolist does not necessarily make a profit. He may earn a super profit or normal profit or even produce at a loss in the short run.

15.6.1. Monopoly Equilibrium

Under monopoly, only one business unit constitutes the whole industry. As such, the industry equilibrium and the business units equilibrium will be the same. The main goal of a monopolist is to maximise profit, the equilibrium is attained at the point where, MR = MC (the point at which profit is maximised). The monopolist will continue to produce an additional quantity of output until MR is equal to MC.

There are two basic conditions for the equilibrium of the monopoly business unit:

1. MC = MR
2. MC curve cuts the MR curve from below

15.6.2. Equilibrium with Maximising Profits and Minimising Losses

In the short run, a monopolist may make a profit or incur a loss. The reasons for incurring loss during the short run may be many. The time available for the monopolist to make adjustments for the change in demand and cost conditions may not be sufficient. The monopolist may reduce the price of the product substantially to prevent potential rivals to enter the business. In such cases, the objective is to prevent competition and make profits in the long run. But in the short run, the business unit may need to experience losses. Figure 15.2 shows the short-run equilibrium output at which the monopolist maximises profit. The intersection of the MC curve and MR curve at point E represents the equilibrium point. The equilibrium output is OQ at OP price. The PRST is the profit zone where R is the revenue at OP price for OQ quantity. S is the average cost per unit. Since the average cost per unit is lower than the revenue generated per unit, the business unit earns profit to the tune of PRST.

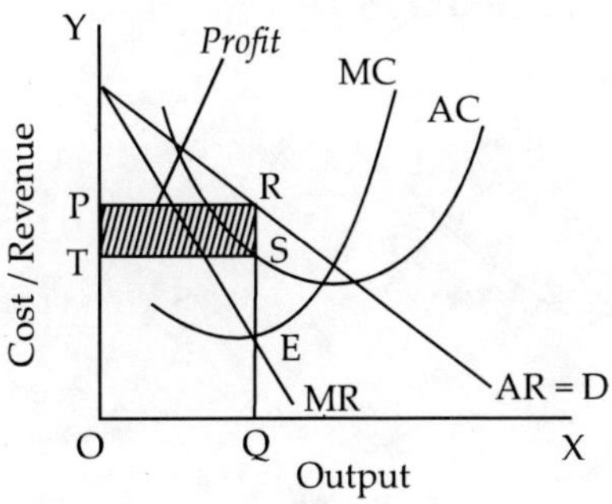

Figure 15.2. Maximising profit

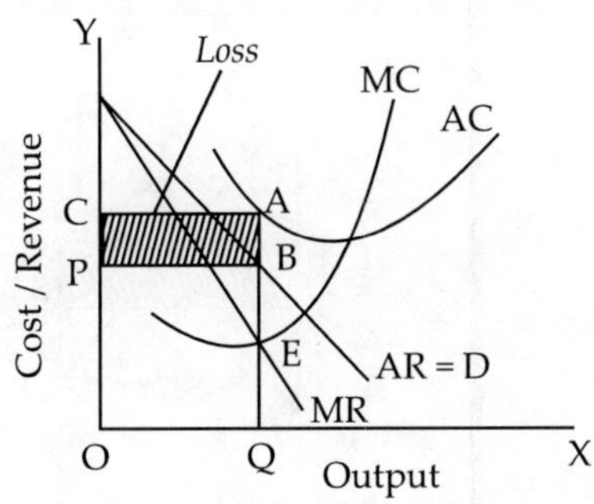

Figure 15.3. Minimising loss

As mentioned already there is a possibility of making a loss by the monopolist during a short period. The cost and revenue curves of the business unit when it is making a loss during a short period are shown in Figure 15.3. The OQ is the quantity produced at the equilibrium point E. The revenue generated at the OP price for OQ quantity is indicated by point B. The average cost per unit indicated by A is more than the revenue generated per unit. Therefore, the business unit incurs losses to the tune of CAPB.

Under monopoly conditions, the business unit is a price maker rather than a price taker. It doesn't mean that he can sell any quantity in the market by setting the price at any level. At a given point of time, a monopolist can either fix the price or fix the quantity to be sold. But both the decisions cannot be done simultaneously. If the monopolist chooses to fix the price then the business unit has to take the demand whatever is generated in the market to that price. On the other hand, if the monopolist chooses to sell a certain quantity of the product then he has to adjust the price according to the demand pattern in the market.

15.7. PRICE-OUTPUT DETERMINATION IN THE LONG RUN

One of the characteristics of a monopoly is barriers for the new business units into the industry. The barriers may be an exclusive control over raw materials needed for the production of products or exclusive right to produce a certain product (patent) or to sell in a certain market. The monopolistic business unit makes long-run adjustments in the scale of the plant as per the market conditions. In case, the demand for the product is limited, the monopolist can afford to produce output at sub-optimum scale. If the market size is large and permits to expand output, then the monopolist would build an optimum scale of plant and would produce the products at minimum cost per unit. However, the monopolist would not stay in the business, if he makes losses for long. The long-run equilibrium of a monopolistic business unit is shown in Figure 15.4.

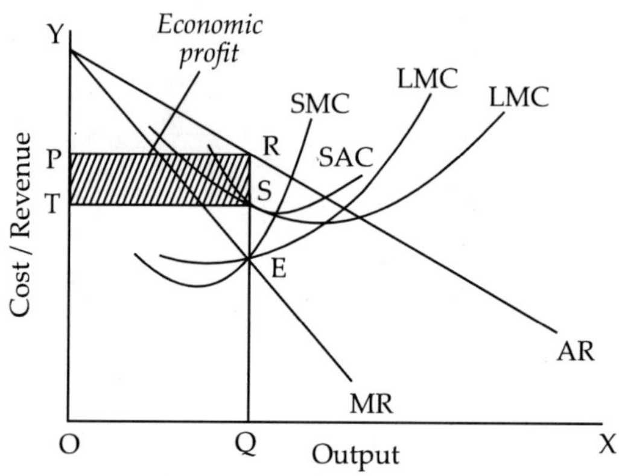

Figure 15.4. Long-run equilibrium

In the long run, all the factors of production including the size of the plant are variable. A monopoly business unit will maximise profit at that level of output for which long-run marginal cost (LMC) is equal to the marginal revenue (MR) and the LMC curve intersects the MR curve from below. The business unit is in equilibrium at point E where LMC = MR and LMC cuts the MR curve from below. QR is the equilibrium price and OQ is the equilibrium output.

At OQ level of output, the long-run average cost per unit (LAC) is QS, whereas the price per unit of the product is OP. PRST represents supernormal profit. It may be noted that at the equilibrium output, OQ, the plant is not being fully utilised. The long-run average cost (LAC) is not minimum at this level of output, OQ. The business unit can expand production to the optimum scale of the plant only when the demand for the product increases.

15.8. SUMMARY

- A monopoly is a unique situation where a particular individual or business unit is the only supplier of that product.
- The basic causes of the monopolistic market are control over raw materials, efficiency in production, public interest, economies of scale, and legal restrictions.
- The important features of a monopoly are single business unit/sole supplier, no close substitutes, a large number of buyers, monopoly is a price maker, barriers for entry of new business units, and restricted supply of products.
- The barriers to entry can be classified as economic, legal and deliberate barriers.
- A monopoly has complete control over the supply of a product in the market and can fix the price of a product at will.
- The demand curve of the monopoly equates with average revenue (AR) curve and slopes downwards which implies that if the high prices are set by the monopolist, the demand will fall.
- In the short run, a monopolist will maximise profits by producing the quantity of output that equates marginal cost (MC) and marginal revenue (MR).
- The two basic conditions for the equilibrium of the monopoly business unit are MC = MR, and MC curve cuts the MR curve from below.
- In the short run, at a given point of time, a monopolist can either fix the price or fix the quantity to be sold.
- In the long run, the monopolistic business unit makes long-run adjustments in the scale of the plant as per the market conditions.
- A monopoly business unit will maximise profit at that level of output for which long-run marginal cost (LMC) is equal to marginal revenue (MR) and the LMC curve intersects the MR curve from below.

SHORT ANSWER QUESTIONS

1. Define a monopoly.
2. What are the legal restrictions under monopoly?
3. Write a short note on monopoly equilibrium.
4. What are the barriers of monopoly?

ESSAY ANSWER QUESTIONS

1. What is a monopoly? Discuss the causes of monopoly.
2. Explain the key features of a monopolistic competitive market.
3. Explain the significance of AR and MR curves under monopoly.

4. Describe the price-output determination in a monopolistic market structure.
5. Explain the price-output determination under monopoly.

FILL IN THE BLANKS

1. Monopoly is the highly __________ market structure.
2. The monopoly emerged out of economies of the scale factor is called a __________.
3. __________ allows the holder to exercise his market power.
4. __________ can provide an opportunity to monopolise the market of a product/service.
5. In the long run, all the factors of production including the size of the plant are __________.
6. Under monopoly, the marginal revenue is greater than average revenue. (T/F)
7. In monopoly conditions, the business unit is a price maker. (T/F)
8. In the long run, the LMC curve cuts the MR curve from below. (T/F)

Answers

1. Imperfect
2. Natural monopoly
3. Intellectual property
4. Legal rights
5. Variable
6. False
7. True
8. True

MULTIPLE-CHOICE QUESTIONS

1. The ability to increase the price of a product above the marginal cost without losing the customers is:
   (A) Market power (B) Market research
   (C) Market efficiency (D) Market situation
2. Which of the following is not a cause of monopoly?
   (A) Legal restrictions (B) Economies of scale
   (C) No close substitutes (D) Control over raw materials
3. Which of the following is not a barrier of monopoly?
   (A) Economic barriers (B) Legal barriers
   (C) Deliberate actions (D) Natural barriers
4. The basic condition for the equilibrium of the monopoly business unit is:
   (A) MC = MR (B) MC > MR
   (C) MC < MR (D) AR = MR
5. Under monopoly conditions, the business unit is a price:
   (A) Taker (B) Maker
   (C) Controller (D) Checker

Answers

1. A 2. C 3. D 4. A 5. B

REFERENCES

1. Dean, Joel. (1951). *Managerial Economics.* New York: Prentice-Hall, Inc.
2. Dwivedi, D.N. (2015). *Managerial Economics* (8th Edition). New Delhi, India: Vikas Publishing House Pvt. Ltd.
3. Ferguson, C.E. (1972). *Macroeconomic Theory*. (Richard D. Irwin, Illinois, 1972).
4. Herberger, A.C. (1954). *Monopoly and Resource Allocation.* American Express Review.
5. Koutsoyiannis, A. (1975). *Modern Microeconomics.* London: The Macmillan Press Ltd.
6. Lerner, A.P. (1934). The concept of monopoly and measurement of monopoly power. *The Review of Economic Studies,* 1(3), 157-175.
7. Marshall, A. (1920). *The Principles of Economics* (8th Edition). London: Macmillan.
8. Robinson, J. (1934). The economics of imperfect competition. *Journal of the Royal Statistical Society,* 97(4), pp. 671-674.
9. Varshney, R.L. & Maheswari, K.L. (2014). *Managerial Economics.* New Delhi, India: Sultan Chand & Sons.

Chapter

16 Monopolistic Competition

LEARNING OBJECTIVES

After studying this chapter, you should be able to understand:

- concept of monopolistic competition;
- features of perfect competition;
- price-output determination in short run; and
- price-output determination in the long run.

16.1. INTRODUCTION

Monopolistic competition refers to a market structure in which a large number of sellers sell differentiated products that are close substitutes of each other. Monopolistic competition is a mixture of both perfect competition and monopoly. Edward E. Chamberlin (1933) developed the theory of monopolistic competition, which presents a more realistic picture of the actual market structure and the nature of competition. It exists when there are many business units and each one produces such products that are close substitutes of each other or if many sellers produce differentiated products. For example, a wide range of consumer goods like soap, toothpaste, computer, television, cigarette, etc., are subject to a large degree of product differentiation as a means of attracting customers.

Definitions of monopolistic competition

Author	Definition
Joe S. Bain (1966)	Monopolistic competition is a market structure found in the industry where there is a large number of small sellers, selling differentiated but close substitute products.
Lim Chong-Yah (1967)	Monopolistic competition is a market situation where there are many producers but each one offers a slightly different product.
Leftwitch (1969)	Monopolistic competition is a market situation in which there are many sellers of a particular product, but the product of each seller is in some way different in the minds of consumers from the product of every other seller.

16.2. FEATURES OF MONOPOLISTIC COMPETITION

The monopolistic competition combines the elements of both perfect competition and monopoly. The main features of monopolistic competition are:

1. Large number of business units/sellers
2. Large number of buyers
3. Product differentiation
4. Freedom of entry and exit
5. Elastic demand

1. **Large number of business units/sellers:** There are a large number of business units or sellers relatively small in size, operate under monopolistic competition. A relatively small fraction of the total market is shared by each business unit or seller. The industry consists of many sellers who are independent and follow independent pricing policy. However, no single seller can influence the market demand or price significantly.
2. **Large number of buyers:** In a monopolistic competitive market, a large number of buyers make relatively small size orders. The buyers have their brand preferences and tastes. No single buyer can influence the overall market demand or price of the product.
3. **Product differentiation:** The distinctive feature of a monopolistic competitive market structure is product differentiation. The producers/sellers try to differentiate the marketing offer to take advantage of a monopoly to the extent possible. They try to differentiate products through unique features (colour, shape, size, brand, composition, quality, trademark, packaging, durability, etc.), benefits, advertising, customer relations, after-sales service, innovation, and so on. A single producer/ seller may also introduce a variety of products differentiating each other in the same product category as close substitutes.
4. **Freedom of entry and exit:** Under monopolistic competition, the business units are relatively free to enter the market and exit from the market. There will not be any restrictions for entering into the business or to leave the business at the will of the producers.
5. **Elastic demand:** Due to a differentiated product, each business unit possesses partial monopoly power, and therefore, the demand is elastic. There will be marginal tolerance for the price changes among loyal consumers. Once the change in price crosses the tolerance limit, the loyal customers consider switching over to other brands. Therefore, the price elasticity of demand exists in the monopolistic competitive structure.

16.3. PRICE - OUTPUT DETERMINATION

Under monopolistic competition, every business unit tries to maximise profit by way of product differentiation and by developing a monopoly-like situation in the market. Product innovation and market promotion are the key strategies to ensure a loyal consumer base and to increase market turnover. The price-output relations depend upon the demand and cost conditions of the product. Each business unit is free to determine the price and output of a product. As the ultimate goal is profit maximisation, the business unit continues to increase the quantity of production until the point at which marginal revenue equals marginal cost (MR = MC).

16.4. SHORT-RUN EQUILIBRIUM OF A BUSINESS UNIT

As the business units produce differentiated products in a monopolistic competitive market, each business unit does not have a perfectly elastic demand for its products. In such a market, each business unit is free to determine the price of its products. Therefore, the demand curve is sloping downwards (AR = D). The elasticity of demand increases as and when the differentiation between the products decreases. Two possible conditions may emerge in the short run for a business unit under monopolistic competition. The business unit may earn supernormal profits due to higher favourable market conditions. It may incur losses when market conditions are not favourable to the business unit and the time available to adapt to the situation is not sufficient.

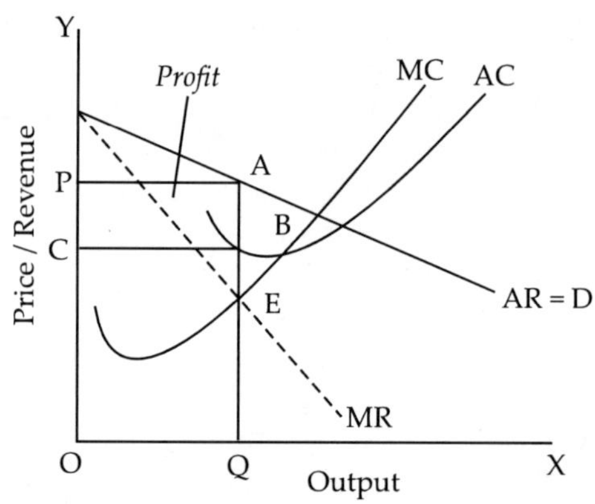

Figure 16.1. Short-run equilibrium of a business unit–supernormal profit

Figure 16.1 represents the situation in which the business unit makes a supernormal profit in the short run. It shows the demand curve is flat and sloping downwards. The short-run average cost curve is U-shaped. The price-output determination is done to achieve short-run equilibrium of an individual business unit. Two conditions emerge under short-run equilibrium:

1. MC = MR
2. The MC curve cuts the MR curve from below.

Figure 16.1 shows the profit maximisation, where the MC curve cuts the MR curve at point E (MC = MR). Thus, the point is called the equilibrium point. At this point, the equilibrium price is OP and equilibrium output is OQ. Here, per unit cost is BQ, per unit supernormal profit (price-cost) is BA or CP, and total supernormal profit is PCBA.

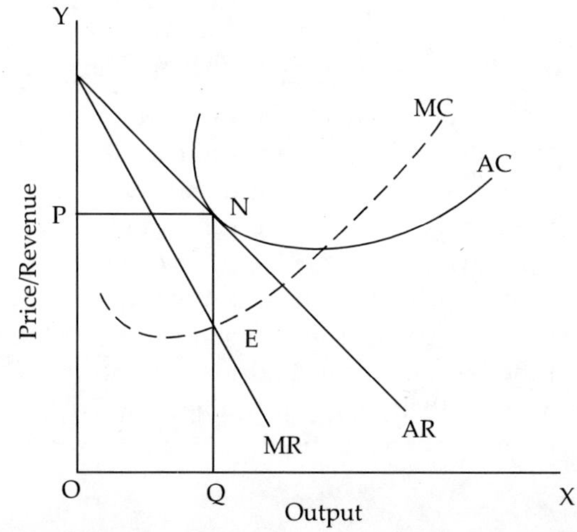

Figure 16.2. Short-run equilibrium of a business unit–normal profit

If the price of the product is equal to AC, the business unit will earn a normal profit. Figure 16.2 shows that MC is equal to MR at point E. This is the equilibrium point where the equilibrium output is OQ and price is OP. At this point, AC is NP and AR is also NP, i.e., AC=AR. Thus, the business unit will earn only normal profits.

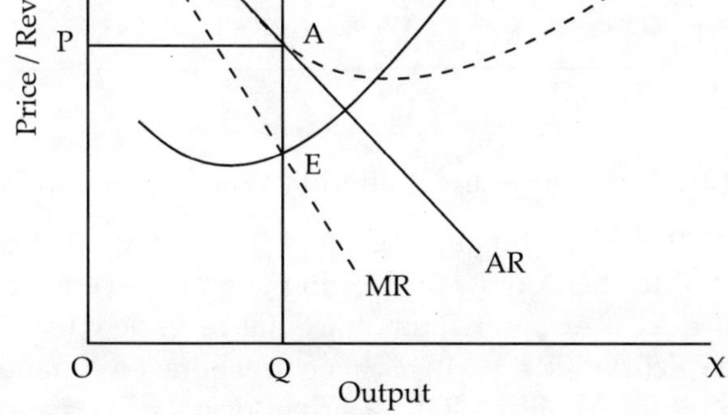

Figure 16.3. Short-run equilibrium of a business unit – losses

Figure 16.3 depicts a business unit incur losses in the short run. In such conditions, the per unit cost BQ is higher than the price AQ of the business unit. Thus, BQ > AQ (or OP) and therefore, the loss per unit is BQ – AQ = AB. The total loss incurred is BAPC.

16.5. LONG-RUN EQUILIBRIUM OF A BUSINESS UNIT

In the long run, competitive conditions change due to market dynamics. If the business units are making supernormal profits in the short run, many new business units enter the market to make higher profits. As these business units enter, the profits per business unit decrease as the total demand gets shared between a larger number of business units. Hence, competition becomes intensive and business units will compete with each other for acquiring market share. The demand is shared and the situation will continue until the business units end up with normal profits. At this point, business units reach their long-run equilibrium. To get equilibrium in the long run, the business unit has to fulfil two conditions:

1. MR = MC
2. AR = AC

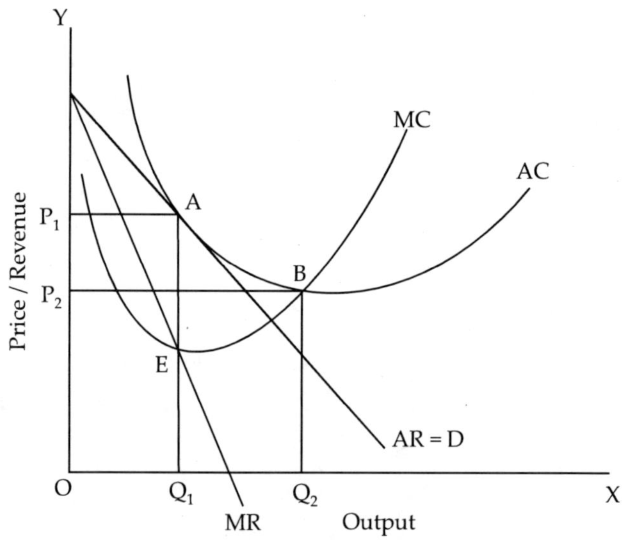

Figure 16.4. Long-run Equilibrium of a business unit

From Figure 16.4 it can be observed that the average cost curve (AC) will be tangential to the downward sloping average revenue curve (AR) at point A (AR = AC). At point E the marginal revenue curve is equal to the marginal cost curve (MR = MC). This corresponds to quantity Q_1 and price P_1. At equilibrium (MR = MC), all supernormal profits are zero since the AR = AC. Therefore, all business units earn zero supernormal profits or earn only normal profits. The AC curve is tangential to the AR curve at higher than its minimum point, B. OQ is the equilibrium output and OP is the equilibrium price.

If the business units are incurring losses in the short run, some adjustments will take place in market conditions. The business units that cannot bear losses in the short run may opt for exit from the business. With the exit of some business units, the demand for the products of remaining business units will increase and the business units may earn normal profits. Therefore, the market dynamics ensure normal profits to the business units in the long run under monopolistic competitive conditions.

16.6. SUMMARY

- Monopolistic competition refers to a market structure in which a large number of sellers sell different products that are close substitutes of each other.
- The main features of monopolistic competition are a large number of business units/sellers, a large number of buyers, product differentiation, freedom of entry and exit, and elastic demand.
- In monopolistic competition, every business unit tries to maximise profit by way of product differentiation and by developing a monopoly-like situation in the market.
- The price-output relations depend upon the demand and cost conditions of the product.
- Each business unit is free to determine the price and output of a product.
- Under short-run equilibrium, two conditions emerge, i.e., MC = MR, and the MC curve cuts the MR curve from below.
- To get equilibrium in the long run, the business unit has to fulfil two conditions, viz., MR = MC and AR = AC.
- If the business units are incurring losses in the short run, some adjustments will take place in market conditions.

SHORT ANSWER QUESTIONS

1. What is monopolistic competition?
2. Write a short note on the short-run equilibrium of a business unit.

ESSAY ANSWER QUESTIONS

1. What are the features of a monopolistic competitive market?
2. Explain how price-output can be determined in the short run.
3. Discuss the long-run equilibrium under monopolistic competition.

FILL IN THE BLANKS

1. Monopolistic competition is a mixture of both perfect competition and __________.
2. In monopolistic competition, every business unit tries to maximise profit by way of __________.
3. The price-output relations are dependent upon the demand and __________ conditions of the product.
4. The elasticity of demand increases as and when the differentiation between the products __________.
5. The business unit may earn __________ profits due to higher favourable market conditions.
6. The short-run average cost curve is __________.
7. In short run, the demand curve is flat and slopes __________.
8. In monopolistic competition, a single buyer can influence the overall market demand or price of the product. (T/F)
9. Under monopolistic competition, no single seller can influence the market demand or price significantly. (T/F)

Answers

1. Monopoly
2. Product differentiation
3. Cost
4. Decreases
5. Supernormal
6. U-shaped
7. Downward
8. False
9. True

MULTIPLE-CHOICE QUESTIONS

1. A market structure in which a large number of sellers sell different products that are close substitutes of each other is called:
   (A) Monopoly (B) Monopolistic competition
   (C) Perfect competition (D) Oligopoly
2. Which one of the following is a feature of monopolistic competition?
   (A) Large number of business units
   (B) Inelastic demand
   (C) Few numbers of sellers
   (D) Few numbers of buyers
3. In monopolistic competition, the demand for a product is:
   (A) Unitary (B) Inelastic
   (C) Elastic (D) Zero
4. Under short-run equilibrium, the MC curve cuts the MR curve from:
   (A) Above (B) Below
   (C) Upwards (D) Beyond
5. To get equilibrium in the long run, the business unit has to fulfil two conditions:
   (A) MR = MC and AR = AC (B) MR > MC and AR = AC
   (C) MR < MC and AR = AC (D) MR = MC and AR > AC

6. In the long run monopolistic competitive conditions the business units incur:
   (A) Supernormal profits (B) Abnormal profits
   (C) Usual profits (D) Normal profits

Answers

1. B 2. A 3. C 4. B 5. A
6. D

REFERENCES

1. Bain, J.S. (1967). Chamberlin's impact on microeconomic theory. *Monopolistic Competition Theory: Studies in Impact; Essays in Honor of Edward H. Chamberlin*, New York: John Wiley, 147-176.
2. Chamberlin, E.E. (1933). *Theory of Monopolistic Competition.* Cambridge, Mass, Harvard University.
3. Chamberlin, E.H. (1949). *Theory of Monopolistic Competition: A Re-orientation of the Theory of Value.* Oxford University Press, London.
4. Chong-Yah, L. (1967). *Economic Development of Modern Malaya.* Oxford University Press.
5. Cohen, K.J. & Cyert, R.M. (1976). *Theory of the Firm.* New Delhi: Prentice-Hall of India.
6. Douglas, Evan, J. (1970). *Managerial Economics: Theory, Practice and Problems.* N.J: Prentice Hall, Inc.
7. Dwivedi, D.N. (2015). *Managerial Economics* (8th Edition). New Delhi, India: Vikas Publishing House Pvt. Ltd.
8. Leftwich, R.H. (1969). *An Introduction to Economic Thinking.* Holt, Rinehart and Winston.
9. Robinson, J. (1953). Imperfect competition revisited. *The Economic Journal*, 63(251), 579-593.
10. Samuelson, P.A. (1967). The monopolistic competition revolution. In Robert E. Kuenne (Eds.) *Monopolistic Competition Theory: Studies in Impact, Essays in Honor of Edward H. Chamberlin.* New York: John Wiley & Sons.
11. Telser, L.G. (1968). Monopolistic competition: Any impact yet?. *Journal of Political Economy*, 76(2), 312-315.

Chapter

17 Oligopoly

LEARNING OBJECTIVES

After studying this chapter, you should be able to understand:

- concept and sources of oligopoly;
- types of oligopoly market;
- features of oligopoly market; and
- different oligopoly markets.

17.1. CONCEPT OF OLIGOPOLY

The term 'oligopoly' derives from two Greek words, 'oligo' which means 'a few' and 'polan' means 'seller'. Thus, it is referred to as a market of a few sellers. Oligopoly is the form of imperfectly competitive market structure in which there are a few business units/sellers, producing/selling either homogeneous products or products which are a close but not perfect substitutes of each other. If the business units are selling identical products it is referred to as pure or homogeneous oligopoly. For example, business units producing cement, chemicals, steel, gas, sugar, etc., fall under homogeneous oligopoly. When the business units sell differentiated or heterogeneous products, it is known as a differentiated oligopoly. For example, the business units of automobiles, computers, soft drinks, refrigerators, TV sets, tobacco, etc., fall under differentiated oligopoly.

Oligopoly is a situation where a few large business units compete against each other and there is an element of interdependence in the decision making of these business units. Any pricing decision taken by one business unit will affect the trade of the competitors. Each business unit in oligopoly has to take into account the price being charged by the other units. If they follow live-and-let-live policy without getting into price wars, all the business units will make reasonable profits provided that the market conditions are positive. Since the number of business units is small, there is every possibility that they enter an agreement informally to follow a price policy that maximises their benefits.

For instance, the telecommunication sector in India with Airtel, Jio, Idea, BSNL, and a few other small players, is having a large number of buyers. The prices of mobile services and broadband services used to be high before the entry of Jio. The Jio made a sensational entry with a price substantially lower than the then prevalent prices of the competitors. The competing companies are a way forced to bring down the prices to match closely if not exactly the price of Jio to protect their market position. Therefore, under oligopoly situation, one seller can influence the business of other sellers either positively or negatively. Cut-throat competition or price wars lead to a situation where all the business units may suffer and end up with losses. The business units generally work for a common agreement to avoid such unhealthy competitive situations.

17.2. SOURCES OF OLIGOPOLY

The prime sources of oligopoly market are:

1. Economies of scale
2. Free but limited entry
3. Legal restriction
4. Established business units
5. Control over supply
6. Government policies
7. Product differentiation
8. Pricing

1. **Economies of scale:** In an oligopoly, the entire market is shared by a few business units. Thus, large-scale production is a possibility which ensures economies of scale.
2. **Free but limited entry:** Huge capital investments and specialised inputs are required to enter an oligopolistic market, which stands as a barrier to entry for other business organisations. Though the entry to the industry is free, very few will enter due to the above reasons.
3. **Legal restriction:** A few business units may own a patent for the exclusive right to commercialise or produce a product or use a particular production process restricting new entrants in the market.
4. **Established business units:** Existing business units may have loyal customers based on product quality and service. Therefore, new business units may find it difficult to establish themselves in the market and face competition from the existing business units.
5. **Control over supply:** A few business units may own or control the entire supply of required raw materials in the production of a product. New entrants may face difficulty in finding alternative materials to produce the product.
6. **Government policies:** The government may give the franchise to only a few business units to operate in the market.
7. **Product differentiation:** An existing business unit that has already convinced its customers that their product is significantly better than new entrants will not have an advantage over others.

8. **Pricing:** By way of fixing low prices to the products, the existing business units may discourage entry of new business units into the market. The market may not be attractive to the new entrants.

17.3. TYPES OF OLIGOPOLY

1. **Pure oligopoly or perfect oligopoly:** Pure oligopoly occurs when the product is homogeneous. This type of oligopoly tends to process raw materials or produce intermediate goods that are used as inputs by other industries. For example, aluminium, petroleum, and steel industries.
2. **Differentiated or imperfect oligopoly:** Differentiated oligopoly occurs when products sold are based on product differentiation. For example, talcum powder.
3. **Partial or full oligopoly:** Oligopoly is partial when the industry is dominated by one large business unit which is considered or looked upon as the leader of the group. The dominating business unit will be the price leader. In a full oligopoly, the market will be conspicuous by the absence of price leadership.
4. **Open and closed oligopoly:** In an open oligopoly market, new business units can enter the market and compete with the existing business units. But, in a closed oligopoly entry is restricted.
5. **Collusive and competitive oligopoly:** When a few business units of the oligopoly market come to a common understanding or act in collusion with each other either in fixing price or output or both, it is a collusive oligopoly. When there is an absence of such an understanding among the business units and they compete with each other, it is called a competitive oligopoly.
6. **Syndicated and organised oligopoly:** Syndicated oligopoly refers to that situation where the business unit sells its products through a centralised syndicate. Organised oligopoly refers to the situation where the business units organise themselves into a central association for fixing prices, output, quotas, etc.

17.4. FEATURES OF OLIGOPOLY MARKET

The main features of an oligopoly market structure are:

1. Few sellers/business units
2. Difficult for entry
3. Indeterminate demand curve
4. Interdependence of business units
5. Advertising and selling costs

6. Complex market structure
7. Price rigidity

1. **Few sellers/business units:** There are relatively a small number of sellers under oligopoly market structure selling identical or different products. Each seller controls a large part of the demand and the policies of every seller influence the price and output of the industry as a whole. Any decision taken by one business unit influences the actions of other business units in the industry.
2. **Difficult for entry:** Under oligopoly, the entry is not easy for new entrants. The new business units cannot enter the market as the existing business units have a complete hold over the market conditions and the business units are also reluctant to leave because of the huge investment made by them. Therefore, entry into an oligopoly market is risky and the new entrants may need to wait for long to make profits.
3. **Indeterminate demand curve:** Under oligopoly market structure, the shape of the demand curve is broken and is indeterminate because the business units cannot assume that the rival business units will not make a change in their price policy in response to change in price affected by it. Thus, the fact that the reaction pattern of the rival business units is indeterminate leaves the demand curve in an indeterminate position.
4. **Interdependence of business units:** As there are only a few business units, any step taken by one business unit to increase sales by reducing price or change product design or increase advertisement expenditure will affect the sales of other business units in the market. So, the decisions of all the business units in the industry are interdependent.
5. **Advertising and selling costs:** In an oligopoly, each business unit pursues an aggressive and defensive marketing strategy to control the market. Advertising plays a greater role in the oligopoly market when compared to other market systems. The huge expenditure on advertising and sales promotion techniques is needed both to retain the present market share and to increase it.
6. **Complex market structure:** The market structure of oligopoly is quite complex. As there is a possibility of rival business units to end rivalry by working out some policy of collusion and the collusive oligopoly manifests itself in the form of a combination of rival business units to fix the same price and also share in output as in case of cartels. Besides it, non-collusive oligopoly is also found in practice which presents a complex market structure.

7. **Price rigidity:** In the oligopoly market, the prices remain rigid. Price rigidity and price war are the common features of an oligopoly market structure. Each business unit retaliates and acts according to the actions of the other business units and a tug of war starts between them which is better known as 'price war' which further paves the way to price rigidity. If one business unit reduced the price it is with the intention of attracting the customers of other business units in the industry. To retain their consumers, they will also reduce the price. Thus, the pricing decision of one business unit results in a loss to all the business units in the industry.

17.5. OLIGOPOLY MODELS

In the case of oligopoly, there is no general theory of oligopoly as it is difficult to attribute a single type of interaction among the business units. Thus, several models of various degrees of realism have evolved over a period of time with different behavioural assumptions regarding the interactions among business units. Some of these models have become standard and are explained below:

1. The Cournot model
2. Bertrand's model
3. Edgeworth model
4. Chamberlin's oligopoly model
5. Kinked demand curve model
6. Collusion model - The Cartel
7. Price leadership model

17.5.1. The Cournot Model

A formal model was first introduced by a French economist Augustin Cournot in 1838. This model highlights the interdependence of the existing business units in an industry as duopoly operates. The general assumption is that the production by the two business units would be equal to the production by the entire industry. The key feature of the model is that each business unit tries to maximise its profit by assuming that other business units hold its output constant at the existing level.

The Cournot model was about two business units selling spring mineral water in the same market. This model relates to the business units producing homogeneous products. The model assumed that:

- the two business units were operating mineral springs without incurring any cost of production;
- each business unit decides its level of output assuming that the other business unit would not change its output accordingly;
- business units face a demand curve with a constant negative slope; and

- the conjectural variation between the two business units in the industry was zero.

In other words, the business units decide the amount of output which is most profitable to produce in the light of rival's output and assumes that it will remain constant.

Equilibrium determination

The price-output determination in the Cournot model can be described with the following illustration. The demand curve confronting the two producers of the mineral water is the straight line DD as shown in Figure 17.1. The maximum daily output of each mineral spring is OQ and QD. Thus, the total output of both the springs is OD which is offered for sale in the market, where the price will be zero. If there was a perfect competition, the long-run equilibrium price would have been zero and the actual output produced is equal to OD. This is because the cost of production is assumed to be zero, the price must also be zero to provide a zero profit long-run equilibrium under perfect competition.

If the first business unit started as a sole producer of the mineral water in the market, he will produce daily OQ output at a price of OP. Since the costs are zero, the whole of total revenue OQAP will represent profits. If the second business unit enters the market at this stage, it finds that the first business unit is producing OQ quantity of output. Based on the Cournot's assumption, the second business unit believes that the first business unit will continue producing OQ (equal to half of OD) quantity of output, regardless the level of he decides to produce.

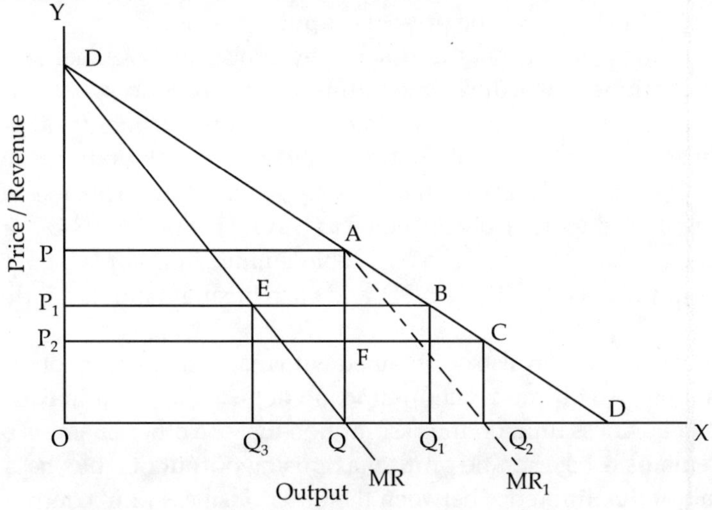

Figure 17.1. Cournot model: Price output determination

Given this belief, the best that the second business unit can do is to regard segment AD as the demand curve confronting him. With his demand curve AD and corresponding marginal revenue curve MR2, the second business unit will produce QQ_2 (equal to half of QD) quantity of output. Thus, the total output will be $OQ + QQ_2 = OQ_2$, and as a result, the price will fall to OP_2 or CQ_2 per unit. The total profits made by the two business units will be OQ_2CP_2 which are less than OQAP. Out of total profits OQ_2CP_2, profits of the first business unit will be $OQFP_2$ and profits of second business unit will be QQ_2CF. Thus, entry into the market by the second business unit and producing output OQ_2, the first business unit's profits have been reduced. The first business unit will review the situation and assume that the second business unit will continue to produce output OQ_2. Therefore, the first business unit can best do is to produce 1/2 ($OD - OQ_2$) by reducing the output.

Accordingly, the second business unit will increase its output. With this move, the first business unit will find its profits reduced. This process of adjustment and readjustment will continue and the first business unit being forced gradually to reduce its output and the second business unit being able to increase its output gradually until the total output OQ_1 is produced (i.e., 2/3 OD) and each is producing the same amount of output equal to 1/3 OD. Thus, the first business unit produces OQ_3 quantity of output and the second business unit produces Q_3Q_1 quantity of output and $OQ_3 = Q_3Q_1$. Throughout this process of adjustment and readjustment, each business unit assumes that the other will keep its output constant at the present level and then always finds its maximum profits by producing output equal to 1/2, (OD – the present output of the other).

As seen, the first business unit starts by producing OQ (equal to 1/2 OD) and continuously reduces the output until it produces OQ_3, i.e., 1/3 OD (equal to 1/2 OQ_1). On the other hand, the second business unit begins by producing $1/4^{th}$ of OD and continuously increases the output until it produces Q_3Q_1, i.e., 1/3 OD (equal to 1/2 OQ_1). Thus, the two business units together will produce total output equal to 1/3 OD + 1/3 OD = 2/3 OD (equal to OQ_1). Thus, in Cournot's model, stable equilibrium is reached when total output produced is $2/3^{rd}$ of OD and each business unit is producing $1/3^{rd}$ of OD.

Cournot solution can also be obtained with reaction functions of the two business units. An output reaction function depicts the profit maximising output of a business unit, on the assumption that the other business unit's output remains constant. The profit maximising output of a business unit is one-half of the difference between the other business unit's output and the market demand for output at which price equals marginal cost. This is called the reaction function of a business unit. This output at which price equals marginal cost (MC) is the maximum output which can be produced because any output beyond this will cause the price to go below marginal cost (which is equal to AT under constant cost conditions) and will therefore not be worthwhile to produce.

Criticism

Cournot model of oligopoly is perhaps the first model which describes the behaviour of an individual business unit under conditions of monopoly and competition. Therefore, it has occupied an important place in economic theory as a reference model or as a starting point of explaining the behaviour of the individual business unit under the oligopolistic market structure. Although this model yields a stable equilibrium, it has been criticised. The model assumes that while deciding its output each business unit believes that its rival will hold output constant at the present level whatever output it might produce. This is a logical error in Cournot's model. Further, by assuming that oligopolist, will think that his rival will continue producing the current level of output. Cournot model ignores the mutual interdependence between the business units which is the chief characteristic of oligopoly, Thus, Cournot model provides a solution for oligopoly problem by removing from it its most important feature.

17.5.2. Bertrand's Model

Joseph Bertrand, a French mathematician, criticised Cournot's model and proposed a substitute model in 1883. According to Bertrand, there is no limit to the fall in price since each business unit can always lower the price by underbidding the other business unit. Therefore, increasing the supply of output until the price becomes equal to his unit cost of production. In Bertrand's model, business units first set the price of the product and then produce the output which is demanded at that price. Here, each business unit assumes that his rival will keep his price constant at the present level whatever price he might himself set. Thus, the business units adjust the price and not output.

Further, it is not necessary that the business units know the exact market demand of their products, or should have an identical view about the market demand. It is sufficient for each business unit to know that they can capture the whole market by undercutting his rival. The other assumptions of Bertrand's model are the same as those of Cournot's model though their implications may be different. Thus, in Bertrand's model the products produced and sold by the two business units are completely identical and in no way different. Its implications are that if a business unit underbids the other, it can conquer the whole market. Further, the two business units have identical costs and also work under constant marginal cost. Moreover, the productive capacity of the business units is unlimited, that is, there is no limit to their increase in the supply of output up to the maximum requirement of demand.

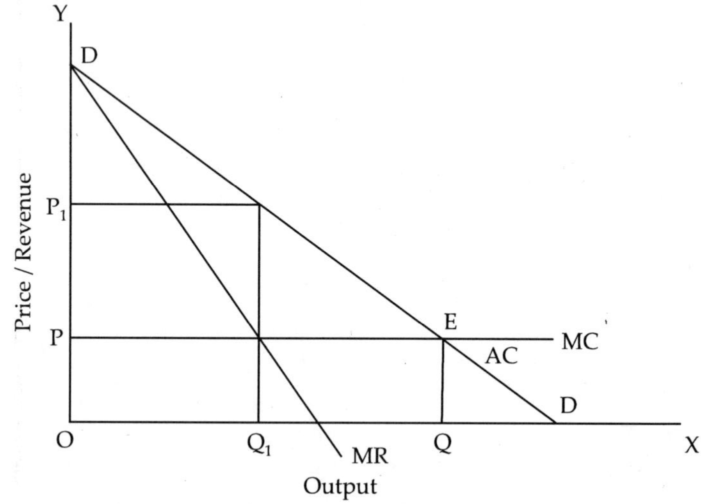

Figure 17.2. Bertrand's oligopoly model

Bertrand's model is illustrated in Figure 17.2. For instance, there are two business units, A and B. The market demand curve for the product produced by them is given by linear curve DD. Suppose that the business unit A starts the business first as a sole producer and sets the price at the monopoly level, which is the most profitable. This monopoly price is P_1 and produces OQ_1 quantity of output which is half of the perfectly competitive output assuming constant average and marginal cost equal to OP.

Suppose the business unit B also enters the market with the same product and assumes that A will continue to charge the same price P_1, irrespective of whatever price it might set. Further, business unit B finds that it can capture the whole market by slightly undercutting the price and thereby make a substantial amount of profits. Accordingly, B sets a price slightly lower than A's price P_1 and as a result gets the entire demand of the product. Hence, the sales of business unit A fall to zero. Now threatened with the loss, the business unit A will reconsider its price policy assuming that B will continue to charge the present price. Thus, there are two alternatives for the business unit A. First, the business unit may match the price-cut made by B and charge the same price. In this case, it will secure half the market, the other half going to the business unit B. Secondly, it may undercut B and set a slightly lower price than that of B. But again, the business unit B will be forced to undercuts.

This price war will continue until the price falls to the competitive levels, i.e., equal to average or marginal cost of production. At this stage, neither of them would like to cut the price further because total cost would exceed total revenue and incur losses, or raise the price as they would lose the entire market to another business unit under the assumption that the other will continue to charge the same lower price. Thus, when the price has fallen to the competitive level of the average cost of production, neither of the business units would have any incentive to lower the price further or to raise it and, therefore, the equilibrium has been achieved. In Bertrand's model, equilibrium is achieved when as a result of price war market price has fallen to the average cost of production and the combined equilibrium output of the two business units is equal to the competitive output.

17.5.3. Edgeworth Model

Francis Y. Edgeworth, a French economist introduced a model based on Bertrand's model in 1889. The model assumed that each business unit believes that its rival will continue to charge the same price as it charged. Under this assumption taking the example of Cournot's mineral springs with zero cost of production, the model found that no determinate equilibrium would be reached in oligopoly. The main difference between Edgeworth's model and Bertrand's model is that in the Bertrand model, the productive capacity of each business unit is practically unlimited so that it could satisfy any amount of demand. But in Edgeworth's model, the productive capacity of each business unit is limited so that neither of the business units can meet entire demand at the lower price ranges.

Each business unit accepts as much demand for the product at a price as it can meet. The products don't have to be perfectly homogeneous, the products can be close substitutes so that a slight price differential is sufficient for a good proportion of customers to switch from a higher priced product to a lower priced product.

Comments over the above classical models of oligopoly

The three classical models of oligopoly assume that the business units have zero conjectural variation, that is, while deciding the output or price policy, each business unit believes that its rival will hold output or price constant at the present level of output. Further, a business unit remains unshaken in this erroneous belief even when it constantly finds itself to be proved incorrect since the rival does react and changes output or price even after such action. This is a chief logical error in classical models. By assuming zero conjectural variation on the part of the oligopolists, classical models ignore the mutual interdependence which is the chief characteristic of an oligopoly. Thus, classical models provide a solution to the oligopoly problem.

17.5.4. Chamberlin's Oligopoly Model

Chamberlin E.H. (1933) criticised the behavioural assumption of Cournot, Bertrand and Edgeworth that the oligopolists behave independently in the sense that they ignore their mutual dependence and while deciding about their output or price assume that their rivals will keep their output or price constant at the present level. According to Chamberlin, oligopolists behave quite intelligently as they recognise their interdependence and learn from the experience when they find that their action causes the rivals to react and adjust their output level. This realisation of mutual dependence on the part of the oligopolists leads to the monopoly output being produced jointly and charging of the monopoly price. In this way, maximisation of joint profits and stable equilibrium is achieved by the oligopolists even though they act in a non-collusive manner. Given identical costs, they will also equally share these monopoly profits.

Profit-maximising equilibrium under oligopoly

The process of achieving stable equilibrium under oligopoly is illustrated in Figure 17.3. The model considers two producers, A and B, with zero cost of production and assumes that the market demand curve for the product is linear. MD represents the linear market demand curve for the homogeneous product of the business units. As in Cournot's model, suppose producer A is the first to start production. He will view the whole market demand curve MD facing him and corresponding to it MR_a is the marginal revenue curve. To maximise his profits, he will equate marginal revenue with marginal cost (which is here taken to be equal to zero). It can be observed that he will be in equilibrium by making MR = MC when he produces OQ output (i.e., half of OD) which is, in fact, the monopoly output and will fix price equal to OP.

Now, suppose producer B enters the market, assumes that producer A would continue to produce OQ output and views ED portion of the market demand curve as the relevant demand curve facing him and corresponding to it MR_a is the marginal revenue curve. With marginal cost being equal to zero, for maximum profits he will produce half of QD, that is, QL or at point L at which his marginal revenue curve MR intersects the Y-axis along which output is measured. With aggregate output OL (OL = OQ of A + QL of B), the price will fall to the level LK or OR with the result that profits earned by producer B will be equal to the area of rectangle QLKT, and due to the fall in price, the profit of producer A will decrease from OPEQ to ORTQ.

However, from this point onwards the producers learn from their experience that they are interdependent. With the realisation of mutual

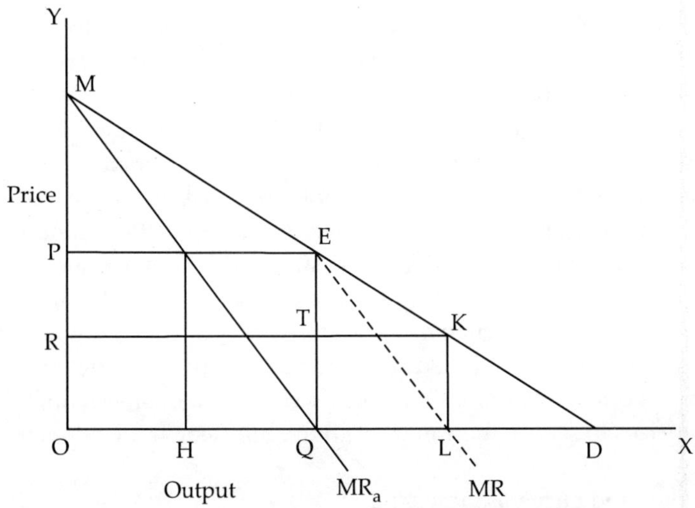

Figure 17.3. Profit-maximising equilibrium under oligopoly

dependence, producer A decides to produce output OH equal to output QL of producer B and half of the monopoly output OQ so that the aggregate output of both of them is the monopoly output (OQ = OH of A + QL of B). With OQ as the aggregate output level, the price will rise to QE or OP. Business unit B also realises that in view of interdependence it is in the best interest for both of them to produce half of the monopoly output and will maintain output at the QL or OH level which is half of the monopoly output. Thus, each producer producing half of the monopoly output will result in maximisation of joint profits though they do not enter into any formal collusion. In this way, Chamberlin explains that the business units behaving intelligently and realising their interdependence reach a stable equilibrium and together produce monopoly output and charge monopoly price each sharing profits equally.

17.5.5. Kinked Demand Curve Model

The kinked demand curve of oligopoly was developed by Paul M. Sweezy in 1939. The model focuses on the behaviour of oligopolistic business units, instead of emphasising the price-output determination. The model advocates that the behaviour of oligopolistic business units remains stable when the price and output are determined. This implies that an oligopolistic market is characterised by a certain degree of price rigidity or stability, especially when there is a change in prices in a downward direction. For example, if a business unit under oligopoly reduces the price of products, the competitor business units would also follow it and neutralise the expected gain from the price reduction. On the other hand, if the business unit increases the price, the competitors would also cut down their prices. In such a case, the organisation that has raised its prices would lose some part of its market share.

The kinked demand curve model explains the reason for price rigidity under oligopolistic market situations. Therefore, to understand the kinked demand curve model, it is important to note the reactions of rival business units on the price changes made by respective oligopolistic business units. There can be two possible reactions of rival business units when there are changes in the price of a particular business unit. The rival business units would either follow price cuts, but not price hikes or they may not follow changes in prices at all. A kinked demand curve represents the behaviour pattern of oligopolistic business units in which rival business units lower down the prices to secure their market share, but restrict an increase in the prices.

A kinked demand curve assumes that:

- if one business unit reduces the prices, then other business units would also cut their prices,
- if one business unit increases the prices, then other business units would not follow an increase in prices, and
- there is always a prevailing price.

A kinked demand curve model is explained with the help of Figure 17.4.

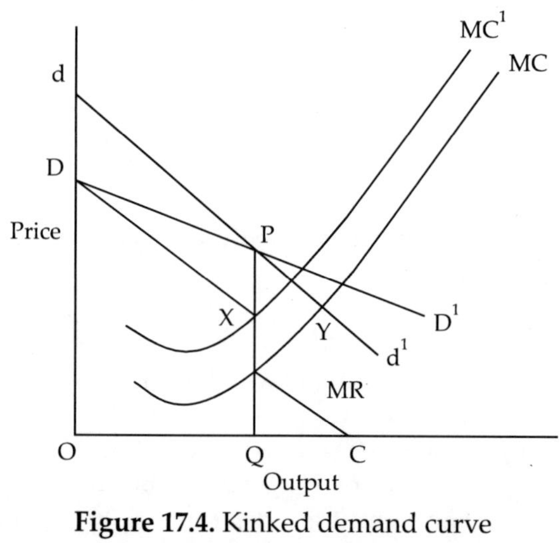

Figure 17.4. Kinked demand curve

The slope of a kinked demand curve differs in different conditions, such as price increase and price decrease. In this model, every business unit faces two demand curves. In the case of high prices, a business unit faces a highly elastic demand curve, which is dd[1] in Figure 17.4. On the other hand, in case of low prices, the business unit faces the inelastic demand curve, which is DD[1]. Suppose the prevailing price of a product is PQ and one of the business units makes changes in its prices, then there can be three reactions of rival business units.

First, when a business unit increases its prices, its demand curve would shift to dd′ from DD[1]. In such a case, consumers would switch to rivals, which would lead to a fall in the sales of the business unit. In addition, the dP portion of dd′ would be more elastic, which lies above the prevailing price. On the other hand, if price falls, the rivals would also reduce their prices, thus, the sales of the business unit would be less. In such a case, the demand curve faced by the oligopolistic business unit is PD[1], which lies below the prevailing price.

Secondly, rival business units will not react with respect to changes in the price of the oligopolistic business unit. In such a case, the business unit would face DD[1] demand curve. Thirdly, the rival business unit may follow the price cut, but not a price hike. If the business unit increases the price and rivals do not follow it, then consumers may switch to rivals. Thus, the rivals would gain control over the market. Thus, the oligopolistic business unit would be forced from dP demand curve to DP demand curve, so that it can prevent losing its customers. This would result in producing the kinked demand curve. On the other hand, if the business unit reduces the price, the rival business unit would also reduce prices for securing their customers. Here, the relevant demand curve is Pd′. The two parts of the demand curve are DP and Pd[1], which is DPd[1] with a kink at point P.

Let us draw the MR curve of the oligopolistic business unit. The MR curve would take the discontinuous shape, which is DXYC, where DX and YC correspond directly to DP and Pd[1] segments of the kinked demand curve. The equilibrium point is attained when MR = MC. In Figure 17.4, the MC curve intersects MR at point Y where at output OQ. At point Y, the business unit would achieve maximum profit. Now, if cost increases, the MC curve would move upwards to MC. In such a case, the business unit cannot increase the prices. This is because if the business unit increases the prices, the rival business unit would decrease their prices and gain the market share. Moreover, the profits would remain the same between point X and Y. Thus, there is no motivation for increasing or decreasing prices. Therefore, price and output would remain stable.

However, the kinked demand curve model is criticised by various economists. The model emphasises price rigidity but does not explain price itself. It assumes that rival business units only follow price decrease, which does not hold true empirically. The model ignores non-price competition among business units. Non-price competition can be in terms of product differentiation, advertising, and other tools used by business units to promote their sales. Further, the model ignores the application of price leadership and cartels, which account for a larger share of the oligopolistic market.

17.5.6. Collusion Model: The Cartel

In oligopolistic market conditions, the business units are indulged in high competition with each other, which may lead to price wars. For avoiding such type of problems, the business units enter into an agreement regarding uniform price-output policy. This agreement is known as collusion, which is opposite to competition. Under collusion, the business units are involved in collaboration with each other to take combined actions for keeping their bargaining power stronger against consumers.

According to Samuelson (1947), "Collusion denotes a situation in which two or more business units jointly set that price or output, divide the market among them, or make other business decisions." Thomas J. Webster (2003) expressed that collusion represents a formal agreement among business units in an oligopolistic industry to restrict competition to increase industry profits. The benefits of collusion to business units are:

- It helps the business units to increase their performance.
- It helps the business units in preventing uncertainties.
- It provides opportunities to prevent the entry of new business units.

The agreement of collusion formed may be tacit or formal in nature. A formal agreement among competing for business units is known as a cartel. In other words, the cartel can be defined as a group of organisations that together make pricing and output decisions.

According to Khemani and Shapiro (1993), "Cartels are productive structures involving multiple producers acting in unison that allow producers to exercise monopoly power." In the words of Boyes and Melvin (1994), a cartel is an organisation of independent business unit, whose purpose is to control and limit production and maintain or increase prices and profits. According to Webster (2003), a cartel is a formal agreement among the business units in an oligopolistic industry to allocate market share and/or industry profit.

Under cartels, the price and output determination is done by the common administrative authority, which aims at equal profit distribution among all member business units under cartel. The total profits are distributed in proportion as decided among member business units. The most famous example of a cartel is the Organisation of the Petroleum Exporting Countries (OPEC), which has shared control of petroleum markets.

Price and output decisions under cartels

Assume that two business units that have formed a cartel. The price and output decisions of two business units and industry are shown in Figure 17.5.

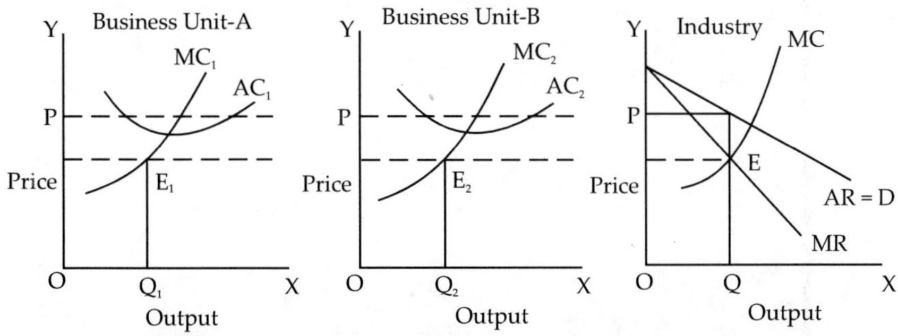

Figure 17.5. Cartel-price and output determination

In Figure 17.5, AR is the aggregate demand curve of both the business units and MC curves are the addition of MC_1 and MC_2 curves of business units A and B, respectively. The total output of the industry is determined according to MR and MC of the industry. OQ and OP are the equilibrium price and output of the industry. Now, this output will be allocated among the business units. This can be done by drawing a horizontal line from equilibrium point E of industry, towards MC curves of business units A and B. The points of intersection E_1 and E_2 are the equilibrium levels of the business units, A and B, respectively. OQ_1 is the equilibrium output of business unit A and OQ_2 is the equilibrium output of business unit B. Thus, $OQ_1 + OQ_2 = OQ$. These levels of outputs ensure the maximum joint profits of member business units.

17.5.7. Price Leadership Model

The business units in the oligopolistic market are not happy with price competition among themselves. They try various methods to maximise joint profits. Price leadership is one of the means which provides relief to the business units from the strains of price competition. The business units in the oligopolistic industry (without any formal agreement) accept the price set by the leading business unit in the industry and move their prices in line with the prices of the leading business unit. The acceptance of price set by the price leader business unit maximises the total profits of each business unit in the oligopolistic industry.

The main assumptions of price leadership model under oligopoly are:

- There are two business units, A and B, in the market.

- The output produced by the two business units is homogeneous.
- The business unit A being the low-cost business unit or a dominant business unit acts as a leading business unit.
- Both of the business units face the same demand curve.
- Each of the two business units has an equal share in the market.

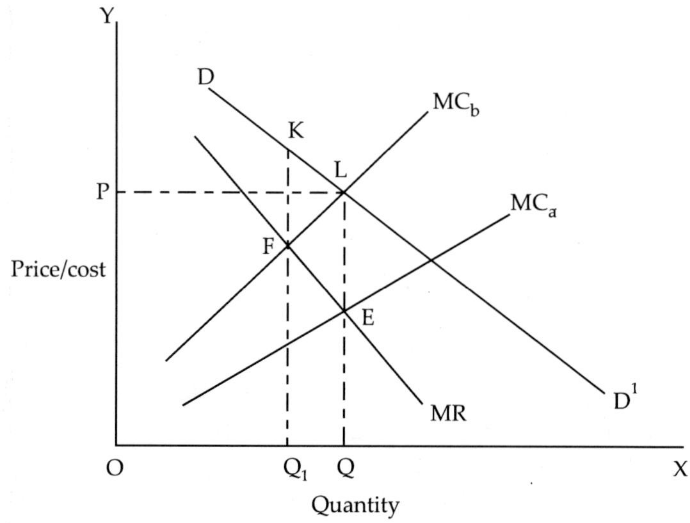

Figure 17.6. Price and output determination under price leadership

Figure 17.6 shows the price-output determination under leadership model. DD[1] is the demand curve which is faced by each of the two business units. MR is the marginal revenue curve of each business unit. MC_a is the marginal cost of business unit A and MC_b is the marginal cost of business unit B. The model assumes that business unit A is low-cost than business unit B. As such the MC_a lies below MC_b. The leader business unit using the marginalistic rule of MC = MR is in equilibrium at point E. The business unit A maximises profits by selling output OQ and setting price QP or QL. The business unit B is in equilibrium at point F where, MC_b = MR. The business unit B maximises profits by producing OQ_1 output and selling it at Q_1K price. The business unit B has to compete for business unit A in the market, if the business unit B fixes the price Q_1K per unit, it will not be able to compete with business unit A which is selling goods at QL price per unit.

Hence, the business unit B will be compelled to follow the leader business unit A. The business unit B will also charge QL price per unit as set by the business unit A. The business unit B will also produce OQ output like the business unit A. Thus, both the business units will charge the same price QL and sell each of them OQ output. The business unit A being the low-cost business unit will maximise profits by selling OQ output at QL price. The profits of the business unit B are lower than of business unit A because its costs of production are higher than of business unit-A.

17.6. SUMMARY

- Oligopoly is the form of an imperfectly competitive market where a few business units/sellers, produce/sell either homogeneous products or products which are a close but not perfect substitutes of each other.
- When the business units sell differentiated or heterogeneous products, it is referred to as differentiated oligopoly.
- The prime sources of oligopoly market are economies of scale, free but limited entry, legal restriction, established business units, control oversupply, government policies, product differentiation, and pricing.
- The various types of oligopoly are pure oligopoly or perfect oligopoly, differentiated or imperfect oligopoly, partial or full, open and closed, collusive and competitive oligopoly, and syndicated and organised oligopoly.
- The main features of an oligopoly market structure are few sellers/ business units, difficult for entry, indeterminate demand curve, the interdependence of business units, advertising and selling costs, complex market structure, and price rigidity.
- The Cournot Model was developed by a French economist Augustin Cournot in 1838. It assumes that the production by the two business units would be equal to the production by the entire industry. The key feature is that each business unit tries to maximise its profit by assuming that other business units hold its output constant at the existing level.
- Bertrand model assumes that there is no limit to the fall in price since each business unit can always lower the price by underbidding the other business unit. Therefore, increasing the supply of output until the price becomes equal to his unit cost of production.
- Edgeworth's model assumed that each business unit believes that its rival will continue to charge the same price as it charged. The productive capacity of each business unit is limited so that neither of the business units can meet the entire demand at the lower price ranges.
- According to Chamberlin's model, oligopolists behave quite intelligently as they recognise their interdependence and learn from the experience when they find that their action causes the rivals to react and adjust their output level. This realisation of mutual dependence on the part of the oligopolists leads to the monopoly output being produced jointly and charging of the monopoly price.

- The kinked demand curve of oligopoly was developed by Paul M. Sweezy in 1939. The model advocates that the behaviour of oligopolistic business units remains stable when the price and output are determined. This implies that an oligopolistic market is characterised by a certain degree of price rigidity or stability, especially when there is a change in prices in a downward direction. This model explains the reason for price rigidity under oligopolistic market situations.
- In collusion model, the business units are involved in collaboration with each other to take combined actions for keeping their bargaining power stronger against consumers. Collusion represents a formal agreement among business units in an oligopolistic industry to restrict competition to increase industry profits. A formal agreement among competing for business units is known as a cartel.
- Under price leadership model, the business units in the oligopolistic industry (without any formal agreement) accept the price set by the leading business unit in the industry and move their prices in line with the prices of the leading business unit. The acceptance of price set by the price leader business unit maximises the total profits of each business unit in the oligopolistic industry.

SHORT ANSWER QUESTIONS

1. What is oligopoly?
2. List the prime sources of oligopoly.
3. What are the general assumptions of the Cournot model?
4. Discuss the assumption of Edgeworth model.
5. What are the benefits of collusion to business units?
6. Write a short note on Sweezy demand curve model.

ESSAY ANSWER QUESTIONS

1. Explain the types of oligopoly and prime sources of an oligopoly market.
2. Describe the feature of an oligopolistic market structure.
3. What is the importance of the Cournot model? Discuss the price-output determination with an illustration.
4. Briefly explain how equilibrium is achieved in Bertrand's oligopolistic model.
5. Describe the process of achieving stable equilibrium under Chamberlin's oligopoly model.
6. Explain why an oligopolist faces a kinked demand curve with an illustration.
7. What is a collision model? Explain the price and output decisions under cartel.
8. Why business units in oligopoly market decide to agree on collusion?
9. What do you understand by price leadership? Describe the price-output determination under price leadership model.

FILL IN THE BLANKS

1. The business units selling identical products are referred to as _________.
2. Any pricing decision taken by one business unit will affect the trade of the _________.
3. In a closed oligopoly, the entry of business units is _________.
4. The conjectural variation between the two business units in the industry is _________.
5. A substitute oligopolistic model to Cournot's model was proposed by _________.
6. The means of providing relief to the business units from the strains of price competition is _________.
7. Under oligopoly, the entry is not easy for new entrants. (T/F)
8. A kinked demand curve assumes that there is always a prevailing price. (T/F)

Answers:

1. Pure oligopoly
2. Competitors
3. Restricted
4. Zero
5. Joseph Bertrand
6. Price leadership
7. True
8. True

MULTIPLE-CHOICE QUESTIONS

1. When the business units sell heterogeneous products, it is known as:
   (A) Differentiated oligopoly (B) Homogeneous oligopoly
   (C) Imperfect oligopoly (D) Interdependence oligopoly
2. The situation where the business units organise themselves into a central association for fixing prices, output, quotas, etc., is called:
   (A) Syndicated oligopoly (B) Competitive oligopoly
   (C) Organised oligopoly (D) Collusive oligopoly
3. In an oligopoly, the decisions of all the business units in the industry are:
   (A) Dependent (B) Interdependent
   (C) Relevant (D) Irrelevant
4. The Cournot model was propounded in the year:
   (A) 1838 (B) 1848
   (C) 1938 (D) 1883
5. In Cournot's model, the business units face a demand curve with a constant:
   (A) Downward slope (B) Upward slope
   (C) Negative slope (D) Positive slope
6. The kinked demand curve of oligopoly was developed by:
   (A) Paul M. Sweezy (B) F.Y. Edgeworth
   (C) A. Chamberlin (D) Joseph Bertrand
7. A formal agreement among competing for business units is known as:
   (A) Collusion (B) Contract
   (C) Cartel (D) Competition

8. The model advocating the behaviour of oligopolistic business units to remain stable when the price and output are determined is:
   (A) Kinked demand curve
   (B) Price leadership
   (C) Profit maximising
   (D) Price rigidity

Answers

1. A	2. C	3. B	4. A	5. C
6. A	7. C	8. A		

REFERENCES

1. Bertrand, J. (1883). Review of Theorie mathematique de la richesse sociale and of Recherches sur les principles mathematiques de la theorie des richesses. *Journal des Savants*, 67, 499-508.
2. Boyes, W. & Melvin, M. (1994). *Microeconomics.* Boston: Houghton Mifflin.
3. Chamberlin, E.H. (1933). *Theory of Monopolistic Competition.* Cambridge, M.A.: Harvard University Press.
4. Cournot, A. (1838). *Researches into the Mathematical Principles of the Theory of Wealth.* New York: Macmillan.
5. Cournot, A. (1963). *The Mathematical Principles of the Theory of Wealth.* Homewood, Illinois: Richard D. Irwin.
6. Dean, J. (1951). *Managerial Economics.* New York: Prentice-Hall, Inc.
7. Dwivedi, D.N. (2015). *Managerial Economics* (8th Edition). New Delhi, India: Vikas Publishing House Pvt. Ltd.
8. Edgeworth, F. (1889). *The Pure Theory of Monopoly*. Reprinted in Collected Papers relating to Political Economy. 1. Macmillan. 1925.
9. Gupta, G.S. (2017). *Managerial Economics.* New Delhi, India: Tata McGraw-Hill.
10. Khemani, R.S. & Shapiro, D.M. (1993). Glossary of Industrial Organisation Economics and Competition Law, commissioned by the Directorate for Financial, Fiscal and Enterprise Affairs.
11. Mehta, P.L. (2007). *Managerial Economics: Text and Cases.* New Delhi, India: Sultan Chand & Co.
12. Robinson, J. (1934). The economics of imperfect competition. *Journal of the Royal Statistical Society*, 97(4), 671-674.
13. Samuelson, Paul A. (1947). *Foundations of Economic Analysis.* Enlarged edn. 1983. Harvard University Press.
14. Sweezy, P.M. (1939). Demand under conditions of oligopoly. *Journal of Political Economy*, 568-573.

15. Thomas, C.R. & Maurice, S.C. (2016). *Managerial Economics: Foundations of Business Analysis and Strategy*. New York: McGraw-Hill Education.
16. Varshney, R.L. & Maheswari, K.L. (2014). *Managerial Economics*. New Delhi, India: Sultan Chand & Sons.
17. Webster, T.J. (2003). *Managerial Economics: Theory and Practice*. California, USA: Academic Press (Elsevier).

Chapter

18 Pricing Policy

LEARNING OBJECTIVES

After studying this chapter, you should be able to understand:

- concept of pricing and factors influencing pricing decisions;
- objectives of pricing and market structure elements influencing pricing objectives;
- role of costs in pricing;
- government intervention in pricing; and
- policies related to price control/administered pricing.

18.1. CONCEPT OF PRICING

Price is the exchange value of a product or service. It is an agreement between the buyer and seller for exchanging product/service at a value which maybe expressed in terms of money or product/services or partly money and partly product/services. The concept of price is expressed by different names by different persons/organisations for different products and services. Some of the names used to express price are rent, fee, tax, lease, premium, commission, tariff, etc. In a business situation, the seller proposes the offer of product/service at a price which is expected to be acceptable to the buyer. If the offer price is acceptable to the buyer the same will become the final price. If the buyer disagrees with the offer price he/she may bargain for an agreeable price. Therefore, price is an agreed value between the buyer and seller for exchanging the desired value from both ends generally, on a win-win proposition.

In the monopolistic competition scenario, the power is balanced between the buyer and seller. No single buyer or seller can influence the market or can be forced to succumb to pressure or power. Therefore, the exchange will be only on mutual agreement. In the case of monopoly, the power is in favour of the seller, therefore, seller plays a major role in deciding the price and many a time the buyer may be forced to accept the price fixed by the seller. In oligopoly conditions, the power of fixing price also lies mostly with the seller and buyer has to either accept or reject the product. In perfect competition, the demand and supply positions at a given point of time determine the price. As we have discussed price determination under different competitive structures in earlier chapters, this chapter is devoted to discussing pricing in commercial organisations.

Pricing policy refers to the way a business unit fix the prices of its products and services based on costs, value, demand, and competition. Pricing strategy refers to the way in which a business unit uses price to achieve its business goals. Business units first establish a base price to the product and then develop pricing strategies to exploit market situations into their favour. Formulating price policies and setting the price are the most important aspects of managerial decision making. A managerial economist tries to develop the system which contains optimum prices and be consistent with opportunities and constraints. Price is the source of revenue which the business units focus to maximise at every opportune time. Price is also considered the most important device to expand the market. If the price is set at a higher level, the seller may be forced to get himself out of the market. If the price is low, the seller may not be able to cover the costs and as such may incur losses. Therefore, pricing decisions must be made judiciously.

18.2. FACTORS INFLUENCING PRICING DECISIONS

The factors influencing pricing decisions may be broadly categorised as internal factors and external factors. The factors within the control of the business unit are known as *internal factors* and the factors, not in the control of the business unit but influence significantly the pricing decisions are called *external factors*. While formulating pricing policies and strategies it is necessary to take into consideration both internal as well as external factors. These factors are not static but are dynamic in nature. Both the internal factors and external factors change in its form, scale, composition, degree of influence, and flexibility based on changes in the business environment. For example, digitalisation influenced many internal as well as external factors significantly in recent years. Therefore, business units should continuously list the internal and external factors influencing pricing decisions and also the intensity of their influence.

Internal factors

The following are the internal factors that influence pricing decisions:

1. Cost of production
2. Product life
3. Production cycle
4. Product quality
5. Product standardisation
6. Input availability
7. Supply capacity
8. Product innovation
9. Product differentiation

10. The extent of product customization
11. Marketing mix
12. Product life cycle

1. **Cost of production:** The costs incurred for factors of production is the fundamental base for fixing the base price. The cost of inputs, technology, human resources, administration, outsourcing services, maintenance, and other expenditures are not similar to all business units and they vary based on location, experience, property, taxes, managerial efficiency, etc. One of the major challenges of any business unit is to see the cost of production at the minimum possible. Then only it can take advantage over the competition.
2. **Product life:** The life of the end product is another important factor influencing pricing decisions. The pricing for durables, perishables, and services have distinctive influencing factors. Durables can be stored and as such when there is a short of demand, the seller can wait for a few days to find a fair price. In the case of perishables and services, the seller has no option in case of adverse situations except to make adjustments in price to clear the stock or to utilise the full capacity. Thus, the factors influencing the price of vegetables cannot be the same in the case of furniture. Similarly, the factors influencing the pricing of hotels cannot be similar to that of iron.
3. **Production cycle:** A production cycle refers to the duration required to convert the raw materials into finished products. The products with longer production cycles have inputs used at various prices during the production process. By the time the product is completed, the input prices may increase or decrease. Therefore, the changes in input prices affect the final price of the product. The products with relatively very short production cycle can have stable prices of input materials. Thus, the final price of the product reflects the current prices of input materials.
4. **Product quality:** Price and quality have a positive correlation. The general perception of the consumers is that, if the price is high, the quality is high and vice versa. The business unit has to decide the level of quality of the product based on market expectations and accordingly fix the price. A high price with low quality or a low price with high quality proves disastrous to the producer. In the first case, the market rejects the product and the producer ends up with unsold stock. In the second case, the market quickly takes away the product, but the revenues will be lower than the cost of production resulting in huge loss. It is necessary, therefore, to balance product quality with price to optimise business results.

5. **Product standardisation:** Standardisation is vital for manufacturing goods as well as services. Consumer loyalty depends upon how consistent the producers are in the production quality. Thus, producers try to ensure consistent quality in their products and services. When prices of factors of production are consistent there may not be any problem in maintaining production standards and pricing the output. If the factors of production are fluctuating, the producers face many problems in maintaining the standards and offering the product at the same price. As it is not a good strategy of changing prices quite often, the producers struggle to manage the same composition of raw materials and sometimes make minor changes in the composition to see that the ultimate cost of production is not significantly changed. For example, onions in India is one of the key ingredients for food production. The exponential growth of prices of onions in the later part of 2019 created a lot of problems to the food industry to maintain standards of quality without changing the final price.
6. **Input availability:** Business units often face fluctuations in the supply of raw materials and spare parts. At times of shortage of inputs, the producers have to pay higher prices to acquire the required quantities. In such cases, the cost of production will go up. The producer left with no option excepts either to increase the final price of the product or reduce the profit margin to that extent.
7. **Supply capacity:** Production capacity determines the supply capacity of the business unit. Sometimes, it is possible to either stretch or to create excess capacity in a short period to meet the growing demand. Similarly, when demand is falling, the capacity can also be either reduced or used for some other purposes. In such cases, there may not be any impact on prices due to supply capacity. But this kind of situation is limited to a few businesses. In the majority of the cases, when demand is increasing the prices will increase due to the gap between supply and demand and vice versa. Therefore, supply capacity is an important factor influencing pricing decisions.
8. **Product innovation:** The pricing of innovative products does not follow the conventional methods of fixing prices. The innovative product is unique in the market and it will not have any competition for a certain period. Further, the producer incurs expenditure on research and development to design and develop an innovative product. The producer tries to recover the innovation expenditure at the earliest possible opportunity and also to exploit the market

opportunity for the uniqueness of his offering. Thus, there will be a difference in the pricing policy of the existing products and innovative products.

9. **Product differentiation:** Product differentiation is one of the powerful marketing strategies to capture consumer attention and also make them loyal. Under this strategy, the producers introduce products with minor variations to that of competing products. In other words, they add additional values and benefits to create the consumer perception that product 'X' is different from that of product 'Y' in the same category. For example, all brands of toothpaste serve similar core purpose but, each brand is sold stating different values and benefits. In support of product differentiation, the price adjustments will be done to attract and retain customers.
10. **The extent of product customization:** Product customization refers to making the products exactly suitable to every customer by involving customers in the process of production. The degree of customization has a direct relationship with the cost of production. So, the higher the degree of customization, the higher will be the cost of production per unit and vice versa. Accordingly, the price of the product varies.
11. **Marketing mix:** Marketing mix is the holistic strategy adopted by the business units to achieve desired results in the market against the competition. There are four important components in the marketing mix. They are the product, price, place and promotion. The final price of the product depends upon the product strategies, place/distribution strategies, and promotion strategies. The total cost of goods sold can be arrived at only after including the expenditure on these strategic elements. Therefore, market mix strategy is an important influencing factor in fixation of the final price.
12. **Product life cycle:** The product life cycle consists of four important stages such as introduction, growth, maturity and decline. The market conditions are different in different stages of the life cycle. At the introduction stage, the cost of the promotion will be very high and distributors demand higher margins. As such the costs will be higher than the revenues. Despite incurring losses, the producer may not increase the price because it adversely affects the demand for the product. In the growth stage, the sales are very positive, the revenues generate and business make huge profits as the market is ready to take his product. At this stage, the higher price result in higher margin which becomes an attraction to the competitors to enter into the business. So, a careful analysis is

required to change the prices at this stage. In the maturity stage, the sales growth declines due to the entry of competitors. The producer may not have a choice of increasing the price. On the other hand, he has to add additional values to the product without increasing the price to defend market share. As a result, profits will decline. In the declining stage, there will be a decline in the sales as well as profit margin due to the fact that the consumers switch over their loyalties either to the competitors or to the new innovative products that can better satisfy their needs. The pricing strategy at this stage will be influenced by several factors.

External factors

The following are the external factors that influence pricing decisions:

1. Product demand
2. The intensity of competition
3. Distribution channels
4. General economic conditions
5. Government policy
6. Reaction of consumers
7. Suppliers
8. Risk associated
9. Brand image
10. Prices of substitute products
11. Import policy and customs duty
12. Foreign exchange rates

1. **Product demand:** The law of demand states that there is an inverse relationship between price and demand. As per the law, if the price is increased the demand will fall and if the price is reduced the demand will rise. The price elasticity of demand measures the degree of change in demand with the change in prices. Business units try to fix up prices at a higher level when the demand is inelastic. On the other hand, they are cautious in changing the price, if the price elasticity of demand is high.
2. **The intensity of competition:** Business units may face competition from multiple angles. According to Micheal Porter, there are at least five forces from which business units may face competition. They are: threat from new entrants, bargaining power of buyers, bargaining power of suppliers, threat of substitute products, and rivalry among the existing competitors. The influence of competition on pricing decisions cannot be overemphasised. The more the intensity of competition the more the stability in pricing. No single

seller initiates a price change due to the reason that a minor change will attract serious reaction from the competitors. If the competition is remote, the business units will have relative freedom in fixing the prices.

3. **Distribution channels:** Business units depend on distribution channels to reach the ultimate group of customers. Distribution channels charge a margin for creating place and time utility to the product. In the case of a new product, the distributors demand a higher margin, whereas for the established products they may not charge higher margin as it is easier to sell an established brand than a new brand. The final price of a product is inclusive of distributors' margin and therefore, the choice of the distribution channel, the distribution strategy, the brand image of the product, and the margin are the factors that influence pricing decision of a product/ service.
4. **General economic conditions**: The general economic conditions such as inflation, depression, trade cycles, export-import policy, tax system, and so on also influence the price of a product significantly.
5. **Government policy**: While taking a pricing decision, a business unit has to take into consideration the taxation policy, trade policies, etc., of the government. For example, the introduction of GST (Goods and Services Tax) impacted the pricing of a large number of products in the country.
6. **Reaction of consumers:** The price fixed for the product should be accepted by the consumers. If the business unit fails to convince the customers, the value for the price they pay, the consumers may not prefer to buy the product. If the negative reaction is found from the consumers against the price of the product, the business unit should immediately respond in the form of adjusting the price as per the expectations of the consumers. In case of failure to do so, the business unit will face problems in marketing their products and services.
7. **Suppliers:** Suppliers are those who supply raw materials and spare parts to the business units. If the prices of such products are changing either positively or negatively, that will impact the price of the final product.
8. **Risk associated:** The conditions in the market cannot be predicted accurately. Many uncertain factors influence the market. If the risk associated with the marketing of a product is high, the business unit tries to charge a higher price. When low is risk associated with the product then the product will be priced low.

9. **Brand image:** Brand image is an intangible asset of a business unit. If the brand has a positive image and many loyal consumers, the business unit can behave like a monopoly and fix the price accordingly. Price is used as one of the key factors to develop a brand image and also to protect the established brand image. Thus, brand image has a direct influence on pricing decisions.
10. **Prices of substitute products:** If a product is having close substitutes then the pricing decision depends upon the prices of substitutes. The consumers compare the prices of the product with that of substitute products in taking purchase decisions. If the price of the product is higher compared to substitute products, the consumer may switch loyalty. Thus, while making pricing decisions the prices of substitute products have to be taken into consideration.
11. **Import policy and customs duty:** The import policy of the government influences the supply of the product and as such influences the pricing decisions. When the government senses the demand-supply gap for a product, it will try to import to fill the gap. In such a case, the prices will come down to the normal level. Customs duty is used to control supply from other countries to protect the interests of domestic producers. Thus, the import policy, as well as customs duty, play an important role in fixing the prices.
12. **Foreign exchange rates:** When business units are engaged in the export of finished products or importing raw materials and/or spare parts from other countries, they have to transact through foreign exchange. The foreign exchange rates are dynamic and therefore, impact the prices of imported or exported products.

18.3. OBJECTIVES OF PRICING

Pricing decisions are usually considered a part of the general strategy for achieving a broadly defined goal. Before determining the price itself, the management should decide the objectives. While setting the price, the business unit may aim at one or more of the objectives. The market conditions sometimes are not favourable to all the business organisations. They may face a continuous decline in sales for a long time due to either slow down in economic growth or negative economic growth. Under such circumstances, the business units price the products not to make profits but to survive in the business. They continue to reduce the price until they reach shutdown point. At the shutdown point, the out-of-pocket costs will be more than or equal to the revenues. Therefore, in abnormal conditions survival also becomes one of the objectives of pricing. In normal business conditions, the pricing objective can be broadly classified as:

1. Profit oriented objectives
2. Sales oriented objectives
3. Competition oriented objectives

1. **Profit oriented objectives:** One of the key objectives of any business unit is to make profits. The profit oriented objectives are two types: target return on investment and maximisation of profits.
   - **(a) Target return on investment:** Every business unit works for achieving a satisfactory return on investment. This objective can be realised only through pricing. The price set for the product should be capable of generating adequate revenues that ensure the target return on investment.
   - **(b) Maximisation of profits:** Profit maximisation is yet another profit oriented objective. However, the business units have to decide whether to achieve this objective in the short run or the long run. Some products may not have long life and therefore, the business tries to exploit the market at the earliest and maximise its profits in the short run. On the other hand, some products can have a very long life and there will be enough opportunity for the business unit to maximise profit in the long run.
2. **Sales oriented objectives:** Every business unit aims to achieve sales as per the targets and beyond. The volume of sales is an indicator of the status of the product in the market. A relatively higher sales consistently makes the product leader in the market. Price is the most powerful instrument used by marketers to influence sales. The sales oriented objectives of pricing are sales growth and growth in market share.
   - **(a) Sales growth:** Continuous growth in sales is an indicator of success in the marketing of products and services. High growth rates in sales can be achieved by manipulating prices of the products. As a result, sometimes, the business units may need to sacrifice some part of the profits in the short run. But in the long run, this strategy of using pricing for sales growth helps the business unit to earn higher revenues.
   - **(b) Growth in market share:** Market share of a product indicates the position of the product compared to the other brands in the market. Every business unit tries to enhance the market share of its products. Price is used as a strategic weapon for triggering growth in market share.

3. **Competition oriented objectives:** When a business unit enters into a market with its products/services, it is inevitable to face competition. It has to evolve a strategy against the competition within the ambit of its vision and mission. The competition oriented objectives are of two types: meeting the competition, and non-price competition.
   (a) **Meeting the competition:** Consumers compare prices of competing products with the products of a business unit. As every consumer tries to maximise his/her benefits, their choice would be to select the product available at a relatively low price. Therefore, the business units cannot fix the price in isolation, they have to take into consideration the prices of the competitors. The safest strategy is to fix the price on par with the competition so that there will not be any reactive actions from the competition.
   (b) **Non-price competition:** When competition is severe, the business units may not prefer to play games with pricing. To prove an advantage over the competition, the business units may opt for non-price competition. The factors such as aggressive consumer promotion, trade promotion, image building, customer support, customer relationship management, etc., are used to create additional value to the product.

18.4. MARKET STRUCTURE ELEMENTS INFLUENCING PRICING OBJECTIVES

The elements of market structure influence significantly the pricing objectives. The business unit has to understand these elements while setting the pricing objectives. The elements of market structure are not static but are dynamic. Therefore, a continuous flow of information on the elements is essential for making the right decisions. The following are the market structure elements that influence the pricing decisions.

1. Extent of differentiation
2. Level of concentration
3. Size of the market (number of customers and competitors)
4. Existing profit margins
5. Form of competition (perfect competition, oligopoly, monopoly, monopolistic competition)
6. Degree of government intervention
7. Consumers' price elasticity
8. The extent to which customers are informed about the existing prices

9. The extent to which customers are informed about the existing products or services offered in the market
10. Barriers to entry and exit from the market
11. Rate of technological change

18.5. ROLE OF COSTS IN PRICING

Cost data are the most important component in the price setting process. Costs must be relevant to the pricing decision. There should not be any underestimation or overestimation of costs. The factors such as sales levels, costs of production, marketing, and administrative costs are all parts of strategic pricing decision. The ability and willingness of the target consumers also will be taken into consideration for deciding the final price. The cost concepts are important considerations to decide the relevant costs to be applied for a product. The choice of cost concept depends upon the internal factors as well as external factors. When the product is produced using the idle capacity of a business unit, only variable costs recovery is sufficient to get breakeven. In such a case, the fixed costs are already recovered from the existing capacity utilisation. When the product is part of the total production schedule for various products then the average cost of production forms the basis for price fixation.

Generally, the cost of production sets the lower limit for the price of a product while market opportunity sets the higher limit. Business units try to variate the prices of the products as per the demand of the situation. If favourable market conditions are existing, the business units try to exploit the opportunity by rising the price to the level of market acceptance. When the supply is more than the demand or when substitute products are available at a lower price or the competitors are using low price strategy or the product reached the decline stage in the life cycle, the business units have to reduce price as per the trends in the market. However, the lower limit of reduction of the price will be decided by the costs incurred for production and the type of cost concept used to determine the production cost.

There are two mutually exclusive approaches the business units follow for price determination and recovery of costs. They are cost based pricing and demand based pricing.

1. **Cost based pricing:** Under this approach, the business units identify the relevant costs of a product and the cost per unit stands as the basis for price fixation. The objective is to recover the costs totally and also to earn profits as per the policy of the business unit. The seller tries to influence the market to buy the product at the price

already fixed taking into consideration their business interests. This kind of pricing is producer oriented. It does not take into consideration the market conditions. This approach is generally used by ancillary units, producers of machinery and equipment, spare parts, premium products, and customised products. In the case of fast moving consumer goods (FMCG) and mass consumption products, this kind of pricing may not be suitable.

2. **Demand based pricing:** The relationship between demand and price is well established all over the world. In the consumer market, generally, demand influences prices. Therefore, if a business unit wants to make its presence in the market it has to sell the products at the price that is acceptable to the market. So, consumers have no consideration for the cost incurred by the seller. Their interest will be on the value they are getting against their sacrifice. Under such circumstances, the business unit has to work backwards to see that the cost of production is less than the market price and also make sure that the costs of marketing are recovered and a reasonable profit margin is ensured. To achieve this the business units have to re-engineer their cost system by way of eliminating wastages, enhancing the productivity, developing an ideal material mix, using appropriate technology, and achieving a high level of managerial efficiency.

18.6. GOVERNMENT INTERVENTION IN PRICING

The government plays an important role in the pricing of certain products/ services in the interest and well-being of society. The government may choose to intervene in the price mechanism when a change in the allocation of resources is needed and when the government perceives that it is necessary for an improvement in economic and social welfare. All the political parties intervene in the economy to influence the allocation of scarce resources for optimising social benefit. The aims of government intervention in markets include stabilisation of prices, ensuring producers/ farmers with a minimum income, to control excessive prices of products that impact social welfare, and to discourage undesirable products/ encourage desirable products.

There are several ways through which the government influences product pricing. These are categorised as direct and indirect government interventions.

1. **Direct Government Intervention:** The government may choose to intervene directly in product pricing as per the demands of different situations. The most common direct intervention is in agricultural

products. The forms of government intervention in markets are categorised as minimum prices, maximum prices, and administered pricing.

(a) **Minimum prices:** The government announces a minimum price to such products where the producers are exploited by the middlemen. It involves setting the lower limit for the price. The producer is guaranteed to get the price announced by the government for the produce. The minimum price sometimes leads to surplus. In such a case, the government has to purchase the unsold produce from the producers and store it for distribution at a later stage. It may become costly for the government.

(b) **Maximum prices:** When prices of certain products are increasing beyond a proportion, the government intervenes and announces maximum prices for such products. The maximum price involves putting a limit on any increase in the price. The maximum price declaration will not allow the monopoly power to the suppliers to increase the price beyond a particular point.

(c) **Administered pricing:** Under this policy, the government intervenes against the market forces of supply and demand. The government dictates the price of a product/service and the sellers are forced to offer the products in the market on that price only.

2. **Indirect Government Intervention:** The government intervenes in the pricing through the imposition of various taxes such as excise duty, sales tax and customs duty, corporate taxation, etc. When necessary, the government may announce subsidies or tax holidays to certain business sectors or certain regions. The government may also announce minimum wages for the labour which impacts the cost of production. Such measures indirectly influence the pricing of products and services.

18.7. PRICE CONTROL/ADMINISTERED PRICING

Administered pricing and/or price controls are formulated and implemented within the broad framework of the general economic policy of the government. Price control is a direct measure of achieving certain economic goals such as welfare, equity, and stability.

It is the responsibility of the government to take measures to control prices when they are impacting the welfare of the population. The government may choose to control the prices either formally or informally. The government may advise the associations of industry/ business units to control the prices. Based on the advice, the industry/business units will agree to regulate the price voluntarily as per the limits directed by the government. Sometimes, the government may choose to interfere directly to control the prices. Then the government issues a statutory order fixing the price of the product/service and all business units and sellers should follow the same.

The price control may be total or partial. The total stock of output will be sold at the government fixed price under the total price control system. Generally, in the case of public sector monopolies total price control system is used. Under partial price control, the price for a part of the production of a product will be fixed by the government directly and arrange for its distribution. The remaining stock is allowed in the open market for sale at a price determined by the market forces. The partial price control system is also called *dual pricing.*

18.8. SUMMARY

- Price is an agreement between the buyer and seller for exchanging product/service at a value which may be expressed in terms of money or product/services or partly money and partly product/services.
- Pricing policy refers to the way a business unit fixes the prices of its products and services based on costs, value, demand, and competition.
- Pricing strategy refers to how a business unit uses price to achieve its business goals.
- The factors influencing pricing decisions may be broadly categorised as internal factors and external factors.
- The internal factors influencing pricing decisions are the cost of production, product life, production cycle, product quality, product standardisation, input availability, supply capacity, product innovation, product differentiation, the extent of product customisation, marketing mix, and product's life cycle.
- The external factors influencing pricing decisions are product demand, the intensity of competition, distribution channels, general economic conditions, government policy, the reaction of consumers, suppliers, the risk associated, brand image, prices of substitute products, import duty and customs duty, and foreign exchange rates.
- The pricing objective can be broadly classified as profit oriented, sales oriented, and competition oriented.
- The profit oriented objectives are target return on investment and maximisation of profits.
- The sales oriented objectives of pricing are sales growth and growth in market share.

- The competition oriented objectives are meeting the competition and non-price competition.
- The government may choose to intervene in the price mechanism when a change in the allocation of resources is needed and when the government perceives that it is necessary for an improvement in economic and social welfare.
- There are direct and indirect ways through which the government influences product pricing.
- The direct forms of government intervention in markets are categorised as minimum prices, maximum prices, and administered pricing.
- The government intervenes in the pricing through the imposition of various taxes such as excise duty, sales tax and customs duty, corporate taxation, etc.
- Administered pricing and/or price controls are formulated and implemented within the broad framework of the general economic policy of the government.
- It is the responsibility of the government to take measures to control prices when they are impacting the welfare of the population.

SHORT ANSWER QUESTIONS

1. Explain the concept of pricing.
2. What are the internal factors influencing pricing decisions?
3. List the external factors influencing pricing decisions.
4. What are profit oriented objectives of pricing?
5. Write a short note on sales oriented objectives of pricing.
6. Briefly explain the competition oriented objectives.
7. What is administered pricing?

ESSAY ANSWER QUESTIONS

1. Discuss the factors influencing pricing decisions and the intensity of their influence.
2. What is the pricing? Elucidate the objectives of pricing in detail.
3. What is the role of costs in pricing? Explain the approaches business units follow for price determination.
4. Describe the ways through which the government influences product pricing.
5. Explain the formulation of price controls for the economic policy of the government.
6. What are the market structure elements influencing pricing objectives? Explain.

FILL IN THE BLANKS

1. The exchange value of a product or service is called ________.
2. The factors within the control of the business unit are known as ________.
3. The duration required to convert the raw materials into finished products is ________.
4. The first stage of product's life cycle is ________.
5. At the shutdown point, the ________ costs will be more than or equal to the revenues.
6. The intangible asset of a business unit is ________.
7. High growth rates in sales can be achieved by ________ prices of the products.
8. The partial price control system is also called ________.
9. ________ will charge a margin for creating place and time utility to the product.
10. Business units will try to fix up prices at a higher level when the demand is ________.

Answers

1. Price
2. Internal factors
3. Production cycle
4. Introduction
5. Out-of-pocket
6. Brand image
7. Manipulating
8. Dual pricing
9. Distribution channels
10. Inelastic

MULTIPLE-CHOICE QUESTIONS

1. The source of revenue which the business units focus to maximise at every opportune time is:
   (A) Cost (B) Price
   (C) Money (D) Cash
2. The factors which are not in the control of the business unit but influence significantly the pricing decisions are called:
   (A) External factors (B) Internal factors
   (C) Pricing factors (D) Control factors
3. Which one of the following is an internal factor influencing the pricing decisions?
   (A) Product demand (B) Production standardisation
   (C) Distribution channels (D) Government policy
4. Making the products exactly suitable to every customer by involving customers in the process of production is referred to as:
   (A) Customer satisfaction (B) Production process
   (C) Product customisation (D) Customer perception
5. The approach where the business units identify the relevant costs of a product and the cost per unit stands as the basis for price fixation is:
   (A) Cost based pricing (B) Demand based pricing
   (C) Strategy based pricing (D) Competitor based pricing

6. Which one of the following is a profit oriented objective of pricing?
   (A) Sales growth (B) Non-price competition
   (C) Maximisation of profits (D) Growth in market share
7. When the government intervenes against the market forces of supply and demand it is called:
   (A) Administered pricing (B) Maximum price
   (C) Minimum price (D) Government price
8. The way a business unit fixes the prices of its products and services based on costs, value, demand, and competition are called:
   (A) Pricing value (B) Pricing control
   (C) Pricing decisions (D) Pricing policy
9. How a business unit uses price to achieve its business goals is referred to as:
   (A) Pricing strategy (B) Pricing policy
   (C) Agreement pricing (D) Innovation pricing
10. Which one of the following external factor influences the pricing decisions?
   (A) Product quality (B) Brand image
   (C) Supply capacity (D) Marketing mix

Answers

1. B	2. A	3. B	4. C	5. A
6. C	7. A	8. D	9. A	10. B

REFERENCES

1. Dean, J. (1968). *Managerial Economics.* New Delhi, India: Prentice-Hall of India Private Limited.
2. Dwivedi, D.N. (2015). *Managerial Economics* (8th Edition). New Delhi, India: Vikas Publishing House Pvt. Ltd.
3. Gupta, G.S. (2017). *Managerial Economics.* New Delhi, India: Tata McGraw-Hill.
4. Kotler, P. (1984). *Marketing Management: Analysis, Planning, and Control.* New York: Prentice-Hall, Inc.
5. Maheswari, Y. (2012). *Managerial Economics.* New Delhi, India: PHI Learning.
6. Mehta, P. L. (2007). *Managerial Economics: Text and Cases.* New Delhi, India: Sultan Chand & Co.
7. Mithani, D.M. (2010). *Managerial Economics.* Mumbai, India: Himalaya Publishing House Pvt. Ltd.
8. Perloff, J.M. (2012). *Micro Economics* (6th Edition). Boston, MA: Pearson Education Inc.
9. Rees, H. (2017). *Managerial Economics.* USA: Library Press.
10. Salvatore, D. & Rastogi, S.K. (2016). *Managerial Economics.* New Delhi, India: Oxford University Press.

11. Samuelson, W.F. & Marks, S.G. (2012). *Managerial Economics* (7th Edition). Hoboken, New Jersey: John Wiley & Sons, Inc.
12. Thomas, C.R. & Maurice, S.C. (2016). *Managerial Economics: Foundations of Business Analysis and Strategy*. New York: McGraw-Hill Education.
13. Varshney, R.L. & Maheswari, K.L. (2014). *Managerial Economics*. New Delhi, India: Sultan Chand & Sons.
14. Webster, T.J. (2003). *Managerial Economics: Theory and Practice*. California, USA: Academic Press (Elsevier).

Chapter

19 Pricing Methods and Strategies

LEARNING OBJECTIVES

After studying this chapter, you should be able to understand:

- the methods of pricing;
- cost and competition based pricing;
- market based pricing and geographic pricing;
- new product pricing and price leadership; and
- product life cycle pricing.

19.1. METHODS OF PRICING

The first step in the pricing process is the setting of pricing objectives. Once the pricing objectives are finalised the next step is to select the pricing method. A business unit has various options for selecting a pricing method. Prices are based on three dimensions that are cost, demand, and competition. The business unit can use any of the three dimensions or a combination of them. Therefore, the pricing methods used by the business unit are cost based pricing, competition based pricing, and market based pricing. The pricing methods help the business unit to arrive at the basic price for a product/service. The final price depends upon various other factors which influence the marketing environment from time to time.

1. Cost based pricing
2. Competition based pricing
3. Market based pricing

19.2. COST BASED PRICING

This method is also called *cost-plus pricing* or *mark-up pricing*. The cost-plus pricing is the traditional and simplest pricing method used by many business units. In this method, the producer sets the price that covers the cost of producing the product plus enough profit to allow the business unit to earn its target rate of return. Cost-plus pricing is used primarily because it is easy to calculate and requires information from internal sources only. Cost-plus pricing is often considered the most rational approach to achieve desired profits. There are two steps involved in cost-plus pricing. The first is to determine the cost of production of a product (both fixed cost and variable cost). The second step is to determine the mark-up over costs.

Cost-plus pricing is followed by many business units due to its specialities such as simple to understand, flexible, ensure return on investment, and provides adequate funds for the development of business. This method is highly suitable for single product manufacturers or limited product manufacturers. The calculation of total cost for a single product manufacturer is very easy compared to a multi-product manufacturer. There are many joint costs and overheads which are to be shared among various products in multi-product manufacturing. In such a case, it is very difficult to find out the exact cost of production of a product. Further, the choice of the cost concept and cost behaviour patterns against the volume of operation and composition of factors of production complicate the ascertainment of exact cost. However, cost-plus pricing is popularly adopted by micro, small and medium enterprises.

There are criticisms of this pricing method. It is criticised as the producer oriented pricing method. This method does not take into consideration the market demand for the product and the price-demand relationship. The impact of market forces is totally ignored in this pricing method.

19.3. COMPETITION BASED PRICING

Producers have to face competition in the market. Competitors try to influence the target market to buy their products. Thus, there will be a fight between and among competitors to convince the customers and to make them loyal. Therefore, one has to be careful and strategic to reach the target customers successfully. Competition may be direct or indirect, close or distant, strong or weak, or good or bad. One has to study and understand the competition and plan accordingly. The most popular weapon used by competitors to fight with others is the price. It is because of this reason, competition based pricing assumed significance. There are three options to set prices against the competition. They are:

1. Pricing above the competition
2. Pricing on par with the competition
3. Pricing below the competition

1. **Pricing above the competition:** This method is highly challenging and involves high risk. When the business unit decides to fix the price above the competition level it has to convince the customer with the reasons for making them pay a higher price. If the product is having unique and innovative value over the competitive products, consumers may prefer to pay more. It all depends upon how the producer creates additional values to the customer and also how they convince the customers.

2. **Pricing on par with competition:** Most of the business units in a competitive market do not have sufficient power to set prices above their competitors. They follow live and let live policy. They don't challenge the competitors and try to follow them. This approach is to avoid price wars and continue the business in a harmonious environment. It is very easy to follow the competitor as the producer need not do any exercise to arrive at a price. This is also called *going rate pricing*. Producers follow it when there is a degree of price leadership in the market and there is a degree of collusion between and among the business units. This is criticised as a defensive strategy. Marketers are respected when they are offensive in the market rather than defensive.
3. **Pricing below the competition:** This method is also called *predatory pricing*. It is aggressive pricing with undercutting intent to drive out competitors from a market. Predatory pricing is an act of setting prices low in an attempt to eliminate the competition. It is illegal under anti-trust laws, as it makes markets more vulnerable to a monopoly. Business units may create barriers to entry for new competitors or engage in unethical production methods to minimise costs to eliminate competition. They may even incur losses in the short run to make the business unattractive to the new entrants and lossmaking for the late entrants. Once all of them withdraw from the business, then the business unit increases the price and recovers losses. Pricing below the competition often leads to price wars. In the short run, the price wars can be beneficial for consumers because of the lower prices. In the long run, it may not be beneficial as the business unit that wins the price war, effectively putting its competitor out of business, will emerge as a monopoly and exploit the customers. If predatory pricing leads to an increase in monopoly power, then it will harm the public interest because it leads to higher prices in the long term.

19.4. MARKET BASED PRICING

This is also known as *customer oriented pricing*. The key determinant of price is what customers are willing to pay. This strategy is more difficult than cost based pricing because the customers themselves may not have the ability to judge the right price for them. Consumers generally use reference prices or their experience to judge the reasonability of the price of a product. All the consumers may not have similar information, knowledge, experience, judgement capability, attitude, intentions and motives, need pressure and purchasing power. Therefore, finding a common line of acceptance or rejection is close to impossible. Marketers try to segment consumers to identify some homogeneous factors relating to price and value perceptions.

There are two ways to understand the accepted price of consumers. One way is to conduct market research and based on the data and inferences the marketers can estimate the acceptable price. The success rate in this approach may not be very high as consumer research has its limitations in predicting the behaviour of consumers. The second way is experimentation. The marketers select different markets and introduce products at different prices at the same time or introduce the same product in the same market – changing prices at different time intervals to study consumer responses. This approach though takes more time but the results would be dependable. However, this method is costly and time consuming. Competitors will know closely the pricing strategy of the business unit and they will develop counter-strategies.

19.5. GEOGRAPHIC PRICING

When different prices are set for different locations or countries, it is called *geographic pricing*. Business units often land in confusion whether to charge higher prices to distant consumers due to high transportation costs or charge a low price to attract additional business. However, business units develop an equation of price, demand and revenue to achieve the business goals. Geographic pricing is one of the important options in arriving at the basic price of a product. The following are the geographic pricing methods.

1. Uniform delivered pricing
2. Basing-point pricing
3. F.O.B. (Free On Board) pricing

1. **Uniform delivered pricing:** Under this method, the business unit makes the product available at a price common in all locations. Whether the buyer is close to the factory or at a distance the price of the product remains the same. There are two approaches followed under this method. They are postage stamp pricing and zonal pricing. *Postage-stamp pricing* means delivered prices are common to all buyers irrespective of their location. This method is followed when the transportation cost is insignificant. This pricing method provides access to all markets in different locations to the business units. *Zonal pricing* means delivered prices that are uniform within specified locations which are called zones. The entire market will be divided into parts which are called zones taking into consideration the transportation costs. The prices of the products marginally vary between and among zones as the price includes the average transport cost of the zone.

2. **Basing point pricing:** Basing point pricing is an alternative to uniform delivered pricing. Under this method, the location of the production unit(s) will be taken as a base point. Business units may follow *single basing point pricing* or multiple basing point pricing. Under single basing point pricing, all production units regardless of location, arrive at the delivered price by adding transportation cost to the base price of the product. Under *multiple-basing point pricing,* several production centres are identified as basing points. The delivered price is arrived at by adding transportation cost to the nearest basing point.
3. **F.O.B. (free on board) pricing:** Under F.O.B. pricing, products are priced at the production unit based on the cost of production and profit margin. The buyer will bear the transportation costs.

19.6. NEW PRODUCT PRICING

Pricing policy in respect of a new product depends on whether or not close substitutes are available. Depending on whether or not close substitutes are available, in pricing a new product, generally, two kinds of pricing strategies are suggested, viz., price skimming, and price penetration.

1. **Price skimming:** Introduction of a product into a market with a policy of relatively high prices and heavy promotional expenditure is called *price skimming* strategy. Some business units use this strategy as a successful formula for certain products that are having some distinctive features. The reasons for the success of this strategy include:

(a) Demand is expected to be more price inelastic in the beginning than when the market for the product grew to a higher scale. In the early stages of the product life cycle, the product will have a few close rivals and therefore, the cross-elasticity of demand will be lower. Promotional elasticity, on the other hand, will be quite high for products with high unit prices.

(b) Producers favour this strategy due to the reason that high initial price for a product can be used as a device for breaking the market into segments based on the price elasticity of demand. The initial high price provides an opportunity for the sellers to skim the cream of the market that is relatively insensitive to price. Further, the sellers can scale down prices to tap successively more elastic markets.

(c) When it is difficult to measure demand elasticity, price skimming serves as testing price during the stage of exploration. The business units can continue experimentation by lowering the price at different levels in different markets until they find a price that can create adequate demand for the product.

(d) The business units prefer price skimming when they need to generate high revenue to meet the initial investment and expenditure towards the production of a product.

Business units cannot use price skimming strategy for all the products. This strategy is used successfully only when certain favourable conditions exist in the market. The following are the desirable conditions for using price skimming strategy effectively.

1. The product should be innovative and there should not be any close substitute.
2. The production of the product requires a high level of investment and, therefore, it may not be possible for competitors to enter the market.
3. The product should aim at the premium market which is price inelastic.
4. The product should be capable of creating esteem value to higher income group people.
5. If the producer is having a patent right or exclusive right to produce the product, this strategy is highly suitable.
6. If the product is having a very short expected life, this pricing strategy is suitable.

2. **Penetration pricing:** An alternative pricing strategy for the business units for the introduction of new products is *penetration pricing*. Under this strategy, the product will be introduced with a low initial price. The objective of the business unit is to maximise the profit in the long run by way of achieving high turnover and high market share. This strategy is suitable when:

(a) Demand is price elastic.
(b) Easy to enter into the market by competitors.
(c) There is a threat for potential competition.
(d) No market restrictions.
(e) Product is aimed at the mass market.
(f) The business unit aims at a normal profit.
(g) Economies of large-scale production are available to the business unit with the increase in sales.
(h) The product is accepted easily and adopted by consumers.

Business units prefer penetration pricing strategy when they expect the life of the product longer. When the product is offered at a lower price, which otherwise, yields a lower profit margin, the business may not be attractive to the competitors. They will study the market acceptance of the product and its revenue generating capacity over a period, and then only decide whether to enter or not into the market with such a product. By the time the competitors decide to enter into the market, the business unit which introduced the product will have an established accepted market. Such business unit will have an advantage over competitors in terms of cost of production due to economies of scale, market leadership, low marketing costs, and customer loyalty. Further, the capital investment for the new entrants will be higher due to inflation and, therefore, it will be difficult to get the expected return on investment (ROI) facing competition from the existing player. Therefore, penetration pricing strategy safeguards the marketability of the product for a long time and also ensures the maximisation of profits.

19.7. PRODUCT LIFE-CYCLE PRICING

The product life cycle is the sequence of strategies used by business units as the product goes through its life cycle. The life cycle of a product is generally divided into four stages: introduction, growth, maturity, and decline. Figure 19.1 depicts the four stages of a product's life cycle. The stages in the life cycle of a product are identified based on two variables. They are in total sales and profits. The sales curve and profit curve is shown in the figure helps in identifying the stage of the life cycle of a product in the market.

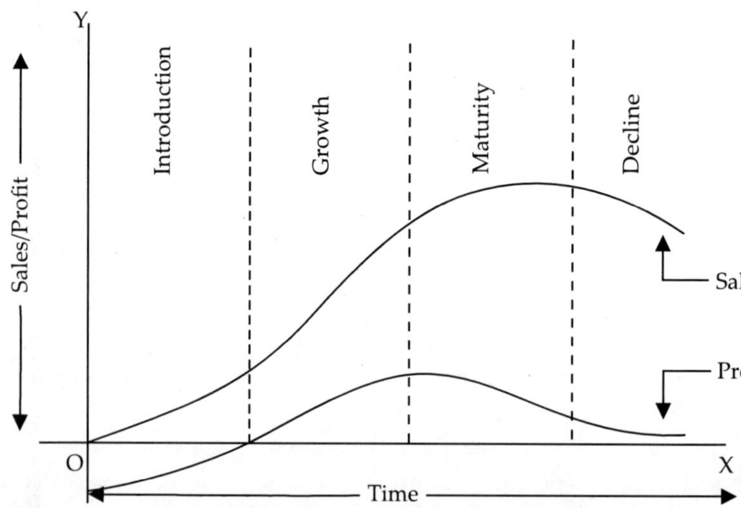

Figure 19.1. Stages in product life cycle

1. **Introduction stage:** At the introduction stage, the business unit faces lot of challenges. It has to create awareness about the product in the market which involves heavy expenditure on promotion. The sales will be low and record a slow growth rate in the beginning. The revenue earned will be less than the expenditure covering the cost of production, marketing costs, and promotion costs. Once the business unit is successful in gaining consumer acceptability and loyalty, the sales pick up well and record a relatively higher growth rate. Once the turnover generates enough revenues to meet all the expenses and generate some profit, the introductory stage of the product gets concluded and the growth stage begins.
2. **Growth stage:** The beginning of the growth stage provides positive signals to the business unit. The sales grow at a faster rate, new customers will add to the existing, marketing and promotional expenditure per unit will reduce significantly, the profit margin per unit increases, and no serious competitive threat will be there in the market. During this stage, the profits reach their peak stage. So, this is the most desirable market situation and therefore, every business unit desires to have the longest period of the growth stage. However, it is not possible to enjoy this facility for more than a specified period as the market structure will find competitive forces to disturb the situation. Attracted by the profits, the competitors try to enter into the market with an improved product or marketing offer. The competitor's entry will impact the growth of sales as the sales growth is shared by the new entrants. The business unit has to respond to the competitive threat and, therefore, may add new features or benefits to the existing product. Additional promotional efforts and additional features without increasing the price leads to a reduction in profit margin and thereby, reduction in profits. So, the profit curve starts declining due to competition. When a product reaches such a situation, the growth stage gets concluded and maturity stage begins.
3. **Maturity stage:** The maturity is the stage in which sales continue to increase but at a lower rate up to a certain period and then total sales eventually becomes constant. The business unit faces severe competition from many players who enter the market with a differentiated market offers. To face the challenges of the competitors the business unit may need to reduce the price, add new features without adding price, or use both the strategies simultaneously. These measures may protect the sales turnover but cause in the reduction of profits. Therefore, their will be a continuous decline in the profit curve during this stage. The business unit will try all

possible ways to defend the market share and its position in the market. It will try to stretch this period as long as possible. When inevitable happens the profit curve will touch its zero levels, the sales curve slopes downward at a faster rate, then it can be concluded that the maturity stage is over and the product has entered the declining stage.

4. **Decline stage:** This stage is highly undesirable to the business unit. The market environment towards the product will be highly unfavourable. The sales curve declines at a faster rate and the business unit incurs losses. It is time to decide the withdrawal of the product from the market.

The pricing strategies vary from stage to stage over the life cycle of a product depending on the market conditions. Business units have to use an appropriate pricing strategy to manage product life cycle effectively to the advantage of the business.

19.8. PRICE LEADERSHIP

In a market situation, not all business units change prices simultaneously. One business unit takes the initiating role in all price changes, and the other business units react either by matching the leader's price or with price differentials. Price leadership generally can be observed in a well established stable industry with standardised products or in industries where there are considerable product differentiations.

Price leadership is in a way a tacit concurrence by the majority of the business units in the industry with the wisdom of leaders pricing decision. One business unit by virtue of its leadership in different fronts takes the lead of changing the price which is acceptable to all other business units. The other business units try to follow the leader to avoid price wars. A business unit gets acceptability from other business units as a price leader when it possesses the following three requisites.

1. A substantial share of the market.
2. A reputation for sound pricing decisions.
3. The ability to take initiative by critically assessing the business environment.

19.9. SUMMARY

- A business unit has various options for selecting a pricing method based on three dimensions: cost, demand, and competition.
- The pricing methods used by the business unit are cost based pricing, competition based pricing, and market based pricing.

- In the cost based pricing method, the producer sets the price that covers the cost of producing the product plus enough profit to allow the business unit to earn its target rate of return.
- Mark-up pricing involves determining the cost of production of a product and the mark-up over costs. It is highly suitable for single product manufacturers and/or limited product manufacturers.
- Cost-plus pricing is followed by many business units due to its specialities such as simple to understand, flexible, ensures return on investment, and provides adequate funds for the development of business.
- In the competition based pricing method, the producer sets the prices based on the level of competition in the market.
- There are three options to set prices against the competition. They are pricing above the competition, pricing on par with the competition, and pricing below the competition.
- Pricing below the competition method is aggressive pricing with undercutting intent to drive out competitors from a market.
- In the market based pricing method, the prices are fixed based on what the customers are willing to pay. It is also known as customer oriented pricing.
- There are two ways to understand the accepted price of consumers. One way is to conduct market research and the second way is experimentation.
- When different prices are set for different locations or countries, it is called geographic pricing.
- The basic geographic pricing methods are uniform deliver pricing, basing-point pricing, and F.O.B. (Free On Board) pricing.
- Under uniform delivered pricing method, the business unit makes the product available at a price common in all locations.
- Postage-stamp pricing means delivered prices are common to all buyers irrespective of their location, and zonal pricing means delivered prices that are uniform within specified locations which are called zones.
- In single basing point pricing, all production units regardless of location, arrive at the delivered price by adding transportation cost to the base price of the product.
- In multiple basing point pricing, several production centres are identified as basing points and the delivered price is arrived by adding transportation cost to the nearest basing point.
- In free onboard pricing method, the products are priced at the production unit based on the cost of production and profit margin.

- Introduction of a product into a market with a policy of relatively high prices and heavy promotional expenditure is called price skimming strategy.
- When it is difficult to measure demand elasticity, price skimming serves as testing price during the stage of exploration.
- Price skimming strategy is used successfully only when certain favourable conditions exist in the market.
- In a penetration pricing strategy, the product will be introduced with a low initial price. The objective of the business unit is to maximise the profit in the long run by way of achieving high turnover and high market share.
- The product life cycle is the sequence of strategies used by business units as the product goes through its life cycle. The life cycle of a product is generally divided in four stages: introduction, growth, maturity, and decline.
- At the introduction stage, the business units have to create awareness about the product in the market which involves heavy expenditure on promotion. The revenue earned will be less than the expenditure covering the cost of production, marketing costs, and promotion costs.
- In growth state, the sales grow at a faster rate, new customers will add to the existing, marketing and promotional expenditure per unit will reduce significantly, the profit margin per unit increases, and no serious competitive threat will be in the market.
- The maturity is the stage in which sales continue to increase but at a lower rate up to a certain period and then total sale eventually becomes constant. The business unit faces severe competition from many players who enter the market with a differentiated market offers.
- In the declining stage, the market environment towards the product will be highly unfavourable, the sales curve declines at a faster rate and the business unit incurs losses.
- Price leadership is in a way a tacit concurrence by the majority of the business units in the industry with the wisdom of leaders pricing decision.
- A business unit gets acceptability from other business units as price leader when it possesses a substantial share of the market, a reputation for sound pricing decisions, and the ability to take initiative by critically assessing business environment.

SHORT ANSWER QUESTIONS

1. What is cost based pricing?
2. Write a short note on market based pricing.

3. Define geographic pricing.
4. Write a brief note on penetration pricing.
5. What is meant by price skimming?
6. What is the product life cycle?

ESSAY ANSWER QUESTIONS

1. Explain the methods of pricing a product by a business unit.
2. What is competition based pricing? Discuss the options to set prices against the competition.
3. Describe the geographic pricing methods in detail with suitable examples.
4. What is the new product pricing? Explain the strategies adopted in pricing a new product.
5. Discuss the stages involved in product life cycle pricing.
6. Explain why the business units need to adopt a price leadership strategy.

FILL IN THE BLANKS

1. Prices are based on three dimensions that are cost, demand, and __________.
2. Cost based pricing method is also called __________.
3. Mark-up pricing method is highly suitable for __________ product manufacturers.
4. Cost based pricing method does not consider the __________.
5. The most popular weapon used by competitors to fight with others is __________.
6. Pricing on par with competition is referred to as __________ strategy.
7. The method of pricing below the competition is called __________.
8. Market based pricing method is also known as __________.
9. Customer oriented pricing method is time consuming and __________.
10. When the products are priced at the production unit based on the cost of production and profit margin, it is called __________.
11. When the location of the production unit(s) is taken as base point it is called __________.
12. The business units prefer price skimming when they need to generate high __________.
13. Business units prefer penetration pricing strategy when they expect the life of the product to be __________.
14. The pricing strategy adopted by business units for the introduction of new products is __________.
15. In growth stage, the profits reach its __________.
16. In maturity stage, they will be a continuous __________ in profit curve.

Answers

1. Competition
2. Mark-up pricing
3. Single
4. Price-demand relationship
5. Price
6. Defensive

7. Predatory pricing
8. Customer oriented pricing
9. Costly
10. F.O.B pricing
11. Basepoint pricing
12. Revenue
13. Longer
14. Penetration pricing
15. Peak
16. Decline

MULTIPLE-CHOICE QUESTIONS

1. The producer sets the price that covers the cost of producing the product plus enough profit to allow the business unit to earn its target rate of return, is called:
   (A) Multi-product pricing (B) Cost-plus pricing
   (C) Market based pricing (D) Strategy based pricing
2. Cost based pricing method is referred to as:
   (A) Customer oriented pricing method
   (B) Market oriented pricing method
   (C) Producer oriented pricing method
   (D) Product oriented pricing method
3. Cost-plus pricing primarily requires information from:
   (A) Internal sources
   (B) External sources
   (C) Both internal and external sources
   (D) Market sources
4. The fixation of prices on par with the competition is referred to as:
   (A) Going concern pricing (B) Going rate pricing
   (C) Product pricing (D) Strategic pricing
5. The act of setting prices low in an attempt to eliminate the competition is called:
   (A) Legal pricing (B) Monopoly pricing
   (C) Collusion pricing (D) Predatory pricing
6. When the delivered prices are common to all buyers irrespective of their location it is:
   (A) Postage-stamp pricing (B) Zonal pricing
   (C) Base-point pricing (D) Free onboard pricing
7. When all production units regardless of location, arrive at the delivered price by adding transportation cost to the base price of the product, it is:
   (A) Uniform delivered pricing
   (B) Marginal delivered pricing
   (C) Multiple-basing point pricing
   (D) Single-basing point pricing
8. The strategy of introducing a product into a market with a policy of relatively high prices and heavy promotional expenditure is called:
   (A) Penetration pricing (B) Price skimming
   (C) Promotional pricing (D) Market pricing

9. Under the penetration pricing strategy, the product will be introduced with:
   (A) Low price (B) Towering price
   (C) Moderate price (D) High price
10. Which one of the following is not a suitable condition for adopting a penetration pricing strategy?
    (A) Easy to enter into the market by competitors
    (B) There is a threat for potential competition
    (C) Demand is price inelastic elastic
    (D) No market restrictions
11. In which stage, the sales will be low and record a slow growth rate.
    (A) Introduction (B) Growth
    (C) Maturity (D) Decline
12. The stage where sales continue to increase but at a lower rate up to a certain period and then total sale eventually becomes constant is:
    (A) Saturation (B) Growth
    (C) Maturity (D) Diminishing
13. A tacit concurrence by the majority of the business units in the industry with the wisdom of leaders pricing decision is called:
    (A) Price leadership (B) Loss leader pricing
    (C) Market pricing (D) Consumer oriented pricing

Answers

1. B	2. C	3. A	4. B	5. D
6. A	7. D	8. B	9. A	10. C
11. A	12. C	13. A		

REFERENCES

1. Alhabeeb, M.J. & Moffitt, L. J. (2013). *Managerial Economics: A Mathematical Approach.* New Jersey: John Wiley & Sons, Inc.
2. Baye, M. (2000). *Managerial Economics & Business Strategy.* Boston: Irwin/McGraw-Hill.
3. Cowen, T. & Tabarrok, A. (2013). *Modern Principles of Economics* (2nd Edn). New York, NY: Worth Publishers.
4. Dean, J. (1968). *Managerial Economics.* New Delhi, India: Prentice-Hall of India Private Limited.
5. Dwivedi, D.N. (2015). *Managerial Economics* (8th Edn). New Delhi, India: Vikas Publishing House Pvt. Ltd.
6. Hibdon, J.E. (1969). *Price and Welfare Theory.* McGraw Hill.
7. Hirschey, M. (2009). *Managerial Economics* (12th Edn). USA: South-Western Cengage Learning.
8. Kishtainy, N. & Abbot, G. (2012). *The Economics Book* (1st Edn.). New York [N.Y.]: DK Pub.

9. Kotler, P. (1984). *Marketing Management: Analysis, Planning, and Control.* New York: Prentice-Hall, Inc.
10. Maheswari, Y. (2012). *Managerial Economics.* New Delhi, India: PHI Learning.
11. Mansfield, E. (1975). *Microeconomics: Theory/Applications.* New York: W.W. Norton & Co.
12. Mehta, P.L. (2007). *Managerial Economics: Text and Cases.* New Delhi, India: Sultan Chand & Co.
13. Perloff, J.M. (2012). *Micro Economics* (6th Edn). Boston, MA: Pearson Education Inc.
14. Rees, H. (2017). *Managerial Economics.* USA: Library Press.
15. Salvatore, D. & Rastogi, S. K. (2016). *Managerial Economics.* New Delhi, India: Oxford University Press.
16. Samuelson, W.F. & Marks, S. G. (2012). *Managerial Economics (7th Edn).* Hoboken, New Jersey: John Wiley & Sons, Inc.
17. Spencer, M.H. & Siegelman, L. (1959). *Managerial Economics: Decision Making and Forward Planning.* Homewood, Illionous: Richard D., Irwin, Inc.
18. Stiglar, G.J. (1953). *Theory of Price.* New York: The Macmillan Co.
19. Thomas, C.R. & Maurice, S.C. (2016). *Managerial Economics: Foundations of Business Analysis and Strategy.* New York: McGraw-Hill Education.
20. Varshney, R.L. & Maheswari, K.L. (2014). *Managerial Economics.* New Delhi, India: Sultan Chand & Sons.
21. Webster, T.J. (2003). *Managerial Economics: Theory and Practice.* California, USA: Academic Press (Elsevier).
22. Wilkinson, N. (2005). *Managerial Economics: A Problem-solving Approach.* Cambridge, UK: Cambridge University Press.

Chapter

20 Promotional Pricing: Discounts and Discrimination

LEARNING OBJECTIVES

After studying this chapter, you should be able to understand:

- concept of promotional pricing and various options;
- concept of price discounts and its types;
- product line pricing and its methods;
- problems of product line pricing; and
- concept of price discrimination, its advantages and conditions.

20.1. PROMOTIONAL PRICING

Business units cannot stick on to one price all the time and for all markets. As the revenue of the business unit depends upon the price and demand of a product, they have to decide prices suiting to the situations to exploit the demand and to generate the desired revenue. Promotional pricing is one such strategic option to the business units to manipulate demand through pricing strategy. Promotional pricing strategies may vary from product to product, market to market, time to time, and situation to situation. The business unit has to carefully study and examine the market trends and situations particularly, the competitive conditions while deciding the price for promoting sales. The following are some of the options.

1. **Leader pricing:** It is also called *loss leader pricing*. This strategy is mostly used by retailers to attract a large number of customers to their retail outlets. The retailer offers huge discounts or price offs on a few products and promotes well to create awareness among the target customers. The retailers are prepared to incur a loss on the identified products with an anticipation that the customers who visit the retail outlet will not confine only to the identified loss leader products, but also purchase other products available in the outlet. They will cover the losses by way of generating a larger turnover by selling other products to the same customers.
2. **Special occasion pricing:** Business units will identify special occasions during which the customers prefer to make purchases either due to cultural requirement or habitual or family traditions or religious requirements. During such occasions, a special price may be offered to attract the customers and also to make them buy large quantities.

3. **Special customer pricing:** Business units may offer special prices to certain customers who are either regular or very important or large size buyers or opinion leaders.
4. **Cash discounts:** Cash rebates are offered in a specific period to stimulate sales of the products. Business units, particularly, choose this strategy during slack seasons.
5. **Low-interest financing:** This strategy is popularly used by retailers to stimulate demand for high priced consumer goods. It is one of the popular strategies followed by the automobile industry throughout the world.
6. **Payment terms:** Retailers offer liberal payment terms suitable to different customer segments. EMI (equated monthly instalment) facility, zero-interest loans, daily instalment, part-payment, credit card payment, gold saving schemes are the popular payment strategies used by the retailers.
7. **Warranty and service:** The business units can promote sales by offering a free or low-cost warranty or service contract.
8. **Psychological discounting:** Under this strategy, the business unit sets an artificially high price and then offers substantial savings to the customers on the purchase of the product. The retailer first increases the price and then offers a discount on the increased price. The consumers get attracted by the percentage of discount and purchase the product. They may not know that they purchased the product either at the original price or even by paying a little more than the original price.
9. **Psychological pricing:** This also called charm pricing or odd pricing. Under this strategy, the price of the product is fixed in odd numbers like Rs. 199.95. This is to create a psychological impression on the consumers that they are charged less than what they are paying for the product. This strategy is popularly used in footwear, mobiles, electronics, textiles, and many more consumer goods adopt this kind of strategy.

20.2. PRICE DISCOUNTS

Business units may not have favourable market situations all the time to sell the desired quantities of their products. Price discount is the strategic option to scale up the turnover or to defend the sales volume or to arrest the decline in sales. A discount is a reduction in the selling price of a product or service. There are six types of price discounts commonly used by the sellers. They are:

1. Quantity discounts
2. Trade discounts
3. Seasonal discounts
4. Cash discounts

1. **Quantity discounts:** This strategy is used to increase sales quantity. The buyers are encouraged to purchase product in large quantities and thereby they can get some discount over the actual price. The quantity discounts may be offered as non-cumulative or cumulative discounts. The non-cumulative discount is independent for each purchase. The buyer may purchase the same product number of times from the seller. In such a case, the discount is calculated on each purchase separately. The cumulative discount is offered for the quantity purchased over a definite period.
2. **Trade discounts:** These discounts are meant for middlemen who play an important role in promoting sales of the product. Trade discounts are also called *functional discounts*. Generally, trade discounts are offered in percentage terms over the quantity ordered by the middlemen.
3. **Seasonal discounts:** These discounts are offered for the products which have only seasonal demand. During the season the products will have demand in the market whereas during the off-season period the sales will fall sharply. To attract consumers during off-season periods, price discounts are offered.
4. **Cash discounts:** The purpose of the cash discount is to encourage buyers to pay cash at the earliest and to discourage credit purchases or longer repayment of the credit. Under this discount, the cash purchases are given higher discount. In the case of credit sales, the maximum credit period which carries discount at differed rates will be specified and after the period the seller may charge penal interest. For example, if a buyer pays cash fully after the purchase he may be given a 5% discount. If the credit is for 10 days, the buyer may get a 3% discount. If the credit period is 11 to 20 days, the buyer may get a 2% discount. After 20 to 30 days, there won't be any cash discount to the buyer. But after 30 days, the buyer may be charged interest for the amount due.

20.3. PRODUCT-LINE PRICING

Product-line pricing refers to setting prices for multiple products offered by a business unit in coordination with one another. The business unit will not take the individual product separately for fixation of the final price, but it will take the holistic perspective of all the products and their marketability. If the business unit offers more than one product/service, it will take into consideration the impact of the price of one product/service on the demand of other products/services offered by it in the same market. Therefore, the knowledge of interrelationships between multiple products in terms of costs as well as demands is necessary to determine prices to different products. Business units often face problems in establishing relationships among the products in a group/category. The following are the methods of product-line pricing.

Methods of product-line pricing

1. **Prices proportional to full costs:** This method is a cost based fixation of prices. The total costs of production will be allocated to different products and based on the full cost plus the net profit margin, the price of a product will be finalised. This method is criticised on the ground that it does not take into consideration the demand conditions.
2. **Prices proportional to incremental costs:** Incremental costs are the costs incurred for producing the additional quantity of units. These costs are directly traceable to the product. Under this method, business units produce the same percentage of contribution-margin for all the products over incremental costs. This method is criticised on the ground that it does not take into consideration the demand and competitive situations. Further, the allocation of common costs arbitrarily was also subject of the criticism.
3. **Prices with profit margins proportional to conversion costs:** Conversion costs are the costs incurred for converting raw materials into finished products. Such costs include labour costs and overheads. Fixation of prices based on conversion costs represents the value-added or the real contribution of the business unit.
4. **Prices which produce contribution margin depending upon the elasticity of the demand of different market segments:** Buyers belonging to premium segments are usually less price sensitive compared to buyers of the mass market. The business units try to exploit the disparity by way of charging higher profit/margin to the premium segment and low profit/margin to the mass market.
5. **Prices related to the stage in the product life cycle:** A product may pass through different stages in its life cycle. There are four stages identified in the life cycle of a product such as: introduction, growth, maturity, and decline. The market conditions are different in each of the stages. The business units have to charge different prices in different stages of the product life cycle to manage the life cycle to achieve optimum results.

20.4. PROBLEMS OF PRODUCT-LINE PRICING

The specific problems related to product-line pricing are:

1. Pricing products with different size
2. Special order pricing
3. Spare parts pricing
4. Pricing of leases
5. Pricing for licences
6. Pricing complementary products

1. **Pricing products with different size:** The pricing of products with different size, generally has certain problems.
   (a) **Fixing a uniform price for different sizes:** This practice is common where buyers' benefits do not vary with size. The products in which cost variations due to differences in size are marginal, the business units prefer to offer products of different sizes at a uniform price. For example, footwear industry, generally, offers different sizes of the same model at a uniform price.
   (b) **Fixing different prices for different sizes:** When business units incur additional expenditure due to the increase in sizes, they are forced to charge different prices for different sizes. If the business units charge the price proportionate to additional cost incurred, it does not fall under price discrimination. But in practice, it is found that the business units charge disproportionately to different sizes of the products based upon consumer demand. In this case, how the size is defined, is a matter of concern. The size may be in volume, length and width, weight, etc. To establish the pattern of relationship between price and size, it is necessary to understand the freedom of buyer to substitute one size of the product for the other. In such a case, the two sizes face compete with each other. The business unit may find it beneficial to charge a lower price for the larger size compared to the smaller one when there are economies of scale. It is to persuade the buyer to go for the larger size.
2. **Special order pricing:** Special orders are generally, customised. The production of goods/services will takes place as per the specifications of customers. Business units generally, charge differently to the special order goods/services. The common practice is to estimate the normal full cost and adding the desired profit to fix the price. The decision of pricing for special order goods/ services depends upon three important factors.

1. The maximum price that can be charged without the risk of losing the order/customer.
2. The minimum price at which the business unit can accept considering the other options such as: utilisation of idle capacity, alternative use of human resources, opportunity cost, etc.
3. The adjustments in price required in the short run are desirable because of the long-run future benefits.

3. **Spare parts pricing:** The business units producing durable goods generally face the problem of pricing spare parts. While deciding the price for spare parts, the business units consider the following issues:
   - The competitive condition in the market. If the business unit is a monopoly, then it has the freedom to fix the price. In the case of other competitive conditions, the price fixation should be as per the demand patterns of the market.
   - Some ancillary industries may specialise in the production of spare parts. Such business units offer keen competition to the original manufacturer. They may also charge prices lower than the manufacturer of original spare parts. In such a case, the ancillary units have to be considered competitors for spare parts.
4. **Pricing of leases:** Price determination for the equipment/space given on lease depends upon factors such as the cost of equipment, availability and accessibility, location, purpose, user characteristics, time period, life of the equipment, residual value, etc. The space at shopping malls, movie theatres, airports, railway stations, and so on, will get premium price compared to many locations in the same city. If the user is government, corporation, charitable institution, and certain customer categories, the price of the equipment may differ significantly. The cost of production, marketing and service costs of the equipment will set the minimum price limit. The business unit can also decide minimum rent to use as a price barrier to discourage the use of equipment by such customers who cannot exploit the potential use of equipment.
5. **Pricing of licences:** In the case of granting licences or charging a royalty for the use of patents, the business units have to consider the following issues:

1. If the cost of developing the patent is a sunk cost, the incremental costs of administering the patent have to be taken into consideration.
2. The maximum price limit should depend upon the benefits of the licensee.

3. The possibility of potential competition, infringement of patents and the intervention of government have to be considered while fixing minimum and maximum price limits.

6. **Pricing complementary products:** A decrease in the price of one product may lead to an increase in demand for the other product, in the case of complementary products. Therefore, a business unit may find it profitable to fix a lower price to the product. Sometimes, it may prefer to incur a loss on some products, if the business unit believes that it can sell another complimentary product at a higher margin. The objective is to take advantage of the cross-elasticity of the demand among the products. The business units may adopt loss leader pricing or they may go for tied sales. Loss leader pricing is used to attract a large number of customers to the stores by offering some products at a lower price (by incurring a loss on them). The seller aims to recover the loss and also get profits by the sale of other products. In the case of tied sales, the highly demanded products are tied with slow moving products and thereby, the entire stock can be cleared. The price will be fixed in such a way that the buyer perceives a higher benefit for the tied sales.

20.5. PRICE DISCRIMINATION

Price discrimination refers to the practice by a seller of charging different prices from the same buyer or different buyers for the same product or service without a corresponding difference in the cost. Price discrimination may be done at three levels. They are:

1. **First-degree price discrimination:** Under this approach, the price charged to each customer depends upon the intensity of his/her demand. Therefore, the seller charges a separate price from every customer.
2. **Second-degree price discrimination:** Under this approach, the price charged from the buyer depends upon the volume of purchase. If the buyer places an order for the small quantity he/she will be charged a relatively higher price compared to the buyer who places an order for larger quantity.
3. **Third-degree price discrimination:** When sellers charge different prices from different classes of customers it is called third-degree price discrimination. The sellers apply this type of price discrimination in different ways. The following are the ways through which the sellers discriminate the buyers:
   (a) **Customer-segment pricing:** Charging different prices to different customer segments/groups.

(b) **Product-form pricing:** Producers do offer the same product in different sizes, packages, designs, colours, etc. If the seller charges different prices which are not proportionate to the costs, it is called discriminated product-form pricing.

(c) **Image pricing:** Different products will have different brand images. If the seller uses the brand image of a product to fix the price, it is called image pricing.

(d) **Channel pricing:** In the distribution products to the market, the business units use different channels. Some channels are used to reach the premium segment and some to reach the mass market. The producers choose to charge different prices from different channels. Such practice is called channel pricing.

(e) **Location pricing:** The same product is priced differently at varied geographic locations although the cost of offering at each location is the same.

(f) **Time pricing:** If the seller fixes different prices in different seasons, days, or hours, it is called time pricing.

20.5.1. Objectives of Price Discrimination

Business units try to achieve the following objectives through price discrimination.

1. To exploit consumer surplus in favour of the business unit.
2. To minimise or prevent surpluses.
3. To expand the market base.
4. To optimise capacity utilisation.
5. To maximise profits.
6. To attack competitors or to defend the competition.
7. To maximise sales turnover.

20.5.2. Conditions for Price Discrimination

The following are the conditions required for the implementation of price discrimination.

1. **Multiple demand elasticity:** The demand elasticity should be different against variables such as income, location, substitutes, tastes and preferences, etc.
2. **Market segmentation:** It is necessary to divide the total market into segments in such a way that the demand elasticity is different in each segment.
3. **No reselling:** The seller should ensure that there is no possibility of resale of goods from the lower to the higher price sub-market.

20.6. SUMMARY

- Promotional pricing is a strategic option to the business units to manipulate demand through pricing strategy.
- As the revenue of the business unit depends upon the price and demand of a product, they have to decide prices suiting to the situations to exploit the demand and to generate the desired revenue.
- The different options of promotional pricing are: leader pricing, special occasion pricing, special customer pricing, cash discounts, low-interest financing, payment terms, warranty and service, psychological discounting, and psychological pricing.
- In leader pricing, the retailer offers huge discounts or price offs on a few products and promotes well to create awareness among the target customers.
- During special occasions, a special price may be offered to attract the customers and also to make them buy large quantities.
- Under psychological pricing, the business unit sets an artificially high price and then offers substantial savings to the customers on the purchase of the product.
- Psychological pricing creates an impression on the consumers that they are charged less than what they are paying for the product.
- Price discount is the strategic option to scale up the turnover or to defend the sales volume or to arrest the decline in sales.
- The six types of price discounts commonly used by the sellers are quantity discounts, trade discounts, seasonal discounts, and cash discounts.
- Under quantity discounts, buyers are encouraged to purchase product in large quantities and thereby they can get some discount over the actual price.
- Trade discounts are meant for middlemen who play an important role in promoting sales of the product.
- Seasonal discounts are offered for the products which have only seasonal demand.
- Cash discounts are provided to encourage buyers to pay cash at the earliest and to discourage credit purchases or longer repayment of the credit.
- Product-line pricing refers to setting prices for multiple products offered by a business unit in coordination with one another.
- The methods of product-line pricing are, prices proportional to full costs, prices proportional to incremental costs, prices with profit margins proportional to conversion costs, prices which produce

contribution margin depending upon the elasticity of the demand of different market segments, and prices related to the stage in the product life cycle.

- The specific problems related to product line pricing are pricing products with different size, special order pricing, spare parts pricing, pricing of leases, pricing for licences, and pricing complementary products.
- The pricing of products with different size, generally have certain problems like fixing uniform price irrespective of different sizes and fixing different prices for different sizes.
- When the production of goods/services takes place as per the specifications of customers and are charged differently to the special order goods/services it is called special order pricing.
- In spare parts pricing, the business units will consider the competitive condition of the market and some ancillary industries specialised in spare parts.
- Price determination for the equipment/space given on lease depends upon factors such as the cost of equipment, availability and accessibility, location, the purpose, user characteristics, the time period, the life of the equipment, residual value, etc.
- In the case of granting licences or charging a royalty for the use of patents, the business units have to consider the incremental costs of administering the patent, maximum price limit, and the possibility of potential competition.
- While pricing complementary products, the business units may adopt loss leader pricing or they may go for tied sales.
- Price discrimination refers to the practice by a seller of charging different prices to the same buyer or different buyers for the same product or service without a corresponding difference in the cost.
- The ways through which the sellers discriminate the buyers are customer -segment pricing, product-form pricing, image pricing, channel pricing, location pricing and time pricing.
- The conditions required for the implementation of price discrimination are multiple demand elasticity, market segmentation, and no reselling.

SHORT ANSWER QUESTIONS

1. Define leader pricing.
2. What is psychological discounting?
3. Distinguish between trade discounts and cash discounts.
4. Write a short note on product-line pricing.
5. Explain pricing products with different size.

6. What is special order pricing?
7. What conditions are required for the implementation of price discrimination?

ESSAY ANSWER QUESTIONS

1. What is promotional pricing? Discuss the options available under promotional pricing.
2. Define price discounts. Explain the types of price discounts commonly used by the sellers.
3. What is meant by product line pricing? Explain the methods of product-line pricing.
4. Describe the specific problems related to product line pricing.
5. What is price discrimination? Explain the objective of price discrimination.
6. Describe the three levels of price discrimination through which the sellers discriminate the buyers.

FILL IN THE BLANKS

1. Loss leader pricing is referred to as _________.
2. A reduction in the selling price of a product or service is called _________.
3. Quantity discount strategy is used to increase _________.
4. Trade discounts are also called _________.
5. The discounts offered for the products which have only seasonal demand is called _________.
6. The strategy of setting prices for multiple products offered by a business unit in coordination with one another is _________.
7. The practice of charging different prices to the same buyer or different buyers for the same product is called _________.
8. If the seller charges different prices which are not proportionate to the costs, it is called _________ pricing.

Answers

1. Leader pricing
2. Discount
3. Sales
4. Functional discount
5. Seasonal discount
6. Product-line pricing
7. Price discrimination
8. Product form

MULTIPLE-CHOICE QUESTIONS

1. The strategy where a business unit sets an artificially high price and then offers substantial savings to the customers on the purchase of the product is:
   (A) Psychological pricing (B) Psychological discounting
   (C) Cash discounts (D) Low-interest financing
2. Psychological pricing is also called :
   (A) Charm pricing (B) Leader pricing
   (C) Term pricing (D) Special customer pricing

3. The discount offered for the quantity purchased over a definite period is:
   (A) Fixed discount (B) Infinite discount
   (C) Cumulative discount (D) Non-cumulative discount
4. The discounts meant for middlemen who play an important role in promoting sales of the product are:
   (A) Trade discounts (B) Cash discounts
   (C) Quantity discounts (D) Mass discounts
5. The strategic option to scale up the turnover or to defend the sales volume or to arrest the decline in sales is:
   (A) Product discount (B) Sales discount
   (C) Customer discount (D) Price discount
6. The costs which are incurred for producing an additional quantity of units is called:
   (A) Additional costs (B) Incremental costs
   (C) Traceable costs (D) Conversion costs
7. If the seller fixes different prices in different seasons, days, or hours, it is called:
   (A) Time pricing (B) Image pricing
   (C) Channel pricing (D) Location pricing
8. Which one of the following is not an objective of price discrimination?
   (A) To minimise or prevent surpluses
   (B) To expand the market base
   (C) To maximise profits
   (D) To minimise sales turnover
9. Which one of the following is the condition required for the implementation of price discrimination?
   (A) Customer segmentation (B) Reselling
   (C) Market segmentation (D) Maximise surplus

Answers

1. B	2. A	3. C	4. A	5. D
6. B	7. A	8. D	9. C	

REFERENCES

1. Baye, M. (2000). *Managerial Economics & Business Strategy*. Boston: Irwin/McGraw-Hill.
2. Cowen, T. & Tabarrok, A. (2013). *Modern Principles of Economics* (2nd Edn). New York, NY: Worth Publishers.
3. Dean, J. (1968). *Managerial Economics.* New Delhi, India: Prentice-Hall of India Private Limited.
4. Dwivedi, D.N. (2015). *Managerial Economics* (8th Edn). New Delhi, India: Vikas Publishing House Pvt. Ltd.
5. Hibdon, J.E. (1969). *Price and Welfare Theory.* McGraw Hill.

6. Hirschey, M. (2009). *Managerial Economics* (12th Edn). USA: South-Western Cengage Learning.
7. Kotler, P. (1984). *Marketing Management: Analysis, Planning, and Control.* New York: Prentice-Hall, Inc.
8. Krugman, P.R. & Obstfeld, M. (2003). Economies of scale, imperfect competition and international trade. *International Economics: Theory and Policy*. Chapter 6, pp. 120-159. Pearson Education India.
9. Maheswari, Y. (2012). *Managerial Economics.* New Delhi, India: PHI Learning.
10. Mehta, P.L. (2007). *Managerial Economics: Text and Cases.* New Delhi, India: Sultan Chand & Co.
11. Perloff, J.M. (2012). *Micro Economics* (6th Edn). Boston, MA: Pearson Education Inc.
12. Phillips, R. (2005). *Pricing and Revenue Optimization.* Stanford University Press.
13. Rees, H. (2017). *Managerial Economics.* USA: Library Press.
14. Salvatore, D. & Rastogi, S.K. (2016). *Managerial Economics.* New Delhi, India: Oxford University Press.
15. Samuelson, W.F. & Marks, S.G. (2012). *Managerial Economics* (7th Edn). Hoboken, New Jersey: John Wiley & Sons, Inc.
16. Stiglar, G.J. (1953). *Theory of Price.* New York: The Macmillan Co.
17. Thomas, C.R. & Maurice, S.C. (2016). *Managerial Economics: Foundations of Business Analysis and Strategy.* New York: McGraw-Hill Education.
18. Varshney, R.L. & Maheswari, K.L. (2014). *Managerial Economics.* New Delhi, India: Sultan Chand & Sons.

Chapter

21 Price Forecasting

LEARNING OBJECTIVES

After studying this chapter, you should be able to understand:

- concept of price forecasting;
- specific price movements;
- nature of product and market conditions; and
- prospective supply and demand.

21.1. INTRODUCTION

Business units often experience the problem of change in the prices of raw materials and other factors of production, in the fixation and maintenance of selling price. The price fluctuations may be due to general economic conditions or due to scarcity and intense competitive conditions. To avoid surprises and to adopt a systematic price change for the products/services, business units find price forecasting as a useful method. Price forecasting involves the projection of changes in prices of raw materials and other factors of production for a definite future period by way of assessing the factors responsible for such price changes, and the direction of change in such factors. Price forecasting helps the business units to plan price changes of its products/services in advance and work out for profit maximisation.

For the purpose of price forecasting, business units closely monitor three important factors besides others. They are:

1. Specific price movements
2. Nature of product and market conditions
3. Prospective supply and demand of the product

21.2. SPECIFIC PRICE MOVEMENTS

The specific price movements of products can be traced particularly during seasonal demand and supply variations, and cyclical fluctuations.

1. **Seasonal demand and supply variations**: Some products have seasonal demand and some products have seasonal supply. The products such as woollen clothes, umbrellas, raincoats, cotton fabrics, air conditioners, and so on will find a sharp rise in demand during certain seasons. Similarly, the supply of many agricultural products is limited to certain seasons. The prices of products

having seasonal demand are influenced by the supply conditions and the same is true with the products having seasonal supply. The business units develop marketing strategies to influence the demand for seasonal products positively during off-season periods by making adjustments in price. They may offer the products at a lower price during the off-season periods in a market or they may export to such locations where different season exists. In the case of the products, supply is limited to a particular season, it is difficult to manage continuous supply throughout the year.

The business unit may need to have a large storage capacity, special measures for protecting the product and maintaining quality, and high level of investment. The cost of storage and maintenance will add to the procurement/production cost. During the season, due to the high level of supply, the business unit has to charge a lower price to match the prices of the competitors. During the other seasons, they have to fix a different price to recover additional expenditure. The business units can face the challenges created by seasonal demand variations and supply variations only when they have a reliable forecast that supports the price forecasting.

2. **Cyclical fluctuations :** As per the economic theory, business cycles occur over a period of time. During business cycles, the prices of the products/services fluctuate significantly. In a cyclical period, a boom is followed by a recession and then by depression. The price fluctuations during different stages of the business cycle are not similar for all products. In some products, the price changes are highly fluctuating, while the price fluctuations are marginal in some other products. There may not be any change in the prices of some products. Therefore, to make a price forecast during different stages of the business cycle, it is necessary to have the data and information related to the extent to which the price of a product responds to the changes in economic conditions. It is also necessary to forecast the general economic conditions in the market.

Sometimes, business cycles occur due to false expectations of price changes by a substantially large number of independent producers. Such cycles are known as *cobweb cycles*.

Cobweb cycles: Prof. Nicholas Kaldor proposed Cobweb theory in 1934. According to the theory, farmers plan independently to produce more quantity when higher prices in future are expected. Further, new farmers produce the same product with a similar expectation. As a result, the aggregate output increases substantially in the future leading to a fall in prices. Discouraged with the fall in prices, as they could not sell the products at the expected price and the loss incurred due to lower price realised, the producers plan to produce less quantity in future. The cumulative effect of smaller output plans of individual farmers creates a shortage of output for the next season. Due to the shortage of supply, the prices rise. The farmers may again plan for a larger production. The expansion and contraction of output due to individual producer price forecast create cyclical fluctuations of cob-web type. The length of the period of the cycle is usually two production periods or longer.

21.3. NATURE OF PRODUCT AND MARKET CONDITIONS

A successful price forecasting involves understanding of the nature of the product and its market conditions. The price of a given product fluctuates quite differently to that of another product due to fundamental differences in supply and demand conditions and the nature of the product. Therefore, understanding the nature of the products and their supply and demand characteristics in the market is useful in making a reliable price forecast. The following are important considerations to the nature of the product and market conditions for price forecasting.

1. **Main product or by-product:** The price forecasting depends upon whether it is the main product or a by-product. The production of a by-product depends largely on the quantity of the production of the main product. Therefore, the output of the by-product is insensitive to price changes of the main product. Since the by-products are linked to the main product and are not produced for their own sake, their cost of production is not relevant for price forecasting.
2. **Nature of demand:** The nature of the demand for a product in the market is an important factor for price forecasting. If the demand for a product is inelastic, a given change in the supply will bring less change in the price than when the demand for the product is elastic.
3. **Change in price of related goods:** The price forecasting of a product depends on the prospective changes in the prices of the related products (substitutes and complementary products). If prices of substitute products are expected to rise, the price of the product under consideration can also be predicted to increase, and vice versa. If the prices of complementary products are expected to increase, it will reduce their demand and the product under consideration may also experience a decrease in demand.
4. **Cost of raw material:** The prices of many products depend upon the prices of the raw materials. The producer not only considers

the prices at which the raw materials are purchased but the current prices of those raw materials. Price determination of goods produced would, therefore, require forecasting of the price of concerning raw materials. The expected increase in the prices of raw material will influence the price forecasting of the finished products.

5. **Influence of supply and demand on price:** The expected supply of the product and expected changes in demand are important factors for price forecasting. For example, in the case of agricultural products, the conditions for change in demand and the conditions for the change in the supply are different. The supply cannot be adjusted in the short run for the changes in demand. Therefore, the price forecaster focuses on the analysis of supply. In the case of manufactured products, supply can be adjusted to a greater extent to the changes in demand. Therefore, the key emphasis will be on demand analysis. For some products, the relative importance of supply and demand changes seasonally.
6. **Changes in the supply of product:** When demand for a product is changing, the nature and extent of the price depend upon the conditions of production capacity, the extent of unused production capacity and the availability of transportation and other resources. Sometimes, the business units may not be able to increase supply to respond fully to the changes in demand, i.e., either they may take more time to respond or they may not be able to increase the supply as much as the change in demand. In the case of raw materials, the response of supply to changes in demand is generally slow. Where supply response is faster, the price change is slower and vice versa. This fact needs to be considered while price forecasting.
7. **Extent of competition:** The extent of competition in the market also determines the extent to which accurate price forecasting can be made. If the industry is led by one dominant business unit, price policy of that dominant business unit becomes the basis for price forecasting. In the case of cut-throat competition in the market, it would not be easy to arrive at a reliable price forecast.
8. **Setting price in domestic and global market:** The price forecasting becomes more difficult when business units have a presence in domestic as well as global markets. The market conditions in international markets differ significantly to that of domestic markets. Both the markets may be influence each other in supply as well as demand determinants. The price forecaster has to understand and analyse carefully all such factors.
9. **Predictable and controllable supply:** If the supply of a product is predictable it is relatively easy for price forecasting. If the changes in

supply are unpredictable and beyond control, the price forecasting is very difficult. For example, an increase in the supplies of crude oil which is highly uncertain. The element of the unpredictability of supply makes the price outlook uncertain.

10. **Government intervention and policies:** Government intervention is common in the case of some products like steel, pharmaceuticals, cement, transport, communications, banking, insurance, etc. The price fixation, as well as changes in prices of such products, is subject to the approval of the government and within the particular policy framework existing at that time. If the government policy changes, their prices are also readjusted accordingly, so the price forecaster should understand, analyse and predict changes in the government policy towards the product under consideration.
11. **International trade barriers:** International trade barriers are subject to changes as per the changing situations internationally. Some changes may help a product to widen the market base. For some products, the market may become narrow. If there are any new import duties or other trade barriers on a particular product, then the business unit has to take into account such changes.

21.4. PROSPECTIVE SUPPLY AND DEMAND

In price forecasting, the study of prospective supply and demand conditions of a product is essential. The supply and demand conditions for the future shall be estimated accurately. For example, if the forecast is made for a period of six months, the probable changes in supply and demand of the product under consideration for the ensuing six months have got to be estimated carefully.

21.4.1. Prospective Supply

While estimating prospective supply the following points may be noted:

1. The current volume of production of the product should be compared with the total productive capacity to ascertain the excess productive capacity in the industry. A larger excess of capacity may create a tendency towards overproduction and acts as a restraint upon a rise in price.
2. The existing cost-price relationship may also determine prospective supply. There may be a tendency among business units producing a product to curtail or suspend their operations when its price has fallen below the variable cost of production. As a result, the overall perspective of supply would decline. On the other hand, when price exceeds the variable cost the business units may prefer to produce more quantity of output.

3. In the case of agricultural products, estimates of prospective supply made by the departments of agriculture and statistics, affect the market prices. Good crop reports lead to a decline in prices while adverse crop reports lead to an increase in prices.

21.4.2. Prospective Demand

The prospective demand for a product is determined by the nature of the need for that product, the willingness of the buyers to buy that product and their purchasing power. The important points to be noted in this regard are given below.

1. The volume of consumption of a particular product over the past several years would give an idea about the likely consumption in the future. However, in the case of durable products or luxuries, if the consumption in the immediate past has been below the average consumption, there is likely to be a greater demand in the immediate future and vice versa.
2. The desire backed up by purchasing power creates real demand. The estimation of prospective demand should consider the data on wage payments and prospective conditions of employment. These data are especially important in the case of consumer goods/ services.
3. As regards industrial products, for estimating the prospective demand, important data to be studied are the liquidity of industrial buyers, and the credit and capital market conditions, including the policies of investors and bankers.
4. Sometimes, even a high price becomes attractive when it is expected that a still-higher price will prevail in future. Indeed, during such times business units make all efforts to purchase as much as possible.

21.5. SUMMARY

- Business units often experience price fluctuations due to general economic conditions or due to scarcity and intensive competitive conditions.
- Price forecasting involves the projection of changes in prices of raw materials and other factors of production for a definite future period by way of assessing the factors responsible for such price changes, and the direction of change in such factors.
- The specific price movements of products can be traced particularly during seasonal demand and supply variations, and cyclical fluctuations.

- The prices of products having seasonal demand are influenced by the supply conditions and the same is true with the products having seasonal supply.
- The business units can face the challenges created by seasonal demand variations and supply variations only when they have a reliable forecast that supports the price forecasting.
- During business cycles, the prices of the products/services fluctuate significantly. The price fluctuations during different stages of the business cycle are not same for all products.
- To make a price forecast during different stages of the business cycle, it is necessary to have the data and information related to the extent to which the price of a product responds to the changes in economic conditions.
- Sometimes, business cycles occur due to false expectations of price changes by a substantially large number of independent producers. Such cycles are known as *cobweb cycles* as proposed by Prof. Nicholas Kaldor in 1934.
- The important considerations to the nature of the product and market conditions for price forecasting are main product or by-product, nature of demand, change in the price of related goods, cost of raw material, influence of supply and demand on price, changes in the supply of the product, extent of competition, setting price in domestic and global market, predictable and controllable supply, government intervention and policies, and international trade barriers.
- While estimating prospective supply the current volume of production of the product should be compared with the total productive capacity to ascertain the excess productive capacity in the industry.
- The prospective demand for a product is determined by the nature of the need for that product, the willingness of the buyers to buy and their purchasing power.

SHORT ANSWER QUESTIONS

1. Write a short note on price forecasting.
2. What are cyclical fluctuations?
3. What are cobweb cycles?
4. Distinguish predictable and controllable supply.
5. How prices are set in the domestic and global market?
6. What points can be considered while estimating prospective supply?

ESSAY ANSWER QUESTIONS

1. Explain in detail the specific price movements of products.
2. Describe the important considerations to the nature of the product and market conditions for price forecasting.
3. Explain the prospective supply and demand conditions of a product in price forecasting.
4. Discuss the purpose of forecasting price of products by the business units.

FILL IN THE BLANKS

1. Price forecasting helps the business units to plan price changes and work out for profit __________.
2. The cost of storage and maintenance will add to the __________ cost.
3. During business cycles, the prices of the products/services __________.
4. When business cycles occur due to false expectations of price changes by a substantially large number of independent producers, it is known as __________.
5. A successful price forecasting involves understanding of the nature of the product and its __________.
6. The prices of many products depend upon the prices of the __________.

Answers

1. Maximisation
2. Procurement
3. Fluctuates
4. Cobweb cycle
5. Market conditions
6. Raw materials

MULTIPLE-CHOICE QUESTIONS

1. In a cyclical period, a boom is followed by:
   (A) Recession (B) Depression
   (C) Introduction (D) Growth
2. Cobweb theory was proposed by
   (A) Phillip Kotler (B) Adam Smith
   (C) Nicholas Kaldor (D) Joel Dean
3. The length of the production period of the cycle is usually:
   (A) One or more (B) Two or more
   (C) Three or more (D) Four or more
4. Cobweb cycle theory was developed in the year:
   (A) 1934 (B) 1924
   (C) 1928 (D) 1932
5. Where the supply response is faster, the price change is:
   (A) Faster (B) Slower
   (C) Higher (D) Lower

Answers:

1. A 2. C 3. B 4. A 5. B

REFERENCES

1. Cowen, T. & Tabarrok, A. (2013). *Modern Principles of Economics (2nd Edn)*. New York, NY: Worth Publishers.
2. Dean, J. (1968). *Managerial Economics.* New Delhi, India: Prentice-Hall of India Private Limited.
3. Dwivedi, D.N. (2015). *Managerial Economics* (8th Edn). New Delhi, India: Vikas Publishing House Pvt. Ltd.
4. Hirschey, M. (2009). *Managerial Economics* (12th Edn). USA: South-Western Cengage Learning.
5. Kotler, P. (1984). *Marketing Management: Analysis, Planning, and Control.* New York: Prentice-Hall, Inc.
6. Maheswari, Y. (2012). *Managerial Economics.* New Delhi, India: PHI Learning.
7. Mehta, P.L. (2007). *Managerial Economics: Text and Cases.* New Delhi, India: Sultan Chand & Co.
8. Perloff, J.M. (2012). *Micro Economics* (6th Edition). Boston, MA: Pearson Education Inc.
9. Salvatore, D. & Rastogi, S.K. (2016). *Managerial Economics.* New Delhi, India: Oxford University Press.
10. Stiglar, G.J. (1953). *Theory of Price.* New York: The Macmillan Co.
11. Thomas, C.R. & Maurice, S.C. (2016). *Managerial Economics: Foundations of Business Analysis and Strategy.* New York: McGraw-Hill Education.
12. Varshney, R.L. & Maheswari, K.L. (2014). *Managerial Economics.* New Delhi, India: Sultan Chand & Sons.

Chapter

22 Profit Policies

LEARNING OBJECTIVES

After studying this chapter, you should be able to understand:

- concept and characteristics of profit;
- kinds, functions of profit and role of profit;
- theories of profit and profit policy; and
- factors influencing and limiting profit policy.

22.1. CONCEPT OF PROFIT

Profit is considered an incentive for undertaking entrepreneurial function. It is regarded as a reward for risk-taking. Profit is referred to as the surplus of total revenue over the total cost. In other words, it is the reward or returns accruing to the entrepreneur who can keep the total cost below the total revenue. One of the major goals of a business unit is to make a profit. Business units try to exploit every possible opportunity to generate more and more profits. Many of them consider the purpose of business is to make profits. The entire organisational effort of every business unit focuses on generating profit from every activity. It is not just making some profit, the business unit's work for making more and more profits every year. They want to achieve growth in profits to satisfy their shareholders.

Profit means different things to different people. The word profit is regarded in a different sense by business units, accountants, employees, tax collectors, public, investors, and economists. In a general sense, profit is regarded as an income of the proprietors/ shareholders. Similarly, wages for the labourers, rent to the owners of any land or building and interest to the investors of the capital of a business are perceived as profit by the respective groups. To an account, profit means the excess of revenue overall paid out costs including both manufacturing and overhead expenses. In accountancy, profit or business income means the profit of a business including its non-allowance expenses.

In economics, pure profit is called profit. Pure profit may be defined as a residual left after all contractual costs have been met, including the transfer costs of management, insurable risks, depreciation and payment to shareholders, sufficient amount to maintain investment at its current level. Therefore,

Pure profit = Total revenue – (Explicit costs + Implicit costs)

Economic or pure profit creates provision for depreciation, insurable risks, and required minimum payments to investors in preventing them from withdrawing their investment/capital. Pure profit is associated to be a short-term phenomenon for a business unit. It does not exist in the long run, especially under perfect market conditions. Due to the existence of imperfect market conditions, pure profit may either be positive or negative for a single business unit in a single year. Economic profit also takes into account the implicit or imputed costs. The implicit cost is also called an *opportunity cost*. If an entrepreneur uses his labour in his own business, he foregoes his income or salary, which he might have earned by working as a manager in another business unit. Similarly, by using assets like land and building for his own business, he foregoes the market rent, which might have earned otherwise. All these foregone incomes such as interest, salary and rent, are called opportunity costs or transfer costs. Accounting profit does not consider the opportunity cost.

Profit is the reward for entrepreneurial ability and goes to the entrepreneur of the business unit. Profit is residual of income over and above all economic cost, both explicit and implicit, that results from the operation of a business. It is the return for the business unit or investors for risk-taking. The following are some of the definitions of profit by economists.

Definitions of profit

Author	**Definition**
J. Von Thunen (1826)	Profit is the residue after deduction of interest, insurance for risk and wages for management.
J.A. Schumpeter (1934)	Profit is the reward for the work of entrepreneur or it is a payment for risks, uncertainties and innovations.
Henry Grayson (1954)	Profit may be considered a reward for making innovations, a reward for accepting risks and uncertainties, a result of imperfections in the market. Any one of these conditions or a combination of them can give rise to economic profit.
J. K. Mehta (1962)	The element of uncertainty introduces a fourth category of sacrifice in the productive activities of man in a dynamic world. This category is risk-bearing or uncertainty bearing. It is remunerated by profit.
H. Speight (1964)	Profit is commonly said to be a payment for risk-bearing.

22.2. CHARACTERISTICS OF PROFIT

The characteristics of profit are:

1. Profit is the residual income.
2. Higher the risk, higher the profit.
3. Profit is always uncertain and indeterminate.
4. Profit always bears dynamic fluctuations.
5. Profit may be positive, zero or negative.
6. Profit occurs by keeping total cost below total revenue.
7. It is the ability of entrepreneur, i.e., able entrepreneur will earn more profit.

22.3. KINDS OF PROFIT

Profit is generally classified under the following heads:

1. Gross profit
2. Net profit
3. Normal profit
4. Supernormal profit

1. **Gross profit:** Gross profit or total profit is the residual income which accrues when total explicit costs are deducted from total revenue or total sales proceeds of the business unit. Explicit cost means the visible cost of production, which includes the cost of raw material, wages, salary, power, etc. In financial accounting terms, gross profit is the difference between total revenue and direct cost.

   Gross profit = Total revenue – Total cost

2. **Net profit:** Net profit or economic profit is the reward paid to the entrepreneur for taking the risk in the process of production, bearing uncertainty, and reward for innovations. It is that residual income which accrues when explicit and implicit costs are deducted from total revenue. Implicit cost is also called *invisible cost of production,* which includes advertising cost, transport cost, etc. In accounting terms, net profit is referred to as the difference between direct and indirect costs and total revenue.

   Net profit = Total revenue – (Explicit cost + Implicit cost)

   or

   Net profit = Total revenue – (Direct cost + Indirect cost)

3. **Normal profit:** The concept of normal profit was propounded by Alfred Marshall. It includes the production cost of the business unit. According to this concept, the business unit can recover cost only. In other words, the business unit can recover variable cost and not the fixed cost. Thus, it is said to be in normal profit situation or no profit no loss situation. It is the minimum amount which an entrepreneur must get to survive in the market.

4. **Supernormal profit:** The income accrued over and above normal profit is called supernormal profit. It accrues to the entrepreneur when he succeeds in keeping total cost below the total revenue. In other words, when average revenue is greater than the average cost, the business unit earns a supernormal profit or abnormal profit. Supernormal profit is generally a short-term phenomenon. In the long run, business units earn only normal profits due to imperfect competitive conditions. However, in the case of a monopoly market, the business unit may even earn supernormal or abnormal profit in the long run.

22.4. FUNCTIONS OF PROFIT

According to Peter F. Drucker, profit serves three main purposes of a business unit. They are:

1. A measure of performance
2. Premium to cover costs to stay in business
3. Ensuring the supply of future capital

1. **A measure of performance:** Profit measures the net effectiveness and soundness of business efforts. When a business unit earns a higher profit, it indicates that the business is being run successfully. Indeed, profit is far from being the perfect measure of business efficiency, but it is the best indicator of the general efficiency of a business unit.
2. **Premium to cover costs to stay in business:** Profit is the premium that covers the costs of staying in business. These costs include replacement costs, obsolescence market, and technical risks and uncertainty.
3. **Ensuring supply of future capital:** Profit ensures the supply of future capital for innovation and expansion. Directly, by providing the means of self-financing out of retained profits and indirectly, through providing sufficient inducement for new external capital which will optimise the business units' capital structure and minimise its cost of capital.

22.5. ROLE OF PROFIT

Profit is a crucial earning expected in business. Profitability is an index of the success of business in an economy. Though, in reality, business units rarely avoided the objective of profit maximisation, they do expect and try for a high level of profit. A reasonably high level of profit is essential to play its positive role in the market economy as well as the economy as a whole on various counts. The various aspects of profit are:

1. Shareholders' benefit
2. High business reputation
3. High capacity to perform R&D
4. Prudency against risks
5. Ploughing back for growth
6. Corporate tax revenue
7. Business sustainability
8. Better employment
9. Virtuous cycle
10. Market signals
11. Resource allocation

1. **Shareholders' benefit:** Profit is the reward for shareholders' investment initiative. Shareholders receive high dividends when the business units earn high profits. The higher the profit earned by the business unit, the higher will be the returns of the shareholders. Therefore, the main objective of the business units is to maximise the profits.
2. **High business reputation:** A high dividend paid from high profit enhances the image of the business unit in the share market. Tata, Birla, Ambani, and such other large business houses have earned their business reputation because of the high profitability of their business units.
3. **High capacity to perform R&D:** When substantial profit is earned by a business unit, it can put more funds in its research and development (R&D) programme. This makes it possible to acquire, improve and adopt better technology and enhance the efficiency scale of the business unit.
4. **Prudency against risks:** Part of profit may be retained as a reserve fund that may provide a cushion to the business unit for risk-bearing and self-dependence in bad times of economic downturn.
5. **Ploughing back for growth:** High-profit earnings enable the business unit to invest further using own resources for the expansion and growth of the business. Retained profits would become an important source of internal finance to launch upon new capital investment projects and business enlargement.
6. **Corporate tax revenue:** When business units earn more profit, the government receives high yields in the form of corporate tax. The revenue generated by corporate taxes will help in the development of the economy.
7. **Business sustainability:** A profit making business unit can deal with cyclical ups and downs of the business more comfortably and remain in a sustained position.

8. **Better employment:** A profit making business unit can offer better facilities and rewards to employees, such as bonus, recreation facilities, increments, etc.
9. **Virtuous cycle:** There is a virtual cycle of risks and profit management in a dynamic business system. A business unit expects to earn high returns by taking high risk involving ventures. When high profits are earned, the business unit gains more confidence and develops the capacity to bear further high risks and earn more profits.
10. **Market signals:** Supernormal profits earned by the business units imply business potentiality of growth in a dynamic market economy. It indicates the chance of entry for the new business units in a competitive situation.
11. **Resource allocation:** Usually, the rate of returns expected in the channels of business guide the business units to allocate their business resources into the production activity. For instance, if the profit range is higher for two-wheelers rather than cars, the automobile business unit may shift its focus from car to two-wheelers production. Profit diverts scarce business resources to flow where returns are expected to be high and better. This would mean the optimisation of resource allocation to meet business goals in a better way.

By and large, profit has a positive role to play in a dynamic market economy. Profit is a legitimate earning of genuine entrepreneurship in serving the community through want fulfilling activity. Hence, the lowest risk taking business community deserves respect and dignity in a free economic society.

22.6. THEORIES OF PROFIT

The concept of profit is better understood if different theories of profit analysed. The following are the nine popular theories on profit.

1. Walker's rent theory
2. Taussig's wage theory
3. Hawley's risk bearing theory
4. Knight's uncertainty bearing theory
5. Clark's dynamic theory
6. Schumpeter's innovation theory
7. Marginal productivity theory
8. Socialist/labour exploitation theory
9. Monopoly power theory

22.6.1. Walker's Rent Theory of Profit

Rent theory was advocated by American economist Francis L. Walker in 1887. This theory is based on the concept of net profit. Walker stated that profit is the rent for exceptional abilities exhibited by the entrepreneur over others. Rent is the difference between the yields of the least and the most efficient entrepreneurs. Walker computed profit by comparing the abilities of the marginal and super marginal entrepreneur. As rent is considered the reward for the use of land, in the same way, profit is treated as the reward for ability. As pieces of land differ in their fertility, an entrepreneur also differs in his ability. An able entrepreneur is defined as a super marginal entrepreneur in the theory and his ability is compared to that of the marginal entrepreneur who sells his product on just cost and earns no or little profit. Thus, profit is the rent for the ability of the entrepreneur.

Criticism

1. Profit does not always arise due to ability; other factors (macro-variables) are also responsible for profit.
2. Rent is generally positive and in some cases, it may be even zero, while profit may be positive, zero, and even negative.
3. A marginal entrepreneur does not exist in the real world.
4. Profit arises in a dynamic economy, where changes take place continuously and not in a static economy.
5. This is a short period theory where profit enters into the price, which is not possible in the long period.

22.6.2. Wage Theory of Profit

Wage theory was proposed by American economist F. W. Taussig (1891 & 1910). According to the theory, profit is similar to wage, which is given to the entrepreneur for the services rendered by him/her in the business. This theory explains the similarity between labour and entrepreneur. Just as the labour gets wages for the services rendered in the business, an entrepreneur gets profit in the business for providing services. Thus, this theory emphasises that profit is a type of wage for the entrepreneur.

But this theory has ignored the fact that labour does not take any risk whereas, an entrepreneur takes the risk. Therefore, an entrepreneur is justified to have profit. This theory also ignores that labour will get wages under all circumstances but this is not applicable in case of profit.

Criticism

1. Wages are always positive, but it is not essential that profit is always positive. It may be positive, zero, or even negative in dimension.

2. Labour and entrepreneur are not similar. Labour is generally performing the tasks assigned to them by the entrepreneurs. Whereas, entrepreneurs create work which involves a lot of physical and mental exercise.
3. This theory does not explain the profit received by the shareholders, who may not render any service.
4. Labour does not undertake any risk, but an entrepreneur undertakes risk so there is no similarity between labour and entrepreneur.

22.6.3. Risk Theory of Profit

Risk theory was propounded by American economist F.B. Hawley in 1893. In a business unit, the risk may occur due to obsolescence of a product, a sudden drop in prices, unavailability of specific materials, introduction of a better substitute by a competitor and risks due to fire, war, etc. Hawley considered risk an unavoidable factor of production and business units who take risk are more likely to earn better profits. Therefore, profit is considered a reward for taking risk. If any entrepreneur of a business unit undertakes risk, he will find a chance to have profit, and if he is not prepared to take any risk, he may not be able to have more profit. Thus, this theory is based on the basic principle that higher the risk, higher the profit and lower the risk, lower the profit. As per the theory, profit consists of two parts:

- Compensation for actual or average loss supplementing the various classes of risk.
- A reward for facing the consequences of being exposed to risk in entrepreneurial activities.

Hawley assumed that profits arise from factor ownership as long as it involves risk. In case of absence of risks, an entrepreneur would cease to be an entrepreneur and would not receive any profit. In this theory, profits arise from uninsured risks of the business unit. The amount of reward cannot be determined until the uncertainly ends with the sale of the products of a business unit.

Criticism

1. There is no direct relationship between risk and profit.
2. Profit does not arise due to risk rather accrues due to the avoidance of risk.
3. Profit does not arise due to all types of risk.
4. It does not measure the volume of profit generated for taking the risk.

22.6.4. Uncertainty Bearing Theory of Profit

Uncertainty bearing theory was propounded by American economist Frank H. Knight during 1921. According to this theory, profit is the reward for bearing uncertainty. This theory is also known as *Knight's theory of profit,* as he lays down the difference that profit does not arise from all types of risk. So, he divided risk under two heads namely, foreseen and unforeseen risks.

1. **Foreseen risks** are those risks which can be predicted and can be covered through insurance. It includes the risk of fire, theft, etc. It is also referred to as *calculable risk.*
2. **Unforeseen risks** refer to those risks which cannot be predicted and cannot be covered through insurance. It includes government policy, business cycles, competitive risk, technical risk, etc. It is also referred to as *incalculable risk.*

According to Knight, profit arises due to non-insurable risk. As this risk cannot be foreseen and no insurable company is ready to cover these risks, these are called *non-insurable risk* or *uncertainty bearing risk.* Uncertainty makes decision making critical for an entrepreneur. If the decisions taken by entrepreneur attest to be accurate, the business unit makes a profit. Thus, according to Knight, profit arises from the decisions taken and implemented under the conditions of uncertainly. The profits may also arise as a result of the increase in the degree of monopoly, holding of stocks that give rise to windfall gains and introduction of new techniques or innovations.

Criticism

1. Uncertainty bearing is not a factor of production.
2. Profit is not the only reward for uncertainty bearing.
3. This theory does not measure the volume of profit.
4. This theory explains only sudden and causal explanation of profit.

22.6.5. Dynamic Theory of Profit

Dynamic theory was propounded by American economist J.B. Clark (1891). According to Clark, profit always arises in a dynamic economy and not in a static economy. The basic reason for profit in a dynamic economy is continuous changes in the economy. In the case of a static economy, everything is predictable with absolute accuracy. No surprises and the activities of the previous year will be repeated in the current year. The value generated due to production activity will be shared by the factors of production. As a result, the price will be equal to its cost and there will be no profit. The static economy is ideal and imaginary. In the real world, the environment is dynamic and change is a continuous process.

Clark identified five changes that continuously take place in the dynamic economy and are responsible for profit. They are:

1. continuous change in population;
2. continuous changes in techniques of production;
3. continuous changes in the supply of capital;
4. continuous changes in the structure of the business unit; and
5. continuous changes in tastes, preferences, and habits of consumers.

According to Clark, only those business units will survive, develop and incur profit, which can adopt these changes and satisfy consumer needs. The business units which do not accept these changes cannot survive and generate any profit. The major function of entrepreneurs or managers in dynamic economic conditions is to take advantage of changes and promote their business by expanding their sales and reducing the cost of production. A dynamic economy is characterised by the following features:

- Increase in population.
- Increase in capital.
- Improvement in production techniques.
- Changes in the forms of the business unit.

Clark stated that profit is an intangible sum that entrepreneurs can grasp but cannot retain. It slips through their fingers and bestows itself on all members of the society. This results in a rise in demand for factors of production and therefore, rise in factor prices and subsequent rise in the cost of production. Due to a rise in the production costs and a subsequent fall in the selling price of the products, the profits of a business unit vanish. The disappearance of profit does not mean that profit arises in the dynamic economy once only, but it means that the managers take the advantage of the changes taking place in the economy and thereby make profits continuously.

Criticism

1. Every change does not bring profit.
2. The static economy does not exist in the real world.
3. This theory does not give any importance to uncertainty bearing and risk involved.
4. It does not measure the volume of profit.

22.6.6. Innovation Theory of Profit

The innovation theory was developed by American economist Joseph A. Schumpeter. By innovation, Schumpeter means adopting new techniques of production, as a result of which production cost would tend to decline and it will lead to an increase in profit. If a business unit wants to increase the level of profit, it can either increase the price of the product, or reduce the cost of production.

The first strategy may not be appropriate, as it promotes competition in the market. If the business unit increases the price of the product, the competitors may not increase the price. As a result, the demand for the product of the business unit will fall, which will further reduce the profit margin. The second way is to increase the volume of profit. This profit will keep on accruing until the consumers stop accepting this innovation. Thus, it can be said that the profit which accrues due to innovation lapses. Hence, this theory explains that profit accrues to the business unit only because of innovations and not due to any other reason.

Schumpeter argued that the process of economic development can be supplemented by aspects such as the emergence of interest and profits, and the repetition of trade cycles. To explain the phenomenon of economic development and profit, Schumpeter starts from the state of a stationary equilibrium, which is characterised by the equilibrium in all the spheres. Under the conditions of stationary equilibrium, the total receipts from the business are exactly equal to the cost. This means that there will be no profit. The business units can earn profits through the introduction of innovations in the production process and the techniques used in the supply of products. The following are some of the activities included in innovations:

- Introduction of a new product or a new method of production.
- Identifying the new sources of procuring raw materials.
- Innovativeness in organising the industry with new techniques.
- Identifying new markets and target consumers.

Criticism

1. Innovation theory ignores the risk factor of the entrepreneur.
2. Profit does not accrue due to innovations only.
3. This theory fails to measure the volume of profit.
4. This theory relates to a short period only.

22.6.7. Marginal Productivity Theory

This theory explains that reward for every factor of production can be decided by the marginal productivity of that factor of production. The theory assumes entrepreneurial ability as one of the factors of production. According to this theory, the value of entrepreneurial ability, i.e., profit is decided by the marginal productivity of the entrepreneur. The supply of entrepreneurial ability is scarce, and it depends on how much an entrepreneur earn in an industry or his income, i.e., transfer income and opportunity cost. The supply of entrepreneurial ability cannot be increased or decreased easily. Supply being scarce, able entrepreneurs earn huge profits due to higher marginal productivity. Under conditions of perfect competition, profits of an entrepreneur tend to equal to his marginal productivity. But perfect competition is nowhere found in the real world.

Criticism

1. The assumption of the theory that all entrepreneurs are of the same type with equal skills is not correct.
2. The marginal productivity theory is a one-sided argument. It confers more emphasis on demand side and ignores the supply side.
3. This theory is based on the assumption of perfect competition and in real situation perfect competition does not exist.
4. This theory does not consider windfall profits.
5. It is difficult to determine the marginal productivity of an entrepreneur because in case there is only one entrepreneur.

22.6.8. Socialist Theory of Profit

The socialist theory of profit was propounded by American economist Karl Marx (1818-1883). According to this theory, the value of a product is determined by labour itself involved in the process of production. It is also referred to as *labour exploitation theory*. Under a capitalist economy, a major part of total produce is grabbed by capitalists and a small portion of the produce is given to the labour. The major portion which is taken away by the capitalists is referred to as *surplus value*. Therefore, the main reason for accruing profit is the exploitation of labour by capitalists, termed legalised robbery.

This will result in a division of the economy into two parts, i.e., haves and have-nots. The first category enjoys at the cost of the second. But the second category will struggle due to exploitation and will go for strikes and lockouts. They will demand higher wages and other amenities of life. Therefore, in the long-run profit will tend to fall.

Criticism

1. The theory explains that labour is the sole factor which is responsible for accruing profit, which is incorrect. There are several other factors which are engaged in production, along with labour.
2. Profit is not just the outcome of exploitation of labour, rather it is due to the ability of the entrepreneur.
3. The theory ignores the risks and uncertainty bearing.

4. The theory does not consider the windfall profits.
5. The theory does not provide any means to measure the volume of profit.

22.6.9. Monopoly Theory of Profit

Monopoly is a market situation in which there is a single seller of a product without a close substitute. Monopoly market may arise due to sole ownership of raw materials, economies of scale, legal sanction, protection, mergers and acquisitions. A monopolist may earn a pure profit, which is also called *monopoly profit*. A monopoly maintains earning of pure profit in the long run by using its monopoly powers. A monopolist enjoys the power of controlling supply and price and prevents the entry of competitors by reducing the prices of the products in the market.

22.7. PROFIT POLICY

Profit is a necessity for survival and growth. Different business units adopt different policies to achieve business unit goals. Generally, business units adopt two types of policies, i.e., profit maximisation and fair profit policy.

22.7.1. Profit Maximisation Policy

According to this policy, the main aim of every business unit is to maximise its profit. This policy outlines that profit is the only reward to measure the efficiency of a business unit. In other words, a business unit is said to be ideal, only when it maximises profit. The fundamental assumption of economic theory is that the basic objective of every business unit is to maximise profits. However, business units often plan profit maximisation in the long run for various other reasons. They may try to achieve some benefits with the long-term profit maximisation plan such as restraining competition, maintaining management control, discouraging wage demands, and avoiding antitrust suits. Many big business units do not operate on the principle of profit maximisation in terms of marginal costs and revenues. They set standards or targets of reasonable profits.

Criticism

1. This is a vague policy. This theory does not explain how a business unit can maximise its level of profit.
2. This theory ignores risk and uncertainty factor-essential for every business unit.
3. This theory ignores the time factor. It does not explain how much time is required to maximise profit.

22.7.2. Fair Profit Policy

In the present economic conditions, the business units are adopting a satisfactory profit policy, which further motivates the business unit to remain in business for a longer period. This policy explains a reasonable level of profit, which will enable the business unit to clear all its liabilities and a reasonable amount left, will encourage them to stay in business. The business unit generally adopts this policy for the following reasons:

1. To discourage potential competitors.
2. To restrain wage demands of organised labour.
3. To maintain customer goodwill.
4. To keep control undiluted.
5. To maintain pleasant working conditions.
6. To stay alive in business for a longer period.
7. To fulfil the social obligation.

By keeping these reasons in mind, business units may pursue fair profit policy. This policy is also advantageous from the viewpoint of society.

22.8. FACTORS INFLUENCING PROFIT POLICY

Making a profit is considered the ultimate objective of every business unit. The success of a business unit is largely measured by the amount of profit earned by it. Thus, profit maximisation is the major goal of a business unit. It is to be noted that the modern business units do not accept this view and hold another opinion in this regard. Also, this does not imply that earning a profit is not their objective. Their entire focus is not just on earning profits but on attaining other objectives as well. The factors influencing profit policy are:

1. Industry leadership
2. Restricting the entry
3. Political impact
4. Customer goodwill
5. Wage consideration
6. Liquidity preference
7. Risks and uncertainty bearing
8. Innovations
9. Element of luck or chance
10. Differences in abilities of the entrepreneurs

1. **Industry leadership:** This may comprise either the accomplishment of the maximum sales volume or maintaining maximum product lines. To be a leader in the industry, there has to be a satisfactory level of profit along with the capital invested, labour force employed and volume of output produced.

2. **Restricting the entry:** When a business unit adheres to a policy of restricting its profit, no competitor is expected to enter the market because the profits are not attractive. Reasonable profit which ensures its survival and growth is essential.
3. **Political impact:** A business unit earning huge profits is likely to come under the scanner of the government and thereby attract heavy imposition of the tax upon it.
4. **Consumer goodwill:** Good customer relationship is vital for the survival of every business unit in the market. For maintaining consumer goodwill, business units have to restrict the profit. By upholding low profit, the business units may pursue the goodwill of the consumers.
5. **Wage consideration:** When a business unit earns high profits, it implies that it can pay high wages to its labour force. If the business unit declares high dividends to the shareholders and the labour associations come to know about this, they will naturally demand higher wages, bonus and so forth.
6. **Liquidity preference:** Several business units impart greater prominence to capital soundness. Therefore, the management gives preference to liquidity for maximising the profits of a business unit. Liquidity preference is referred to as the preference to hold cash for meeting the day-to-day transactions of the business unit.
7. **Risks and uncertainty bearing:** It is commonly held that the emergence of profit is attributable to taking risks on the part of the entrepreneurs. The expectation of profit is a necessary prerequisite for starting any new venture by the entrepreneur because every business involves a certain risk. Taking risk is one of the important functions of an organizer. Greater the risk higher should be the gain or profit to induce the entrepreneur to start a business.
8. **Innovations:** Profits may also arise on account of economic innovation. By economic innovation is meant the introduction of a new market, the invention of new methods of production, development of a new source of raw material and new methods of the business unit. The business units which make use of such innovations first can make profits until competitors come forward to do the same. Therefore, economic innovation is the source of profit. In other words, profits arise also because of economic innovation.
9. **Element of luck or chance:** Profits may also arise merely on account of good luck. Certain business units flourish only due to their good luck. Apart from, luck, sometimes profits may arise just by chance. For instance, during war, some countries could get the chance of selling the commodities at a better and higher price in the market.

Such profits would not have been there in the absence of war which gave the chance to the entrepreneurs. Such profits are called the *fortuitous gains.*

10. **Differences in abilities of the entrepreneurs:** The profits may arise mainly on account of differences in the abilities of the entrepreneurs. Profits can be compared with that of rent which arises in the case of land. Just as the superior grade of land earns a surplus over and above the marginal grade land, the entrepreneurs superior in ability earn surplus over and above the earnings of the marginal entrepreneurs. Hence, profits can be referred to as the rent of ability. In other words, profits arise also because of the difference in the abilities of the entrepreneurs.

22.9. FACTORS LIMITING PROFITS

Profit of a business unit can be limited by many factors. Modern business units themselves try to limit the profits on account of the number of reasons. The factors limiting the profits are as follows:

1. Creation of competition
2. Creation of substitutes
3. Heavy taxation
4. Increased wages
5. Increasing the cost of input
6. Ceiling on profits

1. **Competition:** Modern business units usually discourage entry of potential rivals or competitors. Though there are opportunities for making enormous profits. Profits made in the absence of competition do not get distributed among a large number of business units and thus, profits of another individual business units can be limited and evils of excess profits such as inequalities of income and wealth and concentration of economic and political power can be easily avoided.
2. **Substitutes:** Another factor that can limit the profits is the availability of substitutes. When there are a few /no substitutes for the product of a business unit, they can make huge profits. When substitutes are available, the business unit cannot charge a higher price to make more profits as there is a danger that the consumers may shift to substitute products.
3. **Heavy taxation:** Profits may also be limited to avoid heavy taxation. When business units are making huge profits, a part of their profits may be taken employing heavy taxation. Either the existing tax rates may be enhanced or new taxes may be introduced.

4. **Increased wages:** Another reason for limiting profits is the potential demand from workers for an increase in the rate of wages. Labour is the factor of production which contributes the most in the production. When excess profits are made by business units, the working class demands higher wages. The higher profits may be a short term phenomenon but once the wages are increased it may not be possible to reduce.
5. **Increase in the cost of the inputs:** When business units are making a lot of profits, the government can limit them by increasing the cost of various inputs which they use in the production. When the cost of inputs increases, their total cost of production will increase and profits will be reduced. Generally, this method is not used for limiting the profits because any increase in the cost is likely to be shifted on to the consumer by raising the price of the product. However, this is also one of the factors that can limit the profits provided price of the product is controlled.
6. **Ceiling on profits:** Profits can be limited by imposing direct controls such as a ceiling on profits by passing certain laws. This measure of limiting profits may work more effectively in socialistic countries.

22.10. SUMMARY

- Profit is referred to as the surplus of total revenue over the total cost. Profit is residual of income over and above all economic cost, both explicit and implicit, that results from the operation of a business. It is the return for the business unit or investors for taking risks.
- Pure profit may be defined as a residual left after all contractual costs have been met, including the transfer costs of management, insurable risks, depreciation and payment to shareholders, sufficient amount to maintain investment at its current level.
- Gross profit is the residual income which accrues when total explicit costs are deducted from the total revenue or total sales proceeds of the business unit. Net profit is the reward paid to the entrepreneur for taking the risks in the process of production, bearing uncertainty, and reward for innovations.
- Normal profit is the minimum amount which an entrepreneur must get to survive in the market. When average revenue is greater than the average cost, the business unit earns a supernormal profit or abnormal profit.
- The main purposes of a business unit are a measure of performance, the premium to cover costs to stay in business, and ensuring the supply of future capital.

- A reasonably high level of profit is essential to play its positive role in the market economy as well as the economy as a whole on various counts.
- The various aspects of profit are shareholders' benefit, high business reputation, high capacity to perform R&D, prudency against risks, ploughing back for growth, corporate tax revenue, business sustainability, better employment, virtuous cycle, market signals, and resource allocation.
- Rent theory was advocated by American economist Francis L. Walker in 1887. He stated that profit is the rent for exceptional abilities exhibited by the entrepreneur over others. Rent is the difference between the yields of the least and the most efficient entrepreneurs. Profit is computed by comparing the abilities of the marginal and super marginal entrepreneur.
- Wage theory of profit was proposed by American economist F.W. Taussig. The theory states that profit is similar to wage, which is given to the entrepreneur for the services rendered by him in the business.
- Risk theory was propounded by American economist F.B. Hawley in 1893. In a business unit, the risk may occur due to obsolescence of a product, a sudden drop in prices, unavailability of specific materials, introduction of a better substitute by a competitor and risks due to fire, war, etc. Hawley considered risk an unavoidable factor of production and business units who take risk are more likely to earn better profits.
- Uncertainty bearing theory was propounded by Frank H. Knight during 1921. The theory states that profit is the reward for bearing uncertainty and lays down the difference that profit does not arise from all types of risk.
- The dynamic theory of profit was propounded by J.B. Clark. He states that profit always arises in a dynamic economy and not in a static economy. The basic reason for arising profit in a dynamic economy is continuous changes in the economy. Clark stated that profit is an intangible sum that entrepreneurs can grasp but cannot retain.
- The innovation theory was developed by Joseph A. Schumpeter. Innovation refers to adopting new techniques of production, as a result of which production cost would tend to decline and it will lead to an increase in profit. If a business unit wants to increase the level of profit, it can either increase the price of the product, or it can try to reduce the cost of production.
- Marginal productivity theory explains that reward for every factor of production can be decided by the marginal productivity of that factor of production. The theory assumes entrepreneurial ability as one of the

factors of production. The value of entrepreneurial ability, i.e., profit is decided by the marginal productivity of the entrepreneur.

- Socialist theory of profit states that the value of a product is determined by labour itself involved in the process of production. A major part of total produce is grabbed by capitalists and only a small portion of the produce is given to the labour. It is also referred to as labour exploitation theory.
- Monopoly is a market situation in which there is a single seller of a commodity without a close substitute. Monopoly market may arise due to sole ownership of raw materials, economies of scale, legal sanction, protection, mergers and acquisitions. A monopolist may earn a pure profit, which is also called monopoly profit.
- Business units adopt two types of policies, i.e., profit maximisation and fair profit policy. According to profit maximisation policy, the main aim of every business unit is to maximise its profit. Fair policy theory explains a reasonable level of profit, which will enable the business unit to clear all its liabilities and a reasonable amount left, will encourage them to stay in business.
- The factors influencing profit policy are industry leadership, restricting the entry, political impact, customer goodwill, wage consideration, liquidity preference, risk, and uncertainty bearing, innovations, the element of luck or chance, and differences in the abilities of the entrepreneurs.
- The factors limiting the profits are the creation of competition, creation of substitutes, heavy taxation, increased wages, increasing the cost of input, and ceiling on profits.

SHORT ANSWER QUESTIONS

1. Define profit.
2. What is a supernormal profit?
3. What are the functions of profit?
4. Describe the wage theory of profit.
5. Write a short note on the socialist theory of profit.
6. Explain the monopoly theory of profit.
7. Distinguish between gross profit and net profit.
8. Explain the wage theory of profit.

ESSAY ANSWER QUESTIONS

1. What do you understand by the concept of profit? Explain the characteristics of profit.
2. Explain the different kinds of profit with suitable examples.

3. Discuss the role of profit in the success of business in an economy.
4. Describe Walker's rent theory of profit.
5. Explain the risk theory of profit and its assumptions.
6. Discuss the significance of uncertainty bearing theory of profit.
7. What is innovation theory? Explain the features of innovation activity.
8. Explain the marginal productivity theory of profit.
9. Briefly explain the dynamic profit theory proposed by Clark.
10. Define profit policy. Discuss the appropriate policy with reasons.
11. Describe the factors that influence profit policy.
12. Critically examine the factors limiting the profit policy.

FILL IN THE BLANKS

1. Profit is regarded as a reward for __________.
2. The surplus of total revenue over the total cost is called __________.
3. Pure profit is associated to be a __________ phenomenon.
4. The concept of normal profit was propounded by __________.
5. Walker's rent theory of profit was advocated in the year __________.
6. According to uncertainty theory, profit is the reward for bearing __________.
7. The risks which can be predicted and can be covered through insurance are called __________.
8. The innovation theory was developed by __________.

Answers

1. Risk-taking
2. Profit
3. Short-term
4. Alfred Marshall
5. 1887
6. Uncertainty
7. Foreseen risks
8. Joseph A. Schumpeter

MULTIPLE-CHOICE QUESTIONS

1. Economic profit is also referred to as:
   (A) Total revenue (B) Pure profit
   (C) Insurable profit (D) Positive profit
2. Creation of provision for depreciation, insurable risks, and required minimum payments to investors in preventing them from withdrawing their investment/capital is called:
   (A) Economic profit (B) Explicit cost
   (C) Implicit cost (D) Opportunity cost
3. Implicit cost is also called:
   (A) Depreciation (B) Residual income
   (C) Total revenue (D) Invisible cost
4. The income accrued over and above normal profit is called:
   (A) Normal profit (B) Supernormal profit
   (C) Net profit (D) Gross profit

5. Wage theory of profit was advocated by:
   (A) Francis Walker (B) Alfred Marshall
   (C) W. Taussig (D) F.B. Hawley
6. Hawley's risk theory of profit was propounded in the year:
   (A) 1893 (B) 1983
   (C) 1887 (D) 1878
7. Uncertainty bearing theory of profit was propounded by:
   (A) J.B. Clark (B) Frank H. Knight
   (C) Karl Marx (D) H.A. Simon
8. Risks which cannot be foreseen and no insurance company is ready to cover these risks are called:
   (A) Non-insurable risk (B) Certainty bearing risk
   (C) Insurable risk (D) Foreseen risk
9. Which theory assumes entrepreneurial ability as one of the factors of production?
   (A) Innovation theory of profit
   (B) Monopoly theory of profit
   (C) Marginal productivity theory
   (D) Dynamic theory of profit

Answers

1. B	2. A	3. D	4. B	5. C
6. A	7. B	8. A	9. C	

REFERENCES

1. Clark, J.B. (1891). Distribution as Determined by the Law of Rent. *The Quarterly Journal of Economics*, 5(3), 289-318.
2. Cowen, T. & Tabarrok, A. (2013). *Modern Principles of Economics* (2nd Edn). New York, NY: Worth Publishers.
3. Dean, J. (1968). *Managerial Economics.* New Delhi, India: Prentice-Hall of India Private Limited.
4. Dwivedi, D.N. (2015). *Managerial Economics* (8th Edn). New Delhi, India: Vikas Publishing House Pvt. Ltd.
5. Grayson, H. (1954). *Economic Planning under Free Enterprise.* Washington DC: Public Affairs Press.
6. Gupta, G.S. (2017). *Managerial Economics.* New Delhi, India: Tata McGraw-Hill.
7. Hague, D.C. (1969). *Managerial Economics: Analysis for Business Decisions*. Wiley.
8. Hall, R.L., & Hitch, C.J. (1939). Price theory and business behaviour. *Oxford Economic Papers*, (2), 12-45.
9. Hamermesh, D.S. (1986). The demand for labour, in the long run (chapter 8) in *Handbook of Labor Economics,* volume 1, edited by Orley Ashenfelter and Richard Layard. North-Holland, New York.

10. Hawley, F.B. (1893). The risk theory of profit. *The Quarterly Journal of Economics*, 7(4), 459-479.
11. Knight, F.H. (1921). *Risk, Uncertainty and Profit*. Boston & New York: Houghton Mifflin Company.
12. Knight, F. H. (1957). *Risk, Uncertainty and Profit*. (Eighth Impression.). London School of Economics and Political Science.
13. Marshall, A. (1920). *Principles of Economics*. London: Macmillan and Co. Ltd.
14. Marx, K. (1847). Wage labour and capital. In: K. Marx and F. Engels, *Selected Works*, Volume I, Moscow: Foreign Languages Publishing House, 1962.
15. Marx, K. (1867) *Capital*, Volume I, London: Lawrence and Wishart, 1970.
16. Mehta, J.K. (1962). *A Philosophical Interpretation of Economics*. Allen & Unwin.
17. Mehta, P.L. (2007). *Managerial Economics: Text and Cases*. New Delhi, India: Sultan Chand & Co.
18. Schumpeter, J.A. (1934). *The Theory of Economic Development*. Cambridge, Mass: Harward University Press.
19. Simon, H.A. (1959). Theories of decision-making in economics and behavioural science. *The American Economic Review*, 49(3), 253-283.
20. Speight, H. (1964). *Economics: The Science of Prices and Incomes* (Vol. 104). Methuen.
21. Speight, H. (1967). *Economics and Industrial Efficiency: An Introduction to Managerial Economics* (Vol. 201). London; Melbourne, [etc.]: Macmillan; New York: St. Martin›s P.
22. Taussig, F.W. (1891). A contribution to the theory of railway rates. *The Quarterly Journal of Economics*, 5(4), 438-465.
23. Taussig, F.W. (1910). Outlines of a Theory of Wages. *American Economic Association Quarterly*, 11(1), 136-156.
24. Varshney, R.L. & Maheswari, K.L. (2014). *Managerial Economics*. New Delhi, India: Sultan Chand & Sons.
25. Von Thünen, J. (1826). *Isolated State*. Translated by Carla M. Wartenberg.
26. Walker, F.A. (1887). The source of business profits. *The Quarterly Journal of Economics*, 1(3), 265-288.
27. Walker, F.A. (1891). *Land and its Rent*. Little, Brown.

Chapter

23 Profit Planning and Forecasting

LEARNING OBJECTIVES

After studying this chapter, you should be able to understand:

- the concept of profit planning and profit maximisation;
- the concept of break-even analysis and determine break-even point;
- the concept of cost-volume-profit analysis; and
- profit forecasting for a business unit.

23.1. INTRODUCTION

A business unit is considered successful when it earns sound profits and handles risks as well as smartly. A business unit will face several uncertainties. These uncertainties are largely in the form of consumer needs, the varied nature of competition, the nature of most elements of cost and the rapid pace of technological developments. At times, the business unit is uncertain about the likely pattern and the extent of consumer demand for a specific product and this increases the risk faced by the business unit.

The nature of competition is related to either product or price or both factors together. Price competition begins in the market once the competitors find a comfortable position in the market. The business units use price as a strategy to expand its market share. They also work for introducing product varieties, additional features, new applications and benefits to the consumers to intensify product competition. With the passage of time, constant technological enhancements may make production processes completely outdated. If an improved process is available, a business unit can restrict its risk by neglecting its fixed investment. If it does not have access to the improved processes, it may have to go out of business. Hence, a business unit has to prepare fully to face all kinds of risks and uncertainties. Managing risk is highly important as it impacts the profits of the business unit significantly. Therefore, profit planning requires a detailed understanding of the relationship between cost, volume of output and profit.

23.2. PROFIT PLANNING

In modern business, profit earning is not an easy task. Profitability and success of the business depend on the accurate business planning and operation of the business units. Profit planning is essential in the wake of many constraints, limitations and uncertainties existing in the dynamic business environment. Profit planning is considered an art as well as science. It not only requires a systematic analysis of the facts and trends, methodical projections and computations but also creative thinking and strategy. With an appropriate profit planning business units can make profit consistent with the myriad of risk elements encountered. It is the sign of a good business. To earn profit, one has to face risks and one who deals with risks successfully can make a profit. To deal with the risks and to avoid losses one has to plan. It is the essence of profit planning.

Profit planning is an integral element of business policy and planning. Profit policy is programmed through profit planning. Profit planning gives a concrete shape to the profit policy of the business unit. Profit planning is a time-bound action to fulfil this idea of profit policy. Profit is the difference between total sales revenue and the total cost of production. Thus, in profit planning, to regulate the profit, sales volume and input quantity (or costs of production) are to be manipulated. In modern business, profits are controlled by adopting many techniques such as break-even analysis, cost control, profit volume analysis and linear programming.

23.3. PROFIT MAXIMISATION

The conventional goal of a business unit is profit maximisation. It means that the business unit put all its efforts to achieve the highest level of profits either in short-run or in the long run. Price of the product and the demand in the market are the key determinants of profit. Supply of the product is another important factor. Freedom of price fixation for a business unit depends upon the nature of the market structure. In perfect competition, price is determined at the point of equilibrium, where demand equals the supply of a product. The business unit has to maximise its profit only at this market price. In perfect competition business unit is the price taker. In an imperfect competition such as monopoly, oligopoly and monopolistic competition the freedom of price fixation varies with the degree of imperfection in competition. The monopolist will enjoy absolute freedom for fixing the price for products while in monopolistic competition business units enjoy limited freedom to fix the price of the product.

The traditional economic theory assumes that profit maximisation is the only objective of business units. According to this theory, profits must be earned by business to provide for its survival, coverage of risks, growth and expansion. It is a necessary motivating force and it is in terms of profits that the efficiency of a business is measured. It forms the basis of conventional price theory. Profit maximisation is referred to as the most analytical and productive objective of a business unit. The profit maximisation assumption helps in predicting the behaviour of business units and also the behaviour of price and output under different market conditions.

According to this theory, total profit (TP) is the difference between total revenue (TR) and total cost (TC) and is calculated as below:

$$TP = TR - TC$$

where,

TR refers to the total revenue
TC refers to the total cost

The total cost includes fixed cost and variable cost. The cost which remains the same at different levels of output is called fixed cost. The sum of all those costs which vary directly with the level of output is called variable cost. In the context of profit maximisation objective, the difference between total cost (TC) and total revenue (TR) is to be maximised. Two conditions must be fulfilled to maximise the gap between TR and TC. These conditions are divided into two categories, i.e., first-order/necessary condition and secondary/ supplementary condition. These conditions are:

1. The first order/ necessary condition states that marginal revenue (MR) must be equal to marginal cost (MC), i.e., MR = MC. The revenue generated from the production and sale of one additional unit of output is known as marginal revenue (MR), and the cost incurred due to the production of one additional unit of output is known as marginal cost (MC).
2. The secondary/supplementary condition states that the first-order condition must show the decreasing MR and rising MC. The secondary condition is fulfilled only when both the MC is rising as well as the MR is decreasing, i.e., marginal cost curve must intersect marginal revenue from below. This condition is illustrated by point P_2 in Figure 23.1.

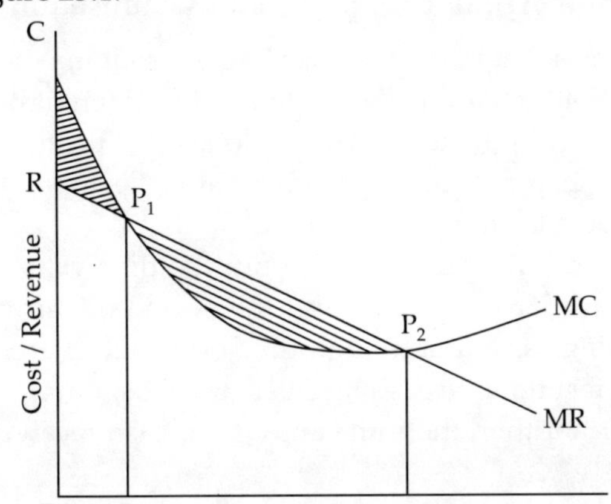

Figure 23.1. Profit maximisation

For example, the total revenue and total cost functions are respectively given as below:

$$TR = TC = f(Q) \qquad ...(I)$$

where Q = quantity produced and sold.

Substituting total revenue and total cost functions in equation (I), profit function can be written as below:

$$TP = f(Q)TR - f(Q)TC \qquad ...(II)$$

With the help of equation (II), the first-order condition and the secondary condition can be understood easily.

23.3.1. Favourable Arguments for Profit Maximisation

The following points are in support of the profit maximisation objective of the business unit:

1. When profit earning is the aim of the business unit then the profit maximisation should be the obvious objective.
2. Profitability is the barometer for measuring the efficiency and economic prosperity of a business unit, thus, profit maximisation is justified on the ground of rationality.
3. Profits are the main source of finance for the growth of the business unit. So, a business unit should aim at maximisation of the profits for enabling its growth and development.
4. Profitability is essential for fulfilling social goals also. A business unit by pursuing the objectives of profit maximisation can also try to maximise the socio-economic welfare.
5. A business unit may be able to survive under unfavourable condition only if it had some past earnings to rely upon.

23.3.2. Unfavourable Arguments for Profit Maximisation

The following points are against the objective of profit maximisation:

1. The term 'Profit' means different things for different people. It may be referred to as short-term profit or long-term profit, total profit or earning per share, profit before tax or after-tax, operating profit or profit available for the shareholders.
2. The theory does not take into account the time value of money. It does not consider the degree and the period of earnings. It treats all the earnings as equal though they occur in different periods. It ignores the fact that the cash received at the beginning of the year is more important than the same amount of cash received at the end of the year.
3. The theory does not consider the risk of the potential flow of earnings. Some projects are riskier than others. Two business units may have

the same expected earnings per share, but if the earning stream in one is riskier, the market share of its share will be comparatively less.

4. The effect of the dividend policy on the market price of the shares is also not considered in profit maximisation. In case, earnings per share are the only objective then the business unit may not think of paying dividends to the shareholders. Instead, the business unit can retain profits in the business or invest the amount in the market which may satisfy the objective.

23.3.3. Reasons for not aiming at Profit Maximisation

The business units generally aim at making profits. The volume of profit made by the business units is regarded as a primary measure of its success. In economic theory, a basic assumption is that the business unit aims at maximising profits. This assumption may not always be true as in practice the business units do not always try to maximise profits due to the following reasons:

1. Attainment of industry leadership.
2. Avert potential competition.
3. Prevent Government's intervention.
4. Retain consumer goodwill.
5. Restrictive demand for a wage increase.
6. Accent on the liquidity of a business unit.
7. Avoiding risk.
8. Changed business structure.

23.4. BREAK-EVEN ANALYSIS

Break-even analysis (BEA) helps to identify the level of output and sales volume required at a given price at which the business unit 'breaks even'. It means the revenues generated out of sales are sufficient enough to cover all costs of production. The break-even point indicates the point at which there is no profit or no loss. Break-even analysis is an important technique to trace the relationship between cost, revenue and profits at the varying levels of output or sales. In BEA, the breakeven point is located at that level of output or sales at which the net income or profit is zero. Various managerial decisions of business units are taken based on the break-even point. The objective of Break-even analysis is to understand the financial relationship among cost, revenue and the rate of output. This is shown in Table 23.1.

Table 23.1. Break-even schedule

Output (units)	Total Revenue (TR in Rs.)	Total Fixed Cost (TFC in Rs.)	Total Variable Cost (TVC in Rs.)	Total Cost (TC in Rs.)	Stage
0	0	100	0	100	Loss
10	50	100	30	130	
20	100	100	60	160	
30	150	100	90	190	
40	200	100	120	220	
50	250	100	150	250	BEP
60	300	100	180	280	Profit
70	350	100	210	310	
80	400	100	240	340	

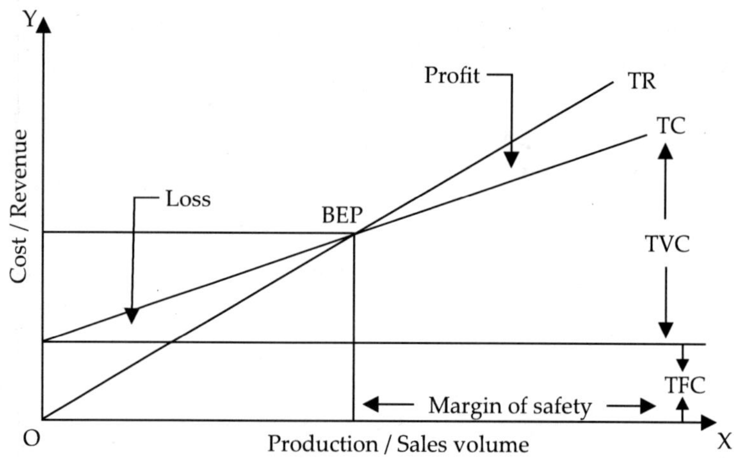

Figure 23.2. Break-even graph

Figure 23.2 shows the break-even point of a business unit, i.e., total revenue (TR) and total costs (TC) are plotted on the vertical axis, where sales or output per period are plotted on the horizontal axis. When the production is 50 units, the total cost and total revenue are equal that is Rs. 250, which is at the intersecting point of the curves. Break-even point always denotes the quantity produced or sold to equalise the revenue and cost. When the business unit produces less than 50 units the revenue earned is less than the cost of production (TR < TC) therefore, the business unit incurs loss which is shown in the graph. Through selling more than 50 units the revenue increases more than the cost of production therefore, the difference between revenue and cost increases and provides profit to the business unit (TR > TC).

23.4.1. Assumptions of Break-even Analysis

The concept of break-even analysis is based on the following assumptions:

1. The production and sales are equal, i.e., the total output produced is sold in the market.
2. The principle of cost variability is valid.
3. All costs can be separated into fixed and variable components.
4. Fixed cost remains same irrespective of the production volume.
5. Variable cost varies with the production. It changes in the same proportion to that of the production. Hence, it has a linear relationship with the production. In other words, the variable cost per unit remains the same.
6. Selling price per unit remains the same irrespective of the quantity sold.
7. Prices paid for input factors will remain the same.
8. Technological methods and efficiency of men and machines will not be changed.
9. Cost control will be neither strengthened nor weakened.
10. Production and sales will be synchronised.
11. Either only one product or several products are being produced and sold, the sales mix will remain constant.
12. Revenue and costs are being compared with a common activity base, e.g., sale value of production or units produced.
13. The efficiency of the plant can be predicted with accuracy.

23.4.2. Significance of Break-even Analysis

Break-even analysis is an important tool for business decision making. It helps in identifying various components of costs and their impact on the profit of a business unit. It helps in arriving at effective decisions relating to product mix, make or buy decisions, etc.:

1. Sales volume can be determined to earn a given amount of return on capital.
2. Profits can be forecasted if estimates of revenue and cost are available.
3. Effect of change in the volume of sales, sale price, cost of production, can be analysed.
4. Choice of products can be made from the available alternatives. Product-mix can also be determined.
5. Impact of increase or decrease in fixed and variable costs can be measured.

6. Inter-business unit comparisons of profitability can be made.
7. Cash break-even chart helps proper planning of cash requirements.
8. Break-even analysis emphasises the importance of capacity utilisation for achieving economies.
9. The margin of safety is a useful measure for business strategy.

23.4.3. Limitations of Break-even Analysis

1. Break-even analysis is based on a fixed cost, variable cost and total revenue. A change in one variable affects the break-even point.
2. All costs cannot be classified as fixed and variable as there are certain semi-variable costs incurred during the production.
3. It is based on a fixed cost, so it is applicable only in the short-run, as in the long-run these costs may change.
4. If business conditions are volatile, break-even analysis may not give stable results.
5. It applies to business units producing single product only as there are problems in the application of multi-product business units.

23.4.4. Application of Break-even Analysis

Break-even analysis (BEA) is a useful and practical technique for profit planning and decision making. It helps the management in internal production control and financial analysis of a business unit. Break-even analysis can be applied for testing the profitability or proposed action, for considering alternatives or for other decision-making purposes. The different areas of its applications are:

1. **Profit planning:** Break-even is a useful tool in profit planning for a business unit. There are four important ways of improving the profit performance of a business unit. It includes increasing the volume of production, increasing the selling price of the product, and decreasing variable cost and fixed costs of the product. Profit planning refers to forecasting for future business operations for attaining maximum profit. The contribution ratio shows the relative profitability of various sectors of business whenever there is a change in the selling price, variable cost, etc.
2. **Introduction of a new product:** The business units can sometimes plan to introduce an entirely new product or add a product to the existing lines of products to utilise idle facilities, capture a new market, expand the existing market share, and for any other marketing purposes. The profitability of the new product has to be identified before launching into the market. Generally, the new product can be manufactured only if it is capable of contributing to the fixed costs and profit after meeting its variable costs.

3. **Level of activity planning:** The break-even analysis will be useful for planning the level of activity or operations to be carried out in the business unit. The decision-makers have to plan the activities in such a manner to maximise the profits. Planning to generate maximum contribution at a particular level of activity will lead to maximising the profitability of a business unit.
4. **Limiting factors:** A business unit produces and sells the products that generate maximum profits under the assumption that they will likely be able to produce any quantity and sell as well in the market. But in real market situations, this becomes impractical as there are several constraints involved during the production and selling process. The constraints include the availability of raw materials, availability of skilled labour, plant capacity, demand for the product, etc. These constraints that reduce the business unit's efforts to produce and sell in unlimited quantities are called limiting factors. The business unit must ascertain the extent to which these factors influence the production process and ensure the maximising of profits. When the business units can determine the contribution ratio and the limiting factors, the relative profitability of different products or processes can be measured with the help of the following formula:

$$\text{Profitability} = \frac{\text{Contribution}}{\text{Limiting Factors}}$$

5. **Make or buy decisions:** A business unit might be having an unused capacity which may be utilised for making parts or similar items instead of buying them from the market. In arriving at such a `make or buy' decision, the cost of manufacturing parts should be compared with the price quoted in the market. If the variable costs are lower than the purchase price then the parts can be manufactured in the business unit itself. Fixed costs are excluded under the assumption that they have been already incurred, and the manufacturing of components involves only variable cost. However, if there is an increase in fixed costs and any limiting factor are operating while producing components that should also be taken into account.
6. **Suitable product mix/sales mix:** A business unit generally plans to select the optimum product mix that generates maximum revenue and profitability. The product mix is the ratio in which various products are produced and sold. The marginal costing technique helps management in making appropriate decisions regarding the

product mix, i.e., in changing the ratio of product mix to maximise profits. The technique not only helps in dropping unprofitable products from the mix but also helps in dropping unprofitable departments, activities, etc.

7. **Pricing Decisions:** Marginal costing techniques help a business unit to decide about the prices of various products in a reasonable approach. Marginal cost refers to the additional cost incurred for producing an additional unit by the business unit.

23.4.5. Determination of Break-even Point

The calculation of the break-even point is the foundation stone of break-even analysis. It may be described as that point of output and sales volume at which the business unit breaks even, i.e., the point where sales revenue equals the cost of making and selling the product. It is a situation where neither profit nor loss is reported. Therefore, this point is also referred to as a 'No profit - No loss' point.

23.4.5.1. Break-even Point

Break-even level can be worked out with the help of the following formulae:

$$\text{B.E.P. (Units)} = \frac{\text{Fixed Cost}}{\text{Contribution (per unit)}}$$

$$(or) = \frac{\text{Fixed Cost}}{\text{Selling Price (per unit)} - \text{Variable Cost (per unit)}}$$

$$\text{B.E.P. (Sales)} = \frac{\text{Fixed Cost}}{\text{Contribution (per unit)}} \times \text{Selling Price (per unit)}$$

$$(or) = \frac{\text{Fixed Cost}}{\text{Total Contribution}} \times \text{Total Sales}$$

$$(or) = \frac{\text{Fixed Cost}}{\text{P / V Ratio}}$$

At the break-even point, the desired profit is zero. Where the volume of output or sales is to be calculated to earn a desired amount of profit, the amount of desired profits has to be added to the fixed cost given in the above formula.

$$\text{Units to Earn a Desired Profit} = \frac{\text{Fixed Cost + Desired Profit}}{\text{Contribution (per unit)}}$$

$$\text{Sales to Earn a Desired Profit} = \frac{\text{Fixed Cost + Desired Profit}}{\text{P / V Ratio}}$$

23.4.5.2. *Contribution*

The difference between the selling price and variable cost (or marginal cost) is known as 'contribution' or `gross margin'. It may be considered some sort of fund from out of which all fixed costs are met. The difference between contribution and fixed cost represents either profit or loss, as the case may be. The contribution is calculated as:

$$\text{Contribution} = \text{Selling Price} - \text{Variable Cost}$$

(*or*)

$$= \text{Fixed Cost} + \text{Profit (or)} - \text{Loss}$$

Thus, profit arises only when the contribution exceeds fixed costs. In other words, the 'No profit - No loss' point can be determined at the level where the contribution is equal to fixed costs incurred by the business unit.

23.4.5.3. *Profit Volume Ratio (P/V Ratio)*

The business units can identify the profitability of its production operations by determining the P/V ratio. P/V ratio explains the relationship between contribution and sales and is generally expressed in the form of a percentage. It is also referred to as contribution-sales ratio' or `marginal income ratio', or `variable-profit ratio'. P/V ratio is the ratio of contribution to sales and is calculated as:

$$\text{P/V Ratio} = \frac{\text{Contribution}}{\text{Sales}} \times 100 \ (or)$$

$$= \frac{\text{Sales} - \text{Variable cost}}{\text{Sales}} \times 100 \ (or)$$

$$= \frac{\text{Fixed cost} + \text{Profit}}{\text{Sales}} \times 100$$

P/V ratio can also be determined by measuring the change in contribution to the change in sales, or a change in profit to a change in sales. An increase in contribution would indicate an increase in profit, as fixed expenses are assumed to be constant at all levels of production.

$$\text{P/V Ratio} = \frac{\text{Change in Contribution}}{\text{Change in Sales}} \times 100 \ (or)$$

$$= \frac{\text{Change in Profit}}{\text{Change in Sales}} \times 100$$

The importance of P/V ratio lies in its use for evaluating the profitability of alternative products, proposals or schemes. A higher ratio shows greater profitability. Management should, therefore, try to increase the P/V ratio by widening the gap between the selling price and the variable costs.

This can be achieved by increasing sale price, reducing variable costs or switching over to more profitable products.

23.4.5.4. The Margin of Safety

The margin of safety is referred to as the difference between the expected profits and the break-even point. The margin of safety is the result of the total actual sales minus the sales at the break-even point. A lower break-even leads to a higher margin of safety and vice versa. The margin of safety can also be expressed as a percentage of total actual sales. The formula is to determine the margin of safety is:

$$\text{Margin of Safety (MoS)} = \text{Total actual sales} - \text{Break-even sales}$$

(*or*)

$$= \frac{\text{Profit}}{\text{P / V Ratio}}$$

$$\text{Margin of Safety (as a Percentage)} = \frac{\text{Margin of Safety}}{\text{Total Actual Sales}} \times 100$$

A higher level of margin of safety denotes that the business unit is sound and can generate profits. When the sales substantially decrease, (but not below break-even sales) some profits might be earned by the business units. A lower margin of safety denotes that when there is a slight decrease in sales, profit position might be affected adversely. Thus, the margin of safety can be used to test the effectiveness of a business unit. To improve the margin of safety, the business units can increase selling prices without affecting demand, reducing fixed or variable costs and replacing unprofitable products with a profitable product.

23.5. COST - VOLUME - PROFIT ANALYSIS

The cost of production depends to a large extent on the volume of output and production mix which in their turn depend inter alia, upon the sale price and demand of the product in the market. The profit of the business unit depends upon the cost of production, sale price and volume of sales. Thus, there is a direct relationship between these three factors. Cost, volume, profit analysis is a device which attempts to determine the effect of changes in cost, volume, product mix and selling price on profits. It analyses the relationships among the factors affecting profits.

23.5.1. Importance of Cost - Volume - Profit Analysis

The study of cost-volume-profit relationship is very useful for the management. This technique provides management with cost and profit data required for-profit planning, policy formulating and decision making. It is only through the use of this technique that the prediction of the probable effect of any contemplated action is made possible. The following are some of its applications:

1. Calculation of profit for different sales volumes.
2. Evaluating the profitability of a product or a price on profits.
3. Computing the effect of contemplated change in selling price on profits.
4. Computing the sales volume required to offset a contemplated price reduction.
5. Measurement of the effect of changes in profit factors.
6. Helping in the preparation of flexible budgets.
7. Useful in making decisions like make or buy decisions, pricing decision, selection of an optimum product mix, selection of the best channel of distribution, etc.
8. Assisting in cost control by evaluating the effect on the cost of changes in volume, methods of production and product mix.

Illustration-1:

The sales of a product are 10,000 units, selling price is Rs. 20 per unit, variable cost is Rs. 10 per unit and fixed costs are Rs. 80,000. Determine break-even point in units and sales revenue. What is the profit earned? What should be the sales for earning a profit of Rs. 60,000?

Solution:

(a) BEP (units) = Fixed cost / Contribution (per unit)
= 80,000 / 10 = 8,000 units

Contribution = Sales (per unit) – Variable cost (per unit)
= 20 – 10 = Rs. 10 per unit

(b) Sales = BEP (units) × Selling Price (per unit)
= 8,000 units × Rs. 20 = Rs. 1,60,000

(c) Sales when profit = Rs. 60,000

S = F + P / S – V
= 80,000 + 60,000 / 20 – 10
= 1,40,000 / 10 = 14,000 units

Sales = 14,000 units × 20 = Rs. 2,80,000

(d) Profit = Sales – VC – FC
= 2,80,000 – (14,000 × 10) – 80,000
= 2,80,000 – 1,40,000 – 80,000
= Rs. 60,000

Illustration-2:

A business unit estimates its fixed costs for the year at Rs. 8,00,000 and its profit target at Rs. 2,00,000. Each unit of product is sold at Rs. 10 and the variable cost per unit is Rs. 8. What sales level must the business unit achieve to realise its profit goal?

Solution:

Sales to get a profit of Rs. 2,00,000

S = F + P / C
= 8,00,000 + 2,00,000 / (10 – 8)
= 10,00,000 / 2
= 5,00,000 units
Sales = 5,0,0000 units × Rs. 10
= Rs. 50,00,000

Illustration-3:

A business unit sells 20,000 units at a selling price of Rs. 30 per unit, variable cost per unit is Rs. 15 and fixed cost is Rs. 2,40,000. Calculate:

(a) BEP in units and value
(b) Margin of safety
(c) Sales to get a profit of Rs. 2,00,000

Solution:

(a) BEP (Units) = Fixed Cost / Contribution (per unit)
= 2,40,000 / (30 – 15)
= 16,000 units
P/V Ratio = Contribution / Sales × 100
= 15/30 × 100
= 0.50 or 50%
BEP (Rs.) = Fixed Cost / PV Ratio
= 2,40,000 / 0.50
= Rs.4,80,000

(b) Margin of Safety (units) = Actual Sales – BEP Sales (units)
= 20,000 – 16,000
= 16,000 units
Margin of Safety (Rs.) = Actual Sales – BEP Sales (Rs.)
= (20,000 units × Rs. 30) – 4,80,000
= 6,00,000 – 4,80,000
= Rs. 1,20,000

(c) Sales to get a profit of Rs. 2,00,000

S = F + P / C

= 2,40,000 + 2,00,000 / 15
= 4,40,000 / 15
= 29,333.33 units
Sales = 29,333.33 units × Rs. 30
= Rs. 8,80,000

Illustration-4:

Calculate the break-even point from the following figures:

Sales	Rs. 40,000
Fixed Expenses	Rs. 10,000
Variable Cost:	
Direct labour	Rs. 6,000
Direct material	Rs. 10,000
Direct expenses	Rs. 4,000

Solution:

P/V Ratio = Contribution / Sales × 100
= (40,000 – 20,000 / 40,000) × 100
= 50%
BEP sales = Fixed cost / PV Ratio
= 10,000 / 0.50
= Rs. 20,000

Illustration-5:

From the following data, you are required to calculate:

(a) P/V Ratio
(b) Break-even sales
(c) Sales required to earn of profit Rs. 2,25,000

Variable costs:	
Direct material	Rs. 3
Direct labour	Re. 1
Direct overheads	Re. 1
Selling price per unit	Rs. 6
Fixed cost	Rs. 45,000

Solution:

(a) P/V Ratio = Contribution / Sales × 100
= 1 / 6 × 100
= 16.67%
Contribution = Sales – Variable cost
= 6 – 5 = Re. 1

(b) Break-even sales = FC / PV Ratio
= 45,000 / 16.67% = Rs. 2,70,000

(c) Sales required to earn a profit of Rs. 2,25,000

Sales = Fixed cost + Required profit / PV Ratio

= 45,000 + 2,25,000 / 16.67%

= Rs. 16,20,000

Illustration-6:

From the following information calculate:

(a) P/V Ratio

(b) Sales required to earn a profit of Rs. 20,000

(c) Profit when sales are Rs. 60,000

Year	Sales (Rs.)	Profit (Rs.)
2011	70,000	7,500
2012	80,000	10,000

Solution:

(a) P/V Ratio = Change in Profit / Change in Sales × 100

= 2,500 / 10,000 × 100

= 25%

Calculation of fixed cost:

P/V Ratio = Fixed cost + Profit / Sales

25% = F + 7,500 / 70,000

F + 7,500 = 70,000 × 0.25

F = 17,500 – 7,500

Fixed cost = Rs. 10,000

(b) Sales required to earn a profit of Rs. 20,000/-

Sales = Fixed cost + Required Profit / PV Ratio

= 10,000 + 20,000 / 25%

= Rs. 1,20,000

(c) Profit when sales are Rs. 60,000

Sales = Fixed cost + Profit / PV Ratio

60,000 = 10,000 + P / 25%

10,000 + P = 60,000 × 0.25

P = 15,000 – 10,000

Profit = Rs. 5,000

Illustration-7:

Business unit budgets for production of 150000 units. The variable cost per unit is Rs. 14 and fixed cost per unit is Rs. 2 per unit. The business unit fixes the selling price to fetch a profit of 15% on cost. Find out:

(a) Break-even point

(b) Profit/volume ratio

(c) If the selling price is reduced by 5%, how does the revised selling price affects the Break-even Point and the Profit/Volume Ratio?

(d)If the profit increase of 10% is desired more than the budget, what should be the sales at a reduced price?

Solution:

Calculation of Contribution per unit:

Selling Price per unit = Total Cost + 15% Profit on cost
= Rs. 16 (Rs. 14 variable cost + Rs. 2 fixed cost) + Rs. 2.40 (15% of Rs. 16)
= Rs. 18.40

Contribution = Selling Price – Variable Cost
= Rs. 18.40 – Rs. 14
= Rs. 4.40

(a) Break-even Point = Fixed Cost /Contribution per unit
= Rs. 2 × 1,50,000 units
= Rs. 3,00,000 / Rs. 4.40
= 68,182 units

(b) Profit/Volume Ratio = Contribution per unit/Selling price / unit × 100
= Rs. 4.40 /Rs. 18.40 × 100
= 23.91%

(c) Reduction in selling price by 5%:

Reduced selling price = Rs. 18.40 – 5% of Rs. 18.40
= Rs. 17.48

Revised contribution = Rs. 17.48 – Rs. 14.00
= Rs. 3.48

Break-even Point = Fixed Cost /Contribution per unit
= Rs. 3,00,000 /Rs. 3.48
= 86,207 units

(d) Desired profit = Rs. 2.40 + 10% of Rs. 2.40
= Rs. 2.64 per unit

Total Profit = Rs. 2.64 × 1,50,000 units = Rs. 3,96,000
+ Total Fixed Costs = Rs. 3,00,000
Total Contribution = Rs. 6,96,000

Quantity to be sold = Total Contribution + Revised Contribution per unit
= Rs. 6,96,000 / Rs. 3.48 = 2,00,000 units

Sales Value = 2,00,000 units × Rs. 17.48
= Rs. 34,96,000

Illustration-8:

A business unit manufactures two products M and N. The business unit wants to drop the product N as it is yielding less contribution per unit and add the product O. By adding the product O, the new fixed cost is likely to be Rs. 2,50,000 and the sales volume will increase to Rs. 18,00,000. Consider the following information and suggest whether the business unit should change the product or not.

Existing Product-mix

Product	Selling price per unit (Rs.)	Variable cost per unit (Rs.)	% of sales
M	80	32	60
N	100	40	40

The total fixed cost during the year is Rs. 2,00,000/- and sales are Rs. 16,00,000/-

Proposed Product-mix

Product	Selling price per unit (Rs.)	Variable cost per unit (Rs.)	% of sales
M	100	40	30
O	120	48	70

Solution:

(a) Existing Product-mix:

Contribution ratio for product M and N = (Selling price – Variable cost/ Selling price) × percentage of total sales

Product M = (80 – 32 / 80) × 0.60
= 0.36

Product N = (100 – 40 / 100) × 0.40
= 0.24

Total contribution ratio for M and N = M + N
= 0.36 + 0.24
= 0.60

Total contribution = Sales × Contribution ratio
= 16,00,000 × 0.60
= Rs. 9,60,000

Profit = Total contribution – Fixed cost
= 9,60,000 – 2,00,000
= Rs. 7,60,000

(b) Proposed Product-mix:

Contribution ratio for product M and O = (Selling price – Variable cost/ Selling price) × percentage of total sales

Product M = (100 – 40 / 100) × 0.30
= 0.18

Product O = (120 – 48 / 120) × 0.70
= 0.42

Total contribution ratio for M and O = M + O
= 0.18 + 0.42
= 0.60

Total contribution = Sales × Contribution ratio
= 18,00,000 × 0.60
= Rs. 10,80,000

Profit = Total contribution – Fixed cost
= 10,80,000 – 2,50,000
= Rs. 8,30,000

Recommendation: The profit in proposed product-mix is higher than the existing product mix and hence, the business unit can change the product mix.

23.6. PROFIT FORECASTING

Profit forecasting means the projection of future earnings taking into consideration all the factors affecting the size of business profits. For example, pricing policies, costing policies, and depreciation, etc. Therefore, profit forecasting is an essential function of any business unit. An effective profit forecasting will lead to successful profit planning.

Profit forecasting involves a careful analysis of the cost and revenue data in terms of the interrelationship between sales volume, prices, variable costs, and fixed costs. A thorough study including proper estimation of both economic and non-economic variables may be necessary for a business unit to project its sales volume, costs and profits for the future. The need for profit forecasting is directly related to the degree of competition faced by the business units. In a monopolistic situation, a business unit need not undertake a serious study of profit forecasting because of the element of control over prices. But in a competitive situation, an exercise in profit forecasting becomes inevitable as the very existence of the business unit in such a condition depends upon its efforts to achieve profits in the long run.

The business unit has to analyse the competitive conditions and the elasticity of demand for the product to expand the sales volume and to get a better price of the product. A multi-product business unit can analyse these factors to plan for the most profitable sales mix. Further, by analysing the cost of each activity like production, selling and distribution, administration as well as research and development, the business unit can identify the areas where there is a scope of reducing the costs.

The business unit can constitute a body to look after the profit improvement to make the profit forecasting exercise more useful. Such a body should look after the following jobs:

1. To decide about the rate of return most profitable to the business unit.
2. To analyse the alternative investment proposals to improve profits.
3. To monitor the implementation of the selected alternative proposals.

23.6.1. Approaches to Profit Forecasting

According to Joel Dean (1968), there are three approaches for forecasting the profit of a business unit. They are:

1. Spot Assessment
2. Break-even analysis
3. Environmental analysis

1. **Spot assessment:** Spot assessment refers to the estimation of profit and loss account for a specified future period by forecasting each element individually. The business units need to make forecasts about the sales volume, prices of products and cost of production while projecting the sales in the market. Profits are considered residuals, and therefore, the errors in the estimation of the various elements of costs and revenue get cumulated while preparing the income and expenditure statement.
2. **Break-even analysis:** Break-even analysis is an imperative tool for forecasting future profits. It is useful in assessing the various costs involved in the production process and make minimum profits. There are two methods of forecasting profit with the help of break-even analysis.
   (a) The analysis identifies the functional relationship between both the cost and revenue to the output, with profits related to output as a residual. Hence, proper planning at output level can maximise the gap between cost and revenue.
   (b) Based on the past data concerning the relationship between output and profit, profits are estimated for the budgeted level of output.
3. **Environmental analysis:** Environment analysis is a process of forecasting based on the external and internal economic factors related to the business unit that affects its performance. It includes predictions of general business operations, government policies, level of prices, etc. The analysis involves assessing the level threats

at an early stage and assists the business unit in developing necessary strategies for its survival. It also helps in identifying the opportunities, such as prospective consumers, new product, segmentation, technology, competitors, and acquire a maximum share of the market.

The three approaches may not be mutually exclusive but can be used together for determining the required information while forecasting profits for a future period. While preparing the profit and loss statement, the functional relationship among cost to output and its other determinants can be used. Similarly, determining the effect of external economic forces on the profitability of the business units can facilitate effective forecasting and improve the accurateness of break-even analysis.

23.7. SUMMARY

- Profit planning is essential in the wake of many constraints, limitations and uncertainties existing in the dynamic business environment. It not only requires a systematic analysis of the facts and trends, methodical projections and computations but also creative thinking and strategy.
- The conventional goal of a business unit is profit maximisation. It means that the business unit put all its efforts to achieve the highest level of profits either in short run or in the long run.
- Profit maximisation theory states that profits must be earned by business to provide for its survival, coverage of risks, growth and expansion. It is a necessary motivating force and it is in terms of profits that the efficiency of a business is measured. Two conditions must be fulfilled to maximise the gap between TR and TC.
- The first order/ necessary condition states that marginal revenue (MR) must be equal to marginal cost (MC), i.e., MR = MC. The secondary/ supplementary condition states that the first-order condition must show the decreasing MR and rising MC.
- The business units may not aim to maximise profits due to attainment of industry leadership, avert potential competition, prevent government's intervention, retain consumer goodwill, restrictive demand for a wage increase, accent on the liquidity of a business unit, avoiding risk, and changed business structure.
- Break-even analysis (BEA) helps to identify the level of output and sales volume required at a given price at which the business unit 'breaks even'. It is an important technique to trace the relationship between cost, revenue and profits at the varying levels of output or sales. The breakeven point indicates the point at which there is no profit or no loss.

- The different areas of its break-even applications are profit planning, the introduction of a new product, level of activity planning, limiting factors, make or buy decisions, suitable product mix/sales mix, and pricing decisions.
- Break-even point is a situation where sales revenue equals the cost of making and selling the product.
- The contribution is referred to as the difference between the selling price and variable cost (or marginal cost).
- P/V Ratio explains the relationship between contribution and sales and is generally expressed in the form of a percentage.
- The margin of safety is referred to as the difference between the expected profits and the break-even point.
- Cost - volume - profit analysis is a device which attempts to determine the effect of changes in cost, volume, product mix and selling price on profits. It analyses the relationships among the factors affecting profits.
- Profit forecasting means the projection of future earnings taking into consideration all the factors affecting the size of business profits. It involves a careful analysis of the cost and revenue data in terms of the inter-relationship between sales volume, prices, variable costs, and fixed costs.
- The various approaches to profit forecasting are spot assessment, break-even analysis, and environmental analysis.

SHORT ANSWER QUESTIONS

1. Briefly explain profit planning.
2. Write a short note on profit maximisation.
3. Define break-even analysis.
4. What are the limitations of break-even analysis?
5. What is a cost-volume-profit analysis?

ESSAY ANSWER QUESTIONS

1. Discuss the objective of profit maximisation and the reasons for not aiming at profit maximisation.
2. Explain the favourable and unfavourable arguments related to profit maximisation.
3. Explain the concept of break-even analysis graphically.
4. Discuss the assumptions and significance of break-even analysis.
5. Describe the different application areas of break-even analysis.
6. What is profit forecasting? Explain the approaches to profit forecasting.
7. From the following information related to Good work and Co., determine (i) Break-even point (units and value), (ii) Variable Cost per unit, and (iii) Selling price per unit.

Profit-Volume Ratio (P/V Ratio) is 20%
Fixed costs Rs. 36,000
Selling price per unit Rs. 150

8. A business unit reported the following results for two periods. Calculate BEP, P/V Ratio, Fixed cost, Variable cost and Margin of safety.

Period	Sales	Profit
I	Rs. 2,00,000	Rs. 20,000
II	Rs. 2,50,000	Rs. 30,000

9. From the following information determine break-even-point. What should be the selling price per unit, if the break-even point is reduced to 6,000 units?
   Selling price per unit is Rs. 30
   Variable cost per unit is Rs. 20
   Fixed expenses are Rs. 54,000
10. A business unit provides the following information:
    Direct material cost per unit Rs. 15
    Direct labour cost per unit Rs. 5
    Fixed overheads Rs. 50,000
    Variable overheads (60% of direct labour)
    Selling price per unit Rs. 30
    Trade discount 5%
    Determine the break-even point and net sales value at this point. Calculate net profits when sales are 10% and 25% above the break-even volume.
11. The business unit sells 8000 units and 9500 units in two successive periods. It incurred a loss of Rs. 11,000 and earned Rs. 10,000 as profit respectively. Assuming the selling price per unit as Rs. 100, determine the fixed cost, break-even point, and the number of units to earn a profit of Rs. 40,000.
12. A business unit produces a single product. The cost data about its product is as follows:
    Selling price per unit Rs. 40
    Marginal cost per unit Rs. 24
    Fixed cost per annum Rs. 16,000
    Calculate:
    (a) P/V ratio
    (b) Break-even sales
    (c) Sales to earn a profit of Rs. 3000
    (d) Profit at sales of Rs. 64,000
    (e) New break-even sales, if the price is reduced by 12%

FILL IN THE BLANKS

1. Profit planning is considered as an art as well as __________.
2. The difference between total sales revenue and the total cost of production is called __________.

3. The cost which remains the same at different levels of output is called __________.
4. The cost incurred due to the production of one additional unit of output is known as __________.
5. A business unit by pursuing the objectives of profit maximisation can also try to maximise the __________ welfare.
6. The point indicating no profit or no loss is called __________.
7. At the break-even point, the desired profit is __________.
8. The difference between the selling price and variable cost is known as __________.
9. The relationship between contribution and sales is expressed by __________.
10. A lower break-even leads to a __________ margin of safety.

Answers:

1. Science
2. Profit
3. Fixed cost
4. Marginal cost
5. Socio-economic
6. Break-even point
7. Zero
8. Contribution
9. P/V Ratio
10. Higher

MULTIPLE-CHOICE QUESTIONS

1. Profit planning is a time-bound action to fulfil this idea of:
   (A) Profit forecasting (B) Profit policy
   (C) Profit maximisation (D) Profit analysis
2. The conventional goal of a business unit is:
   (A) Profit maximisation (B) Wealth maximisation
   (C) EPS maximisation (D) Wealth minimisation
3. The sum of all those costs which vary directly with the level of output is called:
   (A) Total revenue (B) Total cost
   (C) Fixed cost (D) Variable cost
4. The revenue generated from the production and sale of one additional unit of output is known as:
   (A) Marginal revenue (B) Marginal cost
   (C) Average revenue (D) Average cost
5. Forecasting for future business operations for attaining maximum profit is referred to as:
   (A) Financial analysis (B) Profit performance
   (C) Profit planning (D) Financial planning
6. The constraints that reduce the business unit's efforts to produce and sell in unlimited quantities are called:
   (A) Market factors (B) Limiting factors
   (C) Cost factors (D) Contribution factors
7. A contribution is also referred to as:
   (A) Gross margin (B) Net margin
   (C) Marginal cost (D) P/V Ratio

8. The difference between the expected profits and the break-even point is called:
   (A) Contribution ratio (B) Marginal income ratio
   (C) Margin of safety (D) Contribution-sales ratio
9. Projection of future earnings taking into consideration all the factors affecting the size of business profits is known as:
   (A) Break-even analysis (B) Variable-profit ratio
   (C) Spot projection (D) Profit forecasting
10. The process of forecasting based on the external and internal economic factors related to the business unit that affects its performance is called:
    (A) Competitive analysis (B) Environmental analysis
    (C) Economic analysis (D) Business analysis

Answers:

1. B	2. A	3. D	4. A	5. C
6. B	7. A	8. C	9. D	10. B

REFERENCES

1. Antony, R.B. (1960). The trouble with profit maximisation. *Harward Business Review*, 38, 126-134.
2. Cowen, T. & Tabarrok, A. (2013). *Modern Principles of Economics* (2nd Edition). New York, NY: Worth Publishers.
3. Cyert, R., & March, J. (1963). *Behavioural Theory of the Business Unit.* Englewoods Cliffs.
4. Dwivedi, D.N. (2015). *Managerial Economics* (8th Edition). New Delhi, India: Vikas Publishing House Pvt. Ltd.
5. Gardner, F.V. (1971). *Profit Management and Control.* London: MacDonald.
6. Gupta, G.S. (2017). *Managerial Economics.* New Delhi, India: Tata McGraw-Hill.
7. Mehta, P.L. (2007). *Managerial Economics*: *Text and Cases*. New Delhi, India: Sultan Chand & Co.
8. Mehta, U. (1972). Rational basis for determining reasonable price and profit. *The Economic Times*, July 29, p. 7.
9. Simon, H.A. (1959). Theories of decision making in economics and behavioural science. *The American Economic Review*, 49.
10. Varshney, R.L. & Maheswari, K.L. (2014). *Managerial Economics.* New Delhi, India: Sultan Chand & Sons.

Chapter

24 Profit Measurement

LEARNING OBJECTIVES

After studying this chapter, you should be able to understand:

- the concept of profit measurement;
- meaning of depreciation and methods of calculating depreciation;
- the inventory valuation models;
- treatment of capital gains and losses; and
- amortisation of long-term intangible assets.

24.1. INTRODUCTION

The measurement of the amount of profit earned by a business unit during a given period should be done from the management point of view. It is because of the reason that the management of a business unit takes risks under uncertain conditions and also introduces innovations in the market. They take responsibility for the earnings of the shareholders. There are multiple meanings to the term profit as explained in the earlier chapters. Accountants consider profit as business income. There are generally accepted accounting principles (GAAP) which provide different treatments for different items. To measure accounting profit, necessary revenue and cost data are obtained from the accounting books of a business unit. It must be noted that accounting profit may present an overstatement or understatement of actual profit if it is based on the illogical allocation of revenues and costs to a given accounting period. The most important aspects of profit measurement are:

1. Inclusiveness of costs (i.e., items to be deducted from the revenue).
2. Classification of depreciation.
3. Treatment of capital gains and losses.
4. Valuation of assets.

Accountants measure the income of a business unit by identifying the difference between net assets at the beginning of the year and the net assets at the end of the year. The business units prepare a profit and loss account to find the difference between income and expenditure from the activities during the accounting period. The positive difference is called the *net profit* and the negative balance is called a *net loss*. The balance sheet shows the financial status of a business unit representing the assets and liabilities. The net value added or lost can be ascertained through the balance sheet.

Thus, there has been a conceptual conflict between the economists and the accountants in measuring the profit of a business unit. The future role in economic values and business decisions is the key difference in measuring profits. In the view of economists, futurity is the basic source of value of today's assets, so the business units consider the past as irrelevant and are interested in the forecast of the future for taking business decisions. On the contrary, the accountant follows the standards of factuality by reporting the historical facts and ignoring speculations on the future. Accountants consider net income as a historical record of the past, whereas, economists consider it as a speculation of the future. The accountant's concept of income requires consolidation of dated transactions of cash outlays and cash receipts for the measurement of profit.

The economists interpret the balance sheet as the basis for anticipating future earnings of the business unit. Each asset has earning power by itself. The value of this earning power is certainly not less than the price of the asset in the current market. Further, the value of combined assets is greater than the value of the sum of individual assets. This additional value depends on the credibility of the business unit, the quality of the human resources, market reach and credibility, and the image of the leadership. This value, in other words, is called *goodwill* or *going-concern value*. Goodwill in accounts is considered an intangible asset and therefore, is not taken as realised value. The market value of the assets will not be taken by the accountants until the value is realised after the sale of the asset. For the measurement of profit, it is necessary to clarify the concepts of depreciation, inclusiveness of costs to measure profit, treatment of capital gains and losses and valuation of assets.

24.2. DEPRECIATION

Depreciation is the capital cost of assets allocated over the estimated life of an asset. It compensates for the gradual decrease in the value of an asset due to wear and tear, obsolescence, usage and passage of time. Depreciation is a book entry having to reduce the book value of the asset and the profits of the current year for the same amount. It does not affect either current assets or current liabilities. It does not result in the flow of funds as it is a non-fund item. Though depreciation is referred to as an operating cost, there is no actual outflow of cash. The amount of depreciation charged is added to profits while computing funds from operations. However, under certain circumstances, depreciation helps a business unit to affect savings in payment of tax and dividends, and amounts to withholding a part of the funds generated through normal trading operations. Therefore, depreciation can be considered an indirect source of fund.

According to the International Accounting Standards Board (IASB), depreciation is the allocation of the depreciable amount of an asset over the estimated useful life. The useful life is referred to as the period over which a depreciable asset is expected to be used by the business unit.

Economists consider depreciation as capital consumption and there are two discrete ways of charging depreciation. It can be charged either by assuming the value of depreciation of equipment to its opportunity cost, or to its replacement cost that will produce comparable earning. The opportunity cost of an equipment is the most profitable alternate use of that is foregone by putting it to its present use. According to Joel Dean (1951), one method of measuring the opportunity cost is to measure the fall in value during a year. This technique is not feasible when the capital equipment has no alternative use, it can be applied for alternative usable equipment only.

Two main factors contribute to the decline in the usefulness of fixed assets. They are deterioration and obsolescence. Deterioration in the physical wearing out whereas obsolescence refers to the loss of usefulness due to the development of improved equipment or processes, changes in style or other causes not related to the physical condition of the asset. The other causes of depreciation are:

1. The mere passage of time will cause a fall in the value of an asset even if it is not used.
2. An asset may reduce in value because of meeting with an accident.
3. A sudden fall in the market price of the asset reduces its value even if it remains brand new.

24.2.1. Characteristics of Depreciation

The general characteristics of depreciation are:

1. It is a charge against profit.
2. It is an estimated loss of the value of an asset. It is not an actual loss.
3. It is restricted to the working life of the asset.
4. It is a process of allocation and not of valuation.
5. It arises from an internal cause like wear and tear or depletion of an asset. But it is treated as any expense charged against the profit.
6. It is charged on tangible fixed assets. It is not charged on any current asset.
7. It indicates a reduction in service potential.

24.3. METHODS OF DEPRECIATION

The amount of depreciation of a fixed asset is determined to take into account the factors such as its original cost, recoverable cost at the time it is retired from service and the length of its life. Out of these factors, the only factor which is accurately known is the original cost of the asset. The other factors cannot be accurately determined until the asset is retired. They must be estimated at the time the asset is placed in service. The excess of cost over the estimated residual value is regarded as depreciation expenditure during the lifetime of the asset. There are no rules and policies for estimating the useful life of an asset and its residual value at the end of the period. Therefore, these two interrelated factors are affected to a considerable extent by the management policies.

The important methods of calculating depreciation are:

1. Straight-line method
2. Diminishing balance method
3. Sum of years digits method
4. Double declining balance method
5. Annuity method

24.3.1. Straight-line Method

This is the most commonly used method to calculate depreciation. It is also known as the *fixed instalment method.* Under this method, an equal/fixed amount is charged as depreciation on the fixed asset in each of the accounting periods. This fixed amount of depreciation is charged until the value of the asset becomes zero or its salvage value at the end of its estimated useful life. The cost of purchase plus the installation charges, minus the scrap value, is spread over the estimated useful life of the asset to arrive at the annual charge.

This method derives its name from a straight-line graph. This graph is deduced after plotting an equal amount of depreciation for each accounting period over the useful life of the asset. Thus, the annual depreciation amount is computed by dividing the difference of the original cost or book value of the fixed asset and the salvage value by the estimated useful life of the asset. The main advantage of this method is that it is simple and easy to calculate depreciation. Depreciation charge is constant every year, regardless of the extent of use of the asset. This method is criticised on the ground that the depreciation charge remaining the same every year, cost of repairs and maintenance would be increasing as the asset becomes older. The efficiency of the asset declines over the years and therefore, it is unfair to charge the same amount of depreciation every year.

The formula for annual depreciation under the straight-line method is as follows:

Annual depreciation = (Cost of an asset – Salvage value)/Useful life of the asset

where,

Cost of the asset is the purchase price or historical cost.

Salvage value is the value of the asset remaining after its useful life.

Useful life of the asset is the number of years for which an asset is expected to be used by the business unit.

For example, a business unit bought a machine to produce widgets. The cost of the machine is Rs. 30,000 and is expected to have five years. It's salvage value, i.e., the worth of the machine after five years of use is Rs. 5000. Thus, the value of the machine at the beginning of the year will be Rs. 25,000 (Rs. 30,000 – Rs. 5000). The depreciation of the machine is (Rs. 30,000 – Rs. 5000) / 5 years = Rs. 5000 per year (see Table 24.1).

Table 24.1. Depreciation calculation using straight line depreciation

Years	Value of asset at the beginning of the year (in Rs.)	Annual depreciation @20% (in Rs.)	Cumulative Depreciation (Rs.)
1	25,000	5000	5000
2	20,000	5000	10,000
3	15,000	5000	15,000
4	10,000	5000	20,000
5	5000	5000	25,000

Therefore, the machine would depreciate by Rs. 5000 per year under the straight-line depreciation method.

24.3.2. Diminishing Balance Method

This method is also referred to as the *reducing balance method, written down value method, or declining balance method.* Under this method, a fixed percentage of depreciation is charged in each accounting period to the net balance of the fixed asset. This net balance is the value of the asset that remains after deducting accumulated depreciation. In this method, the rate of depreciation is charged on the reducing balance of the asset during the year. The asset value is the one reflected in the books of accounts at the beginning of an accounting period. The book value of the asset is written down to reduce it to its residual value. Accordingly, a higher amount of depreciation is charged during the early years of the asset as compared to the later stages.

Unlike the fixed instalment system, depreciation under this method is not fixed, but gradually decreasing over the years. As such, in the initial periods, the amount will be much higher, but negligible in the later period of the asset. Thus, this method tends to compensate the amount of depreciation on one hand, and repairs and maintenance on the other hand.

This method is also easy to understand, even though the computation of annual depreciation of an asset is a little complicated. This method is best suited to assets such as plant and machinery which have a long life.

The formula for diminishing balance method is:

Depreciation = (Book value of the asset at beginning of the year × Rate of depreciation)/100

For example, if the cost of an asset is Rs. 50,000 and the rate of depreciation is 20%, the depreciation in the first year is Rs. 10,000 (Rs. 50,000 × 20/100). The written down value of the asset at the beginning of the second year will be Rs. 40,000. The depreciation for the second year is Rs. 8000 (Rs. 40,000 × 20/100) and the written down value of the asset at the beginning of the third year will be Rs. 32,000. The depreciation for the third year will be Rs. 6400 (Rs. 32,000 × 20/100) and the written down value of the asset at the beginning of the fourth year will be Rs. 25,600. Similarly, the depreciation will be calculated for the estimated life of the asset. Under this method, the written down value will never be zero. Hence, the asset is assumed to have some scrap value (see Table 24.2).

Table 24.2. Calculation of depreciation using the declining balance method

Years	Value of asset at the beginning of the year (in Rs.)	Annual depreciation @20% (in Rs.)	Cumulative depreciation (in Rs.)
1	50,000	10,000	10,000
2	40,000	8000	18,000
3	32,000	6400	24,400
4	25,600	5120	29,520
5	20,480	4096	33,616

24.3.3. Sum of Years' Digits Method

Another important method of computing depreciation is the sum of years' digits method. This method recognises depreciation at an accelerated rate. Under this method, the depreciable amount of an asset is charged to a fraction over different accounting periods. The fraction is referred to as the ratio between the remaining useful life of the asset in a particular period and the sum of the years' digits. Thus, this fraction indicates that the capital blocked or the benefit derived out of the asset is the highest in the first year. So, as the asset moves towards the end of its useful life, the benefit gained out of such an asset declines. In other words, the highest amount of depreciation is allocated in the first year since no amount of capital has been recovered till then. Consequently, a low amount of depreciation is charged in the last year as a major fraction of invested capital is recovered.

The formula to calculate sum of years' digits depreciation is:

Depreciation = Depreciable Cost × (Remaining useful life of the asset/ Sum of years' digits)

where,

Depreciable cost = Cost of an asset – Salvage value

Sum of years' digits = (n(n + 1))/2 (where, n = useful life of an asset)

For example, a business unit purchases a machine for Rs. 40,000 with an estimated life of 5 years, and then the total years of equipment life are aggregated. Depreciation is then charged at the rate of the ratio of the last year's digits to the total of the years. Therefore, the aggregated years of the equipment's life will be 1 + 2 + 3 + 4 + 5 = 15. The annual depreciation for the first year will be Rs. 13,333 (Rs. 40,000 × 5/15). In the second year, the depreciation amount will be Rs. 10,667 (Rs. 40,000 × 4/15). In the third year, depreciation amount it will be Rs. 8000 (Rs. 40,000 × 3/15), and so on. Thus, at the end of the estimated life, the value of the machine will be zero (refer to Table 24.3).

Table 24.3. Depreciation calculation using sum of years' digits method

Years	Value of asset at the beginning of the year (in Rs.)	Annual depreciation (in Rs.)	Cumulative depreciation (in Rs.)
1	40,000	13,333	13,333
2	26,667	10,667	24,000
3	16,000	8000	32,000
4	8000	5333	37,333
5	2667	2667	40,000

24.3.4. Double Declining Balance Method

This method is a mix of straight-line and diminishing balance method. Under this method, depreciation is charged on the reduced value of the fixed asset at the beginning of the year as in the case of diminishing balance method. However, a fixed rate of depreciation is applied just as in the straight-line method. This rate of depreciation is twice the rate charged under the straight-line method. Thus, this method leads to an over-depreciated asset at the end of its useful life as compared to the anticipated salvage value.

The formula to calculate depreciation under double declining balance method is:

Annual depreciation = 2 × (Cost of an asset – Salvage value)/Useful life of an asset

or

Depreciation = 2 × Cost of the asset × Depreciation rate

For example, the original cost of an asset is Rs. 2,20,000, estimated scrap value is Rs. 20,000, and the estimated working life of the asset is 5 years. Thus, the amount of annual depreciation is calculated as:

Total depreciation = Rs. 2,20,000 – Rs. 20,000 = Rs. 2,00,000

Annual depreciation = Rs. 2,00,000 / 5 = Rs. 40,000

Rate of depreciation under the straight-line method = Rs. 40,000 / Rs. 2,00,000 × 100 = 20%

Therefore, depreciation under DDB method = 2 × 20% = 40%

Table 24.4. Depreciation calculation using double declining balance method

Years	Value of asset at the beginning of the year (in Rs.)	Annual depreciation @ 40% (in Rs.)	Cumulative depreciation (in Rs.)
1	2,20,000	88,000	88,000
2	1,32,000	52,800	1,40,800
3	79,200	31,680	1,72,480
4	47,520	19,008	1,91,488
5	28,512	8512	2,00,000

In the last year, the depreciation is Rs. 8,512, as the asset has a scrap value of Rs. 20,000, i.e., Rs. 28,512 – Rs. 20,000 as shown in Table 24.4.

24.3.5. Annuity Method

Under this method, the amount spent on the acquisition of an asset is regarded as an investment which is assumed to earn interest at a certain rate. Here, the asset account is debited with the amount of interest and credited with the amount of depreciation every year. This interest is calculated on the debit balance of the asset at the beginning of the year. The amount to be written off as depreciation is ascertained from the annuity table and the same depends upon the rate of interest and the period over which the asset is to be written off. The rate of interest and the amount of depreciation are adjusted in such a way that at the end of its estimated useful life, the value of the asset would be reduced to zero or its scrap value.

This method has the advantage of treating the purchase of an asset as an investment within the business, and the same is supposed to earn interest. However, calculations become difficult when additions are made to the asset. The method is suitable only for long leases and other assets to which additions are not usually made and as such in case of machinery this method is not found suitable.

The formula to calculate depreciation under the annuity method is:

Annual depreciation = Value of the asset × Annuity value at a fixed interest

or

$$\text{Depreciation} = (C + Cr)/n$$

where,

n is the total number of years of capital

C is the total capital

r is the interest rate

The amount of depreciation in this method is calculated with the help of annuity table.

For example, a lease is purchased for a term of 4 years by payment of Rs. 1,00,000. It is proposed to depreciate the lease by annuity method charging 4% interest. The annuity of Re. 1 for 4 years at 4% is 0.275490. Thus, the amount of annual depreciation is calculated as:

Depreciation = Rs. 1,00,000 × Re. 0.275490 = Rs. 27,549 (see Table 24.5).

Table 24.5. Depreciation calculation of deprecation using the annuity method

Years	Value of asset at the beginning of the year (Rs.)	Annual depreciation (Rs.)	Cumulative depreciation (Rs.)
1	80,000	22,039	22,039
2	57,961	22,039	44,078
3	35,922	22,039	66,118
4	13,882	13,882	80,000

Therefore, in the fourth year, the interest rate for the lease will be adjusted by Rs. 8,157 (Rs. 22,039 – 13,882).

Thus, it is clear that the amount of profit would depend upon the method of depreciation adopted by the business unit. With the same asset, different business units can show different amounts of depreciation and different amounts of profits.

24.4. VALUATION OF INVENTORY

One of the important aspects of the valuation of inventory is pricing of the issues. Material is issued to production processes. The material in stores may be purchased at different points of time and different prices. Therefore, it is essential to identify the consumption value of the materials. The question is that at what price the issues should be charged. The answer is that the issues should be priced at the same price at which they are purchased. But practically, it is not possible to identify the material issued against every order for production. So, the materials to be issued should be priced by using certain methods depending upon the situation and nature of the manufacturing process. The following are the more practised methods of inventory valuation.

1. First In First Out Method (FIFO)
2. Last In First Out Method (LIFO)
3. Highest In First Out Method (HIFO)
4. Simple Average Cost Method
5. Weighted Average Method

1. **First In First Out (FIFO) Method:** Under FIFO method, the material is taken out of stock for further processing in the order which they are acquired, i.e., the material received first is issued first. Thus, the material in stock at the beginning of a period is issued first and then the issues are made according to the dates of purchases made. The inventory, therefore, appears in the balance sheet at the actual cost price. This method overstates profits at the time of rising prices. This is a logical method which follows the sequence of the issue according to the dates of purchases. The price charged to the issue of inventory will be as per the purchases made from time to time. Therefore, the latest market price will not be charged to consumption. This method is criticised on the ground that when the prices are rising the inventory issues will be charged at lower prices. In the case of falling prices, the inventory issue will carry higher prices compared to the prevailing market price. The closing stock generally will be valued at the latest prices as the material purchased towards the end of the period will be in the stock.
2. **Last In First Out (LIFO) Method:** Under the LIFO method, the stock purchased most recently becomes the cost of the raw material in the current year production. The stock issue will be charged at the price at which the material purchased last. The speciality of this method is that the price of the material issues represents the latest market prices and therefore, consumption value will be close to the market trend. The product cost in such case will be more realistic. The inventory valuation under this method will be at the original price at which materials are purchased. It is because the balance material may belong to earlier batches of purchases. This method of inventory valuation is not acceptable for the preparation of financial accounts.
3. **Highest In First Out (HIFO) Method:** Under this method, the materials with the highest prices are issued first, irrespective of the

date on which they are purchased. This method is used particularly when the market characteristics of the materials are highly fluctuating and inflationary. The business units plan to quickly absorb the cost of material in the product cost to avoid the risk of inflation. Under this method, the product costs tend to be higher due to the reason that the issues are charged at the highest prices. This method is not considered suitable in a competitive environment as the price of the product will be relatively higher and the competitors may not follow this method.

4. **Simple average cost method:** In simple average cost method, the issues are priced at an average rate of the materials purchased without considering the quantity procured. For example, the materials are procured in three lots at prices of Rs. 20, Rs. 24 and Rs. 22. The material will be issued at the average of the three lots prices, i.e., Rs. 20 + Rs. 24 + Rs. 22 = Rs. 66/3 = Rs. 22. This method does not have much prominence as it only considers the prices of different batches but not the quantities purchased in different batches. During the periods of price fluctuations, a simple average cost method is useful but when the price fluctuations are large, this method may not be applicable for pricing the material issues.
5. **Weighted average method:** Under this method, the materials are issued at a price which is an average price of materials purchased. The weighted average price is used to avoid fluctuation in price and reduce the number of calculations. The prices and the quantities of materials purchased are taken into consideration in this method. The weighted average is calculated by dividing the total amount by the total quantity after each receipt. The issue is charged at prices arrived at as per the weighted average.

   For example, when three batches of materials are purchased with quantities of 1000 units at Rs. 15, 1200 units at Rs. 18 and 1500 units at Rs. 20. The weighted average price is calculated as:

   = (1000 units × Rs. 15) + (1200 units × Rs. 18) + (1500 units × Rs. 20)

   = Rs. 15,000 + Rs. 21,600 + Rs. 30,000

   = Rs. 66,600 / 3700 = Rs. 18

   Therefore, the subsequent material issue will be priced at Rs.18. The main advantage of the weighted average method is that it evens out the price fluctuations and reduces the number of computations to be made.

   Thus, it can be observed that there are several methods of pricing of material issues to production processes. Anyone of these can be selected. All these methods have their advantages and limitations and do not reflect the true profit of the business.

Illustration:

From the following information, prepare store ledger using FIFO, LIFO, HIFO, simple average and weighted average method of pricing the issues:

April 1st : Balance in hand 1000 units @ Re. 1 each
April 20th : Received 3000 units @ Rs. 1.25 each
May 10th : Issued 2000 units
May 30th : Received 2000 units @ Rs. 1.5 each
June 15th : Issued 3400 units

Solution:

First In First Out (FIFO) Method

Date	Particulars	Receipts			Issues			Balance		
		Qty.	Rate	Amount	Qty.	Rate	Amount	Qty.	Rate	Amount
April 1st	Opening balance							1000	1.00	1000
April 20th	Receipts	3000	1.25	3750				1000 3000	1.00 1.25	1000 3750
May 10th	Issues				1000 1000	1.00 1.25	1000 1250	2000	1.25	2500
May 30th	Receipts	2000	1.50	3000				2000 2000	1.25 1.50	2500 3000
June 15th	Issues				2000 1400	1.25 1.50	2500 2100	600	1.50	900

Last In First Out (LIFO) Method

Date	Particulars	Receipts			Issues			Balance		
		Qty.	Rate	Amount	Qty.	Rate	Amount	Qty.	Rate	Amount
April 1st	Opening balance							1000	1.00	1000
April 20th	Receipts	3000	1.25	3750				1000 3000	1.00 1.25	1000 3750
May 10th	Issues				2000	1.25	2500	1000 1000	1.00 1.25	1000 1250
May 30th	Receipts	2000	1.50	3000				1000 1000 2000	1.00 1.25 1.50	1000 1250 3000
June 15th	Issues				2000 1000 400	1.50 1.25 1.00	3000 1250 400	600	1.00	600

Highest In First Out (HIFO) Method

Date	Particulars	Receipts			Issues			Balance		
		Qty.	Rate	Amount	Qty.	Rate	Amount	Qty.	Rate	Amount
April 1st	Opening balance							1000	1.00	1000
April 20th	Receipts	3000	1.25	3750				1000 3000	1.00 1.25	1000 3750
May 10th	Issues				2000	1.25	2500	1000 1000	1.00 1.25	1000 1250
May 30th	Receipts	2000	1.50	3000				1000 1000 2000	1.00 1.25 1.50	1000 1250 3000
June 15th	Issues				2000 1000 400	1.50 1.25 1.00	3000 1250 400	600	1.00	600

Simple Average Cost Method

Date	Particulars	Receipts			Issues			Balance		
		Qty.	Rate	Amount	Qty.	Rate	Amount	Qty.	Rate	Amount
April 1st	Opening Balance							1000	1.00	1000
April 20th	Receipts	3000	1.25	3750				4000		4750
May 10th	Issues				2000	1.125	2250	2000		2500
May 30th	Receipts	2000	1.50	3000				4000		5500
June 15th	Issues				3400	1.375	4675	600		825

Working notes:

- On May 10th the rate of the issue is computed by taking the simple average of the rates of Re. 1 and Rs. 1.25, i.e. (1 + 1.25)/2 = Rs. 1.125.
- On June 15th the rate is computed by taking the simple average of the rates of Rs. 1.25 and Rs. 1.50, i.e. (1.25 + 1.50)/2 = Rs. 1.375. The earlier rate of Re. 1 is not taken into consideration as the material quantity has been issued and is not there in the stock as on 15th June.

Weighted Average Method

Date	Particulars	Receipts			Issues			Balance		
		Qty.	Rate	Amount	Qty.	Rate	Amount	Qty.	Rate	Amount
April 1st	Opening balance							1000	1.00	1000
April 20th	Receipts	3000	1.25	3750				4000		4750
May 10th	Issues				2000	1.19	2380	2000		2370
May 30th	Receipts	2000	1.50	3000				4000		5370
June 15th	Issues				3400	1.34	4564.5	600		805.5

Working notes:

- On May 10th the rate of the issue is computed by taking the weighted average of the prices and quantities, i.e., 4750/4000 = Rs. 1.19.
- On June 15th the rate is computed by taking the weighted average of the prices and quantities, i.e., 5370/4000 = Rs. 1.34.

24.5. TREATMENT OF CAPITAL GAINS AND LOSSES

Capital gains refer to any profits or gains arising out of the transfer of a capital asset effected in the previous year. Capital gains are chargeable under income tax. The capital gains are deemed to be the income of the previous year. Capital gains are categorised in two ways such as capital asset and transfer.

1. **Capital asset:** A capital asset refers to any kind of property held by an assessee. The assessee may or may not be connected with a business or profession. A capital asset held by an assessee for not more than 36 months immediately preceding the date of its transfer is called a *long-term capital asset.*
2. **Transfer:** Capital gains may result due to the transfer of a capital asset from one entity to the other. The entity may be a person, business unit or a company. Such transfer of capital asset takes place under different circumstances. The following are some examples:
   - When a capital asset is sold, exchanged or relinquished.
   - When the rights on the asset are extinguished.
   - As per the law, the assets are acquired under compulsion.
   - When the owner of the capital asset converted it into the stock-in-trade of a business unit.
   - When a zero-coupon bond is matured or redeemed.

The expenditure incurred in connection with such transfer plus the indexed cost of acquisition and the cost of any improvement in the capital asset considered will be deducted while computing the income chargeable under the head 'capital gains'. In case the net result under capital gains is a loss, the loss shall be carried forward to the following assessment year. Such a loss will be set off in the following manner:

1. If the net result is a loss in case of any short-term capital asset, such loss is allowed to be set-off against income, if any, for that assessment year.
2. If the net result is a loss in case of any long-term capital asset, such loss is allowed to be set-off against income, if any, for that assessment year.
3. The net loss is not allowed to set-off against income under capital gains if the loss is under any other head.
4. Unabsorbed losses can be carried forward to the subsequent assessment year up to a maximum of eight assessment years.
5. The short-term capital loss is permitted to set-off against short-term capital gain as well as a long-term capital gain.
6. The long-term capital loss can be set-off against long-term capital gain only.

Capital gains and losses are regarded as windfalls. A fluctuation in the prices of the stock market is one of the most common sources of windfalls. According to Joel Dean (1951), capital losses are greater than capital gains in a progressive society. Many of the capital losses are insurable and the excess becomes the capital gain. The profit of a business unit is also affected by the way capital gains and losses are treated in accounting. Dean (1968) stated that not recording windfalls until they are turned into cash by purchase or sale of assets is the sound accounting policy since it is never clear until then exactly how large the windfalls are. In practice, some business units do not record capital gains until it is realised in money terms, but they do write off capital losses from the current profit. The use of different policies results in different profits. But, an economist is not concerned with the accounting practice or principle, which is followed in recording past events. An economist is concerned mainly with what happens in future.

The shareholders expect an increase in the market value of the equity shares held by them over some time. Capital gain refers to the profit resulting from the sale of capital investment, i.e., the equity shares in case of shareholders. For example, if a shareholder purchases a share for Rs. 40 and later on sells it for Rs. 60 the amount of capital gain is Rs. 20. According to economists, the management should be aware of the approximate magnitude of such windfalls before they are accepted by the accountants. This would help take the right decision concerning those assets, which are affected by the use of policies given by economists. In the case of unrealised capital gains, there is almost unanimity that they should not be included in the profits. If there is a revaluation of property, the gain resulting therefrom is usually transferred to capital reserve.

24.6. AMORTISATION OF LONG-TERM INTANGIBLE ASSETS

The fixed assets are classified as tangible and intangible assets. The tangible fixed assets are fixed in nature with a long lifespan and can be seen, touched and felt. For example, land, building, furniture, plant and machinery, etc. The intangible fixed assets can be classified as:

1. The assets having a limited lifespan such as patents, copyrights, leasehold, licences, permits, etc.
2. The assets having an unlimited lifespan such as goodwill, trademarks, preliminary expenses, etc.

Amortisation is the systematic allocation of the depreciable amount over its useful life of an intangible asset. In the case of intangible fixed assets like goodwill, etc., a certain amount of total costs is charged against periodic revenues. Depreciation includes amortisation of intangible assets with pre-estimated effective lives. Amortisation or writing off such assets is made to account for the deterioration of their economic values. The useful life shall not exceed 10 years from the date the asset is available for use. However, the amortisation period should be revised accordingly but in no case, it would equal to inappropriate delay to later years.

In general, for each class of intangible asset is assessed by:

1. The useful life and amortisation rates, amortisation method, gross carrying amount and the accumulated amortisation including impairment loss at the beginning and end of the reporting period, and a reconciliation of the carrying amount.
2. The class of intangible asset and use by the business unit information on impaired intangible asset is also considered.
3. The carrying amount and remaining amortisation period of any individual asset is materialised as a whole.
4. The existence and the carrying amount of intangible assets whose title is restricted and the carrying amount of intangible asset pledged as security for liabilities.
5. Amount of commitments for the acquisition of intangible assets such as research and development (R&D) expenditure and other information encouraged to disclose a description of the only fully amortised intangible asset but still in use.

For example, a business unit bought a trademark for Rs. 50 lakh and estimated the trademark's remaining life to be 14 years. Its unamortised cost was Rs. 35 lakh. The business unit decided to amortise the trademark over the maximum period allowed. Thus, to determine the accumulated amortisation, the intangible assets are initially measured at cost. Therefore, the business unit should amortise the trademark at its original cost of Rs. 50 lakh. The unamortised cost on the seller's books, i.e., Rs. 35 lakh is irrelevant to the buyer. Though the remaining useful life of the trademark is 14 years, intangible assets are amortised over a maximum period of 10 years only. Therefore, the maximum amortisation expense and accumulated amortisation are Rs. 5 lakh (Rs. 50 lakh / 10 years).

The internally generated computer software also can be recognised as an asset on satisfying the conditions like:

- The technical feasibility to make it available for internal use.
- Ability to perform individual functions.
- Ability to generate future economic benefit.
- Availability of technical, financial and other resources to complete the development and use.
- Reliability in measuring the expenditure on software development.

For computer software, considering the fact of technological change and obsolescence, it is 3-5 years of useful life, which needs to be reasoned in the disclosure. The expenditure for purchasing, developing, maintaining and enhancing hardware related to the website are accounted for. The expenditure may be incurred internally when developing, enhancing and maintaining its website in the context of planning, application and infrastructure development, graphical design and content development and operating stage. These are directly attributable or allocable on a reasonable basis to creating, producing and preparing the asset for the intended use. The nature of each activity should be evaluated to decide website stage of development.

24.7. SUMMARY

- To measure accounting profit, necessary revenue and cost data are obtained from the accounting books of a business unit. It must be noted that accounting profit may present an overstatement or understatement of actual profit if it is based on the illogical allocation of revenues and costs to a given accounting period.
- The most important aspects of profit measurement are inclusiveness of costs, classification of depreciation, treatment of capital gains and losses, and valuation of assets.
- Depreciation is regarded as the capital cost of assets allocated over the estimated life of an asset. It is to compensate for the gradual decrease in the value of an asset due to wear and tear, obsolescence, usage and passage of time. The two main factors contributing to the decline in the usefulness of fixed assets are deterioration and obsolescence.

- The amount of depreciation of a fixed asset is determined to take into account the factors such as its original cost, recoverable cost at the time it is retired from service and the length of its life.
- The important methods of calculating depreciation are the straight-line method, diminishing balance method, the sum of years digits method, double declining balance method, and annuity method.
- Straight-line method is the most commonly used method to calculate depreciation. It is also known as a fixed instalment method. Under this method, an equal/fixed amount is charged as depreciation on the fixed asset in each of the accounting periods. This fixed amount of depreciation is charged until the value of the asset becomes zero or its salvage value at the end of its estimated useful life.
- In the diminishing balance method, the rate of depreciation is charged on the reducing balance of the asset during the year. The asset value is the one reflected in the books of accounts at the beginning of an accounting period. The book value of the asset is written down to reduce it to its residual value.
- Under the sum of year's digits method, the depreciable amount of an asset is charged to a fraction over different accounting periods. The fraction is referred to as the ratio between the remaining useful life of the asset in a particular period and the sum of the years' digits.
- Double declining balance method is a mix of straight-line and diminishing balance method. Under this method, depreciation is charged on the reduced value of the fixed asset at the beginning of the year as in the case of diminishing balance method.
- In the annuity method, the amount spent on the acquisition of an asset is regarded as an investment which is assumed to earn interest at a certain rate. Here, the asset account is debited with the amount of interest and credited with the amount of depreciation every year. This interest is calculated on the debit balance of the asset at the beginning of the year.
- The highly practising methods of inventory valuation are First In First Out Method (FIFO), Last In First Out Method (LIFO), Highest In First Out Method (HIFO), simple average cost method, and weighted average method.
- Under the FIFO method, the material is taken out of stock for further processing in the order which they are acquired, i.e., the material received first is issued first. Thus, the material in stock at the beginning of a period is issued first and then the issues are made according to the dates of purchases made.
- Under the LIFO method, the stock purchased most recently becomes the cost of the raw material in the current year . The speciality of this method is that the price of the material issues represents the latest

market prices and therefore, consumption value will be close to the market trend.

- Under HIFO method, the materials with the highest prices are issued first, irrespective of the date upon which they are purchased. This method is used particularly when the market characteristics of the materials are highly fluctuating and inflationary.
- In simple average cost method, the issues are priced at an average rate of the materials purchased without considering the quantity procured.
- Under the weighted average method, the materials are issued at a price which is an average price of materials purchased. The weighted average price is used to avoid fluctuation in price and reduce the number of calculations. The prices and the quantities of materials purchased are taken into consideration in this method.
- Capital gains refer to any profits or gains arising out of the transfer of a capital asset effected in the previous year. Capital gains are chargeable under income tax. Capital gains are categorised in two ways such as capital asset and transfer.
- Capital gains and losses are regarded as windfalls. A fluctuation in the prices of the stock market is one of the most common sources of windfalls. According to economists, the management should be aware of the approximate magnitude of such windfalls before they are accepted by the accountants. This would help take the right decision concerning those assets, which are affected by the use of policies given by economists.
- Amortisation is the systematic allocation of the depreciable amount over its useful life of an intangible asset. It is charged on tangible fixed assets but not on current assets. In the case of intangible fixed assets like goodwill, etc., a certain amount of total costs is charged against periodic revenues.

SHORT ANSWER QUESTIONS

1. Define depreciation.
2. What are the characteristics of depreciation?
3. Write a short note on the sum of years' digits method.
4. Explain simple average cost method.
5. Briefly explain the concept of transfer.
6. What is amortisation?
7. Explain the assessment of intangible assets.

ESSAY ANSWER QUESTIONS

1. Explain the concept of profit measurement in detail.
2. Explain the methods of depreciation with suitable examples.
3. Distinguish between the straight-line and diminishing balance method.

4. Describe the double declining balance method of calculating depreciation.
5. Explain the annuity method of depreciation with an illustration.
6. Discuss the mostly practised methods of inventory valuation.
7. Describe the treatment of capital gains and losses with examples.
8. Discuss the accounting process of amortisation of long-term intangible assets.
9. A business unit purchased the machine for Rs. 2,00,000. The estimated life of the machine is 5 years. It was estimated that the scrap value of the machine would be Rs. 50,000 at the end of the fifth year. Calculate depreciation using a fixed instalment method and the sum of years' digits method.
10. A business unit purchased a plant for Rs. 10,000 and spent Rs. 2000 as erection charges. The estimated life of the plant is 5 years. Calculate the amount of depreciation @15% per annum under the written down value method.
11. A lease is purchased for a term of 5 years by payment of Rs. 1,40,000. Calculate the depreciation amount of the lease by annuity method charging 5% interest.
12. Consider a piece of equipment that costs Rs. 2,50,000, with an estimated useful life of 8 years and a salvage value of Rs. 25,000. Depreciate the equipment using double declining balance depreciation.
13. From the following information, prepare store ledger using FIFO and LIFO methods of pricing the issues:
    June 1st : Opening balance 2000 units @ Rs. 11 each
    June 8th : Received 3200 units @ Rs. 15 each
    June 13th : Received 1200 units @ Rs. 14 each
    June 14th : Issued 2500 units
    June 20th : Issued 1500 units
    June 23rd : Received 1750 units @ Rs. 16 each
    June 30th : Issued 3400 units
14. Prepare store ledger using simple cost and weighted average cost methods of pricing the issues:
    August 1st : Balance in hand 300 units @ Rs. 24 each
    August 6th : Receipt of 220 units @ Rs. 26 each
    August 12th : Issues of 240 units
    August 17th : Receipts of 450 units @ Rs. 27.5 each
    August 21st : Issues of 275 units
    August 28th : Receipts of 345 units @ Rs. 24.5 each
    August 31st : Issued 480 units

FILL IN THE BLANKS

1. Accountants consider profit as business __________.
2. The financial status of a business unit representing the assets and liabilities is called __________.
3. Economists consider net income as a __________ of the future.
4. The excess of cost over the estimated residual value during the lifetime of the asset is regarded as __________.

5. Straight-line method also is known as __________.
6. Diminishing balance method is suitable to assets having __________ life-span.
7. The method where the amount spent on the acquisition of an asset is regarded as an investment which is assumed to earn interest at a certain rate is __________.
8. FIFO method __________ profits at the time of rising prices.
9. The method where the stock issue will be charged at the price at which the material purchased last is called __________.
10. Capital gains and losses are regarded as __________.
11. The systematic allocation of the depreciable amount over its useful life of an intangible asset is called __________.

Answers:

1. Income
2. Balance sheet
3. Speculation
4. Depreciation
5. Fixed instalment method
6. Long
7. Annuity method
8. Overstates
9. LIFO
10. Windfalls
11. Amortisation

MULTIPLE-CHOICE QUESTIONS

1. The capital cost of assets allocated over the estimated life of an asset is called:
   (A) Amortisation (B) Depreciation
   (C) Opportunity cost (D) Replacement cost
2. Economists consider depreciation as:
   (A) Capital consumption (B) Deterioration
   (C) Obsolescence (D) Speculation
3. When a fixed amount of depreciation is charged until the value of the asset becomes zero or its salvage value at the end of its estimated useful life, it is called:
   (A) Diminishing balance method
   (B) Fixed rate method
   (C) Straight-line method
   (D) Fixed cost method
4. When a fixed percentage of depreciation is charged in each accounting period to the net balance of the fixed asset, it is called:
   (A) Reducing balance method (B) Fixed instalment method
   (C) Annuity method (D) Annual decreasing method
5. Under which method, the depreciable amount of an asset is charged to a fraction over different accounting periods.
   (A) Diminishing balance method
   (B) Double declining balance method
   (C) Sum of years' digits method
   (D) Written down value method

6. Under which method, the material in stock at the beginning of a period is issued first and then the issues are made according to the dates of purchases made.
   (A) Simple average (B) LIFO
   (C) HIFO (D) FIFO
7. Any profits or gains arising out of the transfer of a capital asset effected in the previous year are called:
   (A) Capital revenue (B) Capital expenditure
   (C) Capital gains (D) Capital structure
8. A fluctuation in the prices of the stock market is one of the most common sources of:
   (A) Windfall (B) Capital loss
   (C) Capital set-off (D) Magnitude

Answers:

1. B	2. A	3. C	4. A	5. C
6. D	7. C	8. A		

REFERENCES

1. Besanko, D.A. & Braeutigam, R.R. (2011). *Micro Economics* (4th Edn). New Jersey: John Wiley & Sons, Inc., Hoboken.
2. Cowen, T. & Tabarrok, A. (2013). *Modern Principles of Economics (2nd* Edn). New York, NY: Worth Publishers.
3. Dean, J. (1968). *Managerial Economics.* New Delhi, India: Prentice-Hall of India Private Limited.
4. Dean, Joel. (1951). *Managerial Economics.* New York: Prentice-Hall, Inc.
5. Dwivedi, D.N. (2015). *Managerial Economics* (8th Edn). New Delhi, India: Vikas Publishing House Pvt. Ltd.
6. Gupta, G.S. (2017). *Managerial Economics.* New Delhi, India: Tata McGraw-Hill.
7. Hirschey, M. (2009). *Managerial Economics* (12th Edition). USA: South-Western Cengage Learning.
8. Knight, F.H. (1957). *Risk, Uncertainty and Profit.* (Eighth impression.). London School of Economics and Political Science.
9. Marshall, A. (1920). *Principles of Economics.* London: Macmillan and Co. Ltd.
10. Mehta, P.L. (2007). *Managerial Economics: Text and Cases.* New Delhi, India: Sultan Chand & Co.
11. Salvatore, D. & Rastogi, S.K. (2016). *Managerial Economics.* New Delhi, India: Oxford University Press.
12. Varshney, R.L. & Maheswari, K.L. (2014). *Managerial Economics.* New Delhi, India: Sultan Chand & Sons.

Chapter

25 Inflation

LEARNING OBJECTIVES

After studying this chapter, you should be able to understand:

- concept of inflation;
- types and theories of inflation;
- measures of measuring inflation; and
- effects of inflation and measures to control inflation.

25.1. CONCEPT OF INFLATION

Inflation is a quantifiable degree at which the average price level of select goods and services increases over a period of time. Inflation is often expressed as a percentage, which indicates a fall in the purchasing power of a country. Inflation is a phenomenon in which a general increase in prices and a decline in purchasing is witnessed. Economists define that inflation does not emerge until price increase averages are less than 5% per year for a sustained period.

Definitions of Inflation

Author	Definition
G. Crowther (1957)	Inflation is a state in which the value of money is falling, i.e., prices are rising.
A.C. Pigou (1941)	Inflation exists when money income is expanding more than in proportion to the increase in earning activity.
Harry G. Johnson (1963)	A substantial increase in prices.
Milton Friedman (1971)	Inflation is a steady and sustained rise in prices.
Gardner Ackley (1953)	Inflation is a persistent and appreciable rise in the general level of prices.

25.2. TYPES OF INFLATION

Based on the rapidity with which prices rise, inflation may be classified into four types as shown in Figure 25.1.

1. **Creeping inflation:** Creeping inflation is the trifling form of inflation and is not reflected to cause any ill effects on the economy. It is a situation where the inflation of an economy increases slowly but continuously over a period and its effect is observed after a long

period. Creeping inflation is believed to be an inescapable moment of economic development. When prices rise by not more than 3% in a year, such a situation is described as creeping inflation.

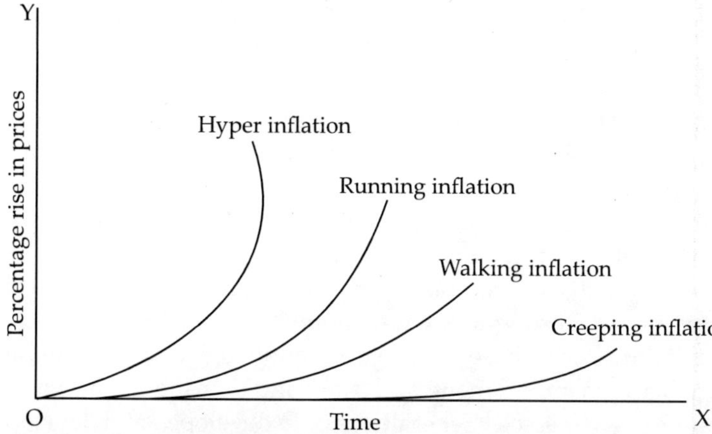

Figure 25.1. Types of inflation

2. **Walking inflation:** Walking inflation is the subsequent stage of inflation. It is a situation where prices rise moderately and the annual inflation rate is in a single digit. This type of inflation rate makes the government cautious to initiate necessary steps to control before it increases. Once creeping inflation lasts over a decade and prices escalate not more than 3% to 10%, it is described as walking inflation.
3. **Running inflation:** Running inflation is a situation where the prices of products and services increase at a rate of the two-digit or three-digit rate per annum. It is also known as *galloping inflation* and *jumping inflation*. Running inflation is at the time when the speed of price rises further intensifies, walking inflation gets adapted into running inflation which would record not more than 10% to 20% upsurge in prices over a period of time.
4. **Hyper inflation:** Hyper inflation is quick and usually uncontrollable currency depreciation causing the prices of products and services to shoot up in a short period. It quickly decreases the real value of the local currency, as the price of products and services increases. Although there is no precise limit, hyper inflation typically describes the inflation rate that surpasses 50%.

Inflation is further classified as:

1. **Demand-pull inflation:** In the market economy, the money flow is directly proportional to the flow of goods and services. In this

scenario, money chases more relatively to less quantity of goods and services. Surplus demand for goods and services rationally drives up the prices. Such inflation, as a consequence of greater money outflow, is called demand-pull inflation. In other words, when demand for goods and services are more than their supply, the price of such goods and services increases.

2. **Cost-push inflation:** This refers to a situation where prices persistently escalate because of mounting costs. Cost-push inflation is witnessed when certain aspects of production particularly wage earners try to proliferate their share of total merchandise by raising their prices. A growth in factor prices entails to an increase in the overall cost of production and subsequently a rise in the price level. Inflation once set in motion due to cost-push in one industry or sector spreads throughout the economy.
3. **Stagflation:** It is a phase where persistently high inflation combined with high unemployment and stagnant demand in a country's economy is witnessed. Generally, in both developed and developing countries, the combined phenomenon of both demand-pull and cost-push inflation can be observed. One of these situations is in the form of stagflation under which economic stagnation, in the form of low rate of growth, combines with the increase in the general price level. This happens in developing countries when average demand intensifies at a fast rate due to high public spending and spreading out of credit money, the aggregate cost rises due to higher wages resulting from pressure from labour groups thus, linking cost-push effect with demand-pull inflation.

25.3. CAUSES OF INFLATION

The inflation causes due to the following two reasons:

- Increase in money income
- Fall in the production

25.3.1. Increase in Money Income

Inflation emerges on account of the increase in money incomes of certain sections of the community without any corresponding increase in their productivity giving rise to an increase in the aggregate demand for goods and services which cannot be at current prices by the total available supply of goods and services in the economy. The following are the factors responsible for the increase in money income:

1. Monetary and credit policy of the government
2. Increase in the velocity of money

3. Credit policy of commercial banks
4. Deficit financing
5. Increase in unproductive expenditure
6. Import of foreign capital
7. Financial disorder
8. Favourable balance of payments
9. A rise in import price

1. **Monetary and credit policy of the government:** When the governments of developing countries fall short of financial resources for the implementation of their development programmes, the governments float new currency into circulation. The circulation of new currency is the result of monetary policy. The circulation of the new currency increases monetary income but no increase is noticed in the real income. This creates an inflationary situation in the economy.
2. **Increase in the velocity of money:** Increase in the propensity to consume in the society and the fall in liquidity preference of the people increases the velocity of money. Increase in the velocity increases the monetary income of the people, which creates an inflationary situation in the economy.
3. **Credit policy of commercial bank:** Commercial banks with the help of their credit policy create an inflationary situation in the economy. When the demand for credit increases, commercial banks by reducing their cash reserve ratio can create the credit. This credit creation policy of the bank increases the quantity of money flow which further results in inflation.
4. **Deficit financing:** It refers to the financing of the excess expenditure over total revenue receipts of the government. The financing of this excess expenditure is covered with the help of issue of new currency to circulation. This issue of the new currency increases monetary income, which results in the inflationary situation in the economy.
5. **Increase in unproductive expenditure:** Supply may suddenly decrease on account of some natural calamities or some similar things. Flood, drought, diseases of crops, etc., can reduce the supply of essential goods and feed inflationary forces.
6. **Import of foreign capital:** When a country continuously imports foreign capital or borrows heavy loans from outside, the inflationary forces start emerging in the economy. This increases monetary income.
7. **Financial disorder:** When the government fails to collect the full amount of levied taxes, the number of unaccounted money

increases. In the absence of any control on this unaccounted money, undue pressure is built on demand of goods and services. This increases the price level in the country and the situation of inflation starts emerging.

8. **Favourable balance of payments:** As a result of favourable balance of payments (i.e., excess of exports over imports), the supply of foreign exchange increases in the country. The increase in foreign exchange reserve creates an inflationary situation in the economy.
9. **Rise in import price:** If the prices of importable products rise, it leads to imported inflation. If the imported products are inputs or raw materials in domestic products such as crude oil, the cost of production would rise in general resulting in higher domestic prices and inflation.

25.3.2. Fall in Production

The following are the factors responsible for a fall in the production of goods and services:

1. Natural factors
2. Increase in population
3. Black marketing and hoarding
4. Shortage of raw material
5. Industrial unrest
6. Trade and fiscal policy of the government
7. Shortage and bottlenecks in productive process

1. **Natural factors:** Floods, droughts, famine, earthquake, and similar happenings reduce the supply of essential goods in the market. Due to these natural factors, production goes down but the monetary income remains constant. This feeds inflationary forces in the economy.
2. **Increase in population:** When the population of the country increases at a faster rate and production of the goods and services remains constant or grows at a slow rate, the scarcity of such goods is realised. This scarcity results in an increase in prices, and thus inflation.
3. **Black marketing and hoarding:** Sometimes inflation is caused by black marketing and hoarding. The commodities which are in demand are hoarded by the traders and businessmen. As a result, their prices rise and it leads to inflationary conditions.
4. **Shortage of raw material:** Sometimes due to shortage of raw material, production and supplies of goods are adversely affected. This increases prices of such goods and the occurrence of inflation.

5. **Industrial unrest:** Many a time production is adversely affected by industrial unrest like strikes and lockouts. This reduces the supply of essential goods and feeds inflationary forces.
6. **Trade and fiscal policy of the government:** To boost exports and reduce imports, governments make the necessary changes in trade policy. As a result of such changes exports start increasing at the cost of the domestic economy. This creates a shortage of essential goods in the economy and domestic price level starts rising.
7. **Shortage and bottlenecks in productive process:** In developing countries, structural inadequacy leads to a shortage of inputs and resources, which in turn, would result in inflation.

25.4. THEORIES OF INFLATION

Two foremost theories describe inflation where there is a rapid growth rate of money income. They are the quantity theory and the Keynesian-type theory. The quantity theory of money underscores the quantity of money as the factor of demand; the Keynesian-type theory finds the factors of demand and the level of money income from a wide perspective.

1. **Quantity theory of money:** The quantity theory of money explains the theory of the price rise vis-à-vis theory of aggregate demand. If the supply of money is consistent for the purchase of goods, an increase in the money supply may not be proportionate to the increase in total spending. If the economy is growing at a faster rate, it increases spending means. The increase in spending means raises the price level of products/services and results in inflation. Thus, under these circumstances, inflation continues as long as and as fast as the money supply is expanding. However, inflation culminates when the money supply stops increasing.
2. **Keynesian-type theory:** Keynes has expressed demand analysis in terms of the concept of "inflationary gap". Keynes presented the theory to highlight the significance of the flow of money income in coercing the general price level. He wanted to show the eminence of fiscal measures such as taxation and borrowing in wiping the inflationary gap. Inflationary gap is defined as an excess of anticipated expenditure over the available output at base prices. Anticipated expenditures are measured concerning consumption, savings pattern and the technological structure.

25.5. METHODS OF MEASURING INFLATION

Inflation can be measured in terms of a wholesale price index (WPI) method and consumer price index (CPI) method.

1. **Wholesale price index (WPI):** Wholesale price index is the price of a descriptive set of wholesale goods. The WPI depends on the price of goods and services in the wholesale market. WPI comprises a complete set of commodities. WPI does not include services and non-tradable merchandises. This is different from core inflation in which the products that have unstable prices are not considered.
2. **Consumer price index (CPI):** Consumer price index measures the changes in the price level of consumer goods and services purchased by the household sector. It reflects the cost of living for a uniform group of consumers. There are four CPI categories in India. It includes CPI for industrial workers, CPI for agricultural labour, CPI for rural labour and CPI for urban non-manual employees. Consumer price index is considered a more realistic measure of inflation than the wholesale price index.

25.6. EFFECTS OF INFLATION

Inflation affects all the sections of society. While for the rich it brings good fortune, for the poorer sections, it may prove to be disastrous. Inflation initially activates the economy. According to Keynes, inflation has not only diminished the capacity of the investing class to save but has destroyed the atmosphere of confidence which is a condition of willingness to save. However, continuous inflation shakes the foundation of the economic system which makes the rich richer and the poor poorer. Effects of inflation can be divided into four heads.

25.6.1. Effect of Inflation on Different Sections of Society

Inflation does not influence all sections of society similarly. While a section of society may tend to gain, another section would invariably lose. The effect of inflation on different sections of society can be discussed as follows:

1. **Producers:** In this category, industrialists, traders, farmers, and employers are included. Inflation is a boon to the producers because it serves as a tonic for business enterprise. During inflation, corporate and non-corporate profits rise sharply and businessmen react to these rising prices by building up inventories.
2. **Investors:** Investors could be classified into two categories. Investors dealing in speculative activities (equity shares) and investors in fixed interest yielding securities (bonds and debentures). The former category of investors gains during inflation because dividend on equities increases with an increase in prices and corporate earnings.

Investors in fixed interest yielding securities have to be content with the fixed income and they cannot share the fruits of prosperity in the economy arising as a result of inflation. Thus, investors in fixed interest yielding securities may tend to lose during inflation.

3. **Consumers:** Every individual in society is a consumer. The consumer is the worst sufferer during inflation because their purchasing power goes down with the increase in prices.
4. **Wage and salary earners:** People getting fixed income, i.e., wages and salaries, pensioners, suffer most during inflation. Although with an increase in the price level, wages and salaries rise, they do not rise in the same proportion in which the cost of living rises. This results in fall in real wages and as a result, the living standard of fixed income class declines.
5. **Debtors and creditors:** During inflation, debtors are the gainers and the creditors are the losers. The debtor when borrowed money before inflation had set in it commanded more purchasing power than what it commands during inflation. So, when the money is returned, the creditor receives less in real terms.

25.6.2. Other Effects of Inflation

1. **Redistribution of wealth:** During inflation, inequality in society arises. Wage and salary earners and consumers had to suffer a lot during inflationary situations, because of the high rise in prices. Thus, during inflation, the rich become richer and the poor become poorer.
2. **Increase in government expenditure:** During inflation, government expenditure rises tremendously. It is because the government has to pay higher wages to its employees and the cost of various projects under construction also increases.
3. **Increasing tax revenue to the government:** In a progressive tax system, the government can add to its tax revenue simply on account of increasing money incomes. Since tax liabilities are based on money incomes, therefore, taxpayers keep moving into higher income brackets, for tax purpose without any addition of their real incomes. In such a situation, the government collects more revenue without increasing tax rates or imposition of new taxes. Hence, taxpayers are worst affected during the inflationary situation.
4. **Increase in public debts:** During the inflationary period, the governments generally find that their tax receipts are lagging behind their requirements of expenditure. As a result, the government

has to resort to borrowing. But it is found that with the progress of inflation, it becomes increasingly difficult to borrow from the market.

5. **Distortion of financial institutions:** Inflation has the effect of distorting financial institutions. Inflation is a monetary phenomenon. Interest is an integral part of the monetary and credit structure. During inflation, when the interest rate starts moving upwards, financial institutions are put to great difficulties as they had to pay the increased interest rates on the matured liabilities immediately. The revision of their receipts from interest takes time, while their interest expenses start increasing more rapidly. This disrupts the smooth functioning of financial institutions.
6. **Hoarding of goods:** In anticipation of the rise in prices, during the inflationary situation, both traders and consumers start hoarding essential goods. The traders hoard essential commodities to make higher profits or to sell scarce items in the black market.
7. **Stimulation to speculative activities:** On account of the uncertainty generated by a continuous rise in the price level, inflation gives stimulus to speculative activities. Producers and traders, during this period, try to maximise their profit with the help of speculative activities.
8. **Fall in saving rate:** Inflation affects saving activity in society. The savers find that the value of their saving is getting eroded on account of inflation. Though the rate of interest goes up, the fall in the value of money will be more than the additional income from the interest. Therefore, the savers become net losers.
9. **Adverse balance of payments:** Inflation leads to a balance of payment difficulties. Because of increased prices, exports start declining due to failure to face competition. The rate of exchange also moves against the home currency and results in increasing trade deficit. However, inflationary conditions can impose severe balance of payment problems upon developing countries.
10. **Employment effect:** During inflation, more employment is generated because the producers in anticipation of larger profits expand the size of the output.

25.6.3. Moral Effect

The moral effect of inflation is not positive. Inflation when wipes out savings, the affected persons may tend to work against the government rules and regulations and they may not follow societal values and ethics.

They try to adopt illegal and immoral ways of making money. Inflation is said to be the powerful agent of evil practices. It is a paradise for speculators and profiteers who are enriched through no effects of their own, partly at the expense of wage earners.

25.6.4. Social and Political Effect

Inflation has certain social and political effects. Inflation promotes inequality in society and divides it into rich and poor categories. The widening gap between the rich and the poor creates class conflict. There are many incidences in the history of such happenings.

25.7. MEASURES TO CONTROL INFLATION

The effects of inflation are economically unsound, politically dangerous, socially disastrous and morally indefensible. It generates inequalities of wealth, paralyses the machinery of wealth production and even as a source of revenue it soon gets dried up. It is, therefore, obvious that inflation is a serious disease which needs to be effectively controlled before it is too late. The subject of controlled inflation can be viewed from two angles: the general controls and the explicit controls. The general control is concerned principally with currency and credit fixing. Different measures can be adopted to control inflation. These measures can be grouped into three categories:

1. Monetary measures
2. Fiscal measures
3. Policy measures

25.7.1. Monetary Measures

Monetary measures are real-time pragmatic tools in which the flow of money and credit is checked. These are usually quantitative measures like bank rates, statutory supplies and open market exercises, and qualitative measures like margin requirements, moral persuasion, in which a discursive strategy is followed to change their policies that suggest a set of principles to pressurise individuals, groups, or nation-states. It is a situation used by various business units for diverse purposes.

In such a situation where the Reserve Bank of India (RBI) wants to regulate inflation, it adopts any one or more of these measures. Government is compelled to sell its securities in the open market and takes away liquidity from the public. This pulls down the balances with the banks, which in turn, decreases liquidity in the economy and brings down the market prices to control inflation. Similarly, banks raise interest rates of statutory reserve funds through which the RBI has complete control over liquidity and credit and finally market prices. The degree to which these measures will be effective rests on the concentration of investment demand. The raising of statutory reserve ratio is an extensively used phenomenon in India but the outcome of this extent also be determined by the banking behaviour of people. However, in countries where banking is not widely spread and all money is not rapidly banked, the result will be much lesser.

The following are the monetary measures which help in controlling the inflationary situation.

1. **Making rupee note issue policy strict:** The central bank should adopt strict rupee note issue policies so that it may not issue additional money. For making note issue more stringent, the gold or foreign exchange reserve should be enhanced. Adoption of such measures makes note issue system a difficult one. These measures also check the inflationary situation.
2. **Issue of new currency:** When the inflation reaches an uncontrollable level, the government issues new currency and squeezes old currency out of circulation. These measures are also called demonetisation. It is an unusual method of controlling inflation.
3. **Control on credit money:** To control inflation, it is essential to control credit money also. For this purpose, the central bank of the country adopts the following measures:
   - **(a) Increase in bank rate:** Bank rate is the rate of which the central bank rediscounts the bills of a commercial bank or at which it extends financial accommodation to the commercial banks. If there is much expansion of credit in the banking system, in such cases to control credit central bank increases bank rate. Increase in bank rate checks the rising inflationary situation
   - **(b) Open market operations:** Another method to check inflation is the central bank of the country resorts to selling government securities to the public and the banks. When the public and the banks purchase the securities, they have to make payments for these securities to the central bank. The result is that the cash moves from the commercial banks to the central bank. This reduces the ability of commercial banks to create credit.
   - **(c) High reserve requirement:** The central bank to reduce the money supply in the economy increases the limit of the reserve requirement of commercial banks. This method prevents the commercial bank from forming a basis for further credit expansion.

25.7.2. Fiscal Measures

Government, to control such a situation, would take certain steps about taxation, expenditure and public borrowings. The economy of a country is determined by the taxes and the size of disposable income by the public. An accurate tax strategy is then in place to avoid tax cuts or to hike the existing tax rates to minimise the purchasing capacity by the people and thus decrease the demand on prices. These economic implements have been comprehensively adopted as tools to regulate inflation in India. The liberal income tax system, a mechanism to control public expenditure, the introduction of fresh taxes has improved profits of various public sector units, which led to control inflation. The following fiscal measures can be adopted by the government for combating inflation:

1. **Taxation:** During inflation, efforts should be made to reduce the size of disposable income in the hands of the public. This can be done either by imposing new taxes or by increasing the existing rates of taxation. This will leave less money supply with the public.
2. **Government expenditure:** To control inflation, the government should reduce its expenditure especially the unproductive expenditure. Any drastic cut in the government expenditure to curb inflationary situation may land the economy in the slump.
3. **Balanced budget:** To control the inflationary situation, the government should adopt the policy of balanced budget because deficit budget further increases inflation in the economy. In the case of the inflationary boom, the government should also try to prepare a surplus budget.
4. **Increase in savings:** To provide a positive incentive to promote savings which will reduce outlays and curb inflation, the government should have in its budgetary policy incentives for savings also.
5. **Increase in public debts:** To check inflation, the government should also issue debentures and bonds and encourage the people for its purchase. By issue of debentures and bonds, the government can take back additional purchasing power. The amount collected by the government through these sources should be utilised in productive channels.
6. **Control on investment:** During inflation, in anticipation of the future rise in prices, traders and industrialists increase their investment activities. Such investment increases the money supply in the market and this increase in the money supply further increases inflation. Hence, to check inflation, the government should control unusual investments in the economy.

7. **Overvaluation of currency:** An overvaluation of domestic currency in terms of foreign currencies also serves as an anti-inflationary measure. This will discourage exports and encourage imports, resulting in an increase in the domestic supply of goods in the economy. This will check the rise in prices.
8. **Income and prices policy:** Another method to control inflation is to evolve a policy of incomes and prices. The wages should be linked to productivity. Similarly, the factorial incomes, in general, are to be related to their marginal product. The excessive rise in income of factors of production has to be avoided. Scrutiny on prices should also be pursued. Thus, by controlling factor incomes and unwarranted price rise, inflation can be cured.
9. **Other fiscal controls:** Other fiscal measures for the control of inflation are the introduction of rationing system, reducing exports, fixing of the price of essential commodities by the government and shifting of productive resource to the production of more sensitive goods, etc.

25.7.3. Policy Measures

It is a well known fact that inflation perpetrates great travail on the under-privileged people and disrupts society morally, socially, economically, and politically. Hence, there is a necessity for controlling inflation. Inflation cannot be controlled by conventional actions. It requires a strong minded and resolute action plan from all corners. In addition to the above-mentioned fiscal and monetary measures, the following measures can be adopted for controlling inflation.

1. **Increase in production:** By increasing production, the inflationary pressure can be reduced. Increase in production increases the supply of goods, which helps in stabilising prices.
2. **Price control and rationing system:** The government can control the rise in prices by eliminating unnecessary price rise or by putting a ceiling on prices of selected products or services. The government can also impose price control along with rationing of the products/services.
3. **Export-import control:** By restricting exports and promoting imports, the government can increase the supply of goods in the country. This helps in controlling the rise in prices.
4. **Public distribution system:** The public distribution system in the country should be strengthened. So, the products are made available at reasonable prices.

From an economic point of view, inflation is less harmful to the economy up to a certain extent. Inflation is referred to a state in which the value of money is falling and the prices are rising. These increased prices will increase national income and per capita income. This will signify an improvement in the living standard. But it will have a positive result only when it remains in a controlled stage. But as soon as it reaches the galloping or running inflation stage, it will show the bad effects. It will have the negative consequences of the increase in inequality, artificial prosperity, invisible robbery, degrades moral values, and the promotion of corrupt practices in the economy. Therefore, inflation beyond a point is unjust.

25.8. SUMMARY

- Inflation is a quantifiable degree at which the average price level of select goods and services increases over a period of time. It is a phenomenon in which a general increase in prices and a decline in purchasing are witnessed.
- Based on the rapidity with which prices rise, inflation may be classified as creeping inflation, walking inflation, hyperinflation, and running inflation. Inflation is further classified as demand-pull inflation, cost-push inflation, and stagflation.
- Creeping inflation is the trifling form of inflation and is not reflected to cause any ill effects on the economy. Walking inflation is the subsequent stage of inflation. It is a situation where prices rise moderately and the annual inflation rate is a single digit. Running inflation is a situation where the prices of products and services increase at a rate of the two-digit or three-digit rate per annum. Hyperinflation is quick and usually uncontrollable currency depreciation causing the prices of products and services to shoot up in a short period.
- Demand-pull inflation is witnessed when the demand for goods and services are more than their supply, the prices of such goods and services increases.
- Cost-push inflation is witnessed when certain aspects of production particularly wage earners try to proliferate their share of total merchandise by raising their prices.
- Stagflation is witnessed when persistently high inflation combined with high unemployment and stagnant demand is in a country's economy.
- The inflation causes due to the increase in money income and a fall in production.
- The factors responsible for the increase in money income are monetary and credit policy of the government, increase in the velocity of money

credit policy of commercial banks, deficit financing, increase in unproductive expenditure, import of foreign capital, financial disorder, a favourable balance of payments, and a rise in import price.

- The factors responsible for a fall in the production of goods and services are natural, increase in population, black marketing and hoarding, shortage of raw material, industrial unrest, trade and fiscal policy of the government, and shortage and bottlenecks in the production process.
- The quantity theory of money explains the theory of the price rise vis-à-vis theory of aggregate demand. If the supply of money is consistent for the purchase of goods, an increase in the money supply may not be proportionate to increase in total spending.
- Keynes has expressed demand analysis in terms of the concept of "inflationary gap". The theory highlights the significance of the flow of money income in coercing the general price level. He wanted to show the eminence of fiscal measures such as taxation and borrowing in wiping the inflationary gap.
- Inflation can be measured in terms of a wholesale price index (WPI) method and consumer price index (CPI) method.
- The effect of inflation on different sections of society is producers, investors, consumers, wage and salary earners, debtors and creditors.
- The other effects of inflation include redistribution of wealth, increase in government expenditure, increasing tax revenue to the government, increase in public debts, distortion of financial institutions, hoarding of goods, stimulation to speculative activities, fall in saving rate, adverse balance of payments, and employment effect.
- The moral effect of inflation is not positive. Inflation when wipes out savings, the affected persons may tend to work against the government rules and regulations and they may not follow societal values and ethics. Inflation has certain social and political effects. Inflation promotes inequality in society and divides it into rich and poor categories.
- The effects of inflation are economically unsound, politically dangerous, socially disastrous and morally indefensible. Different measures can be adopted to control inflation. These measures monetary measures, fiscal measures, and policy measures.
- Monetary measures are quantitative measures like bank rates, statutory supplies and open market exercises, and qualitative measures like margin requirements, moral persuasion, in which a discursive strategy is followed to change their policies that suggest a set of principles to pressurise individuals, groups, or nation-states.
- The monetary measures which help in controlling the inflationary situation are making rupee note issue policy strict, control on credit money, and issue of new currency.

- Under fiscal measures, the government would take certain steps about taxation, expenditure and public borrowings. An accurate tax strategy is then in place to avoid tax cuts or to hike the existing tax rates to minimise the purchasing capacity by the people and thus, decrease the demand on prices.
- The fiscal measures can be adopted by the government for combating inflation are taxation, government expenditure, a balanced budget, increase in savings, increase in public debts, control on investment, overvaluation of currency, income and prices policy, and other fiscal controls.
- The policy measures that can be adopted for controlling inflation increase in production, price control and rationing system, export-import control, and public distribution system.

SHORT ANSWER QUESTIONS

1. What is meant by inflation?
2. Write a short note on stagflation.
3. Explain the Keynesian-type theory of inflation.
4. What is quantity inflation theory of money?
5. What are the methods of measuring inflation?
6. What are the moral and social effects of inflation?
7. List the policy measures of controlling inflation.

ESSAY ANSWER QUESTIONS

1. Define inflation. Explain the types of inflation based on their rapidity in price rise.
2. Discuss the factors responsible for the increase in money income due to inflation.
3. Describe the factors responsible for a fall in the production of goods and services.
4. Discuss the effect of inflation on different sections of society.
5. Explain the different measures which can be adopted to control inflation.
6. Discuss the fiscal measures adopted by the government for combating inflation.

FILL IN THE BLANKS

1. A quantifiable degree at which the average price level of select goods and services increases over some time is called __________.
2. A situation where prices rise moderately and the annual inflation rate is a single digit is called __________.
3. A situation where prices persistently escalate because of mounting costs is __________ inflation.

4. The circulation of new currency is the result of __________.
5. An excess of anticipated expenditure over available output at base prices is referred to as __________.
6. The price of a descriptive set of wholesale goods is referred to as __________.
7. The changes in the price level of consumer goods and services purchased by the household sector are measured by __________.
8. The government can also impose price control along with __________ of the products/services.

Answers:

1. Inflation
2. Walking inflation
3. Cost-push
4. Monetary policy
5. Inflationary gap
6. Wholesale price index
7. Consumer price index
8. Rationing

MULTIPLE-CHOICE QUESTIONS

1. A situation where the inflation of an economy increases slowly but continuously over a period and its effect is observed after a long period is called:
   (A) Running inflation (B) Hyperinflation
   (C) Creeping inflation (D) Walking inflation
2. Running inflation is also known as:
   (A) Galloping inflation (B) Moderate inflation
   (C) Demand-pull inflation (D) Cost-push inflation
3. The situation where the demand for goods and services is more than their supply, the prices of such goods and services increases are called:
   (A) Stagflation (B) Jumping inflation
   (C) Cost-push inflation (D) Demand-pull inflation
4. Which one factor is not responsible for the increase in money income?
   (A) Monetary and credit policy of the government
   (B) Trade and fiscal policy of the government
   (C) Increase in the velocity of money
   (D) Increase in unproductive expenditure
5. Which one factor is not responsible for a fall in the production of goods and services?
   (A) Increase in population (B) Black marketing and hoarding
   (C) Shortage of raw material (D) A rise in import price
6. In Keynesian-type theory, demand analysis is expressed in terms of:
   (A) Inflationary gap (B) Economic gap
   (C) Productive gap (D) Demand gap
7. A is Which situational measure used by business units for diverse purposes.
   (A) Policy measure (B) Inflation measure
   (C) Monetary measure (D) Fiscal measure

Answers:

1. C	2. A	3. D	4. B	5. D
6. A	7. C			

REFERENCES

1. Ackley, G. (1953). The Theory of Inflation. *Kyklos*, 6(3), 269-272.
2. Bronfenbrenner, M. & Holzman, F.D. (1963). Survey of inflation theory. *The American Economic Review*, 53(4), 593-661.
3. Crowther, G. (1957). *Balances and Imbalances of Payments*. Harvard University, Graduate School of Business Administration.
4. Dwivedi, D.N. (2015). *Managerial Economics* (8th Edn). New Delhi, India: Vikas Publishing House Pvt. Ltd.
5. Friedman, M. (1971). Government revenue from inflation. *Journal of Political Economy*, 79(4), 846-856.
6. Geetika., Ghosh, P. & Choudhury, P. (2008). *Managerial Economics* (1st edn.). New Delhi: Tata McGraw-Hill.
7. Johnson, H.G. (1963). A survey of theories of inflation. *Indian Economic Review*, 6(3), 29-69.
8. Keynes, J.M. (1936). *The General Theory of Employment, Interest and Money*. London, UK: Palgrave Macmillan.
9. Keynes, J.M. (2010). Inflation (1919). In *Essays in Persuasion* (pp. 57-58). Palgrave Macmillan, London.
10. Marshall, A. (1920). *Principles of Economics* (8th Edn). London: Macmillan.
11. Mehta, P.L. (2007). *Managerial Economics: Text and Cases*. New Delhi, India: Sultan Chand & Co.
12. Peterson, H.C., Lewis, W.C. & Jain, S.K. (2005). *Managerial Economics* (4th Edn). New Delhi: Pearson Education.
13. Pigou, A.C. (1941). Types of war inflation. *The Economic Journal*, 51(204), 439-448.
14. Varshney, R.L. & Maheswari, K.L. (2014). *Managerial Economics*. New Delhi, India: Sultan Chand & Sons.

Chapter

26 Business Cycles

LEARNING OBJECTIVES

After studying this chapter, you should be able to understand:

- concept and characteristics of business cycles;
- phases, types and theories of business cycles;
- causes and effects of business cycles; and
- measures to control business cycles.

26.1. CONCEPT OF BUSINESS CYCLES

Business often goes through expansions, recessions, contractions and recovery of aggregate economic activity. The ups (expansions) and downs (contractions) in aggregate economic activity are common in all the economies. The period of high income, output and employment are called the period of expansion, upswing or prosperity. The period of low income, output and employment are expressed as contraction, recession, downswing or depression. In free-market capitalist economies, the period of economic prosperity or expansion is alternatively shown with the period of contraction or recession. These alternating periods of expansion and contraction in economic activity are known as *business cycles*. They are also referred to as *trade cycles*.

Business cycles are short-term fluctuations in the macroeconomic variables such as total national output, income and employment, widespread expansion or contraction in most sectors of the economy. A business cycle is a series of economic activities that pass through phases of prosperity and depression. However, business units take the challenges with effective planning and decision making at the right time during different phases of the business cycle. Business cycles influence business decisions. The cycles affect not only the economy in general but each business unit.

26.2. CHARACTERISTICS OF BUSINESS CYCLES

Every business unit in any form has to go through different phases of economic expansion and contraction. The business atmosphere is dynamic and the changes in the business environment have a substantial impact on business practices. The trend of periodicity in prosperity, as well as depression, is called business cycles and the business cycles have some common characteristics. The features of business cycles are:

Definitions of business cycle

Author	**Definition**
J.M. Keynes (1957)	A business cycle is composed of periods of good trade characterised by rising prices and low unemployment percentages alternating with periods of bad trade characterised by falling prices and high unemployment percentages.
R.A. Gordon (1952)	Business cycles consist of recurring alternations of expansion and contraction in aggregate economic activity, the alternative movements in each direction being self-reinforcing and pervading virtually all parts of the economy.
Frederic Benham (1939)	A business cycle may be considered rather badly as a period of prosperity followed by a period of depression. It is not surprising that economic process should be irregular trade being good at some time and bad at others.

1. The fluctuation of aggregate economic activity
2. Alteration of expansion and contraction in economic activity
3. Co-movement
4. Self-reinforcing
5. Degree of regularity
6. Presence of crisis
7. International in character

1. **The fluctuation of aggregate economic activity:** Business cycles refer to the fluctuations in aggregate economic activity rather than fluctuations in a single specific economic variable. It occurs not only in the production of goods and services but also in other variables such as employment, investment, consumption, rate of interest and price level simultaneously.
2. **Alteration of expansion and contraction in economic activity:** A trade cycle is characterised by alteration of economic expansion (prosperity) and contraction (depression). They are repetitive and periodic. The period of prosperity is followed by depression which again is followed by a period of prosperity. This indicates that the movement is wave-like, but not an erratic fluctuation.
3. **Co-movement:** Business cycles do not take place in just a few sectors or just a few economic variables. Expansions or contractions take place at the same time in several economic activities. Thus, although some industries are more sensitive to the business cycles than the rest, the level of output and employment in most business sectors tends to fall in recession and rise in expansion. Many other economic variables like prices, productivity, investment and

government purchases also have regular and predictable patterns of behaviours throughout the business cycle. The tendency of many economic variables to move together in a predictable way over the business cycle is called co-movement.

4. **Self-reinforcing:** The nature of a trade cycle is self-reinforcing. Each upswing or downswing feeds on itself and generates further movement (change) in the same direction until its direction is reversed by external forces. Thus, the process of expansion and contraction is a cumulative self-reinforcing in nature.
5. **Degree of regularity:** A trade cycle has a degree of regularity. The upswing of a trade cycle may be longer than the downswing or vice versa, but it maintains regularity.
6. **Presence of crisis:** A trade cycle is characterised by the presence of a crisis, i.e., peak and low are not symmetrical. In the words, the change from upward to downward may be more sudden and violent than is the change from downward to upward movement. Consequently, the peak of the trade cycle is pointed with steep bends on either side whereas low has a gently sloping swing.
7. **International in character:** When business fluctuations occur in a country, it will be spread all over the world because the economies of various countries are inter-dependent. For example, if there is a recession in the USA or China or Japan, which are very active in international trade, will cause a fall in demand for imports from other countries whose exports would be adversely affected causing recession.

26.3. PHASES OF THE BUSINESS CYCLES

Business cycles have divergent phases. These phases have been named differently by different economists.

The following are the diverse levels of business cycles:

1. Prosperity (boom, expansion)
2. Recession (deflation)
3. Depression (slump)
4. Recovery (revival)

1. **Prosperity:** According to Haberler (1952), prosperity is a state of affairs in which the real income consumed, real income produced and the level of employment are high or rising, and there are no idle resources or unemployed workers or very few of either. This means that the deployment of the labour force to its fullest volume is comprehended in the prosperity phase. More and more new equipment is used for business operations. The value of the production upsurges during this period. The supplementary

workforce is engaged at higher wages. During a business spread, both production and employment increase until full employment of resources and production is at its peak. Thus, everything seems to be glorious through the state of prosperity.

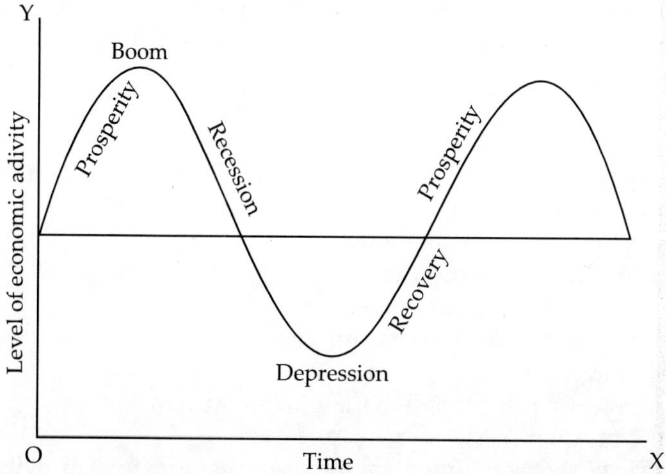

Figure 26.1. Phases of the business cycle

Prosperity witnesses:

- Demand expansion
- Increased production
- A rise in merchants stock
- High prices and profits
- Increased supply of money
- Increase in foreign trade
- Declining unemployment

2. **Recession:** According to Lee (1955), a recession once started tends to build upon itself much as a forest fire. Once underway, it tends to create its drafts and give internal impetus to its destructive ability. The end of the period of prosperity is the beginning of a recession. Recession is a situation where a slowdown or a massive contraction occurs in economic activities. This slowdown in economic activities influences economic growth. A substantial plunge in expenditure leads to recession. When an economy is facing a recession, business transactions and returns decrease substantially and arrest the expansion of businesses.

Recession witnesses:

- Reduced capital investment.
- Downward trend in supply and demand.

- Accumulation of stocks.
- Slowdown in business.
- Unemployment and underemployment.
- Decline in income, expenditure, prices, and profits.
- Laying-off of many business units.

3. **Depression:** Depression is a long-term decline in economic activity in one or more economies. Harberler (1952) stated that depression is a situation where the real income consumed or volume of production per head and the rate of employment are decreasing, and there are idle or unused resources. The period of depression is the worst phase of the business cycle and leads to dissatisfaction.

Depression witnesses:

- Increase in the unemployment rate.
- Decrease in demand for products.
- Decline in production volumes.
- Low wages and reduced purchasing power.
- Decline in interest rates.
- Profits are reduced due to fall in the prices of products.
- Selling the products/services below the cost.

4. **Recovery:** Recovery or revival shows the beginning of growth in the output of the economy after the worst phase of depression. Recovery is a turning point from depression to expansion. The increase in investment with new hopes in business induces an increase in consumption. As a result, industries start producing more and the total capacity is put into full use. Employment of human resources increases and the rate of unemployment falls. The demand slowly picks up. Recovery may be initiated by innovation or investment. The idle workers come forward to work at low wages and as a result, the prices will be at the lowest. The consumers who postponed their consumption during the depression period now start consuming. The economic activity starts picking up.

Recovery witnesses:

- Rise in demand and production.
- Increase in income.
- A rise in prices and profits.
- A rise in investment and employment.

26.4. THEORIES OF BUSINESS CYCLE

The following are different theories of the business cycle:

1. Climatic theory
2. Innovation theory
3. Psychological theory

4. Pure monetary theory
5. Keynes theory
6. Hicksian theory
7. Under-consumption theory
8. Monetary over-investment theory
9. Multiplier-accelerator interaction theory

1. **Climatic theory:** The climatic theory is one of the oldest explanations of business cycles. It is also referred to as *sun-spot theory*. It was developed by W. Stanley Jevons in 1878. Sun-spots are storms on the surface of the sun caused by violent nuclear explosions that affect changes in climatic conditions. The theory relates to the business cycle to climatic variations due to sun-spots produced fluctuations in agricultural output. There may be good agriculture yield resulting in enhanced income in the segment due to upright and promising conditions. This increased income may generate further demand for industrial goods.
2. **Innovation theory:** This theory was proposed by Joseph A. Schumpeter in 1939. According to Schumpeter, modernisation in business units is the main foundation for business cycles. Introduction of new products, modern technology, creation of markets, and use of the new form of raw material is known as innovation. Innovative methods of production necessitate setting up of new machinery which leads to further demand and employment which escalates economic activity. Competitor business units respond to the changes and introduce improved products. Allied businesses also start growing. Subsequently, over a period the supply surpasses demand causing a descending trend in the business unit. Thus, the introduction of innovative approaches leads to a spurt in pecuniary activities for some period and after that leads to recession.
3. **Psychological theory:** According to A.C. Pigou (1927), there are surfs of optimism and pessimism in the human mind. Fluctuations in human psychology and particularly the attitude of the business people are responsible for business cycles. When a slight price rise is felt, the human cognizance turns out to be optimistic. The top business units, in anticipation of a further increase in price and profitability, expand their businesses. This kind of attitude leads to the overall growth of the economy. This, in turn, changes the cost dynamics of production which may lead to the reduction in profit margins. Low profits discourage new investments and skepticism creeps in the minds of the businessmen. As a result, business

deteriorates and recession leads to depression. Once the price of inputs descends, prospects of profitability surge, optimism grows and recovery begins. It is a fact that business environments are extremely inclined by the psychosomatic reactions of the producers.

4. **Pure monetary theory:** According to R.G. Hawtrey (1927), monetary factors are responsible for the business cycle which is purely a monetary phenomenon. Monetary theories of the business cycle are directly proportional to monetary effects. Business units depend mostly upon commercial banks for taking credits to meet working capital requirements towards procurement of capital inputs and for payment of salaries. During the prosperity stage of the business cycle, bank loans are in upsurge. In this scenario, bank advances are most lucrative and the rival banks also embolden this trend. Consequently, production, employment and incomes increase, leading to further demand for bank credit. Banks are overwhelmed to multiply credit. Thus, it will lead to the expansion of the business. However, at the peak of the boom, banks come out intending to avert any inflationary state emerging, reverse their lending strategy and turn out to be vigilant in their lending and keep production under the lens. As a consequence, the business growth process is adversely affected. Traders are forced to run down their stock to encounter the situation. They sometimes terminate orders of business inputs. Thus, the economy takes a reverse direction.
5. **Keynes' theory:** As per J.M. Keynes (1930), variations in peripheral efficiency of capital are accountable for the business cycles. This theory is based on two aspects. They are the series of potential revenues from outlay in the innovative capital assets and the additional price of new capital assets. These two elements are centred on the psychology of investors. Marginal efficiency of capital means a predictable level of profit from a new unit of capital. When marginal efficiency is high, investment, employment and income will grow and leads to the expansion of the business. When production surpasses demand, the marginal efficacy of capital will decline and investments also show the declining trend. Production and employment will be negatively affected, leading to depression. Thus, business cycles are instigated by instabilities in the marginal efficiency of capital.
6. **Hicksian theory:** J.R. Hicks (1950) stated that business cycles take place as a result of economic growth. He advocated the interrelationship of business cycle theory and growth theory. Hicks took the multiplier and acceleration effects to quantify the

initial rise in investment. The collective effects of multiplier and accelerator are extremely stronger than the separable effects of the multiplier or the accelerator. The multiplier effect displays an initial investment in an economy that generates income not only equal to it but in the manifold. The multiplier theory evaluates the effect of growth in investment upon the level of income. The acceleration effect indicates that increase in income brought about by the rise in investment encourages more investment.

7. **Under-consumption theory:** Under-consumption theory of business cycles was developed way back 1930s. Economists like Sismondi, Hobson, Marx and Malthus are associated with the under-consumption theory of business cycles. The key feature of all the variants of the under-consumption theory is that money incomes are not adequate in the consumption of goods and services, since, in a capitalist society, the majority of people are poor. They cannot afford to purchase more goods. Hence, the demand for goods will be less than the supply. The prices will fall and lead to depression. According to this theory, consumption is responsible for business cycles.
8. **Monetary over-investment theory:** According to F.A. Hayek (1933), fluctuations in investment are the reason for business cycles. Such fluctuations bring about variations in consumers income. Hayek puts the entire blame of crisis on the over-issue of loans. The monetary over-investment theory focuses on the role of imbalance between the desired and actual investments in economic fluctuation. In other words, excess of an actual investment than the desired investment. According to him, the significance of the rate of interest lies in its outcome on unplanned changes in the structure of production. The changes in the structure of production are the main causes of business cycles.
9. **Multiplier accelerator interaction theory:** The post-Keynesian period economists focused on the importance of multiplier and accelerator concepts in determining business cycles. P.A. Samuelson introduced the multiplier accelerator interaction model in 1939 that represents the interaction between these two concepts. He stated the process of interaction between multiplier and accelerator for creating income, increasing consumption and demand for investment. He also stated the role of these two factors for economic fluctuations. The model analyses the concepts of autonomous investment and derived investment to analyse the fluctuations. *Autonomous investment* arises due to exogenous factors like the

new product, production methods, and market conditions. *Derived investment* arises due to increase in the investment of capital goods produced with increase in the demand for consumer goods.

When autonomous investment occurs in an economy, the income of the people rises and the process of multiplier begins. When income levels increase, the demand for consumer goods also increases depending on the marginal propensity to consume. The supply of consumer goods should satisfy the demand for consumer goods. This is possible when the production technique is capable to produce a large quantity of products/services. This encourages the business unit to invest more to develop advanced production techniques and increase production for meeting consumer demand. Thus, the consumption affects the demand for investment resulting in the acceleration process and a further increase in income level. If the business unit has no excess production capacity, then its existing capital will be inadequate to meet the increased demand. Therefore, the business unit should go for new investment to meet the growing demand.

26.5. CAUSES OF BUSINESS CYCLES

During the last several years, philosophers and economists have attributed various causes to business cycles. According to Samuelson (1967), business cycles are classified as external and internal factors.

26.5.1. External Factors

The external factors focus on the causes of fluctuations in the business cycles outside the economic system. The external factors include natural factors, wars, revolutions, political events, gold discoveries, population explosion, migrations, discoveries and innovations. These factors change the level of national income by affecting either the investment or consumption component of aggregate demand.

1. **Natural factors:** Trade cycles may take place due to certain natural reasons. For example, during the period of less rainfall, agricultural productivity is badly affected. It causes a shortage of industrial raw material and therefore, industrial production also decreases. If this situation persists for some time, it reduces economic activities in the whole economy. On the other hand, good weather conditions lead to an increase in agricultural activities and the expansion of economic activities.
2. **Wars:** During wars, all the available economic resources are utilised for the production of weapons which greatly affect capital and

consumer goods. The fall in production decreases income, profits which further creates unemployment. The economic activity slows down.

3. **Post-war period:** In the post-war period, the level of consumption and investment goes upward. Both the government and individuals are involved in the construction (houses, roads, bridges, etc.) and production activities. All these activities increase the value of output and as a result income and employment goes upward.
4. **Political factors:** In developing countries, governments are changed frequently. The new government formulates new policies and abandons the policies of previous governments. This creates uncertainty in the economy and causes business activities to slow-down. On the other hand, when businessmen feel the continuity of the existing political setup, it builds up confidence in them and promotes investment in new projects. This causes upturn in the business cycle.
5. **Scientific development:** Another cause of the business cycle is scientific development. Every day new products are introduced to markets such as mobiles, laptops, etc. These products require a huge amount of investment in research and development through which new technology of production is adopted. All this increases income, employment and profit, etc., and plays an important part in the revival of the economy.
6. **Gold discoveries:** The discoveries of gold mines stimulate the volume of international trade and help in adjusting trade deficit, loans, etc. The rising incomes lead to an expansion in economic activity.
7. **Population expansion:** An abnormal increase in population is also a major cause of economic problems. When the population increases at a higher rate than the increase in national output, it becomes difficult to employ all human resources. Such a situation usually brings about the recession in the economy.

26.5.2. Internal Factors

The internal factors relate to the mechanisms within the economic system itself which will give rise to self-generating business cycles. The expansion leads to recession and contraction, whereas, the contraction will lead to revival and expansion. It is a quasi-regular, repeating, and never-ending chain. The internal factors influencing business cycle are psychological, money supply, over investment, over-saving or under-consumption, competition, innovations, and the marginal efficiency of capital.

1. **Psychological factors:** According to Pigou (1927), the alternating waves of 'optimism' and 'pessimism' are the sole causes of industrial fluctuations. He traces cyclical fluctuations to the tendency of businessmen to react excessively to the changing conditions of the economy. Over-production and under-production in the alternating periods are caused due to this tendency. When the businessmen are optimistic about future market conditions they take up investment. Here, the expansion phase of the business cycle starts which ultimately ends in a boom. On the contrary, the pessimism reduces investment, production, employment and shifts to a downward trend in business activity.
2. **Money supply:** Hawtrey (1927) and other monetarists regard business cycles as a purely monetary phenomenon. According to them, cyclical fluctuations are caused by the expansion and contraction of bank credit. If there is an expansion in money and credit supply, there will be a rise in economic activity. If there is contraction there will be a downfall in economic activity.
3. **Over-investment:** Hayek (1933) identified that the root cause of business cycles is over investment. It is bank loans which lead to over-investment in capital goods industries relative to consumer goods industries that ultimately bring depression in the economy. When the total money supply exceeds the amount of voluntary savings, it leads to an increase in the investment activity and ultimately to a boom. But banks cannot continue to give credit for long due to the shortage of voluntary savings. As a result, production declines which leads to depression.
4. **Over-saving or under-consumption:** Business cycles are caused by over-saving or under-consumption. These wide disparities of income and wealth lead to depression in the country. The rich people are not able to spend their entire income, so they save more and invest more in producing consumer goods. On the other hand, the poor people have low incomes or wages, so their demand for consumer goods is low which means that there is under-consumption. Thus, over-saving leads to the production of consumer goods in large quantities and to a boom. The low wages of industrial labour bring a fall in the demand for consumer goods. Stocks get accumulated at the current level of prices, which leads to a fall in the prices of consumer goods and the income of the producers. As a result, it leads to depression.
5. **Competition:** The main cause of business cycles is competition in an economy. Competition leads to over-production and ultimately

to a crisis (depression). Competition and profits lead to over-production and surplus of products in the market and to fall in prices. On the other hand, the race to produce more and get more profit increases the demand for factors of production. Competition among producers to hire more factors raises their prices. Thus, the cost rises, which raise the prices of products. Demand falls and there will be accumulated stocks of products which eventually lead to a fall in prices and leads to depression.

6. **Innovations:** According to Schumpeter (1939), innovations in the structure of an economy are the source of economic fluctuations. The cyclical upswing is set in motion when the business units start investing in innovation of a new product. This enables them to make profits and create a cumulative expansion in the economy. When there is an excess of new products in the market, their prices fall, and profit margins of business units are reduced. Some business units cut down the production and other business units are forced into liquidation. Thus, the economy enters into depression phase.
7. **Marginal efficiency of capital (MEC):** According to Keynes (1957), changes in the rate of the marginal efficiency of capital are responsible for the business cycle. When the rate of the marginal efficiency of capital gets higher the expansion phase of the trade cycle commences. There is a contraction phase when the rate of the marginal efficiency of capital is lower.

There are also other causes of business cycles which are different in different countries and these also vary at different phases of the business cycle. For example, an act of terrorism may cause a recession in the affected country. Similarly, the situation of law and order, economic policies, level of literacy and social behaviour of people are all different factors which determine the prosperity or poverty of a nation.

26.6. EFFECTS OF BUSINESS CYCLES

Business units are affected differently by cyclical fluctuations owing to the divergent nature of their businesses. The effects on business units during the expansion phase usually differ from the effects in the contraction phase. For example, during revival and expansion, the business units' demand rises rapidly as a result of which selling prices rise more rapidly than costs do and the profit margins also rise. So, business units and merchants largely feel happy during the expansion phase.

During the phase of recession, business units and merchants find their inventories unusually high, which also depreciate fast in their value at that time. Since these excessive inventories are usually made up of finished goods rather than of raw material, more money gets locked up in inventories. Some business divisions are not capable to pay their debts and get liquidated. To meet these business obligations, they are compelled to sell their goods at relatively low cost, resulting in a loss.

At the time of depression, these predicaments are expected to remain and might get strengthened owing to the fixed charges of all costs which the business units have to bear helplessly. Business units may cut the output, retrench workforce and purchase lesser raw material, but overhead costs cannot be abridged. The financial losses suffered thereby land the business units in crucial exertion, though business units can make the indispensable adjustments to overcome the hard effects of cyclical fluctuations.

26.7. MEASURES TO CONTROL BUSINESS CYCLES

The measures that can be adopted to resolve the problems arising out of business cycles are categorised into two types:

1. Preventive measures
2. Relief measures

26.7.1. Preventive Measures

Preventive measures are intended to provide relief from suffering grave losses in recession and contraction phases of the business cycle. These measures are usually adopted during the business expansion phase for regulating purchases, protecting the assets and to avoid imprudent credit expansion. These measures can be embraced only if the business managers are familiar with the relationship between cyclical changes in general business and cyclical changes in the business of the given enterprise. They should also understand the nature of the cyclical price movements in the purchases and sales of a particular business relative to the general business cycle. If a business manager has analysed these statistics, steps can be taken to develop a strategy of adapting to the business cycle.

The different preventive measures alongside the effects of the business cycle are:

1. Conservation of assets during expansion by avoiding an undue increase in plant and equipment, and dividends.
2. Management of machinery and plants to its optimum use in such a way to avoid a decrease in overhead costs and to ensure an increase in business production.
3. Inventories should be regulated to avoid unnecessary inventories and consumption commitments over and above the accessible financial resources.

4. Capital assets of a business unit should be conservative to meet future requirements.

26.7.2. Relief Measures (Curative Measures)

Relief measures are to speed up the recovery process consequent upon contraction. The following steps can be adopted to reduce the effect of contraction of a business unit:

1. Reduction in costs of manufacturing products through rationalisation of production processes and quick liquidation of inventories.
2. Improving the quality of finished products, the adoption of marketing techniques for augmenting demand.
3. Developing the plant, labour and business unit as a whole to make it more efficient.
4. Introduce new sales promotion techniques to enhance sales.
5. Introduce new products to avoid idle capacity of machinery and plant and other production facilities.

26.8. SUMMARY

- Business cycles are short-term fluctuations happening in the macroeconomic variables such as total national output, income and employment, widespread expansion or contraction in most sectors of the economy. A business cycle is a series of economic activities that pass through phases of prosperity and depression.
- The features of business cycles are the fluctuation of aggregate economic activity, alteration of expansion and contraction in economic activity, co-movement, self-reinforcing, degree of regularity, and presence of crisis.
- Business cycles have divergent phases. These phases are prosperity, recession, depression, and recovery.
- Prosperity is a state of affair in which the real income consumed, real income produced and the level of employment are high or rising, and there are no idle resources or unemployed workers or very few of either. The deployment of the labour force to its fullest volume is comprehended in the prosperity phase.
- Recession is a situation where a slowdown or a massive contraction occurs in economic activities. This slowdown in economic activities influences economic growth. A substantial plunge in expenditure leads to recession.
- Depression is a long-term decline in economic activity in one or more economies. It is a situation where the real income consumed or volume of production per head and the rate of employment is decreasing, and there are idle or unused resources.

- Recovery or revival shows the beginning of growth in the output of the economy after the worst phase of depression. The increase in investment with new hopes in business induces an increase in consumption. As a result, industries start producing more and the total capacity is put into full use.
- The climatic theory relates to the business cycle to climatic variations due to sun-spots produced fluctuations in agricultural output.
- Innovation theory states that modernisation in business units is the main foundation for business cycles. Innovative methods of production necessitate setting up of new machinery which leads to further demand and employment which escalates economic activity.
- The psychological theory states that fluctuations in human psychology and particularly the attitude of the business people are responsible for business cycles. When a slight price rise is felt, the human cognizance turns out to be optimistic. This kind of attitude leads to the overall growth of the economy.
- Monetary theories of the business cycle are directly proportional to monetary effects. Business units depend mostly upon commercial banks for taking credits to meet working capital requirements towards procurement of capital inputs and for payment of salaries. As a consequence, the business growth process is adversely affected.
- Keynes theory states that variations in peripheral efficiency of capital are accountable for the business cycles. This theory is based on two aspects. They are the series of potential revenues from outlay in the innovative capital assets and the additional price of new capital assets.
- Hicksian theory states that business cycles take place as a result of economic growth. It advocates the interrelationship of business cycle theory and growth theory. Hicks took the multiplier and acceleration effects to quantify the initial rise in investment.
- Under-consumption theory of business cycles states that money incomes are not adequate in the consumption of goods and services, since, in a capitalist society, the majority of people are poor. They cannot afford to purchase more goods. Hence, the demand for goods will be less than the supply.
- Monetary over-investment theory states that fluctuations in investment are the reason for business cycles. Such fluctuations bring about variations in consumers' income. In other words, excess of an actual investment than the desired investment.
- Multiplier accelerator interaction theory states the process of interaction between multiplier and accelerator for creating income, increasing consumption and demand for investment. The model analyses the concepts of autonomous investment and derived investment to analyse the fluctuations.

- Business cycles are classified as external and internal factors. The external factors focus on the causes of fluctuations in the business cycles outside the economic system. It includes natural factors, wars, the post-war period, political factors, scientific development, gold discoveries, and population expansion.
- The internal factors relate to the mechanisms within the economic system itself which will give rise to self-generating business cycles. It includes psychological factors, money supply, over-investment, over-saving/under-consumption, competition, innovations, and the marginal efficiency of capital.
- Business units are affected differently by cyclical fluctuations owing to the divergent nature of their businesses. The effects on business units during the expansion phase usually differ from the effects in the contraction phase.
- The measures that can be adopted to resolve the problems arising out of business cycles are preventive and relief measures. Preventive measures are intended to provide relief from suffering grave losses in recession and contraction phases of the business cycle. Relief measures are to speed up the recovery process consequent upon contraction.

SHORT ANSWER QUESTIONS

1. What are business cycles?
2. Write a short note on pure monetary theory.
3. Explain the Hicksian theory of the trade cycle.
4. What are the different preventive measures of the business cycle?
5. Describe the external factors influencing business cycles.

ESSAY ANSWER QUESTIONS

1. Define the business cycle. Explain the characteristics of business cycles.
2. Describe the different phases of the business cycle with graphical representation.
3. Discuss the different theories of the business cycle.
4. Explain the multiplier accelerator interaction theory.
5. What the internal and external are factors causing business cycle? Explain.
6. Describe the effect of cyclical fluctuations owing to the divergent nature of businesses.
7. Explain the measures that can be adopted to resolve the problems arising out of business cycles.

FILL IN THE BLANKS

1. These alternating periods of expansion and contraction in economic activity are known as __________.
2. Business cycles have __________ phases.

3. A substantial plunge in expenditure leads to __________.
4. A long-term decline in economic activity in one or more economies is called __________.
5. The climatic theory is also referred to as __________.
6. The innovation theory was proposed by __________.
7. A predictable level of profit from a new unit of capital is called __________.
8. The measures usually adopted during the business expansion phase for regulating purchases is __________.
9. Relief measures are also referred to as __________.

Answers:

1. Business cycles
2. Divergent
3. Recession
4. Depression
5. Sun-spot theory
6. Joseph A. Schumpeter
7. Marginal efficiency
8. Preventive measure
9. Curative measures

MULTIPLE-CHOICE QUESTIONS

1. The period of high income, output and employment are called the period of:
   (A) Depression (B) Recession
   (C) Upswing (D) Downswing
2. In which stage, deployment of the labour force to its fullest volume is comprehended.
   (A) Prosperity (B) Depression
   (C) Recovery (D) Deflation
3. The situation where a slowdown or a massive contraction occurs in economic activities is:
   (A) Revival (B) Recession
   (C) Recovery (D) Expansion
4. The stage of prosperity is also referred to as:
   (A) Slump (B) Contraction
   (C) Expansion (D) Premium
5. The climatic theory was developed by
   (A) Joseph A. Schumpeter (B) A.C. Pigou
   (C) R.G. Hawtrey (D) W. Stanley Jevons
6. In psychological theory, when a slight price rise is felt, the human cognizance turns out to be:
   (A) Optimistic (B) Pessimistic
   (C) Negative (D) Gloomy
7. Which theory advocated the interrelationship of business cycle theory and growth theory?
   (A) Keynes' Theory (B) Hayek's Theory
   (C) Hicksian Theory (D) Schumpeter Theory

8. Which measures are intended to provide relief from suffering grave losses in recession and contraction phases of the business cycle?
   (A) Relief (B) Preventive
   (C) Reprive (D) Sanguine

Answers:

1. C	2. A	3. B	4. C	5. D
6. A	7. C	8. B		

REFERENCES

1. Benham, F. (1939). *Economics: A General Textbook for Students*. London: Sir Issac Pitman & Sons Ltd.
2. Bowman, M.J. & Bach, G.L. (1949). *Economic Analysis and Public Policy*. New York: Prentice Hall Inc.
3. Clark, J.J. & Chen, M. (1963). *Business Fluctuations, Growth and Economic Stabilization*. New York: Random Edn.
4. Dauten, C.A. (1961). *Business Cycles and Forecasting*. Cincinnati: Southern-Western Publishing Co.
5. Dewett, K.K. (1964). *Modern Economic Theory*. Premier Publishing Co.
6. Dwivedi, D.N. (2015). *Managerial Economics* (8th Edn). New Delhi, India: Vikas Publishing House Pvt. Ltd.
7. Gordon, R.A. (1952). *Business Fluctuations*. New York: Harper and Brothers Publishers.
8. Haberler, G. (1952). *Prosperity and Depression*. New York, UN.
9. Hamberg, D. (1951). *Business Cycles*. New York: The Macmillan Company.
10. Hawtrey, R.G. (1927). The monetary theory of the trade cycle and its statistical test. *The Quarterly Journal of Economics*, 41(3), 471-486.
11. Hayek, F.A. (1933). *Monetary Theory and the Trade Cycle*. New York: Harcourt, Brace & Co.
12. Hayek, F.V. (1933). Monetary Theory and the Trade Cycle (N. Kaldor & HM Croome, Trans.). Jonathan Cape, London. (Reprinted by AM Kelley, New York, 1975.).
13. Hicks, J.R. (1950). *A Contribution to the Theory of the Trade Cycle*. London: Oxford University Press.
14. Jevons, W.S. (1878). Commercial crises and sun-spots. *Nature*, 19, 33-37.
15. Jevons, W.S. (1882). The solar-commercial cycle. *Nature*, 26, 226-228.
16. Keynes, J. M. (1930). *The Great Slump of 1930*, Nation and Atheneum, reprinted in *The Collected Writings of John Maynard Keynes*, Vol. IX: *Essays in Persuasion* (1972), London: Macmillan.

17. Keynes, J.M. (1936). *The General Theory of Employment, Interest and Money*. London, UK: Palgrave Macmillan.
18. Keynes, J.M. (1957). *The General Theory of Employment: Interest and Money*. London: Macmillan.
19. Kuznets, S. (1935). *Relation between Capital Goods and Finished Products in Business Cycle*. New York: Columbia University Press.
20. Lee, W.W. (1955). *Economic Fluctuations*. Illinois: Richard D. Irwin Inc.
21. Maurice, W.L. (1955). *Economic Fluctuations: An Analysis of Business Cycles and Other Economic Fluctuations* (The Irwin Series in Economics). Illinois: Richard D. Irwin Inc. Homewood, III, 1955.
22. Mehta, P.L. (2007). *Managerial Economics: Text and Cases*. New Delhi, India: Sultan Chand & Co.
23. Pigou, A. (1927). *Industrial Fluctuations*. London: MacMillan & Co. Ltd.
24. Pigou, A.C. (2013). *The Economics of Welfare*. Palgrave Macmillan.
25. Samuelson, P.A. (1939). Interactions between the multiplier analysis and the principle of acceleration. *The Review of Economics and Statistics*, 21(2), 75-78.
26. Samuelson, P.A. (1967). *Economics*. New York: McGraw Hill.
27. Schumpeter, J.A. (1939). *Business Cycles* (Vol. 1, pp. 161-174). New York: McGraw-Hill.
28. Shapiro, E. (1978). *Macroeconomic Analysis*. NY: Harcourt Publishers Ltd.
29. Spencer, M.H. (1968). *Managerial Economics*. Illinois: Richard D. Irwin Inc.
30. Varshney, R.L. & Maheswari, K.L. (2014). *Managerial Economics*. New Delhi, India: Sultan Chand & Sons.
31. Wesley, C.M. (1972). *Business Cycles: The Problem and its Setting*. New York: National Bureau of Economic Research.

Chapter

27 National Income

LEARNING OBJECTIVES

After studying this chapter, you should be able to understand:

- concept and meaning of national income;
- aggregates and measurement of national income;
- methods of measuring national income;
- two-, three- and four-sector models of national income; and
- assumptions and determination of the equilibrium level of income.

27.1. CONCEPT OF NATIONAL INCOME

National income is the monetary value of all the finished goods and services delivered by a country over one year. National income comprises an array of goods and services of diverse nature. Since these goods and services are quantified in different physical forms, it is not possible to add them in terms of quantitative units altogether. Thus, it cannot be said that national income is so many millions of metres of cloth, so many million litres of milk, etc. Therefore, the common measure used for national income is money.

National income is used to measure the economic growth of a nation. By comparing the national income figures of different periods of a country, one can study whether its economy is growing or not. The analysis of national income helps the policy makers and architects of a country to understand whether they can achieve success in their efforts in promoting development and if so, to what extent. Thus, national income can be considered a measure or sign of economic growth of a country.

The human resource and capital of a country using its natural resources produce annually a certain amount of goods and services. The value of such output in terms of money is called national income of the country. Two things must be noted to understand national income. First, it determines the market value of annual output, i.e., national income as an economic measure. Secondly, all goods and services produced for any given period in a year must be taken into account only once for computing national income accurately. National income only includes the market price of all finished goods and services and disregards the dealings involving intermediary goods or services.

The idea of national income has attracted the attention of economic philosophers and policy-makers since the inception of economic thought.

The following are some of the definitions of national income by renowned economists and institutions.

Definitions of national income

Author	Definition
Alfred Marshall (1920)	National income is the labour and capital of a country, acting on its natural resources produce annually a certain net aggregate of commodities, material and immaterial including services of all kinds and net income due on account of foreign investment must be added in. This is a true net national income or revenue of the country or the national dividend.
A.C. Pigou (1946)	National income or dividend is that part of the objective income of the community including, of course, income derived from abroad which can be measured in money.
Irving Fisher (1930)	The national income consists solely of services as received by ultimate consumers, whether from their material or their human environment.
Colin Clark (1937)	National income for any period consists of the money value of the goods and services becoming available for consumption during that period, reckoned at their current selling prices, plus additions to capital reckoned at the prices paid for the new capital goods, minus depreciation and obsolescence of the existing capital goods, and adding the net accretion of, or deducing the net drawings upon stocks, also reckoned at current prices.
National Income Committee of India	A national income estimate measures the volume commodities and services turned out during a given period, counted without duplication.

There are three different perspectives on understanding the concept of national income. They are:

- **Production perspective:** Under this perspective, national income is the total of the money value of the net flow of all the final goods and services produced by residents within the country and abroad, during a financial year.
- **Income perspective:** Under this perspective, national income is the total of factor incomes earned by normal residents of a country in the form of rents, wages, interest and profit in a year.
- **Expenditure perspective:** Under this perspective, national income is the net expenditure on goods and services flowing during a year from the nation's production into the hands of consumers or end-users.

27.2. AGGREGATES OF NATIONAL INCOME

The following are the combinations related to national income.

1. **Gross domestic product at market price (GDP_{MP}):** It refers to the total of value added by all producing units within the domestic territory of a country during an accounting year, inclusive of depreciation and estimate at market price.
2. **Net domestic product at market price (NDP_{MP}):** It refers to the market value of the final goods and services produced by all producing units within the domestic territory of a country during an accounting year, excluding depreciation.

$$NDP_{MP} = GDP_{MP} - \text{Depreciation}$$

3. **Gross domestic product at factor cost (GDP_{FC}):** It refers to the total of factor income (rent, wages, interest and profits) generated within the domestic territory of a country in an accounting year, along with depreciation and excluding net indirect taxes.

$$GDP_{FC} = GDP_{MP} - \text{Net indirect taxes}$$

4. **Net domestic product at factor cost (NDP_{FC}):** It refers to the total of factor incomes generated within the domestic territory of a country during an accounting year excluding depreciation and net indirect taxes.

$$NDP_{FC} = GDP_{MP} - \text{Depreciation} - \text{Net indirect taxes}$$

5. **Gross national product at market price (GNP_{MP}):** It is the total of the market value of the final goods and services produced within the domestic territory of a country during an accounting year and also includes net factor income from abroad.

$$GNP_{MP} = GDP_{MP} + \text{Net factor income from abroad}$$

6. **Net national product at market price (NNP_{MP}):** It is the total of the market value of the final goods and services produced within the domestic territory of a country during an accounting year, exclusive of depreciation and net factor income from abroad.

$$NNP_{MP} = GDP_{MP} - \text{Depreciation} + \text{Net factor income from abroad}$$

7. **Gross national product at factor cost (GNP_{FC}):** It is the total of factor cost of final goods and services produced within the domestic territory of a country during an accounting year, inclusive of depreciation and net factor income from abroad excluding net indirect taxes.

$$GNP_{FC} = GDP_{MP} + \text{Net factor income from abroad} - \text{Net indirect taxes}$$

8. **Net national product at factor cost (NNP_{FC}):** It is the total of factor cost of final goods and services produced within the domestic territory of a country during an accounting year, exclusive of depreciation and net indirect tax, and inclusive of net factor income from abroad.

   $NNP_{FC} = GDP_{MP}$ – Depreciation - Net indirect tax + Net factor income from abroad
9. **National disposable income:** It is the income from all sources (earned income as well as transfer payments from abroad) available to residents of a country for consumption expenditure or for saving during a year. It is calculated as:

   Net national disposable income = National income + Net indirect taxes + Net current transfers from abroad

   Gross national disposable income = Net national disposable income + Depreciation
10. **Personal income:** It is the income received by the individuals in a year. The whole national income does not reach the hands of the individuals. The national income only after making some deductions in the form of corporate taxes, social security contribution, etc., is available for distribution among individuals. Transfer payments must be added with national income to arrive at personal income. The various allowances provided by the government in the form of unemployment allowance, old-age pension, widow pension, etc., are the transfer payments.

27.3. MEASUREMENT OF NATIONAL INCOME

National income is generally measured in terms of money. It is computed in two ways:
- National income at current prices
- National income at constant prices

1. **National income at current prices:** It is referred to as nominal national income. It is the money value of all the final goods and services at current prices, i.e., the prices prevailing in that particular accounting year. For example, when goods and services produced during the year 2019-20 are valued at prices by considering base as the same year 2019-20, it will be called national income at current prices.
2. **National income at constant prices:** It is referred to as real national income. It is the money value of all the final goods and services produced in a year measured at fixed prices, i.e., by considering

prices of the base year. For example, when goods and services produced during the year 2019-20 are valued at the prices by considering the base year as 2009-10, it is called national income at constant prices.

27.4. METHODS OF MEASURING NATIONAL INCOME

In any economy, the production gives rise to income. Income, in turn, gives rise to the demand for goods and services. The rise in demand for goods and services gives rise to expenditure. The rise in expenditure leads to a further rise in production. This is the development cycle representing phases from production to production as shown in Figure 27.1.

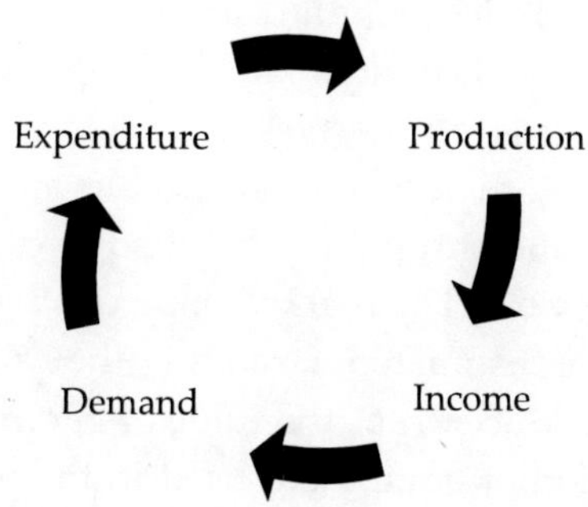

Figure 27.1. The production to the production cycle

The circular flow of production, income, demand and expenditure represents three correlated phases, namely, production, distribution and disposition. These three phases empower to look at national income in three ways, i.e., the flow of goods and services, flow of income on goods and services, and flow of expenditure on goods and services. To quantify each phase, it is necessary to have diverse data from various sources and methods for calculation and analysis. To quantify the phase of production, the sum of net values added by all the producing business units of the country will be ascertained. To quantify the phase of the income distribution, the data related to the generation of production of goods and services are necessary. Finally, to quantify the phase of disposition, the sum of expenditures of the three spending units in the economy such as government, consumer households, and producing enterprises should be considered. The following are the three methods of measuring national income.

1. Value added method (product method)
2. Income method
3. Expenditure method

27.4.1. Value Added Method

Value added (VAD) method measures the influence and role of each producing enterprise in the domestic territory of the country. It is also referred to as *product method*. This method involves:

1. Identifying the producing enterprise and categorising them into industrial segments according to their nature of the activity.
2. Assessing the net value contributed by each producing enterprise as well as each industrial sector and adding up the net value of all the sectors.

Producing business units are broadly classified into three main sectors:

- *Primary sector* including agriculture and all allied activities.
- *Secondary sector* includes manufacturing units.
- *Tertiary sector* includes services like banking, insurance, transport and communication, trade , professions, etc.

These sectors are further divided into sub-sectors and each sub-sector is further divided into specific groups. This method of computation is done from an output point of view. The market value of all goods and services produced in a year is thus, estimated. From this, the value of raw material purchased from other producers, i.e., the value of intermediate goods, will be deducted. Depreciation of equipment used in the production process will also be deducted. The net income from foreign trade, i.e., exports minus imports will be added.

27.4.2. Income Method

The factors of production involved in production activities are paid for their value generation in the form of factor income. Thus, various forms of income generation activities are: land generates rent, labour gets wages, capital generates interest and an entrepreneur gets profits. In other words, whatever is produced by a producing unit is distributed among various factors of production for their contributed value. The income earned by all the factors of production forms the subject matter of calculation of national income by income method. The factors of production used by all production units and the income generated by their use constitute national income.

This method is an approach from the distribution point of view. All the incomes received by the individuals in the form of wages, interests, rents and profits are added in this method. The income of self-employed people is also considered.

27.4.3. Expenditure Method

The various sectors like household sector, business sector, government sector, etc., either spend their incomes on consumer goods and services or save a part of their income or spend a part of their income on non-consumption goods (capital goods). Overall expenditure in an economy comprises expenditure on financial assets, on goods produced in the preceding periods, on raw materials and intermediate goods and services and final goods and services produced in the current period.

Under this system, all the expenditures incurred on goods and services during a year are computed. These expenses may be for consumption purpose and/or for investment purpose. All the consumption expenditure and investment expenditure of individuals, institutions and government are taken into account. Further, the contribution from international trade, i.e., exports minus imports will be added.

27.5. TWO-SECTOR MODEL OF NATIONAL INCOME

The two-sector model of income determination of an economy includes household and business sectors. This model is proposed by J.M. Keynes. The Keynesian theory of the determination of national income is pertinent in the short run only as the stock of capital, techniques of production, the efficiency of labour, the size of the population, forms of business units have been anticipated to stay constant. Further, in this model of income determination, the theory presumes that the price level in the economy remains unaffected. Keynes focused on the simple two-sector model of determination of national income and arrived at conclusions regarding policy construction.

Assumptions

Income determination in a closed economy is built on the following assumptions:

1. The economy is a two-sector economy in which only consumption and investment expenditures take place. The total output, therefore, is the sum of consumption and investment expenditure.
2. Investment refers to net investment after depreciation.
3. Closed economy and as such there are no exports or imports.
4. No corporate business units and therefore the question of corporate undistributed profits do not arise.
5. No taxes and as a result disposable personal income equals to the net national product (NNP).
6. No transfer payments.
7. No government and investment are autonomous.

8. There will be less than the full employment level of output.
9. The price remains constant until full employment level is attained.
10. Stable money wage rate.
11. Stable consumption function.
12. Fixed rate of interest.
13. Short-run analysis.

The above-mentioned assumptions drive to the conclusion that the national income can be determined by the equality of aggregate demand and aggregate supply or by the equality of saving and investment. Aggregate demand (aggregate expenditure) is the summation of consumption expenditure on newly produced consumer goods by households and their services (C), and investment expenditure on newly produced capital goods and inventories by businessmen (I). Thus, it can be denoted as:

Aggregate demand (Aggregate expenditure) = Consumption expenditure + Investment expenditure

Consumption expenditure = Expenditure by households

Investment expenditure = Demand for expenditure on capital goods by business units

Following identities are shown:

$$Y = C + I \qquad ...(27.1)$$

Personal income:

$$Y_d = C + S \qquad ...(27.2)$$

But

$$Y = Y_d$$

$$C + I = C + S$$

$$(or)$$

$$I = S$$

where,

Y = National income
Y_d = Disposable income
C = Consumption
S = Saving
I = Investment

In the above identities, C + I relate to consumption and investment expenditures which denote aggregate demand of an economy. C is the consumption function which specifies the relation between income and consumption expenditure. In Figure 27.2, the consumption function is presented by the slope of the curve C which represents MPC (marginal propensity to consume). 'I' refers to autonomous investment demand. If the demand for investment (I) is added to consumption function (C), then C + I becomes the aggregate demand function.

The aggregate supply of an economy can be represented as C + S. With the total consumption expenditure consumer goods and services are produced and with aggregate savings, investments are made in capital goods for facilitating production. The equality of aggregate demand and aggregate supply (C + I = C + S) or the equality of saving and investment (S = I) determines the equilibrium level of national income in any economy. These two approaches are explained with the help of Figures 27.2 and 27.3.

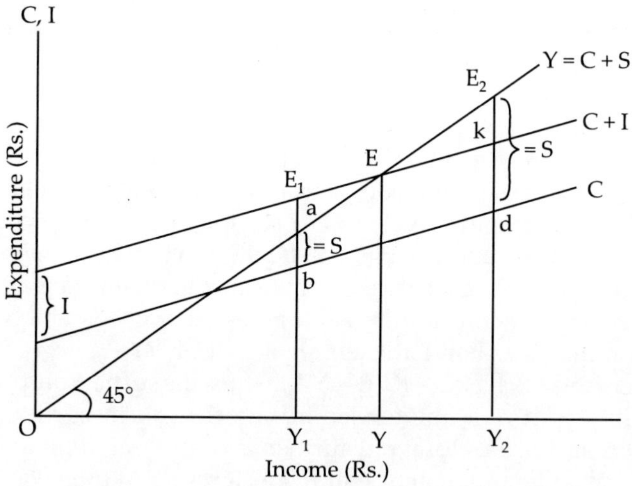

Figure 27.2. Income-expenditure approach

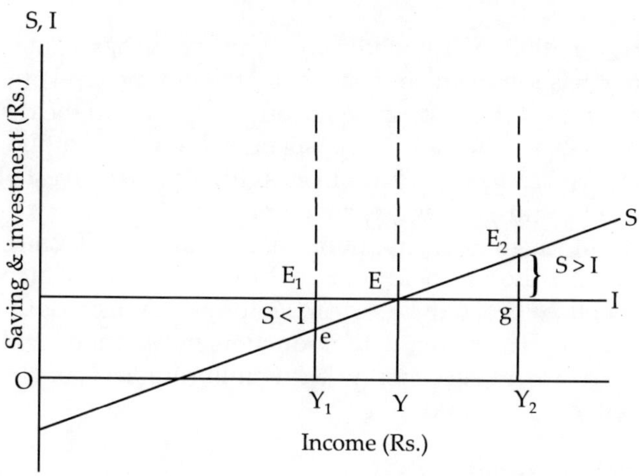

Figure 27.3. Saving-investment approach

Equality of aggregate demand and aggregate supply

The point at which the aggregate demand function (curve) intersects the aggregate supply function is the equilibrium level of national income. In

Figure 27.2, C + I represents the aggregate demand function. It is the sum of the consumption function (C) the investment demand (I). The 45° line shows the aggregate supply function (Y = C + S). The aggregate demand function C+I intersects the aggregate supply function Y = C + S at the point E and the equilibrium level of income OY is determined. Assuming a disequilibrium in aggregate demand and supply of the economy, disequilibrium can exist either when aggregate demand exceeds aggregate supply or aggregate supply exceeds aggregate demand of a business unit. Therefore, in such conditions, how will the equilibrium level of income be restored in the two situations.

Let us take an example where the aggregate supply exceeds aggregate demand. This is represented by OY_2 level of income. The aggregate output or supply is Y_2E_2 and aggregate demand is Y_2k. The disposable income is OY_2 (= Y_2E_2). At the income level of OY_2, consumer spending will be Y_2d on consumption goods and savings will be dE_2. To buy investment goods the business units try to make investments equal to dk. In such a case, the aggregate demand for consumption and investment goods will be at $Y_2d + dk = Y_2k$. on the other hand, the aggregate supply (Y_2E_2) is greater than aggregate demand Y_2k by $kE_2 = (Y_2E_2 - Y_2k)$. Thus, the surplus output worth kE_2 will be in the form of unintended inventories. Business units reduce production in such cases to avoid further inventory accumulation. The output, income and employment will fall as a result and the equilibrium level of income is restored at OY. At point E the aggregate supply equals the aggregate demand.

The second situation of disequilibrium occurs when aggregate demand exceeds aggregate supply which is shown by the income level of OY_1. The aggregate demand is Y_1E_1, the aggregate output is Y_1a and the disposable income is OY_1 (= Y_1a). The consumers spend Y_1b on consumption goods and save ba at this income level. The business units plan to invest bE to buy investment goods. Thus, the aggregate demand is $Y_1b + bE_1 = Y_1E_1$ which is greater than the aggregate supply of goods, $Y_1a + aE_1$. To meet excess demand worth aE1 the business units reduce inventories matching this amount. Further to control reduction in inventories, the business units try to increase production. The increase in production, income and employment will result in growth in the economy. The equilibrium level of income OY will be restored at E.

Equality of saving and investment

The equilibrium level of income can also be shown by the equality of saving and investment functions. When aggregate supply (C + S) equals aggregate demand (C + I), the equilibrium level of income is determined in an economy. As such the intended (or planned) saving also equals intended (or planned) investment. This can be shown algebraically as:

$$C + S = C + 1$$
$$S = I$$

The equilibrium level of income in terms of the equality of saving and investment is shown in Figure 27.3, where I represents the autonomous investment function and S is the saving function. The equilibrium level of income OY is determined at point E where saving and investment functions intersect. At any time disequilibrium occurs because of inequality between saving and investment, forces will operate to restore equilibrium. Suppose, the income level is OY_2 which is above the equilibrium income level, OY, at this income level of OY_2, savings exceed investment by gE_2. It means that people are consuming and spending less. Thus, the aggregate demand is less than the aggregate supply. This will lead to the accumulation of unintended inventories with businessmen. Further to control the accumulation of inventories, the business units try to reduce production. The reduction in production, income and employment continues until the equilibrium level of income (OY) is restored at E where, S = I.

If the income level is below the equilibrium level, investment exceeds saving (OY_1 level of income when investment Y_1E_1 exceeding savings). The excess of planned investment over planned saving indicates that the aggregate demand will exceed aggregate supply by eE_1. Since the aggregate output is below the aggregate demand, the business units will reduce inventories. To arrest further decline in inventories, the business units will increase production. Consequently, output, income and employment will increase in the economy and the equilibrium level of income (OK) will again reach at point E.

27.6. THREE-SECTOR MODEL OF NATIONAL INCOME

The three-sector model of national income was developed by adding the government sector to the two-sector model. Thus, the three sectors involved in this model are the household sector, business sector and government sector. The government escalates aggregate demand by spending on goods and services, and by collecting taxes. The three-sector model incorporates the role of government with its expenditure and taxation in the determination of national income.

Government Expenditure

The analysis of two-sector model deals with the determination of equilibrium level of national income by the consumption function and autonomous investment demand. In the analysis, the role of government expenditure in the determination of national income is not taken into account. In all economies, including the free-market capitalist economies like the USA, UK, Japan, etc., the government expenditure on goods and services plays an important role in the determination of national income. Hence, it should be included in the analysis while determining the income. It is pertinent to note that the government expenditure on various heads such as highways, public parks, education, health services, etc., is governed by the deliberation of promoting employment, encouraging social welfare, and growth in the economy. It does not depend on the income level of the economy. In the three-sector economy, the income generating effects of government expenditure will be taken into consideration. The following equation explains the equilibrium level of national income.

$$Y = C + I + G$$

By adding government expenditure (G) to the saving and investment equation, it will be:

$$Y = C + I + G$$

$$Y = C + S \; [S = Y - C]$$

$$I + G = S$$

Both the equations are illustrated in Figures 27.4 and 27.5. In Figure 27.4, C + I + G refers to the new aggregate demand curve which intersects the aggregate supply curve 45° line at point E_1 where OY_1 is the equilibrium level of income. This income level is greater than the income level of OY without including government expenditure.

Similarly, according to the concept of saving and investment, the new investment curve (I + G) intersects the saving curve S at point E_1 in Figure 27.5. Consequently, the income level OY_1 is more than the income level OY without government expenditure. It should be noted that by adding government expenditure to consumption and investment expenditure (C + I), the national income increases by YY_1 which is more than the government expenditure, $\Delta Y > G$. This is due to the multiplier effect which depends upon the value of marginal propensity to consume (MPC) or marginal propensity to save (MPS), where, MPC or MPS < 1.

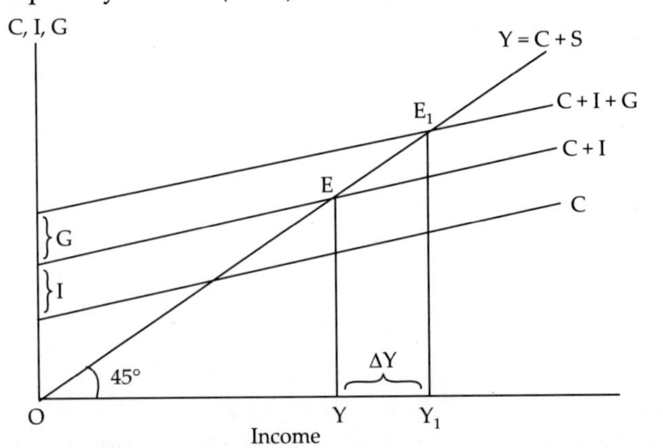

Figure 27.4. Three-sector income-expenditure approach

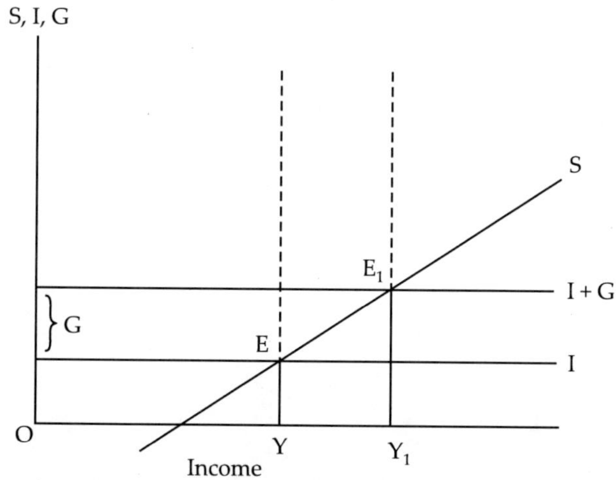

Figure 27.5. Three-sector saving and investment approach

Taxation approach

The effects of taxes on the level of national income need to be analysed. When the government imposes a tax, the amount of tax is reduced from the national income and what remains is the disposable income. Thus,

$$Y - T = Y_d$$

where,

Y refers to national income

T refers to tax

Y_d refers to disposable income.

The disposable income (Y_d) becomes less than national income (Y) by the amount of tax (T), i.e., $Y_d < Y$. With a decrease in disposable income, people will reduce their expenditure on consumption. This leads to a reduction in the national income, as it will depend on the tax rate and the value of marginal propensity to consume (MPC). Based on the above assumptions where the government expenditure is constant, the effects of taxes on national income are illustrated in Figures 27.6 and 27.7.

The effect of lump-sum tax on income is depicted in Figure 27.6. The equilibrium level of income without taxation is at point E where the aggregate demand curve (C + I + G) intersects the aggregate supply curve 45° line and the income level OY is determined. By imposing a lump-sum tax, the consumption function is reduced by the amount of tax. Accordingly, the aggregate demand curve C + I + G shifts downwards to C_1 + I + G and intersects the aggregate supply curve 45° line at point E_1. This results in the reduction of income level from OY to OY_1. Thus, the national income is reduced by YY_1 by imposing the lump-sum tax.

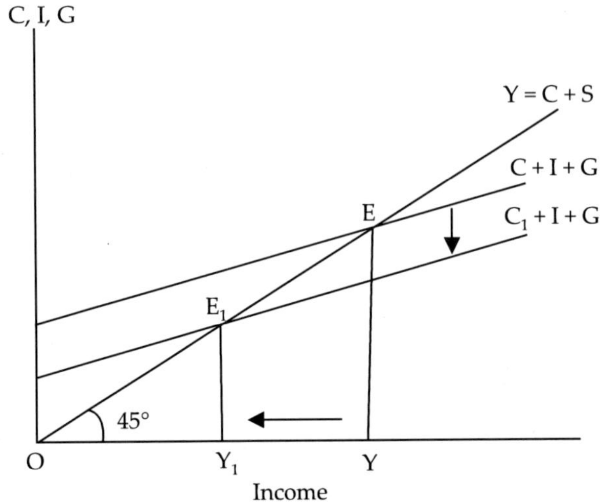

Figure 27.6. Effect of a lump-sum tax on income

Consider a proportional tax which is imposed on income at a constant percentage. In this situation, with a rise in the tax rate, the consumption and national income will decrease, and with a fall in the tax rate, the consumption and national income will increase. This effect of the tax rate on income level is shown in Figure 27.7.

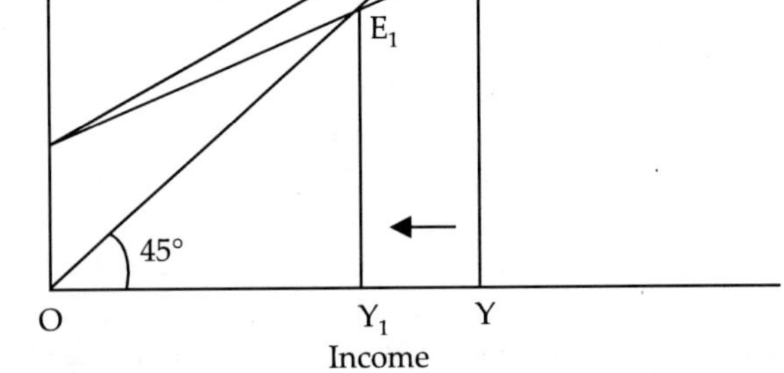

Figure 27.7. Effect of a lump-sum tax on income

The aggregate demand curve (C + I + G) before the imposition of tax intersects the aggregate supply curve 45° line at point E and the income level OY is determined. After imposing the tax, the C + I + G curve shifts downward to C_1 + I + G due to a fall in consumption. It intersects the 45°

line (Y = C + S) at point E_1, and the equilibrium level of national income is reduced from OY to OY_1 (YY_1).

Effect on Saving and Investment

The effect of tax on saving and investment also determines the equilibrium of national income as indicated below:

$$Y = C + I + G$$

and

$$Y = C + S + T$$

$$Y = C + I + G = C + S + T$$

(or)

$$K = I + G = S + T$$

Therefore, the equilibrium of national income is achieved, when planned investment (I) plus government expenditure on goods and services (G) equals the planned saving (S) plus tax (T). I + G are inflows or injections in the national income and S + T are outflows or leakages. Figure 27.8 shows the equilibrium of national income. Here, E is the equilibrium point before imposing the tax where S and I + G curve intersect each other and the income level OY is determined. When the tax is imposed, the S curve shifts upward to the left as S + T and the new equilibrium point E_1 is achieved with I + G and the national income falls from OY to OY_1 (YY_1).

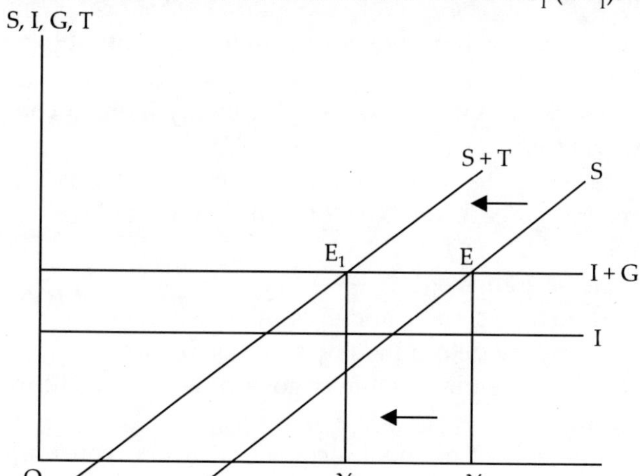

Figure 27.8. Three-sector taxation approach

27.7. FOUR-SECTOR MODEL OF NATIONAL INCOME

In the four-sector model of determination of national income, the foreign trade sector is added to the three sectors, viz., households, business units and government. Foreign trade, i.e., the volume of exports and imports of the country also affects the level of national income of a country. The Keynesian model of determination of national income is extended by including the effect of exports and imports of a country on the generation of income. For example, the exports of India represent foreign demand and generate income for the Indians. On the other hand, imports represent the demand for foreign goods by the Indians and generate incomes for the people of other countries. Therefore, imports tend to reduce domestic aggregate expenditure. It follows that national income will depend on the net exports, i.e., the exports minus imports (X – M) where, X stands for exports and 'M' for imports. The exports and imports of a country depend to a great extent on the level of economic activity (i.e., the level of output and income of the country).

While determining the national income in an open economy, it may be noted that government expenditures are like investments as they raise the demand for goods. They are injections in the national income. The impact of exports and imports is similar to that of government expenditure. Exports are considered injections due to the reason they increase the demand for goods in the economy. Imports are considered leakages in the national income as they represent the supply of goods.

Assumptions

The following are the assumptions for the determination of income in an open economy:

1. International trade in the domestic economy is small compared to total world trade.
2. Existence of less than full employment in the economy.
3. The general price level is stable until full employment level is reached.
4. Exchange rates are fixed.
5. There are no tariffs, trade and exchange restrictions.
6. Gross exports are determined by external factors.
7. Exports (A), investment (I) and government expenditure (G) are autonomous.
8. The components of national income (Y) such as consumption (C), imports (M), savings (S) and taxes (I) are fixed in proportion and their relationships are linear with national income.

Based on these assumptions, an open economy will be in equilibrium when its national expenditure (E) is equal to its national income (Y). Therefore, the equilibrium level of income can be shown in the form of an equation.

$$Y = E = C + I + G + (X - M)$$

Determination of Equilibrium Level of Income

When the growth of industrial output is rapid, it will generate greater demand for imported materials. On the other hand, the higher industrial growth would also cause exports to rise provided there is a demand for goods abroad. However, in the Keynesian model of income determination, exports and imports are considered autonomous, i.e., independent of income, being determined outside the model. Further, as mentioned above, the increase or decrease in aggregate expenditure or demand due to exports and imports depends on the net exports, i.e., X – M which can be written as NX. If the net exports are positive, there will be an addition to the aggregate demand or expenditure or a country. On the other hand, if the net exports are negative, there will be a decrease in the aggregate expenditure.

When net exports (NX) are included in the analysis, the following equation for the equilibrium level of income can arrive.

$$Y = C + I + G + (X - M)$$

where,

$$C = a + b\,(Y - T)$$

$$Y = a + bY - bT + I + G + NX$$

(or)

$$Y\,(1 - b) = a - bT + I + G + NX$$

Hence,

$$Y = 1/(1 - b)\,(a - bT + I + G + NX)$$

Thus, the equilibrium level of income is the sum of all fixed autonomous expenditures (i.e., $a - bT + I + G + NX$) times the value of multiplier $(1/1 - b)$. In the four-sector model, national income can be determined when saving gap between consumption and income is equal to the sum of investment, government expenditure and net exports (i.e., $I + G + NX$).

27.8. SUMMARY

- National income is the monetary value of all the finished goods and services delivered by a country over one year. It comprises an array of goods and services of diverse.
- National income comprises two aspects. First, it determines the market value of annual output, i.e., national income as an economic measure. Secondly, all goods and services produced for any given period in a year must be taken into account only once and not more than once for computing national income accurately.
- There are three different perspectives on understanding the concept of national income. They are production perspective, income perspective, and expenditure perspective.

- Gross domestic product at market price refers to the total of value added by all producing units within the domestic territory of a country during an accounting year, inclusive of depreciation and estimate at market price.
- Net domestic product at market price refers to the market value of the final goods and services produced by all producing units within the domestic territory of a country during an accounting year, excluding depreciation.
- Gross domestic product at factor cost refers to the total factor income generated within the domestic territory of a country in an accounting year, along with depreciation and excluding net indirect taxes.
- Net domestic product at factor cost refers to the total of factor incomes generated within the domestic territory of a country during an accounting year excluding depreciation and net indirect taxes.
- Gross national product at market price is the total of the market value of the final goods and services produced within the domestic territory of a country during an accounting year and also includes net factor income from abroad.
- Net national product at market price is the total of the market value of the final goods and services produced within the domestic territory of a country during an accounting year, exclusive of depreciation and net factor income from abroad.
- Gross national product at factor cost is the total of factor cost of final goods and services produced within the domestic territory of a country during an accounting year, inclusive of depreciation and net factor income from abroad excluding net indirect taxes.
- Net national product at factor cost is the total of factor cost of final goods and services produced within the domestic territory of a country during an accounting year, exclusive of depreciation and net indirect tax, and inclusive of net factor income from abroad.
- National disposable income is the income from all sources available to residents of a country for consumption expenditure or for saving during a year.
- Personal income is the income received by the individuals in a year. The national income only after making some deductions in the form of corporate taxes, social security contribution, etc., will be available for distribution among individuals.
- National income is generally measured in terms of money. It is computed in two ways, i.e., at current prices (nominal national income) and constant prices (real national income).
- Nominal national income is the money value of all the final goods and services at current prices. Real national income. It is the money value

of all the final goods and services produced in a year measured at fixed prices.

- The circular flow of production, income, demand and expenditure represents three correlated phases, namely, production, distribution and disposition. These three phases empower to look at national income in three ways, i.e., the flow of goods and services, flow of income on goods and services, and flow of expenditure on goods and services.
- There are three methods of measuring national income. They are value added method, income method, and expenditure method.
- Value added (VAD) method measures the influence and role of each producing enterprise in the domestic territory of a country. The income earned by all the factors of production forms the subject matter of calculation of national income by income method. Under the expenditure method, all the consumption expenditure and investment expenditure of individuals, institutions and government are taken into account.
- The two-sector model of income determination of an economy includes household and business sectors. The Keynesian theory of the determination of national income is pertinent in the short run only as the stock of capital, techniques of production, the efficiency of labour, the size of the population, forms of business units have been anticipated to stay constant.
- The national income can be determined by the equality of aggregate demand and aggregate supply or by the equality of saving and investment. Thus, aggregate demand (aggregate expenditure) = Consumption expenditure (C) + Investment expenditure (I).
- The three-sector model of national income was developed by adding the government sector to the two-sector model. Thus, the three sectors involved in this model are the household sector, business sector and government sector. The three-sector model incorporates the role of government with its expenditure and taxation in the determination of national income.
- The equilibrium of national income is achieved, when planned investment (I) plus government expenditure on goods and services (G) equals the planned saving (S) plus tax (T). I + G are inflows or injections in the national income and S + T are outflows or leakages.
- In the four-sector model of determination of national income, the foreign trade sector is added to the three sectors, viz., households, business firms and government. Foreign trade, i.e., the volume of exports and imports of the country also affects the level of national income of a country.

- An open economy will be in equilibrium when its national expenditure (E) is equal to its national income (Y). Therefore, the equilibrium level of income can be shown in the form of an equation. Thus, $Y = E = C + I + G + (X - M)$.

SHORT ANSWER QUESTIONS

1. What are the different perspectives of national income?
2. What is national disposable income?
3. Write a note on personal income.
4. What are the assumptions of the two-sector model of national income?
5. Explain the effects of taxation on saving and investment.
6. List the assumptions of four-sector model of national income.

ESSAY ANSWER QUESTIONS

1. Explain the concept of national income in detail.
2. Discuss the different combinations of aggregates of national income.
3. Describe the general ways to measure national income.
4. Discuss the different methods of measuring national income.
5. What is the two-sector model of national income? Explain the equality of aggregate demand and aggregate supply.
6. What is the three-sector model of national income? Explain the determination of the equilibrium of national income.
7. Explain the four-sector model of national income? Discuss the determination of the equilibrium level of income.

FILL IN THE BLANKS

1. The common measure used for national income is __________.
2. National income is used to measure the __________ growth of a nation.
3. Gross national disposable income is referred to as net national disposable income plus __________.
4. The income from all sources available to residents of a country for consumption expenditure or for saving during a year is called __________.
5. The income received by the individuals in a year is called __________.
6. National income at current prices is also referred to as __________.
7. Value added method is also referred to as __________ method.
8. A two-sector model of income determination was proposed by __________.
9. With a decrease in disposable income, people will __________ their expenditure on consumption.
10. In the Keynesian model of income determination, exports and imports are considered __________.

Answers:

1. Money
2. Economic
3. Depreciation
4. National disposable income

5. Personal income
6. Nominal national income
7. Product
8. J.M. Keynes
9. Reduce
10. Autonomous

MULTIPLE-CHOICE QUESTIONS

1. Under which perspective, national income is the total of factor incomes earned by normal residents of a country in the form of rents, wages, interest and profit in a year.
   (A) Production (B) Income
   (C) Expenditure (D) Demand
2. Net domestic product at market price is denoted as:
   (A) $NDP_{MP} = GDP_{MP}$ – Depreciation
   (B) $NDP_{MP} = GDP_{MP}$ – Income
   (C) $NDP_{MP} = GDP_{MP}$ – Expenditure
   (D) $NDP_{MP} = GDP_{MP}$ – Interest
3. Gross domestic product at factor cost is calculated as:
   (A) $GDP_{FC} = GDP_{MP}$ – Direct taxes
   (B) $GDP_{FC} = GDP_{MP}$ – Taxable income
   (C) $GDP_{FC} = GDP_{MP}$ – Net indirect taxes
   (D) $GDP_{FC} = GDP_{MP}$ – Indirect expenses
4. The total of factor incomes generated within the domestic territory of a country during an accounting year excluding depreciation and net indirect taxes is called:
   (A) Net domestic product (B) Gross domestic product
   (C) Gross national product (D) Net national product
5. Net national product at market price is referred to as:
   (A) $NNP_{MP} = GDP_{MP}$ – Indirect taxes + Net factor income from abroad
   (B) $NNP_{MP} = GDP_{MP}$ – Indirect taxes – Net factor income from abroad
   (C) $NNP_{MP} = GDP_{MP}$ – Depreciation – Net factor income from abroad
   (D) $NNP_{MP} = GDP_{MP}$ – Depreciation + Net factor income from abroad
6. National income at constant prices is also known as:
   (A) Nominal national income (B) Real national income
   (C) Net national income (D) National disposable income
7. Which method measures the influence and role of each producing enterprise in the domestic territory of the country?
   (A) Income method (B) Expenditure method
   (C) Valued added method (D) Revenue method
8. The two sectors considered in the determination of the two-sector model of income are:
   (A) Household and business (B) Household and government
   (C) Business and government (D) Government and foreign trade

Answers:

1. B 2. A 3. C 4. A 5. D
6. B 7. C 8. A

REFERENCES

1. Abraham, W.I. (1969). *National Income and Economic Accounting*. NJ: Prentice-Hall.
2. Clark, C. (1937). National income at its climax. *The Economic Journal*, 47(186), 308-320.
3. Clark, C. (2019). *National Income and Outlay*. Routledge.
4. Cowen, T. & Tabarrok, A. (2013). *Modern Principles of Economics* (2nd Edn). New York, NY: Worth Publishers.
5. Dwivedi, D.N. (2015). *Managerial Economics* (8th Edn). New Delhi, India: Vikas Publishing House Pvt. Ltd.
6. Ferguson, C.E. (1972). *Macroeconomic Theory*. (Richard D. Irwin, Illinois, 1972).
7. Fisher, I. (1930). The *Theory of Interest: As Determined by Impatience to Spend Income and Opportunity to Invest it*. Clifton: Augustusm Kelly Publishers.
8. Froyen, R.T. & Perez, S.J. (1990). *Macroeconomics: Theories and Policies* (No. 339 F7 2005.). Macmillan.
9. Gupta, G.S. (2017). *Managerial Economics*. New Delhi, India: Tata McGraw-Hill.
10. Keynes, J.M. (1936). *The General Theory of Employment, Interest and Money*. London, UK: Palgrave Macmillan.
11. Kuznets, S. (1946). Introduction to "National Income: A Summary of Findings". In *National Income: A Summary of Findings* (pp. 1-2). NBER.
12. Marshall, A. (1920). *Principles of Economics* (8th Edn). London: Macmillan.
13. Marshall, Alfred. (1890). *Principles of Economics*. London: Macmillan.
14. Mehta, P.L. (2007). *Managerial Economics: Text and Cases*. New Delhi, India: Sultan Chand & Co.
15. Pigou, A.C. (1946). *Income: An Introduction to Economics*. London: Macmillan & Co.
16. Pigou, A.C. (1951). Real income and economic welfare. *Oxford Economic Papers*, 3(1), 16-20.
17. Pigou, A.C. (2013). *The Economics of Welfare*. Palgrave Macmillan.
18. Samuelson, P.A. (1950). Evaluation of real national income. *Oxford Economic Papers*, 2(1), 1-29.
19. Sen, A. (1976). Real national income. *The Review of Economic Studies*, 43(1), 19-39.
20. Shapiro, E. (1978). *Macroeconomic Analysis*. NY: Harcourt Publishers Ltd.
21. Varshney, R.L. & Maheswari, K.L. (2014). *Managerial Economics*. New Delhi, India: Sultan Chand & Sons.

Chapter

28 Goods & Services Tax (GST)

LEARNING OBJECTIVES

After studying this chapter, you should be able to understand:

- concept of GST and dual GST model;
- IGST model and the concept of supply;
- GST Council, GST levy and collection;
- GSTN and composition scheme; and
- Exemptions and benefits of GST

28.1. CONCEPT OF GST

Goods and Services Tax (GST) was the largest indirect tax reform in the history of India introduced on 1st of July, 2017 through GST Act, 2017. GST covers to the whole of India including the State of Jammu and Kashmir. According to the Article 366 (12A) of Constitution of India, Goods and services tax refers to the tax on supply of goods or services, or both, except taxes on supply of alcoholic liquor for human consumption. The objective of GST is to eliminate the complexity in the tax system in the country and to implement one tax for one nation philosophy. The reform mandated integration of the entire nation's diverse tax portfolio into a single taxation system. GST provides a single interface for over crore taxpayers for their tax compliance functions. Goods and Services Tax Network (GSTN) was established to build a platform to serve the needs of a diverse set of stakeholders.

Destination principle is the basis for GST to levy consumption based tax. Taxing the supply of goods or services at the point of consumption is the basic concept of GST. Both goods and services are covered in the comprehensive tax regime of GST. At each stage of the supply chain, the tax is collected on value added. The GST paid on the procurement of goods and services can be set off against the tax payable on the supply of goods or services.

Value Added Tax (VAT) was introduced as indirect tax in the Indian taxation system on April 1, 2005, replacing the then existing sales tax to make India a single integrated market. It is commonly expressed as a percentage of the total cost. For example, if a product costs Rs. 100 and there is a VAT of 15%, the end-user pays Rs. 115 to the trader. The trader keeps Rs. 100 and remits Rs. 15 to the government. However, the Goods and Services Tax (GST), has replaced the central and state indirect taxes such as VAT, excise duty and service tax.

An example of a 10% VAT in sequence through a chain of production might occur as follows. A producer of electronic spare parts purchases raw materials of various metals from a supplier. The metal supplier is regarded as the seller in the production chain. The supplier charges the producer Rs. 100 plus a 10% VAT, and then sends the 10% VAT to the government. The producer uses the raw materials to make electronic spare parts, which it then sells to a mobile manufacturing business unit for Rs. 200 plus a 20% VAT. The producer of spare parts sends 10% of the VAT collected to the government and retains the other 10%, which reimburses it for the VAT it previously paid to the metal supplier.

The mobile manufacturer adds value by making its mobile phones, which it then sells to a mobile retailer for Rs. 300 plus a 30% VAT. The manufacturer pays 10% of the VAT to the government and retains the 20% of the VAT collected to reimburse the mobile manufacturer for the VAT it has paid to the electronic spare parts producer. Finally, the mobile retailer sells a phone to a consumer for Rs. 500 plus a 40% VAT, where 20% is paid to the government and the remaining 20% is retained with the retailer. Thus, the VAT paid at each sale point along the way represents 10% of the value added by the seller.

28.1.1. Calculation of VAT Paid at Each Stage of Purchase/Production

A motorbike manufacturer purchases raw materials for Rs. 5.50, which includes a 10% VAT. After completing the manufacturing of the parts, they are purchased by the assembler for Rs. 11, which includes a VAT of Re. 1. The manufacturer receives Rs. 11, of which he pays Re. 0.50 to the government. The full Re. 1 VAT is not paid to the government, as the manufacturer will keep the portion of VAT that he paid to the seller of the raw materials. As the manufacturer paid Re. 0.50 in VAT to the seller of the raw materials, he is required to pay only a VAT of Re. 0.50 (Re. 1 – Re. 0.50) to the government (i.e., the incremental VAT).

Similarly, VAT paid at each stage of purchase/production can be calculated by subtracting the VAT that's already charged from the VAT at the latest stage. The total VAT is ultimately passed on to the final buyer(s), as the persons at the previous stages of purchase are reimbursed for the VAT they have paid. The final consumer pays the entire sum of the VAT paid by the other buyers at prior stages as shown in Table 28.1. The final consumer's VAT can also be calculated by multiplying the price by the VAT rate (i.e., Rs. 30 × 10% = Rs. 3).

Table 28.1. VAT calculation

Stage of purchase	Cost (Rs.)	VAT charged (Rs.)	VAT paid (Rs.)
Purchase of raw materials	5.00	0.50	0.50
Purchase after manufacturing	10.00	1.00	0.50
Purchase after assembling	15.00	1.50	0.50
Wholesale	20.00	2.00	0.50
Retail	30.00	3.00	1.00
VAT charged to the customer			3.00

Thus, GST is a tax levied on goods and services at each point of supply. It is a national level tax based on value-added principle just like state level value added tax (VAT) which was imposed as a tax on the sale of inter-state goods.

For example, under VAT regime, a consultant is charged 15% service tax on services of Rs. 1,00,000. The output tax will be Rs. 15,000 (Rs. 1,000,000 × 15%). Further, if he purchases office provisions for Rs. 30,000 paying a VAT of 5%, the tax will be charged Rs. 1500 (Rs. 30,000 × 5%). Thus, the consultant has to pay Rs. 16,500 (Rs. 15,000 + Rs. 1,500). Under GST regime, GST on service of Rs. 1,00,000 @ 18% is Rs. 18,000. Deduct GST on office provisions of Rs. 1500 (Rs. 30,000 × 5%). Thus, the net GST payable is Rs. 16,500 (Rs. 18,000 – Rs. 1500).

28.1.2. Cascading Tax Effect

GST is a value added tax imposed on the sale of goods or services or both, where the burden is borne by the final consumer. It is a destination-based consumption tax offering a comprehensive and continuous chain of the tax credit. GST brings a uniform tax structure all over India and eliminates the cascading effect of the tax. The cascading tax effect is also called "tax on tax". The cascading effect occurs due to the reason that a product is taxed at every stage of production and distribution until it is finally sold to the consumer. In other words, every succeeding transfer of product is taxed inclusive of the taxes charged on the preceding transfer. The end-user has to accept the burden of multiple taxes charged at every stage of production. In the earlier indirect tax regime, the centre, states and local governments used to have powers to levy varied taxes. The central government used to formulate tax laws for the products and services under the Union List. The state governments used to formulate tax laws for the products and services under the State List. The central and state governments used to formulate tax laws for the products and services under the concurrent list. The centre levies the income tax, excise duty, service tax, and central sales tax (CST), securities transaction tax whereas states levy VAT/sales tax, entry tax, state excise tax, property tax, agricultural tax, and grant tax. The cascading effect increased the tax burden on Indian goods and made them less competitive in the international market. It is considered one of the main drawbacks of the Indian taxation system. The example of the cascading effect is given in Table 28.2.

Table 28.2. Cascading effect

Distribution channel	**Before GST**	**After GST**
Manufacturer		
Cost	100	100
Tax @ 10%	10	10
Total selling price to wholesaler	110	110
Wholesaler		
Cost	110	110
Adds profit	40	40
Total	150	150
Tax @ 10%	15	4
	(10% tax on the total)	(GST tax is on profit, i.e., 10% on Rs. 40 and not on total)
Total selling price to retailer	165	154
Retailer		
Cost	165	154
Adds profit	75	75
Total	240	229
Tax @ 10%	24	7.5
	(10% tax on the total)	(GST tax is on profit, i.e., 10% on Rs. 75 and not on total)
Total selling price to the customer	**264**	**236.5**

28.2. ADOPTION OF DUAL GST MODEL

The ideologies of GST are almost common in all the countries. There are certain differences in implementing the GST model depending on the persistent existence of exemptions and special arrangements to meet specific objectives. The point of difference arises from adopting various approaches in defining the jurisdiction of consumption and taxation. There are several variations in the application process of GST along with the different interpretations of the same concepts, various approaches to time of supply and its interaction with the place of supply, different classifications of services and intangibles, and inconsistent treatment of mixed supplies, around the world. Different countries follow a different model of GST based upon their own legislative and administrative structure and their requirements.

India has introduced the dual GST model due to its unique federal nature. The federal system refers to relations between the centre and the states of India as provided in Part XI of the Indian constitution. The Constitution of India specifies the distribution of legislative, administrative and executive powers between the union government and the states of India. Under the GST model, tax is levied concurrently on a common base, i.e., supply of goods or services or both by the centre as well as the states. GST levied by the centre is called Central GST (Central tax/CGST). The GST levied by the states is called State GST (State Tax/SGST). The GST (State Tax/SGST) levied by Union Territories without legislature is called UTGST (Union territory tax). CGST & SGST / UTGST shall be levied on all taxable intra-state supplies. The GST levied for inter-state supplies of goods and/or services is called IGST.

The following are the details:

1. **Central Goods and Services Tax Act, 2017 (CGST):** CGST imposed and collected by the Central Government. It is a source of revenue to the Central Government of India on intra-state supplies of taxable goods/services or both.
2. **State Goods and Services Tax Act, 2017 (SGST):** The State Governments/Union Territories with State Legislatures (viz., Delhi and Pondicherry) impose and collect SGST on intra-state supplies of taxable goods or services or both. It is one of the revenue sources of the respective State Government.
3. **Union Territory Goods and Services Tax (UTGST):** The Union Territories without State Legislatures, impose and collect UTGST on intra-state supplies of taxable goods or services or both.
4. **Integrated Goods and Services Tax (IGST):** IGST is governed by the IGST Act. IGST applies to the supply of goods and/or services in cases of imports and exports from India. Under IGST, exports are zero-rated and tax is shared by the central and state government on prescribed proportion.

The Indian GST system has its uniqueness in many ways. Apart from India, Brazil is the only country in the world which follows a similar dual GST System. In India, GST has been rolled out as a uniform taxation system all across the nation by removing entry barriers between states.

In Canada, though the GST scheme closely resembles that of India, it failed to achieve consensus among states. As a result, the GST was made optional, not mandatory. States are free to adopt or reject GST. In India, GST is uniformly applicable all over India including the State of Jammu and Kashmir.

28.3. TAXES SUBSUMED UNDER GST

The different taxes subsumed under GST can be classified as central taxes and state taxes. These include:

1. **Central taxes:** The central taxes subsumed under GST are Central Excise Duty, Duties of Excise (Medicinal and Toilet Preparations), Additional Duties of Excise (Goods of Special Importance), Additional Duties of Excise (Textiles and Textile Products), Special Additional Duty of Customs (SAD), Additional Duties of Customs (commonly known as CVD), Service tax, and cess and surcharges related to supply of goods/services.
2. **State taxes:** The state taxes subsumed under GST are State VAT, Central Sales Tax, Purchase Tax, Luxury Tax, Entry Tax (All forms), Entertainment Tax (except those levied by the local bodies), Taxes on advertisements, Taxes on lotteries, betting and gambling, and State cesses and surcharges as they relate to supply of goods or services.

28.4. INTEGRATED GOODS AND SERVICES TAX (IGST) MODEL

IGST is levied and collected by the central government on all taxable inter-state transactions of goods/services. IGST is a mechanism designed to monitor the inter-state trade of goods and services and to ensure the SGST component accrues to the consumer state. IGST maintains the integrity of the input tax credit (ITC) chain in inter-state supplies. ITC refers to the tax paid by the buyer on the purchase of goods or services. Such tax, which is paid at the time of purchase and reduced from liability payable on outward supplies, is known as an input tax credit. In other words, the input tax credit is the tax reduced from the output tax payable on account of sales.

For example, a manufacturer purchased goods worth Rs. 20,000 on which GST at 18% was Rs. 3600. He sold goods worth Rs. 30,000. The GST payable at 18% is Rs. 5400. The net GST payable and input GST credit is as follows:

Outward GST payable = 5400
Less: GST paid on purchases = 3600

Net GST payable = 1800

Therefore, Rs. 3600 reduced is input tax credit availed that has been paid on purchases.

The IGST model is the unique contribution of India in the field of VAT. As per the IGST model, the centre will levy IGST (Integrated Goods and Service Tax) which is CGST plus SGST on all inter-state supply of goods or services or both. The IGST rate would broadly be equal to CGST plus SGST rate. The decision on IGST or CGST + SGST while raising invoices is shown in Figure 28.1.

The major advantages of IGST model are:

1. Maintenance of uninterrupted ITC chain on inter-state transactions.
2. Absence of upfront payment of tax for the inter-state supplier or recipient.
3. No refund claim in exports as ITC is used while paying the tax.
4. Self-monitoring model.
5. The model takes 'business to business (B2B)' as well as 'business to consumer (B2C)' transactions into an account.

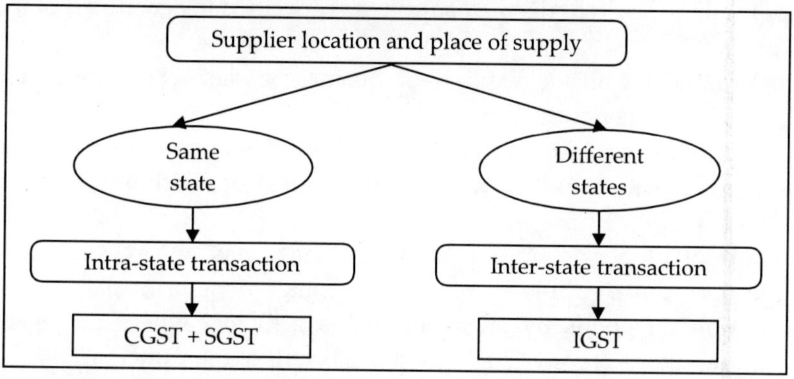

Figure 28.1. Decision on IGST or CGST + SGST while raising invoices

28.5. CONCEPT OF SUPPLY

Supply is the point of taxation or the taxable event under GST. The term supply is referred to with the following traits:

1. Supply should be of goods or services.
2. Whatever is not goods/services (like money, securities, etc.) is not supply.
3. It must be echoed that only movable property is taken as goods.
4. Barters and exchanges would be leviable under GST.
5. Licences, leases, rentals with or without transfer of the right to use are considered supply and leviable to GST.

6. Supply should be made for a consideration which could be in the form of money or otherwise.
7. Supply includes the flow of money from a 3rd party on behalf of the receiver.
8. Deposit is not a consideration unless specifically applied to by the supplier.
9. Supply should be made in the course of the continuance of the business.
10. Any supply made for personal consumption or in personal capacity does not entice GST.
11. The supply shall be made by a taxable person, who is registered or is liable to be registered under the Act.
12. Supply between both non-taxable parties is not leviable to GST.
13. Supply could be made to a non-taxable person also.

28.5.1. Activities to be Treated as Supplies

There are a few activities which, even without consideration are interpreted as supply, also known as deemed supplies as specified in Schedule-I of the GST Act, 2017.

1. Permanent transfer/disposal of business assets where input tax credit has been availed on such assets.
2. Supply of goods/services/both between related persons or between distinct persons, when made in the course or continuance of the business.
3. Supply of goods by a principal to his agent where the agent undertakes to supply such goods on behalf of the principal.
4. Supply of goods by an agent to his principal where the agent undertakes to receive such goods on behalf of the principal.
5. Import of services by a taxable person from a related person or any of his other establishments outside India.

According to the Schedule-II of the Central Goods & Services Tax Act, 2017, certain activities which are to be treated as supply of goods and services are:

1. Transfer of title in goods under an agreement where the property in goods passes at a future date on payment of full consideration.
2. Renting of immovable property.
3. Permanent transfer/disposal of goods forming part of business assets by or under the directions of the person carrying on the business whether or not for consideration. Any goods forming a part of business assets will be deemed to be transferred in the

continuance of business, before any person ceases to be a taxable person, except when the business is transferred as a going concern or the business is carried on by a personal representative who is deemed to be a taxable person.

4. Supply of goods by any unincorporated association or body of persons to an unincorporated member thereof for cash, deferred payment or other valuable consideration.
5. Any transfer of right in goods or undivided share in goods without the transfer of title.
6. Any lease, tenancy, easement, licence to occupy land or any lease or letting out of the building including a commercial, industrial or residential complex for business or commerce, either wholly or partly.
7. Any treatment or process which is applied to another person's goods.
8. Temporary transfer or permitting the use or enjoyment of any intellectual property right.
9. Development design, programming, customisation, adaptation, upgradation, enhancement, implementation of information technology software.
10. Agreeing to the obligation to refrain from an act, or to tolerate an act or a situation, or to do an act.
11. Transfer of the right to use any goods for any purpose (whether or not for a specified period) for cash, deferred payment or other valuable consideration.
12. Where, by or under the direction of a person carrying on a business, goods held assets or used for business are put for any private use or made available to any person for any use other than for business, at the direction of the person carrying on the business, whether or not for a consideration.
13. Construction of a complex, building, civil structure or a part thereof, including a complex or building intended for sale to a buyer, wholly or partly, except where the entire consideration has been received after issuance of the completion certificate, where required, by the competent authority or after its first occupation, whichever is earlier.
14. Supply of goods, as a part of any service or in any manner, being food or any other article for human consumption or any drink (other than alcoholic liquor for human consumption), where such supply or service is for cash deferred payment or other valuable consideration.

28.5.2. Activities not to be Regarded as Supply

According to the Schedule-III of CGST Act, 2017, there are certain activities which cannot be treated as a supply of goods or services. These are:

1. Services rendered by the employee to the employer.
2. Duties performed by any individual as a Chairperson/Member/ Director in a body established by the Central/State Government or local authority and not considered as an employee.
3. Functions performed by the Members of Parliament, State Legislature, Panchayats, Municipalities and other local authorities.
4. Duties performed by any individual holding any position in fulfilment of the provisions of the Constitution.
5. Services by any Court/Tribunal established under law.
6. Services such as funeral, burial, crematorium or mortuary including transportation of the deceased.
7. Sale of land or building as per the clause (b) of Schedule-II.
8. Actionable claims, other than lottery, betting and gambling.

28.5.3. Composite Supply

According to Chapter-I of the Central Goods and Services Tax (CGST) Act, 2017, Section 2(30), *composite supply* refers to the supply made by a taxable person to a recipient consisting of two or more taxable supplies of goods/ services/both or any combination thereof, which are bundled and supplied in conjunction with each other in the ordinary course of business, one of which is a principal supply.

For example, on purchasing a smart TV, the accessories like remote control, wire, wall mount, other accessories, warranty and the annual maintenance services are provided to the customer. It is evident that smart TV is the principal supply and the other accessories are all ancillary services. The composite supply will be charged at the rate which applies to the principal supply as shown in Table 28.3.

Table 28.3. Tax under composite supply

Smart TV with accessories, warranty with annual maintenance services	= Rs. 1,00,000
GST (smart TV) @ 28%	= Rs. 28,000
Invoice value	= Rs. 1,28,000

28.5.4. Mixed Supply

According to Section 2(74) of CGST Act, 2017, mixed supply means two or more individual supplies of goods/services, or any combination thereof, made in conjunction with each other by a taxable person for a single price where such supply does not constitute a composite supply.

For example, buying the consolidated package of beauty products which includes shampoo, comb, conditioner, nail polish, lipstick and tooth powder. It is evident that the products can all be independently supplied and any one of them cannot be singled out as a principal supply and these are deliberately bundled and sold together. The mixed supply will be charged at the rate applicable to the supply that attracts the highest rate of tax from within the consolidated package as shown in Table 28.4.

Table 28.4. Tax under mixed supply

Items	**Rs.**
Bottles of Shampoo (GST @ 28%)	3000
Bottles of Conditioners (GST @ 28%)	2000
Comb (GST @ 5%)	300
Hair Dryer (GST @ 28%)	1500
Lipstick set (GST @ 28%)	2000
Nail Polish (GST @ 28%)	1000
Tooth Powder (GST @ 12%)	800
Consolidated Value of Supply	10,600
GST (highest rate 28%)	2968
Invoice value	13,568

28.6. GOODS & SERVICES TAX (GST) COUNCIL

According to the Constitution (One Hundred and First Amendment) Act, 2016, Article 279A (4), the President by order constitute a council to be called the Goods and Services Tax Council. GST Council is a constitutional body for making recommendations to the Union and State Government on issues related to GST. The Council is expected to make recommendations to the Union and the States on key issues related to GST, like the goods and services that may be subjected or exempted from GST, model GST laws, principles that govern the place of supply, threshold limits, GST rates including the floor rates with bands, special rates for raising additional resources during natural calamities/disasters, special provisions for certain states, etc. The GST Council will ensure harmonisation on aspects of GST between the centre and the states and also among the states.

GST Council is the first constitutional federal body vested with powers to take all major decisions relating to GST. The Council consists of 33 members. Two members represent the Centre and 31 members represent from 28 states and 3 union territories with legislation. The members of the Council include Union Finance Minister (as chairperson), Union Minister of States in charge of revenue or finance (as a member), and the ministers of states in charge of finance or taxation or other ministers as nominated by each state government (as members). The members of the GST Council shall choose one amongst themselves to be the Vice-Chairperson of the Council for such period as they may decide. The vision of the Council is to establish highest standards of co-operative federalism in the functioning of GST Council. The mission of the council is to evolve by a process of wider consultation, a Goods and Services Tax structure, which is an information technology-driven and user friendly.

The GST Council will determine the procedure of performance of its functions. Every decision of the Council shall be taken at a meeting, by a majority of not less than three-fourths of the weighted votes of the members present and voting. The principles followed for the purpose are:

- the vote of the Central Government shall have a weightage of one-third of the total votes cast; and
- the votes of all the State Governments taken together shall have a weightage of two-thirds of the total votes cast, in that meeting.

The GST Council shall make recommendations to the Union and the States on:

1. taxes, cesses and surcharges levied by the Union, the States and the local bodies which may be subsumed in the goods and services tax;
2. goods and services that may be subjected to, or exempted from the goods and services tax;
3. model Goods and Services Tax Laws, principles of levy, apportionment of Goods and Services Tax levied on supplies in the course of inter-state trade or commerce under article 269A and the principles that govern the place of supply;
4. threshold limit of turnover below which goods and services may be exempted from goods and services tax;
5. rates including floor rates with bands of goods and services tax;
6. any special rate or rates for a specified period, to raise additional resources during any natural calamity or disaster;
7. special provision to the States of Arunachal Pradesh, Assam, Jammu and Kashmir, Manipur, Meghalaya, Mizoram, Nagaland, Sikkim, Tripura, Himachal Pradesh and Uttarakhand; and
8. any other matter relating to the goods and services tax, as the Council may decide.

28.7. GST LEVY AND COLLECTION

GST is levied at the point of supply, that is, at the time and place of supply and that's when the liability to charge GST arises. As per the CGST Act, 2017, GST would be levied on the transaction value.

- **Tax rates on goods:** Rates are broadly 0.25%, 3%, 5%, 12%, 18% and 28% and that is split into CGST and SGST equally for intra-state sales and fully leviable as IGST for Inter-state sale.
- **Tax rates on services:** Rates are broadly 5%, 12%, 18% and 28% and that is split into CGST and SGST equally for intra-state sales and fully leviable as IGST for inter-state sale.

The GST council has fitted over 1300 goods and 500 services under four tax slabs of 5%, 12%, 18% and 28% under GST. This is aside from the tax on gold that is kept at 3% and rough precious and semi-precious stones that are placed at a special rate of 0.25% under GST. The list of various GST slab rates in India is presented in Table 28.5.

In the 41st GST Council, on 27th August 2020, a discussion between the Centre and States regarding compensating states for the shortfall in revenue was held. As per the Central Goods and Services Act, the Centre has guaranteed payment for the loss of revenue in the first five years of the GST implementation (2017). The Centre has given states the option of getting loans through the Reserve Bank of India (RBI) for the deficit arising due to the implementation of GST.

Table 28.5. List of various GST slab rates in India, 2020

No tax	Goods	No taxes will be levied on goods like sanitary napkins, deities made of stone, marbles or wood, rakhis without any precious metals like gold, silver, raw material used in brooms, Sal leaves and fortified milk, fruits, vegetables, bread, salt, bindi, curd, sindoor, natural honey, bangles, handloom, besan, flour, eggs, stamps, printed books, judicial papers, newspapers, etc.
	Services	All hotels and lodges who carry a tariff below Rs. 1000 are exempted from taxes under GST. The list also includes IMM courses and bank charges on the savings account, Jan Dhan Yojana.
GST Tax Slab of 5%	Goods	The goods which will attract taxation of 5% under GST include skimmed milk powder, fish fillet, frozen vegetables, coffee, coal, fertilisers, tea, spices, pizza bread, kerosene, ayurvedic medicines, agarbatti, sliced dry mango, insulin, cashew nuts, unbranded namkeen, lifeboats, Ethanol (solid biofuel pellets), handmade carpets and other handmade textile floor coverings (including namda/gabba), hand-made braids and ornamental trimming in the piece.

Contd.

	Services	Small restaurants along with transport services like railways and airways, standalone AC non-AC restaurants and those which serve liquor, takeaway food, restaurants in hotels with a room tariff less than Rs. 7500 (no input credit for these restaurants), will come under this category. Special flights for pilgrims (Economy Class) come under 5%.
GST Tax Slab of 12%	Goods	Items coming under the tax slab of 12% include frozen meat products, butter, cheese, ghee, pickles, sausage, fruit juices, namkeen, tooth powder, medicine, umbrella, instant food mix, cell phones, sewing machine, man-made yarn, handbags including pouches and purses; jewellery box, wooden frames for painting, photographs, mirrors, etc, ornamental framed mirrors, brass kerosene pressure stove, art ware of iron, etc.
	Services	Business-class air tickets will attract a tax of 12% under GST. The slab also includes movie tickets priced under Rs. 100.
GST Tax Slab of 18%	Goods	As mentioned above, most of the items are part of this tax slab. Some of the items are flavored refined sugar, cornflakes, pasta, pastries and cakes, detergents, washing and cleaning preparations, safety glass, mirror, glassware, sheets, pumps, compressors, fans, light fitting, chocolate, preserved vegetables, tractors, ice cream, sauces, soups, mineral water, deodorants, suitcase, brief case, vanity case, oil powder, chewing gum, hair shampoo, preparation for facial make-up, shaving and after-shave items, washing powder, refrigerators, water heaters, washing machines, televisions (up to 68 cm), vacuum cleaners, paints, hair shavers, hair curlers, hair dryers, scent sprays, lithium-ion batteries, detergent, stones used in flooring, marble & granite, sanitaryware, leather clothing, wristwatches, cookers, stoves, cutlery, telescope, goggles, binoculars, oil powder, cocoa butter, fat, artificial fruits, artificial flowers, follage, physical exercise equipment, musical instruments and their parts, stationery items like clips, some diesel engine parts, some parts of pumps, electrical boards, panels, wires, razor and razor blades, furniture, mattress, cartridges, multi-functional printers, door, windows, aluminium frames, monitors and television screens, tyres, power banks for lithium-ion batteries, video games, carriage accessories for disabled, etc.
	Services	Restaurants located inside hotels with tariffs of INR 7500 and above, outdoor catering (input tax credit to be available), movie tickets priced above Rs. 100, actual bill

		of hotel stay below Rs. 7500, IT and Telecom services and financial services along with branded garments will be part of this tax slab.
GST Tax Slab of 28%	Goods	Over 200 goods will be taxes at a rate of 28%. The goods which will be part of this category under GST are sunscreen, pan masala, dish washer, weighing machine, paint, cement, vacuum cleaner. Other items include automobiles, hair clippers, and motorcycles.
	Services	As mentioned above, five-star hotels, whose actual bill of a hotel stay above Rs. 7500, movie tickets, betting on casinos and racing will come under this category.

28.8. GOODS AND SERVICES TAX NETWORK (GSTN)

Goods and Services Tax Network (GSTN) is a registered non-profit non-government private limited company under Section 25 of the Companies Act, 1956 and 2013. Technology has been the mainstay for GST in India. GST being a destination-based tax, the inter-state trade of goods and services (IGST) is expected to provide a robust settlement mechanism between the centre and the states. This is possible only in the presence of a strong IT infrastructure and service backbone which enables capture, processing and exchange of information amongst the stakeholders (including taxpayers, states and central governments, accounting offices, banks and RBI). To serve the purpose, the Goods and Services Tax Network (GSTN) was introduced on March 28, 2013, in India. GST Network is a 100 per cent government-owned company from September 26, 2018.

28.8.1. Functions of the GSTN

GSTN was assigned the functions related to the creation of common and shared IT infrastructure for taxpayers. The following are the detailed functions of GSTN:

1. Facilitating registration and filing of returns.
2. Forwarding the returns to central and state authorities.
3. Computation and settlement of IGST.
4. Matching of tax payment details with banking network.
5. Providing various MIS reports to the central and the state governments based on the taxpayer return information.
6. Providing analysis of taxpayers' profile.
7. Running the matching engine for matching, reversal and reclaim of the input tax credit.

All statutory functions of the tax officials under GST remain unchanged like approval of registration, assessment, audit, appeal, enforcement, MIS/

reports, etc., will remain with the respective tax departments. The GSTN will integrate the common GST portal with the existing tax administration IT systems and also build interfaces for taxpayers. Further, the GSTN develops back-end modules like assessment, audit, refund, appeal, etc., for 19 states and UTs (Model-II States). The CBEC and Model-I States (15 states) will themselves develop their GST back-end systems. Integration of GST front-end system with back-end systems will be completed and tested well in advance for a smooth transition.

28.9. COMPOSITION SCHEME

Composition scheme has been formulated for small businessmen being the supplier of goods and services. The objective of the scheme is to ensure simplicity and reduce compliance cost for the small taxpayers. Under the scheme, a person with turnover up to Rs. 1.5 crore (Rs. 75 lakh in states of Arunachal Pradesh, Manipur, Meghalaya, Mizoram, Nagaland, Sikkim, Tripura and Uttarakhand) needs to pay a tax equal to 1% to 5% on the turnover and needs to file the returns annually with quarterly payment from the financial year 2019-20 onwards.

Composition scheme has also been formulated for the supplier of services, i.e., the persons/enterprises not eligible under the current composition scheme. Under the scheme, a person with turnover up to Rs. 50 lakh need to pay a tax equal to 6% on the turnover and shall file returns annually with quarterly payment from the financial year 2019-20 onwards. The aggregate turnover refers to the sum of taxable supplies, exempt supplies, zero-rated supplies, and inter-state supplies. The Reverse Charge Mechanism (RCM) supplies are not included in this scheme, as these would be added to the turnover of the unregistered supplier. In the reverse charge mechanism, the liability to pay tax is on the recipient of supply of goods or services instead of the supplier of such goods or services in respect of notified categories of supply.

28.9.1. Conditions and Restrictions of Composition Scheme

1. The supplier who opts for composition levy cannot raise tax invoice. The composition levy is an alternative method of charging of tax designed for small taxpayers whose turnover is up to Rs. 75 lakhs (Rs. 50 lakhs in case of few states). Therefore, they need not collect any tax on supply.
2. The recipient of such supplies cannot claim any input-tax credit (ITC) on supplies from such suppliers who have opted for composition levy.

3. Similarly, even they cannot claim any ITC (input-tax credit) on the inward taxable supplies.
4. A person opting for the scheme shall mention on the invoices issued that he has opted for such a scheme.
5. A person shall also mention composition taxable person on every notice board displayed at the place of business.
6. The following cannot opt for composition levy:
   - Supplier of services (except food & restaurant services)
   - Supplier of exempt goods
   - Supplier of inter-state supplies
   - E-commerce operators
   - Manufacturers of ice cream, pan masala and tobacco

The tax rate prescribed for different categories of registered persons under the scheme is shown in Table 28.6.

Table 28.6. Tax rates under composition scheme

Sl. No.	Registered person	CGST rate	SGST rate	Total tax
1.	Manufacturers (other than manufacturers of goods as may be notified by the Government)	0.50%	0.50%	1%
2.	Restaurant services, i.e., suppliers of food/ drink for human consumption (other than alcoholic liquor for human consumption)	2.50%	2.50%	5%
3.	Traders or any other supplier eligible for composition levy	0.50%	0.50%	1%

The GST under composition scheme is not collected from the customers. It is the facility for hassle-free compliance. The composition levy is applicable under one PAN (permanent account number), and for all businesses under that PAN or none. This implies, that it is not allowed for some businesses under normal levy and some under composition levy. Once the turnover reaches the threshold of Rs. 1.5 crore, the composition levy is transformed into the normal levy. There is no hassle of maintaining accounts and compliances under GST. A simple quarterly return is to be filed under this scheme.

For example, a trader having a revenue of Rs. 55,00,000 inclusive of GST at 5% has purchases amounting to Rs. 42,00,000 (GST at 5% extra). Book-keeping and GST compliance costs are Rs. 2,00,000 and other administrative costs are Rs. 60,000. The trader now wants to switch to composition levy. The comparison between the normal levy and composition levy is shown in Table 28.7.

Table 28.7. Tax under normal levy and composition levy

Normal levy		**Composition levy**	
Revenue	55,00,000	Revenue	55,00,000
Less: GST	2,61,905	Less: GST	Nil
Net revenue	52,38,095	Net Revenue	55,00,000
Less: Purchases	42,00,000	Less: Purchases	44,10,000
Bookkeeping	2,00,000	Bookkeeping	1,00,000
Other costs	60,000	Other costs	60,000
		GST Liability	55,000
Profit	**7,78,095**	**Profit**	**9,30,000**
Payable	2,61,905	**GST Liability**	**55,000**
ITC	2,00,000	(1% of Turnover)	
GST liability	**61,905**		
Cash flow	7,16,190	Cash flow	9,30,000

Calculation Notes:

1. When a trader opts for composition levy, the GST liability will not exist. The trader can charge the full amount which was charged inclusive of GST earlier.
2. For normal levy, the GST included in sales is 55,00,000 × 5/105
3. The ITC is available in case of normal levy and not for composition levy. Hence, the taxes (input) are a part of purchase costs and the output is @ 1% of the turnover in case of composition levy.

Since the book-keeping costs are substantially lower in case of composition levy, the profits and cash flows are higher and hence, the trader should be advised to switch to Composition Levy.

28.10. EXEMPTIONS UNDER GOODS & SERVICES TAX

Governments offer exemptions which are based on goods and services consumed by low-income people, people living in disadvantaged regions and so on. Central government has the power to grant an exemption on goods and/or services in the public interest generally or by special order. A general exemption is granted by notification and is available to all persons. It may be absolute or conditional. Such exemption may be total or partial.

An ad-hoc exemption shall be granted to persons under certain exceptional situations through a special order communicating to the party seeking exemption. For example, charitable trusts, educational institutions, scientific, research, defense, etc. Central government has the power to interpret by an explanation the provisions of the notification or order at a later date but within one year which has retrospective effect.

Exempt supply has been defined as the supply of any goods/services/ both, which attract a NIL rate of tax, or which may be wholly exempt from tax, and therefore, includes non-taxable supplies. Essential goods/services have been exempted. These are unbranded atta/besan/maida, milk, eggs, curd, fresh vegetables, healthcare, education, services by the government (except post office, transport of goods/passengers, etc.), services by RBI, services by ESIC/EPFO, and services by IRDA and SEBI.

28.11. BENEFITS OF GST

The overall benefits of GST are:

1. Implementation of One Nation One Tax.
2. Dropping of multiple indirect taxes such as VAT, CST, Service tax, CAD, SAD, and Excise.
3. Removal of cascading effect of taxes, i.e., removes tax on tax.
4. Enhanced ease of doing business.
5. Reduction in the cost of production will lead to an increase in demand and an increase in supply.
6. GST will boost exports and manufacturing activity, generate employment and will lead to economic growth.

The benefits of GST with reference to different sectors are:

1. Benefits to Central Government

(a) A unified common national market can be created, giving a boost to foreign investment and Make in India campaign.

(b) The cascading effect of taxes can be mitigated as input tax credit is available across goods and services in all stages of supply.

(c) Laws, procedures and rates of tax between the centre and states and across states can be harmonised.

(d) Environment for compliance can be improved as all returns are to be filed online, input credits verified online, encouraging more paper trail of transactions at all levels of the supply chain.

(e) Uniform SGST and IGST rates will reduce the incentive for tax evasion.

(f) Greater certainty to the taxation system due to common procedures for registration of taxpayers, a refund of taxes, uniform formats of tax return, common tax base, a common system of classification of goods and services.

(g) Greater use of IT will reduce human interface between the taxpayer and the tax administration, and help in reducing corruption.

2. Benefits to State Governments

(a) Expansion of the tax base as they will be able to tax the entire supply chain from manufacturing to retail.
(b) Authority to tax services, which will boost state revenues.
(c) GST will favour consuming states as it is a destination-based consumption tax.
(d) Improve the overall investment climate in the states.
(e) Uniform tax rates will reduce the incentive for tax evasion.
(f) Higher compliance levels of the taxpayers will contribute to increased revenue collection of the states.

3. Benefits to Trade and Industry

(a) Simpler tax regime with fewer exemptions.
(b) Increased ease of doing business.
(c) Reduction in multiplicity of taxes.
(d) Elimination of double taxation on certain sectors like works contract, software, hospitality sector.
(e) No cascading of taxes.
(f) Reduction in compliance costs.
(g) More efficient neutralization of taxes especially for exports.
(h) Simplified and automated procedures for various processes such as registration, returns, refunds, tax payments, etc.
(i) The average tax burden on the supply of goods/services is likely to decline.

4. Benefits for Common Consumers

(a) Simpler tax system.
(b) Reduction in prices of goods and services due to the elimination of cascading.
(c) Uniform prices throughout the country.
(d) Transparent taxation system.
(e) No cascading effects.
(f) Reduced burden of tax on goods.
(g) Transparent final price of goods.
(h) Reduction in prices of commodities and goods in the long run.

5. Benefits to Entrepreneurs

(a) The units having aggregate annual turnover of more than Rs. 20 lakh (Rs. 10 lakh in certain cases) in case of a supplier of services and Rs. 40 lakh (Rs. 20 lakh in certain cases) in case of a supplier of goods have to be registered under GST.

(b) Single registration under GST in one state.
(c) An additional benefit under composition scheme.
(d) Seamless national market access across the country.

6. Benefits to the Exporters

(a) Reduction in the cost of locally manufactured goods and services.
(b) Boost to Indian exports due to reducing the compliance cost.

7. Promote Make in India

(a) Help to create a unified common national market for India, giving a boost to foreign investment and Make in India initiative.
(b) Prevent cascading of taxes and make products cheaper, thus, boosting aggregate demand.
(c) Harmonisation of laws, procedures and rates of tax will boost export and manufacturing activity, generate more employment and thus increase GDP with gainful employment leading to substantive economic growth.
(d) Help in poverty eradication by generating more employment and more financial resources.
(e) More efficient neutralisation of taxes especially for exports.
(f) It will also improve the overall investment climate in the country which will naturally benefit the development in the states. Uniform CGST & SGST and IGST rates will reduce the incentive for evasion by eliminating rate arbitrage between neighbouring states and that between intra-state and inter-state supplies.
(g) The average tax burden on companies is likely to come down.

8. Ease of Doing Business

(a) Simpler tax regime with fewer exemptions along with a reduction in multiplicity of taxes will lead to simplification and uniformity.
(b) Reduction in compliance costs and therefore, lesser investment of resources and manpower in maintaining records.
(c) Simplified and automated procedures for various processes such as registration, returns, refunds, tax payments.
(d) Common GSTN portal facilitates the less public interface between the taxpayer and the tax administration.
(e) Improve the environment of compliance as all returns to be filed online, input credits to be verified online, encouraging more paper trail of transactions.
(f) Common procedures for registration of taxpayers, a refund of taxes, uniform formats of tax return, common tax base, a common system of classification of goods and services will lend greater certainty to the taxation system.

28.12. IMPLEMENTATION OF GST

The Union and State governments have taken appropriate measures for the implementation of GST across the country. The GST revenue for the financial years from July 2017 to March 2020. The increase in GST revenue is a clear indication of the success of the implementation of this tax regime. The GST revenue was Rs. 7.40 lakh crore in 2017-18. It was Rs. 11.77 lakh crore in the following financial year. In 2019-2020 the GST revenue has gone up to Rs. 12.11 lakh crore (Figure 28.2). The problems between the centre and states are amicably resolved. The GST is becoming stronger year by year and the tax on various items are modified as per the demands of the business environment.

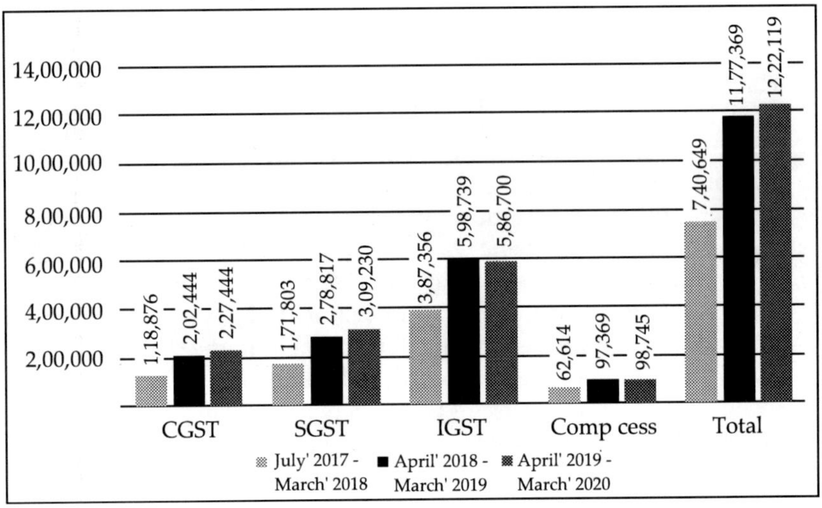

Source: https://www.gstn.org.in/

Figure 28.2. Trends in GST collection in Rs. crore (FY 2017-2020)

28.13. SUMMARY

- Goods and services tax (GST) refers to the tax on supply of goods or services, or both, except taxes on supply of alcoholic liquor for human consumption.
- The GST paid on the procurement of goods and services can be set off against the tax payable on the supply of goods or services.
- Value Added Tax (VAT) is an indirect tax expressed as a percentage of the total cost. It is paid at each sale point.
- GST is a destination-based consumption tax offering a comprehensive and continuous chain of the tax credit. It brings a uniform tax structure all over India and eliminates the cascading effect of the tax.

- The cascading effect occurs due to the reason that a product is taxed at every stage of production and distribution until it is finally sold to the consumer.
- There are several variations in the application process of GST along with the different interpretation of the same concepts, various approaches to time of supply and its interaction with the place of supply, different classifications of services and intangibles, and inconsistent treatment of mixed supplies, around the world.
- India has introduced the dual GST model due to its unique federal nature.
- Under the GST model, tax is levied concurrently on a common base, i.e., supply of goods or services or both by the Centre as well as the States.
- GST levied by the Centre is called Central GST (Central tax /CGST). The GST levied by the States is called State GST (State Tax /SGST).
- The GST (State Tax / SGST) levied by Union Territories without legislature is called UTGST (Union territory tax). CGST & SGST / UTGST shall be levied on all taxable intra-state supplies.
- The GST levied for inter-state supplies is called IGST. IGST is a tax levied on all inter-state supplies of goods and/or services.
- As per the IGST model, the Centre will levy IGST (Integrated Goods and Service Tax) which is CGST plus SGST on all inter-state supply of goods or services or both.
- Supply is the point of taxation or the taxable event under Goods & Services Tax.
- Composite supply refers to the supply made by a taxable person to a recipient consisting of two or more taxable supplies of goods/services/ both or any combination thereof, which are bundled and supplied in conjunction with each other in the ordinary course of business, one of which is a principal supply.
- Mixed supply means two or more individual supplies of goods/services, or any combination thereof, made in conjunction with each other by a taxable person for a single price where such supply does not constitute a composite supply.
- Goods & Services Tax Council is a constitutional body for making recommendations to the Union and State Government on issues related to Goods and Service Tax.
- The GST Council is expected to make recommendations to the Union and the States on key issues related to GST, like the goods and services that may be subjected or exempted from GST, model GST laws, principles that govern the place of supply, threshold limits, GST rates including the floor rates with bands, special rates for raising additional resources during natural calamities/disasters, special provisions for certain states, etc.

- The tax rates on goods are broadly 0.25%, 3%, 5%, 12%, 18% and 28% and that is split into CGST and SGST equally for intra-state sales and fully leviable as IGST for inter-state sale.
- The tax rates on services are broadly 5%, 12%, 18% and 28% and that is split into CGST and SGST equally for intra-state sales and fully leviable as IGST for inter-state sale.
- Goods and Services Tax Network (GSTN) is a registered non-profit non-government private limited company under Section 25 of the Companies Act, 1956 and 2013.
- GSTN is assigned the functions related to the creation of common and shared IT infrastructure for taxpayers.
- Composition scheme has been formulated for small businessmen being the supplier of goods and services. The objective of the scheme is to ensure simplicity and reduce compliance cost for the small taxpayers.
- In the reverse charge mechanism, the liability to pay tax is on the recipient of supply of goods or services instead of the supplier of such goods or services in respect of notified categories of supply.
- Governments offer exemptions which are based on goods and services consumed by low-income people, people living in disadvantaged regions and so on.
- An ad-hoc exemption shall be granted to persons under certain exceptional situations through a special order communicating to the party seeking exemption.

SHORT ANSWER QUESTIONS

1. Define GST.
2. Write a short note on VAT.
3. What is cascading effect?
4. What are the benefits of GST?
5. What are the taxes subsumed under GST?
6. What are the advantages of IGST model?
7. Describe the concept of supply.
8. Which activities are not to be treated as supply?
9. What are the exemptions under GST?

ESSAY ANSWER QUESTIONS

1. Explain the concept of GST and cascading effect with an illustration.
2. Describe the ideology of adopting dual GST model in India.
3. Explain the integrated goods and services tax model and the decision to taken while raising invoices.
4. Describe the concept of supply. Explain the activities to be treated as supply of goods and services.

5. Explain the composite supply and mixed supply with illustrations.
6. Discuss the role of GST council in making recommendations to the Union and the States.
7. Explain the benefits of GST with reference to different sectors.
8. Discuss the various GST slab rates applicable in India.
9. What is a GSTN? Discuss the functions of GST network.
10. What is composition scheme? Explain the conditions and restrictions of composition scheme.

FILL IN THE BLANKS

1. At each stage of the supply chain, the tax is collected on _____.
2. Cascading tax effect is also known as _____.
3. The tax levied on all inter-state supplies of goods and/or services is called _____.
4. The tax reduced from the output tax payable on account of sales is known as _____.
5. The GST council consists of _____ members.
6. A registered non-profit non-government private limited company is called _____.

Answers:

1. Value-added
2. Tax on tax
3. IGST
4. Input-tax credit
5. 33
6. GSTN

MULTIPLE-CHOICE QUESTIONS

1. The basis for GST to levy consumption based tax is:
   (A) Incremental principle (B) Destination principle
   (C) Consumption principle (D) Compliance principle
2. VAT was introduced as indirect tax into the Indian taxation system in:
   (A) 2005 (B) 2004
   (C) 2006 (D) 2007
3. The tax paid by the buyer on the purchase of goods or services is called:
   (A) Input-tax debit (B) Income-tax credit
   (C) Inter-state credit (D) Input-tax credit

Answers:

1. B 2. A 3. D

REFERENCES

1. GSTN Act. Retrieved from https://www.gstn.org.in/gst
2. Overview of GST. Retrieved from https://economictimes.indiatimes.com/overview-of-goods-and-services-tax-gst/articleshow/58574706.cms? utm_source=contentofinterest&utm_medium=text&utm_campaign=cppst

3. GST Council Meetings. Retrieved from http://www.gstcouncil.gov.in/meetings
4. GST Council. Retrieved from http://www.gstcouncil.gov.in/gst-council
5. GST-An update. Retrieved from http://gstcouncil.gov.in/sites/default/files/GST-an_update_030819.pdf
6. The Gazette of India. http://gstcouncil.gov.in/sites/default/files/CGST.pdf
7. Central Goods and Services Tax (CGST) Rules, 2017. https://www.cbic.gov.in/resources//htdocs-cbec/gst/CGST_10092018.pdf
8. The CGST Act, 2017. http://legislative.gov.in/actsofparliamentfromtheyear/central-goods-and-services-tax-act-2017
9. GST 3 Years of Commitment. A Statistical Report on Completion of 3 years of GST. Retrieved from https://www.gstn.org.in/assets/mainDashboard/Pdf/3YearReport.pdf
10. Jaiswal, S. (2017). *Removing Cascading Effect of Taxes.* Retrieved from https://www.cbgaindia.org/wp-content/ uploads/ 2017/ 08/ Removing-Cascading-Effect-of-Taxes-GST.pdf

Chapter

29 Demonetisation

LEARNING OBJECTIVES

After studying this chapter, you should be able to understand:

- concept and features of demonetisation;
- motives of the third demonetisation in India;
- reasons for demonetisation and its impact on Indian economy;
- sector-wise impact of demonetisation and its criticisms; and
- impact of demonetisation on GDP and digitisation.

29.1. INTRODUCTION

Demonetisation is one of the strategies to control the monetary system in an economy. The objective of demonetisation can be curbing corruption, fake currency, illegal activities and making cashless economy. It is an act of withdrawing a currency unit of its status as legal tender. As a result of demonetisation, there will be a change in national currency. The current form or forms of money is pulled from circulation and retired, often to be replaced with new notes or coins. This strategy is used only in special situations as this decision creates a lot of disturbance in money transactions and create problems for the population. The government has to plan carefully the remedies to resolve the problems that arise due to demonetisation and take measures to strengthen the financial system of the economy.

29.2. FEATURES OF DEMONETISATION

1. Demonetisation is considered the most powerful tax administration measure. People with black money have to necessarily declare their unaccounted wealth and pay taxes at a penalty.
2. It indicates the government's firm resolve that tax evasion will no longer be tolerated or accepted.
3. It leads to channelising savings into the formal financial system. Though much of the cash that has been deposited in the banking system is bound to be withdrawn some of the new deposit schemes offered by the banks will continue to provide a base loan, at lower interest rates.
4. Demonetisation helps in promoting digital transactions facilitating transparency and control in the financial system. Further, it helps in improving tax compliance.

There are arguments against the promotion of digital transactions as it requires the use of smart phones for customers and point of sale (PoS) machines for merchants, which depend on internet connectivity. On the contrary, these disadvantages are counter-balanced by the argument that it helps people into the formal economy, thereby increasing financial saving and reducing tax evasion.

29.3. DEMONETISATION IN INDIA

Demonetisation as a measure of monetary reform was used on different occasions in India in varied forms. The currency ban was first introduced in 1946. The currency notes of Rs. 1000 and Rs. 10,000 which were introduced in 1934 and 1938 respectively, were removed from circulation. The ban did not impact the common man seriously due to non-accessibility of currency of such higher denomination. However, the government reintroduced the notes in 1954 along with a new Rs. 5000 note. The second ban on currency came in 1978. The currency notes of Rs. 1000, Rs. 5000 and Rs. 10,000 were made out of circulation. The sole aim of the ban was to curb black money generation in the country (Pimputkar, 2016).

The third ban on currency was introduced in 2016. The Government of India announced demonetisation of all Rs. 500 and Rs. 1000 bank notes of the Mahatma Gandhi series. The issuance of new Rs. 500 and Rs. 2,000 banknotes in exchange for the demonetised bank notes was also initiated. This initiative impacted the common man seriously as it led to eighty-six per cent of the money in circulation invalid. Almost the entire population of India were forced to deposit the invalid currency in the banks. The banks could not respond to the demands, and therefore, restrictions were placed on cash withdrawals and the convertibility of domestic money and bank deposits.

29.4. MOTIVES OF THE THIRD DEMONETISATION

Demonetisation has both positive and negative effects. Many people argue that demonetisation alone cannot fight the parallel economy and eliminate black money. Several other measures are required to change the economy for good (Munimji, 2017). The following are the motives for demonetisation:

1. Demonetisation would facilitate the government to seize the accumulated wealth due to undeclared income in the economy and thereby eliminate the black economy.
2. This is a decisive blow against corruption.
3. Elimination of counterfeit currency in the economy.

4. Pushing India toward a modern digitised economy by creating an environment wherein people are compelled for digital payments. The growth in digitised payments would convert a larger part of the informal Indian economy into the organised and formal sector.
5. By forcing people to convert their old cash into the new currency through the banking system, unaccounted money can be brought into the formal tax network and generate greater digital footprints to track individuals and business units.

After an extended counting process, the Reserve Bank of India announced that over 99 per cent of the demonetised currency had been returned to it through the commercial banks. It is to be noted that within a year of demonetisation, currency in circulation in the economy was also back to its pre-demonetisation level.

29.5. REASONS FOR DEMONETISATION

The main reason for the demonetisation are:

1. Eradication of black money
2. Removal of fake currency
3. Promotion of online transactions
4. Contribute to the growth of GDP

1. **Eradication of black money:** Demonetisation was described as a bold and revolutionary action of the government of India to curb black money and eliminate the parallel economy in the country. Persons with black money can be identified with this move. Some business enterprises like property dealers, jewellers, foreign currency dealers, private moneylenders generally hold huge amounts of unaccounted money in form of currency notes which creates a parallel economy in the country. The illegal currency has reached the bank accounts through direct or indirect channels.
2. **Removal of fake currency:** Fake currency notes have been rooted out from the economy with the demonetisation. Withdrawing highest currency notes out of them will have a serious impact on the fake currency syndicates, thus, putting an end to the terror funding in Jammu and Kashmir, Naxalite hit states and north-eastern states. Demonetisation was like a surgical attack on a fake currency circulation and it has converted fake currency notes into mere pieces of paper.
3. **Promotion of online transactions:** One of the significant motives of demonetisation was to promote cashless/digital economy. More and more cash-less or less-cash transactions will lead to more disclosure of income which will increase the direct tax collections. Electronic

mode of payment like online transaction, payment through e-applications, e-wallets, e-banking, usage of debit and credit cards, etc., can be encouraged to have more transparent transactions.

4. **Contribute to the growth of GDP:** Though demonetisation may negatively impact certain sectors like real estate and property, construction, and household consumption in the short run, it is believed that long-term benefits for GDP growth will outweigh the short-term transitional impact.

29.6. IMPACT OF DEMONETISATION ON INDIAN ECONOMY

There are both positive as well as negative impacts of demonetisation on the Indian economy.

The positive impact of demonetisation:

1. **Elimination of black money:** Demonetisation on a single stroke choked the black money. Out of the total currency of Rs. 17 lakh crore, Rs. 3 lakh crore was estimated as black money. The demonetisation decision resulted in the collection of huge deposits with the bank. All unaccounted money has either been deposited into the banks with the heavy penalty or been simply destroyed.
2. **Strengthening the economy:** Demonetisation has proved to be a turning point for the economy as it cleaned up the black money and brought more borrowings to the treasury. Investment opportunities have also been revived and gave a boost to infrastructure and the manufacturing sector. A huge amount of money deposited in banks, which in turn, helped to reduce interest rates and lower income tax rate.
3. **Control on hawala transactions:** Demonetisation was a big thrash to the hawala racketeers. In hawala money is transferred without its actual movement. Hawala had become the route to facilitate money laundering and terror funding. Hawala rackets run on black money. The withdrawal of black money from the economy was like a surgical strike to hawala operations.
4. **Purging of counterfeit currency:** One of the objectives of demonetisation was to eliminate counterfeit Indian currency. Indian Statistical Institute (ISI) reported that at any given point of time fake currency notes amounting to Rs. 400 crore were in circulation in the economy and around Rs. 70 crore fake currency notes are pushed into the country every year. But the real number could be much

larger. With demonetisation decision to ban old currency notes of Rs. 500 and Rs. 1000 notes and replacing them with new ones sucked the circulation of fake currency. As new currency notes have come with highly advanced security features which are barely possible to replicate.

5. **Terror financing:** The main sources of terror financing are counterfeit currency and hawala. Fake currency is circulated by the network of hawala operators. These hawala operators have a link with gamblers and smugglers of arms and drugs. Indirectly, they all end up financing terrorism. Besides, the terrorists obtain huge money by donations routing such as money through hawala transactions. The government claimed that all channels of terror financing are closed with the control in the circulation of counterfeit currency and hawala operators.
6. **Attack on Maoism:** Maoist sympathisers have declared demonetisation as an undeclared financial emergency. The currency ban proved to be a serious attack on the Maoists movement. Black money is considered the major source of fund for Maoists. Maoists raise crores of rupees through extortion. Such unaccounted money is used to purchase arms and ammunition.

The negative impact of demonetisation:

1. **Liquidity crisis**: People of India particularly lower and middle-income groups faced liquidity problem as it became difficult to get a sufficient amount of cash to fulfil their basic needs. These sections mainly depend on cash to meet their daily needs. The total circulation of Rs. 500 rupee notes constituted nearly 49 per cent of the currency in terms of value.
2. **Loss of well-being:** The lower-middle- and lower-class population earn income from the occupations such as daily wage labourers, small traders, and low income-generating resources. These sections lost their income due to the scarcity of cash for a long time. Cash crunch made firms to cut their labour cost and thus reduce the income of the lower middle class.
3. **Consumption:** Cash shortage adversely affected the consumption behaviour of the people. The consumers became cautious in spending and tried to limit their cash transactions to essentials. As the digital mode of transactions is limited to a few sellers and most of the consumer segments particularly lower and middle-income segments are not familiar with digital transactions, sales of small retailers affected significantly.

4. **A decrease in GDP:** Withdrawal of the highest currency notes reduces the growth rate of the economy. Demonetisation reduced consumption pattern, income, investment, etc. This resulted in the slowdown of the economic growth rate.
5. **Interest rate and bank deposits:** Deposits in banks increased in short term due to demonetisation. However, in the long run, people plan investments and the money will flow out of the banks again. As these are not voluntary savings aimed to get interest, they will be withdrawn by the savers as soon as the supply of new currency takes place. This indicates that new savings are only for short-term which may be encashed at the appropriate time in future. It may not be said that demonetisation will generate big savings in the banking system in long term, this may reduce interest rates in short but not in the long term.
6. **Unaccounted money:** One of the main reasons behind demonetisation was to curb unaccounted money but only a small portion of the unaccounted money is stored in the form of cash. Most of the unaccounted money is kept in the form of land, gold and buildings, etc. Hence, the amount of unaccounted money deposited with the banks is only up to the amount of cash deposited.

29.7. SECTOR-WISE IMPACT OF DEMONETISATION

1. **Real estate and property:** The real estate sector is one of the most affected sectors by the currency note ban. Demonetisation has finished the businesses of the majority of the builders as a major portion of their transaction depends on cash rather than banks transfer or cheque transactions. As like other sectors, marginal builders are adversely impacted due to the high involvement of cash component in payment in this sector.
2. **Gems & jewellery:** The substantial portion of the payment by customers involves cash for purchasing jewellery so the impact of demonetisation in this sector is quite high. Demonetisation made people with less cash available in their hands for fulfilling their daily needs let alone purchasing jewellery. Smaller retailers in the unorganised sector were the most to be impacted which reduced the demand for jewellery. Many jewellers started selling gold at more than their market price to take advantage of banned notes which resulted in income tax raids on such jewellers. Notices were issued to many jewellers. This sector is seriously hit by demonetisation as buyers prefer to pay in cash.

3. **Banks:** Banks have proved to be the backbone of this entire process of demonetisation and also the biggest beneficiaries. As on the direction of the government, old notes have to be exchanged with the new ones, this resulted in the increased liquidity position of banks which could be utilised for lending. Both deposit and lending rates have been cut by many banks.
4. **Media and entertainment industry:** Currency ban adversely impacted the media and entertainment industry as it resulted in lesser number of viewers. The major portion of the drop was seen in the lower middle class. The sudden decision of demonetisation affected the film industry as well. This brought the production of films to a halt. Also, the new and small players in the industry were most affected by demonetisation.
5. **Hospitality and tourism:** Due to demonetisation, Indian tourism industry was severely impacted as the majority of spending is in cash. Most of the luxury foreign trips sponsored by black money came to a halt. Due to the cash crunch, local tourism was also affected. The unorganised sector was the most impacted with the inability to make payment in cash.
6. **Luxury items:** Demonetisation impacted this sector seriously. Majority of the people generally spend their unaccounted money on luxuries. After the note ban, luxury segments and allied business-like clothing, electronics, the luxury car faced a huge setback.
7. **Automobiles:** Demonetisation also affected the automobile industry. The major decline in demand was seen in two-wheelers business as compared to four-wheelers/luxury cars because buyers prefer to pay in cash for buying a two-wheeler. The used car industry is another segment affected by the demonetisation wherein a sudden decrease in sales has been reported by several dealers.
8. **Retail:** The cash crunch led to low consumer demand for many products. Since cash is the favourable mode of payment in buying daily needs, which in turn, result in the number of cash transactions. The impact of demonetisation on small and the unorganised traders is higher than on the organised sector.
9. **Agriculture:** In the agriculture sector, sales, distribution, marketing and transport and such other factors are dominantly cash-dependent. Demonetisation disrupted the supply chain and as a result, this sector has severely been impacted by huge wastage of perishables. The small farmers selling their products on daily basis to the wholesale centres, mandis and the consumers have also been impacted by demonetisation.

10. **Labour-intensive sectors:** To pay daily wage labourers, a huge amount of cash is required. Limitations on the withdrawal amount from the banks affected the weekly payments to contract personnel in mining, textile and leather industries.

29.8. CRITICISMS ON DEMONETISATION

There are two types of criticism against the demonetisation. One group of critics mostly from left parties criticised demonetisation highlighting its disastrous consequences for the peasants, petty producers, and labourers in general. The other group of critics including former Prime Minister Manmohan Singh highlighted its deleterious effect on the country's GDP growth rate.

The former criticism has not been unaware of, or silent about, its deleterious effect on growth as it is an attack on the petty production sector which is so important for an economy like ours cannot but affect its growth rate adversely. And the latter, it would be churlish to suggest, is unaware of, or unconcerned about, the sufferings of the working people under demonetisation. Nonetheless, there is a difference of focus and emphasis between the two, one highlighting the effects on people directly, and the other the effects on GDP growth, one focusing on the condition of the people, and the other on the size of the heap of things (Patnaik, 2018).

Former Reserve Bank of India (RBI) governor Raghuram Rajan stated the fact that, while the growth rate of the world economy was picking up, India's growth rate, being linked to it under the neo-liberal regime, should also have increased, had, on the contrary, slowed down. Further, attributed this fact to the effects of demonetisation and the introduction of the Goods and Services Tax. He suggested, like all neo-liberals, that his concern with the growth rate was derived from his concern about employment, and hence about the people, that India had to have a higher growth rate than 7 per cent per annum if it was to make a dent on its unemployment problem, but demonetisation and GST had brought down the growth rate below that figure (Lahiri, 2020).

Therefore, emphasising GDP growth, apparently for promoting the people's interest by creating larger employment opportunities, serves to de-legitimise all peoples' struggles, and to legitimise instead all sorts of concessions being offered to capital for undertaking investment. The profits of the capitalists are seen to arise because of the inherent properties of the means of production themselves, rather than from the appropriation of surplus value through using the labour power of the workers in the process of production. Exactly, in the same way, GDP nationalism, which attributes mysterious powers to things, provides an ideological justification for ordering society in a manner most favourable to the big bourgeoisie.

Further, the planning was very poor and disorganised. The Rs. 2000 note was being printed only two months before November 8, 2016. The Rs. 500 currency note which was more than 45 per cent of the total currency was printed a couple of weeks before the note ban. This highly belated printing of currency notes led to the massive cash crunch, which hit the economy very hard. Before demonetisation India was growing at 7.6 per cent of GDP. By January 2017, the IMF estimated that GDP growth had dropped to 6.6 per cent, within just two months.

The Government of India was very slow in remonetisation of the economy. It imported only 8000 metric tonnes of currency paper for the printing of currency notes in 2016. In 2017, it imported 27,500 metric tonnes for currency paper from eight foreign companies. Without adequate currency paper, there could be no printing of notes. So, further delay in remonetisation may have led to a greater loss of potential cash flows and hit the economy hard. It continues to be facing a severe cash crunch, which will further dampen possibilities of economic growth.

People in support of demonetisation argue that it is necessary to expose black money. However, it is estimated by economists that the black money in India constitutes only 5 to 7 per cent of the total cash in the economy. Black assets are found to be mostly in real estate, gold, jewellery, shares, etc. Further, a significant proportion of such assets is kept in tax havens like the Cayman Islands, Dubai, the Virgin Islands, Singapore, etc. It was argued that the note ban would hit corruption hard. That too has not happened. So, as numerous economists in India and abroad have pointed out there appears to be no causal link between high-end currency notes and corruption (Chenoy, 2017).

29.9. IMPACT OF DEMONETISATION ON GDP

While the move was initially hailed as courageous and transformative by some sections of the society, the mood rapidly gave ground to widespread concerns regarding:

1. the preparedness of the Reserve Bank of India (RBI) to manage the process of remonetising the economy;
2. the potential of demonetisation to achieve the stated goals; and
3. the costs of the move for the Indian economy.

With six years having passed since the enactment of the policy, the shreds of evidence suggest point to demonetisation having mostly failed to achieve its stated objectives. The goal of eradicating black wealth and corruption by demonetising currency was problematic from the start, given the widespread acknowledgement of the fact that undeclared income is seldom held for long periods in terms of cash. Moreover, demonetising currency, which attacks a stock, does little to impede the fresh creation of undeclared income, which is a flow problem. The second goal of destroying counterfeit currency also did not impact the economy given the very low-estimated counterfeit currency in circulation in India.

Figure 29.1 depicts the path of the tax/GDP ratio in India from 2005. The Figure 29.1 plots direct and indirect tax ratios separately. Direct taxes are primarily composed of personal income taxes and corporate taxes. Indirect taxes are comprised of sales taxes, customs duties, and excise duties. The vertical lines on the graphs mark the fiscal years in which demonetisation and the Goods and Services Tax were introduced. Demonetisation occurred in the fiscal year 2016-2017, while GST happened in the fiscal year 2017-2018.

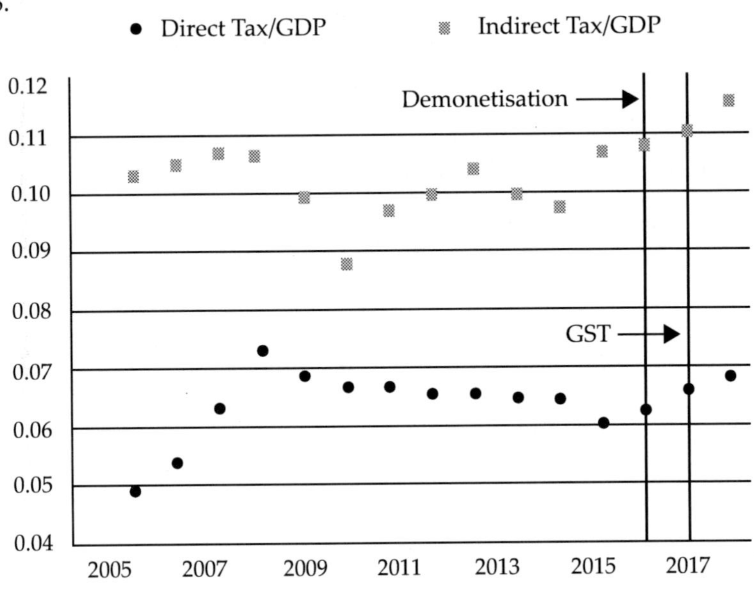

Source: Reserve bank of India & Central board of direct taxes (2019)

Figure 29.1. Demonetisation: Tax revenues & GDP

The direct taxes typically account for just about one-third of overall tax revenues in India. This is due to the very small number of individual and other non-corporate taxpayers in India (around 44 million in 2017, less than 10 per cent of the labour force). The abysmal state of direct taxes has been a long-running public finance concern in India. It partly reflects the low income of most of the workforce but is also indicative of extensive tax evasion. There does appear to be a mild increase in both the direct and indirect tax/GDP ratios in 2017 relative to 2016 (the fiscal year before demonetisation). However, the figure also shows that both the direct and indirect tax ratios in 2018 were not very different from their past trends.

Thus, the direct tax ratio in India has been stable between 6 and 7 per cent since 2010. Its levels in 2018 and 2019 were 6.7 and 6.9 per cent, respectively.

Interestingly, these levels for the direct tax ratio are below the levels it reached in 2008-2009. The indirect tax/GDP ratio has been on a gradually rising path except for declines in 2014 and 2015. Neither demonetisation nor Goods and Services Tax (GST) appear to have pushed the indirect tax/GDP ratio off its recent trend path. A conclusive assessment of the impact of demonetisation on tax revenues would require a few more years of data, as well as decoupling the effects of Goods and Services Tax from demonetisation.

Figure 29.2 shows the time paths of three different measures of money, i.e., M_0, M_1, and M_2. The units are in millions of rupees. M_0 measures the currency in circulation, plus deposits by bankers and others with the Reserve Bank of India. M_1 includes currency, demand deposits with the banking system, and other deposits with the RBI. M_2 adds savings deposits of post office savings banks to M_1. By the end of March 2017, both M_1 and M_2 were just 2.1 and 2.9 per cent below their October 2016 levels. In contrast, M_0 remained 15 per cent below its pre-demonetisation level. In January 2018, M_0 recovered to its pre-demonetisation level.

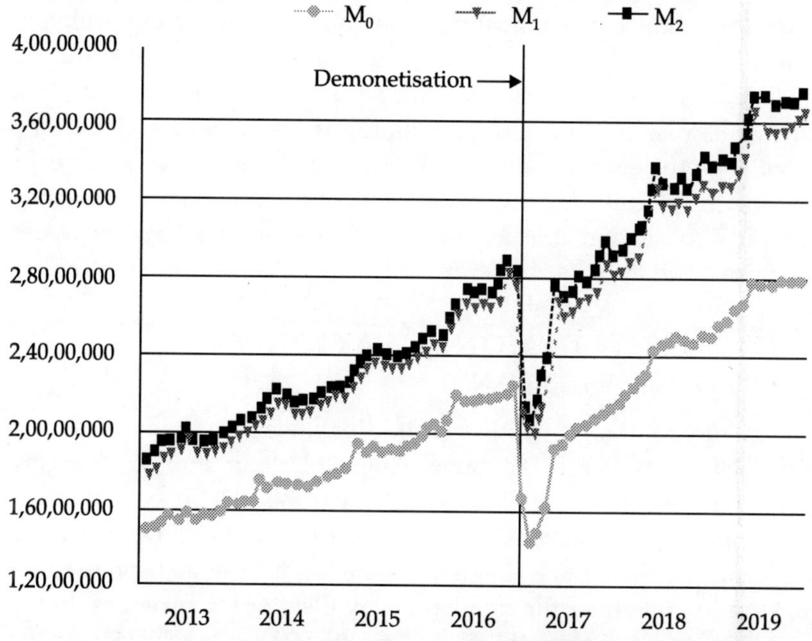

Source: Reserve Bank of India (2019)

Figure 29.2. Demonetisation: Money stocks

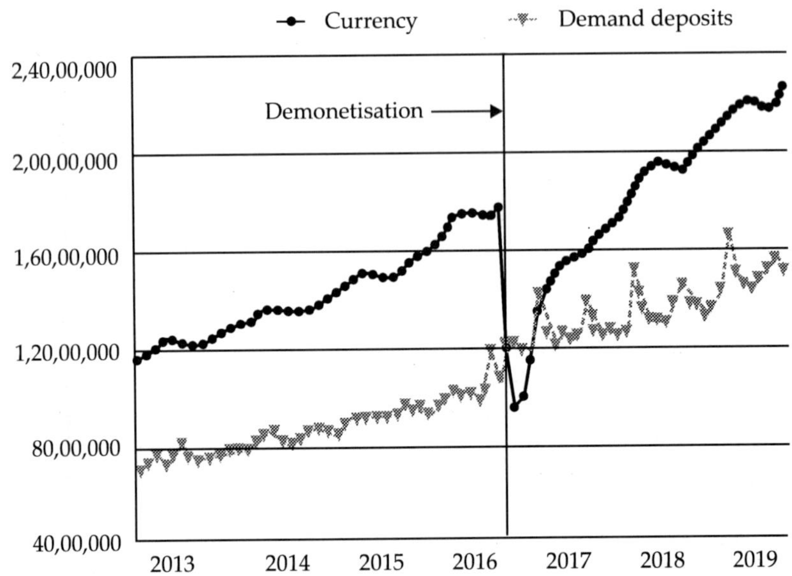

Source: Reserve Bank of India (2019)

Figure 29.3. Demonetisation: Cash and deposits

Figure 29.3 shows the contrasting behaviour of currency in circulation and bank deposits which comprise saving and checking deposits during the episode. Currency in circulation fell by around 8.4 trillion rupees while bank deposits rose by a meagre 1.5 trillion rupees between October (the last month before demonetisation) and December 31, 2016 (the last date for exchanging the old bills for new ones). Most of the demonetised currency was instead deposited in time deposits, which rose by over 4 trillion rupees during this period.

29.10. IMPACT OF DEMONETISATION ON DIGITISATION

An examination of the growth in digitised payments, in the tax base and tax revenues, suggests that the move achieved little in terms of changing the pre-demonetisation trends in these measures. Digitised payments were growing exponentially in India before 2016, and they have continued on the same nonlinear trend. There is no such systematic impact of demonetisation on either the number of tax filers or tax revenues. In the relatively short period since the demonetisation, these conclusions on the time trends in digital transactions and taxes should be viewed as tentative. On the cost side, there appears to be strong evidence that demonetisation reduced output and employment, especially in the informal sector. However, these losses were likely temporary rather than being permanent. In short, demonetisation appears to have failed the cost-benefit analysis of public policy initiatives, it had little success in achieving its stated goals while having imposed significant costs on the public.

Demonetisation has induced the public to switch out of cash transactions which influenced the rise in the velocity of money. The velocity of money is defined as the ratio of nominal GDP to the stock of money. It captures the speed with which money circulates in the economy to buy the flow of goods being produced. The estimated value of velocity depends on the measure of money that one uses. The narrower the measure of money, the larger the measured velocity will be. Here it is not in the level of velocity, but rather its movements around and after the time of demonetisation are considered.

Figure 29.4 shows the measured velocity for three different monetary aggregates ranging from the M_0, which is the narrowest to M_1 and M_2, which is the broadest.

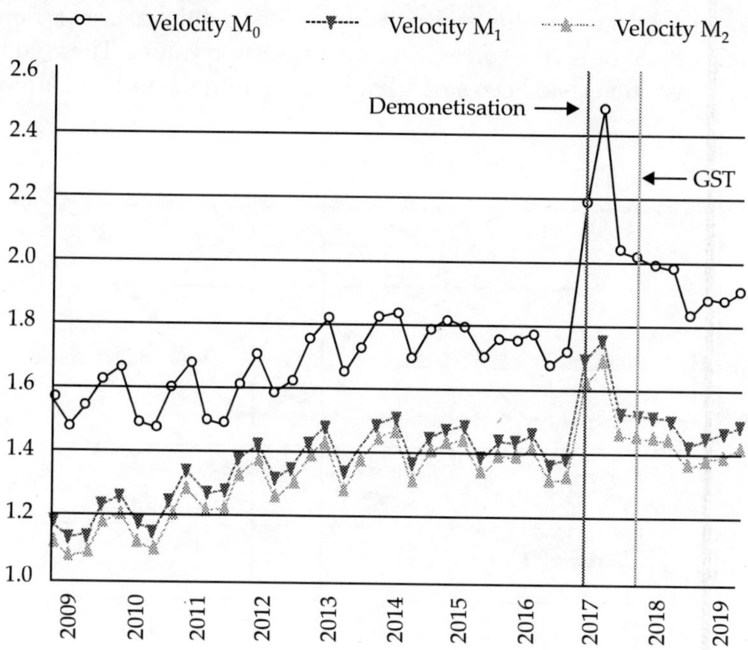

Source: Reserve Bank of India (2019)

Figure 29.4. Demonetisation and velocity of money

- First, the biggest increase in velocity around the demonetisation period was for M_0, which is the narrowest measure of money. The velocity of

M_1 rose as well but less than for M_0. Movements in the velocity of the broader measures of money were extremely muted by contrast; indeed, measures of velocity associated with broader measures of money than M_2 showed almost no change in response to demonetisation.

- Second, after three quarters, all the velocity measures returned to their near-term trend levels. It would appear that initially there was some substitution from cash into other payment methods for transactions in response to the monetary shock. Once things normalised, however, the public returned to their usual usage of cash for transactions purposes.

An alternative approach to measuring the effect of demonetisation on digitisation is to examine directly the time paths of digital transactions in the economy. The effect of demonetisation on the digitisation of the Indian economy can be expressed by the evolution of digital and traditional transactions, both in terms of volumes and value. Traditional transactions are transactions that involve either paper clearing or card transactions at automatic teller machines, while all other transactions are classified as digital.

Figure 29.5 shows the volume of both digital and traditional transactions, while Figure 29.6 shows the corresponding transaction values. The volume of digital transactions had been steadily growing in India and had almost

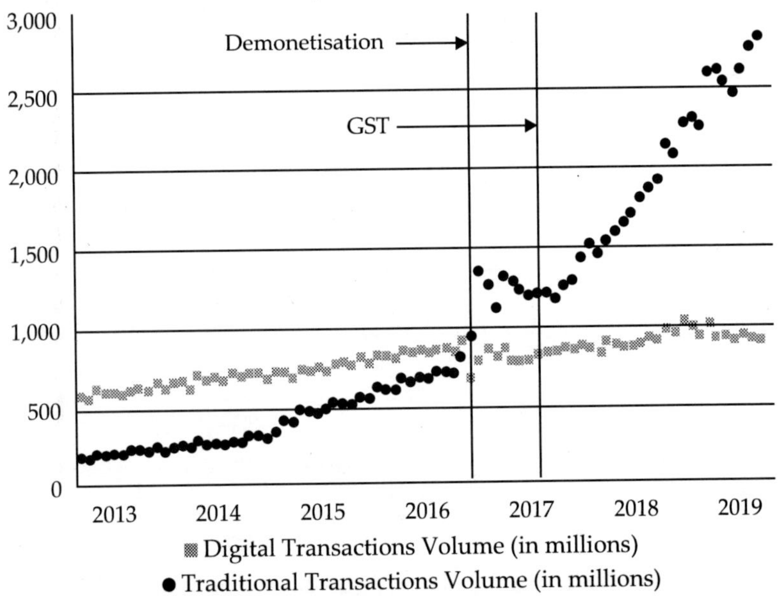

Source: Reserve Bank of India (2019)

Figure 29.5. Transaction volumes

caught up with the volume of traditional transactions. The volume of digital transactions had almost matched with the traditional transactions by October 2016. The demonetisation of November 2016 resulted in a positive impact on the digital transactions and therefore, the volume of digital transactions registered an upward trend. In contrast, there is a drop in the volume of traditional transactions. These patterns lived short and in subsequent months the traditional transactions volume returned to its pre-demonetisation level. The volume of digital transactions did fall back to a little extent from its levels during the demonetisation months but stayed well above its pre-demonetisation level. The digital transactions have exceeded traditional transactions consistently both in level and growth rate after 2017. The value of digital transactions is larger and growing faster than traditional transactions for the last ten years.

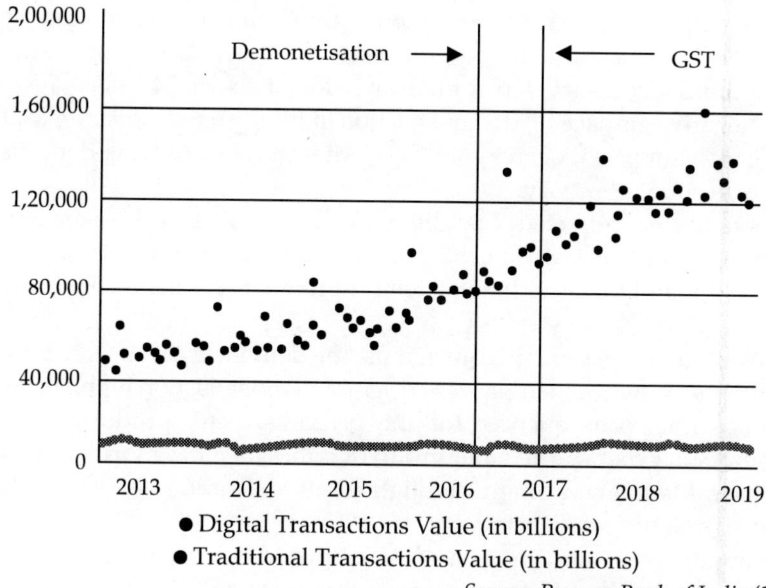

Source: Reserve Bank of India (2019)

Figure 29.6. Transaction values

Basing on the factual information it can be concluded that demonetisation might have induced the people of India to use digital payment methods for smaller value transactions relative to the pre-demonetisation period.

29.11. SUMMARY

- Demonetisation is an act of withdrawing a currency unit of its status as legal tender. The current form or forms of money is pulled from circulation and retired, often to be replaced with new notes or coins.

- Demonetisation is considered the most powerful tax administration measure. It leads to channelising savings into the formal financial system.
- Demonetisation helps in promoting digital transactions facilitating transparency and control in the financial system.
- The currency ban was first introduced in 1946. The currency notes of Rs. 1000 and Rs. 10,000 were removed from circulation.
- The second ban on currency came in 1978. The currency notes of Rs. 1000, Rs. 5000 and Rs. 10,000 were made out of circulation.
- The third ban on currency was introduced in 2016. The Government of India announced the demonetisation of all Rs. 500 and Rs. 1000 banknotes of the Mahatma Gandhi series.
- The main reason for the demonetisation is the eradication of black money, removal of fake currency, promotion of online transactions, and contribute to the growth of GDP.
- The positive impact of demonetisation is the elimination of black money, strengthening the economy, control on hawala transactions, elimination of counterfeit currency, terror financing, and attack on Maoism.
- The negative impact of demonetisation liquidity crisis, loss of well-being, consumption, decrease in GDP, interest rate and bank deposits, and unaccounted money.
- Demonetisation affected the different sectors like real estate and property, gems and jewellery, banks, media and entertainment industry, hospitality and tourism, luxury items, automobiles, retail, agriculture, and labour-intensive sectors.
- There are two types of criticism against the demonetisation. One group of critics mostly from left parties criticised demonetisation highlighting its disastrous consequences for the peasants, petty producers, and labourers in general. The other group of critics including former Prime Minister Manmohan Singh highlighted its deleterious effect on the country's GDP growth rate.
- The impact of demonetisation on GDP includes the preparedness of the Reserve Bank of India to manage the process of remonetising the economy, the potential of demonetisation to achieve the stated goals and the costs of the move for the Indian economy.
- An examination of the growth in digitised payments, in the tax base and tax revenues, suggests that the move achieved little in terms of changing the pre-demonetisation trends in these measures.

SHORT ANSWER QUESTIONS

1. What is demonetisation?
2. What are the features of demonetisation?

3. Describe the reasons for demonetisation.
4. Explain the motives of the third demonetisation in India.

ESSAY ANSWER QUESTIONS

1. 'Demonetisation is a measure of monetary reform'. Explain.
2. Explain the impact of demonetisation on the Indian economy.
3. Explain the impact of demonetisation on different sectors.
4. Discuss the criticisms against the demonetisation in India.
5. Describe the impact of demonetisation on GDP.
6. What is the impact of demonetisation on digitisation?

FILL IN THE BLANKS

1. A strategy to control the monetary system in an economy is __________.
2. The second ban on currency notes was first introduced in __________.
3. In 2016, the Government imported __________ metric tonnes of currency paper.
4. In 2017, the GoI imported currency paper from __________ foreign companies.
5. The composition of personal income taxes and corporate taxes is called __________.

Answers:

1. Demonetisation
2. 1978
3. 8000
4. Eight
5. Direct taxes

MULTIPLE-CHOICE QUESTIONS

1. An act of withdrawing a currency unit of its status as legal tender is known as:
   (A) Tax evasion (B) Remonetisation
   (C) Demonetisation (D) Transition
2. The currency ban was first introduced in the year:
   (A) 1946 (B) 1948
   (C) 1978 (D) 2016
3. Demonetisation is a decisive blow against:
   (A) Digitisation (B) Corruption
   (C) Taxation (D) Consumption
4. Which one of the following is a positive impact of demonetisation?
   (A) Strengthening the economy
   (B) Loss of well-being
   (C) Liquidity crisis
   (D) Decrease in GDP

5. Which one of the following is a negative impact of demonetisation?
   (A) Control on hawala transactions
   (B) Purging of counterfeit currency
   (C) Terror financing
   (D) Consumption
6. The composition of sales taxes, customs duties, and excise duties is known as:
   (A) Direct taxes (B) Indirect taxes
   (C) Corporate taxes (D) Goods and Services Tax

Answers:

1. C	2. A	3. B	4. A	5. D
6. B				

REFERENCES

1. Chenoy, K.M. (2017). A Theoretical Critique of Demonetisation. Retrieved from https://www.thecitizen.in/index.php/en/News Detail/index/4/9755/A-Theoretical-Critique-of-Demonetisation.
2. Economic Survey Analysis on Demonetisation. Retrieved from https://iasscore.in/topical-analysis/economic-survey-analysis-on-demonetisation
3. Demonetisation Impact on GDP. Retrieved from https://www.motilaloswal.com/blog-details/the-demonetization-impact-on-gdp-may-actually-be-beneficial../1374
4. Karthik. K.V. What Demonetization may mean for the Indian economy. Retrieved from https://www2.deloitte.com/in/en/pages/finance/articles/what-demonetization-may-mean-for-the-indian-economy.html
5. Lahiri, A. (2020). The great Indian demonetization. *Journal of Economic Perspectives,* 34(1), 55-74.
6. Munimji. (2017). Advantages and Disadvantages of Demonetisation. Retrieved from https://www.munimji.co.in/academic/blogs/13-general/198-advantages-and-disadvantages-of-demonetisation.html
7. Patnaik, P. (2018). Demonetisation: Criticism and Criticism. Retrieved from https://www.newsclick.in/demonetisation-criticism-and-criticism
8. Pimputkar, S. (2016). India's History with Demonetisation: From 1946 to 2016. Retrieved from https://www.freepressjournal.in/cmcm/indias-history-with-demonetisation-from-1946-to-2016.

Chapter

30 Information Economics

LEARNING OBJECTIVES

After studying this chapter, you should be able to understand:

- concept of information economics;
- the scope of information economics;
- concepts of supply chain, market selection, segmentation and distribution; and
- selection of human resources, signalling, screening for choice and control mechanism.

30.1. INTRODUCTION

Information economics studies the allocation of information for making economic decisions and the impact of the imperfect allocation of information on economic analysis and economic development. The information economics, also called, 'economics of information' is a part of microeconomic theory. It studies how information and information systems affect an economy and economic decisions. The concept of information economics was introduced by George Akerlof, Michael Spence and Joseph Stiglitz in 1970. They became Nobel Prize winners in 2001 for their analysis of markets with asymmetric information applying the concept of information economics. In the words of Stiglitz (1985), "Information economics is the extent to which markets and other institutions process and convey information. Many of the problems of markets and other institutions result from costly information, and many of their features are responses to costly information".

30.2. CONCEPT OF INFORMATION ECONOMICS

Information economics studies the possibility of imperfect information in an economy which will result in asymmetric information. It questions the relevance of the assumption under perfect competition which states that everyone has access to complete and perfect information relating to prices of products and services in an economy. Everyone will have equal information on all market participants, products available, their utility as well as cost. However, in the real world where we find substantial developments in economic markets, perfect and complete market information to all is close to impossible. Imperfect/asymmetry information leads to purchase decision making in the majority of the occasions. The information asymmetry takes place in situations where one person or a party has access to better or more information than the other. The person or party having more or better information will be in an advantageous position in handling situations. On the other hand, people with imperfect information tend to get exploited. The information asymmetry can lead to cover that can imbalance transaction due to the reason that the other party does not have complete information on the utility and cost functions.

We are in the age of information. Information explosion is taking place due to the technological advancements in information and communication throughout the world. Information management became one of the key challenges to business units. Everyone realised that information is power and the person with timely, adequate, and reliable information can take right decisions at the right time. The quality of the decisions of the managers depends upon the quality of information input. The asymmetry in information affects the quality of decision making significantly. Therefore, business units invest heavily on the development of an effective management information system that ensures a continuous flow of qualitative information to the decision makers.

Let us examine the market conditions under asymmetric/imperfect information. In the presence of imperfect information, both suppliers and consumers seek more and more information for making purchase decisions. Marketers use advertising as a response to imperfect information. They try to communicate the features of the product, price, availability, and other benefits to the target audience in favour of their products and services. Business units use sales personnel as well as intermediaries to spread information sought by the customers. The information on competing products, substitutes, marketing strategies of competitors, the specific needs and desires of the people in a locality, demographic information, change in income levels, and other related information inputs help the business unit to handle market situations effectively.

For a transaction to take place there must be at least two persons or parties willing to exchange products/services at a value agreed upon. When the two persons or parties do not have the same or similar information about the transaction it is called *information asymmetry*. It happens when one party is having more information than the other. Information asymmetry also occurs when all the participants in the transaction do not have perfect knowledge. Information asymmetry is quite common in market situations. Often the consumers make purchase decisions with insufficient information on various products and services. As a result, they are emotionally influenced by making choices. Marketers try to exploit the incomplete/asymmetric information status of the consumers by way of aggressive promotion using celebrities and other emotional influencers. The information asymmetry leads to exploitation, improper allocation of resources, under utilisation of resources, high risk of failure, and opportunity costs. It is a known fact that the markets function well and fair transactions take place when market information is perfect. However, the rapid growth of information and communication technologies around the world and the generation of huge quantities of information could not able to resolve the problem of information asymmetry in the economy as well as market situations. As such the exploitation of the people with information gaps is continuing.

30.3. SCOPE OF INFORMATION ECONOMICS

To understand the dimensions of information economics and the impact of information asymmetry, it is necessary to examine the following seven aspects.

1. Supply chain
2. Market selection, segmentation and distribution
3. Selection of human resources
4. Signalling
5. Screening for choice
6. Control mechanism

30.4. SUPPLY CHAIN

A supply chain is a network between the business units and its suppliers to produce and distribute a specific product or service. The entities in the supply chain include producers, vendors, warehouses, transportation companies, distribution centres, and retailers. The functions in a supply chain include product development, marketing, operations, distribution, finance, and customer service. Supply chain management results in lower costs and a faster production cycle. The supply chain members may face different types of asymmetric information. For example, a party may have private information about demand, cost, quality, or disruption that cannot be observed by the whole system but can affect the performance of the system.

Information asymmetry exists within the supply chain. Information updating or sharing can overcome or mitigate the negative effects of information asymmetry. Due to decentralised supply chain operations, and involvement of many independent participants at different locations and business goals, information asymmetry is likely to present among supply chain members. The information related to supply as well as demand will be asymmetrically distributed among the supply chain members, and therefore, there is a scope for exploitation. In supplier-retailer channels, the retailer can collect more information on demand, whereas the supplier can collect more information on the supply side of the resources. The detailed information on supply and demand is not known to both the supply chain members. As a result, ineffective information sharing happens which leads to information asymmetry within the supply chain.

There has been a growing interest in improving performance and supply chain efficiency for all members of a supply chain through information sharing. In many cases, supply chain players make decisions with limited information. A significant benefit of information sharing is that the shared information (i.e., consumer demand information, sales trend and point-of-sale data, etc.) improves information accuracy and distribution planning. Information sharing initiatives such as collaborative planning, forecasting, and replenishment (CRFR), radio frequency identification (RFID) technology, supply chain management integration, and efficient consumer response (ECR) facilitate sharing of information among the supply chain players.

Information sharing between two business units selling complementary products is not always beneficial for each business unit. If the total profit for the two business units in the information sharing is less than the total profit in the non-information sharing, then information sharing is not a beneficial strategy. Therefore, only a strategic alliance is the best choice all the time. The manufacturer and the retailer can benefit from information sharing only when the manufacturer's forecast is higher than the retailer's forecast. If the manufacturer's forecast is lower than the retailer's forecast, the manufacturer would benefit from information sharing while the retailer would not. The retailer would voluntarily share its information with the manufacturer only if the cost of adding value is lower than the threshold value.

30.5. MARKET SELECTION, SEGMENTATION AND DISTRIBUTION

Business units have to rightly identify the markets to sell their products and services. The economy consists of different markets such as consumer markets, industrial markets, government markets, international markets, short-term markets, long-term markets, primary markets, secondary markets, product-specific markets (vegetables, shares, bullion, etc.), regulation based markets (regulated and unregulated), etc. The selection of the market to serve is a critical decision which requires information from various sources. The quality of the decision depends upon the adequacy and accuracy of the information available. Quite often the business units face the problem of information asymmetry in the selection of markets and face a lot of problems to settle down. Many of the information sources are likely to be external organisations as it is costly and time taking for the business units to collect comprehensive information for market selection. Therefore, information asymmetry affects significantly the market selection.

Business units may offer their products/services to the undifferentiated market or a differentiated market. When the consumers are homogeneous, the undifferentiated market strategy works out. But in reality, it is close to impossible to find a purely homogeneous market. Therefore, business units tend to go for market segmentation. Market segmentation is dividing the market into parts in such a way that each part is homogeneous in all significant aspects. To divide the market into segments, the business unit has to collect information on different aspects such as substantiality, measurability, accessibility, response rates, demographic information, geographic information, and psychographic information. The success of market segmentation depends upon the availability of timely and sufficient information on all the factors. Business units often experience information asymmetry in market segmentation as well as facing competition. The business unit having better information will gain more through market segmentation compared to the business units with inadequate market information.

Distribution channels are the marketing intermediaries that take a product from a manufacturer to the end-users. They provide a variety of services. A central feature of distribution channels is that the retailer is closer to the consumer than the manufacturer. Therefore, he is often better informed about demand conditions than the manufacturer. A retailer with poor quality of information is unlikely to form an information-sharing alliance with the manufacturer and the better the quality of the information the more likely the retailer will like information sharing to occur.

30.6. SELECTION OF HUMAN RESOURCES

Employers often are not clear about the quality of potential candidates aspiring to join the organisation. In such a case, hiring candidates can be risky. In case of difficulty in firing employees due to legal and other problems or heavy investments are required to train the candidates, the risk of wrong selection will be very high. Labour markets, therefore, operate in an environment where there is asymmetric information. When an employer does not know the candidate's actual and comprehensive skill set, the candidate may take advantage and exaggerate his or her true competencies to get the job.

The recruitment and selection of employees are, therefore, very critical to the business units. Many business units face problems with employees in different ways. The problems are such as low level of job skills than expected, attitude problems, behavioural problems, learning inefficiency, inability to work with teams, low morale and motivation, and resistance to change. The information asymmetry at the time of recruitment and selection leads to hiring problematic employees. The job-seeking candidates try to project only positive information and try to hide negative information. There are no dependable sources for the business units to understand comprehensively the prospective candidates and, therefore, face problems. Business units generally, hire professional organisations to take up the recruitment and selection process to minimise the information gaps.

30.7. SIGNALLING

Signalling refers to an idea that one person conveys some credible information about himself/herself to another person, maybe the higher authority. The theory of signalling was developed by Michael Spence in 1973. The theory is based on observations related to gaps existing between organisations and prospective employees. The signalling theory is found useful in human resource management, business, and financial markets. According to Spence's job-market signalling model, present and potential employees send signals about their skills and abilities to the employer by showing academic qualifications, performance and learning experience.

Michael Spence proposed that going to college can function as a credible signal of an ability to learn. Assuming that people who are skilled in learning can finish college more easily than unskilled people, then by attending college, skilled people signal their skill to prospective employers. When information asymmetry is in existence in the business unit, employees should try to signal their qualities and competencies to the employer to resolve the asymmetry. The employees must know the ways through which they can transmit such information credibly. The credentials communicated to the employer are used to distinguish between low skilled employees and skilled employees.

30.8. SCREENING FOR CHOICE

The theory of screening was proposed by Joseph E. Stiglitz in 1975. According to this theory, the under-informed person adopts different ways to induce the other person to reveal the required information. A set of questions are prepared in such a way that the other person can find the optimal choice only by using his/her private information.

Screening is used in hiring employees when both the candidate and the organisation do not know the true skills of the candidate. Several screening tests are developed to assess the abilities and potential of the candidates. The tests such as cognitive ability tests, physical ability tests, aptitude tests, personality tests, talent assessment tests, English proficiency tests, honesty and integrity tests, polygraph tests, emotional intelligence testing, sample job task tests, and medical tests are conducted as per the needs of the job. Screening may also be done at the time of identifying the right persons for promoting to decision making jobs. Screening can be beneficial to both the business unit as well as the employees. Having a reliable knowledge of their abilities, the employees can demand a higher salary/remuneration. The business unit can increase their profits and achieve higher growth if it places able employees in the right jobs.

30.9. CONTROL MECHANISM

The business units must develop control mechanisms to ensure the plans are implemented properly and effectively. The effectiveness of the control system depends upon the internal information sources, reporting system, frequency of reporting, feedback, and the communication and information flow designed in the business unit. The employees try to report positives without any problem, but in the case of negatives, they may not report accurate information with a fear of punishment. In such a case, information asymmetry affects control mechanisms. When there is personal bias in reporting, information asymmetry will result. Therefore, care has to be taken in identifying reporting personnel and designing reporting systems to avoid information asymmetry.

In the increasingly complex and dynamic world, collection of information and generating knowledge has become an economic activity. The information is a valuable asset to those who possess it. The economics of information is concerned with how information along with the quality and value affects an economy and economic decisions. The basic assumption of microeconomics models is that the information is freely and equally accessible to all agents. Such an assumption is unrealistic. In the real world, information is costly and access to information is asymmetric. Business units, as well as consumers, often struggle to have complete and reliable information to interact with each other. Information economics, therefore, has the highest relevance in microeconomics.

30.10. SUMMARY

- Information economics studies the allocation of information for making economic decisions and the impact of the imperfect allocation of information on economic analysis and economic development.
- It studies how information and information systems affect an economy and economic decisions.
- Information economics studies the possibility of imperfect information in an economy which will result in asymmetric information.
- It questions the relevance of the assumption under perfect competition which states that everyone has access to complete and perfect information relating to prices of products and services in an economy.
- To understand the dimensions of information economics and the impact of information asymmetry, seven aspects are examined.
- They include supply chain, market selection, segmentation and distribution, selection of human resources, signalling, screening for choice, and control mechanism.
- A supply chain is a network between the business units and its suppliers to produce and distribute a specific product or service. Information asymmetry exists within the supply chain.
- The selection of the market to serve is a critical decision which requires information from various sources. The business unit having better information will gain more through market segmentation compared to the business units with inadequate market information.
- Employers often are not clear about the quality of potential candidates aspiring to join the organisation. Labour markets operate in an environment where there is asymmetric information.
- Signalling refers to an idea that one person conveys some credible information about himself/ herself to another person, maybe the higher authority.
- Screening theory states that the under-informed person adopts different ways to induce the other person to reveal the required information.
- The effectiveness of the control system depends upon the internal information sources, reporting system, frequency of reporting, feedback, and the communication and information flow designed in the business unit.

SHORT ANSWER QUESTIONS

1. What is the information asymmetry?
2. Define information economics.
3. Write a short note on supply chain.

4. What is meant by signalling?
5. Explain the concept of screening.
6. Write a short note on control mechanism.

ESSAY ANSWER QUESTIONS

1. Explain the possibility of imperfect information in an economy which results in asymmetric information.
2. Examine the various aspects to understand the impact of information asymmetry.
3. Discuss the role of the supply chain in information economics.
4. Explain the market selection, segmentation and distribution process during information asymmetry.

FILL IN THE BLANKS

1. Information economics is a part of __________ theory.
2. A network between the business units and its suppliers to produce and distribute a specific product or service is called __________.
3. Labour markets operate in an environment where there is __________ information.
4. The signalling theory was introduced in the year __________.
5. The theory of screening is proposed by __________.

Answers:

1. Microeconomic
2. Supply chain
3. Asymmetric
4. 1973
5. Joseph E. Stiglitz

MULTIPLE-CHOICE QUESTIONS

1. The study of the possibility of imperfect information in an economy that results in asymmetric information is called:
   (A) Information asymmetry (B) Information economics
   (C) Imperfect allocation (D) Economic decisions
2. The undifferentiated market strategy works out when the consumers are:
   (A) Satisfied (B) Dissatisfied
   (C) Heterogeneous (D) Homogeneous
3. Dividing the market into parts in such a way that each part is homogeneous in all significant aspects is referred to as:
   (A) Market segmentation (B) Market penetration
   (C) Market selection (D) Market analysis
4. An idea that one person conveys some credible information about himself/herself to another person, maybe the higher authority is called:
   (A) Screening (B) Signalling
   (C) Recruitment (D) Selection

5. The theory of signalling was developed by:
   (A) Joseph E. Stiglitz (B) Edward Lazear
   (C) Michael Spence (D) Peter F. Drucker
6. Which of the following is used for hiring employees when both the candidate and the organisation do not know the true skills of the candidate?
   (A) Signalling (B) Screening
   (C) Cognitive tests (D) Emotional intelligence

Answers:

1. B	2. D	3. A	4. B	5. C
6. B				

REFERENCES

1. Akerlof, G. (1970). The market for 'Lemons': Quality uncertainty and the Market Mechanism. *Quarterly Journal of Economics, 84,* 353-374.
2. Baumeister, R.F. (2011). Self and identity: A brief overview of what they are, what they do, and how they work. *Annals of the New York Academy of Sciences,* 1234(1), 48-55.
3. Drucker, P.F. (1954). *Making Decisions: Practice of Management.* New York: Free Press.
4. Lewin K. (1951). *Field Theory in Social Science: Selected Theoretical Papers* (ed. Cartwright D). New York: Harper & Row.
5. Lewin, K. (1947). *Field Theory in Social Science.* New York: Harper & Row.
6. Spence, M. (1973). Job market signaling. *The Quarterly Journal of Economics,* 87(3), 355-374.
7. Stiglitz, J.E. (1975). The theory of screening, education, and the distribution of income. *American Economic Review,* 65(3), 283-300.
8. Stiglitz, J.E. (1985). Information and economic analysis: a perspective. *The Economic Journal,* 95, 21-41.
9. Stiglitz, J.E. & Weiss, A. (1992). Asymmetric information in credit markets and its implications for macro-economics. *Oxford Economic Papers,* 44(4), 694-724.

Chapter

31 Personnel Economics

LEARNING OBJECTIVES

After studying this chapter, you should be able to understand:

- concept of personnel economics;
- internal and external labour markets; and
- scope of personnel economics.

31.1. CONCEPT OF PERSONNEL ECONOMICS

Personnel economics is the application of economic and mathematical approaches and econometric and statistical methods to traditional questions in human resource management (Lazear, 2008). Personnel economics deal with personnel management within business units and labour markets. It includes economic issues related to managerial, supervisory and non-supervisory workers. The study of human resource management practices like compensation, hiring practices, training, and teamwork in a business unit constitutes an integral part of personnel economics.

Personnel economics is different from sociological and psychological approaches to the study of organisational behaviour and human resource management. It analyses the use of labour (constitutes the major part of production costs in many business units) by formulating relatively simple and testable relationships. It also analyses the labour costs in the context of market equilibrium, rational maximising behaviour, and economic efficiency. Personnel economics provides answers for many issues like variations in pay to workers within business units, compressed pay, performance-based payments, the relationship between pay and promotions, teamwork, incentives, etc. Personnel economists offer new tools to analyse these issues and offer suitable solutions.

31.2. INTERNAL AND EXTERNAL LABOUR MARKETS

Internal labour markets are those where workers are hired to higher levels from within the organisation. The wages are determined internally without any market pressure. External labour markets imply that workers move somewhat fluidly between business units and wages are determined by some aggregate process where business units do not have significant discretion over wage setting. Although internal promotion being important, a significant part of labour is taken from the external market which affects both wage setting and hiring patterns. In a free labour market, external factors discipline the business units in setting wages.

There are two kinds of fluidity in modern labour markets. They are ex-ante fluidity and ex-post fluidity. Ex-ante fluidity refers to the flexibility of labour markets for workers at the start of a career. Even in the presence of strong internal labour markets, external labour markets compete seriously at the time of hiring personnel for the entry-level positions. Ex-post fluidity refers to fluidity of the labour market with a fair amount of tenure in an organisation. The workers employed eventually tend to settle down and remain with the same employer for a significant part of their career. A variety of factors may influence the continuation with a business unit. The incentive structures, the positive work environment, promotion policy, welfare measures, etc., convert the employees as business unit-specific human capital. One potential implication of ex-post rigidity is that wages do not move with the market.

Lazear and Oyer (2003) stated that even in the economic environment where wage and employment determination are constrained by institutional factors, external labour markets are prevalent and forceful. Although promotion from within is the rule at higher-level positions in most business units, positions are often filled from outside the business unit, and the wages paid are those determined by the general market conditions, not by the business unit.

31.3. SCOPE OF PERSONNEL ECONOMICS

Personnel economics focuses on different aspects of human resource management. They are:

1. Manpower planning
2. Recruitment and selection
3. Training and skill development
4. Structure of the organisation
5. Job design
6. Compensation system and rewards
7. Employee turnover and employee retention
8. Employee's performance appraisal
9. Employer-employee relationship

31.4. MANPOWER PLANNING

Manpower planning is the process of estimating the optimum number of people required to complete a task or achieve the goals of a business unit within a specified time. It helps the business unit to assess its future manpower needs. It helps the management of a business unit to identify the right people to the right job, and proper utilisation of human resources for the achievement of organisational objectives. According to E.W. Vetter (1964), manpower planning is the process by which the management determines how a business unit should make from its current manpower position to its desired manpower position. Through planning,the management strives to have the right number and the right kind of people, at the right place, at the right time, doing the right things. As a result, both individuals and organisations receive maximum long-run benefits.

The main objectives of manpower planning are:

- Forecast human resource requirements
- Optimization of labour cost
- Recruitment and selection
- Management of change
- Achievement of organisational goals
- Optimum utilisation of human potential
- Human resource development
- Promotion of employer-employee relationship
- Identification of future training and development needs
- Minimisation of wages and salary costs
- Avoid shortage or surplus of staff

The HR department will assess the skills required for employees to perform each job at the desired level. Such an assessment will help HR in estimating its future demand and supply against different positions. An effective manpower plan will provide various mechanisms designed to get rid of talent gaps, which may exist between the organisation's supply of labour and its demand for the same. Manpower planning is a dynamic process and requires adjustments as per the prevailing conditions of the labour market.

Manpower planning is done as per the organisational goals and objectives. The process of manpower planning involves:

(a) Analysis of current manpower
(b) Formulation of a recruitment plan
(c) Projecting future organisational structure and future manpower requirements
(d) Development of employment programmes
(e) Designing training programmes

31.5. RECRUITMENT AND SELECTION

Recruitment refers to the search of the prospective employees suitable to the job requirements as per the job specifications. It is an activity that brings together the candidates with jobs on hand and the candidates seeking jobs.

According to Edwin B. Flippo (1976), recruitment is the process of searching for prospective employees and stimulating and encouraging them to apply for jobs in a business unit. There are two sources of recruitment, i.e., internal and external sources.

Internal sources include promotion, transfer, past employees, internal advertisements, and in certain cases demotion. The advantages of internal sources are: it improves morale, promotes loyalty, and economy in recruitment and training costs.

The external sources include media advertisements, employment exchanges, campus recruitment, personnel consultants, professional bodies, private recruitment agencies, recommendations of the existing employees, telecasting, factory gates, casual callers, unsolicited applicants, walk-ins, electronic job portals like Naukri, Monster, LinkeDin, Times jobs, etc., central application file, labour unions, labour contractors, and reference from former employees. The external sources of recruitment are costly and time consuming. However, it facilitates a wider choice and accessibility to skilled candidates.

Selection is the process of choosing the right candidates from among the applicants as per the job requirements. The steps in the scientific selection process include screening and shortlisting of applications based on the set criteria, the conduct of written examination, preliminary interview, group discussions, aptitude tests, intelligence tests, achievement tests, personality, interest and preferences (PIP) tests, projective tests, final interview if necessary as per the need of the job. It also includes medical examination, reference checks, final selection, job offer, and appointment.

The recruitment and selection process are crucial stages in personnel economics. This process aims at balancing the cost of human resource against the value generated by them. The cost efficiency in the human resource can be achieved through efficient policies of recruitment and selection.

31.6. TRAINING AND SKILL DEVELOPMENT

Training is an organised activity for increasing the knowledge and skills of people for a definite purpose. Business units have to introduce changes to match the changes in the business environment. For the purpose, they have to prepare the human resources to adapt themselves to the changes and also to become creative in introducing changes. This requires training continuously. The training and skill development requires a systematic procedure for transferring technical know-how to the employees to enhance their knowledge levels and develop skills for undertaking specific jobs with proficiency. According to Edwin B. Flippo, training is the act of increasing the knowledge and skills of an employee for doing a particular job.

The objectives of the training are to bridge the gap between the existing performance ability and desired performance. The key objectives of the training are:

(a) Imparting basic knowledge and skill to the new employees.
(b) Exposing the latest concepts, information and techniques and developing the skills in particular fields to the existing employees.
(c) Developing the second line of officers to take up more responsible positions.
(d) Imparting customer education to all the employees.
(e) Facilitating organisational change.
(f) Developing job related positive attitudes among employees.
(g) Preventing manpower obsolescence in the business unit.
(h) Enhancing the level of morale, enthusiasm, work spirit and work culture among employees.

The following methods are generally used to provide training.

1. **On-the-job training methods:** This type of training is imparted on the job and at the workplace where the employees are expected to perform their duties. On-the-job training methods include job experience, job rotation, coaching, job instruction, committee assignments, internship training, temporary promotions, and special study.
2. **Off-the-job training methods:** This type of training is imparted outside the workplace. Off-the-job training methods include case studies, role play, special courses and lectures, conferences and seminars, programmed instruction, brainstorming, vestibule training, apprenticeship training, in-basket exercise, business games, work shadowing, computer based training, behaviour modelling, sensitivity training, and multiple management.

Training and skill development involve costs to the business units. When we look at the benefits of timely and quality training the costs involved in it look very small. Business units should systematically and professionally identify the training needs and select appropriate training methods. The services of experts including the qualified and experienced persons from the business units should be used to train the employees. The results of the training can be assessed through different methods to ensure the expenditure incurred in training yielded good results. Business units should consider the amount spent on training as an investment and the trained personnel continue to perform well in future also and transform as the human capital of the unit. Business units will gain a competitive advantage in the market with uniquely skilled manpower.

31.7. STRUCTURE OF THE ORGANISATION

The organisational structure provides a framework for managers and other employees to perform various functions. It facilitates the workflow in the business unit. The roles and responsibilities, superior-subordinate relationships, and reporting system are clearly defined in the organisational structure. The performance of the business unit greatly depends upon the design of the organisational structure. A good organisational structure should not be static but dynamic. It should be subject to change from time to time in the light of changes in the business environment.

There are two types of structural variables: horizontal structure and vertical structure. The horizontal structure indicates a division of labour while vertical structure indicates the line authority and unity of command. Various management concepts influence the formation of organisational structure. They are centralisation, decentralisation, formalisation, specialisation, stratification and standardisation.

An organisational structure may be mechanistic and organic. The mechanic model of organisational structure is preferred by the business units which are not influenced by frequent technological, product and market changes. They generally maintain a constant pattern. The organic structure model is flexible and prone to frequent changes in technology, market environment and product/product attributes. The organic structures use delegation of authority at various levels, provide autonomy at the work environment and decentralisation of power to achieve the goals.

Within a formal organisation setup, informal business units emerge. The reason is that every business unit is filled with people having different needs and desires, competencies, attitudes, beliefs, perceptions, motivations, social and cultural backgrounds, and career objectives. They cannot be placed under the formal system all the time which expect all the employees to follow rules and regulations as prescribed by the formal organisational structure. The triggering of social instincts in employees and common issues and problems promote the formation of informal organisation structure. This structure also will be having norms, leadership and working ethics.

31.8. JOB DESIGN

Job design is the process of deciding on the contents of a job in terms of its duties and responsibilities. It creates a match between job requirements and human attributes. The main objective of job design is to integrate the needs of the individual and the requirements of the organisation. Needs of employees include job satisfaction in terms of interest, challenge and achievement. Organisational requirements are high productivity, technical efficiency and quality of work. The following are various job design techniques.

1. **Job simplification:** In this technique, jobs are broken down into small parts called tasks. The tasks are repeatedly performed by the same individual. Thus, the worker achieves a high level of proficiency in the assigned task.
2. **Job enlargement:** In this technique, two or more simple tasks are combined and allotted to an employee. More tasks are added to a job to make the employee learn to perform a variety of simple tasks.
3. **Job rotation:** It refers to the technique where the employee is periodically rotated from one job to another within the work design. It involves moving employees among different jobs over a period of time. In job rotation, workers get opportunities to do different jobs within a short period as they are rotated from one job to another.
4. **Job enrichment:** Job enrichment entails skill development and is a challenge. It entails inbuilt motivation, absolute control over the job and opportunities for growth and learning. Enriched jobs offer intrinsic value to the worker and promote motivation among the individuals doing the job.

31.9. COMPENSATION SYSTEM AND REWARDS

Compensation is the reward given to the employees for their labour. Compensation can be given in two forms: direct compensation and indirect compensation. Direct compensation consists of the base wage and incentives. Indirect compensation includes benefits that are mandated by law and those that employers provide voluntarily. The decisions on compensation influence the quality and composition of human resources in the business unit. Relatively high compensation offer attracts a quality workforce and also keep them motivated and retained. The compensation also can be used to recognise, appreciate and treat the employees fairly and equitably. The compensation system of the business units should be dynamic and follow market trends. The system should ensure accurate calculation of earnings owed to each of the employees for purposes like overtime, performance rewards, incentive payments and allowances, by the employer and make sure that pay is distributed in time and with proper records. The system should control costs, comply with the statutes and be easy to administer.

The different types of compensation plans are given below.

1. **Incentive based compensation plan:** Incentive refers to the inducements offered to get better output from the employees. Incentive schemes are used to enhance the motivation level of the

employees to earn more. Incentives tend to influence individuals to stretch their capacities and personal objectives and carry out special tasks and take initiative. Incentive compensation provides a proportionate reward for employee performance. Incentives are not part of the base wage but it is paid in addition to the base wage to an employee or a group of employees based on performance. While individual incentive plans encourage competition among employees, group or plant-wide incentive plans encourage co-operation and direct the efforts of all employees toward achieving overall organisational objectives.

2. **Skill based compensation:** Under skill based compensation, the employees are paid based on the special skills possessed by them. It is an additional pay as recognition for formal certification of the employee's mastery of skills, knowledge, and/or competencies. Skill is acquired and observable expertise in performing tasks but not the job held by them.
3. **Team based compensation:** This type of compensation is paid to teams. The performance of members of the team is recognised and rewarded through team based compensation. Many business units have recognised the importance of close cooperation and mutual development in a workgroup. They want to encourage employees to work as a team by offering incentives based on the overall performance of the team.
4. **Performance based compensation:** This type of compensation is purely based on meritocracy and the result of employee's performance. It is paid in addition to the regular wages. This system is to recognise meritorious employees and motivate them to work better all the time. It encourages internal competition among employees to perform better and gain more.

31.10. EMPLOYEE TURNOVER AND EMPLOYEE RETENTION

Employee turnover refers to the number or percentage of employees leaving the business unit. Employees may leave the business unit voluntarily due to personal reasons, dissatisfaction on job or work environment or for a better opportunity in some other business unit. Sometimes employees are forced to leave the business unit involuntary due to variety of reasons. The management of the business unit may fire some employees to downsize the employment, to introduce machines as a replacement to human resource, or due to low productivity of specific employees or for any other reason as per the rules of the business unit. Therefore, voluntary turnover occurs when an employee chooses to leave the business unit, and involuntary turnover occurs when the employer decides for the employee to leave the business unit.

Employee turnover for any reason impacts business and profits. The business units may be required to pay continuing benefits or severance pay and also incur the cost of hiring new employees. This may result in lost productivity and lost revenue. Therefore, the reasons for employee turnover need to be analysed systematically and measures must be initiated to keep it at the lowest possible. Turnover is measured for individual business units and the industry as a whole. If a business unit is having a high turnover relative to its competitors, it indicates that employees of that business unit have a shorter average tenure than those of others in the industry. High turnover may be harmful to the productivity of the business unit if skilled workers are often leaving and the worker population contains a high percentage of apprentice workers.

Employee turnover may be internal or external. Internal turnover involves employees vacating the current positions to taking new positions in the same business unit. Internal turnover may lead to both positive and negative effects on the business unit. If the internal turnover increases the morale of the employees due to movement to the desired task or promotion to a higher position, it gives a positive impact. On the other hand, if the internal movements are for punishment or to less important positions, it may create negative effects. Internal turnover can be moderated and controlled by HR mechanisms by introducing sound HR policies. Internal transfers should be treated as an opportunity to help employees in their career growth.

Retention is the process through which a business unit ensures that its employees don't quit their jobs. Employee retention refers to the various policies and practices that make the employees attached to a business unit for a longer period. Retaining skilled employees is vital to the success of a business. A high rate of employee turnover can result in a loss of knowledge and skills, and can negatively impact a company's bottom line.

The following are some ways through which the business units can achieve employee retention:

(a) Reward employees' contributions.
(b) Fair and competitive compensation package.
(c) Free flow of communication and encouragement for new ideas.
(d) Effective training programmes to enhance skills development, learning, and career growth.
(e) Support through welfare measures.
(f) Leadership opportunities.
(g) Align employees' interests with company's growth plans.

31.11. EMPLOYEE'S PERFORMANCE APPRAISAL

Performance appraisal is a technique of evaluating the work performance and behaviour of employees at the workplace with the help of the quantitative and qualitative aspects of job performance. Performance appraisal involves a systematic and periodic assessment of employee's performance impartially to find out his/her excellence in performing the job and also to identify the potential of the employee to take up a better job. Performance appraisal helps the employees in self-improvement and self-development. It helps the management in certain important HR decisions such as placement, promotions, transfer, and training and development.

Steps in the appraisal of employee's performance:

1. Establishing performance standards
2. Communicating performance expectations to employees
3. Measuring actual performance
4. Comparing actual performance with standards
5. Discussing the appraisal with the employee
6. Initiating corrective action

The methods used for evaluating employee's performance are classified into two broad categories. They are traditional methods and modern methods.

1. **Traditional methods** are used for rating the personality traits of individuals:such as initiative, dependability, drive creativity, integrity, intelligence, and leadership potential are appraised by using the following methods.
   (a) **Ranking method:** It is the oldest and simplest method of performance appraisal in which an employee is compared with all others to place an order of worth. The employees are ranked from the highest to the lowest or from the best to the worst.
   (b) **Grading method:** In this method, certain standards/grades are identified and established in advance. In general, the standards like outstanding, satisfactory and unsatisfactory are established to evaluate the performance of employees.
   (c) **Man-to-man comparison method (paired rating):** In this method, each employee is compared with other employees on a one-on-one basis. The rater is provided with a set of slips each coining pair of names to select one employee whom he/she considers the best out of the two. The number of times an employee is compared as better compared to others determines the final ranking.
   (d) **Graphic rating scale method:** The graphic rating scale (also known as linear rating scale) is one of the most popular and simplest techniques for appraising performance. In this

method, scales are established for several identified traits. The list of traits and generally a five-point scale of job performance characteristics of each trait are provided to the employees. The rater rates each appraisee on the given scale. The assigned values for the traits are then totalled to arrive at the final performance score of an employee.

(e) **Check-list method:** In this method, a series of statements/ questions are given to the rater to answer in either 'yes' or 'no'. Each statement/question carries a weightage in relationship to their importance.

2. **Modern methods:** The modem methods of performance appraisal emphasise on the work performance of the employee relating to job achievements. These methods are relatively more objective compared to traditional methods. The modern methods of performance appraisal are given below.

   (a) **Management by objectives (MBO):** The concept of MBO was conceived by P.F. Drucker (1954). It is the process whereby the superior and subordinate managers of a business unit jointly identify its common goals. They define the major areas of responsibility of each individual and the expected results. An MBO programme consists of four main steps like goal setting, performance standard, comparison, and periodic review.

   (b) **Assessment centre method:** The main objective of this method is to test employees in a social situation, using several assessors and a variety of procedures. For the purpose, job related simulations are used. These simulations involve characteristics that managers feel are important to job success. The assessors observe and evaluate participants as they perform activities commonly found in higher-level jobs.

   (c) **Behaviourally anchored rating scales (BARS):** This method, also called behavioural expectation scales, uses rating scales for the statements of effective and ineffective behaviour of employees. The scales represent a range of descriptive statements of behaviour varying from the least to the most effective. A rater must indicate which behaviour on each scale best describes an employee's performance.

   (d) **Cost accounting method:** This method evaluates an employee's performance based on the monetary benefits the employee yields to the business unit. This is ascertained by establishing a relationship between the costs involved in retaining the employee, and the benefits generated by him/her.

(e) **360° appraisal:** In 360-degree feedback appraisal system, an employee's performance is appraised by his superiors, subordinates, peers, and customers with whom he/she interacts during the job. All appraisers provide information or feedback on the employee. Such information is compiled to prepare individualised reports and presented to the employees being rated. The appraisee then meets the appraiser, i.e., superior, subordinates or peers and shares the information they feel is pertinent and useful for developing a self-improvement plan. In the 360-degree method, performance appraisal is based on all-around feedback, therefore, an employee is likely to be more correct and realistic.

(f) **720° appraisal:** 720-degree feedback is doing 360-degree appraisal twice to comprehensively appraise the performance of an employee. After the 360-degree appraisal, the employee is expected to make adjustments in behaviour or work performance. On conducting 360-degree appraisal again to the same employee the management can ascertain whether the first appraisal is useful in improving the performance of the employees or any support is needed to help the employee to reach his/her potential.

31.12. EMPLOYER-EMPLOYEE RELATIONSHIP

The employer and employee enter into the bondage of relationship once a person is legally connected with the business unit (employer) as an employee. This relationship exists individually as well as collectively. The employer and employee's direct relationship will be at the individual level, and the relationship between the employer's associations and trade unions is called collective relations. In collective relations, the state also takes part by way of imposing regulations. Therefore, employer-employee relations are multi-dimensional and include regulated, unregulated, institutionalised, organised and unorganised sectors. The relationship between these two parties depends upon attitudes and approaches towards each other. These relations are a part of social relations.

According to V.B. Singh (1968), the employer-employee relations system in a country is conditioned by economic and institutional factors. The economic factors are: economic system, capital structure, labour markets and technology. The institutional factors include the state policy, labour laws, trade unions, social institutions, HR policies and procedures, compensation system, and welfare measures. The central and state governments play an important role in regulating employer-employee relations by way of legislations, rules, agreements, court judgements, and executive mechanism. The government also sets up different administrative mechanisms such as wage boards, labour courts, tribunals and other bipartite and tripartite bodies. The purpose of such state mechanisms is to maintain healthy relations between employers and employees.

The scope of employer-employee relations includes redressal of grievances, employees participation in decision making, collective bargaining, settlement of industrial disputes and ethical code and discipline. A positive relationship between employers and employees leads to higher motivation and employee engagement. A strong employer-employee relationship has many benefits like increased productivity for the business unit; enhance employee loyalty and morale, and a healthy and conflict-free work environment.

31.13. SUMMARY

- Personnel economics is the application of economic and mathematical approaches and econometric and statistical methods to traditional questions in human resources management.
- Internal labour markets are those where workers are hired to higher levels from within the organisation.
- External labour markets imply that workers move somewhat fluidly between business units and wages are determined by some aggregate process where business units do not have significant discretion over wage setting.
- Personnel economics focuses on different aspects of human resource management. They are manpower planning, recruitment and selection, training and skill development, the structure of the organisation, job design, compensation system and rewards, employee turnover and employee retention, employee's performance appraisal, and the employer-employee relationship.
- Manpower planning is the process of estimating the optimum number of people required to complete a task or achieve the goals of a business unit within a specified time. It helps the management of a business unit to identify the right people to the right job, and proper utilisation of human resources for the achievement of organisational objectives.
- Recruitment refers to the search of the prospective employees suitable to the job requirements as per the job specification. Selection is the process of choosing the right candidates from among the applicants as per the job requirements. The recruitment and selection process are crucial stages in personnel economics.

- Training is an organised activity for increasing the knowledge and skills of people for a definite purpose. Business units should systematically and professionally identify the training needs and select appropriate training methods. Business units will gain a competitive advantage in the market with uniquely skilled manpower.
- The organisational structure provides a framework for managers and other employees to perform various functions. The performance of the business unit greatly depends upon the design of the organisational structure.
- Job design is the process of deciding on the contents of a job in terms of its duties and responsibilities. The main objective of job design is to integrate the needs of the individual and the requirements of the organisation.
- Compensation is the reward given to the employees for their labour. The compensation system of the business units should be dynamic and follow market trends.
- Employee turnover refers to the number or percentage of employees leaving the business unit. They may leave voluntarily due to personal reasons, dissatisfaction on job or work environment or for a better opportunity in some other business unit. Retention is the process through which a business unit ensures that its employees don't quit their jobs.
- Performance appraisal is a technique of evaluating the work performance and behaviour of employees at the workplace with the help of the quantitative and qualitative aspect of job performance.
- The employer and employee enter into the bondage of relationship once a person is legally connected with the business unit (employer) as an employee. A strong employer-employee relationship has many benefits like increased productivity for the business unit; enhance employee loyalty and morale, and a healthy and conflict-free work environment.

SHORT ANSWER QUESTIONS

1. What is personnel economics?
2. Write a short note on the structure of an organisation.
3. What is the employer-employee relationship?

ESSAY ANSWER QUESTIONS

1. What are internal and external labour markets? Explain.
2. Explain the significant aspects of HRM in personnel economics.
3. Discuss the role of training and skill development in personnel economics.

4. Describe the impact of employee turnover and employee retention on organisational success.
5. What is performance appraisal? Explain the techniques of appraising employees performance.

FILL IN THE BLANKS

1. The flexibility of labour markets for workers at the start of a career is referred to as ________.
2. Manpower planning helps the business unit to assess its ________ manpower needs.
3. An organised activity for increasing the knowledge and skills of people for a definite purpose is called ________.
4. Organisational structure facilitates the ________ in the business unit.
5. The compensation system of the business units should be ________.
6. When the employer decides for the employee to leave the business unit, it is ________ turnover.
7. The concept of MBO as was conceived by ________.

Answers:

1. Ex-ante fluidity
2. Future
3. Training
4. Workflow
5. Dynamic
6. Involuntary
7. P.F. Drucker

MULTIPLE-CHOICE QUESTIONS

1. The fluidity of the labour market with a fair amount of tenure in an organisation is called:
   (A) Ex-ante market (B) Ex-post market
   (C) Ex-ante fluidity (D) Ex-post fluidity
2. The process of estimating the optimum number of people required to complete a task or achieve the goals of a business unit within a specified time is called:
   (A) Employee turnover (B) Manpower planning
   (C) Organisational planning (D) Manpower positioning
3. The activity that brings together the candidates with jobs on hand and the candidates seeking jobs is known as:
   (A) Recruitment (B) Job specification
   (C) Job description (D) Selection
4. A good organisational structure should be:
   (A) Static (B) Dynamic
   (C) Rigid (D) Flexible
5. The structure is preferred by the business units which are not influenced by frequent technological, product and a market change is:
   (A) Formal structure (B) Informal structure
   (C) Organic model (D) Mechanic model

6. The process of deciding on the contents of a job in terms of its duties and responsibilities is called:
   (A) Job design (B) Job simplification
   (C) Job enlargement (D) Job rotation
7. The compensation includes benefits that are mandated by law and those that employers provide voluntarily are called:
   (A) Voluntary (B) Non-voluntary
   (C) Indirect (D) Direct
8. Behaviourally anchored rating scales (BARS) are also called :
   (A) Behavioural accounting scales
   (B) Behavioural expectation scales
   (C) Behavioural assessment scales
   (D) Descriptive rating scales

Answers:

1. D	2. B	3. A	4. B	5. D
6. A	7. C	8. B		

REFERENCES

1. Akerlof, G. (1970). The market for 'Lemons': Quality uncertainty and the Market Mechanism. *Quarterly Journal of Economics, 84*, 353-374.
2. Akerlof, G. (1976). The economics of caste and of the rat race and other woeful tales. *The Quarterly Journal of Economics*, 90, 599-617.
3. Baumeister, R.F. (2011). Self and identity: A brief overview of what they are, what they do, and how they work. *Annals of the New York Academy of Sciences*, 1234(1), 48-55.
4. Drucker, P.F. (1954). *Making Decisions: Practice of Management*. New York: Free Press.
5. Drucker, P.F. (1954). *The Practice of Management*. New York, NY: Harper Business.
6. Flippo, E.B. (1976). *Principles of Personnel Management*. McGraw-Hill.
7. Herzberg, F. (1964). The motivation-hygiene concept and problems of manpower. *Personnel Administration*.
8. Herzberg, F. (1966). *Work and the Nature of Man*. New York: World Publishing.
9. Lazear, E. (2008). Personnel economics. *The New Palgrave Dictionary of Economics*, 6, 380-384.
10. Lazear, E. & Oyer, P. (2004). Internal and external labor markets: a personnel economics approach. *Labour Economics*, 11(5), 527-554.
11. Lewin K. (1951) *Field Theory in Social Science: Selected Theoretical Papers* (ed. Cartwright D). New York: Harper & Row.
12. Lewin, K. (2013). *Principles of Topological Psychology*. Read Books.

Chapter

32 Behavioural Economics

LEARNING OBJECTIVES

After studying this chapter, you should be able to understand:

- concept of behavioural economics;
- dimensions of behavioural economics;
- concept of learning organisation; and
- disciplines and dimensions learning organisation.

32.1. CONCEPT OF BEHAVIOURAL ECONOMICS

The concept of behavioural economics was introduced by Richard H. Thaler (1980), Nobel Prize winner. The study of behavioural economics analyses the effects of psychological, cognitive, emotional, cultural and social factors on the individual and the decisions of the business units. Economics is concerned with how people behave. The standard economic theory (neo-classical economics) assumes that people always make choices that are rational and maximise their welfare. When choices are made over different periods, people will choose the option that gives the best outcome over their lifetime. Even in the absence of perfect information, people will choose the option that results in the highest welfare based on the available information.

Behavioural economics states that people do not always make choices that maximise their benefits . People often get into time pressure in making purchase decisions. They compromise on certain information requirements and try to compromise to save the situations. They may reinforce the same decision of purchasing a product without going for market information related to the availability of new products or better products when they are pressed with time. Behavioural economics does not assume people irrational, but it assumes that it is not possible to become rational in purchase decisions all the time. There are many other factors which emotionally influence people to take decisions.

Behavioural economics focuses on understanding the behaviour of the people that consistently deviate from standard economic theory. It examines and tests the biases and influences that impact the behaviour of individuals and their choices. Behavioural economics analyses the response of the people to the market stimulations in real situations. The disciplines such as psychology and economics are used to understand why people make irrational decisions in different situations and the reasons for deviations from the predictions of economic models.

Thaler and Sunstein (2008) proposed the Nudge theory to explain how small interventions can encourage individuals to make different decisions. A nudge is a technique used by choice makers to change the behaviour of an individual without reducing the number of choices available. Nudges can, however, be manipulative, to the detriment of individuals. For example, a supermarket can create an environment, where attention can be drawn to certain products to encourage consumers to spend money. They can influence the impulsive behaviour of the consumers and sell many products which are not in the planned list of the consumers.

32.2. DIMENSIONS OF BEHAVIOURAL ECONOMICS

The various dimensions of behavioural economic are:

1. Individuals are influenced by others' behaviour.
2. Habits influence behaviour.
3. People can be motivated to choose the right things.
4. The self-concept: – behaviour based on self-perception.
5. People try to avoid losses.
6. The readiness to change depends upon the involvement of people.

1. Individuals are influenced by others' behaviour

Human beings learn many things by observing and imitating others. The parents, family members, friends, relatives, neighbours, and others in society influence the behaviour of individuals significantly. Many a time, people seek approval either directly or indirectly from others on their lifestyle and behaviour. Social acceptance is an important consideration in formulating lifestyle and also consumer behaviour. Particularly, in unfamiliar and complex situations, people tend to observe the behaviour of others and learn the way to handle the situation.

Neo-classical economics does not take into account the direct influence of society and others on individual behaviour. The basic assumption of the theory was that the people independently learn to decide what they need and want. This theory assumes that people are rational thinkers and analyse situations taking full information on available options.

The behavioural economic theory, on the other hand, assumes that other people influence the behaviour of other individuals. Every person learns mostly by observation and imitation of others in the society. It doesn't mean that the economic behaviour of the people depends upon the learnings from others. The individuals study and understand the behaviour of others and are also influenced by their behavioural determinants such as personality, motivation, perception, attitudes and beliefs.

The neo-classical economic analysis helps the policy-makers to devise a system for short term. To design an economic system for a long period, the policy-makers have to consider the changing preferences of individuals due to many intervening variables and shifts in individuals behaviour.

2. Habits influence behaviour

Habits refer to an acquired pattern of behaviour indicated by involuntary and frequent repetition. They are the dispositions of thoughts and feelings of an individual and his/her mental makeup. Habits drive an unconscious and compulsive behaviour of individuals which provide increase facility of performance.

Habits are hard to change. Many of our regular day-to-day works are performed without any conscious effort repeatedly in a similar way because we know that the best solutions can be gained either by personal experimentation or by learning from others' experience. Once we perceive comfort with the solution, we tend to implement the same repeatedly. This process is called *habituation*. Though neo-classical economists do not recognise the existence of habits and reinforced behaviour of people, the psychologists repeatedly emphasise the fact that the frequency of past behaviour influences the current behaviour.

Habits can also be changed when there is a strong influencing reward for change in behaviour. Business units struggle hard in changing the habits of the customers. They have to unfreeze the subconscious actions of the target individuals and influence them to receive new things to the conscious level by explaining the merits of alternative behaviour.

3. People can be motivated to choose the right things

Motivation is the process of satisfying the needs and desires by the individuals. It is an inner process that begins with the awareness of needs which creates a sense of tension in an individual and forces him/her to act upon for the satisfaction of that need. The unfulfilled need generates action tendencies and drives the person to formulate a goal that is capable of satisfying the need. Motivation is the result of the interaction between the individual and the situation. Individuals may differ in their needs, attitudes, perceptions and motivational drives. From the business units point of view, motivation is the willingness to exert high levels of efforts towards the business unit's goals, conditioned by the effort and ability to satisfy some individual needs. When an employee is motivated by the nature of the work rather than the compensation from the work, it can be said that the work is intrinsically motivating the employee. Extrinsic motivation is based on the secondary outcomes of work like pay or reputation. When work is not comfortable or liked by the employee, it is more likely that outcomes like money, fame, power, etc., may motivate the employee to do such work. The motivating factors other than work are called extrinsic motivators.

Abraham Maslow has proposed the need hierarchy to explain the order of the needs the people try to satisfy. He has developed a pyramid model wherein five levels of needs are identified. They are physiological needs, safety and security needs, social needs, esteem needs, and self-actualisation needs. Based on the economic status of an individual, the order of needs will be selected for satisfaction. The people with an income just sufficient for sustenance will try to satisfy the physiological needs. When there is a growth in income, people try to satisfy the next order needs. The underlying message of this theory is that human beings try to move to satisfy the higher-order needs all the time.

Herzberg's two-factor theory of motivation states that the common features of competing products become hygiene factors to the consumers. They are not capable of influencing the consumer to prefer a product for purchase. The motivational factors are the differentiators between and among the competing products. The consumers consider such differentiators and get motivated to buy such products.

The behavioural economics advocates that people can be motivated towards economic activities. The economic rewards result in positive motivation, whereas, the punishments, negative outcomes, and relatively low rewards result in negative motivation. Both financial and non-financial factors influence the motivational behaviour of the people.

4. The self-concept:behaviour based on self-perception

Every individual has a self-perception of behaviour, abilities, unique characteristics, thoughts, feelings and personality. Such an understanding is called self-concept. People develop self-concept right from childhood and continue to modify over time based on learnings. Self-concept is not fixed but it is active and dynamic. It can be influenced by many social situations and knowledge about self through experimentation. According to Roy Baumeister (2011), a social psychologist, self-concept should be understood as a knowledge structure. People pay attention to themselves, noticing both their internal states and responses and their external behaviour. Through such self-awareness, people collect information about themselves. Self-concept can be categorised into four types: self, ideal self, social self, and ideal social self.

1. **Actual self** is a cognitive structure consisting of all self-describing attributes that a person is aware of. These attributes may be developed through self-evaluations or evaluations provided by others in society. People develop self-image based on self-description attributes such as physical factors, social roles, and personality traits. The self-image may not be matching to the reality. Some will develop inflated self-image and some may develop an under-rated

self-image. People also tend to evaluate themselves with that of others in formulating actual self-concept.

2. **Ideal self** refers to the self one would like to be. This is the perception of an individual about how people should behave based on standards of aspirations. People form ideal self basing on the counselling they receive from parents, teachers, and others close to them right from childhood. They influence an individual to develop an ideal personality and also define what an ideal personality is. Individuals dream of certain qualities and work for acquiring them to the best possible extent. There may be a gap between the real self and the ideal self. In some cases, there will be a very wide gap and in some cases, the gap may be narrow.
3. **Social self** concept is the image that one individual believes what others think about him/her. Every individual is part of the society and the perceptions of the society on him/her are important to develop social relationships and networking. Based on the social self-concept individuals can identify the people with whom they can develop relationships and know what is desirable to develop a relationship with the people who do not have positive perceptions of the person.
4. **Ideal social self** concept is the desired social self of an individual. It is the expectation of a person as to how others should perceive him/her and develop an image. When individuals find any kind of deviations in other's perceptions, they may try to work on to bridge the gaps or to modify the behaviour.

Self-concept is a useful analysis for the business units to understand target customers and to plan activities that are capable of influencing them in favour of the organisation. Though it is very difficult to study and establish the facts of the self-concept, business units strive to collect such information as it plays an important role in strategic decision making.

5. People try to avoid losses

No one wants to incur losses in the business. Profit making is one of the key objectives of any business unit. However, business units incur losses sometimes when market conditions are not favourable. The uncertainties in the business environment sometimes create problems and lead to losses. But the management of business units struggles to face the situations and work out strategies to avoid losses. Therefore, the behavioural economics assumes that people try to avoid losses to the best possible extent. Business and risk go hand in hand. Some business units take higher risks and some business units prefer to take only minimal risks. Business analysts believe that higher the risk, higher is the profit, and lower the risk, lesser is the profit.

Risk-taking is the controlled behaviour of the management due to perceived uncertainty about the outcome. It is based on the expectations related to possible benefits or expenditure for taking up certain activities. Behavioural economics states that people will go out of their way to avoid losses. They put more effort into preventing a loss than to gain something. Therefore, the behaviour of the people towards profit and towards losses will not be the same.

6. The readiness to change depends upon the involvement of people

Change management is one of the major challenges of the business units, particularly to those in a highly competitive environment. A business unit operates in an open system and it has to interact with the prevailing business environment. The changes in the environment have to be monitored continuously and necessary measures should be taken to incorporate such changes in the internal systems, sub-systems and processes. Employees do not want to disturb their comfort zones in the workplace and therefore, try to resist change whenever it is contemplated. The changes may be in technology, organisational structure, working processes, work environment, organisational policy and even the roles of different employees. When employees perceive the change beneficial, they accept it willfully. If they suspect the increase in work pressure or any other problem, they resist such change.

Business units should workout strategies to implement changes with the acceptance of employees. They have to follow a systematic procedure to see that the employees are willfully participating in the change process and show involvement. According to Kurt Lewin (1947), there are three stages in the process of transforming the business unit from the present position to the changed position. The three stages in the change process are unfreezing, moving, and refreezing.

The purpose of unfreezing is to make individuals ready for change. To be successful in this stage, business units have to communicate in advance to all the employees about the kind of change they want to implement. There should not be any surprises to the employees as far as the introduction of change is concerned. Unfreezing requires the creation of an environment which unfolds the fears of psychological safety due to proposed change, and motivates employees for readiness to change.

The second stage in the change process is moving. It means incorporating the change process. The management of the business units should develop step by step implementation process by involving employees. A lot of efforts are needed to convince employees to take up the process or change effectively. They may need to be trained on various new skills, counsel psychologically, and provide access to learn.

The third stage in the change process is refreezing. It is the process of integrating new behaviours into the personality and attitude of the individual. Refreezing refers to stabilization and achieving balance in the behaviour of employees towards change. Refreezing takes place when the new behaviour is adopted in the normal way of life. The change in behaviour must be permanent.

32.3. LEARNING ORGANISATION

Learning organisation theory was introduced by Peter Senge in 1990 through his research paper 'The Fifth Discipline: The Art and Practice of the Learning Organisation'. As per the theory "people continually expand their capacity to create the results they truly desire, where new and expansive patterns of thinking are nurtured, where collective aspiration is set free, and where people are continually learning to see the whole together."

A learning organisation has the skills to change an individual's behaviour to form new ideas, information and understanding through creation, gathering and transfer of information based on a continuous learning cycle. It is essential for the employees to be open to innovation and learning and to increase service quality. Learning organisations have been gaining importance in all fields and institutions in terms of reforming information and adapting to change (Volante, 2010). Gaining awareness of the characteristics of learning organisations can result in dynamism and innovation, as well as increased motivation and enthusiasm in the business units.

In the digital age where information is power, learning can be understood as an effective process of collecting, developing and transferring information. The concept of the learning organisation has been linked to innovation and performance in business units. The ability to introduce or respond to change and the capability of introducing continuous improvements to meet the challenges in the environment depends upon the ability of the business units to learn. Thus, business units that enable learning will be able to keep abreast with developments and improvements in the current business environment to operate successfully and to exploit business opportunities.

Business units have multiple and intricate networks of relationships. These relationships are sustained through communication and feedback with varying degrees of interdependence. This requires qualified and skilled employees working for the organisation with involvement and commitment. Developing intellectual capital of the workforce is the challenge to the business units in light of the rapid pace of changes in the business environment and technology. Due to such changes, the business units are forced to train and retrain the employee's number of times. The business units face several key changes that focus attention on efficiency concerning delivery methods. New opportunities are being offered by information technology (IT) which could facilitate major changes in the delivery of training and provide greater flexibility for learning (Littejohn and Watson, 2004).

A futuristic perspective drives us to the conclusion that the business units may not survive without transforming themselves as communities of learning. Continuous improvement is necessary to survive and grow and such improvements require a commitment to learning. Finding the right solutions to the problems, introducing new products, and reengineering processes require understanding the global scenario in a new perspective and act accordingly. In the absence of learning, organisations and individuals simply repeat old practices. Change remains cosmetic, and improvements are short-lived.

32.4. FIVE DISCIPLINES OF THE LEARNING ORGANISATION

The learning organisation perspective has gained importance in business management. According to Senge (2001), the most successful business units are learning organisations and that the ability to learn faster than competitors is the only sustainable advantage. It might, therefore, be reasonable to assume that being a learning organisation would manifest itself in an excellent performance, given that this must be a key area of competitive advantage. Senge (1990) developed five interrelated dimensions that are considered vital to building organisations that can truly learn.

The five components of the learning organisation were conceptualised to help people become active participants in understanding their real self and shaping themselves for the future. Imitation of best practices of some organisations may not contribute to learning. On the other hand, such practice leads to dependency and partial successes as the nuances of each organisation differ. Therefore, understanding thoroughly and responding to changes in the environment is important. It is necessary to follow the five disciplines which include mental models, personal mastery, shared vision, team learning, and systems thinking to develop a learning organisation.

1. Mental Models

Mental models refer to the state of mind of an individual in understanding the people through deeply ingrained assumptions/generalisations. These are the lenses through which individuals view the world around them.

A clear understanding of mental models helps individuals to examine the internal process of understanding and develop a mirror picture of the outcome of the internal process. They have to bring such pictures to the fore and scrutinise them. Then they are capable of sharing their thinking with others and expose it to their influence. This kind of process helps them to correct their view about people and situations.

A learning environment requires an open culture that promotes inquiry seeking new information and trust. It is necessary to promote learning as a lifestyle of the employees. At the same time, it is also very important to influence the employees to unlearn unwanted values. Thus learning and unlearning are the two different processes the business units should put in practice as per the demand of the situations. If the business unit is to develop a capacity to work with mental models, then the employees must learn new skills and develop new orientations.

2. Personal Mastery

It is also termed self-leadership. Personal mastery is the process of regulating self and behaviour towards a vision duly aligning with personal values. It requires constant self-learning and understanding the reality of the situations. In other words, personal mastery is a set of principles and activities that help a person to learn, develop personal vision, and perceive the world with a realistic perspective. Personal vision must be objective and the purpose is clearly defined.

Individuals striving for personal mastery are committed to life-long learning, and ever-increasing proficiency in their work, which they approach almost like a work of art. They are particularly interested in understanding how their actions affect others around them. Their goal is to attain expertise which can be shared with others, not to dominate others. They focus their energies on desired results. Their mind is open to finding innovative and creative solutions to problems. People with a high level of personal mastery are acutely aware of their strengths and weaknesses.

3. Shared Vision

When an individual vision is translated into a shared picture of the future of an organisation or a working group it is called a shared vision. A vision conceptualised by an individual is shared with others in the organisation and gets acceptance of the same or with minor modifications. This kind of shared vision is powerful because it is accepted by all and more importantly all participate in finalising the vision of the organisation. Such a vision provides the focus and energy for subsequent team learning. The development of a shared vision is important in motivating the employees to learn, as it creates a common identity. The traditional organisational structures create some hindrances for shared vision as organisational vision is imposed from the top in such organisations. Therefore, a flat decentralised organisational structure is convenient for promoting a shared vision.

4. Team Learning

Team learning is a process in which teams of employees think together and arrive at a consensus on the ways to achieve organisational goals. Teamwork provides learning to all the members of the team as everyone with his/her intellect contributes to problem-solving. That is the reason why modern organisations emphasise on building teams and facilitating teamwork. Team learning starts with a conversation. The conversations will be effective when all the members of the team respect each other as equals, have open-mindedness, positive attitude and a resolve to find solutions to the problem on hand. Good teams are often in conflict, the free flow of conflicting ideas is essential for creative thinking. When teams are truly learning, they can produce extraordinary results.

5. Systems Thinking

Systems thinking is nothing but considering the four disciplines (mental models, personal mastery, building shared visions, and team learning) as interrelated parts of a process and exploring the possibilities of integrating them as a coherent body of theory and practice. In modern management theory, organisations are viewed as systems comprised of interrelated parts and actions. Systems thinking states that all the characteristics of an organisation must be transparent to become a learning organisation.

32.5. DIMENSIONS OF LEARNING ORGANISATION

According to Watkins & Marsick (1993, 1997), the learning organisation is an integrative model, where learning is a continuous process, used strategically, and is integrated with overall work processes. Learning organisation integrates both structure and people as they leverage learning at three levels: individual, team and organisational system. At the individual level, continuous learning opportunities should be created, facilitating members of the organisation to acquire knowledge and skills. At the team level, individuals learn as teams, focusing on collaboration and teamwork. This is followed by learning at the organisation level incorporating individual and group learning and capture all in standard operating procedures, work processes, operations manuals, information systems, and the organisational culture. Learning at the organisational level is described as the most difficult, and least practised by business units as it requires effective systems to capture and share learning, and gaining organisational consensus and commitment from all employees through empowering them toward a collective vision, increasing the performance of a business unit (Watkins & Marsick, 2003).

Watkins & Marsick (1997) suggested that the design of a learning organisation requires six action imperatives including empowering people toward a collective vision, promoting inquiry and dialogue, encouraging collaboration and team learning, creating continuous learning opportunities, connecting the organisation to the environment, and establishing systems to capture and share learning. These action imperatives are expected to take place at four different levels for continuous learning and change. The four levels are individual level through continuous learning, the team level by way of collaboration, organisation level through empowerment and designing systems, and societal levels by connecting to the environment.

32.6. SUMMARY

- Behavioural economics states that people do not always make choices that maximise their benefits though they wanted to. People often get into time pressure in making purchase decisions. They compromise on certain information requirements and try to compromise to save the situations.
- The various dimensions of behavioural economics are individuals are influenced by others' behaviour, habits influence behaviour, people can be motivated to choose the right things, the self-concept – behaviour based on self-perception, people try to avoid losses, and the readiness to change depends upon the involvement of people.
- Human beings learn many things by observing and imitating others. The behavioural economic theory assumes that other people influence the behaviour of individuals.
- Habits refer to an acquired pattern of behaviour indicated by involuntary and frequent repetition. Habits can also be changed when there is a strong influencing reward for change in behaviour.
- Motivation is the process of satisfying the felt needs and desires by the individuals. The behavioural economics advocates that people can be motivated towards economic activities. The economic rewards result in positive motivation, whereas, the punishments, negative outcomes, and relatively low rewards result in negative motivation.
- Self-concept is a useful analysis for the business units to understand target customers and to plan activities that are capable of influencing them in favour of the organisation.
- Risk-taking is the controlled behaviour of the management due to perceived uncertainty about the outcome. Behavioural economics states that people will go out of their way to avoid losses.

- Change management is one of the major challenges of the business units, particularly to those in a highly competitive environment. Business units should workout strategies to implement changes with the acceptance of employees.
- A learning organisation has the skills to change an individual's behaviour to form new ideas, information and understanding through creation, gathering and transfer of information based on a continuous learning cycle. The most successful business units are learning organisations and that the ability to learn faster than competitors is the only sustainable advantage.
- The five disciplines of the learning organisation include mental models, personal mastery, shared vision, team learning, and systems thinking to develop a learning organisation.
- The dimensions of learning organisation require six action imperatives including empowering people toward a collective vision, promoting inquiry and dialogue, encouraging collaboration and team learning, creating continuous learning opportunities, connecting the organisation to the environment, and establishing systems to capture and share learning.

SHORT ANSWER QUESTIONS

1. Define behavioural economics.
2. What are the dimensions of a learning organisation?
3. What are mental models?
4. Write a short note on personal mastery.
5. Describe learning organisation.

ESSAY ANSWER QUESTIONS

1. What is behavioural economics? Discuss the Nudge theory.
2. Explain the various dimensions of behavioural economics.
3. What is a learning organisation? Explain the five disciplines of a learning organisation.

FILL IN THE BLANKS

1. The concept of behavioural economics was introduced by __________.
2. The process of satisfying the felt needs and desires by the individuals is called __________.
3. The perception of an individual about how people should behave based on standards of aspirations is called __________.
4. The process of regulating self and behaviour towards a vision duly aligning with personal values is called __________.

5. When an individual vision is translated into a shared picture of the future of an organisation or a working group it is called a_________.

Answers:

1. Richard H. Thaler 2. Motivation
3. Ideal self 4. Personal mastery
5. Shared vision

MULTIPLE-CHOICE QUESTIONS

1. A technique used by choice makers to change the behaviour of an individual without reducing the number of choices available is called:
   (A) Nudge (B) Impulsive
   (C) Choice (D) Behaviour
2. The need hierarchy motivation theory was proposed by:
   (A) Roy Baumeister (B) Fredrick Herzberg
   (C) Abraham Maslow (D) Douglas McGregor
3. A cognitive structure consisting of all self-describing attributes that a person is aware of is called:
   (A) Actual self (B) Ideal self
   (C) Social self (D) Ideal social self
4. The process of integrating new behaviours into the personality and attitude of the individual is called:
   (A) Unfreezing (B) Refreezing
   (C) Moving (D) Freezing
5. The state of mind of an individual in understanding the people through deeply ingrained assumptions are called:
   (A) Personal mastery (B) Shared vision
   (C) Mental model (D) Systems thinking
6. Personal mastery is also termed as:
   (A) Self-leadership (B) Team leaning
   (C) Self-learning (D) Personal vision

Answers:

1. A 2. C 3. A 4. B 5. C
6. A

REFERENCES

1. Akerlof, G. (1976). The economics of caste and of the rat race and other woeful tales. *The Quarterly Journal of Economics*, 90, 599-617.
2. Baumeister, R.F. (2011). Self and identity: A brief overview of what they are, what they do, and how they work. *Annals of the New York Academy of Sciences*, 1234(1), 48-55.
3. Herzberg, F. (1964). The motivation-hygiene concept and problems of manpower. *Personnel Administration*.

4. Herzberg, F. (1966). *Work and the Nature of Man*. New York: World Publishing.
5. Maslow, A. H. (1943). A theory of human motivation. *Psychological Review*, 50(4), 370.
6. Senge, P.M. (1990). *The Fifth Discipline: The Art and Practice of the Learning Organisation*. New York, NY: Doubleday.
7. Senge, P.M. (1996). Leading Learning Organisations: The Bold, the Powerful, and the Invisible, in Hesselbein, F., Marshall, R., Bechkard, R. (eds.) *The Leader of the Future* (pp. 41-57). New York, NY: Jossey-Bass.
8. Senge, P.M. (2001). The learning organisation. In W.E. Natemeyer & J.T. McMahon (Eds.), *Classics of Organisational Behaviour* (3rd Edn.; pp. 468-472). Prospect Heights, IL: Waveland Press.
9. Thaler, R.H. (2015). *Misbehaving: The Making of Behavioral Economics*. New York: W.W. Norton & Company.
10. Thaler, R.H. & Sunstein, C.R. (2008). *Nudge: Improving Decisions about Health Wealth and Happiness*. New Haven, CT: Yale University Press.
11. Thaler, R.H. & Sunstein, C.R. (2003). Behavioral economics, public policy, and paternalism: Libertarian paternalism. *American Economic Review, Papers and Proceedings*, 93, 175-179.
12. Volante, L. (2010). Assessment of, for, and as learning within schools: Implications for transforming classroom practice. *Action in Teacher Education*, 31(4), 66-75.
13. Watkins, K.E. & Marsick, V.J. (1993). *Sculpting the Learning Organisation: Lessons in the Art and Science of Systemic Change*. San Francisco, CA: Jossey-Bass.
14. Watkins, K.E. & Marsick, V.J. (1997). *Dimensions of the Learning Organisation Questionnaire*. Warwick, RI: Partners for the Learning Organisation.
15. Watkins, K.E. & Marsick, V.J. (2003). *Making Learning Count! Diagnosing the Learning Culture in Organisations*. Thousand Oaks, CA: Sage Publications.

Index

I

J

K

L

M